JESUS AND THE
ZEALOTS

BY THE SAME AUTHOR

The Fall of Jerusalem and the Christian Church
Time and Mankind
Man and his Destiny in the Great Religions
Creation Legends of the Ancient Near East
History, Time and Deity
Jesus and the Zealots
The Judgment of the Dead

'Whose is this image and superscription? And they said unto him, Caesar's'
(Mark xii. 16). A silver *denarius* of the Emperor Tiberius. The type of coin
probably used in the Tribute Money incident. (*Enlarged reproduction,
reproduced by courtesy of the Manchester Museum.*)

JESUS AND THE ZEALOTS

A STUDY OF THE POLITICAL
FACTOR IN PRIMITIVE
CHRISTIANITY

S. G. F. BRANDON

CHARLES SCRIBNER'S SONS
NEW YORK

Think not that I came to bring peace on the earth:
I came not to bring peace, but a sword.

(Matt. x. 34)

A–11.68 [MC]

PRINTED IN THE UNITED STATES OF AMERICA

Library of Congress Catalog Card Number 68–57073

CONTENTS

LIST OF ILLUSTRATIONS

Frontispiece: 'Whose is this image and superscription? And they said unto him, Caesar's' (Mark xii. 16).

Plates I–XII *are between pages* 144 *and* 145.

ACKNOWLEDGEMENTS

The author gratefully acknowledges the permission kindly given by the following persons, institutions and publishers to reproduce material of which they own the copyright: Professor Y. Yadin, the Hebrew University, Jerusalem, for photographs from the *Israel Exploration Journal*, vol. xv, reproduced here on the Plates illustrating Masada; The Israel Department of Antiquities and Museums for the photograph of the Pilate inscription exhibited in the Israel Museum, Jerusalem; Dr D. E. Owen, Director of the Manchester Museum, for the photographing of coins in the Museum; Verlag Anton Schroll, Vienna, for plates from L. Curtius and A. Nawrath, *Das Antike Rom*; Messrs William Heinemann Ltd. for quotations from H. St J. Thackeray's translation of Josephus in the Loeb Classical Library; The Institut d'Études slaves, Paris, for the quotation from P. Pascal's translation in *La Prise de Jérusalem de Josèphe le Juif*.

PREFACE

No responsible scholar will lightly undertake to write on the question whether Jesus of Nazareth became involved in the Jewish resistance movement against Rome. For he knows that to many people, whose beliefs and principles he may deeply respect, the very asking of the question will cause offence and suggest a distressing scepticism about that which is sacred. For them there is no question to discuss: the incarnated Son of God could never have taken part in Jewish-Roman politics. His mission to save mankind by his own vicarious death was part of a divine plan that transcended space and time, and it could not have become involved in, and conditioned by, the political relations of Jews and Romans in first-century Judaea.

The theological presuppositions which underlie this judgement are very ancient, and their origins can be traced back to the first century. But, from the beginning, they were essentially interpretations, inspired by current theological concepts, of certain historical facts. For, however impressive may be the metaphysical structure and content of Christian theology, its authority ultimately derives from certain events that are alleged to have occurred in Judaea during the procuratorship of Pontius Pilate, who had been appointed to this office by the Emperor Tiberius.

This fact is recognised every time the Creed is recited, in the words 'suffered under Pontius Pilate'.[1] But the reference to the death of Jesus 'under Pontius Pilate' does not just attest the historicity of the Crucifixion; it also implies a fatal involvement of Jesus with this Roman governor of Judaea. It means that Jesus was put to death on his orders. Now, of the many charges on which a Roman governor at this time might have put a Jew to death, that on which Jesus was executed is of peculiar significance. It was a charge of sedition against the Roman government in Judaea. There can be no doubt that this was the charge on which he was condemned, for it is attested by all four Gospels. Hence, whatever may be the theological evaluation of the crucifixion of Jesus, its cause constitutes a historical problem. In its simplest form it may be expressed by the question: why did the Roman governor of Judaea decide to execute Jesus for sedition?

[1] *passus sub Pontio Pilato, crucifixus,*...

The question is, of course, not a new one. In fact the first of the Christian Gospels, the Gospel of Mark, tried to answer it. This Markan answer was accepted and elaborated by the other Evangelists, and it has become the traditional interpretation of the historical cause and circumstances of the Crucifixion. But is it the right answer? The development of New Testament criticism has shown, with ever-increasing evidence, that the New Testament documents must be evaluated in terms of the ideas and needs of the particular communities in which, or for which, they were originally written. This has meant that the Markan account of the trial and crucifixion of Jesus has to be viewed primarily with reference to the *Sitz im Leben* of the Christian community in which it originated, and not as an objective historical record of what actually happened in Jerusalem on the first Good Friday. And the other Gospel accounts must be similarly interpreted. When the traditional Gospel explanation of the death of Jesus is so studied, it soon becomes evident that apologetical factors have decisively shaped the presentation of the events which had their tragic culmination on Golgotha.

The Roman execution of Jesus does, therefore, constitute a historical problem which demands the attention of historians. It is, because of the nature of the relevant data, a highly complex problem, as the following study will amply show. Its study requires an acute and careful interrogation of the evidence, with a firm resolve to eschew any facile, and, above all, any sensational, solution that may suggest itself. It is the belief of the present writer that such an investigation not only is especially necessary now, in the light of the new evaluation of the Zealots, but that it also will help in understanding the historical Jesus, who chose a Zealot for an apostle, and who died crucified between two men, probably Jewish resistance fighters, who had challenged Rome's sovereignty over Israel.[1]

I desire to put on record my gratitude to the University of Manchester for making it possible for me to visit sites in Israel and Jordan connected with the history of the fateful years from A.D. 6 to 70. I gladly take the opportunity also of thanking Professor Y. Yadin of the Hebrew University, Jerusalem, for kindly arranging

---

[1] The present work forms a sequel to my book *The Fall of Jerusalem and the Christian Church*, although it deals with the earlier period. As will quickly become obvious in the study, the problem of Jesus and the Zealots can only be approached by working backwards from the post-A.D. situation.

for my visit to Masada, and to Mr Avraham Fagin for his kindness and courtesy in explaining the excavations of this great fortress, made both tragic and glorious. by Zealot faith and fortitude in A.D. 73. Masada survives as the most authentic and moving memorial that links us with those years which saw the rise of Christianity and the end of the Jewish national state, in which Jesus and his disciples were nurtured and lived their lives.

Once again I wish to thank my friend and colleague, Rev. D. Howard Smith, for his valuable help, so freely given, in reading through the manuscript and offering much useful criticism and advice. Dr M. Wallenstein kindly assisted in checking the Hebrew typography. I should also like to record my gratitude to Dr Cecil Roth and Dr Paul Winter for generously supplying me, during a period of many years, with offprints of their publications. I desire also to express my appreciation here of Martin Hengel's magisterial study entitled *Die Zeloten*. Although I have dissented from his interpretation on a number of points, the notes will show how greatly I am indebted to him.

To the kind cooperation of Professor F. C. Thompson, the Hon. Keeper of Coins and Medals, and Mr H. Spencer, Chief Technician, of Manchester Museum, I owe the fine photographs of Roman and Jewish coins in the Museum. Mr S. Roberts, the Deputy Librarian, and Mr G. A. Webb, of the Arts Library of Manchester University, kindly arranged the reproduction of certain of the illustrations. The Israel Department of Antiquities and Museums kindly provided the photograph of the *Pilatus* inscription recently found at Caesarea.

I have welcomed the opportunity of publishing this book through the Manchester University Press, because it has given me once again the kind and efficient assistance of the Secretary, Mr T. L. Jones, and of other members of its staff. I am also grateful to the reader of the University Printing House, Cambridge, for many useful suggestions for improving the text.

S. G. F. BRANDON

Manchester University
August 1966

ABBREVIATIONS

A.L.U.O.S.	*Annual of Leeds University Oriental Society.*
B.A.	*The Biblical Archaeologist*, American Schools of Oriental Research, Cambridge, Mass.
Bauer, *Wörterbuch*	Bauer, W., *Griechisch-Deutsches Wörterbuch zu den Schriften des Neuen Testaments*, 2. Aufl. Giessen, 1928.
B.C.	*The Beginnings of Christianity*, edited by F. J. Foakes Jackson and Kirsopp Lake. 5 vols., London, 1920–33.
B.-h. H.-wb.	*Biblisch-historisches Handwörterbuch*, hrg. Bo Reicke und L. Rost, 3 Bände, Göttingen, 1962.
Bilderatlas	*Bilderatlas zur Religionsgeschichte*, hrg. H. Haas, Leipzig–Erlangen, 1924–30.
B.J.R.L.	*The Bulletin of John Rylands Library*, Manchester.
C.A.H.	*The Cambridge Ancient History.*
D.S.H.	*Habakkuk Pesher.*
E.R.E.	*Encyclopaedia of Religion and Ethics*, ed. J. Hastings, 12 vols. and index vol. Edinburgh, 1908–26.
E.T.	English Translation.
H.J.	*The Hibbert Journal*, London.
H.Th.R.	*The Harvard Theological Review.*
I.C.C.	*International Critical Commentary.*
I.E.J.	*Israel Exploration Journal*, Jerusalem (Israel).
I.L.N.	*The Illustrated London News.*
J.B.L.	*The Journal of Biblical Literature*, Philadelphia (Penn.).
J.E.	*The Jewish Encyclopaedia*, New York, 1901.
J.J.S.	*The Journal of Jewish Studies*, London.
J.Q.R.	*The Jewish Quarterly Review*, Philadelphia (Penn.).
J.R.S.	*Journal of Roman Studies*, London.
J.S.S.	*The Journal of Semitic Studies*, Manchester.
J.T.S.	*The Journal of Theological Studies*, Oxford.
New Comm. N.T.	*A New Commentary of Holy Scripture*: section on the New Testament.

N.T.	*Novum Testamentum*, Leiden.
N.T.S.	*New Testament Studies*, Cambridge.
O.C.D.	*The Oxford Classical Dictionary*, Oxford, 1949.
Peake's Commentary[2]	*Peake's Commentary on the Bible*, 2nd ed. 1962.
P.G.	*Patrologia Graeca*, ed. J. Migne.
P.L.	*Patrologia Latina*, ed. J. Migne.
R.A.C.	*Reallexikon für Antike und Christentum*, hrg. T. Klauser, Bände I–VI (continuing), Stuttgart, 1950–66.
R.G.G.[3]	*Religion in Geschichte und Gegenwart*, 3. Aufl. hrg. K. Galling, Bände I–VI, Tübingen, 1957–62.
R.H.P.R.	*Revue d'Histoire et Philosophie religieuses*, Strasbourg.
R.H.R.	*Revue de l'Histoire des Religions*, Paris.
R.Q.	*Revue de Qumran*, Paris.
R.S.V.	American Revised Standard Version of the Bible.
R.Th.P.	*Revue de Théologie et de Philosophie*, Lausanne.
S.B. *Kommentar*	Strack, H. L. and Billerbeck, P., *Kommentar zum Neuen Testament aus Talmud und Midrasch*, 4 Bände, Munich, 1922–8.
Schürer, *G.J.V.*	Schürer, E., *Geschichte des jüdischen Volkes im Zeitalter Jesu Christi*, 3 Bände, Leipzig, 1898–1901.
Th.Wb.	*Theologisches Wörterbuch zum Neuen Testament*, hrg. G. Kittel, Stuttgart, 1932.
V.C.	*Vigiliae Christianae*, Amsterdam.
V.T.	*Vetus Testamentum*, Leiden.
Z.N.T.W.	*Zeitschrift für die neutestamentliche Wissenschaft*, Berlin.

CHAPTER 1

'SUFFERED UNDER PONTIUS PILATE': THE PROBLEM OF THE ROMAN EXECUTION OF JESUS

Ironic though it be, the most certain thing known about Jesus of Nazareth is that he was crucified by the Romans as a rebel against their government in Judaea. The fact is recorded in the four Christian Gospels,[1] and the execution, on the order of Pontius Pilate, is mentioned by the Roman historian Tacitus, writing early in the second century.[2] The Christian attestation is particularly significant. That the founder of their faith had been put to death on a charge of sedition could hardly have been invented by Christians; for such a fact obviously caused the Roman authorities to view the faith with suspicion, as Tacitus' statement shows.[3] The early Christians had, indeed, a strong motive for suppressing so embarrassing a fact; that they did not do so surely attests both its authenticity and notoriety.

The fact itself, in terms of current Romano-Jewish relations in Judaea, was not particularly remarkable. The Jewish historian Josephus records numerous instances, during the period concerned, of the crucifixion of Jewish rebels by the Romans.[4] But what makes

---

[1] Mark xv. 1–2, 15–20, 26, 32; Matt. xxvii. 11–31, 37; Luke xxiii. 1–25, 38; John xviii. 29–xix. 24. Cf. I Tim. vi. 13.

[2] *Annales*, xv. 44: 'Auctor nominis eius Christus Tiberio imperitante per procuratorem Pontium Pilatum supplicio adfectus erat.' Although Tacitus does not specify the form of execution, 'supplicium' could well mean crucifixion. In *Hist.* II. 72; IV. 11, Tacitus refers to crucifixion as 'supplicium servile' (i.e. a 'despicable death'). On the authenticity of the passage, and its source, cf. M. Goguel, *Life of Jesus* (London, 1933), pp. 94–7; Ch. Guignebert, *Jésus* (Paris, 1933), p. 16, who is typically very cautious: cf. Ed. Meyer, *Ursprung und Anfänge des Christentums* (Stuttgart and Berlin, 1921–3), I, 209, n. 1; P. de Labriolle, *La réaction païenne* (Paris, 1934), p. 39. See also H. Fuchs, 'Tacitus über die Christen', *V.C.* I (1950), 82–8.

[3] 'repressaque in praesens exitiabilis superstitio rursum erumpebat, non modo per Judaeam, originem eius mali,...' Cf. de Labriolle, *La réaction païenne*, pp. 38–41. Cf. B. H. Streeter, 'The Rise of Christianity', *C.A.H.* XI, 254–6; H. Furneaux, *The Annals of Tacitus*, II, 374–5.

[4] *The Jewish War*, II. 75 (=*Ant.* XVII. 295), II. 241 (=*Ant.* XX. 129), 241, 306, 308; V. 449–52; VII. 202; *Life*, 421–2 (an interesting case of taking down

the Christian accounts of the crucifixion of Jesus specially notable, as records of historical fact, is that they represent Jesus as being innocent of the charge on which he was condemned. Although they vary in some details, the four Gospel accounts agree in showing that Jesus was falsely accused of sedition by the Jewish authorities, and that these authorities also forced the Roman governor, Pontius Pilate, against his better judgement, to condemn and execute him.[1]

These Gospel accounts are circumstantial, and, on a cursory reading, they present a convincing case for the innocence of Jesus. And such a presentation is not intrinsically improbable: similar instances of the miscarriage of justice and judicial murder could be cited from all periods of history.[2] Whether the Roman procurator, Pontius Pilate, was a man likely to have yielded in such a way to the pressure of Jewish leaders and a Jewish mob, could certainly be questioned in the light of what Josephus tells us of his character and attitude to the Jews.[3] Such a contention need not, however, be explored at this point, since more serious ground for doubting the Gospel presentation is actually provided by that presentation itself.

It here becomes necessary to note that the earliest account of the trial and crucifixion of Jesus is that contained in the Gospel of Mark. The fact is of considerable importance, because this account undoubtedly provided the basic framework of the later accounts of the Matthaean and Lukan Gospels.[4] But that is not the whole significance of the fact. The Gospel of Mark, by virtue of its being the first of the Gospels, represents a new departure in what had hitherto been Christian practice.[5] Such a change naturally suggests an effective

three of the crucified, of whom one survived). 'Die Kreuzigung wurde zur bevorzugten Hinrichtungsart, vermutlich weil sie unter römischer Herrschaft überhaupt das verbreitetste Exekutionsmittel war' (M. Hengel, *Die Zeloten*, Leiden, 1961, p. 265). Cf. P. Winter, *On the Trial of Jesus* (Berlin, 1961), pp. 62–6.

[1] Mark xv. 9–14; Matt. xxvii. 18–25; Luke xxiii. 4–23; John xviii. 38–40, xix. 4–16.

[2] E.g. the trials of Naboth, Socrates, and Joan of Arc.

[3] See below, pp. 68–9; for Philo's estimate also.

[4] Cf. B. H. Streeter, *The Four Gospels* (London, 1924), pp. 157–69; V. Taylor, *The Gospel according to St Mark* (London, 1952), p. 11 ('Significant of the stability of critical opinion is the fact that, in a modern commentary, it is no longer necessary to prove the priority of Mark'); T. W. Manson, *Studies in the Gospels and Epistles* (Manchester University Press, 1962), pp. 20–1; C. S. C. Williams, 'The Synoptic Problem', *Peake's Commentary*[2], 653 b–d; B. W. Beare, *The Earliest Records of Jesus* (Oxford, 1962), pp. 14–15.   [5] See chapter 3.

cause: in other words, that this Gospel was produced in response to the needs, or under the impetus, of some specific situation. The identification of such a situation is likely to be a task of considerable intricacy, seeing that the document contains no formal statement about its origin or purpose. At this juncture it will, however, suffice to note that the general consensus of expert opinion dates the composition of the Gospel of Mark for the period A.D. 60–75, and locates it in the Christian community at Rome.[1] In the light of these considerations, it would be reasonable, therefore, on a priori grounds, to suppose that the Markan account of the trial and crucifixion of Jesus may have been influenced by the situation from which the Gospel took its rise at Rome. With that possibility in mind, we are now in a better position for evaluating that cause for doubt concerning the nature of the Markan record of the condemnation of Jesus to which reference was made above.

According to Mark, after hearing the accusations of the Jewish leaders, and having made his own interrogation, Pilate was impressed by both the innocence and bearing of Jesus.[2] However, before making known his decision, he was petitioned by the Jewish people to adhere to his custom of releasing a prisoner to them at the Passover, which was then about to be celebrated.[3] Desiring to save Jesus, but evidently under pressure from the Jewish leaders, Pilate seizes the opportunity which this custom thus presented. But, instead of simply releasing Jesus as the amnestied prisoner, he causes the crowd to choose between Jesus and another prisoner, Barabbas, who was a notorious rebel recently involved in some violent act of insurrection. The crowd, prompted by the chief priests, ask for Barabbas and demand the crucifixion of Jesus.[4] The account of the incident thus greatly magnifies the culpability of the Jews, both leaders

---

[1] Cf. Taylor, St Mark, p. 32; R. McL. Wilson, 'Mark', Peake's Commentary[2], 696 b. See also chapter 3.

[2] Mark xv. 5, 10. Mark does not, significantly, explain why Pilate interpreted the chief priests' action as motivated by envy (διὰ φθόνον).

[3] Mark xv. 6–8. καὶ ἀναβὰς ὁ ὄχλος ἤρξατο αἰτεῖσθαι καθὼς ἐποίει αὐτοῖς: the statement suggests that the crowd took the initiative concerning the observation of the custom. Matt. xxvii. 17 seems to indicate that the initiative was Pilate's, while Luke xxiii. 18 gives the impression that the crowd suddenly demanded Barabbas in the place of Jesus. The crowd (ὄχλος) suddenly appears in Mark's account, as a factor in the condemnation of Jesus, without explanation. See below, pp. 260–1.

[4] Mark xv. 9–15. It is interesting that the expression in v. 15, τὸ ἱκανὸν ποιῆσαι ('to satisfy'), is one of Mark's Latinisms; cf. Taylor, St Mark, p. 583, below, pp. 221, 260.

and people, for the death of Jesus—they are depicted as preferring a bloodstained revolutionary to Jesus, whom they condemn innocently to bear the penalty that Barabbas justly deserved. But, to obtain this effect, Mark presents Pilate, a Roman governor, not only as criminally weak in his failure to do justice, but as a fool beyond belief. For, if he had truly sought to save Jesus, he could surely have done nothing worse to defeat his purpose than to offer the Jewish crowd a choice between Jesus and Barabbas. To them Barabbas was a patriot who had risked his life against their hated Roman rulers,[1] whereas Jesus, according to Mark, had advised them to pay tribute to these Romans.[2] To have offered the people such a choice, with the intention of saving Jesus, was the act of an idiot. The result was a foregone conclusion: inevitably Barabbas was preferred.

The Barabbas episode has long been a matter of debate among New Testament scholars; for it is suspect both on the ground of the intrinsic improbability of such a custom existing in so unruly a province as Judaea and because there is no other evidence for it.[3] However, quite apart from such serious considerations, Mark's presentation of the episode, as we have seen, is so manifestly absurd that it suggests some explanation other than that of lack of logic. The clue to that explanation surely lies in the impression created by a cursory reading of the episode. As we have noted, it dramatically attests the guilt of the Jews for the crucifixion of Jesus. And it does so by representing Pilate as recognising that Jesus was innocent of the charge of sedition, but as being forced by the Jews to condemn and execute him. In other words, the account explains that, though Jesus was crucified as a rebel by the Romans, he was guiltless of such a crime; the accusation, and its tragic consequence, resulted from Jewish malice.

Mark's presentation of the Barabbas episode looks, accordingly, as though it were designed to show that, despite the fact of his execution by the Romans, Jesus had not truly been a rebel against their

---

[1] It is significant that Mark describes the killing that had resulted from the obviously anti-Roman revolt, in which Barabbas had been involved, as murder (ἐν τῇ στάσει φόνον πεποιήκεισαν). The use of this opprobrious term indicates from which side Mark is writing: the Jews would undoubtedly have seen such killings (probably of Romans) in a somewhat different light, as all subjugated people view the deaths of their oppressors at the hands of their patriots.

[2] Mark xii. 13–17: see below, pp. 227, 270–1.

[3] See the discussion of the issue on pp. 258–9.

4

government in Judaea. The fact, in other words, is not denied; but its significance is explained away—the crucifixion had been a tragic miscarriage of justice, for which the Jews were essentially responsible. The Barabbas episode is not, however, an isolated instance of Jewish malice against Jesus, according to Mark; in fact, it was the culminating act of the intention which the Jewish leaders had long had to destroy him.[1]

Now, it could well be that Jesus had been the victim of such an intention which had been accomplished in this way. However, since its achievement thus involved the most ludicrous conduct on the part of Pilate, as we have seen, we may reasonably question the accuracy of Mark's account. Since the Barabbas episode, as described by him, has the effect of explaining away the political significance of the Roman execution of Jesus, it may fairly be asked whether this was Mark's intention. To attempt an answer to this question inevitably involves investigation of the situation which produced the Markan Gospel, especially since, as we have noted, its production was a novel undertaking.

Other questions also suggest themselves as we consider the consistency and implications of Mark's account of the trial and crucifixion of Jesus. There is the curious fact that the Jewish authorities, who plan to destroy Jesus, arrest him and eventually condemn him to death for blasphemy. But at his trial the only charge brought against him was that of threatening to destroy the Temple and replace it miraculously by one 'made without hands'. This strange charge fails through a conflict of evidence among the witnesses concerned, who are described as bearing 'false witness' (ἐψευδο-μαρτύρουν) against Jesus.[2] His condemnation is only secured by his answering affirmatively to the high priest's question: 'Art thou the Messiah, the Son of the Blessed?' This answer is adjudged a self-attested blasphemy, meriting death.[3] However, instead of ordering

---

[1] E.g. Mark iii. 6, xii. 12, xiv. 10–11. Cf. S. G. F. Brandon, *The Fall of Jerusalem and the Christian Church* (London, 1951), pp. 187–8, and 'The Apologetical Factor in the Markan Gospel', *Studia Evangelica* (Berlin, 1964), II, 34–46; below, pp. 248 ff.

[2] Mark xiv. 55–9. Cf. Taylor, *St Mark*, pp. 565–6; Brandon, *Fall of Jerusalem*, pp. 38–90, and 'The Date of the Markan Gospel', *N.T.S.* VII (1960–1), 135; see also below, pp. 234, 251–3.

[3] Mark xiv. 61–4. The addition of ὁ υἱὸς τοῦ εὐλογητοῦ to ὁ Χριστός should be noted, since it attributes divinity to the Messiah contrary to current Jewish practice. That the equation is Mark's, as is also his attribution of a direct affirmative to Jesus in his reply to the high priest's question, is

his execution according to the Mosaic Law, the Jewish authorities, after consultation among themselves, take their prisoner to the Roman procurator, Pontius Pilate, accusing him, apparently, on a number of counts, of sedition according to Roman law.[1] Mark does not explain this surprising course of action; but, according to the later Johannine account, the Jewish authorities were themselves unable to execute a person guilty of a capital offence, such as blasphemy was in Jewish law.[2] This alleged inability of the Jewish authorities has been seriously questioned by modern scholars.[3] However that may be, it is important for us to notice that in this original Markan account no explanation is given of why the Jewish authorities did not themselves execute Jesus, but handed him over to Pilate on a different charge—the charge of sedition, on which he was in fact executed by the Romans.

Mark's evident concern to show that the Roman crucifixion of Jesus was really an unfortunate accident, and that the true responsibility for his death lay with the Jewish leaders, justifiably causes suspicion on other grounds also. From the Jewish point of view, it would surely have been an honourable thing for Jesus, a Jew, to have met death at the hands of the heathen Romans, who had imposed by force their wicked rule upon Israel, the Chosen People of God. To his fellow-countrymen Jesus would have been a martyr for Israel, one of a glorious succession of such witnesses who had suffered for

consistent with his theme so concisely stated in i. 1: 'The beginning of the gospel of Jesus Christ, the Son of God.' Accordingly, it is more probable that the simple ἐγώ εἰμι given as Jesus' answer in the principal MSS represents Mark's original text here than the σὺ εἶπας ὅτι ἐγώ εἰμι of the group of MSS favoured by Taylor, St Mark, p. 568. Moreover, it seems more likely that later scribes would have sought to bring Mark xiv. 62 into line with Matt. xxvi. 64 and Luke xxii. 70 than that the extra words should have been omitted later in the MSS which give the simple affirmative.

[1] Mark xv. 1-3. The use of the plural πολλά in describing the chief priests' accusation suggests that they specified more than one instance of sedition. It is difficult to see how the adverbial use of πολλά here can be justified (cf. Bauer, Wörterbuch², 662-1, 1104-β). Such an interpretation is in fact contradicted by Pilate's subsequent admonition to Jesus: 'behold how many things (πόσα) they accuse thee of' (xv. 4). Cf. Taylor, St Mark, p. 579.

[2] John xviii. 31-2. The reason given here looks suspiciously like an *ex eventu* explanation for the fact that the execution of Jesus took the form of crucifixion by the Romans, whereas the Jews are represented as responsible for his death.

[3] E.g. Winter, On the Trial of Jesus, pp. 75-90. See also below, p. 117, n. 1.

the Holy Nation's freedom from heathen domination since the days of the Maccabees.[1] Accordingly, we may again wonder why Mark is at such pains not only to establish the essential responsibility of the Jews for the crucifixion of Jesus, but also to prove that the Romans recognised his innocence.

This curious preoccupation of Mark, to show that the Jewish authorities, not Pilate, were really responsible for the death of Jesus, must also be seen against the background of somewhat similar events during this period of politico-religious unrest in Judaea. The Jewish historian Josephus records a number of instances, which we must note in greater detail later,[2] of Messianic pretenders who roused the people with promises of deliverance and were destroyed by the Romans. In none of these cases did the Jewish authorities arrest them, condemn them for blasphemy and hand them over to the Romans. Why they should have acted so with Jesus, as Mark describes them as doing, is, therefore, the more remarkable.

At this point it becomes necessary that we notice that in the Markan Gospel, while Jesus is recognised as the Messiah of Israel, he is also accorded a far higher status, namely, that of the Son of God. Thus, for example, the Gospel itself is entitled 'Beginning of the gospel of Jesus Christ, the Son of God';[3] and Jesus is represented as affirming the high priest's question, 'art thou the Messiah (*Christos*), the Son of the Blessed?'—a formulation that departs from current Jewish practice in according divine status to the Messiah:[4] and the Roman centurion on Calvary witnesses to Jesus' divinity as he dies.[5] In other words, it must be remembered that, although appearing to give a factual account of events that took place in Judaea during the procuratorship of Pontius Pilate, Mark is really describing the career of a divine being, the Son of God. Now, in this divine role, Jesus obviously had a universal significance such as he could not have had as the Messiah of Israel—for example, to the Gentile

---

[1] Cf. E. Lohmeyer in *Congrès d'Histoire du Christianisme* (Paris, 1928), II, 121–32; C. K. Barrett, 'The Background of Mark 10: 45', *New Testament Essays*, ed. A. J. B. Higgins (Manchester, 1959), pp. 5, 11–15; Hengel, *Die Zeloten*, pp. 261–8.　　　　　　　　[2] See pp. 110, 112–13, 115.

[3] Mark i. 1. Cf. E. Hoskyns and N. Davey, *The Riddle of the New Testament* (London, 1931), p. 95. Taylor, *St Mark*, p. 152, thinks that there are strong reasons for accepting υἱοῦ θεοῦ as genuine, despite its omission from certain MSS. On the question whether this was the original beginning of the Markan Gospel see Manson, *Studies in the Gospels and Epistles*, pp. 30–2.

[4] See p. 5, n. 3 above. Cf. S. Mowinckel, *He That Cometh* (Oxford, 1958), pp. 293–4, 367–70.

[5] Mark xv. 39. See below, pp. 279–80.

Christians of Rome, for whom Mark wrote, so essentially Jewish a conception as that of Messiah could have had little appeal or meaning. The question may, therefore, be reasonably asked whether this factor also might have affected Mark's obvious concern about Jesus' death as a rebel. For, quite apart from the political embarrassment of such a fact for a new religion, it is understandable that a death which resulted from the hatred of those who would not accept his divinity might be deemed more spiritually fitting for one regarded as the Son of God. Here again is an issue that can only properly be decided, if at all, after a careful appraisal of the *Sitz im Leben* of the Markan Gospel. But, pending that evaluation, it will be useful to look a little more closely at the implications of Jesus' role as the Messiah.

If Jesus had claimed to be the Messiah and had been recognised as such by his followers, as Mark relates, then, on Mark's showing, Jesus must have had a very different conception of Messiahship from that which was then current.[1] Thus, instead of leading his people against the hated Romans, he is represented as endorsing their rule in Judaea: for he recognises the duty of the Jews to pay tribute to Caesar.[2] This issue, as we shall see in detail later, was the basic test of Jewish patriotism: for payment of this tribute was tantamount to denying Yahweh's absolute sovereignty over Israel—it was the issue on which the Zealots, the nationalist action party, were prepared to die.[3]

However, unless Jesus had made his position clear on the tribute question, and thereby with regard to the Roman rule, only during his last days at Jerusalem, it is passing strange that, according to Mark, he had been acclaimed on his entry into the Holy City as the Messiah in an unmistakably political sense.[4] Such acknowledgement would surely have never been given to him, if it were known that his attitude was so favourable towards the Romans. But the inconsistency thus implicit in this aspect of Mark's presentation of Jesus extends also in other directions. The celebrated 'Cleansing of the Temple' is

---

[1] Cf. Mowinckel, *He That Cometh*, *ibid*. See also below, pp. 346–7.
[2] Mark xii. 13–17. See pp. 227, 270–1.
[3] See chapter 2.
[4] Mark xi. 8–10: Εὐλογημένη ἡ ἐρχομένη βασιλεία τοῦ πατρὸς ἡμῶν Δαυείδ. 'Eine Messiaslegende, die vielleicht schon im palästinensischen Christentum entstanden ist, ist die Geschichte vom Einzug in Jerusalem Mk. 11, 1–10' (R. Bultmann, *Die Geschichte der synoptischen Tradition*, Göttingen, 1957, p. 333). Cf. Taylor, *St Mark*, pp. 456–7; Mowinckel, *He That Cometh*, p. 292. See below, p. 349.

depicted in an idealistic manner as being effected by Jesus alone, inspired by an apposite text from holy scripture.[1] But it is obvious, on a moment's reflection, that the actual event must have been very different. The money exchange in the Temple, and the selling of sacrificial animals, formed a valuable preserve of the sacerdotal aristocracy, who were, incidentally, inclined to be pro-Roman in the interests of their own position.[2] An attack on this business was tantamount to an attack on the property and authority of these magnates; it was, moreover, calculated to cause a fracas in which many of Jesus' supporters and others were likely to join, occasioning violence and pillage. To have initiated such action does not accord with a pacific attitude, and it is probable that the Jewish authorities, if they had not already done so, began to view Jesus with serious concern; and it would seem that the Romans also would not have remained ignorant of the incident, since the Roman garrison in the Antonia fortress overlooked the Temple courts.[3]

The dangerous aspects of this incident would naturally have been connected also, in the minds of the authorities, with the Messianic salutations with which Jesus had been greeted on his triumphal entry into Jerusalem, which, according to Mark, had occurred on the day before the Cleansing of the Temple.[4] But that is not all: the Markan record also shows that the popular support which Jesus had at this time was such that the Jewish authorities feared to arrest him

[1] Mark xi. 15–18.

[2] Cf. R. Eisler, ΙΗΣΟΥΣ ΒΑΣΙΛΕΥΣ ΟΥ ΒΛΣΙΛΕΥΣΑΣ (Heidelberg, 1929–30), II, 491–9; A. T. Olmstead, *Jesus: in the Light of History* (New York, 1942), pp. 91–3; J. Jeremias, *Jerusalem zur Zeit Jesu* (Göttingen, 1958), I. Teil, pp. 54–5.

[3] The Roman troops stationed in the Antonia quickly observed the assault on Paul in the Temple courts and intervened; Acts xxi. 31–3. On the position of the Antonia see Josephus, *War*, v. 238–46. Cf. E. Schürer, *Geschichte des jüdischen Volkes im Zeitalter Jesu Christi* (Leipzig, 1898–1901), I, 464–5. It is interesting to observe that Taylor, *St Mark*, p. 463, after describing the action of Jesus as 'a spirited protest against injustice and the abuse of the Temple system', asserts, without explanation, that 'His action was not revolutionary'. Cf. V. Eppstein, 'The Historicity of the Gospel Account of the Cleansing of the Temple', *Z.N.T.W.* 55 (1964), pp. 46–7; J. Klausner, *Jesus of Nazareth* (London, 1929), pp. 313–15.

[4] Mark xi. 11–15. The statement in *v.* 11 that, on the day of the triumphal entry, Jesus had gone into the Temple, and having 'looked round about on all things', left without comment or action, is curious. Was περι-βλεψάμενος πάντα an act of reconnoitring for action on the morrow? See below, p. 333, n. 3.

publicly.[1] And when they were given the opportunity of seizing him secretly, they sent a heavily armed party to do so.[2] Their anticipation of violence was justified; armed resistance was offered in Gethsemane.[3] To these significant indications concerning the last fateful days in Jerusalem there must be added also that of the fact that among the twelve disciples of Jesus was a member of the Zealots, the nationalist action party—a fact which Mark, incidentally, tries to conceal from his Roman readers.[4]

In the light of this evidence we may justly wonder, therefore, whether Mark's presentation of Jesus, as publicly endorsing the Roman rule in Judaea, is really consistent with the tradition of Jesus as the Messiah, on which he obviously draws in his Gospel. In other words, we must ask whether Jesus had not, after all, been regarded as the Messiah because his words and actions substantially conformed to current expectations. Such a possibility would certainly account more convincingly for his crucifixion by the Romans than the patently inadequate explanation provided by Mark. It would also mean that Mark had indeed a very strong reason for trying to explain away the significance of the Roman execution: thus again we are brought back to the problem which the Markan account constitutes in this connection.

If, then, we have reason for thinking that behind Mark's presentation there lies a somewhat different tradition of Jesus as the Messiah, we must seek to discern the original nature of this earlier tradition. To this end it is natural that we should ask whether there exists any information about Jesus, antedating this Markan portrait, which will enable us to distinguish between Mark's interpretation and the original tradition which he used. One obvious source at once suggests itself, namely, the Epistles of Paul; for these antedate the Markan Gospel by at least a decade, and probably more. But, as soon as we turn to these documents, we find that our problem grows immensely more difficult. Even making the fullest allowance for the fact that in these letters Paul was dealing with *ad hoc* problems, mostly of a pastoral nature, arising in the communities concerned, the whole atmosphere of the faith seems different therein from that

---

[1] Mark xi. 18. It is to be noted that the Jewish authorities are described here as fearing Jesus (ἐφοβοῦντο γὰρ αὐτόν), not the crowds who were impressed by his teaching. Cf. Bultmann, *Gesch. d. syn. Trad.* p. 66.

[2] Mark xiv. 10–11, 43.

[3] Mark xiv. 47–8. On this crucial episode see below, pp. 340–1.

[4] Mark iii. 18. This fact is discussed at length on pp. 243–5.

evident in Mark. By making a diligent search, scholars have assembled a number of allusions and reminiscences in Paul's Epistles of the Jesus portrayed in the Gospels;[1] but not only is the harvest a very meagre one, that the search has to be made at all witnesses to the fact that Paul's conception of Jesus was virtually independent of the career of that Jesus who lived in Palestine during the first three decades of the present era.[2] Thus, although Paul's writings contain abundant and essential reference to the crucifixion of Jesus, except for one doubtful instance,[3] no mention is made in them of the historical circumstances of the event. But the problem involved here is more than one of silence; for, in his most explicit statements about the Crucifixion, Paul attributes it to the daemonic powers that rule the lower universe.[4] This detachment of the Crucifixion from its historical context, and the endowing of it with a supernatural significance, is consistent with Paul's conception of Jesus. He clearly regarded the historical Jesus, the Christ *kata sarka* in his terminology, as the temporary incarnation of a pre-existent divine being, whom he variously calls 'the Lord of glory', 'the Lord', and 'the Son of God'.[5]

[1] Cf. H. J. Schoeps, *Paulus: die Theologie des Apostels im Lichte der jüdischen Religionsgeschichte* (Tübingen, 1959), pp. 48–51 (E.T. pp. 55–8); R. Bultmann, *Theology of New Testament* (London, 1959), I, 188–9; F. F. Bruce, 'Hebrews', *Peake's Commentary*[2], 812*f–g*.

[2] Cf. W. Schmithals, 'Paul und der historische Jesus', *Z.N.T.W.* 53 (1962), pp. 146–8; S. G. F. Brandon, *History, Time and Deity* (Manchester University Press, 1965), pp. 150–1, 159–71.

[3] I Thess. ii. 14–15. The reference is vague, the Jews only being mentioned as killing (ἀποκτεινάντων) Jesus. On its genuineness, which has been questioned, cf. J. Moffatt, *Introduction to the Literature of the New Testament* (Edinburgh, 1933), p. 73.

[4] I Cor. ii. 6–8; see also Col. ii. 14–15. The expression, in the Corinthian passage, 'rulers (*archontes*) of this age' does not mean the Roman and Jewish authorities who, according to the Gospels, were responsible for the crucifixion of Jesus. The expression denotes the daemonic powers who, in the contemporary astralism and Gnostic thought, were believed to inhabit the planets and so control the destinies of men and the world beneath them. Cf. M. Dibelius, 'Archonten', *R.A.C.* I, 631–3; H. Lietzmann, *An die Korinther, I–II* (Tübingen, 1923), pp. 11–13; A.-J. Festugière, *La Révélation d'Hermès Trismégiste* (Paris, 1950–4), I, 89–96; J. Seznec, *La survivance des dieux antiques* (London, 1940), pp. 35–46; Schoeps, *Paulus*, p. 9; R. Bultmann, *Urchristentum im Rahmen der antiken Religionen* (Zürich, 1949), pp. 211–12; Brandon, *Man and his Destiny in the Great Religions* (Manchester University Press, 1962), pp. 190–3, 213–16; *History, Time and Deity*, pp. 166–9.

[5] E.g. τὸν κύριον τῆς δόξης (I Cor. ii. 8); ὁ κύριος (Phil. ii. 11); υἱὸς θεοῦ (Rom. i. 4). There is much reason for concluding that the titles 'Kyrios'

His incarnation and crucifixion he sees as part of a divine plan to save mankind from enslavement to the daemonic powers who, he believed, controlled the world and the destinies of men.[1]

That so transcendental a conception of Jesus, integrated into an esoteric soteriology unparalleled in contemporary Jewish thought, should have developed within some two decades of his crucifixion by the Romans, constitutes one of the fundamental problems of the study of Christian Origins. Diverse though the numerous interpretations are, which modern scholars have advanced in explanation, on two points there has been general agreement, namely, that Paul's own personal genius played a formative part in the conception, and that the influence of his teaching profoundly affected subsequent Christian thought.[2] From the point of view of our own subject, however, it is important to notice two further things. Although he uses the word 'Christ' as if it were a personal name of Jesus, and one so well known as to need no explanation, Paul appears to be little concerned with Jesus as the Messiah of Israel.[3] This lack of concern can be readily understood, since his letters are addressed to Christian communities composed mainly of Gentiles, to whom the essentially

and 'the Son of God' for Jesus were already current in the Hellenistic Christian communities before Paul wrote: cf. Bultmann, *Theology of New Testament*, I, 124–33. It must not be forgotten, however, that Paul had already taught in these communities (except that at Rome) before writing his letters to them: the fact that he uses these titles in his letters as an established terminology does not mean that he may not have originally introduced and explained them to his converts.

[1] I Cor. ii. 6–9. Cf. Brandon, *Man and his Destiny*, pp. 213–16; *History, Time and Deity*, pp. 159–71. This appears to be Paul's most comprehensive soteriological scheme: the propitiatory soteriology, outlined in Rom. iii. 23–6, is left too vague in its terms of reference.

[2] This is attested by the very fact that Paul's writings occupy a far greater space in the New Testament canon than those attributed to any other Apostle. On Paul's influence on Mark cf. B. W. Bacon, *Jesus and Paul* (London, 1921), pp. 16, 143–54; J. Moffatt, *Intro. to N.T.* pp. 235–6; Taylor, *St Mark*, pp. 16–17, 125–9; Brandon, *Fall of Jerusalem*, pp. 200–1. An essential factor in the problem of Paul's influence on post-Apostolic Christianity was undoubtedly the delay of the *Parousia* and the consequent readjustment of belief which was thus necessitated. Cf. M. Werner, *Die Entstehung des christlichen Dogmas* (Bern and Tübingen, 1941), pp. 139–44 (E.T. pp. 52–5); Brandon, *History, Time and Deity*, pp. 183–8.

[3] The qualification which he adds (κατὰ σάρκα) when mentioning the Davidic descent of Jesus in Rom. i. 3 is significant. 'La foi en Jésus Messie a contraint Paul à dissocier l'œuvre messianique dont il avait hérité l'idée du judaïsme et à en réserver toute une partie pour le retour du Seigneur' (M. Goguel, *La naissance du Christianisme*, Paris, 1946, p. 254).

Jewish concept would have had little appeal. However, what is more significant is that already Jesus was being presented to the Gentiles primarily as a divine being, whose true role transcended the historical circumstances of his earthly life. This presentation seems also to have been recognised by Paul as designedly different from the traditional one current among the original Jewish disciples of Jesus. Thus we find him describing to the Galatian Christians the divine purpose, as he saw it, manifest in his own amazing conversion: 'it was the good pleasure of God...to reveal his Son in me, that I might preach him among the Gentiles.'[1] And he refers to himself as having been 'intrusted with the gospel of the uncircumcision, even as Peter with *the gospel* of the circumcision'.[2] It becomes intelligible, therefore, why the interpretation of the nature and work of Jesus which was presented to the Gentiles, should be one that did not attach essential importance to the historical circumstances of his life and death. How Mark later, writing for the Christians of Rome, came to present Jesus as a historical figure, set in a specific historical context, is a problem which we shall have to investigate together with

[1] Gal. i. 15 f. 'Seine Berufung zum Glauben fiel für ihn mit seiner Berufung zum Apostel zusammen, so wie diese für seine Bewußtsein sich mit seiner Sendung an die Heiden deckt' (H. Schlier, *Der Brief an die Galater*, Göttingen, 1962, p. 54).

[2] Gal. ii. 7. The logic of Paul's statement here has clearly been recognised by a number of scholars who have sought to reduce its seriousness for the traditional view of Christian Origins. As far back as 1865, J. B. Lightfoot explained that Paul's statement 'denotes a distinction of sphere and not a difference of type', and he quoted in support Tertullian, *Praescr. Haer.* 23: 'Inter se distributionem officii ordinaverunt, non separationem evangelii, nec ut *aliud* alter sed ut aliis alter praedicarent' (*Epistle to the Galatians*, p. 109). Schlier, *Der Brief an die Galater*, p. 76, however, cites the same passage of Tertullian in support of his view: 'Es ist das "Heiden-Evangelium" gemeint, aber nicht als ein inhaltlich besonderes Evangelium, sondern als das Evangelium, das unter ihnen verkündet wird.' Cf. F. F. Bruce, 'When is a Gospel not a Gospel?', *B.J.R.L.* 45 (1963), p. 330. But these interpretations overlook the evidence of Gal. ii. 2, where Paul states that he felt obliged to submit τὸ εὐαγγέλιον ὃ κηρύσσω ἐν τοῖς ἔθνεσι to the judgement of the 'pillar' apostles of Jerusalem. It is scarcely credible that Paul should have felt himself so obliged, if his 'gospel' was essentially the same as that of the Jerusalem Church. It must be noted, moreover, that the distinction between a 'gospel of the circumcision' and a 'gospel of the uncircumcision' was undoubtedly Paul's own. The Jerusalem Christians clearly recognised only one 'gospel', i.e. their own, which they did not hesitate to teach to Paul's own converts, as his Epistles abundantly show. Cf. Brandon, *Fall of Jerusalem*, pp. 60–1; 'Tübingen Vindicated?', *H.J.* LVIII (1960), 380–2; *Man and his Destiny*, pp. 195–7.

those others we have already encountered.[1] But we must remember that, despite his circumstantial portrait of the historical Jesus, Mark was also, like Paul, describing one whom he believed to be divine and whose life was given as a 'ransom for many'.[2]

We see, then, still more of the complexity of the main problem with which we are concerned. Seeking an earlier presentation than that of the Markan Gospel, we find that a conception of Jesus was already current in the Gentile churches which was essentially esoteric and virtually uninvolved with the historical circumstances of his crucifixion. But we are also acquainted thereby with a fact of very great significance: this interpretation was distinguished by Paul from that held by the Jewish Christians who formed the original community of believers in Jerusalem. Accordingly, another avenue of investigation appears to open to us. What Paul calls the 'gospel of the circumcision' would seem to offer a more primitive interpretation, unaffected by those concepts and that terminology which made his 'gospel' suitable for Gentile needs. And it would seem likely, too, that this Jerusalem tradition would be more concerned with Jesus as the Messiah of Israel, and so less embarrassed by the fact that the Romans had executed him as a rebel against their government.

When we inquire about this Jerusalem tradition, we find ourselves again frustrated; for it has not been preserved in any direct and certain form, and the reason for this only increases the complexity of the problem confronting us. The Christian church in Jerusalem disappeared completely after the destruction of the city by the Romans in A.D. 70. A later tradition claims that its members escaped *en masse*, before the catastrophe, and found shelter in Pella, a city of the Decapolis.[3] This tradition, when subjected to a critical analysis, appears to be a pious legend originated by a Christian community that later claimed to be descended from the original Mother Church of the faith.[4] But, whatever the origin of this tradition, what is certain beyond doubt is that the Church of Jerusalem did cease to exist as the recognised source and centre of Christianity after A.D. 70. This

---

[1] See chapter 3.
[2] Mark x. 45.
[3] The tradition, in variant forms, is given by Eusebius (*Ecclesiastical History*, III. v. 2–3) and Epiphanius (*adversus Haereses*, XXIX. 7, cf. XXX. 2. 2; *de Mensuris et Ponderibus*, xv). It is usually assumed that these later writers derived their information from the second-century Hegesippus; but this is far from certain. See next note.
[4] Cf. Brandon, *Fall of Jerusalem*, pp. 168–73, 176–7, 264: for further discussion see below, pp. 208–17.

is a fact of key importance; for before that date, as the Epistles of Paul and the Acts of the Apostles abundantly testify,[1] the authority of the Jerusalem Church was unchallenged in all matters of faith and discipline. If this Church had indeed migrated elsewhere before the Roman siege, it would surely have continued to enjoy its prestige among Christians; as did, for example, among the Jews, the rabbinical school founded by Rabbi Johanan ben Zakkai at Jamnia after his flight from the doomed metropolis.[2] Complete disappearance in such circumstances, therefore, constitutes a problem which may have some significant implications. Thus, for example, it may be asked: did the Jerusalem Church perish because its members chose to make common cause with their countrymen, in their last desperate stand against the avenging might of heathen Rome? The answer to that question, whatever it may be, is likely to shed much light upon the attitude of the Jewish Christians, and also Jesus himself, towards the national hope for liberation from the Roman yoke; but once more we have to do with an issue demanding long and involved investigation.[3]

Marking thus another problem for later study, as we chart the proportions of our subject, we may continue our present task by observing that not only did the Jerusalem Church disappear, but its records perished with it. No document survives that can be identified with certainty as originating, directly and unchanged, from that primitive community of disciples. This fact, however, does not mean that we are completely without evidence of what they believed and taught about Jesus. The author of the Markan Gospel clearly drew on traditions that must have derived from the original disciples and followers of Jesus, however he may have presented them for the end he had in view. The Matthaean and Lukan Gospels are also recognised as containing traditions, other than those used by Mark, which may well emanate from Christian communities in Palestine.[4] The

[1] E.g. Rom. xv. 31; I Cor. xvi. 1–3; Gal. i. 17–19, ii. 1–13; Acts viii. 14–17, xi. 20–3, 27, xii. 25, xv. 1–32, xviii. 22, xxi. 15–26.

[2] Cf. G. F. Moore, *Judaism* (Cambridge, Mass., 1927), I, 83–4; J. Derenbourg, *Essai sur l'histoire et la géographie de la Palestine* (Paris, 1857), pp. 282–3; W. D. Davies, *The Setting of the Sermon on the Mount* (Cambridge, 1964), pp. 256 ff.; A. A. T. Ehrhardt, *The Framework of the New Testament Stories* (Manchester University Press, 1961), pp. 112–16.

[3] See below, pp. 208–17.

[4] Cf. C. S. C. Williams in *Peake's Commentary*[2], 656 *b*, K. Stendahl, 'Matthew', *Peake's Commentary*[2], 673 *b*, G. W. H. Lampe, 'Luke', *Peake's Commentary*[2], 715 *c*.

fact that these Gospels follow the narrative framework of Mark means that they were probably influenced by his interpretation of Jesus. However, since they wrote some ten years or more later, it is possible that they were not under pressure from the same situation as that which produced the Markan Gospel. Two significant indications that this was so are afforded by the Gospel of Luke. Mark, as we have noted, disguised the fact from his Roman readers that a Zealot was included among the disciples of Jesus by describing him as a Cananaean;[1] the Lukan writer, however, states frankly that he was a Zealot—it would seem that, when he wrote, the term 'Zealot' no longer had the embarrassing connotation that it had for Mark.[2] Luke similarly records an incident that Mark might well have deemed it politic to suppress, namely, that Jesus took the precaution of seeing that his disciples were armed before going to Gethsemane.[3]

The Gospel of John, though not adhering to the Markan chronological framework and being much later in date, appears to know a tradition concerning Jesus that must be primitive and authentic.[4] According to this tradition, during his Galilaean ministry, the miracles of Jesus caused so great an impression on the people that there was a concerted movement to proclaim him king: 'Jesus therefore perceiving that they were about to come and take him by force, to make him king (ἵνα ποιήσωσιν αὐτὸν βασιλέα), withdrew again into the mountain alone.'[5] The account suggests that Jesus was the unwilling subject of the popular excitement which his display of supernatural power had occasioned, and that he eluded the intent of the crowd. It is, however, significant that this popular enthusiasm was so strong and that it took a political form. That this enthusiasm is not to be dismissed as a typical reaction of simple-minded folk, two subsequent passages in the Johannine Gospel prove by showing that this incident and others were deemed to be politically serious by the authorities, both Jewish and Roman. Thus the increasing concern of the Jewish leaders about Jesus is described: 'The chief priests therefore and the Pharisees gathered a council, and said, What do

[1] See p. 10. See also pp. 243–5.
[2] Luke vi. 15; Acts i. 13. See below, p. 316.
[3] Luke xxii. 35–8. Mark xiv. 47 discreetly refers to the armed action of an unidentified bystander (εἷς δέ τις τῶν παρεστηκότων). Cf. *Fall of Jerusalem*, pp. 102–3; below, pp. 306–7.
[4] Cf. C. H. Dodd, *The Fourth Gospel* (Cambridge, 1954), pp. 444–53; *Historical Tradition in the Fourth Gospel* (Cambridge, 1963), pp. 24, 97–8, 120; C. K. Barrett, 'John', *Peake's Commentary*[2], 737c. See below, pp. 318–20.
[5] John vi. 15.

we? for this man doeth many signs. If we let him thus alone, all men will believe on him: the Romans will come and take away both our place and our nation.'[1] It is to be noted that in this passage the Jewish authorities are represented as being disturbed only by the political danger that Jesus constituted; nothing is said of his teaching as undermining the spiritual authority of the priesthood or his claims as being a blasphemous offence to the principles of Judaism. This view is consistent also with the theme that runs throughout the trial of Jesus by Pilate, namely, of the kingship of Jesus.[2] Although this kingship is represented as of a supernatural character, the Jews insist on its seditious aspect: 'every one that maketh himself a king speaketh against Caesar'.[3]

The Johannine presentation of Jesus sharply defines a problem that is implicit in the accounts of the Synoptic Gospels. It is constituted by the fact that these documents agree in representing Jesus as insulated from the political unrest which was so profoundly agitating contemporary Jewish society. Such insulation would, in itself, be strange in one who doubtless claimed to be, and was certainly recognised as, the Messiah, since the hostility felt towards the Roman government was essentially inspired by religious principles. Palestine was the Holy Land of Yahweh's Chosen People, in which he had settled their ancestors after wonderfully delivering them from their bondage in Egypt. Yahweh was the true owner of the land, and the Temple at Jerusalem was his sacred place of residence on earth. The Jews, as his people, had to serve him alone with their lives and their goods. Hence the Roman government over Judaea was an abiding challenge to Yahweh's sovereignty, and the tribute exacted by that government was a constant affront to the most sacred obligation of Israel to its God.[4] That Jesus should have acted and taught in a way that caused

---

[1] John xi. 47–8.
[2] John xviii. 33–9, xix. 12, 14–15, 19–22. Cf. Dodd, *Historical Tradition*, pp. 112, 115.
[3] John xix. 12. Cf. Brandon, *Fall of Jerusalem*, pp. 124–5.
[4] Even though, in his account of the Tribute question (xii. 13–17), Mark represents the Pharisees and Herodians as setting a trap for Jesus, it is significant that he describes their question as one that might properly be asked of one who teaches 'the way of God'. And Josephus, despite his hatred of the Zealots, admits that their founder's refusal to pay tribute was based upon his acceptance of Yahweh's absolute sovereignty (*War*, ii. 118). Cf. S. G. F. Brandon, 'Recent Study of the Sources for the Life of Jesus', *The Modern Churchman*, n.s. ii (1958–9), 164–5; Hengel, *Die Zeloten*, pp. 84–5, 93–7, 102–3, 136–44. See pp. 47–9.

him to be recognised by many as the Messiah, and yet have remained free from involvement in so vital an issue, surely passes understanding.

John does indeed suggest, as we have seen, that Jesus had, on one occasion, to take energetic action to avoid the compromising enthusiasm of the crowds. But we may legitimately wonder how such evasive action could have been maintained. Jesus evidently continued to exercise a public ministry, which makes it difficult to see how his Messianic reputation could have survived his presumably constant frustration of popular hopes. On the other hand, according to the Johannine record itself, it was not just one isolated and abortive incident but a certain continuity of action which caused the Jewish authorities to regard Jesus as politically dangerous.[1]

This problematic Johannine evidence reinforces that of a similar import provided by the Markan and Lukan Gospels, which we have already noted. These documents, together with Matthew, thus reveal incidentally many facts which indicate that the conduct of Jesus may have afforded real cause for his followers' belief that he was the Messiah who would 'restore the kingdom to Israel',[2] and consequently caused him to be suspect to the authorities, both Jewish and Roman. Such a situation would indeed be more consistent with his ultimate crucifixion as a rebel against Rome than the inherently improbable Markan picture of the Roman execution of one who publicly endorsed the Roman rule.

But, if the conduct of Jesus had in fact so compromised him with the authorities, we are still faced with a problem. If we allow that Jesus might have been considered politically dangerous, and consequently executed, his case would have been similar to that of several other claimants to Messiahship during this period. Yet, whereas their deaths negated their Messianic claims and they were quickly forgotten,[3] the followers of Jesus continued to believe that he

---

[1] According to John xi. 47–8, the Jewish authorities were moved to plan the death of Jesus because he did 'many signs' (πολλὰ... σημεῖα), which were calculated to cause the masses (πάντες) to believe on him. The nature of these σημεῖα was such that it led the authorities to fear that 'the Romans will come and take away both our place and our nation'.

[2] Acts i. 6; cf. Luke xxiv. 21. See below, pp. 327 ff.

[3] Judas of Galilee, the founder of the Zealot movement, probably advanced Messianic claims, and it seems certain that Menahem, his son, did: cf. Hengel, *Die Zeloten*, pp. 298–9. It seems likely that the Theudas of Acts v.

was truly the Messiah. The traditional, and also the obvious, explanation for this remarkable difference is the Resurrection experiences of the disciples. Whatever the nature of those experiences, the disciples became convinced that Jesus had been raised from the dead and that they had made contact with him.[1] Now, since current Messianic belief did not envisage the death and resurrection of the Messiah,[2] the disciples had to readjust their ideas concerning Jesus to the new situation that confronted them. Before his crucifixion they had recognised him as the Messiah who would redeem Israel. Accordingly, there must have been that in his words and deeds which had persuaded them thus. His death at the hands of the Romans, however, was a shocking contradiction of their hopes.[3] If Jesus were the Messiah, he had died without accomplishing his mission. The conviction, stemming from their Resurrection experiences, that he was alive again, still left them with the problem of the unfulfilment of their expectations of him. The evidence of the

36, who claimed εἶναί τινα ἑαυτόν, was a Messianic pretender (cf. Josephus, *Ant.* xx. 97–9), as was also the Egyptian (Jew) mentioned by Josephus (*Ant.* xx. 169–72, *War*, II. 261–3), who, however, disappeared after the failure of his *coup*: cf. Acts xxi. 38. In the light of more recent studies, the commentators in *B.C.* IV, 276, do not seem justified in their categorical assertion: 'Until Bar Cochba there was no Messianic pretender.' Cf. Mowinckel, *He That Cometh*, pp. 284–5; Hengel, *Die Zeloten*, pp. 235–9. An exception to the statement in the text may perhaps be provided by the 'Teacher of Righteousness', whose memory was treasured by the Qumrân community. Whether he was regarded as the Messiah by his followers has not been established; however, he seems to have lived before the period concerned here: cf. A. Dupont-Sommer, *Les écrits esséniens découverts près de la Mer Morte* (Paris, 1959), pp. 369–79; M. Black, *The Scrolls and Christian Origins* (London–Edinburgh, 1961), pp. 160–3; H. H. Rowley, 'The Qumran Sect and Christian Origins', *B.J.R.L.* 44 (1961), pp. 124–9. See below, pp. 112–13.

[1] This fact was shrewdly appreciated by that uncompromising historian of Christian Origins, Ch. Guignebert, when he wrote: 'Si la foi en la Résurrection ne s'était pas établie et organisée, il n'y aurait pas eu de Christianisme' (*Jésus*, p. 662). Cf. Goguel, *La naissance du Christianisme*, pp. 41–104.

[2] Cf. J. Klausner, *From Jesus to Paul* (London, 1942), pp. 139–40; Moore, *Judaism*, I, 551–2; Ch. Guignebert, *Le monde juif vers le temps de Jésus* (Paris, 1935), pp. 191–8; Schürer, *G.J.V.* II, 553–6; J. Brierre-Narbonne, *Le Messie souffrant dans la littérature rabbinique* (Paris, 1940), pp. 1–2; Mowinckel, *He That Cometh*, pp. 327–30; W. Förster, *Palestinian Judaism in New Testament Times*, E.T. (Edinburgh, 1964), pp. 199–200.

[3] See the poignant statement put into the mouth of Cleopas: ἡμεῖς δὲ ἠλπίζομεν ὅτι αὐτός ἐστιν ὁ μέλλων λυτροῦσθαι τὸν Ἰσραήλ (Luke xxiv. 21).

New Testament documents shows that the readjustment of their faith took the form of a revised version of Jesus' Messianic role. That role was still to be achieved in terms of his restoring 'the kingdom to Israel'. The death, that had so unexpectedly interrupted that fulfilment, was explained in terms of Isaiah's Suffering Servant, so that Jesus was seen as a martyr for Israel at the hands of the heathen.[1] Hence, it would appear that the original Jewish disciples, after the crucifixion, came to acquire a twofold conception of their Risen Master. To them he remained essentially the Messiah of Israel, on whom the national hope was concentrated: he would shortly return, with supernatural power and glory, to redeem Israel from oppression and to give it sovereignty over the Gentiles.[2] As a martyr for Israel, he had suffered, as many Jewish patriots had done before him, witnessing to the wickedness of the heathen Romans and the faithlessness of those Jews who had rejected and betrayed him.[3]

Such an evaluation of Jesus was consistent with contemporary Jewish ideas and aspirations; it represents an intelligible reassessment of Jesus after the tragedy of his crucifixion and the Resurrection experiences of his disciples. But for us it still leaves unanswered the question of the personal involvement of Jesus in ideas and actions of such a character as to cause the Romans finally to execute him as a rebel against their government. That others so interpreted his words and deeds as to recognise him as the Messiah, as did his followers, or as a dangerous Messianic pretender, as did the Jewish and Roman authorities, does not necessarily tell us what were his own intentions. Apart from Mark's manifest desire to explain away the significance of the Roman execution, the tradition is curiously ambivalent about the attitude of Jesus to the use of force: his recorded sayings and actions signify variously both pacifism and violence.[4] That the true character and intention of a man of outstanding genius can be mistaken equally by followers and opponents is only too well attested

---

[1] See Mark x. 45; Luke xxiv. 25–7; Acts viii. 26–9. Cf. C. K. Barrett in *New Testament Essays*, pp. 1–18; Brandon, *Man and his Destiny*, pp. 201–4. See also below, pp. 177–82.

[2] Mark xiii. 24–7; Matt. xix. 28, xxiv. 30, xxv. 31; Acts i. 6. Cf. Meyer, *Ursprung*, III, 216–19; Brandon, *Fall of Jerusalem*, pp. 84–5; M. Simon, *Recherches d'histoire judéo-chrétienne* (Paris–La Haye, 1962), pp. 9–11.

[3] Cf. I Cor. xv. 3; Acts iii. 13–15, iv. 24–8, v. 29–31, xiii. 26–8. See also Matt. xxiii. 29–39, and Bultmann, *Gesch. d. syn. Trad.* p. 120, Ergänzungsheft, p. 16.

[4] E.g. Matt. v. 9, 39, xxvi. 52; Luke vi. 27–9; Matt. x. 34f., xxi. 12–13; Luke xii. 51f., xix. 45–6, xxii. 36; Mark xi. 15–16; John ii. 13–17.

in history: what was the real Akhenaten, or Zarathustra, or Mani, or even Paul?

This ambiguity of evaluation, which is to be discerned even in the brief survey of the evidence made here, indicates something of the complexity and intractability of the problem that confronts us under the title of 'Jesus and the Zealots'. But this aspect of the problem does not represent the only difficulty with which we shall be faced in our task; for we have to make an assessment not only of Jesus in the context concerned, but also of the Zealots in contemporary Jewish life and in relation to Jesus. The nature of the Zealot movement, its ideals and influence are not immediately apparent in the relevant sources; for, as we shall see, various forces operated to obscure the real situation.[1] However, the problems involved here concerning Zealotism are today essentially of an academic character; but the same cannot be said of those that attend the evaluation of the attitude of Jesus to contemporary Jewish politics, even when the historian seeks to undertake the task as a subject of academic study. Since the issue involved here is a very serious one, it will be well to consider it now at the outset of our investigation; a realistic appreciation here of certain preconceptions that have long affected an assessment of this aspect of Jesus may perhaps prevent misunderstanding later.

The issue is a very ancient one. We have already met what was probably the first expression of concern about it in the Markan Gospel. As we have noted, and must investigate at length later, Mark seeks to show that Jesus was not implicated in the Jewish nationalist cause against Rome. His exact reasons for trying to show this we have yet to determine; but here we must recall that Mark was not describing the career of a historical personage, but of one whom he regarded as the Son of God. After the Gospel of Mark was written, the status of Jesus was gradually exalted until it was defined in formal credal statements as being essentially that of God, incarnated in human form.[2] Moreover, since the purpose of that incarnation was to effect the salvation of mankind, the human career of Jesus was endowed with a unique transcendental significance. Accordingly, whatever may have been Mark's original motive in representing Jesus as uninvolved in Jewish aspirations for national

[1] See chapter 2.
[2] Cf. Werner, *Die Entstehung des christlichen Dogmas*, pp. 302–88 (E.T. pp. 120–61); J. N. D. Kelly, *Early Christian Creeds* (London, 1950), pp. 66–82.

freedom, theological considerations later made it unthinkable that one who was both God and Saviour of the world could have concerned himself with such mundane and questionable issues. Until the development of critical research into the New Testament writings during the last century, it is not surprising, therefore, that the attitude of Jesus to his people's subjugation to Rome was not a subject that occupied the attention of Christian scholars. So far as Jewish history during the New Testament period was known, that knowledge was derived from the writings of Josephus, who was concerned to represent the Jewish catastrophe of A.D. 70 as the outcome of Zealot activity which he condemned as brigandage and fanaticism.[1] Moreover, the anti-Semitism that permeated Christendom readily saw in the Roman destruction of Jerusalem the punishment of God upon those who slew His Son.[2]

It is significant that in what may be regarded as the first critical study of the life of Jesus the political aspect of his Messiahship was boldly asserted. In his *Von dem Zwecke Jesu und seiner Jünger*, Hermann Samuel Reimarus interpreted Jesus' preaching of the coming of the Kingdom of God as incitement to revolt against the government of Rome.[3] Since the publication of that work, the political factor has from time to time been emphasised in interpretations of the career of Jesus, the most notable instance being that of Robert Eisler in 1928–9.[4] Such interpretations have naturally been vigorously repudiated

---

[1] See chapter 2.

[2] It is, ironically, the most Jewish of the Gospels, namely, Matthew, that develops a philosophy of history designed to explain the Jewish catastrophe of A.D. 70 as divine punishment for the crucifixion. It unwittingly provided Christian anti-Semitism with its scriptural justification in the cry of the Jewish crowd, 'His blood be on us, and on our children' (xxvii. 25). Cf. Brandon, *The Fall of Jerusalem*, pp. 227–30, see also pp. 206–7; M. Simon, *Verus Israel* (Paris, 1948), pp. 245–63, 273–4.

[3] The most important parts of his work were first published, after his death, by Lessing in 1774. Cf. A. Schweitzer, *The Quest of the Historical Jesus* (London, 1910), pp. 14, 16–20; H. Hohlwein, 'Reimarus', *R.G.G.*[3], v, 937–8.

[4] ΙΗΣΟΥΣ ΒΑΣΙΛΕΥΣ ΟΥ ΒΑΣΙΛΕΥΣΑΣ (*Die messianische Unabhängigkeitsbewegung vom Auftreten Johannes des Täufers bis zum Untergang Jakobs des Gerechten. Nach der neuerschlossenen Eroberung von Jerusalem des Flavius Josephus und den christlichen Quellen*, 2 Bände. The abbreviated English version is entitled *The Messiah Jesus and John the Baptist* (*according to Flavius Josephus' recently discovered 'Capture of Jerusalem' and other Jewish and Christian sources*), ed. A. H. Krappe (London, 1931). The 'recently discovered' *Capture of Jerusalem* of Josephus was constituted by an Old Slavonic version which differs from the extant Greek text. For an account of Eisler's work and the

22

by orthodox Christian scholars as basically unsound and inspired by an animus against Christianity.[1] Some Christian scholars have indeed given serious attention to the more obvious indications of a political element in the trial and execution of Jesus;[2] but their approach to the issue has always been too clearly made from a firm conviction that the Divine Saviour could not have concerned himself with contemporary Jewish politics—if he did touch upon them, it was only by way of warning and to urge his hearers to seek spiritual values beyond them.[3]

controversy caused by it, cf. Brandon, *Fall of Jerusalem*, pp. 114–19, 122–3, 261. A French translation of the Slavonic Josephus appeared in 1934, 1938: *La Prise de Jérusalem de Josèphe le Juif* (Texte Vieux-Russe publié intégralement), ed. V. Istrin and A. Vaillant, trans. P. Pascal, 2 tomes (Paris). See below, pp. 364–8.

[1] An objective evaluation of the political factor in Christian Origins has indeed been bedevilled by hostility towards the Christian religion, e.g. K. Kautsky (*Foundations of Christianity*, London, E.T., 1925) represented Jesus as a rebel engaged in a first-century Marxian class-struggle. The comment of the Roman Catholic scholar G. Ricciotti (*Flavio Giuseppe*, Turin, 1937, I, 94) on Eisler's work is significant in this connection: 'Perchè, dunque, tanto chiasso attorno alla pubblicazione dell'Eisler? Certamente per ragioni non scientifiche ma di altro genere, e che quindi non ci riguardano più (ad esempio potrebbe darsi che, trattandosi di documenti russi, ne favorissero la diffusione le autorità dei Sovieti, supponiamo per mecenatismo nazionale, oppure per altre mire non speculative ma pragmatiche; ad ogni modo siamo sempre fuori del campo della pura scienza).'

[2] A notable example is O. Cullmann, *Der Staat im Neuen Testament* (1956), (E.T.) *The State in the New Testament* (London, 1957).

[3] A typical instance of this occurs in H. Conzelmann's article on Jesus Christ in the latest (3rd) edition of the great encyclopaedic *Die Religion in Geschichte und Gegenwart*, III (1959). Commenting upon the Tribute Money episode, he declares: 'Mann kann nicht den Gehorsam gegen den Kaiser und denjenigen gegen Gott miteinander verrechnen. Daß man dem Kaiser geben solle, was des Kaisers ist, und Gott, was Gottes ist, meint nicht eine Relativierung (etwa daß beide Ansprüche ein Stück weit gleichberechtigt seien): Jesus weist gerade auf die *Absolutheit* des Gehorsams gegen *Gott*. Weil man ihm unbedingt gehorchen muß, kann man seinen Namen nicht benützen, um ein weltliches, politisches Programm zu decken: man kann ihn nicht als gegebene Größe benützen, auch nicht zugunsten des "erwählten Volkes"' (640–1). C. J. Cadoux in *The Historic Mission of Jesus* (London, 1941) recognised that 'it is inherently probable that Jesus concerned himself with the political condition of Israel of his time' (p. 163). However, his evaluation of the issue is decisively affected by his confessionist approach; he also failed to appreciate the religious significance of Zealotism. See the catena of similar quotations in *Peake's Commentary*[2], 708 c.

Another factor also seems to have operated in this connection, at least in Britain. Josephus' evaluation of the Zealots as brigands and fanatics, who by political murder and sabotage pushed their nation into its fatal revolt against Rome, evoked a ready acceptance from people proudly conscious of their imperial mission of bringing well-ordered government and civilisation to non-European nations. Accordingly, to those troubled by revolutionaries, whether Russian, Irish or Indian, who threatened the stability of Western capitalist society or British rule, the character and activities of the Zealots in first-century Palestine seemed only too familiar. There was no disposition to consider their cause against imperial Rome sympathetically; and this attitude seems, in turn, to have produced an instinctive abhorrence for any suggestion that Jesus could have sympathised with such subversive elements in Judaea. The Second World War has, however, apparently wrought a change of sentiment: the admiration and encouragement given to 'resistance' groups in various Nazi-occupied lands seem to have stirred a new and sympathetic interest in the Zealots.[1] This change of attitude is beginning to show itself in New Testament study;[2] but with what result remains yet to be seen.

Despite a greater readiness now frankly to face the problems that inevitably result from regarding a historical person as the incarnation of God, there is still a curious reluctance even to consider the possibility that Jesus might have had political views.[3] Although the suggestion would be vigorously repudiated that Jesus was unpatriotic, the logic of what patriotism meant to a Jew living under Roman rule in Judaea is never faced out. Yet it has to be recognised that the

[1] Cf. W. R. Farmer, *Maccabees, Zealots and Josephus* (New York, 1957), pp. 24–44; C. Roth, 'The Zealots—a Jewish Religious Sect', *Judaism*, 8 (1959), pp. 33–40; Hengel, *Die Zeloten*, *passim*. Significant also is the universal interest awakened by the recent excavations of the Zealot fortress of Masada, which the state of Israel plans to restore as a Jewish national shrine (cf. *The Times*, 6 January 1965, p. 8). See also Y. Yadin, Preface (p. 3) to *Masada* by M. Livneh and Z. Meshel (Tel Aviv, 1966).

[2] See p. 23, n. 2 above. Cf. *Peake's Commentary*², 614*d*, 694*k*; R. H. Pfeiffer, *History of New Testament Times, with an Introduction to the Apocrypha* (New York, 1949), p. 36; Förster, *Palestinian Judaism in New Testament Times*, pp. 88–91, 107–8. See also W. R. Farmer's evaluation of Hengel's *Die Zeloten* in *N.T.S.* IX (1962–3), 395–9.

[3] See p. 23, n. 3 above. Cf. H. G. Wood, 'Interpreting This Time', *N.T.S.* II (1955–6), 262–6; W. Barclay, *Jesus as They Saw Him* (London, 1962), pp. 158–9; E. Stauffer, *Jesus and His Story* (London, 1960), p. 92; M. Simon, *Sectes juives au temps de Jésus* (Paris, 1960), p. 120.

Roman domination was imposed and maintained by force; it was, moreover, a heathen administration closely associated with the worship of false gods; and its officers were frequently unjust, corrupt and cruel.[1] To tolerate, still less endorse such a rule, could by no conceivable interpretation of the word be judged patriotic. A shrewd appreciation of what revolt would cost in bloodshed and material loss might, indeed, counsel a passive acceptance; but it would also mean the passive acceptance of injustice, and consequent national and religious degradation. Such a policy of acceptance was adopted by some Jews, of whom Josephus was a well-known example; but Josephus has generally been despised by Jew and Christian alike as unpatriotic and mean.[2] If Jesus had been regarded as the Messiah, indeed had himself claimed to be this long hoped-for deliverer of Israel, he could surely not have avoided pronouncing on the question of the legitimacy of the Roman rule over Israel. What his verdict would have been is surely obvious also.

If theological considerations make it necessary to prejudge the historical situation and to decide that Jesus could not have involved himself in a contemporary political issue, the judgement must accordingly be seen for what it is. In making it, the criteria are theological, not historical. Such an evaluation of Jesus may be deemed theologically necessary and sound; but it will surely concern another Jesus than he who lived in Judaea when Pontius Pilate was procurator, under whom he suffered crucifixion as a rebel against Rome.

[1] Cf. Schürer, *G.J.V.* I, 482–507, 564–85; A. Momigliano, 'Rebellion within the Empire', *C.A.H.* x, 849–55; Hengel, *Die Zeloten*, pp. 109–10, 222.

[2] The prayer, which Josephus describes himself as addressing to God, when he decided to surrender at Jotapata, is very eloquent in this context: 'I willingly surrender to the Romans and consent to live; but I take thee to witness that I go, not as a traitor (προδότης), but as thy minister' (*War*, III. 354). The reaction of his fellow Jews was very natural: they tried to kill him on this and other occasions. Cf. F. J. Foakes Jackson, *Josephus and the Jews* (London, 1935), pp. xii, xv–xvi, 33–4, 258; B. Niese, 'Josephus', *E.R.E.* VII, 570*b*, 571*b*, 575*b*; Brandon, 'Josephus: Renegade or Patriot?', *History Today*, VIII (1958), 830–6.

CHAPTER 2

THE ZEALOTS: THEIR ORIGIN
AND IDEALS

We have already remarked on the irony of the fact that the execution
of Jesus as a rebel against Rome is the most certain thing we know
about him. There is a strange irony also, as we shall see, in the fact
that his birth is made, in one Gospel, to coincide with the census
ordered by the Romans when, in the year A.D. 6, Judaea was for the
first time incorporated into their empire. For this census, required
for the assessment of tribute, brought home to the Jews, in a very
concrete manner, the humiliating fact of their subjection to a
foreign power; it was, moreover, the cause of the first act of rebellion
against their heathen masters and the founding of a party, the
Zealots, who were destined some sixty years later to lead their people
into the fatal war of independence against Rome.

The synchronising of the birth of Jesus with this census is made in
the Gospel of Luke.[1] It conflicts with the dating implied by the
Matthaean Gospel, and it raises other problems which New Testament scholars have long sought to resolve.[2] With such problems of
chronology we are not directly concerned here; it is enough for us to
note that the life of Jesus of Nazareth coincides with the first three of
the seven decades of Romano-Jewish relations which culminated in
the catastrophe of A.D. 70. In other words, his life was lived in a land
where a bitter hatred was felt between the rulers and the ruled;
where resentment steadily deepened and tension mounted as Jewish
intolerance reacted to Roman maladministration. The conflict,
moreover, was not limited to certain places or classes of society;
clashes occurred everywhere, and, since politics and religion were
essentially one for a people who deemed themselves a holy nation,
the issue concerned every Jew, and none who was loyal to his
ancestral faith could insulate himself from it. A careful evaluation of
this conflict, both in regard to its constitutive factors and its chrono-

---

[1] Luke ii. 1–6.
[2] Matt. ii. 1. Cf. E. Klostermann, *Das Matthäusevangelium* (Tübingen, 1927),
pp. 11–13, 18; F. Schmidtke, 'Chronologie', *R.A.C.* III, 49–50; F. X.
Steinmetzer, 'Census', *R.A.C.* II, 969–72; Lampe in *Peake's Commentary*[2],
720 a–c. See below, p. 29.

logical sequence, is, accordingly, a necessary preparation for an inquiry into Jesus' involvement in his people's cause against Rome.

If the tradition preserved in Matthew ii. 1–23 be sound, Jesus was born a few years before Herod the Great died in 4 B.C.[1] The death of this monarch marked the end of an epoch in Jewish history. Since 129 B.C., when under Maccabaean leadership the Seleucid rule had finally been thrown off, the Jews had enjoyed national independence. It is true that the intervening years had witnessed much bitter internal strife and foreign intervention, and Herod had been hated for his Idumaean descent, his cruelty and pagan tastes. But the Jews had not felt themselves a subject people, they were not compelled to pay tribute to a foreign government, nor did they experience the humiliation of seeing foreign troops garrisoning their land. They had much reason to hate Herod; but at least he had professed the Jewish faith, had generally respected their religious scruples, and had rebuilt their Temple on a most magnificent scale: moreover, his long reign had given them an unusual period of peace and economic prosperity.[2]

Herod's death not only marked the end of this state of affairs, but the events that immediately followed revealed to the percipient that the hated Idumaean had long shielded the Jews from the brute reality of Roman power. As a client prince, Herod could not dispose of his kingdom without the consent of the Roman emperor. He had nominated his son Archelaus to succeed him in the kingship; but Archelaus and other members of the Herodian family had to journey to Rome and wait for the imperial decision.[3] Meanwhile in Palestine the Jews were in open revolt. The motive of the rising is not made clear by Josephus, who is our informant of these events. According to him the trouble was started by the depredations of the imperial procurator Sabinus, who had moved in to secure Herod's very considerable property, presumably for the emperor.[4] At the festival of Pentecost that year, i.e. 4 B.C., an armed conflict broke out in

---

[1] Jos. *Ant.* XVII. 191; *War*, I. 665. Herod died shortly before the Passover in 4 B.C. (Jos. *Ant.* XVII. 213; *War*, II. 10), i.e. end of March to beginning of April. Cf. E. Schürer, *G.J.V.* I, 415, n. 167.

[2] Cf. A. Momigliano in *C.A.H.* x, 330–2; A. H. M. Jones, *The Herods of Judaea* (Oxford, 1938), pp. 152–4; S. G. F. Brandòn, 'Herod the Great', *History Today*, XII (1962), 240–1; F. C. Grant, *The Economic Background of the Gospels* (Oxford, 1926), pp. 36–46.

[3] Jos. *Ant.* XVII. 18, 219–27; *War*, I. 664, II. 1.

[4] Jos. *Ant.* XVII. 221–3; *War*, II. 16–18.

Jerusalem between the great crowd of Jewish pilgrims and the Roman forces under Sabinus. Some indication of the Jewish purpose is given by a message which, according to Josephus, the insurgents sent to the Roman procurator. They called upon Sabinus to withdraw: 'and not to stand in the way of men who after such a lapse of time were on the road to recovering their national independence (τὴν πάτριον αὐτονομίαν)'.[1] The implication of this statement is that the Jews were now seeking national independence, having lost it during the reign of Herod. This interpretation of Herod's rule very probably represented the Jewish mind at this juncture; but it is likely that 'national independence' denotes an ideal, stemming from a cherished tradition of the heroic days of David and the Maccabees. Moreover, since Josephus records the name of no leader of the Jewish insurgents on this occasion at Jerusalem, it would seem that the revolt was inspired by a commonly shared ideal, which must have derived from the national belief that Israel must be autonomous in order to serve Yahweh, its divine sovereign lord.[2]

Although the Jerusalem insurgents had no recognised leader, revolts broke out in other parts of the country under men whose names are recorded by Josephus. The most notable of these was one Judas, son of an Ezekias, whom Josephus describes as a 'brigand-chief' (archilēstēs) who had formerly operated in Galilee and had been suppressed by Herod, then a young man serving his father Antipater, the vizier of Hyrcanus, the last of the Hasmonaean rulers.[3] The fact that Herod had been summoned before the Sanhedrin, to answer for his having executed this 'brigand-chief' and his followers, suggests that this Ezekias had a greater significance for the Jews than Josephus' description of him indicates, and that they had mourned his death.[4] This suggestion is strengthened by the fact that some forty years later a son of the same Ezekias, namely, Judas, plays a leading role in the unrest that followed the death of Herod. According

---

[1] War, II. 53 (ἐλευθερίαν τὴν πάτριον, Ant. XVII. 267).

[2] Josephus (Ant. XVII. 304–14; War, II. 84–91) represents a Jewish delegation as begging Augustus to deliver their country from the evils of Herodian rule by joining it to the province of Syria. However, the logic of their religion could find fulfilment only in a theocracy. Cf. W. O. E. Oesterley, History of Israel (Oxford, 1932), II, 383–4; Hengel, Die Zeloten, pp. 330–1; Schürer, G.J.V. I, 453–4.

[3] Jos. Ant. XVII. 271–2; War, II. 56.

[4] Jos. Ant. XIV. 159; War, I. 204. Cf. Schürer, G.J.V. I, 348–9, 420–1; Jones, The Herods of Judaea, pp. 28–31; Klausner, Jesus of Nazareth, pp. 140–2; Hengel, Die Zeloten, pp. 319–22.

to Josephus, at the head of a powerful band of desperate men (ἀνδρῶν ἀπονενοημένων), Judas broke into the Herodian palace at Sepphoris in Galilee and seized the property and arms stored there. His exploits caused him to be greatly feared; he is also reported to have aspired to royalty (3ηλώσει βασιλείου τιμῆς)[1]—a rather surprising ambition, but, as we shall see, one having perhaps a peculiar significance.

These uprisings were finally suppressed by Varus, the governor of Syria, who, with two legions, came to the rescue of the Roman troops, hard pressed in Jerusalem. The punishment inflicted on the captured rebels was savage: two thousand of them were crucified.[2] If the Matthaean chronology is to be trusted, Jesus was a young child when all this happened, and was perhaps in Egypt. However, the memory of those two thousand crucifixions must often have been recalled with deep emotion by those among whom his boyhood was spent; doubtless also, when taken to Jerusalem, he saw the burnt-out porticoes of the Temple and heard of the Roman fury that had destroyed them.[3]

If Jesus had been born before the death of Herod in 4 B.C., he would certainly have been old enough to be aware of the events which convulsed Jewish life in A.D. 6. In that year Judaea and Samaria were placed under direct Roman rule. The emperor Augustus finally made this decision after Archelaus, whom he had appointed ethnarch of these territories in 4 B.C., had convinced him of his inability to rule efficiently.[4] And so, for the first time, the Judaean Jews found themselves, as a subject people, in immediate contact with Roman officials, appointed to govern their land in the interests of Rome and according to Roman ideas.

To implement the imperial decision, a census was necessary to assess the economic resources of the land and its people for the payment of tribute. Augustus ordered P. Sulpicius Quirinius, the legate of Syria, to which province Judaea and Samaria were now annexed, to undertake the task. To assist him, and to remain as governor of the new territories, Coponius was appointed as procurator (ἐπίτροπος), with full powers, including that of inflicting the penalty of death.[5] The reaction of the Jews to the census was immediately

---

[1] *Ant.* XVII. 272.
[2] Jos. *Ant.* XVII. 295; *War*, II. 75.
[3] Jos. *Ant.* XVII. 261–4; *War*, II. 49–50.
[4] Jos. *Ant.* XVII. 342–4, 355; *War*, II. 111, 117. Cf. Schürer, *G.J.V.* I, 450–4.
[5] Jos. *Ant.* XVII. 1–21; *War*, II. 117. In the *Ant.* the powers of Coponius as procurator are defined as ἡγησόμενος Ἰουδαίων τῇ ἐπὶ πᾶσιν ἐξουσίᾳ; in the *War* as μέχρι τοῦ κτείνειν λαβὼν παρὰ Καίσαρος ἐξουσίαν. Cf.

hostile; but, according to Josephus, they were dissuaded from active resistance by the high priest Joazar.[1] Josephus' account of the matter is, however, curiously inconsequential; for, after telling of the pacification of the people, he proceeds to relate how a certain Judas of Galilee, supported by a Pharisee named Saddok, caused a revolt.[2] But, instead of going on to describe what happened, he uses his account of the teaching and aims of these rebel leaders as a kind of text on which to discourse upon the evils of the movement which stemmed from these men, and which, according to him, led finally to the Jewish catastrophe of A.D. 70. Since Josephus is almost our sole informant of these events and their consequences, it is necessary to examine carefully both what he tells us about them and how he tells us of them.

Josephus describes the events of A.D. 6 in two works. The earlier account, which is the shorter, is contained in his *History of the Jewish War against the Romans*. This work was published between A.D. 75 and 79, under imperial patronage, to record the victories of the emperor Vespasian and his son Titus.[3] Since the real theme of this work is the war which started in A.D. 66, the antecedent period is dealt with in a summary fashion. The other account, in his *Antiquities of the Jews*, belongs to a work, published in A.D. 93-4, in which Josephus sought to explain the history and institutions of his people to Graeco-Roman society, which tended to view the Jews with dislike and mistrust.[4] This work is designed to cover Jewish history up to the outbreak of the war against Rome, and is, consequently, fuller for the period

Schürer, *G.J.V.* I, 455–6; Jones, *The Herods of Judaea*, p. 170, who thinks that the Jews probably regarded the equestrian rank of the procurator as a slight, and that the procurators lacked the assurance of a governor of patrician rank. On the title of procurator see below, p. 66, n. 4.

[1] Jos. *Ant.* XVII. 3.

[2] *Ant.* XVII. 4–6; cf. *War*, II. 118, which does not mention the intervention of Joazar.

[3] See Josephus' own account of his *War* in his *Life*, 361–7. Cf. H. St J. Thackeray, Loeb ed. of Josephus, *The Jewish War*, I, vii–xii; Niese in *E.R.E.* VII, 571a–572a; R. Eisler, ΙΗΣΟΥΣ ΒΑΣΙΛΕΥΣ ΟΥ ΒΑΣΙΛΕΥΣΑΣ, I, xl: Ricciotti, *Flavio Giuseppe*, I, 28, 30–1, 43–53. Josephus professed that he also wrote to provide the Jews 'beyond the Euphrates' with an accurate account of the cause and course of the war, in order to dissuade them from any hostile action against Rome (*War*, I. 2–6).

[4] *Ant.* I. 5–9, 14–17, XX. 259–68. Cf. St J. Thackeray, Loeb edition of Josephus, *Jewish Antiquities*, IV, vii–viii; Niese in *E.R.E.* VII, 572a–575b; Ricciotti, *Flavio Giuseppe*, I, 97–102; R. J. H. Shutt, *Studies in Josephus* (London, 1961), pp. 11–12, 120–1.

with which we are now concerned.[1] It has, however, a similar tendency to that which finds expression in the *Jewish War*, namely, to explain the disaster which befell Israel in A.D. 70 as due essentially to the pernicious activity of Sicarii, or Zealots, or 'brigands', as Josephus chooses variously to call these alleged culprits.[2] Since this interpretation of Josephus is of basic significance for our proper understanding of Jewish history during the lifetime of Jesus and the infancy of the Church, we must, as previously stated, examine his statements about the origin and aims of those so designated, in detail.

The relevant passage in the *Jewish War* reads: 'Under his [i.e. the procurator Coponius] administration, a Galilaean, named Judas, incited his countrymen to revolt, upbraiding them as cowards for consenting to pay tribute to Rome and tolerating mortal masters, after having God for their lord (καὶ μετὰ τὸν θεὸν οἴσουσι θνητοὺς δεσπότας).[3] This man was a sophist (σοφιστής) who founded a sect of his own (ἰδίας αἱρέσεως), having nothing in common with the others.'[4] The 'others', to whom reference is made here, as the immediate sequel shows, were the Pharisees, Sadducees, and the Essenes, whom Josephus describes as three forms of Jewish philosophy (παρὰ 'Ιουδαίοις ...φιλοσοφεῖται)—a designation undoubtedly intended for his Gentile readers.[5]

This short statement can be supplemented by two other incidental references which Josephus makes to this Judas elsewhere in the *Jewish War*. In recounting the events that marked the beginning of the revolt in A.D. 66, he tells of a certain Menahem, 'son of the Judas surnamed the Galilaean—that redoubtable doctor (σοφιστὴς δεινότατος) who in old days, under Quirinius, had upbraided the Jews for recognizing the Romans as masters when they already had

---

[1] The sources used by Josephus for the period with which we are concerned are obviously various. For the Herodian period, up to the beginning of the reign of Archelaus, he undoubtedly depended mainly on the writings of Nicolaus of Damascus. After that the situation is obscure: he probably had access to the records of Agrippa II; besides these he must have drawn upon both native and Roman material. Cf. Niese in *E.R.E.* VII, 574b–575a; Schürer, *G.J.V.* I, 53, 84–5; Ricciotti, *Flavio Giuseppe*, I, 150–1; F. J. Foakes Jackson, *Josephus and the Jews*, pp. 249–50, 255–6; Hengel, *Die Zeloten*, pp. 8, 12–16.

[2] *Ant.* XVIII. 6–10, 24–5.

[3] According to J. B. Fischer ('The term ΔΕΣΠΟΤΗΣ in Josephus', *J.Q.R.* XXXIX, 136), Josephus used δεσπότης for אדני, in the sense of the 'Master of the Universe'.

[4] *War*, II. 118 (trans. H. St J. Thackeray, Loeb ed. *Josephus*, II, 367, 369).

[5] *War*, II. 119. Cf. Ricciotti, *Flavio Giuseppe*, II, 240, note *in loc.*

God ('Ρωμαίοις ὑπετάσσοντο μετὰ τὸν θεόν) '.[1] In describing the last stand at Masada of the Sicarii, whose name we must consider later, Josephus records that their leader was Eleazar, 'a descendant of the Judas who, as we have previously stated, induced multitudes (οὐκ ὀλίγους) of the Jews to refuse to enrol themselves, when Quirinius was sent as censor to Judaea'.[2]

We see, then, that, writing for his imperial patrons shortly after the Jewish War, Josephus chose thus to represent the origin of that sect or party which he held to be chiefly responsible for the disaster that had befallen his nation and had caused so much suffering and trouble to the Romans. Of the founder of the movement he says nothing overtly hostile or condemnatory beyond describing him as δεινότατος, a term which can mean 'terrible', 'strange', 'powerful', or 'clever'. More remarkable perhaps is the fact that he twice calls Judas a σοφιστής, which may reasonably be translated as a learned man or teacher—such a designation, in the contemporary Jewish society, would surely mean one learned in the Torah and a skilled expounder of it.[3] Such a character would be in keeping with the principle upon which, according to Josephus, Judas based his exhortation to his countrymen not to pay the tribute. That principle was the absolute sovereignty of Yahweh, the god of Israel. To recognise the Roman lordship would accordingly be tantamount, for the Jews, to disloyalty to their divine lord. In other words, Judas obviously conceived of Israel as a theocracy, and he was prepared to face the practical consequences of that conception, namely, to refuse to recognise and support the alien power that had possessed itself of Judaea, the holy land of Yahweh.[4] Moreover, as a teacher of his people, he felt obliged to make clear to them the religious significance of their act, if they paid tribute to Rome, and to exhort them to resist the powerful foreigner who demanded it of them. Such a description of Judas and his teaching, brief though it is, is sufficient to show that the party or movement which he founded was essentially religious in inspiration and purpose.

Two other points must be noticed about these statements concern-

---

[1] War, II. 433 (trans. Thackeray, Josephus, II, 493).
[2] War, VII. 253 (trans. Thackeray, Josephus, VII, 577).
[3] Cf. G. R. Driver, The Judaean Scrolls (Oxford, 1965), pp. 251, 472–3; C. Roth, The Historical Background of the Dead Sea Scrolls (Oxford, 1958), pp. 7, 54, 60, 73; Hengel, pp. 90–1, 338–9 (on the possibility of Judas' being a בֶּן־תּוֹרָה according to Rabbinic tradition); see also Klausner, Jesus of Nazareth, p. 205; Eisler, ΙΗΣΟΥΣ ΒΑΣΙΛΕΥΣ, I, 53, II, 67; Ricciotti, Flavio Giuseppe, II, 201, n. on 648.   [4] See below, pp. 37, 48–50.

ing Judas in the *Jewish War*. Although he tells nothing of the outcome of the revolt, Josephus implies that Judas gained a large measure of popular support, which is further indicated by the fact that he looks back to Judas some seventy years later as a significant political figure.[1] In the three passages concerned here, it is to be noted that Judas is presented alone as the founder of a sect which had nothing in common with those already existent, namely, the Pharisees, the Sadducees and the Essenes. As we shall next see, this part of the presentation is contradicted by the later account given in the *Antiquities of the Jews*.

The much longer passage in the *Antiquities* is curiously constructed;[2] for, beginning as a record of the events of A.D. 6, it seems to slip unconsciously into a digression on what Josephus took to be the main cause of the disastrous revolt of the Jews against Rome. After this lengthy statement, Josephus seems to have forgotten that he has said nothing about the outcome of the movement initiated by Judas and Saddok; instead he passes on to describe what he calls the other three philosophical sects of the Jews. The significance of the passage will be best appreciated by first giving it *in extenso*, and then commenting upon it.

After telling how the high priest Joazar persuaded the Jews to submit quietly to the census, Josephus continues:

But a certain Judas the Gaulanite, of the city of Gamala,[3] assisted by (προσλαβόμενος) a Pharisee, Saddok, stirred up sedition. They maintained that this census would lead to nothing less than complete slavery, and they called upon the people to vindicate their liberty. They argued that, if they succeeded, they would enjoy the consequences of their good fortune, and, if they failed, they would at least have the honour and glory of having shown a greatness of spirit. Moreover, God would more surely assist them in their undertaking, if, inspired by such ideals, they spared no effort to realise them.[4] Since the people heard them gladly, their reckless enterprise made

---

[1] Thus, writing of Eleazar who commanded Masada during the siege in A.D. 73, he describes him as ἀπόγονος Ἰούδα τοῦ πείσαντος Ἰουδαίους οὐκ ὀλίγους, ὡς πρότερον δεδηλώκαμεν, μὴ ποιεῖσθαι τὰς ἀπογραφάς, ὅτε Κυρίνιος τιμητὴς εἰς τὴν Ἰουδαίαν ἐπέμφθη (*War*, VII. 253).

[2] *Ant.* XVIII. 1–10.

[3] Judas seems generally to have been known as 'the Galilaean' (Jos. *Ant.* XVIII. 23, XX. 202; *War*, II. 118, 433; cf. Acts v. 37). Hengel, *Die Zeloten*, p. 337, n. 3, suggests that Judas was brought up at Gamala, after the death of his father Ezekias, and later returned to Galilee. See the critical note *in loco* in B. Niese's edition of the text, IV, 140. Cf. L. H. Feldman in Loeb ed. of Josephus, IX, 5, n. *f*.

[4] μὴ ἐξαφίωνται πόνου (φόνου) τοῦ ἐπ' αὐτοῖς. See Feldman's note *b* in *Josephus*, IX, 7.

much progress, and there was no evil that did not stem from them and from which the people were afflicted beyond description: wars, from the unceasing violence of which none was spared; loss of friends who might have lightened our sufferings; large-scale brigandage (ληστηρίων τε μεγάλων ἐπιθέσεσιν); the murder of important persons—it was all done on the pretext of the common good; but, in reality, it was motivated by personal gain. Whence arose seditions and political assassinations, sometimes of fellow-countrymen, who fell victims to their internecine fury and fanatical resistance to their enemies, and sometimes of their enemies; famine almost beyond endurance; the taking and destruction of cities, until this revolt finally delivered even the Temple of God to the fire of the enemy. So vast a changing and overthrow of national institutions brought destruction on those they involved. For Judas and Saddok, by introducing and establishing among us a fourth philosophical sect (τετάρτην φιλοσοφίαν), and winning many adherents, immediately filled the land with troubles and planted the roots of the evils that flourished there later. Of this philosophy (φιλοσοφίας), which was unknown before then, I shall say little, chiefly because it has been the support given to it by the youth that has caused the ruin of our land.[1]

Josephus then proceeds to describe the other three philosophical sects of the Jews, namely, the Pharisees, the Sadducees, and the Essenes,[2] after which he returns to what he calls the fourth sect:

The fourth philosophical sect was founded by this Judas the Galilaean. Its sectaries associated themselves in general with the doctrine of the Pharisees; but they had an invincible love of liberty, for they held God to be their only lord and master. They showed an indifference towards the tortures of their parents and friends, in their resolve to call no man master (μηδένα ἄνθρωπον προσαγορεύειν δεσπότην). Since so many people have witnessed the unshakable fortitude, with which they have borne all these ills, I shall say nothing more of them; for I fear, not that what I have said on the subject will be doubted, but, on the contrary, that my words give too feeble an idea of the contempt with which they accepted and bore suffering. This madness began to grow serious among our people during the procuratorship of Gessius Florus, who by his excessive violence caused them to revolt against the Romans. Such, then, are the philosophical sects which exist among the Jews.[3]

In this section of the *Antiquities*, it certainly appears that Josephus was so concerned with what he held to be the pernicious influence of these sectaries in subsequent Jewish affairs that he not only forgets to say what happened to their founders, but he omits even to name the sect or movement itself. His identification of the activity of these sectaries as the chief cause of the Jewish revolt against Rome in A.D. 66 is, without doubt, a factor of key importance in evaluating

---

[1] The latter part of this sentence is difficult to construe: cf. Feldman, *Josephus*, IX, 9, n. *b*.
[2] *Ant.* XVIII. 11-22.   [3] *Ant.* XVIII. 23-5.

what he says about them, both here and elsewhere in his writings. Moreover, since Josephus is almost our sole informant on these sectaries, it is obvious that we must look very carefully at what he says and also at his reason for saying it.

As we have noted, Josephus wrote his first work, *The Jewish War*, to commemorate the victories of his imperial patrons, Vespasian and Titus, over his own nation. He found himself cast for this surely invidious task in consequence of the ambiguous role which he had played in the Jewish War against Rome. A young man of priestly descent and Pharisaic connections, he had been appointed in the year 66 by the insurgent leaders in some capacity to organise the defence of Galilee against the expected punitive action of the Romans. His conduct in this connection was suspect, as his later *apologiae* eloquently attest.[1] There he had clashed with those whom he calls 'brigands' (ληϲταί), but who were, as we shall see, Zealots or members of his so-called 'fourth philosophical sect'. These patriots evidently suspected him of half-heartedness, if not disloyalty, to the national cause—a suspicion which was notably confirmed when, after the siege of Jotapata, he went over to the Romans, having assumed the role of prophet to predict Vespasian's elevation to the emperorship.[2] Acting as a kind of adviser on Jewish affairs and liaison officer to Titus, the emperor's son, he witnessed the final agony of his people and the Roman destruction of Jerusalem and its Temple. His fortunes being now bound up with his imperial patrons, he lived in Rome as their protégé and the chronicler of their victories. Writing of his *Jewish War*, he proudly records that 'so anxious was the Emperor Titus that my volumes should be the sole authority from which the world should learn the facts, that he affixed his own signature to them and gave orders for their publication'.[3] However, Josephus was not wholly a renegade: a complex character, he still remained loyal to his ancestral faith and concerned with the good of his people. Probably the most charitable thing that can be said about him is also the truest. It is that he was too intelligent to be moved by the fanatical faith that swept his fellow-Jews into revolt against Rome. He had been to Rome, and he had

---

[1] Very significant in this connection is *War*, III. 432–42. The *Life* is largely concerned with defending his conduct in Galilee. Cf. Eisler, ΙΗΣΟΥΣ ΒΑΣΙΛΕΥΣ, I, xxxvii–xli; *The Messiah Jesus*, pp. 24–30; Ricciotti, *Flavio Giuseppe*, I, 21–2, 28–9, 37–9, 39–42.

[2] *War*, III. 392–408; cf. *Life*, 412.

[3] *Life*, 363 (trans. Thackeray, *Josephus*, I, 135); cf. *Against Apion*, I. 50.

shrewdly appraised Roman power. Even after the unexpected defeat of the Roman forces under Cestius Gallus in 66,[1] he knew that Rome would surely return with irresistible power and crush the puny nation that had dared to challenge its *imperium*.[2] The religious hopes of his people, as they found expression in Messianism, he was prepared to rationalise, actually seeing in the elevation of Vespasian to the imperial power while in Palestine, the fulfilment of the *Shiloh* prophecy of Gen. xlix. 10 concerning the coming of a world-ruler out of Judah.[3]

It is accordingly intelligible that, viewing the disasters that had befallen his people from his own peculiar point of view, Josephus had little sympathy for those whose teaching and actions had led the Jews into their fatal conflict with the invincible might of Rome. Moreover, in his writings, while primarily concerned to please his imperial patrons, Josephus was also desirous to excuse his people to his Gentile readers, whose natural antipathy to the Jews had been greatly increased by their ferocious conduct during the war. Accordingly, he seeks to depict his fellow-countrymen as the unfortunate dupes of evil-intentioned fanatics, who worked upon their religious feelings and so led them to their doom.[4]

Although his own experience of the Zealots caused him thus to hate them and to blame them for the ruin of Israel, Josephus seems, however, to have been uncomfortably aware of the uncompromising character and power of their religious faith. Very possibly his own cautious conception of religious commitment made him particularly sensitive about the example of those who sacrificed all for their faith. On analysis, his attitude is seen to be curiously ambivalent: the logic of events, as well as the needs of self-justification, caused him to regard the Zealots as dangerous fanatics and to denigrate them as 'brigands'; yet, as a Jew, he could not fail to appreciate that such men had given themselves wholeheartedly to preserve the sovereignty of Yahweh over Israel. Whereas he had shrewdly calculated the might of heathen Rome, they had trusted in the God of their fathers, who was also his God. Hence it would seem that, client of the Roman

---

[1] See below, pp. 135–8.

[2] The assessment of Roman power which he attributes to Agrippa II, in *War*, II. 361–4, undoubtedly represents Josephus' own view.

[3] *War*, VI. 313–15. Cf. Eisler, ΙΗΣΟΥΣ ΒΑΣΙΛΕΥΣ, I, 343, n. 8, II, 603–4; Ricciotti, *Flavio Giuseppe*, IV, 189, n. on 312–13; Schürer, *G.J.V.* I, 613, n. 41. See below, p. 59.

[4] E.g. *Ant.* XVIII. 6–10, 25, XX. 167–72, 256–7; *War*, I. 10–12, VII. 252–74; *Life*, 17 ff. See below, pp. 59, 140–1, 143–4.

Caesars though he was, Josephus could not wholly suppress recognition of the religious motives that had inspired Zealotism. It is fortunate that he acted so; for otherwise we should have been left without means of correcting the general picture that he gives of the Zealots, which in turn would mean that we could not truly understand the environment in which Christianity emerged and by which it was surely conditioned.

We have already commented upon certain aspects of what Josephus tells of Judas and his teaching in his *Jewish War*. We noticed in particular that he calls Judas a *sophist*, by which he evidently meant that he was a teacher, learned in the Torah, in other words, a rabbi. His denunciation of the payment of tribute undoubtedly indicates that he conceived of Israel as a theocracy, so that the recognition of any lord other than Yahweh was tantamount to *lèse-majesté*. This account differs, apart from its brevity, from that in the *Antiquities* in two important particulars. One we have already noticed, namely, the designation of Judas as a *sophist*. However, since the profession of Judas is not mentioned at all in the later work, the difference in this instance probably is not significant, and we have to be thankful that at least in one of his works Josephus gives us this important piece of information about Judas. The other difference is more serious. In the *Jewish War*, Judas appears as the sole founder of what Josephus calls the fourth philosophical sect of the Jews; moreover, he explicitly states that Judas founded his own sect (*idia hairesis*), which had nothing in common with those of the Pharisees, Sadducees, and Essenes.[1] The *Antiquities* account, however, associates a Pharisee, Saddok, with Judas in founding the new sect, and the views of the sectaries are said to agree in general with the doctrine of the Pharisees.[2] Why Josephus should have denied this

---

[1] *War*, II. 118: ἦν δ' οὗτος σοφιστὴς ἰδίας αἱρέσεως οὐδὲν τοῖς ἄλλοις προσεοικώς. Cf. C. Roth, 'The Zealots in the War of 66–73', *J.S.S.* IV (1959), 337.

[2] *Ant.* XVIII. 4, 9, 23: τῇ δὲ τετάρτῃ τῶν φιλοσοφιῶν ὁ Γαλιλαῖος Ἰούδας ἡγεμὼν κατέστη, τὰ μὲν λοιπὰ πάντα γνώμῃ τῶν Φαρισαίων ὁμολογούσῃ, δυσνίκητος δὲ τοῦ ἐλευθέρου ἔρως ἔστιν αὐτοῖς μόνον ἡγεμόνα καὶ δεσπότην τὸν θεὸν ὑπειληφόσιν (23). It would seem that the conjunctive particle δέ, following μέν in the preceding clause, implies a distinction, i.e. that the invincible love of freedom (of the Zealots), and their insistence on the absolute sovereignty of Yahweh, distinguished them from the Pharisees, with whose views they otherwise coincided. Whether Josephus actually intended to suggest that this distinction was absolute would seem doubtful; for it would logically imply that the Pharisees might compromise on the issue of monotheism. It would seem more likely

close connection between the Zealots and the Pharisees, or Pharisaic teaching, in his earlier work is not evident; but it might be reasonable to surmise that the difference was due to a change in Josephus' situation between the writing of the two accounts. The *Jewish War* was written shortly after the fall of Jerusalem and the Roman triumph, when the passions excited by the bitter conflict were still hot and strong. Josephus, himself a Pharisee, would then have had no inclination to record a Pharisaic association with those whom he blamed for his nation's ruin: it would clearly have been less painful, as well as less dangerous, to represent the Zealots as an unfortunate and disastrous aberration from the main traditions of Jewish thought and practice. When, many years later, he sought to present an impressive record of his people's history and institutions, Josephus could look a little more detachedly at the Zealots. Although he still hated them and held them responsible for Israel's sufferings, he no longer felt a need to suppress the Pharisaic connection, and his national pride caused him to commemorate the religious principles of compatriots who so heroically bore the terrible deaths which their fanaticism had brought upon them.[1]

But, even if he thus later admitted this connection with Pharisaism, Josephus still omits to give a name to the followers of Judas and Saddok in the *Antiquities*, as he had omitted to name those of Judas only in the *Jewish Wars*. This omission is very curious, especially when he goes on, in both works, to describe, as we have noted, the

that he meant that Zealot doctrine was more thoroughly theocratic than was that of the Pharisees. However, as Schürer (*G.J.V.* II, 395–6) shows, the logic of the *Erwählungsglaube* inevitably ranged the Pharisees with the Zealots. Cf. S. Angus, 'Zealots', *E.R.E.* XII, 853*b*–854*a*; R. Travers Herford, *The Pharisees* (Boston, 1924), pp. 51–2, 187–90; Förster, *Palestinian Judaism in New Testament Times*, pp. 87–90, 108 ('Zealotism was only a radical form of Pharisaism'); Guignebert, *Le monde juif vers le temps de Jésus*, pp. 217–19, 220–1; A. Stumpf, 'ζηλόω ζηλωτής', *Th.Wb.* II, 886–7; Hengel, *Die Zeloten*, pp. 89–91. Simon (*Les sectes juives au temps de Jésus*, p. 39) maintains that the association of Saddok with Judas had only an individual significance, thus implying that Pharisaism had no essential connection with Zealotism. However, he does describe the Zealots as 'l'aile marchante du pharisaïsme' (*ibid.*). Cf. C. Roth, *Historical Background of the Dead Sea Scrolls*, pp. 23–4, and 'The Pharisees in the Jewish Revolution of 66–73', *J.S.S.* VII (1962), 63–80; Driver, *Judaean Scrolls*, pp. 236, 242–3; B. Salomonsen, 'Some Remarks on the Zealots with Special Regard to the Term "Qannaim" in Rabbinic Literature', *N.T.S.* XII (1966), 166–9, 175.

[1] *Ant.* XVIII. 23–4. In *War*, VII. 417–19 he does pay tribute to the amazing fortitude with which the Sicarii faced torture in Egypt.

other three so-called philosophical sects of the Jews which he clearly distinguishes by name as Pharisees, Sadducees and Essenes. But even more curious is the fact that, in the only place in his works where he does, incidentally, name the followers of Judas, the name he uses is of Roman origin. Towards the end of his *Jewish War*, in describing Eleazar, the leader of the Sicarii, who made a last desperate stand at Masada against the Romans after the fall of Jerusalem, he writes:

He was a descendant of the Judas who, as we have previously stated, induced multitudes of Jews to refuse to enrol themselves, when Quirinius was sent as censor to Judaea. For in those days (τότε γάρ) the Sicarii clubbed together against those who consented to submit to Rome and in every way treated them as enemies, plundering their property, rounding up their cattle, and setting fire to their habitations; protesting that such persons were no other than aliens, who so ignobly sacrificed the hard-won liberty of the Jews and admitted their preference for the Roman yoke. Yet, after all, this was but a pretext, put forward by them as a cloak for their cruelty and avarice, as was made plain by their actions.[1]

In thus naming the followers of Judas as Sicarii, Josephus evidently overlooked the fact that he had earlier assigned the beginnings of the Sicarii to the procuratorship of Felix (A.D. 52–60).[2] In the passage concerned, he tells how a new kind of brigands (ἕτερον εἶδος λῃστῶν) had then sprung up in Jerusalem, who killed their victims in public by stabbing them with short daggers (μικρὰ ξιφίδια), which they concealed in their robes. Since the first to be killed in this way was the high priest Jonathan, these assassinations were clearly political, or more correctly, in this Jewish context, religio-political. The name 'Sicarii' (σικάριοι) was, without doubt, derived from the Latin *sicarius*, meaning one who murdered with a *sica* or dagger, presumably in a sudden clandestine manner.[3] In view of its Latin derivation, it would, accordingly, appear that the name *sicarii* was originally applied by the Romans as a descriptive term, deservedly opprobrious, to those nationalist extremists who then resorted to this method of getting rid of their enemies. That the name became widely used in Palestine as a general designation for members of the extreme action party among the Jews is indicated by

---

[1] *War*, VII. 254–6 (trans. Thackeray, *Josephus*, III, 577, 579).

[2] *War*, II. 254–7. In the parallel account of the murder of Jonathan in *Ant.* xx. 163–5, the 'brigands' (*lēstai*) are not named 'Sicarii'.

[3] Cf. Derenbourg, *Essai sur l'histoire et la géographie de la Palestine*, pp. 280, 475 ff.; Schürer, *G.J.V.* I, 574, n. 31; Hengel, *Die Zeloten*, pp. 47–51; Driver, *Judaean Scrolls*, pp. 183–7, 249. Wellhausen (*Israelitische und Jüdische Geschichte*, 8. Aufl., pp. 331–2) called the Sicarii the 'theokratische Aktionspartei' of the Revolt.

its use in the Acts of the Apostles xxi. 38, where the Roman commander of the Antonia garrison mistakes Paul for a certain Egyptian (Jew), probably a Messianic pretender, who had led four hundred Sicarii (ἄνδρες τῶν σικαρίων) out into the wilderness about this time.[1] The name (סִיקְרִים) also appears in rabbinic sources as a designation for the rebels at Jerusalem during the final siege.[2]

It is significant that in the passage which we have just been considering Josephus describes the Sicarii as being a new kind of brigand (ληστής); for, by his application of 'Sicarii' to the followers of Judas of Galilee, as we have noticed, it follows that he regarded the members of his so-called 'fourth philosophy' as brigands (λη[σ]ταί). The use of this opprobrious term is widespread throughout the writings of Josephus. It was evidently his favourite expression for all forms of violent activity against the established order of the land. However, there is much reason for thinking that Josephus designedly used this term in an indiscriminate manner to denigrate religio-political action of which he did not approve. Throughout this very disturbed period there was undoubtedly, in parts of Palestine, much brigandage that was the work of criminally intentioned desperadoes, and as such it was to be condemned by all responsible persons, both Jews and Romans. But it is evident, from Josephus' own record, that Judas and Saddok had inspired a resistance movement to the Roman occupation which found expression in acts of violence against both the Roman forces and those Jews who supported or cooperated with them. That movement, moreover, as he himself grudgingly admits, was religiously inspired, and its members were prepared to sacrifice themselves for their ideals with the most amazing courage. However, it was natural that those who were concerned with the maintenance of peace and orderly government should not appreciate an altruistic idealism, violent in action, that threatened their own security. As occupying powers, in more recent

---

[1] See below, pp. 110–11.

[2] E.g. Makshirin, i. 6 (H. Danby, *The Mishnah*, p. 759; cf. Derenbourg, *Essai sur l'histoire et la géographie de la Palestine*, pp. 279 f., n. 3). Hengel, pp. 51–2, 68–9, underlines the significance of the fact that, whereas in the second recension of the *Aboth of R. Nathan* it is stated that the Sicarii, before the siege, burnt the corn depots in Jerusalem (cf. Jos. *War*, v. 25; Tacitus, *Hist.* v. 12), in the first recension the Zealots (קנאים) are named as responsible. He also shows (pp. 52–3) that the סיקריקון of the rabbinic Sikarikon law (e.g. Gittin, 5.6) were not the Sicarii, but 'die Günstlinge Roms', who exploited the situation after the war of A.D. 66–70. Cf. Klausner, *Jesus of Nazareth*, pp. 204–5; Roth in *J.S.S.* iv (1959), 334–5.

times, have described resistance fighters among their subject populations as bandits or gangsters, so did the Romans undoubtedly denigrate those Jewish patriots who resisted them.[1] A similar attitude was likely also to have been taken by those Jews, mostly members of the sacerdotal aristocracy or related to the Herodian family, who felt that their own interests were bound up with the maintenance of Rome's rule, which recognised their privileged position and guaranteed its continuance.[2] That Josephus chose to describe the followers of Judas of Galilee as 'brigands' (λῃσταί) also significantly attests his point of view; but it does more, for, by using this opprobrious term, he was able generally to avoid the name by which these men called themselves and were known to the mass of their fellow-countrymen.

This name is 'Zealot' (Ζηλωτής). Josephus does use the name, but without explicitly connecting it with the followers of Judas and always to denote a most vicious group of Jewish rebels at Jerusalem, whose depredations before and during the siege of the city added terribly to the sufferings of the population. His first mention sets the tone of his evaluation of them. In describing how the high priest Ananus endeavoured, during the winter of A.D. 66–7, to reduce the war-fever at Jerusalem, probably with a view to coming to terms with the Romans, he tells of his efforts at 'bending the rebels (τοὺς στασιαστάς) and the madness of the so-called Zealots (τῶν κληθέντων ʒηλωτῶν) to a more salutary policy; but he succumbed to their violence'.[3] His next mention of them is similarly illuminating. Recounting their seizure of the Temple and the attempts of the party of Ananus to dislodge them, he comments upon their name 'Zealots': 'for so they called themselves, as though they were passionately concerned about the good and not excessively zealous (ʒηλώσαντες) for the vilest of deeds.'[4] In the last book of his *Jewish*

---

[1] Hengel, *Die Zeloten*, pp. 43, 323, thinks that Josephus probably took the term λῃσταί over from Nicolaus of Damascus, who used it for the rebels against Herod. He suggests that 'Sicarii' may have been used first by the Romans, when the repressive measures of Felix drove the Zealots underground (pp. 49, 76–7, 357). 'Sicarii', being originally a 'Schimpfwort', used by the Romans, was later adopted by them as a 'Ehrenname' (p. 51). Hengel (p. 36) gives good reason for dismissing the suggestion of K. H. Rengstorf ('λῃστής', *Th.Wb.* IV, 264 ff.; cf. 266, 33 f.) that the לִיסְטִים of Rabbinic literature derive from the λῃσταί of Josephus. Cf. Stumpf, *Th.Wb.* II, 887; Roth in *J.S.S.* IV, 333–7.

[2] On the social aspect of the Zealot movement see below, pp. 56, 132.

[3] *War*, II. 651.   [4] *War*, IV. 161.

War, in summing up the various rebel factions that brought ultimate ruin on Israel, he comes to the Zealots:

In this the so-called Zealots (τὸ τῶν ӡηλωτῶν κληθέντων γένος) excelled, a class which justified their name by their actions; for they copied every deed of ill, nor was there any previous villainy recorded in history that they failed zealously to emulate. And yet they took their title from their professed zeal for virtue (ἀπὸ τῶν ἐπ' ἀγαθῷ ӡηλουμένων), either in mockery of those they wronged, so brutal was their nature, or reckoning the greatest of evils good. Accordingly, these each found a fitting end, God awarding due retribution to them all.[1]

The bitter sarcasm evident in the qualification 'so-called Zealots', and the consequent attempt on each occasion of its use to controvert its meaning, are surely significant. They show how deeply the title 'Zealot' agitated Josephus, and how vehemently he sought to repudiate the implied claim to outstanding zeal for righteousness made by those who professed it. Such a reaction is readily understandable in one whose caution and dexterity caused him to be regarded as a renegade by his people, and whose very record of the Jewish War was made in the service, and to the greater glory, of the Roman victors who had crushed his people. This apparent embarrassment on the part of Josephus about the name 'Zealot', when taken together with other evidence, suggests that the name connoted a claim, and a claim, moreover, that was largely justified, which made the politic historian uncomfortable and desirous of controverting it.[2]

The other evidence comes from two sources. What is probably the earlier is of Christian origin, and is provided by the Gospel of Mark, which may reasonably be dated shortly after A.D. 70, as we shall see later.[3] It is found in the statement that one of the disciples of Jesus, namely, Simon, was called the 'Cananaean'.[4] This strange epithet, obviously of Aramaic origin, Mark, contrary to his custom with regard to Jewish words and customs, does not explain.[5] Fortunately the epithet is later interpreted by the Lukan writer, when recording the names of the disciples, as 'Simon, who was called

---

[1] *War*, VII. 268–70 (trans. Thackeray, *Josephus*, III, 581, 583).
[2] 'Dadurch, daß er [Josephus] die jüdischen Freiheitskämpfer vor und während des Krieges rundweg zu "Räubern" degradierte, konnte er die stolze Eigenbezeichnung "Eiferer" weitgehend vermeiden' (Hengel, *Die Zeloten*, p. 68).
[3] See below, pp. 222 ff.
[4] Mark iii. 18.
[5] Cf. Brandon, *Fall of Jerusalem*, pp. 105, 198–9. See below, pp. 243–5.

Zelotes' and 'Simon the Zealot'.[1] This evidence is definitive on two very important points. It attests both the fact that 'Zealot' had an accepted currency in the time of Jesus, and that 'Cananaean' was the original native name, of which *Zēlōtēs* was the recognised Greek alternative.[2]

The Rabbinic evidence provides an essential clue to the peculiar connotation of the name. A passage in the Tractate Sanhedrin, describing penalties for various offences, reads: 'If a man stole a sacred vessel or cursed by Kosem or made an Aramean woman his paramour, the zealots (קנאין(ה)) may fall upon him.'[3] The precedent for such zealous action against a Jew who had such a liaison with a non-Jewish woman, is, of course, the deed of Phinehas, as recorded in Num. xxv. 6–13. Phinehas is praised by Yahweh, 'in that he was zealous (בְּקַנְאוֹ) with my zeal (אֶת-קִנְאָתִי)'; and the covenant of a

---

[1] Luke vi. 15; Acts i. 13.

[2] The attempt of the editors of *B.C.* I, Appendix A (cf. F. Jackson, *Josephus and the Jews*, pp. 262–5), to prove that the use of 'Zealot' to describe a Jewish party began in A.D. 66, seems to have been inspired by their dislike of the idea that a disciple of Jesus was 'a Zealot, in the sense of belonging to the party of John of Gischala' (p. 425). Consequently, without appreciating the problem constituted by Josephus' ambiguous nomenclature for the Jewish resistance fighters, they base their thesis on the fact that Josephus first uses the word 'Zealot' as a party-name in describing the events of A.D. 66 (the first reference is *War*, II. 651, not IV. 161 (3. 9), as stated, *ibid.* p. 423). However, since the Gospel statement about Simon the Zealot proves that the designation was current in the time of Jesus, they are then reduced to trying to explain the fact away by assuming that ʒηλωτής, as used here, meant only that Simon was 'zealous', or that the Evangelists were mistaken in thinking that the term referred to the political party, of which they had heard, possibly from reading Josephus (*ibid.* p. 425). Cf. Brandon, *Fall of Jerusalem*, p. 105, n. 1; Rengstorf, *Th.Wb.* IV, 889; Hengel, *Die Zeloten*, pp. 72–3, 77; Roth in *J.S.S.* IV (1959), 335, n. 2, 336–7, 343, n. 2; Driver, *Judaean Scrolls*, p. 245.

[3] Sanh. 9. 6, in Danby, *Mishnah*, p. 396; cf. Hengel, *Die Zeloten*, p. 69; Klausner, *Jesus of Nazareth*, pp. 202–3, 204–5; S.B. *Kommentar*, I, 537. Salomonsen is logically justified in his statement (*N.T.S.* XII (1966), 175) that 'qannaim cannot always be regarded as the rabbinic equivalent of the Greek ʒηλωταί'. However, the evidence of Mark iii. 18 is surely decisive for the currency of קנאה as a technical term, signifying a member of the Zealot party, and not just a particularly zealous person. If ὁ Καναναῖος had merely described Simon's nature, Mark would doubtless have given some indication how this disciple was so distinguished for his zeal, and for what he was thus zealous. That, contrary to his custom, he leaves this one Aramaic term unexplained can only mean that its Greek equivalent was ὁ Ζηλωτής, and that to his readers it would mean a member of the Zealot party. See pp. 243–5.

perpetual priesthood is given to him and his posterity, 'because he was zealous for his God (קִנֵּא לֵאלֹהָיו), and made atonement for the people of Israel'.[1]

The evidence of the statement cited from the Tractate Sanhedrin, when seen in connection with its obvious reference to Phinehas, is of the highest significance. It means that those known as the *Ḳannā'im* or *Ζēlōtai* were commonly recognised as men who vigorously punished infringements of the Torah committed by their fellow-Jews, following the scriptural example of Phinehas. In this sense, Phinehas was the traditional prototype of the Zealot; the ascription of this role to him is indeed attested by the Fourth Book of the Maccabees, which probably dates from the first century A.D.[2] A mother of seven Jewish heroes is described as telling her sons how she had been instructed by her father in the glorious traditions of Israel: 'he was accustomed to speak to us of the Zealot Phinehas (ἔλεγεν δὲ τὸν ζηλωτὴν Φίνεες).'[3] But this was not the only example that Phinehas provided. In Num. xxxi. 1 ff., Phinehas appears as the leader specially commissioned to lead Israel in a holy war of revenge against the Midianites: 'And Moses sent them, a thousand of every tribe, to the war, them and Phinehas the son of Eleazar the priest, with the vessels of the sanctuary and the trumpets for the alarm in his hand. And they warred against Midian, as the Lord commanded Moses; and they slew every male.'[4]

Phinehas was, accordingly, the Zealot prototype—the man, 'zealous for his God', who devoted himself wholeheartedly, in rigorous action, both to ensuring his countrymen's complete loyalty

[1] ἀνθ' ὧν ἐζήλωσε τῷ θεῷ αὐτοῦ (LXX). It is perhaps significant that, whereas in the LXX version of the passage ζῆλος and ζηλόω are each used twice, in Josephus' account of the incident (*Ant.* IV. 152–4) neither word appears. When he tells how the example of Phinehas inspired young men, he refers to 'the daring of Phinehas (τῆς Φινεέσσου τόλμης)'. Cf. Hengel, *Die Zeloten*, pp. 160, 166; Roth in *J.S.S.* IV (1959), 336, who cites Midrash Rabbah, Num. xx. 26, telling how Phinehas disguised his intention by hiding the blade of his spear in his garment; cf. *J.J.S.* XI (1960), 175; cf. A. Stumpf in *Th.Wb.* II, 886, 887.

[2] Cf. Schürer, *G.J.V.* III, 393–5; Pfeiffer, *History of New Testament Times*, pp. 215–21.

[3] IV Macc. xviii. 12, in *Apok. u. Pseudepig.* (ed. E. Kautzsch), II, 176. Cf. Hengel, *Die Zeloten*, pp. 164–5.

[4] Num. xxxi. 6–7. Cf. Meyer, *Ursprung u. Anfänge des Christentums*, II, 404; Farmer, *Maccabees, Zealots and Josephus*, pp. 177–80, 183; Hengel, *Die Zeloten*, pp. 165–7; Roth in *J.J.S.* XI (1960), 175; Stumpf, *Th.Wb.* II, 886, 887; Driver, *Judaean Scrolls*, p. 245.

to God's Law and to vindicating Israel by war against the heathen oppressor. Nor was this all: for there is evidence that in certain Jewish circles during this period Phinehas was identified or equated with Elijah.[1] This connection was of considerable consequence, as we shall see, because Phinehas acquired thereby the Messianic or eschatological significance accorded to Elijah in Mal. iv. 5.[2]

Some further evidence, of a curious kind, concerning the beliefs of the Zealots is given by the second-century Christian writer Hippolytus in his *Refutatio omnium haeresium*. Towards the end of an account of the Essenes, which parallels that of Josephus, Hippolytus suddenly enters into a description of certain sectaries, whom he regards as Essenes but designates Zealots or Sicarii:

In the course of time they [the Essenes] have split into four parties, of which each have their own peculiar way of life. The members of one of these parties lay such emphasis upon the precepts that they will never touch a coin on the ground that one should neither carry, nor look upon, nor make an image (ὡς μηδὲ νόμισμα βαστάζειν, λέγοντες μὴ δεῖν εἰκόνα ἢ φέρειν ἢ ὁρᾶν ἢ ποιεῖν). They enter no town, to avoid passing through a gate on which there are statues (ἀνδριάντες); for they hold it to be wrong to pass under statues. Members of the second party, if they hear some man discussing God and His Law, who is uncircumcised, they lie in wait for him, and, when they catch him alone, they threaten him with death, if he will not allow himself to be circumcised; should the man refuse, without compunction, he is killed. For this reason they have acquired the name of 'Zealots'; some call them Sicarii. Adherents of one of the other parties will name no one lord, except

---

[1] The earliest evidence is provided by the so-called *Biblical Antiquities of Philo*, XLVIII. 1: 'Et in tempore eo Finees reclinavit se ut moreretur, et dixit ad eum Dominus...Et nunc exurge et vade hinc, et habita in Danaben, in monte, et inhabita ibi annis pluribus...et non descendes ad homines, iam quousque perveniat tempus', ed. G. Kisch, *Pseudo-Philo's Liber Antiquitatum Biblicarum*, p. 239; cf. M. R. James, *Biblical Antiquities of Philo*, p. 210 and note. The work dates from about A.D. 100, but incorporates earlier material. Cf. James, pp. 29–33; Kisch, pp. 15–18; Hengel, *Die Zeloten*, pp. 167–75; Eisler, ΙΗΣΟΥΣ ΒΑΣΙΛΕΥΣ, II, 83, n. 1, 159, n. 4, *Messiah Jesus*, pp. 310–11.

[2] 'Als zweite große Eifergestalt des Alten Testaments mußte auch Elia für die Zeloten bedeutsam werden. Jene eigenartige Identifizierung von Pinehas und Elia, die wohl im Laufe des 1. Jh. n. Chr. zustande kam, kann am ehesten zelotischen Kreisen zugeschrieben werden, da bei ihnen das größte Interesse an einer solchen Verbindung vorausgesetzt werden darf. Dadurch würde auch die Zurückhaltung der offiziellen rabbinischen Überlieferung gegenüber dieser Tradition und ihre Verbreitung in der volkstümlichen Haggada verständlich' (Hengel, *Die Zeloten*, pp. 180–1). Cf. R. T. Herford, 'The Effect of the Fall of Jerusalem upon the Character of the Pharisees', *Society of Hebraic Studies* (1917).

JESUS AND THE ZEALOTS

God, even if they are tortured or killed.[1] So much have the latter departed from the strict life, that those who have remained loyal to the original customs will have no contact with them; and, should they contact them, they wash themselves immediately, as though they had touched a stranger.[2]

Although it is patent that Hippolytus has here confused the Zealots with the four Essene sects described by Josephus,[3] what he says about Zealot action in connection with the uncircumcised is consistent with their rigorous action, following the example of Phinehas, against transgressions of the Torah—such action is not recorded by Josephus.[4] The objection of the sectaries to image-bearing coins would well reflect Zealot scruples, and is strongly reminiscent of the Tribute Money episode in the Markan Gospel, particularly in the matter of the image and superscription of Caesar which the coin bore.[5] It would, accordingly, seem probable that Hippolytus has here preserved a genuine tradition concerning the Zealots, howbeit with some confusion; and it is notable, moreover, that this tradition stresses the religious motivation of such Zealot action.[6]

In the light of this evidence, various and fragmentary though it is, the reason for Josephus' apparent embarrassment over the name 'Zealot' becomes clear. The name was an honourable one, proudly assumed by those who, following the example of Phinehas, uncompromisingly sought to maintain Israel's absolute conformity to the Torah and its complete loyalty to Yahweh as its sovereign lord. To secure these ideals, they were prepared to resort to violent action against both the Romans, who occupied their land, and those of their countrymen whose acceptance of Roman rule was particularly

---

[1] ἕτεροι δὲ αὐτῶν οὐδένα κύριον ὀνομάζουσι πλὴν τὸν θεόν, εἰ καὶ αἰκίζοιτό τις ἢ καὶ ἀναιροῖτο.

[2] *Refut. omn. haer.* ix. 26 (ed. L. Dunker and F. G. Schneidewin, p. 482). Cf. Hengel, *Die Zeloten*, p. 73; M. Black, *The Scrolls and Christian Origins*, p. 189; F. F. Bruce, *Second Thoughts on the Dead Sea Scrolls* (London, 1956), p. 117; A. Hilgenfeld, *Die Ketzergeschichte des Urchristentums*, pp. 133-6.

[3] *War*, ii. 119-61; cf. *Ant.* xviii. 18-22. Cf. A. Dupont-Sommer, *Les écrits esséniens découverts près de la Mer Morte*, pp. 37-46.

[4] Cf. Hengel, *Die Zeloten*, p. 75.

[5] Mark xii. 16: καὶ λέγει αὐτοῖς· τίνος ἡ εἰκὼν αὕτη καὶ ἡ ἐπιγραφή; see below, pp. 271, 345-9.

[6] Cf. Eisler, ΙΗΣΟΥΣ ΒΑΣΙΛΕΥΣ, ii, 196-7; Ricciotti, *Flavio Giuseppe*, i, 65, n. 3, ii, 240, n. on 119; Hengel, *Die Zeloten*, pp. 73-5. Hengel draws attention (p. 75) to the significance of the statement: ζηλωταὶ καλούμενοι ὑπό τινων δὲ σικάριοι, commenting: 'Wie teilweise in der rabbinischen Überlieferung beziehen sich beide Bezeichnungen — im Gegensatz zum Sprachgebrauch des Josephus — auf eine und dieselbe Partei.'

notable. Such patriots, with whom he had himself become embroiled, Josephus preferred to call 'bandits' or Sicarii, opprobrious terms borrowed from the Roman authorities who naturally regarded them as subversive elements criminally intent on overthrowing their government. Consequently, although he was aware of the religious character of Zealot aims, Josephus sought to denigrate them. In writing of recent Jewish affairs for his Roman readers, it was obviously more politic for him to represent the Zealots as criminals, who misled the Jewish people into making their fatal challenge to Roman power, than as patriots who sacrificed themselves for their ideal of Israel as a theocracy under Yahweh.

From this involved inquiry the proportions of the problem of evaluating Jewish affairs during the crucial period A.D. 6–70 become clearer. The problem has been fundamentally bedevilled by the tortuous apologetic of Josephus—and also, as we shall see, by the almost complete silence of the original Christian sources about Zealotism as an environmental factor of the life of Jesus and the beginnings of the Church. But we have already learned enough to perceive that the movement founded by Judas of Galilee and the Pharisee Saddok in A.D. 6 powerfully affected Jewish life during this period.

Although the census, ordered by Augustus in A.D. 6, was the immediate cause of the founding of the Zealot movement, it would appear that in certain Jewish circles the ideas that inspired it were already existent. Thus, shortly before the death of Herod the Great in 4 B.C., two Pharisees, Judas and Matthias, had incited the people to destroy the figure of a large golden eagle which the king had erected over the main gate of the Temple, in defiance of the Torah injunction against images. Captured and brought before Herod, they boldly declared: 'It is not at all surprising, if we believe that it is less important to observe your decrees than the laws that Moses wrote as God prompted and taught him, and left behind.' They were burnt alive.[1] We have already noted how the insurgents, during the disturbances in Jerusalem at Pentecost in 4 B.C., had called upon Sabinus, the Roman procurator, to withdraw his forces and not oppose men seeking to establish national independence.[2] The death

[1] *Ant.* XVII. 159 (cf. *War*, I. 647–55). Josephus calls these two Pharisees σοφισταί. According to the Slavonic version of Josephus' *War*, Herod had erected the golden eagle in honour of the emperor: cf. *La Prise de Jérusalem* (ed. V. Istrin), I, 117; Thackeray, *Josephus*, III, 642–3. On the significance of the Slavonic version see below, pp. 364–8. Cf. Jones, *Herods of Judaea*, pp. 148–50.   [2] See above, pp. 27–8.

of Herod had clearly occasioned what appears to be a new demand. Josephus does not explain what was then meant by national independence; but, since the insurgents did not want to be ruled either by a Herodian prince or by the Romans, and they had no candidate of their own for the sovereignty, it would seem that the demand was for the establishment of a theocracy. Such an ideal logically stemmed from the conception of the absolute sovereignty of Yahweh over his holy people, Israel. It was the theme of the traditional *Heilsgeschichte*, upon which all Jews were nurtured, and the longing for its realisation found passionate expression in an apocalyptic literature.[1] The implied rejection of a human king, even though a native, probably resulted from experience of Herod's long reign: his death now seemed to afford the chance of dispensing entirely with human monarchs— Yahweh was Israel's only king, with perhaps a godly high priest as his vicegerent on earth.[2]

The theocratic ideal, which seems to have been implied in the demands of the Jerusalem insurgents in 4 B.C., was clearly formulated in the exhortations of Judas and Saddok in A.D. 6.[3] It involved two essentially related principles, namely, recognition of the absolute sovereignty of Yahweh over Israel and the freedom of Israel. The latter did, in fact, constitute the necessary condition for the effective recognition of the divine lordship. And it necessarily followed that, if Israel were not free, then it had to be delivered from its state of subjection and servitude to whatever power had imposed its dominion. In other words, the Zealot ideal of Yahweh's sovereignty inevitably involved resistance, as a religious duty, to the Roman government which treated Judaea as a possession of the emperor and the state of Rome. Hence the census and the tribute were seen as tokens of an

[1] Cf. Schürer, *G.J.V.* II, 538–44; Klausner, *Jesus of Nazareth*, pp. 135–7, 167–73; Guignebert, *Le monde juif*, pp. 168–80; Hengel, *Die Zeloten*, pp. 312–15; Brandon, *History, Time and Deity*, ch. v.

[2] It is indeed ironical that what is probably the earliest and most concise definition of Israel as a theocracy, with the high priest as vicegerent, is given by Josephus (*Against Apion*, II. 185): καὶ τίς [polity] ἂν καλλίων ἢ δικαιοτέρα γένοιτο τῆς θεὸν μὲν ἡγεμόνα τῶν ὅλων πεποιημένης, τοῖς ἱερεῦσι δὲ κοινῇ μὲν τὰ μέγιστα διοικεῖν ἐπιτρεπούσης, τῷ δὲ πάντων ἀρχιερεῖ πάλιν αὖ πεπιστευκυίας τὴν τῶν ἄλλων ἱερέων ἡγεμονίαν; Josephus also seems to have been the first to use the term 'theocracy': ὡς δ' ἄν τις εἴποι βιασά-μενος τὸν λόγον, θεοκρατίαν ἀπέδειξε τὸ πολίτευμα, θεῷ τὴν ἀρχὴν καὶ τὸ κράτος ἀναθείς (*ibid.* 166). On the high priesthood at this period, cf. J. Jeremias, *Jerusalem zur Zeit Jesu*, II, 3–17; C. Roth, 'The Constitution of the Jewish Republic of 66–70', *J.S.S.* IX (1964), 297–301.

[3] *Ant.* XVIII. 4–5, 23; *War*, II. 118. Cf. Hengel, *Die Zeloten*, pp. 94–5, 102–3.

impious slavery, which it was the sacred duty of every loyal Jew to resist.[1] Although, according to Josephus, the high priest Joazar persuaded the people to submit to the census in A.D. 6, there is convincing evidence that the payment of tribute continued to be bitterly resented and was the focus of political discontent. Thus the test question put to a Messianic claimant, as the Gospel record shows, was: 'Is it lawful to give tribute to Caesar, or not? Should we give, or should we not?'[2] Tax collectors (τελῶναι) were equated with heathens (ἐθνικοί) and sinners (ἁμαρτωλοί).[3] The dialogue attributed to Jesus and Peter in Matt. xvii. 25–6 is also significant in this connection, although it is related here to the payment of the Temple tax: 'What thinkest thou, Simon? the kings of the earth, from whom do they receive toll or tribute? from their sons, or from strangers (ἀλλοτρίων)? And when he said, From strangers, Jesus said unto him, Therefore the sons are free (ἐλεύθεροι).'[4] The Jews were, incidentally, seriously behind in their payment of tribute, when the revolt broke out in A.D. 66.[5] This desire for freedom found significant expression also on the coins issued during the war of A.D. 66–70; the inscriptions of some of them read: 'for the Redemption of Zion (לגאלת ציון)'; 'Freedom of Zion (חרות ציון)'.[6]

---

[1] τήν τε ἀποτίμησιν οὐδὲν ἢ ἄντικρυς δουλείαν ἐπιφέρειν λέγοντες [Judas and Saddok] καὶ τῆς ἐλευθερίας ἐπ' ἀντιλήψει παρακαλοῦντες τὸ ἔθνος (*Ant.* xviii. 4). Cf. D. A. Schlatter, *Die Geschichte Israels von Alexander dem Großen bis Hadrian* (Stuttgart, 1925), p. 263; Hengel, *Die Zeloten*, pp. 114–20: 'Das erste zeitlich genau fixierbare Auftreten des hebräischen Begriffs für "Freiheit" fällt bezeichnenderweise in der Zeit des Jüdischen Krieges, und zwar finden wir das Wort חֲרוּת — ein ursprünglich aramäisches Abstraktum — erstmalig auf den jüdischen Aufstandsmünzen' (p. 120). Cf. P. Winter in *R.Q.* IV (1963), 112: 'Their aims and beliefs were fundamentally religious. They were convinced that these aims could be achieved only in a Jewish society that was independent of pagan masters.'

[2] Mark xii. 14–15. See below, pp. 271, 345–9.

[3] Mark ii. 15–16; Matt. ix. 10–11; Luke v. 30. Cf. V. Taylor, *St Mark*, pp. 204–5; Klausner, *Jesus of Nazareth*, pp. 160–1, 187; Schürer, *G.J.V.* I, 478–9.

[4] E. Klostermann, *Das Matthäusevangelium*[2], p. 146, after discussing the historical context of the passage, concludes with much insight: 'In jedem Falle sind also Jesus und die Jünger eigentlich steuerfrei.' Cf. G. D. Kilpatrick, *Origins of Gospel of St Matthew* (Oxford, 1946), pp. 41–2; H. Montefiore, 'Jesus and the Temple Tax', *N.T.S.* XI (1964), 60–71.

[5] Jos. *War*, II. 404, 405.

[6] Cf. A. Reifenberg, *Israel's History in Coins* (London, 1953), pp. 13, 30–1; F. W. Madden, *Coins of the Jews* (London, 1881), p. 198, cf. pp. 203, 206, and *History of Jewish Coinage* (London, 1864), pp. 174–5; Schürer, *G.J.V.* I,

The growth of this theocratic ideal was surely linked with the increasing fervour of that apocalyptic expectation which is so vividly reflected in both Jewish and Christian literature of this period. As the Gospels abundantly show, the original Jewish Christians believed that the end of the present world-order and its supersession by the kingdom of God were at hand. Jesus of Nazareth begins his ministry with words of urgent warning: 'The time is fulfilled, and the kingdom of God is at hand (ἤγγικεν)';[1] and, later, in an apocalyptic discourse, he is represented as assuring his disciples: 'when ye see these things coming to pass, know that it is nigh, *even* at the doors (ἐγγύς ἐστιν ἐπὶ θύραις). Verily I say unto you, This generation shall not pass away, until all these things be accomplished.'[2] This sense of the imminence of the end of the present order permeates the whole Christian outlook prior to A.D. 70, affecting the evaluation of social and economic issues as well as inspiring an intense spiritual fervour.[3] Such ideas and feelings were not peculiar to the Christian movement in Judaea; for its apocalyptic concepts and outlook stemmed from contemporary Jewish life and thought.[4] These ideas, accordingly, afford a valuable guide for understanding aspects of the Zealot movement which, though clearly existent, are not adequately documented in the surviving sources. Thus they make intelligible the apparently suicidal policy of the Zealots in opposing the Roman government. Any shrewd observer of the current situation must have realised, as did Josephus, the utter impossibility of a puny nation, as was Israel, challenging successfully the might of the Roman empire. Israel was not situated on the periphery of the empire, with an unconquered hinterland, as, for example, were the British or Germanic

765–72 (but see also Reifenberg, *Israel's History in Coins*, pp. 15, 36–41 on the identification of the Bar Kochba coins), and Hengel, *Die Zeloten*, pp. 120–2. B. Kanael thinks that silver shekels and half-shekels were quickly issued by the insurgents, 'so that temple dues might be offered in Jewish money' ('Ancient Jewish Coins and their Historical Importance', *B.A.* xxvi, 1963, 57).

[1] Mark i. 15. Cf. Guignebert, *Jésus*, pp. 394–5; Goguel, *Life of Jesus*, pp. 311–12; Brandon, *History, Time and Deity*, pp. 151–2.
[2] Mark xiii. 29–30. Cf. Bultmann, *Gesch. d. synop. Tradition*, p. 130, Ergänzungsheft, p. 19; Taylor, *St Mark*, p. 521.
[3] Cf. Goguel, *La naissance du christianisme*, p. 287; J. Weiss, *Earliest Christianity*, E.T. (New York, 1959), II, 559–61; Bultmann, *Theology of the New Testament*, I, 37–9; Brandon, *History, Time and Deity*, pp. 152–3.
[4] Cf. Schürer, *G.J.V.* II, 496–553; R. H. Charles, *A Critical History of the Doctrine of a Future Life, or Hebrew Jewish and Christian Eschatology* (London, 1913), chh. VII–VIII; S. Mowinckel, *He That Cometh*, pp. 261–450.

peoples: instead, its territory formed the strategic link between the important provinces of Egypt and Syria. An intelligent appreciation of Roman power and interest would show, therefore, that, whatever small-scale successes might be gained initially, Rome would never tolerate the continuing independence of a rebel state in such a vital part of the empire and would put forth her vast strength to crush it.[1] But it was not in their own strength that the Zealots trusted; their trust lay in the God who had so miraculously delivered their ancestors from slavery in Egypt. The history of their people, recorded in a holy scripture, was a veritable *Heilsgeschichte*, abounding with thrilling accounts of how Yahweh had saved those who faithfully and courageously had withstood the impious heathen—from Joshua to Judas Maccabaeus, long and inspiring was the roll of Israel's heroes, whose faith and daring had been so signally rewarded by their God.[2] It is, therefore, a necessary inference that Judas and Saddok, when they called upon their people to withstand the Roman demand, also believed that the kingdom of God was at hand. Even Josephus admits that they expected God's succour, and it is likely that, no less vividly than Jesus, they might have envisaged the intervention of twelve legions of angels.[3]

---

[1] See the speech of Agrippa II to the Jewish insurgents, Jos. *War*, II. 345–401, which probably contains the earliest reference to the sea as Britain's wall of defence (τὸ Βρεττανῶν τεῖχος), in comparison with the walls of Jerusalem (τοῖς Ἱεροσολύμων τείχεσιν), *ibid.* 378; see also VI. 330–1. Cf. M. Cary, *The Geographic Background of Greek and Roman History* (Oxford, 1949), pp. 172–4, 215.

[2] Cf. Farmer, *Maccabees, Zealots and Josephus*, pp. 175–82; Hengel, *Die Zeloten*, pp. 277–80. There is much reason for believing that the Megillath Taanith was in origin a Zealot document, containing an annual reminder of Israel's past victories, in order to encourage resistance to Rome; cf. Farmer, pp. 152–8, 205–9; J. S. Kennard, 'The Jewish Provincial Assembly', *Z.N.T.W.* 53 (1962), p. 46.

[3] Matt. xxvi. 53. Cf. E. Lohmeyer and W. Schmauch, *Das Evangelium des Matthäus* (Göttingen, 1958), p. 365; Farmer, *Maccabees, Zealots and Josephus*, pp. 181–2. This passage is now greatly illuminated by the Qumrân scroll *D.S.W.* Thus, in the final encounter with the *Kittim* (Romans), angel hosts will be engaged as well as men (I. 9–11; cf. XII. 7); cf. Y. Yadin, *The Scroll of the War of the Sons of Light against the Sons of Darkness* (Oxford, 1962), pp. 230–1, 237, 260, 316. On the Zealots' belief that God would cooperate to bless their venture of faith see Jos. *Ant.* XVIII. 5, describing the teaching of Judas and Saddok: καὶ τὸ θεῖον οὐκ ἄλλως ἢ ἐπὶ συμπράξει τῶν βουλευμάτων εἰς τὸ κατορθοῦν συμπροθυμεῖσθαι, ἂν μεγάλων ἐρασταὶ τῇ διανοίᾳ καθιστάμενοι μὴ ἐξαφίωνται πόνου τοῦ ἐπ' αὐτοῖς. (The MSS give φόνου for πόνου: cf. Loeb ed.

The attempt of Judas and Saddok in A.D. 6 obviously failed. Josephus does not tell us of its outcome, although he mentions that it won popular support and made some progress.[1] Its failure appears to have been disastrous, if the evidence of the Acts of the Apostles may be accepted on the point. For, according to its record, more than twenty years later the rabbi Gamaliel recalls: 'After this man [i.e. Theudas] rose up Judas of Galilee in the days of the enrolment, and drew away *some of the* people after him: he also perished (ἀπώλετο); and all, as many as obeyed him, were scattered abroad (διεσκορπίσθησαν).'[2] However, despite this defeat, the movement evidently did not break up and disappear. Josephus, as we have seen,[3] traced the Zealots or Sicarii of the period 66–73 back to Judas, and, although he gives no facts about the movement's history during the intervening years, there are some significant indications of its existence and activity. Thus, we may notice that two sons of Judas were crucified by the procurator Tiberius Alexander (A.D. 46–8),[4] while another son, Menahem, played a leading part in the early days of the revolt of A.D. 66,[5] and the leader of the Sicarii at Masada, Eleazar, was a descendant (ἀπόγονος) of Judas.[6] This information suggests that a kind of dynastic succession was preserved, the right of the founder's family to leadership of the movement being recognised; it also indicates that Zealotism continued as a coordinated movement or party, with some effective form of organisation. Such dynastic succession surely attests that Judas himself must have been a man of dynamic personality and held in high repute. Unfortunately Josephus tells us little about him beyond describing him as a learned man (σοφιστής), probably a rabbi, and suggesting, by his

Josephus, IX, 7, n. *b*.) According to Josephus (*War*, II. 163), the Pharisees also believed that Providence assisted men in their righteous actions (βοηθεῖν δὲ εἰς ἕκαστον καὶ τὴν εἱμαρμένην)—his use of *Heimarmenē* here is clearly due to the fact that he writes for Gentile readers.

[1] καὶ ἡδονῇ γὰρ τὴν ἀκρόασιν ὧν λέγοιεν ἐδέχοντο οἱ ἄνθρωποι, προύκοπτεν ἐπὶ μέγα ἡ ἐπιβολὴ τοῦ τολμήματος,... (*Ant.* XVIII. 6).

[2] Acts v. 37. The value of this statement depends on whether the author of Acts was carelessly following Josephus here or drawing upon some other source. A sure decision is impossible on the extant evidence: what is said of the fate of Judas could be an inference from Josephus' account, for such a fate was obviously probable. Cf. *B.C.* IV, 60–2; Hengel, *Die Zeloten*, pp. 343–4.

[3] See above, pp. 31–40.

[4] *Ant.* XX. 102; see below, pp. 103–4.

[5] *War*, II. 433–4; see below, pp. 131–3.

[6] *War*, VII. 253; see below, p. 133. Cf. Driver, *Judaean Scrolls*, pp. 239–42.

use of the adjective δεινότατος, that he was a redoubtable person.[1] There can be little doubt that this Judas was the same person as the Judas, son of Ezekias, who led a rebel band in Galilee during the disturbances following the death of Herod.[2] Since this Ezekias had been a brigand-chief (archilēstēs), according to Josephus, whose execution by Herod, when a young man, led to his trial before the Sanhedrin, it would appear that Judas was already, in A.D. 6, a man of unique prestige both by reason of his descent and his own exploits. Circumstantial though the evidence is, it would seem that Judas had thus inherited a tradition of resistance to rulers whose Jewish descent and faith were suspect. Opposed to the Herodian succession in 4 B.C., he was moved to a more fundamental and passionate resistance when, in A.D. 6, Judaea passed from the rule of a Herodian prince to that of the heathen emperor of Rome; for objectionable though a Herodian ruler might be, he did not claim to be divine, as did the Roman emperor, and the resources of the Holy Land did not go to support a foreign heathen government. In protesting against Israel's subjection in A.D. 6, Judas was in the true line of succession to the prophets of old and to the Maccabees. His descent from Ezekias, as well as his own earlier activity and reputation, doubtless marked him as an accepted leader of Jewish resistance to Rome, when Judaea came under Roman rule. His death in the ensuing struggle clearly enhanced his reputation, and it ensured that succession of his family to leadership of the movement which he had founded. He was surely venerated as one of the glorious succession of martyrs for Israel.[3]

The connection of Judas with Galilee is significant. He was a

[1] *War*, II. 433. Ricciotti, *Flavio Giuseppe*, II, 323, translates δεινότατος as *esiziale*. If the *midrash* on Eccl. R. on i. 11 refers to Judas, the son of Hishia, then, in Rabbinic tradition, Judas was reckoned a חָסִיד as well as a בֶּן־תּוֹרָה; cf. Klausner, *Jesus of Nazareth*, p. 205; Hengel, *Die Zeloten*, p. 339.

[2] Cf. Schürer, *G.J.V.* I, 486; Klausner, *Jesus of Nazareth*, pp. 156, 162, 205; Hengel, *Die Zeloten*, pp. 337–9; Roth, *Historical Background of the Dead Sea Scrolls*, pp. 6–7. See above, pp. 27–9.

[3] T. Mommsen (*Das Weltreich der Caesaren*, Wien–Leipzig, 1933, p. 369) wrote with great insight on Judas: 'Wenn nicht viele seinem Ruf zu den Waffen folgten und er nach wenigen Monaten auf dem Blutgerüst endigte, so war der heilige Tote den unheiligen Siegern gefährlicher als der Lebende.' Commenting upon the dynastic tradition, J. S. Kennard says that we have to do 'with a clan which for a hundred and thirty-three years submitted to Rome only in death' ('Judas of Galilee and his Clan', *J.Q.R.* XXXVI, 1945, 284).

native of the country, and it was the place where both he and his father had operated their resistance movements. Galilaeans also played a prominent part in the war against Rome.[1] It would, accordingly, appear that, although it did not come under Roman rule at the same time as Judaea, Galilee had a strong tradition of active opposition to governments deemed unfitted to rule in Israel, whether they were of a native dynasty such as the Herodian or of heathen Rome. There is even some evidence that the Zealots were sometimes called Galilaeans;[2] a fact that invests with a special interest the otherwise curious account in the Lukan Gospel that Jesus was once informed about certain 'Galilaeans whose blood Pilate had mingled with their sacrifices'.[3]

At this point we should notice that, although Josephus associates Saddok with Judas in the founding of the Zealot movement, Judas clearly was the more important figure and was the better remembered. However, Saddok's association is important, for it shows that Zealotism was not incompatible with the profession of Pharisaic principles. Josephus tells us that the Pharisees maintained the doctrine of human free-will, but with the corollary that Providence (εἱμαρμένη) cooperated (βοηθεῖν) with each action.[4] Such a view of divine synergism finds notable expression in the exhortation of Judas and Saddok, namely, that God would help their undertaking, if they spared no effort to realise their ideals.[5]

---

[1] Josephus gives a detailed, and very lively, account, which is also clearly very tendentious, of the Galilaeans' activities from the time of his arrival in Galilee to organise its defence (*War*, II. 569 ff.; *Life*, 28 ff.).

[2] The *Mishnah* (Yadaim, 4. 8) seems to preserve, howbeit in a garbled form, some memory of men known as Galilaeans who professed Zealot principles: 'A Galilaean sectary (מִן גָּלִיל) said, "I protest against you, O Pharisees, for you write in a bill of divorce the name of the ruler together with the name of Moses." The Pharisees replied, "We protest against you, O Galilaean sectary, because you write the name of the ruler together with the Name (of God) on the (same) page, and, moreover, you write the name of the ruler above, and (God's) Name beneath; as it is written, And Pharaoh said, Who is Yahweh that I should hearken unto his voice, to let Israel go?"'; cf. Danby, *Mishnah*, p. 785; Klausner, *Jesus of Nazareth*, p. 204; Hengel, *Die Zeloten*, p. 58, see also pp. 57–61. Hengel thinks that Epictetus' reference to the fortitude of the Galilaeans (Arrian, *Discourses of Epictetus*, IV. vii. 6) is probably to be interpreted as a reference to the Zealots; cf. *ibid.* p. 60.

[3] Luke xiii. 1. See below, p. 78. Cf. A. Jaubert, 'Jésus et le Calendrier de Qumrân', *N.T.S.* VII (1961), 11–12.

[4] *War*, II. 163.   [5] *Ant.* XVIII. 5: see above, p. 51, n. 3.

The dispersal of the followers of Judas after his death, and the fact of the continuance of the movement, naturally raise the question of the manner in which further resistance was maintained and from what bases it was directed. Josephus gives a clue when he relates how the various insurgents, during the disturbances of 4 B.C., 'filled all Judaea with ληστρικοῦ πολέμου'.[1] We have noted his tendentious use of 'bandit' (lēstēs) to describe such men; but bandits do not normally conduct war (polemos). It would, accordingly, be reasonable to translate lēstrikos polemos here as 'guerrilla war'—in other words, operations of the kind carried out by resistance groups against the occupying power, most notably in the Peninsular War and the Second World War. The strongholds of such resistance groups were undoubtedly in the desert areas of Palestine: indeed the caves discovered recently in Nahal Hever, near En Gedi, which had been occupied by the forces of Bar Kochba during the revolt of A.D. 132–5, attest the type of refuge and mode of life of those who fought for Israel's freedom a generation or two before.[2] The records of Josephus contain abundant evidence of this Zealot connection with the desert,[3] and it is not without significance that in the Markan Apocalypse Jesus is represented as telling his followers to flee into the mountains when the 'abomination of desolation' stands in the Temple.[4] It would seem likely, however, that members of the Zealot bands did not all permanently reside in their desert hide-outs; as circumstances permitted, they would doubtless have mingled with the ordinary population, very much after the fashion of the resistance groups in other lands and times. Such a situation seems to be suggested by the inclusion of a Zealot among the disciples of Jesus, and it is implied by what Josephus tells of the operations of the Sicarii in Jerusalem.[5]

It would, of course, be unrealistic to suppose that every Zealot was equally inspired by the high self-sacrificing ideals set forth in the

---

[1] *War*, II. 65.
[2] See Y. Yadin, 'Finding Bar Kochbar's Despatches', *I.L.N.* 4 November 1961, pp. 772–5, 11 November 1961, pp. 820–2; cf. 2 December 1961, pp. 972–4. C. Roth has argued that Qumrân became the Zealot centre from the time of Judas: see p. 61, n. 4 below.
[3] Cf. Hengel, *Die Zeloten*, pp. 259–61.
[4] Mark xiii. 14; see below, pp. 230–5.
[5] Mark iii. 18; Matt. x. 4; Luke vi. 15; Acts i. 13: it must, of course, be remembered in this connection that Jesus and his disciples apparently led a wandering life. The Sicarii whose activities Josephus describes in *War*, II. 254–7, *Ant.* xx. 164–5, evidently resided in Jerusalem. Cf. Roth in *J.S.S.* IV (1959), 337.

teaching of Judas and Saddok, as recorded by Josephus. Undoubtedly many lawless and desperate characters were attracted to a movement which enabled them to gratify their instincts for violence and rapacity under the cloak of religious and patriotic zeal: such men have been found in extremist action-parties, no matter how altruistic the ideals professed, in other days and places. Moreover, it is unlikely that Zealotism was a highly organised and disciplined movement. There is evidence, as we have seen, of a kind of dynastic succession stemming from the founder, Judas; but it would seem that organisation must generally have been loose and many groups, sometimes in rivalry to each other, operated under the name of Zealots or Sicarii, or possibly of Galilaeans. The social composition of the movement is also obscure. The founders were men of some standing, Judas being probably a rabbi and Saddok a recognised member of the Pharisees. By the time of the war a considerable body of the priesthood were Zealots or identified themselves with Zealot principles; these men, however, were of the lower orders of the hierarchy and were certainly opposed to the sacerdotal aristocracy which was concerned to maintain the *status quo* and tended to be pro-Roman.[1] There is, indeed, much reason for thinking that among the Zealots there would have been many of the poor and dispossessed: for the tribute would have borne more hardly on the poor than on those with better economic resources.[2] Josephus records an action of the Zealots which significantly attests their social interests. During the disturbances that marked the beginning of the revolt in Jerusalem in A.D. 66, the Sicarii not only destroyed the house of Ananias, the high priest, and the palaces of the Herodian dynasts Agrippa and Bernice, but they burnt also the public archives (τὰ ἀρχεῖα), 'eager to destroy the money-lenders' bonds and to prevent the recovery of debts, in order to win over a host of grateful debtors and to cause a rising of the poor against the rich, sure of impunity'.[3]

Whatever doubtful elements became enrolled in the Zealot ranks and whatever fierce rivalries among the leaders led to the internecine conflicts that Josephus dilates upon, the spirit of fortitude and commitment, with which the Zealots struggled and suffered for their ideals, was astounding—it even drew forth the grudging acknowledgement of the renegade historian.[4] They knew the fate that

[1] See below, pp. 130–2.
[2] Cf. Grant, *Economic Background of the Gospels*, pp. 100–1, 105–6; Hengel, *Die Zeloten*, pp. 89, 341–2.
[3] *War*, II. 427. [4] Jos. *Ant.* XVIII. 23–4; *War*, VII. 417–19.

awaited them, if they fell into Roman hands. Crucifixion was a reality which they had to face personally, and it is possible that Jesus was using a well-known Zealot saying when he said: 'If any man would come after me, let him deny himself, and take up his cross, and follow me.'[1] Indeed, it must, in all fairness, be recognised that, if the endurance of the Christian martyrs attests the strength and sincerity of their faith, the steadfastness, under torture and death, of the Zealots bears a like witness. The following description of the sufferings of the Sicarii rebels, who retreated to Egypt after the fall of Jerusalem, comes not from a Zealot hagiography but from the reluctant pen of Josephus:

Six hundred of them were caught on the spot; and all who escaped into Egypt and the Egyptian Thebes were ere long arrested and brought back. Nor was there a person who was not amazed at the endurance and—call it which you will—desperation or strength of purpose, displayed by these victims. For under every form of torture and laceration of body, devised for the sole object of making them acknowledge Caesar as lord (Καίσαρα δεσπότην ὁμολογήσωσιν), no one submitted nor was brought to the verge of utterance; but all kept their resolve, triumphant over constraint, meeting the tortures and the fire with bodies that seemed insensible of pain and souls that wellnigh exulted in it. But most of all were the spectators struck by the children of tender age, not one of whom could be prevailed upon to call Caesar lord. So far did the strength of courage rise superior to the weakness of their frames.[2]

Josephus witnesses also to the inspired resolution of the Zealots in the speech which he attributes to Eleazar on the eve of the final Roman assault on Masada. Although this speech is certainly a tendentious fabrication whereby the Zealot leader is made to acknowledge the crimes of the Zealots,[3] Josephus undoubtedly had reason for ascribing the sentiment in the following passage to a Zealot who was descended from the founder of the movement: 'Long since, my brave men, we determined neither to serve the Romans nor any other save God, for He alone is man's true and righteous Lord;[4] and now the time is come which bids us verify that resolution by our actions.'[5] And the sentiment was indeed matched by action; for, when the Romans broke into the fortress the next day, nine hundred and sixty corpses

[1] Mark viii. 34. Cf. Schlatter, *Gesch. Israels*, p. 264; Hengel, *Die Zeloten*, p. 266.
[2] *War*, VII. 416–19 (trans. Thackeray, *Josephus*, III, 621, 623).
[3] *War*, VII. 329–33.
[4] μόνος γὰρ οὗτος [God] ἀληθής ἐστι καὶ δίκαιος ἀνθρώπων δεσπότης,...
[5] *War*, VII. 323 (trans. Thackeray, *Josephus*, III, 595).

of men, women and children testified that the Zealots chose death rather than surrender to a heathen lord.[1]

Of special significance for our later study is the evidence of Zealot concern for the holiness of the Temple. As a token of loyalty to their Roman overlord, the priestly aristocracy had instituted the custom of offering sacrifice twice daily in the Temple on behalf of the emperor and the Roman people.[2] This custom was obviously an offence to the more rigorist of the Jews, and in A.D. 66 one Eleazar, son of Ananias the high priest, persuaded the priests to abandon the offering of these sacrifices.[3] Such an act was tantamount to rebellion, and the leading Jewish ecclesiastical and civil authorities sought in vain to prevent it.[4] Eleazar evidently had Zealot sentiments and support, and in the struggle that followed his party, consisting of the lower orders of the priesthood, was quickly reinforced by the Sicarii.[5] After they had gained control of the Temple, the Zealots sought to purify the high priesthood by reverting to the ancient custom of electing the incumbent of that supreme office by lot.[6] The Temple remained their stronghold throughout the siege of the city, they defended it with fanatical courage and many perished there in the final conflagration.[7] Those who fought their way out through the attacking Romans and gained the upper part of the city offered to abandon this to the Romans on condition that they might withdraw, with their families, into the desert (εἰς τὴν ἔρημον)—now that the shrine of Yahweh was desecrated and destroyed, instinctively they

---

[1] War, VII. 389–401. Cf. M. Avi-Yonah, 'Where 960 Zealots Committed Suicide sooner than Submit to a Roman Army of 15,000', I.L.N. 5 November 1955, pp. 784–7, and 'The Archaeological Survey of Masada', I.E.J. VII (1957), 1–60; Y. Yadin, The Excavation of Masada, 1963/64 (Jerusalem, 1965), pp. 16–17, 20–1, 43, 72–3, 90–1; M. Livneh and Z. Meshel, Masada (Tel Aviv, 1966), p. 16.

[2] Jos. War, II. 409. According to War, II. 197, these sacrifices were offered twice daily περὶ...Καίσαρος καὶ τοῦ δήμου τῶν Ῥωμαίων. Josephus (Against Apion, II. 77) says that the expense was borne by the 'whole Jewish community'; according to Philo, Leg. ad Gaium, 157, 317, Augustus had instituted the sacrifices at his own expense. Cf. Philonis Alexandrini Legatio ad Gaium, ed. E. M. Smallwood, pp. 240–1, 311; Schürer, G.J.V. II, 303–4; J. S. Kennard in Z.N.T.W. 53 (1962), pp. 30–2; C. Roth, 'The Debate on the Loyal Sacrifices, A.D. 66', H.Th.R. LIII (1960), 93–7.

[3] Jos. War, II. 409; see below, pp. 130–1.

[4] Jos. War, II. 410, 413–16.

[5] Ibid. 425–6.

[6] Ibid. IV. 153–4; see below, p. 140.

[7] War, VI. 71 ff., 271–3, 278–80, 318–22.

sought the desert, the ancient home of their race. Titus, the Roman commander, naturally refused, and the struggle was fought out to its bitter end amid the ruins of the holy city.[1]

That the Zealots partook of the Messianic hope, looking for the coming of the redeemer foretold in ancient prophecy, is evident from the existence of various Messianic pretenders who seem to have had Zealot connections. It is probable also that the prophecy concerning a world-ruler, mentioned by Josephus, was promulgated by the Zealots. Josephus calls this prophecy an 'ambiguous oracle (χρησμὸς ἀμφίβολος)', and he regarded it as a potent factor in causing the Jews to revolt and persist so stubbornly in their hopeless contest against the might of imperial Rome. He says that the oracle was found in the holy scriptures of his people, but he does not identify the passage concerned. According to him, it was interpreted to mean that 'at that time from their country one should rule the world'.[2] The oracle was naturally understood by the Jews to signify that this world-ruler would be one of their own race. But in interpreting it thus, maintains Josephus, many of their wise men (τῶν σοφῶν) went astray (ἐπλανήθησαν), because the prophecy really concerned Vespasian, who had been proclaimed emperor while in Judaea.[3] This interpretation undoubtedly helped both to satisfy Josephus' conscience and to recommend him to his imperial patrons; but this fact does not detract from the significance of such a prophecy and its influence. If it did indeed help to lead the Jews into war, as Josephus says, it must surely have been formulated into some appeal to revolt, and who, other than the Zealots, were likely to have made such an appeal? Moreover, Josephus contends that the prophecy had thus been erroneously interpreted by 'many of their wise men (sophists)'. This statement indicates that the interpretation was promulgated by a definite group of sophists, and, when we recall that Josephus describes Judas of Galilee as a sophist, it would surely seem most likely

---

[1] Ibid. 277, 351. 'Nachdem der Tempel jedoch von den Römern erobert, entweiht und zerstört worden war, richtete sich ihr Blick wieder auf die Wüste' (Hengel, Die Zeloten, p. 261). According to Driver (Judaean Scrolls, p. 234), the Sicarii who fled to Egypt made their way 'to the old head-quarters of the Zadokite movement', i.e. the Temple at Leontopolis; see below, pp. 292–3.

[2] War, VI. 312–13; ὡς κατὰ τὸν καιρὸν ἐκεῖνον ἀπὸ τῆς χώρας αὐτῶν τις ἄρξει τῆς οἰκουμένης: reference is made to the prophecy by Tacitus, Hist. v. 13 and Suetonius, Vesp. 4.

[3] Cf. Eisler, ΙΗΣΟΥΣ ΒΑΣΙΛΕΥΣ, ΙΙ, 603–8, The Messiah Jesus, pp. 554–61; Ricciotti, Flavio Giuseppe, IV, 189, n. on 312–13.

that the Zealots included many *sophists* or rabbis who found sanction and inspiration for Zealot policy thus in holy scripture.[1]

The likelihood that the Zealots were animated by hopes which passed beyond the freeing of Israel from its servitude to Rome to some concept of world-mastery, is of considerable significance to our subject. In the first place, it may shed light upon that aspect of the Temptation of Jesus, when we come later to inquire into this episode, which took the form of Satan's offer of world-dominion.[2] There are many signs, too, in contemporary apocalyptic of an intense hatred of Rome, not only for its subjugation of Israel, but also for its proud imperial supremacy over all the world.[3] In other words, the destiny achieved by Rome afforded both an ideal and a provocative contrast for the zealous Jew: such world-dominion was thus demonstrated to be possible, and it was surely the right of the Chosen People of God to hold it; yet Israel now lay, a puny subject nation, beneath the Roman eagle. However, a reversal of fortune would come: 'Then shalt thou prosper, O Israel, and ascend on the neck and wings of the Eagle, and the days of the Eagle shall be fulfilled.'[4] Until the revolt in A.D. 66, the Zealots had been able only to conduct a guerrilla warfare against the Romans; but we now know that there were those in Israel who had worked out in considerable detail a plan of campaign against the Gentiles, led by Rome, in a final Armageddon. The *Scroll of The War of the Sons of Light against the Sons of Darkness*, discovered at Qumrân, envisages a six years' struggle between the forces of Israel and the Gentiles, with varying fortune, until God intervenes mightily to give final victory to his people.[5] After this decision, campaigns would be conducted

---

[1] 'Die zugrundeliegende Schriftstelle war nicht ohne weiteres verständlich, denn sie mußte erst durch die σοφοί gedeutet werden. Dies setzt aber für den Deuter ein profetisches Charisma voraus' (Hengel, *Die Zeloten*, p. 243, see also pp. 242–6). On Josephus' use of σοφός and σοφιστής cf. Eisler, ΙΗΣΟΥΣ ΒΑΣΙΛΕΥΣ, I, 53–4.

[2] Matt. iv. 8–10; Luke iv. 5–8. On the significance of the Temptation of Jesus see below, pp. 310–14. Cf. Roth, 'Melekh ha-'olam: Zealot influence in the Liturgy', *J.J.S.* XI (1960), 174–5.

[3] Cf. A. Peretti, *La Sibilla babilonese nella Propaganda ellenistica* (Florence, 1943), pp. 317–61, 453–87; Hengel, *Die Zeloten*, pp. 308–12. The fierce hatred towards Rome which finds such terrible expression in the Christian Apocalypse (Rev. xvii–xviii) probably derives from a Jewish source; cf. R. H. Charles, *The Revelation of St John* (Edinburgh, 1920), II, 54–113.

[4] Ass. Mosis x. 8, in *Apok. u. Pseudepig.* (ed. Kautzsch), II, 327.

[5] Cf. Y. Yadin, *Scroll of the War*, pp. 4, 7–8, 10–13, 20–6. From an analysis of the military and other data, Yadin concludes that this document was

for another twenty-nine years against those nations that had not
been involved in the first conflict.[1] According to the general consensus of specialist opinion, this *Scroll* represented the views of the
Qumrân community, whose members were probably Essenes.[2] On
the relation between this community and the Zealots there has
naturally been much speculation. It is, however, significant that the
settlement at Qumrân appears to have been taken by Roman
assault in Vespasian's campaign of A.D. 68,[3] and the recent excavations at Masada also seem to provide evidence of some close relationship between the Sicarii there and the Qumrân sectaries.[4]

composed 'after the Roman conquest but before the end of Herod's
reign'. The *Kittim*, who head the enemies of the Sons of Light, are
undoubtedly the Romans, *op. cit.* p. 25. Cf. Roth, *Historical Background of
Dead Sea Scrolls*, pp. 76–9; A. Dupont-Sommer, *Les écrits esséniens*, pp. 182–
4; J. T. Milik, *Dix ans de découvertes dans le désert de Juda* (Paris, 1957),
p. 82; Hengel, *Die Zeloten*, pp. 283–7.

[1] Cf. Yadin, *Scroll of the War*, pp. 4, 8, 26 ff.

[2] Cf. M. Burrows, *The Dead Sea Scrolls* (London, 1956), pp. 279–98; H. H.
Rowley, *The Zadokite Fragments and the Dead Sea Scrolls* (Oxford, 1952),
pp. 78–87, and in *B.J.R.L.* 44 (1961), pp. 121–2, 146–7; Dupont-
Sommer, *Les écrits esséniens*, pp. 51–5; Yadin, *Scroll of the War*, p. 246.

[3] R. de Vaux, *L'archéologie et les manuscrits de la Mer Morte* (London, 1961),
pp. 28–33, 86.

[4] According to Professor Y. Yadin, during the recent excavations at Masada
scroll fragments were found identical with a scroll discovered in Qumrân
(Cave IV); it attested that the peculiar Qumrânic calendar was known
at Masada: see *I.L.N.* 31 October 1964, p. 697. A ritual bath (*Miqveh*)
was also found, built according to the meticulous rules of the *halakha* (*ibid.*
p. 696 and fig. 15). See also Yadin in *I.E.J.* xv (1965), 91, 105–8 (on the
finding of a Qumrân document, the *Scroll of the Songs of the Sabbath Sacrifice*).
J. T. Milik has sagely remarked: 'Nous ne serions pas étonnés d'apprendre
que les chefs de la résistance juive aient considéré la Règle de la Guerre
comme un excellent ouvrage de propagande' (*Dix ans de découvertes*, p. 82).
It is significant that, according to Josephus (*War*, II. 567), a certain John
the Essene was among the Jewish leaders at the beginning of the revolt.
Cf. Hengel, *Die Zeloten*, pp. 283–7. It is appropriate to note here that C. Roth
has presented a case for believing that the community that occupied the
site at Qumrân from 4 B.C. to A.D. 68 or 72–3 was Zealot. Roth argues that
Judas of Galilee took over the site, deserted since the earthquake of 31 B.C.,
during the disturbances following the death of Herod the Great. After the
death of Judas in A.D. 6, Qumrân continued to be the headquarters of the
Zealot movement, where its members lived a semi-monastic life; and it was
from there that Menahem, the surviving son of Judas, seized Masada in A.D.
66. Roth identifies Menahem with the Teacher of Righteousness of the
Qumrân scrolls. After the death of Menahem, he believes that the real or
dynastic Zealots retired from Jerusalem, and maintained themselves at
Qumrân and Masada until their extermination by the Romans in 72–3

From the disparate and complex evidence which we have surveyed here, an intelligible and convincing picture begins to emerge of the Zealots and the part which they played in Jewish life during the critical years between A.D. 6 and 73. They appear to represent the concretion or focusing of ideas and aspirations that naturally stemmed from the Yahwist *Heilsgeschichte*. The conception of Israel as a theocracy was basic to Yahwism: that Yahweh had chosen the nation to be his own peculiar people and had given to them the land of Canaan as their home and peculiar possession. The Exodus and the Settlement in the Holy Land constituted the essential pattern of

(*Historical Background of the Dead Sea Scrolls*, pp. 25–35, cf. his 'Historian and the Dead Sea Scrolls', *History Today*, XI (1961), 90–7; also in *J.S.S.* IV, 1959, 338 ff.). The case is a plausible one; but it has not generally commended itself: it is criticised at some length by de Vaux, *L'archéologie*, pp. 91–4, who emphasises that the archaeological evidence proves that occupation of the site at Qumrân ended in June, A.D. 68; cf. Dupont-Sommer, *Les écrits esséniens*, pp. 409–15; see also F. F. Bruce, 'The Dead Sea Habakkuk Scroll', *A.L.U.O.S.* I (1958–9), 20–3; H. H. Rowley, 'The Qumrân Sectaries and the Zealots: an examination of a recent theory', *V.T.* IX (1959), 379–92. J. Allegro (*The Treasure of the Copper Scroll*, New York, 1960, pp. 120–9) has argued that the Zealots took Qumrân forcibly from the Essenes in the spring of A.D. 68 and held it for three months before the Roman assault. According to him, the Copper Scroll, containing information about the burial of the Temple treasure, was made and deposited by the Zealots. This theory implies that the Essenes at Qumrân did not cooperate with the Zealots: cf. his *The Dead Sea Scrolls* (Harmondsworth, 1956), p. 87. Mlle A. Jaubert ('Jésus et le Calendrier de Qumrân', *N.T.S.* VII, 1960–1, 12) regards the Zealots as 'une branche dans la ligne d'un messianisme politique et belliqueux' of the Essenes. Professor G. R. Driver, in a lecture to the Royal Central Asian Society in 1957 (reported in *The Manchester Guardian*, 20 June 1957), has also associated the Qumrân 'Covenanters' with the Zealots. The general burden of the Qumrân evidence seems to indicate that the community there would have supported the Zealots in their venture of faith in challenging the dominion of Rome in the Holy Land. In his recently published (December 1965) *The Judaean Scrolls*, Driver has set forth, at considerable length, a view very similar to that of Roth, identifying the Qumrân Covenanters with the Zealots (pp. 236, 239–43, 244 ff., 251, 266–84, 586–7). Y. Yadin has wisely remarked: 'The discovery of this scroll [of the *Songs of the Sabbath Sacrifice*] at Masada allows us to conclude that the Great Revolt was not restricted to the "Zealot" sect alone: rather, as Josephus also states, many sects of Jewry took part in it, including the sect of the Essenes, either as a whole or in part, or at a certain stage of its development. This is perhaps the most important conclusion to be drawn from the finding of this scroll at Masada, which was one of the few strongholds and places of refuge left at the end of the Revolt' (*Excavation of Masada*, Jerusalem, 1965, p. 108).

Yahweh's providence as manifest in history—of his ability to deliver his people from their enemies and reward their faith.[1] Their subsequent history appeared to repeat this pattern in many dramatic episodes: disloyalty to Yahweh brought on them disaster and subjection to the Gentile; repentance and renewal of faith were rewarded by restoration.[2] The success of the Maccabees was the most recent and glorious demonstration of what zeal for Yahweh could accomplish. Growing discontent under Herod the Great had sharpened the conviction that Israel should be under no other lord than the God who had chosen the nation and so wondrously fulfilled his promises to its ancestors. But, if the rule of Herod had irked, the passing into a state of subjection to the emperor of heathen Rome challenged the very principles of Judaism and outraged the cherished ideal of Israel as a theocracy. The first act of the Roman administration, namely, the census, struck at the very roots of Yahweh's sovereignty over Israel—the holy land of his ancient promise was now regarded as the property of the Roman emperor.[3]

Every pious Jew must have felt the insult to his ancestral faith that the Roman suzerainty constituted. It was, moreover, not just a tacitly implied insult; for, as we shall see, the Romans not only made little attempt to placate the religious susceptibilities of their new subjects, they often designedly outraged them. It was natural, therefore, that the more zealous and courageous felt that loyalty to their national god demanded action, after the example of such heroes of the faith as Phinehas and the Maccabees. Such action could not have been undertaken lightly; for even the most fanatical must have realised the power and resources of the empire whose rule they challenged. As we have seen, although they believed that God would bless their cause, they were prepared to pay for their faith with their lives, and from many the payment was exacted. Undoubtedly many violent and desperate men joined the Zealot bands, and many acts of murder and rapine were committed by them. But Zealotism must be recognised as a true and inherently noble expression of Jewish

[1] Cf. Hengel, *Die Zeloten*, p. 258; Brandon, *History, Time and Deity*, pp. 106 ff.
[2] Cf. Brandon, pp. 119–21, 129–40.
[3] The offence of the census was, in fact, twofold: (i) it constituted a denial of the dearly prized belief that the Holy Land belonged to Yahweh (cf. e.g. Gen. xvii. 8; Deut. xxvi. 4–9; Jos. xxiv. 13); (ii) it contravened the Divine Law (cf. e.g. Exod. xxx. 11–12; II Sam. xxiv: see also Hengel, *Die Zeloten*, pp. 134–6). 'Der Census bringe offensichtliche Sklaverei, Gottes Wille sei es dagegen, daß man ihn als den einzigen Herren über Land und Volk anerkenne' (Hengel, p. 138, cf. p. 141).

religious faith, and one that was sanctioned and inspired by the example of many revered figures of Israel's heroic past. And it is not inappropriate that we should here note the significance of the fact that the modern state of Israel proposes to make the fortress of Masada a national monument; for it is the vigorous resistance, the unflinching faith and courage, and the refusal to surrender, of the Zealots who perished there in A.D. 73, that the Jewish nation today honours and seeks to perpetuate.[1]

[1] Cf. *The Times*, 6 January 1965, p. 8: '"Herod", Dr Yadin observed, "gave Masada its body. The Zealots gave it its soul."'

CHAPTER 3

ISRAEL'S CAUSE AGAINST ROME
A.D. 6–73

As we have already observed, the Zealot movement was founded when Jesus was a boy, possibly when he was about the age of twelve years. He would, accordingly, have been old enough to grasp something of the significance of the Roman census in A.D. 6 and the disturbances that resulted from it. The suppression of Judas of Galilee and the scattering of his followers undoubtedly led to a withdrawal of the hard core of the Zealots to the desert areas of Judaea and Galilee. From such strongholds they probably conducted a guerrilla warfare against both the Romans and their Jewish collaborators in Judaea and the government of Herod Antipas in Galilee; for they would have had little respect or liking for the latter, who was a son of the hated Herod and owed his position to the Roman emperor.[1] There is every reason, therefore, for assuming that Jesus, during his youth and early manhood, grew up with a close acquaintance of the Zealots and their aims and activities. In all probability the memory of Judas was treasured by the Galilaeans, who would have seen in him a martyr for the sacred cause of Israel's freedom. It is likely that many Galilaeans had taken part in the revolt of A.D. 6, and Jesus would have known some of the survivors and the families of those who had perished. To a Galilaean boy or youth those martyred patriots would surely have been his heroes, and doubtless he would often have listened enthralled to tales of Zealot exploits against the hated Romans.

For the particular purpose of our study it will be best to trace out, from A.D. 6, those aspects of Romano-Jewish relations that outraged the religious feelings of the Jews and led ultimately to the fatal rising of A.D. 66. In many of the events concerned, especially in the earlier part of the period, the Zealots do not appear. The reason for this is not clear; but it is probably due to Josephus, who is our chief informant. Their apparent absence from any participation in the events of A.D. 39–40, which was the most crucial episode, as we shall

---

[1] Jos. *War*, II. 94–5; *Ant.* XVII. 317–18. Cf. Schürer, *G.J.V.* I, 431–49; Jones, *The Herods of Judaea*, pp. 176–83.

see, before A.D. 66, is so remarkable as to cause suspicion.[1] However, we are only in a position of knowing that Josephus' record of Jewish affairs between A.D. 6 and 66 is ill-balanced and contains many *lacunae*;[2] the Gospels incidentally witness to political disturbances during the governorship of Pilate which the Jewish historian does not notice.[3] It will, accordingly, be our intention here to underline those happenings which were calculated to affect Jewish life at all levels, and so must have concerned Jesus and his followers during the vital years of his ministry and the infancy of the Church.

Coponius, the procurator concerned with the census, was succeeded about A.D. 9 by Marcus Ambibulus, who was followed in the office by Annius Rufus (*c.* A.D. 12–15).[4] Josephus records no disturbances during these years; indeed, he finds nothing notable at all to record about Jewish affairs at this time. From an action of Pilate later, as we shall see, it would appear that the Romans had so far taken account of Jewish religious susceptibilities as to refrain from bringing military standards, bearing images, into Jerusalem.[5] Perhaps the revolt led by Judas of Galilee had warned them that they had to do with a people whose religious ideas were both strange and fiercely held. In this connection, too, we may notice the cryptic statement of Josephus that Quirinius, the legate of Syria, had deposed

---

[1] See below, pp. 87–8.

[2] Cf. Ricciotti, *Flavio Giuseppe*, I, 150–2; Schürer, *G.J.V.* I, 82–5. See above, pp. 30 ff.   [3] See below, pp. 78–9.

[4] Jos. *Ant.* XVIII. 31. On the title and office of the procurators of Judaea cf. Schürer, *G.J.V.* I, 455–7. Josephus generally uses the term ἐπίτροπος; but a recently found (1961) inscription at Caesarea shows that Pilate was styled *praefectus*, cf. J. Vardaman, 'A New Inscription which mentions Pilate as "Prefect"', *J.B.L.* LXXXI (1962). See Plate II. It would appear that the procurator had a military force at his disposal comprising one *ala* of cavalry and five cohorts of infantry, numbering about 3,000 men in all. These troops seem originally to have formed the *élite* of Herod's army, being known as the Σεβαστηνοὶ τρισχίλιοι. As their name indicates, they came from Sebaste, i.e. Samaria, and as such would therefore have been particularly objectionable to the Jews. These troops were stationed at Caesarea, with one of their cohorts doing garrison duty at Jerusalem. In addition to these forces, there were garrisons in various fortresses. The procurator's troops were intended for the ordinary maintenance of Roman law and order; for military operations on a larger scale the legate of Syria would intervene with legionary troops. Cf. Schürer, I, 460–6; Mommsen, *Das Weltreich der Caesaren*, p. 365; T. R. S. Broughton in *B.C.* V, 439–45; C. H. Kraeling, 'The Episode of the Roman Standards at Jerusalem', *H.Th.R.* XXXV (1942), 265–9.

[5] Jos. *Ant.* XVIII. 55–6. See below, pp. 69 ff.

the high priest Joazar, against whom the people had revolted (καταστασιασθέντα).[1] The action is strange, since Joazar had persuaded his people to submit to the census and thus had given Quirinius cause to be grateful to him. We may well ask whether Joazar's collaboration with the Romans had made him so unpopular with his people that, once he had served his purpose, Quirinius had disposed of him. The transaction looks ominous, and the fact that Josephus provides no explanation renders his record here suspect. Ominous also was the fact that Quirinius not only deposed Joazar from his sacred office, but appointed his successor Ananus—a humiliating reminder, surely, to the Jews that the Romans controlled the appointment of their high priest, who represented them, the Chosen People, on the most sacred occasions before their God.[2]

The significance of Quirinius' action may not have been immediately sensed by the Jews, since it was an unpopular high priest who had thus been deposed. But the true irony of the situation became manifest when the next procurator, Valerius Gratus (A.D. 15–26), deposed and appointed no less than four high priests, ending with the appointment of Caiaphas, who was to achieve undying infamy for the part he played in the trial of Jesus.[3] Josephus tells nothing of the reaction of his people to this shocking degradation of the high priesthood. His silence is surely eloquent, for that reaction, even if it did not find active expression, must have been very bitter. Respect for the Roman nominees who held the sacred office must have sunk low, even to vanishing. It undoubtedly led to an increasing alienation of the people, and the lower orders of the priesthood, from the sacerdotal aristocracy who held office through the favour of the Roman overlord. It also explains the assassination of a later high priest by the Sicarii, the appointment of a new high priest by the Zealots as soon as they gained control of the Temple in 66, and the Zealot sentiments of the subordinate priests.[4] Dependence on Roman favour, moreover, inevitably meant that the sacerdotal aristocracy became increasingly concerned with the maintenance of

---

[1] *Ant.* xviii. 26.
[2] Cf. E. M. Smallwood, 'High Priests and Politics in Roman Palestine', *J.T.S.* xiii (1962), 17–22.
[3] *Ant.* xviii. 34–5. Cf. Schürer, *G.J.V.* ii, 218; Smallwood, *J.T.S.* xiii (1962), 14–15.
[4] See below, pp. 130–1, 140. The unpopularity of the high-priestly families at this period is commemorated, in what appears to be a poetic lament, in the Talmudic tractate Pesahim 57a; see Klausner, *Jesus of Nazareth*, p. 337. Cf. Jeremias, *Jerusalem*, pp. 56–7; Smallwood, *J.T.S.* xiii (1962), 28–9.

Roman government, as its members felt their alienation from their own people. This meant, in turn, that resistance to Rome became a lower-class movement, and it involved hostility also to the Jewish aristocracy.[1] Such social resentment easily combined with the religious patriotism that sought Israel's freedom: hence Zealotism was essentially a popular movement, embodying both the religious and social aspirations and resentments of the 'people of the land'.[2] It will be important to remember this aspect of Zealotism, when we come to evaluate the attitude of Jesus and his disciples towards it. Both Jesus and his disciples were of the 'people of the land' ('am ha-'aretz); and the recorded teaching of Jesus vividly reflects the attitude of the poor towards those 'who wore soft clothing, ate good food, and dwelt in kings' houses'.[3]

The next praefectus or procurator of Judaea was Pontius Pilate, who held the office from A.D. 26 to 36.[4] We are fortunate in being informed of one who played such a key role in the condemnation of Jesus, as well as in contemporary Jewish affairs, by both Josephus and his older contemporary, Philo of Alexandria. It seems that Pilate was particularly detested by the Jews. Philo, quoting from a letter of the Jewish prince Agrippa I to Caligula, describes him as 'naturally inflexible and stubbornly relentless (τὴν φύσιν ἀκαμπὴς καὶ τοῦ αὐθάδους ἀμείλικτος)', and he accuses him of 'acts of corruption, insults, rapine, outrages on the people, arrogance, repeated murders of innocent victims, and constant and most galling savagery'.[5] Josephus, curiously, refrains from any assessment of the conduct and character of Pilate, although his account of two inci-

---

[1] It is significant that, according to Josephus, Zealotism appealed to the youth of the country: περὶ ἧς [his so-called 'Fourth Philosophy'] ὀλίγα βούλομαι διελθεῖν, ἄλλως τε ἐπεὶ καὶ τῷ κατ' αὐτῶν σπουδασθέντι τοῖς νεωτέροις ὁ φθόρος τοῖς πράγμασι συνέτυχε (*Ant.* XVIII. 10). He also states that οἱ ἄνθρωποι received the teaching of Judas and Saddok gladly (*ibid.* 6).

[2] 'Herbeigeführt ist er [the final revolt] viel weniger durch das Verhalten der Römer als durch die Intrigen und die Erpressungen der Aristokratie von Jerusalem, und trägt daher, trotz des religiösen Gewandes, weit mehr den Charakter einer sozialen Revolution und eines Bürgerkrieges als den einer nationalen Erhebung...' (Meyer, *Ursprung u. Anfänge des Christentums*, III, 74, n. 2). Cf. R. Eisler, ΙΗΣΟΥΣ ΒΑΣΙΛΕΥΣ, II, 711, n. 1; Grant, *Economic Background of the Gospels*, pp. 92–110; Brandon, *Fall of Jerusalem*, pp. 155–6; Jeremias, *Jerusalem*, pp. 54–9; Hengel, *Die Zeloten*, pp. 89, 341–2.   [3] Luke vii. 25.

[4] Jos. *Ant.* XVIII. 35; *War*, II. 169. Cf. Schürer, *G.J.V.* I, 487–8. See above, p. 66, n. 4.

[5] *Leg. ad Gaium*, 301 (ed. E. M. Smallwood, p. 128).

dents, for which the procurator was responsible, goes some way to confirming Philo's judgement.

It is unfortunate that Josephus gives no indication of the respective dates of the two incidents concerned; but it may be reasonably inferred that the first occurred shortly after the beginning of his governorship, i.e. A.D. 26. Josephus, in introducing his account of this incident,[1] asserts that Pilate 'led his army from Caesarea and established it for winter-quarters in Jerusalem, for the purpose of destroying the laws of the Jews'.[2] It is not clear from this statement whether Pilate was acting on superior orders or on his own initiative. Since the action he then took represented, as we shall see, a departure from the practice of the preceding procurators, it would seem unlikely that a new governor should have made such a change at the start of his term of office without instructions from those who appointed him. It has been suggested that Pilate was probably carrying out the instructions of Sejanus, the powerful favourite of Tiberius and noted for his anti-Semitic feeling.[3] However, beyond noting the improbability that Pilate was acting on his own initiative, it is impossible to identify the ultimate source of responsibility for the ensuing action. The assertion that Pilate intended to destroy 'the laws of the Jews' logically implies a complete abolition of the foundation of Judaism; but such an undertaking would have been so serious that we may fairly doubt whether Josephus' words are to be taken literally. What seems more likely, from the nature of the action that followed, is that the Roman government thought the time had come to bring the Jews into line with other subject peoples in the acceptance of imperial insignia. In deference to Jewish religious scruples, the former procurators had sent their troops for garrison duty in Jerusalem without the usual emblems on their standards:[4] for these standards bore images of the emperor and other sacred symbols, and they were regarded as cult objects.[5] Pilate now

---

[1] *Ant.* XVIII. 55 ff.; cf. *War*, II. 169 ff. The incident related here comes at the beginning of his account of Pilate's term of government.

[2] *Ant. ibid.*: ἐπὶ καταλύσει τῶν νομίμων τῶν Ἰουδαϊκῶν ἐφρόνησε...

[3] Cf. Derenbourg, *Essai*, p. 198; H. Graetz, *History of the Jews* (London, 1891), II, 139; Schürer, *G.J.V.* I, 492, n. 147; A. D. Doyle, 'Pilate's Career and the Date of the Crucifixion', *J.T.S.* XLII (1941), 192; Philo, *Leg. ad Gaium* (ed. E. M. Smallwood), p. 305.

[4] Jos. *Ant.* XVIII. 56: καὶ διὰ τοῦτο [the Jewish taboo of images] οἱ πρότερον ἡγεμόνες ταῖς μὴ μετὰ τοιῶνδε κόσμων σημαίαις ἐποιοῦντο εἴσοδον τῇ πόλει.

[5] 'Religio Romanorum tota castrensis signa veneratur, signa iurat, signa omnibus deis praeponit. Omnes illi imaginum suggestus in signis monilia

ordered these standards to be taken to Jerusalem, with their images covered (κεκαλυμμένας), and they were introduced under the cover of darkness, possibly with the intention of presenting the Jews with a *fait accompli*.[1]

Josephus' account of the Jewish reaction leaves many points obscure; he appears to be chiefly concerned to emphasise the iniquity of Pilate and the amazing restraint, together with heroic determination to defend their religion, of the Jews. Rather surprisingly, when they discovered that the obnoxious standards were in Jerusalem, the Jews did not immediately demonstrate there, but went *en masse* (κατὰ πληθύν) to Caesarea, the headquarters of the Roman government, whither Pilate had apparently returned. Such a mass movement some sixty miles is certainly a remarkable thing, and one naturally asks how it was organised and led. But Josephus gives no details, nor does he mention who were the Jewish spokesmen in the petition which was then presented to Pilate to remove the standards. The impression given of a well-ordered and well-behaved mass demonstration of protest certainly causes surprise, in view of Jewish reaction when religious principles were involved on other occasions. Moreover, the fact that nothing is said of the leaders of the movement, and no reference is made to the Zealots, reasonably excites suspicion as to whether Josephus has given the full story. However that may be, it is significant that Pilate refused the petition on the ground that to withdraw the standards would be an insult to the emperor (τὸ εἰς ὕβριν Καίσαρι φέρειν).[2] That the action requested by the Jews would indeed have had this aspect emphasises the importance of the question, which we have already noticed, of the original source of the authority for this apparent change of practice.

According to Josephus, the Jewish crowd remained at Caesarea for six days making petition in an orderly, well-behaved manner. Even when threatened with death by Pilate's troops, their resolution and composure remained firm. Being duly impressed by their devotion to their laws, Pilate gave way and ordered the standards to be

crucum sunt' (Tertullian, *Apology*, XVI. 8; cf. Pliny, *Nat. Hist.* XIII. 3 (4). 23; Dionys. Halic. VI. 45. 2; Tacitus, *Ann.* I. 39. 7, II. 17. 2: 'propria legionum numina'). Cf. Eisler, ΙΗΣΟΥΣ ΒΑΣΙΛΕΥΣ, II, 167, n. 2, I, Tafel XXXIV; *O.C.D.* p. 857b; Kraeling in *H.Th.R.* XXXV (1942), 269–76. See also the Qumrân *D.S.H.* VI. 11–14, in A. Dupont-Sommer, *Les écrits esséniens*, p. 274; Bruce in *A.L.U.O.S.* I (1958–9), 13.

[1] Jos. *Ant.* XVIII. 56; *War*, II. 169.
[2] Jos. *Ant.* XVIII. 57.

withdrawn from the holy city.[1] And so, in this edifying manner, the episode ends, and the historian is left asking in vain a number of pertinent questions which the record of Josephus raises but does not satisfy.

A similar feeling of frustration is provoked by the account which Philo gives of another exploit of Pilate, calculated to provoke Jewish feeling. The account occurs in a letter addressed by the Jewish prince Agrippa to the emperor Gaius on an occasion of dire peril to the Jews, as we shall presently see.[2] Although the letter appears in what is essentially a polemical work, condemning the memory of Gaius, there is no obvious reason for doubting its authenticity. It contains, however, much problematical matter, and the fact that the incident is not recorded by Josephus, while it is somewhat reminiscent of his story of the standards, excites suspicion. The two incidents, on analysis, appear to be essentially distinct, and it would seem that the one recalled by Agrippa took place some time after the other.[3] That Agrippa does not cite the incident concerning the

---

[1] *Ibid.* 58–9; *War*, II. 170–1. Cf. W. D. Morrison, *The Jews under Roman Rule* (London, 1890), pp. 141–3.

[2] Philo, *Leg. ad Gaium*, 276 ff. (ed. E. M. Smallwood). 'The letter given by Philo is probably not a verbatim copy of that actually written by Agrippa, but, in accordance with the conventions of ancient historiography, merely reproduces its general contents', Smallwood, p. 292. Cf. E. R. Goodenough, *The Politics of Philo Judaeus* (Yale University Press, 1938), p. 17.

[3] According to Eusebius, *Demonstratio evangelica*, VIII. 2. 122, Philo had related an incident concerning Pilate's installation of imperial images (or standards) in the Temple: Αὐτὰ δὴ ταῦτα καὶ ὁ Φίλων συμμαρτυρεῖ, τὰς σημαίας φάσκων τὰς βασιλικὰς τὸν Πιλᾶτον νύκτωρ ἐν τῷ ἱερῷ ἀναθεῖναι. In his *Ecclesiastical History*, II. v. 7, Eusebius also states that Philo recorded how Pilate had made an attempt on the Temple: περὶ τὸ ἐν Ἱεροσολύμοις ἔτι τότε συνεστὸς ἱερὸν ἐπιχειρήσαντά τι παρὰ τὸ Ἰουδαίοις ἐξόν, τὰ μέγιστα αὐτοὺς ἀναταράξαι. Since Eusebius, in the latter work, had just been recounting Josephus' account of Jewish affairs at this period, it is difficult not to believe that he has ascribed to Philo what Josephus relates. If Philo did, indeed, describe the episode of the standards, probably in a lost work concerning Jewish persecutions during the time of Tiberius, his mention of the Temple in this connection is a problem: Josephus tells only of the offending standards being in Jerusalem, not the Temple. The mention of the Temple could be an addition made by Eusebius; the fact that he specially describes the Temple as ἔτι τότε συνεστός can be equally interpreted to confirm or disprove that he alone was responsible for mentioning it. According to Jerome (*Comm. in Matt.* xxiv. 15), 'τὸ βδέλυγμα τῆς ἐρημώσεως potest...accipi...de imagine Caesaris, quam Pilatus *posuit* in templo'; it would be unwise, however, to assume that this writer was drawing here on some rabbinic source, as has been suggested.

standards in his letter to Gaius may indicate that it did not serve his purpose to do so. If this were so, it would suggest that Agrippa could not claim that Pilate had acted on his own initiative but under orders that ultimately derived from Tiberius.

The incident, which Agrippa recalls in his letter to Gaius, is attributed by him to Pilate's malicious intention of annoying the Jews rather than that of honouring Tiberius.[1] It took the form of setting up on the former palace of Herod in Jerusalem some gilded shields (ἐπιχρύσους ἀσπίδας). They bore no image or emblem, but only a brief inscription, recording the emperor's name and that of the person who dedicated the shields to him.[2] One might have supposed that such objects would have been considered innocuous even by the most pedantic of Jewish legalists. But apparently they were not, and a Jewish delegation, headed by four Herodian princes, petitioned Pilate to remove them; they claimed that the shields violated their native customs (κινεῖν ἔθη πάτρια), which other kings and emperors had respected. When Pilate obstinately refused (στερρῶς δὲ ἀντιλέγοντος), the Jews are represented, in Agrippa's letter, as torn between their loyalty to the emperor and obedience to their religion. They call on Pilate not to cause a revolt (μὴ στασίαζε), nor break the peace (μὴ κατάλυε τὴν εἰρήνην), nor use Tiberius as an excuse for insulting their nation.[3] They challenge Pilate to produce the authority for his action, and threaten to appeal to the emperor, whom they significantly call their master (*despotēs*).[4] This threat is stated to have disturbed Pilate most profoundly, because he feared that his maladministration would thus become known to Tiberius, who would not tolerate such action.[5] It is to be noted

Cf. Schürer, *G.J.V.* I, 489, n. 145, III, 527–9; Smallwood, ed. *Leg. ad Gaium*, pp. 37–43, 302 (ἐπιχρύσους ἀσπίδας...). See also Eisler's interpretation of the different versions, ΙΗΣΟΥΣ ΒΑΣΙΛΕΥΣ, II, 166–7. On the probable date of the incident, see below, p. 75, n. 1.

[1] *Leg. ad Gaium*, 299: οὗτος οὐκ ἐπὶ τιμῇ Τιβερίου μᾶλλον ἢ ἕνεκα τοῦ λυπῆσαι τὸ πλῆθος...

[2] ἐπιχρύσους ἀσπίδας μήτε μορφὴν ἐχούσας μήτε ἄλλο τι τῶν ἀπηγορευμένων, ἔξω τινὸς ἐπιγραφῆς ἀναγκαίας, ἣ δύο ταῦτα ἐμήνυε, τόν τε ἀναθέντα καὶ ὑπὲρ οὗ ἡ ἀνάθεσις (*Leg. ad Gaium*, 299). Smallwood, p. 302, thinks that Pilate himself was the donor of the shields.

[3] μὴ πρόφασις τῆς εἰς τὸ ἔθνος ἐπηρείας ἔστω σοι Τιβέριος (*Leg. ad Gaium*, 301).

[4] *Ibid.* 301. It is not without significance that the Jewish leaders, namely, the chief priests, are also represented in John xix. 15 as strenuously professing their loyalty to the emperor (οὐκ ἔχομεν βασιλέα εἰ μὴ Καίσαρα), in striking contrast to the Zealot attitude, which we have noted.

[5] *Ibid.* 302.

that this is made the chief cause of Pilate's concern, and not that he had acted without imperial authority in the matter of the shields, as is suggested in the earlier part of the letter. In view of our particular interest here in evaluating Pilate's character and policy, the point is important; however, we can only conclude that Philo or his source is obscure in this connection, and that whether this obscurity is intentional or accidental cannot be determined.[1]

The sequel is equally obscure, owing to the extravagance of the language used. The Jewish authorities (οἱ ἐν τέλει) wrote to the emperor about the matter. Tiberius' reaction, directed against Pilate, is described in hyperbole. He was moved by excessive anger, and immediately wrote to the offending procurator, condemning him for his rash innovation in the most uncompromising manner.[2] He ordered him to remove the shields to the temple of Augustus at Caesarea. Agrippa concludes this section of his letter by stressing, for the benefit of Gaius, that in this signal manner the traditional (Roman) policy towards Jerusalem (ἡ πρὸς τὴν πόλιν ἀρχαία συνήθεια) had been maintained.[3]

The account, as it is given in Philo's tractate, presents an edifying tale in which Pilate's viciousness is contrasted with the Jews' firm but orderly resistance to an outrage on their religion; their loyalty to the emperor is also emphasised, as is also his ready and effective support of their privileges. However, on analysis the account is found to be full of difficulties and improbabilities. We have already noticed that it is uncertain whether Pilate was acting solely upon his own initiative in setting up the shields in Jerusalem. It could be that,

[1] Philo's (or Agrippa's) subsequent statements (*ibid.* 303) are equally obscure. Although he had emphasised Pilate's exceeding fear that a Jewish embassy would discover his misdeeds to the emperor, he describes him as continuing in his refusal to accede to the Jewish request for the removal of the shields. Surely, if he knew that he had exceeded his authority in the matter and that his other iniquities would thereby come to light, he would have prevented the sending of the embassy by a discreet concession? His stubbornness, where he is represented as being in a weaker position *vis-à-vis* the Jewish leaders, contrasts strikingly with his abject submission when Caesar's name is invoked by the chief priests, to secure the condemnation of Jesus; cf. John xix. 12–13, 15. See below, pp. 261–2.

[2] *Ibid.* 304–5: ὁ [Tiberius] δὲ διαναγνοὺς οἷα μὲν εἶπε Πιλᾶτος, οἷα δὲ ἠπείλησεν· ὡς δὲ ὠργίσθη, καίτοι οὐκ εὐληπτος ὢν ὀργῇ, περιττόν ἐστι διηγεῖσθαι...μυρία μὲν τοῦ καινουργηθέντος τολμήματος ὀνειδίζων καὶ ἐπιπλήττων...Dr Smallwood ascribes the great anger of Tiberius to Pilate's disregard of his instructions, issued after the death of Sejanus (A.D. 31). Cf. Doyle in *J.T.S.* XLII (1941), 192.

[3] *Leg. ad Gaium*, 305.

resentful of the Jewish victory over the standards, he devised this means of taking his revenge. But it would be equally possible that the setting up of the shields was a normal official act of loyalty to the emperor; moreover, the place where they were displayed was a secular building, used by the Roman administration and thus affording an appropriate setting for such emblems.[1] The grounds for the Jewish complaint are not clear. It is expressly stated that the shields bore no images and had only a very brief dedicatory inscription, giving the names of the emperor and the donor. Since, therefore, the shields did not contravene the aniconic injunctions of the Torah, it would seem that the inscription must have given offence.[2] The only way in which a short inscription might have done this would have been by its containing some reference to the divinity of the emperor. If this were so, we are at once reminded of the denunciation pronounced by Judas, the founder of the Zealots, of accepting human lords (θνητοὺς δεσπότας), when God was their lord.[3]

If the cause of the Jewish objection lay thus in the inscription, we may reasonably infer therefrom that the teaching of Judas of Galilee had taken deep root in the Jewish mind. Such an objection would surely also have been taken to the Roman coins which circulated in Judaea, a fact which must be remembered when we come to evaluate the famous episode concerning the tribute money in the Synoptic Gospels.[4] Such Jewish susceptibility must have been hard for the Romans to understand, still more to tolerate. It is, accordingly, intelligible that Pilate should have interpreted the Jewish request to remove the shields as an insult to the emperor. How Tiberius reacted to the matter, when he learned of it, is obscured, as we have noted, by the extravagant language used in Agrippa's letter. What is, however, significant is the fact that Tiberius did not recall Pilate, as one might suppose he would have

---

[1] W. D. Morrison acutely observed that 'it is hardly to be supposed that the procurator, in the prosecution of his religious policy, was merely gratifying a feeling of personal animosity at the cost of adding immensely to his difficulties as a ruler. Such is not the course which a man of Pilate's experience was likely to adopt' (*The Jews under Roman Rule*, pp. 145–6). Kraeling (*H. Th.R.* xxxv, 1942, 265, 282) dismisses the suggestion that Pilate acted out of personal spite; he thinks that he either was ignorant of what was involved or underestimated Jewish scruples.

[2] Philo says expressly that the shields bore no image: τότε μὲν οὖν ἀσπίδες ἦσαν, αἷς οὐδὲν ἀνεζωγράφητο μίμημα (*Leg. ad Gaium*, 306).

[3] Jos. *War*, ii. 118. Cf. Hengel, *Die Zeloten*, pp. 108–9.

[4] See below, pp. 271, 345–9. See Frontispiece and Plate i.

done, if the procurator had deliberately provoked the situation. That the shields were ordered to be removed suggests that the emperor did not think it worthwhile to cause trouble over such an issue; and such seems to have been the decision of Pilate over the standards.[1] However, both incidents serve to show how intolerant the Jews could be of any affront, or implied affront, to their religious principles. Such sensitivity, together with the readiness to take opposing action, indicates the presence of a strong and effectively organised vigilance about, if not an open resistance to, the Roman administration, and, although no mention is made of them, no other party was more suited to this role than the Zealots.

The second clash between Pilate and the Jews, according to Josephus, arose out of the building of an aqueduct to bring water into Jerusalem.[2] The historian supplies no information about the antecedents of the undertaking. The work was, presumably, necessary; but who was legally responsible for initiating it and meeting its cost is not recorded.[3] Josephus merely states that Pilate did the work and defrayed the cost from the Temple treasury (δαπάνη τῶν ἱερῶν χρημάτων). Whether the work was undertaken without consulting the Jewish civil authorities, or how the money was taken from the sacred coffers, are matters of obvious importance about which the

---

[1] Cf. Morrison, *The Jews under Roman Rule*, pp. 146–7. On the date of the incident concerning the shields Doyle has argued (in *J.T.S.* XLII, 1941, 190–3) that it must have taken place after the fall of Sejanus in A.D. 31, with which date Smallwood, ed. *Leg. ad Gaium*, p. 303, seems to agree; cf. Schürer, *G.J.V.* I, 492, n. 147. Doyle, p. 191, suggests that Antipas had joined in the Jewish protest to Tiberius, and that this action explains the enmity between him and Pilate which Luke xxiii. 12 mentions. From this interpretation he infers that the crucifixion of Jesus probably occurred in A.D. 33.   [2] Jos. *Ant.* XVIII. 60–2; *War*, II. 175–7.

[3] According to Shekalim 4. 2, 'the (upkeep of the) water-channel, the city wall and the towers thereof and all the city's needs were provided from the residue of the Shekel-chamber', trans. H. Danby, *The Mishnah*, p. 155. Cf. Klausner, *Jesus of Nazareth*, p. 164, n. 85; J. Lightfoot, *Horae Hebraicae et Talmudicae* (Oxford, 1859), I, 221. Eisler, ΙΗΣΟΥΣ ΒΑΣΙΛΕΥΣ, I, 219, n. 2, attempted to explain the matter in terms of the differing lengths given by Josephus for the aqueduct, which 'zeigen, daß die Juden die Großzügigkeit und Kostspieligkeit des Planes beanstandeten, während Pilatus, der bei dem Kostenanschlag gewiß auch einen hübschen Zuschlag für seine eigene Tasche mit hineingerechnet hatte, auf seiner Forderung bestand und schließlich das Geld, das man ihm verweigerte, militärisch requiriete'. On the water supply of Jerusalem at this period cf. Schürer, *G.J.V.* I, 490, n. 146; G. A. Smith, *Jerusalem* (London, 1907), I, ch. 5; Jeremias, *Jerusalem*, I, 14; S. Perowne, *The Later Herods* (London, 1958), pp. 52–3.

Jewish historian says nothing. And on the exact cause of the resulting disturbance he is also vague. According to his account in the *Antiquities*, a great multitude of Jews, 'who did not like what was done about the water',[1] assembled to demand that the work be stopped. This statement seems to imply that the Jews, for some reason, objected to the actual construction of the aqueduct, and that they tried to stop the work when it was in progress. The account in the *Wars*, however, appears to connect the ensuing disturbance with Pilate's use of 'the sacred treasure known as *Korbōnas* (τὸν ἱερὸν θησαυρόν, καλεῖται δὲ κορβωνᾶς)'; for the citing of this term indicates the sacrosanct nature of the money.[2] The employment of this money for a secular purpose, no matter how sensible that purpose was, and the possibility that sacrilege was committed in the taking of it from the Temple, would indeed have been potent causes for Jewish anger; and to them perhaps was added resentment that a heathen foreigner should interfere with the time-honoured arrangements of the holy city.

Jewish reaction, according to Josephus, was very violent, and it extended to personal abuse of the procurator himself (ὕβριζον εἰς τὸν ἄνδρα) when he visited Jerusalem. Pilate's counter-measures appear to have been rather odd. One might have expected that a Roman governor would have deployed his troops to quell any further disturbance or interference with the work. However, Josephus describes Pilate as resorting to clandestine ways of punishing or coercing the Jews. His soldiers in disguise, and concealing clubs (σκυτάλας) in their robes, mingled among the protesting Jews, and, on receiving a preconcerted sign, attacked them so violently that many were killed or wounded. The action was effective, and the disturbance (ἡ στάσις) ended.[3]

---

[1] οἱ δ' οὐκ ἠγάπων τοῖς ἀμφὶ τὸ ὕδωρ δρωμένοις πολλαί τε μυριάδες ἀνθρώπων... (*Ant.* xviii. 60).

[2] According to Josephus, *Against Apion*, 1. 167, the oath (εὑρεθείη) *Korban* could be translated into Greek as δῶρον θεοῦ ('God's gift'). Cf. Ricciotti, *Flavio Giuseppe*, ii, 256, n. on 175; Feldman, Loeb ed. of Josephus, ix, 46, n. *b*.

[3] Jos. *Ant.* xviii. 61–2; *War*, ii. 175–7. On reflection a number of other questions on practical issues arise from these reports of Josephus: (i) presumably Pilate's men must have worn Jewish dress, and have either kept quiet or spoken Aramaic, in order to mingle without detection among the Jewish crowd—if they were Samaritans, there would probably have been little language difficulty, (ii) did his arming of them with clubs, and not swords, imply that Pilate sought to avoid fatal casualties?—according to Josephus there were some deaths, (iii) the use of clubs suggests that Pilate planned a police, not a military, operation.

These three encounters between Pilate and the Jews are of immense significance for our evaluation of the origins of Christianity. Two of them, namely, those concerning the standards and the aqueduct, undoubtedly occurred during the lifetime of Jesus.[1] Although the events took place in Judaea, the excitement must have extended into Galilee; moreover, since Jerusalem, with its Temple, was the focus of Jewish national and religious life, pious Jews frequently went there. The Gospels abundantly witness to the importance of Jerusalem for Jesus,[2] and he would certainly have known of these incidents, even if he had not actually been in the city when they occurred. How would he have reacted to them? Would it have been a matter of indifference to him, as a pious Jew, that the holy city was polluted by the images of a heathen lord? Would he not have shared in his fellow-countrymen's sense of outrage that the Temple treasury had been raided by a particularly vicious Roman official?[3] Would he have viewed unmoved the killing and injuring of those who protested against this violation of their sacred Law?[4]

---

[1] The date of the crucifixion of Jesus can only be inferred, not proved, from a mass of conflicting data: the more generally accepted computations range from A.D. 29 to 33; cf. *R.A.C.* III, 50; *R.G.G.*[3], III, 625–6; *Peake's Commentary*[2], 636c; Doyle in *J.T.S.* XLII (1941), 190–3. If Doyle's arguments are accepted, the episode of the shields also occurred before the death of Jesus. Josephus gives no clear indication of when the aqueduct incident happened beyond prefacing his account in the *War* with μετὰ δὲ ταῦτα, i.e. after the trouble over the standards. The *Antiquities* account is followed in the extant text by the famous passage about Jesus (XVIII. 63–4), which will be discussed at length below (pp. 359–64). If Josephus did give some account of Jesus at this point in his narrative, it would seem that the aqueduct affair happened before his crucifixion; the extant account begins: Γίνεται δὲ κατὰ τοῦτον τὸν χρόνον, Ἰησοῦς σοφὸς ἀνήρ... Eisler concluded, after a careful analysis of the statement: 'Aus diesen Parallelstellen [which he cites] ergibt sich m. E. zwingend daß auch in Antiqq. XVIII, 3, 3, §63 γίνεται durchaus nicht absolut mit dem Subjekt Ἰησοῦς τις verbunden gewesen sein kann, da das Verbum derart gebraucht bei Josephus nur "wird geboren" bedeutet, was hier durch den chronologischen Zusammenhang ausgeschlossen ist' (ΙΗΣΟΥΣ ΒΑΣΙΛΕΥΣ, I, 50; cf. pp. 49–51, 85, 87).

[2] E.g. Mark xi. 15–17; Matt. v. 35, xxiii. 37; Luke xiii. 34.

[3] Such a tradition as that preserved in Mark xii. 41–4 implies that Jesus regarded the money cast into the Temple treasury as being given to God. Cf. Matt. xxiii. 16–21.

[4] It has been thought that the mysterious reference in Luke xiii. 4 to those eighteen who were killed by the falling of the tower in Siloam concerns an incident in the aqueduct affair: cf. Morrison, *The Jews under Roman Rule*, p. 148; J. M. Creed, *Gospel according to St Luke* (London, 1929), p. 180;

The Gospels are strangely silent about these events that clearly convulsed Jewish life during the years concerned. They do, however, indirectly attest the existence of some kind of political disturbance at this time. At the time of the trial and crucifixion of Jesus, the Romans were holding certain men who had been involved in insurrection (ἐν τῇ στάσει);[1] two λῃσταί (Josephus' favourite term for Zealots) were crucified with him;[2] the slaughter of certain Galilaeans, 'whose blood Pilate had mingled with their sacrifices', was reported to Jesus;[3] Jesus also referred to the 'violent ones' (βιασταί), who forcibly seized the kingdom of heaven.[4] Across this background of violence Jesus appears to move, untouched and unconcerned by the deep feelings of those whom he sought to prepare for the coming of the kingdom of God. The problem implicit here is to occupy us at length later; but now we must notice one other fact. It is that, at this critical time, Jesus had among his disciples a professed Zealot.[5]

This last fact has another significance. It is strange, as we have

Olmstead, *Jesus in the Light of History*, pp. 147–9. Eisler, ΙΗΣΟΥΣ ΒΑΣΙ-ΛΕΥΣ, II, 516–25, explained the fall of the tower even more imaginatively by supposing that Pilate's forces destroyed it when driving out the armed followers of Jesus. In the Lukan record the incident appears to be associated with Pilate's slaughter of the Galilaeans (xiii. 1–3); but its association is clearly due to its citation as an example of violent and possibly accidental death. On the meaning of such a *Schulgespräch* see below, p. 316, n. 6; cf. Bultmann, *Gesch. d. synop. Trad.* pp. 56–8; Brandon, *Fall of Jerusalem*, p. 106.   [1] Mark xv. 7. See below, pp. 334, 339.

[2] Mark xv. 27. Cf. Hengel, *Die Zeloten*, p. 30; see below, p. 351, n. 1.

[3] Luke xiii. 1–3: 'Es könnte freilich vielleicht auch irgendein früherer Zeloten-Aufstand gemeint sein; denn die Zeloten scheinen gelegentlich als Γαλιλαῖοι bezeichnet worden zu sein (Justin dial. 80; Hegesipp. bei Eus. h.e. IV 22, 7)' (Bultmann, *Gesch. d. synop. Trad.* p. 57). Cf. O. Cullmann, *The State in the New Testament*, p. 14; Hengel, *Die Zeloten*, pp. 61, 344 (who thinks that the passage is too brief to reconstruct the situation concerned). Klausner, *Jesus of Nazareth*, pp. 153, n. 58, 164, n. 86, suggests that Luke has confused Archelaus with Pilate, and that the incident is that recorded by Jos. *Ant.* XVII. 213–18, 237. Cf. Kraeling in *H.Th.R.* XXXV (1942), 286–9. See also pp. 53–4.

[4] Matt. xi. 12. The βιασταί could well refer to the Zealots; cf. A. von Gall, ΒΑΣΙΛΕΙΑ ΤΟΥ ΘΕΟΥ (Heidelberg, 1926), p. 353; Klausner, *Jesus of Nazareth*, p. 206; S. Angus in *E.R.E.* XII, 851 a, n. 7; K. Stendahl in *Peake's Commentary*², 684 e; H. Windisch, *Der messianische Krieg und das Urchristentum* (Tübingen, 1909), p. 35; *Th.Wb.* IV, 888; T. W. Manson, 'John the Baptist', *B.J.R.L.* 36 (1954), p. 406, n. 2. Hengel, *Die Zeloten*, p. 345, favours the view that the term means the 'feindliche Geistermächte'. See below, p. 300, n. 5.   [5] See p. 43, n. 2.

already noticed, that Josephus makes no mention of the Zealots, under any of his designations for them, in connection with the affair of the standards, and neither do they appear in his account of the trouble over the aqueduct. That Agrippa, in his letter to the emperor Gaius, should have refrained from mentioning them as supporting the Jewish protest over the gilded shields, is, of course, understandable; but if, as we concluded, the offence of the shields lay in their inscription, Zealot influence was probably behind the opposition. However, the silence of both Josephus and Philo, or Agrippa, about Zealot activity on the occasions concerned is not really serious. As we have just noted, it is obvious that such activity would not have been mentioned by Agrippa.[1] The accounts of Josephus of the other two incidents are clearly intended to underline the vicious nature of Pilate and the forbearance of the Jews in resisting attacks on their religion; consequently, any part that the Zealots or 'brigands' might have had was best left unmentioned—after all, the writings concerned were addressed to Gentile readers, who were unlikely to be acquainted with such details.

In terms of Romano-Jewish relations, these actions of Pilate were deleterious. They had the effect, moreover, of reinforcing the Zealot case: submission to Rome meant accepting as lord a heathen ruler who claimed to be divine—the fact being flagrantly advertised in the holy city of Yahweh by the display of the standards and inscribed shields. It resulted also in a heathen official, of a particularly detestable kind, being able to commandeer the sacred funds of the Temple for whatever secular project he might determine. The fact that, according to both Josephus and Philo, protests were made by the Jewish authorities and other Jewish magnates would seem to indicate that the logic of the teaching of Judas of Galilee was now being recognised even by those inclined by tradition and self-interest to moderation. It is difficult to estimate Roman reaction. But if Pilate's action in connection with the standards represented a deliberate tightening of official policy after earlier concessions, the imperial government was made to realise the strength of Jewish intransigence where religion was concerned. And the affair of the shields was calculated to inform it, possibly to its surprise, how far Jewish religious susceptibilities extended. Even if the Roman mind had grasped the reason for the Jewish objection to images, it must surely have been baffled when it found that plain shields, bearing only an

[1] This would apply equally to Philo, if the letter is his composition. Cf. Goodenough, *The Politics of Philo Judaeus*, pp. 5 ff.

honorific inscription to the emperor, were equally objects of Jewish abhorrence. Not only could such an attitude be fairly construed as an insult to the emperor and the majesty of Rome, but it could also be interpreted as evidence of how intolerant the Jews could be, if encouraged by earlier concessions.

Pilate's career as procurator of Judaea terminated, according to Josephus, as the result of his action against the Samaritans in a mysterious affair which is indicative of the religious atmosphere of Palestine at this time.[1] Persuaded by some pseudo-prophet or Messiah that the sacred vessels, believed to be hidden by Moses on Mount Gerizim, would be revealed, the Samaritans gathered to ascend their holy mountain.[2] The fact that they came armed to witness the revelation suggests some form of Messianic movement aimed against the Roman government. Whatever the intent may have been, Pilate took prompt action by sending troops to deal with the situation. This they did effectively, killing a number of the Samaritans and capturing others, who were later executed. The Samaritan leaders complained to Vitellius, the legate of Syria, about Pilate's action, protesting that they had had no intention to revolt. Josephus' account of the sequel is rather perplexing. He states that Vitellius ordered Pilate to go to Rome, to explain (διδάξοντα) to the emperor about the accusations of the Jews. Before he reached Rome, Tiberius had died, and Pilate thus passes out of history.[3]

Vitellius, who had sent his friend Marcellus to take over the government of Judaea, arrived there himself by the time of the Passover of A.D. 36. Probably feeling that a conciliatory gesture would be opportune, he handed over to the Jews the vestments of the high priest, which had been held by the secular ruling power since the days of Herod the Great, the use of them being conceded only for the duration of a religious festival.[4] However, this conces-

---

[1] Jos. *Ant.* XVIII. 85–9.

[2] The Samaritans believed that the *Taheb* (Messiah) would reveal the hidden vessels; cf. M. Gaster, *The Samaritans* (London, 1925), pp. 90–1; W. J. Moulton, 'Samaritans', *E.R.E.* XI, 165b–166a.

[3] On the subsequent fate of Pilate cf. Schürer, *G.J.V.* I, 493, n. 151; Meyer, *Ursprung*, I, 205, n. 5. E. M. Smallwood dates Pilate's dismissal to 36–7 (before the Passover), 'The Date of the Dismissal of Pontius Pilate from Judaea', *J.J.S.* v (1954), 20–1.

[4] Jos. *Ant.* XVIII. 90–5; cf. xv. 403–5, where it is stated that the Jews requested Vitellius to give them custody of the vestments, and that Tiberius granted the request when it was referred to him. Cf. M. P. Charlesworth in *C.A.H.* x, 649–50.

sion was balanced by a reminder of Roman power in that the high priest Caiaphas was deposed for some unstated reason and another, Jonathan, appointed in his place.[1]

Vitellius was destined to learn the strength of Jewish religious intolerance for himself. Under orders from Tiberius, in the spring of A.D. 37 he assembled his forces at Ptolemais, in preparation for a punitive expedition against Aretas, king of Petra.[2] According to Josephus, when the Jewish leaders (ἄνδρες οἱ πρῶτοι) learned that he intended to pass through Judaea (διὰ τῆς 'Ιουδαίων), they petitioned him not to go that way; their reason being that the passage of his troops, with their standards, would violate the Jewish law against images.[3] If Josephus means that objection was made on these grounds to passage through Judaea, it would follow that the Jews had extended the range of their prohibition beyond Jerusalem itself; for the earlier incident, involving military standards, had been concerned with their presence in the holy city only. Such a raising of their claim to immunity would be ominous: it could signify that they had been encouraged by their success against Pilate to become even more demanding in their zeal for their faith. Unfortunately it is not clear from the sequel whether Josephus literally meant Judaea by the words διὰ τῆς 'Ιουδαίων; for he states that Vitellius conceded the Jewish request, and that he ordered his troops to proceed by way of the great plain (διὰ τοῦ μεγάλου πεδίου). This description could indicate a route through the Jordan valley, which would have avoided entry into Judaea; but it could also mean the road through the coastal plain, which would actually have passed through Judaea, yet well removed from the area of Jerusalem.[4]

However that may be, the Jewish request was granted. In Josephus' account, Vitellius appears to have been very well disposed to the Jews; for, after sending his army on its way, he visited Jerusalem, together with Herod Antipas, and offered sacrifice there (θύσων τῷ θεῷ), being well received by the Jews. However, during

[1] Jos. *Ant.* XVIII. 95. E. M. Smallwood supposes that Vitellius deposed Caiaphas because, being an associate of Pilate, he was unpopular with the Jews ('High Priests and Politics in Roman Palestine', *J.T.S.* XIII, 1962, 22).

[2] Jos. *Ant.* XVIII. 120. The expedition had been ordered by Tiberius in support of Herod; cf. Jos. *Ant.* XVIII. 109–15. Cf. Jones, *The Herods of Judaea*, pp. 182–3.

[3] Jos. *Ant.* XVIII. 121: οὐ γὰρ αὐτοῖς εἶναι πάτριον περιορᾶν εἰκόνας εἰς αὐτὴν φερομένας, πολλὰς δ' εἶναι σημαίαις ἐπικειμένας.

[4] *Ant.* XVIII. 122. Cf. Schürer, *G.J.V.* I, 494, n. 154.

his three days' stay in the city, he deposed Jonathan, the high priest, and appointed his brother Theophilus in his stead:[1] no reason is given for the change, which would again have reminded the Jews that ultimate power lay with Rome. Before Vitellius left, news arrived of the death of the emperor Tiberius. The legate, accordingly, obliged the Jews to take an oath of allegiance to the new emperor, Gaius.[2]

As we have noted, Vitellius appears in the record of Josephus as remarkably well disposed towards the Jews. This attitude could conceivably have stemmed from a personal liking; but there are reasons for thinking that it was due rather to political necessity. The concession concerning the vestments of the high priest was probably intended to conciliate Jewish opinion, which had been dangerously disturbed by Pilate's severity and violence. The more notable deference to Jewish demands concerning the passage of the Roman army through Judaea is understandable as a politic act by a commander about to plunge into the desert of Nabataea.[3] It would obviously have been dangerous to have a disgruntled people between him and his base in Syria, especially in the event of difficulties in the Arabian campaign. But, even though the demand was conceded, it was likely to affect future relations for the worse. Whether the Jews had stepped up their demand or not in the matter of the passage through Judaea, the fact that they were ready to obstruct a Roman military operation for such a reason was significant. It surely attests that Jewish zeal for the maintenance of religious principles had become so strong that it could lead to action calculated to embarrass the Romans on a critical occasion. The action, moreover, was officially organised. No mention is made of the Zealots in connection with it; but the extreme nature of the demand well reflects the Zealot spirit, and it at least indicates how far the Zealot attitude was finding expression even among the more responsible members of the people. Further, the gaining of this concession, following on that won by their resistance to Pilate, must undoubtedly have greatly strengthened the conviction of the Jews

---

[1] Jos. *Ant.* XVIII. 123. Dr Smallwood (*J.T.S.* XIII, 1962, 22–3) finds the action of Vitellius puzzling, and suggests that, unless Jonathan had offended in some unrecorded way, the legate may have deposed him because he proved to be too popular with the Jews.

[2] Jos. *Ant.* XVIII. 124: ὤρκισεν τὴν πληθὺν ἐπ' εὐνοίᾳ τῇ Γαΐου. According to Philo, *Leg. ad Gaium*, 231, the Jews later claimed that they were the first of all the people of Syria to rejoice at the accession of Gaius.

[3] Cf. Charlesworth in *C.A.H.* x, 649–50.

that faithfulness to God's Law would be rewarded with success.[1] On the Roman side this latest expression of Jewish intransigence must have been noted with particular concern; for it would have seemed to suggest that the earlier concessions made to Jewish religious susceptibilities had been interpreted as weakness, and led to an even more unreasonable demand on a potentially dangerous occasion. The experience would surely have been noted as a warning. It is possible that the deposition of the high priest by Vitellius was intended as a reminder to the Jews of the power of their Roman masters.

The elevation of Gaius to the imperial purple might have augured an even more conciliatory policy towards the Jews, since the Jewish prince Agrippa was a close friend of the new emperor and had even suffered imprisonment on his behalf during the reign of Tiberius.[2] Gaius had, indeed, quickly shown his appreciation by giving Agrippa the tetrarchy of the recently deceased Philip, together with the title of king.[3] However, Gaius was destined to threaten Jewish religion with the most terrible outrage of its sanctity since the days of Antiochus Epiphanes. But before this came to pass, the emperor had given further proof of his affection for Agrippa by adding to his kingdom the tetrarchy of Herod Antipas, whom he had deposed and exiled to Spain.[4] It is worth noting that the long reign of Herod Antipas had afforded the Jews of Galilee immunity from direct subjection to Rome, which was the fate of their compatriots in Judaea. Whether they had appreciated this aspect of Herod's rule is doubtful;[5] but they would have been fully aware of what Roman

[1] Jos. *Ant.* xviii. 5; see above, pp. 33, 51.

[2] Jos. *Ant.* xviii. 143–236; *War*, ii. 178–80. Cf. Schürer, *G.J.V.* i, 549–52; Jones, *The Herods of Judaea*, pp. 184–92; Perowne, *The Later Herods*, pp. 58–67.

[3] Jos. *Ant.* xviii. 237; *War*, ii. 181.

[4] Jos. *Ant.* xviii. 240–55; *War*, ii. 181–3. Agrippa had accused Antipas of treasonable understanding with the Parthians and of having arms for seventy thousand troops. The latter accusation was apparently based on fact, but it is difficult to believe that Antipas seriously contemplated revolt against Rome. Cf. Jones, *The Herods of Judaea*, pp. 195–6; Schürer, *G.J.V.* i, 447–8.

[5] There must have been significance for his audience in the remark which Jesus of Nazareth made concerning (Herod) Antipas: πορευθέντες εἴπατε τῇ ἀλώπεκι ταύτῃ (Luke xiii. 32). The fox figures in a Rabbinic parable as 'the cleverest among the beasts', Berakhoth, fol. 61 b (in *Der babylonische Talmud*, ed. L. Goldschmidt, i, 277). Cf. *J.E.* p. 441; Schürer, *G.J.V.* i, 432, n. 5; Creed, *St Luke*, p. 186; S.B. *Kommentar*, ii, 200–1.

rule meant from the events in Judaea, in which they apparently sometimes became personally involved. However, the appointment of Agrippa in A.D. 39 put off from them the brute reality of immediate contact with the Romans as masters for a few more years.

The idea of the divinity of the emperor, which the astute Augustus had fostered for political reasons, was taken very seriously by Gaius, who was undoubtedly mentally unbalanced.[1] Such a situation was potentially dangerous for the Jews, and it needed only some significant incident to provoke the emperor to the realisation that he had subjects who refused to acknowledge him as divine. The incident was soon provided.

The Gentile inhabitants of Jamnia, learning of the emperor's obsession with the idea of his divinity (περὶ τὴν ἰδίαν ἐκθέωσιν), erected an altar, presumably for offering sacrifice to him. Philo asserts that they did this with the intention of provoking their Jewish fellow-citizens.[2] However that may be, the Jews were provoked to destroy the altar. The matter was duly reported to Rome by the procurator, Capito. Gaius took the Jewish action as a personal insult, and in revenge he ordered the legate of Syria, Petronius, to erect a colossal gilt statue of Zeus (κολοσσιαῖον ἀνδριάντα ἐπίχρυσον) in the Temple at Jerusalem.[3]

No greater outrage of Jewish religion could be conceived: it would

[1] Philo puts the matter very succinctly in the report of the Jewish messengers concerning Gaius: τὴν μὲν ἀνωτάτω καὶ πρώτην αἰτίαν ἴστε, ἣν καὶ πάντες ἴσασιν ἄνθρωποι· θεὸς βούλεται νομίζεσθαι,... (*Leg. ad Gaium*, 198). Cf. Jos. *Ant.* XVIII. 256, XIX. 284–5; Suetonius, *Caligula*, 22; Dio Cassius, LIX. 26, 28. Cf. A. D. Nock, 'Religious Developments from the Close of the Republic to the Death of Nero', *C.A.H.* x, 496–7; J. P. V. D. Balsdon, *The Emperor Gaius*, pp. 160–72.

[2] *Leg. ad Gaium*, 200–1. Jamnia was imperial property, having been bequeathed to Livia by Salome, Jos. *Ant.* XVIII. 31.'Josephus (*Ant.* XVIII. 257–61) makes the trouble that was to occur in Judaea stem directly from Alexandrian anti-Semitism. Cf. Schürer, *G.J.V.* I, 495–503.

[3] Philo, *Leg. ad Gaium*, 203. In the earlier report of Gaius' intention (*ibid.* 188), it is said that he had ordered the erection of a colossal statue (ἀνδριάντα κολοσσιαῖον), namely, of Zeus himself (Διὸς ἐπίκλησιν αὐτοῦ); cf. *ibid.* 265 (Διὸς ἀνδριάντα). In the light of Philo's subsequent statement (*ibid.* 346) that the Temple was to be re-dedicated to 'Gaius, the New Zeus Epiphanes', Dr Smallwood thinks that the statue was to be of Gaius himself in the guise of Zeus (p. 256, n. on 188, Διὸς ἐπίκλησιν αὐτοῦ). Josephus in *War*, II. 185, speaks of the emperor ordering the installation in the Temple of statues of himself (τοὺς ἀνδριάντας αὐτοῦ). Tacitus states briefly: 'dein iussi a C. Caesare effigiem eius in templo locare...' (*Hist.* v. 9).

not only violate the sanctity of Yahweh's chosen shrine, it would also represent his dethronement there by the chief deity of pagan Rome. Obviously violent Jewish reaction was expected, and Petronius was instructed to use a strong military force for the execution of the project.[1] The legate appears to have been convinced from the outset of the folly of the emperor's order. He had reason to fear also that, while he was involved with the fanatical resistance of the Jews, the Parthians might profit by the weakening of the Roman forces on the eastern frontier to invade Syria, especially since they would have the support of the large Jewish population in Mesopotamia.[2] Accordingly, he moved with great caution, hoping perhaps to impress the Jews by his massive preparation that resistance was futile; for he knew that it would be fatal for himself to ask the emperor to cancel his decision.[3]

During the winter of A.D. 39–40, Petronius entered Palestine with two legions and a strong body of auxiliary troops, and took up quarters in Ptolemais. He seems to have played for time: he gave instructions for the making of the statue at Sidon and opened negotiations with the Jewish leaders for a quiet acceptance of the imperial decree.[4] But his worst fears of Jewish intransigence were realised. Although for the moment there was no violence, myriads of Jews flocked to Ptolemais, to assure him that he could execute his commission only at the cost of a general massacre.[5] As the spring of A.D. 40 passed without prospect of a Jewish submission, Petronius again played for time by ordering the artists to take the greatest possible care to achieve a masterpiece of statuary. He wrote to Gaius, giving this as a reason for his delay in executing his orders, and also the necessity of seeing that the harvest was safely gathered in. The emperor accepted the excuse, though secretly infuriated by it.[6] However, the impending disaster seemed, at least for a while, to have been put off by the skilful diplomacy of King Agrippa in Rome. How this was achieved is uncertain, since the accounts of Philo and

---

[1] Philo, *Leg. ad Gaium*, 207–8; Jos. *Ant.* XVIII. 261–2, according to which Petronius had an army of two legions, with auxiliary troops. In the *War*, II. 186, Josephus gives the number of legions as three, plus a large contingent of Syrian auxiliaries.

[2] Philo, *Leg. ad. Gaium, ibid.*, declares that Petronius took half the Euphrates army; cf. Smallwood, p. 268.

[3] Philo, *Leg. ad Gaium*, 209–21.

[4] Philo, *Leg. ad. Gaium*, 222–3.

[5] *Ibid.* 223–45; Jos. *Ant.* XVIII. 263–77; *War*, II. 192–200.

[6] Philo, *Leg. ad Gaium*, 246–60; Jos. *Ant.* XVIII. 278–88; *War*, II. 201–2.

Josephus are greatly at variance, and each contains what seem to be improbable statements.[1] What appears to be clear is that Agrippa succeeded in persuading the emperor to cancel his command for the setting up of the statue in the Temple; but this concession was qualified by a directive that pagan altars were to be set up, without hindrance, by Gentile communities in Judaea.[2] While Agrippa was thus seeking to turn the emperor from his original intent, in Palestine, according to Josephus, Petronius, having failed again to persuade the Jews to submit, decided to risk his own life by asking Gaius to rescind his order. He wrote to Rome, before learning of Agrippa's success; his letter more than undid what Agrippa had achieved. The emperor was so enraged at its contents that he ordered another statue to be prepared in Rome, which he planned to introduce suddenly into Judaea, and he advised Petronius to commit suicide. Fortunately for both the legate and the Jews, death removed Gaius before further action was taken.[3]

The Temple was thus saved from desecration by what seemed to be an act of divine intervention; but the crisis had profoundly moved the Jewish people, and the memory of it was not easily effaced.[4] What Gaius had proposed, another emperor might also undertake.

[1] Philo, *Leg. ad Gaium*, 261–334; Jos. *Ant.* xviii. 289–301. The account in the *War* is abbreviated, nothing being said of Agrippa's intervention.

[2] Philo, *Leg. ad Gaium*, 334: ἐὰν δέ τινες ἐν ταῖς ὁμόροις ἔξω μιᾶς τῆς μητρο-πόλεως [i.e. Jerusalem] ἐθέλοντες βωμοὺς ἢ ἱερὰ ἤ τινας εἰκόνας ἢ ἀνδριάντας ὑπὲρ ἐμοῦ καὶ τῶν ἐμῶν ἱδρύεσθαι κωλύωνται, τοὺς εἴργοντας ἢ παραχρῆμα κολάζειν ἢ εἰς αὐτὸν ἀνάγειν. That Philo denounces this as 'a very grievous fear' (δέος ἀργαλεώτατον), indicates how greatly Jewish intolerance of paganism had developed since the time of Herod the Great, who had, for example, dedicated a temple to Rome and Augustus at Caesarea (Jos. *Ant.* xv. 339).

[3] *Ibid.* xviii. 302–9; *War*, ii. 203. The death of Gaius is not recorded in the extant form of the *Legatio ad Gaium*, but it seems probable that it was commemorated in the lost 'palinode', cf. Smallwood, pp. 324–5. Cf. Goodenough, *Politics of Philo Judaeus*, pp. 18–19; Schürer, *G.J.V.* I, 504–6. According to Philo, *op. cit.* 346, Gaius had planned to make the Temple at Jerusalem into a shrine of his own divinity, namely 'Gaius, the New Zeus made Manifest' (μεθηρμόζετο καὶ μετεσχημάτιζεν εἰς οἰκεῖον ἱερόν, ἵνα Διὸς Ἐπιφανοῦς Νέου χρηματίζῃ Γαΐου). Cf. Smallwood, pp. 141, 315–16.

[4] Josephus (*Ant.* xviii. 306) attributes the death of Gaius to the wrath of God: τὸν Γάιον ἀποσκευασάμενος ὀργῆς ὧν ἐπὶ σεβασμῷ τῷ αὐτοῦ πράσσειν ἐτόλμησε,... Cf. J. S. Kennard, *Politique et Religion chez les Juifs au temps de Jésus et dans l'Église primitive* (Paris, 1927), p. 12; Mommsen, *Das Weltreich der Caesaren*, pp. 372–6.

Thus their subjection to Roman rule contained for the Jews an abiding menace which even the most moderate and accommodating could not disregard. To compromise on the payment of tribute as the law-abiding majority undoubtedly did, feeling that conformity here at least purchased peace and the free practice of their faith, was discreet and tolerable; but the violation of Yahweh's sanctuary by the image of a pagan god or deified emperor was an outrage beyond endurance. Hence the influence of Zealotism must have been greatly strengthened among the population by the experience of this threat in A.D. 39–40. The logic of the Zealot gospel became more apparent: submission to Rome made them virtually the slaves of a heathen ruler, who could impose any of his impious demands upon them.[1] The sudden and violent death of Gaius would also have seemed to confirm the Zealot belief that God would succour those who hazarded their lives for him.[2]

But what of Zealot reaction to this signal threat to Yahweh's honour and Israel's faithfulness? There is a curious silence about these patriots in the records concerned. That Philo should not have mentioned them is understandable; for the theme of his treatise *Legatio ad Gaium* was clearly that of the manifestation of God's providence for Israel.[3] The reason for Josephus' silence was probably more complicated. In his account of the episode he was evidently intent on honouring the memory of Agrippa I, whose son, Agrippa II, was his patron and friend.[4] Since also the purpose of his *Jewish Antiquities* was apologetic, namely, to counteract the strong anti-Jewish feeling provoked by the war of 66–73, this encounter of his people with the insane Gaius could usefully be made to present the Jews in a favourable light. This would obviously be best accomplished by vilifying Gaius, whose memory was universally execrated, and by emphasising Jewish patience and forbearance under so grave a threat: to have recorded any acts of Jewish fanaticism would have detracted from the favourable impression which he sought to create. Accordingly, he depicts the Jews offering themselves as passive victims to Petronius, rather than resort to war, in their refusal to submit to the impious demand of a mad emperor.[5] However, he does

---

[1] See above, pp. 33, 49–51.
[2] Cf. Jos. *Ant.* xviii. 5. In the Megillath Taanith the day of the death of Gaius was noted as one of rejoicing; cf. Derenbourg, *Essai*, pp. 207 ff.; Hengel, *Die Zeloten*, p. 110, n. 4.
[3] Cf. Goodenough, *The Politics of Philo Judaeus*, pp. 12–19.
[4] E.g. *Life*, 362–7.   [5] *Ant.* xviii. 263–78; *War*, ii. 192–201.

let slip the significant fact that Petronius had warned Gaius, in his letter, that the Jews were threatening to make war against his forces (πόλεμον ἄντικρυς ʿΡωμαίοις ἀπειλεῖν), a situation which appears to be confirmed by Tacitus.[1]

It is possible that some reflection of Zealot teaching or policy during this period of acute tension and foreboding has been preserved in an oracle that Mark has incorporated in the apocalyptic discourse in chapter xiii. We shall have occasion presently to examine this discourse in detail, in order to evaluate its place and purpose in the structure of the Markan Gospel.[2] We shall then be concerned with Mark's use of certain traditional material; our attention now is demanded by the question of the possible relevance of verses 14–20 to the events of A.D. 39–40:

But when ye see the abomination of desolation (τὸ βδέλυγμα τῆς ἐρημώσεως) standing where he ought not (let him that readeth understand), then let them that are in Judaea flee unto the mountains: and let him that is on the housetop not go down, nor enter in, to take anything out of his house: and let him that is in the field not return back to take his cloke. But woe unto them that are with child and to them that give suck in those days! And pray ye that it be not in the winter. For those days shall be tribulation, such as there hath not been the like from the beginning of the creation which God created until now, and never shall be. And except the Lord had shortened (εἰ μὴ ἐκολόβωσεν) the days, no flesh would have been saved: but for the elects' sake, whom he chose, he shortened the days.

The passage seems clearly to envisage a specific situation of great crisis that had suddenly been terminated by what was considered an act of divine intervention. The words 'abomination of desolation standing where he ought not' equate an impending act of sacrilege with the notorious desecration of the Temple by Antiochus Epiphanes in 167 B.C., when he set up therein an altar to Zeus.[3] Now,

---

[1] *Ant.* XVIII. 302; there is also a reference to 'brigandage' (ληστεῖαι), stemming from inability to pay the tribute, *ibid.* 274. Goodenough, *The Politics of Philo Judaeus*, p. 18, assumes that there were disturbances in Judaea, probably interpreting *Leg. ad Gaium*, 335 (τοῦτο δὲ οὐδὲν ἦν ἕτερον ἢ στάσεων καὶ ἐμφυλίων πολέμων ἀρχή). Dr Smallwood, p. 313, n. on 335, does not think that the passage will bear this interpretation. According to Tacitus (*Hist.* v. 9), 'dein iussi a Gaio Caesare effigiem eius in templo locare arma potius sumpsere, quem motum Caesaris mors diremit'.

[2] See below, pp. 230 ff.

[3] II Macc. vi. 2. Cf. Jos. *Ant.* XII. 253; M. Noth, *History of Israel*, E.T.² (London, 1960), pp. 366–7. See also Farmer, *Maccabees, Zealots and Josephus*, pp. 93–7. On the significance of Mark's use of the masc. ἑστηκότα here see below, p. 232.

from that time only twice in Jewish history was the sanctity of the Temple violated, or threatened with violation, in this way:[1] in A.D. 39–40 and in A.D. 70—on the earlier occasion, as we have seen, the threat was suddenly removed, but in the year 70 the 'abomination of desolation' was indeed set up in the sacred courts, as we shall have cause to see.[2] Accordingly, the oracle must relate to one of these two occasions. And since, as will be evident later, the words in parenthesis (i.e. 'let him that readeth understand'), following the statement about the 'abomination of desolation', refer to the event of A.D. 70, the oracle must originally have been concerned with the attempt of Gaius in 39–40. This inference is, moreover, confirmed by two other facts. The prayer that the flight might not be made in winter would well accord with the agitation caused by the concentration of the forces of Petronius at Ptolemais in the winter of 39.[3] Then, the sudden ending of the crisis by God's 'shortening of the days' would well describe the Jewish view of the assassination of Gaius in A.D. 40 that so fortunately stopped his insane undertaking.[4]

[1] The innermost sanctuary (τὸ ἅγιον) of the Temple had indeed been violated by the entry of Pompey and some of his troops in 63 B.C., but no pagan emblem had been introduced; cf. Jos. *Ant.* xiv. 72; *War*, i. 152–3; Tacitus, *Hist.* v. 9. When the Temple was captured by a Roman force commanded by Sossius, in support of Herod, in 37 B.C., Herod prevented the violation of the sanctuary (Jos. *Ant.* xiv. 482–3; *War*, i. 354).

[2] See below, pp.143, 231–3, also Brandon, *Fall of Jerusalem*², pp. 173–4, 272, and *N.T.S.* vii (1960–1), 133–4.

[3] Mark xiii. 18: προσεύχεσθε δὲ ἵνα μὴ γένηται χειμῶνος; Jos. *Ant.* xviii. 262. According to Josephus, great numbers of Jews went to Ptolemais, to implore him to desist from his commission.Where they lodged, and whether they suffered from inclement weather, are not recorded. The sense of insecurity was such that the Jews neglected the sowing of their fields (*Ant.* xviii. 272; *War*, ii. 200). There was a drought in A.D. 40, which was relieved by what was regarded as a providential fall of rain (*Ant.* xviii. 285). There is some discrepancy between the dating of Josephus and Philo for the demonstration at Ptolemais. *Leg. ad Gaium*, 249, suggests that it took place at the time of the grain-harvest, i.e. between April and June; see the detailed discussion of the issue by Smallwood, pp. 281–3, n. on 249. Philo describes the Jewish trek to Ptolemais as a mass abandoning of their homes in Jerusalem and elsewhere (ἐξεληλύθεσαν ἀθρόοι καὶ κενὰς τὰς πόλεις καὶ κώμας καὶ οἰκίας ἀπολιπόντες μιᾷ ῥύμῃ συνέτεινον εἰς Φοινίκην (*Leg. ad Gaium*, 225). Philo, like Josephus, says nothing of the practical problems of such a mass movement; presumably it must have had leaders able to arouse the people to such improvident action.

[4] It was so regarded by Josephus (see above, p. 87, n. 2). Cf. *Th.Wb.* iv, 193.

In view of such strong reason for relating the oracle to the events of A.D. 39–40, we may next ask about the source of what is virtually a directive, addressed to the inhabitants of Judaea, prescribing what action should be taken when the offending image is placed in the Temple. Flight into the mountains, which is ordered, surely provides a clue. The mountains (τὰ ὄρη) would be in the desert country where the Zealots had their strongholds, and to which they sought to withdraw after the destruction of the Temple in A.D. 70.[1] The urgency of such a flight, involving the abandonment of personal property, would be characteristic of Zealot faith in the providence of God for those who wholeheartedly committed themselves in his service. The reference to the elect, whom God had chosen (τοὺς ἐκλεκτοὺς οὓς ἐξελέξατο), and for whose sake he intervenes, would aptly express the view which the Zealots held of themselves and of their part in the economy of Yahweh's providence.[2]

If we may thus reasonably interpret this oracle as being of Zealot origin, and related to this supreme crisis in Jewish affairs, we are naturally led on to consider the significance of the fact that it has been preserved by a Christian writer. Now, the view has been set forth by certain scholars that the Markan apocalypse here incorporates an earlier Jewish Christian apocalypse which was composed to meet the situation created by Gaius' attempt to desecrate the Temple in A.D. 39–40.[3] This suggestion raises some interesting questions, very pertinent to our subject. As we have seen, on analysis the passage concerned (*vv.* 14–20) reflects in a remarkable manner the Zealot outlook. But if it is to be interpreted as originating from the Jewish Christians, during the same time of crisis, a significant agreement of attitude between the Zealots and the Jewish Christians

---

[1] See above, pp. 58–9.

[2] There is an unmistakable sense of election in the words which Josephus attributes to Eleazar, the Zealot commander of Masada, when he exhorted his followers to commit suicide: πρῶτοί τε γὰρ πάντων ἀπέστημεν καὶ πολεμοῦμεν αὐτοῖς τελευταῖοι (*War*, VII. 324).

[3] Cf. Streeter, *Four Gospels*, pp. 491 ff.; Moffatt, *Introduction to New Testament*, pp. 207–9; Bultmann, *Gesch. d. synop. Trad.* p. 129, Ergänzungsheft, pp. 18–19; Taylor, *St Mark*, pp. 498–9. G. R. Beasley-Murray (*Jesus and the Future*, London, 1954) has argued at length against this view, since he maintains that the apocalyptic discourse in Mark xiii comes, substantially, from Jesus; he suggests, however, that the discourse 'circulated widely during the terrible days of suspense aroused by Caligula' (p. 245). For a critique of Dr Beasley-Murray's book cf. Brandon, 'The Markan Apocalypse', *The Modern Churchman*, XLIV (1954), 315–23; see also below, pp. 230–2.

is, accordingly, implied. It means that, like the Zealots, the Jewish Christians were so profoundly shocked by the prospect of the desecration of the Temple that they contemplated immediate flight into the mountains. Now we have seen why the Zealots withdrew into such areas of the country: but why should the Jewish Christians also have thought of going there? The obvious answer is that their motive was the same as the Zealots', namely, to withdraw from a centre where Roman authority was too strong and menacing to their religion and maintain their freedom and resistance in a terrain providing places of refuge and security. Next, we may notice that, if the oracle were of Jewish Christian origin, the Jewish Christians must, therefore, have regarded the murder of Gaius as an act of divine intervention, performed specifically on their behalf as the Elect of God; in other words, that they regarded the sudden and unexpected removal of the Roman threat to desecrate the Temple as due to Yahweh's particular favour to them as his Elect in Israel. Such a conception of their status, in such a context, would be very significant. It would indicate that the Jewish Christians saw themselves during this crisis, caused by the Roman emperor's intention to place his image in the Temple, as an elect group of the faithful in Israel after the manner of the seven thousand who refused to bow the knee to Baal in the time of Elijah or the heroic company of the Maccabees who had resisted the impious intention of Antiochus Epiphanes.[1]

If the oracle was, accordingly, of Jewish Christian origin, then in sentiment and policy the Jewish Christians must have been virtually at one with the Zealots during this crisis. If, on the other hand, it should be felt that such a degree of coincidence would have been unlikely, and that similarity of outlook is more adequately to be explained by assuming that the oracle was not actually composed, but adopted, by the Jewish Christians, an almost equally significant situation would be implied. For it would surely mean that there was so much sympathy in outlook between the Jewish Christians and the Zealots that the former thus valued an oracle that expressed the views of the latter. And, moreover, not only valued it at that time, but had preserved the memory of it, so that it could be utilised by Mark some forty years later.

[1] Mark xiii. 20. It is significant that *vv*. 19–20 are replete with Semitisms; cf. Beasley-Murray, *Jesus and the Future*, p. 249; Taylor, *St Mark*, p. 514. Paul's quotation of I Kings xix. 18, in Rom. xi. 4, shows that the idea of a 'Godly Remnant', who resist the heathen, was a familiar concept to Jewish Christians. See also Heb. xi. 17–40.

This apparent evidence of Jewish Christian concern with the crisis of A.D. 39–40 is of great importance in view of the silence of the Acts of the Apostles about the matter. The chronology of Christian Origins is admittedly an insoluble problem in the light of the extant evidence; however, the earlier chapters of Acts, i.e. i–x, appear to document the decade from the crucifixion, i.e. from about A.D. 30 to 40.[1] Now during this period Jerusalem is depicted as the abode of those Jewish Christians who constituted the infant Church. But although they are distinguished by their faith in Jesus as the Anointed One of God, who had been raised to life again, these Christians are represented as continuing to live as orthodox Jews. The Temple was their accustomed place of worship, and among their number were many priests who would have served therein.[2] It is, consequently, significant that Acts, in giving such a picture of the life of the Church during these years, makes no mention whatsoever of the Roman threat to desecrate the Temple, which, as we have seen, so profoundly disturbed Jewish life. This silence appears the more remarkable, if the Markan Apocalypse preserves, as it would seem to do, an oracle that originated from the agitation caused by the crisis of A.D. 39–40. That the Jewish Christian community in Jerusalem should have been profoundly disturbed by the threat is a necessary inference in view of its attachment to the Temple, and it is confirmed by the evidence of Mark xiii. 14–20, if our interpretation is correct. The reason for the silence of Acts is not clear. In view of the apologetical theme of the work, it is understandable that it would have refrained from mentioning any Christian reaction that might be construed as rebellious, especially since active expression of that reaction was cut short by the death of Gaius.[3] However, it has been worthwhile to discuss this silence of Acts about the crisis of A.D. 39–40, because it serves to show that the narrative of Acts cannot be trusted as a wholly complete record of the life of the Jerusalem Church at this period.

The death of Gaius not only freed the Jews from his insane threat to the sanctity of their Temple, but also led to a short interlude of freedom from direct Roman rule. Agrippa now received, as a reward

---

[1] Or, up to the death of Agrippa I (Acts xii. 20–3), which occurred in A.D. 44; cf. Schürer, *G.J.V.* I, 562–4.

[2] Acts ii. 46, iii. 1 ff., v. 12, xxi. 24, 26; vi. 7: πολύς τε ὄχλος τῶν ἱερέων ὑπήκουον τῇ πίστει. Cf. Brandon, *Fall of Jerusalem*, p. 29; H. Lietzmann, *Geschichte der alten Kirche* (Berlin–Leipzig, 1937), I, 54.

[3] Cf. *B.C.* II, 177–87 (the editors); H. J. Cadbury, *B.C.* II, 510; Brandon, *Fall of Jerusalem*, pp. 101, 208–9; E. Haenchen, 'Apostelgeschichte', *R.G.G.*[3], I, 506–7; Lampe in *Peake's Commentary*[2], 772 b.

for the part which he had played in securing the accession of Claudius to the imperial power, the addition of Judaea to the territories over which he already ruled.[1] His kingdom now equalled in extent that over which Herod the Great had reigned. But Agrippa, although of Herodian stock, seems to have won the regard of the Jews to such a degree that his piety is commemorated in Rabbinic literature.[2] This reputation he achieved apparently by a studious devotion to the practice of Judaism.[3] There are, however, two aspects of his reign which are puzzling, but which perhaps on further consideration have a certain significance for our subject. According to the Acts of the Apostles, Agrippa persecuted the Church, or at least some members of it: 'Now about that time Herod the king put forth his hands to afflict certain of the Church. And he killed James, the brother of John, with the sword. And when he saw that it pleased the Jews, he proceeded to seize Peter also.'[4] This statement introduces a long detailed account of the miraculous delivery of Peter from imprisonment and his departure from Jerusalem. This account is followed by a description of the circumstances that led to the death of Agrippa, which agrees in principle with the account of Josephus.[5] On analysis, however, the Acts narrative is found to contain many problems. For example, whereas it gives the briefest possible statement about the martyrdom of James, it relates the escape of Peter at length.[6] Yet, despite the detailed description of Peter's delivery, the place to which this leading Apostle afterwards withdrew is left unnamed as 'another place' (ἕτερον τόπον).[7] This curious vagueness follows the surprising

---

[1] Jos. *Ant.* XIX. 274–5; *War*, II. 206–16.

[2] Bikkurim, III. 4; Sotah, VII. 8 (in Danby, *The Mishnah*, pp. 97, 301); cf. Schürer, *G.J.V.* I, 554–5.

[3] Cf. Derenbourg, *Essai*, p. 217; Schürer, *G.J.V.* I, 554, n. 23, 555, n. 27, 560. Josephus paints a glowing picture of Agrippa's virtues and piety, *Ant.* XIX. 328, 330–1.

[4] Acts xii. 1–3 (Codex Bezae adds ἐν τῇ Ἰουδαίᾳ after ἐκκλησίας in *v.* 1). The words κατ' ἐκεῖνον δὲ τὸν καιρόν may be intended as a chronological adjustment following the mention of the famine in xi. 27–8, if that had occurred after the death of (Herod) Agrippa, recorded in xii. 19–23. Cf. *B.C.* II, 132; Schürer, *G.J.V.* I, 562, n. 44.

[5] *Ant.* XIX. 343–50; Acts xii. 19–23. The author of Acts evidently regarded Agrippa's death as divine punishment for his persecution of the Church. Cf. Schürer, *G.J.V.* I, 562–4; *B.C.* IV, 139–40.

[6] Acts xii. 1–3: 3–19.

[7] Acts xii. 17. For the possibility that the expression was purposely vague, and that Peter's destination was Alexandria, cf. Brandon, *Fall of Jerusalem*, pp. 211–12. See below, pp. 164, 191, 196–8, 297–9.

introduction of another James, who is a person of such importance that he has to be specially informed of Peter's deliverance and departure.[1] The identity of this James can only be deduced: he was James, the brother of Jesus, who quickly emerged as the head of the Jerusalem Church, but about whose identity and antecedents the author of Acts is strangely silent.[2] These indications of the unreliable nature of the record of Acts at this point, although they counsel caution and raise many other questions, do not compel doubt about the presentation of Agrippa as hostile to the Church. However, the laconic statement about Agrippa's hostile action prompts speculation as to its true nature and cause.

According to the record of Acts, until this time none of the Apostles had suffered death at the hands of the Jewish authorities. Certain action had been taken by the high priest and the Sanhedrin to suppress public preaching about Jesus, chiefly, it would seem, because it involved charging these authorities with his death.[3] It is significant also that in what appears to have been an outbreak of popular violence against Stephen, the Apostles had not been molested.[4] Indeed, the general impression created by the earlier chapters of Acts is that the Christian community enjoyed an effective measure of popular respect, if not actual support, and that the Jewish authorities, though minded to suppress or control them, were cautious in dealing with them.[5] This being so, the question naturally rises: why did Agrippa actually kill one of the Apostles and imprison another, apparently intending to execute him also?

It is possible that some clue to Agrippa's action against these two leaders of the Christian community in Jerusalem is to be found in the policy which he was developing before death cut short his reign. Evidence of this policy is of a rather puzzling kind. Agrippa owed his position to Claudius, to whom he was also bound by ties of friend-

---

[1] Acts xii. 17: εἶπέν [Peter] τε· ἀπαγγείλατε ᾽Ιακώβῳ καὶ τοῖς ἀδελφοῖς ταῦτα.

[2] On the significance of the sudden introduction of James, the Lord's brother, into the narrative of Acts without explanation of his identity or antecedents, see Brandon, *Fall of Jerusalem*, pp. 27–8, 45–8, 209–12. Cf. K. L. Carroll, 'The Place of James in the Early Church', *B.J.R.L.* 44 (1961), pp. 49–56.

[3] Acts iv. 1–23, v. 17–40 (βούλεσθε ἐπαγαγεῖν ἐφ᾽ ἡμᾶς τὸ αἷμα τοῦ ἀνθρώπου τούτου, v. 28).

[4] Acts viii. 1. Cf. Brandon, *Fall of Jerusalem*, pp. 29, 89, n. 2; M. Simon, *Les premiers Chrétiens* (Paris, 1952), pp. 41–2.

[5] Acts ii. 37–47, iv. 4, v. 12–16, 24–42, ix. 31, xxi. 20.

ship;[1] yet on two occasions he took action which caused his loyalty to Rome to be suspect. On the first occasion he began to reconstruct the north wall of Jerusalem on such a scale that Josephus declares that, if the work had been completed, it would have been impregnable.[2] The undertaking was brought to an end when Vibius Marsus, the legate of Syria, reported to the emperor on the danger it might have for Roman rule.[3] From what is known of Agrippa, it is improbable that his motive was seditious. But since he was obviously shrewd and far-seeing, his purpose in this undertaking must have been carefully calculated. The northern side of Jerusalem was the weakest: from this direction the city had been taken by Pompey in 63 B.C. and by Herod and Sossius in 37 B.C., and it was destined again to be breached from this side by the army of Titus in A.D. 70.[4] In recognising the vulnerability of Jerusalem here and attempting to rectify it, Agrippa was undoubtedly moved by a real concern for his people's future. Although he would never himself have contemplated revolt, he was surely aware, especially in the light of the recent attempt of Gaius, that some fatal clash between Israel and Rome was inevitable. As one who was, despite his Herodian ancestry and his own earlier profligacy, sincerely devoted to Judaism, Agrippa thus sought to help his people.[5] The other occasion on which he

[1] Jos. *Ant.* XIX. 265–6, 274–5, 309; *War*, II. 213–16. Agrippa's protestations of loyalty figure strikingly on his coins; cf. Madden, *Coins of the Jews*, pp. 133–4, 136–7; Reifenberg, *Israel's History in Coinage*, p. 26; Schürer, *G.J.V.* I, 560–1.

[2] Jos. *Ant.* XIX. 326–7; *War*, II. 218. On the north, or third, wall see Jos. *War*, V. 147–55. Cf. W. F. Albright, *The Archaeology of Palestine* (Harmondsworth, 1949), p. 158; Ricciotti, *Flavio Giuseppe*, II, 270, n. on 218; Perowne, *The Later Herods*, pp. 78–80; *Der Jüdische Krieg*, hrg. Michel u. Bauernfeind, I, 442, n. 119.

[3] This is the explanation given by Josephus in *Ant.* XIX. 326–7; however, in *War*, II. 218 he says that Agrippa died before the wall had reached its projected height, while in *War*, V. 152 he explains that Agrippa desisted from completing the work, lest Claudius should suspect his motive in undertaking so vast a fortification (ἐπὶ νεωτερισμῷ πραγμάτων ὑπονοήσῃ καὶ στάσεως).

[4] Jos. *War*, V. 302 (cf. Thackeray's note *b*, Loeb ed. III, 294).

[5] According to Tacitus, the Jews at this time, by bribery, succeeded in fortifying Jerusalem in preparation for war ('per avaritiam Claudianorum temporum empto jure muniendi struxere muros in pace tamquam ad bellum', *Hist.* V. 4. 2). There seems to be no indication in the sources concerned that Agrippa undertook this work 'for show only', and to give employment, as Jones suggests (*Herods of Judaea*, p. 213). Perowne surmises that Agrippa's money ran out, and that he saved himself from embarrassment by saying that the Romans ordered the work to cease (*The Later Herods*, pp. 77–8).

incurred suspicion was when he invited five princes, who were vassals of Rome, to a conference at Tiberias. The purpose of the conference is not recorded; but the princes ruled territories of great strategical importance for the peace and stability of the eastern provinces of the Roman empire—Commagene, Emesa, Armenia Minor, Pontus and Chalcis.[1] Again, it is improbable that Agrippa was planning a concerted rising against Rome; but it is intelligible that he might have sought to safeguard the future of the Jews by establishing friendly relations with an important group of client princes of Rome.[2]

If Agrippa, therefore, was intent on providing for the future well-being of Israel, any factors within the state that were likely to exacerbate relations with the Romans would be marked for suppression. Now, since there is reason for thinking that the Messianic hopes of the Christians fomented trouble in both Rome and Alexandria during the reign of Claudius,[3] it is understandable that

[1] Jos. *Ant.* XIX. 338–42. M. P. Charlesworth refers in this connection to Agrippa's 'restless intriguing spirit' (in *C.A.H.* x, 680), whereas A. H. M. Jones thinks the motive of the meeting was probably ostentation only (*Herods of Judaea*, p. 214), as does Perowne, *The Later Herods*, p. 81.

[2] Schürer, *G.J.V.* I, 556, sees some significance in these two actions of Agrippa: 'Zu einer pharisäisch-nationalen Politik gehörte auch Lockerung des Abhängigkeitsverhältnisses von Rom. Und auch hierin machte Agrippa wenigstens ein paar schüchterne Versuche.'

[3] 'Iudaeos impulsore Chresto adsidue tumultuantes Roma expulit', Suetonius, *Claudius*, 25; cf. Acts xviii. 2; Dio Cassius, LX. 6; Orosius, VII. cap. vi (*P.L.*, ed. Migne, t. 31, 469). The expulsion of the Jews from Rome would seem to have taken place in A.D. 49 or 50. Cf. *B.C.* v, 459–60; A. Momigliano, *L'Opera dell'Imperatore Claudio* (Florence, 1932), pp. 66, 76; A. D. Nock in *C.A.H.* x, 500–1; V. M. Scramuzza in *B.C.* v, 295–6; Eisler, IHΣΟΥΣ ΒΑΣΙΛΕΥΣ, I, 132, n. 4; Klausner, *Jesus of Nazareth*, pp. 60–1; F. F. Bruce, 'Christianity under Claudius', *B.J.R.L.* 44 (1962), p. 317. Evidence of Jewish agitation, possibly of Messianic inspiration, in Alexandria is provided by the letter of Claudius to the Alexandrians; cf. *Select Papyri* (Loeb Classical Library, ed. A. S. Hunt and C. C. Edgar), II, 86, ll. 96–100. Cf. H. Idris Bell, *Jews and Christians in Egypt* (London, 1924), pp. 25, 29, and *Cults and Creeds in Graeco-Roman Egypt* (Liverpool, 1953), pp. 78–9 (it is curious that Bell should say that 'there is not a word in Claudius' letter to suggest any religious conflict in the Jewish community', when he admits that it is not credible 'that Christian visitors to Alexandria should not seek to spread the Gospel there'. What otherwise would Claudius have meant by condemning the Jews, who accept compatriots who come from Syria καθάπερ κοινήν τινα τῆς οἰκουμένης νόσον ἐξεγείροντας?). It is surely significant that similar language was employed by the rhetor Tertullus against Paul in accusing him of being

Agrippa should have sought to deal with the source of the movement in his own kingdom. That he should have begun by proceeding against James and Peter is surely significant; for both had been members of the inner circle of Jesus' disciples and both were characterised as men disposed to energetic action.[1] The execution of James by the sword (μαχαίρῃ) suggests the penalty for a political offence, since stoning was the mode of punishment for those guilty on a capital charge against the religious law.[2] The statement in Acts that the death of James pleased the Jews (ἀρεστόν...τοῖς 'Ιουδαίοις) is probably due to the well-known anti-Semite tendency of the author of the work, and is not to be interpreted as signifying popular approval.[3] The Jews whom the execution was likely to have pleased would have been the Jewish authorities who were blamed for the crucifixion of Jesus.[4] That Agrippa's action was not welcomed by the people is suggested by the note in Acts that Agrippa postponed the execution of Peter until after the Passover, when the crowds of pilgrims had left the city.[5]

one κινοῦντα στάσεις πᾶσι τοῖς 'Ιουδαίοις τοῖς κατὰ τὴν οἰκουμένην (Acts xxiv. 5, see also xvii. 6). Cf. Brandon, *Fall of Jerusalem*, p. 222; Pfeiffer, *History of New Testament Times*, p. 177; A. Piganiol, *Histoire de Rome* (Paris, 1949), pp. 264–5; A. Ehrhardt, *Framework of New Testament Stories*, pp. 94–5; W. den Boer, 'Claudius', *R.A.C.* III, 180–1; E. M. Smallwood, 'Jews and Romans in the Early Empire', *History Today*, xv (1965), 236 ff.; Bruce, *B.J.R.L.* 44 (1962), pp. 311–13, 315; Simon, *Recherches d'histoire judéo-chrétienne*, pp. 20–9 (this is a wholly sound 'minimum definition' of the issue; but surely in the light of Suetonius, *Claud.* 25, the Roman authorities could not have been so entirely ignorant that some Jewish agitation centred on a Messianic figure).

[1] Cf. O. Cullmann, *Petrus: Jünger-Apostel-Märtyrer* (Zürich–Stuttgart, 1960), pp. 25–43, E.T. pp. 23–40; Brandon, *Fall of Jerusalem*, pp. 44 ff.

[2] Cf. Sanhedrin, 7. 4, in Danby, *The Mishnah*, p. 391. Of beheading it is said 'they used to cut off his head with a sword as the government [i.e. the Romans] does', *ibid.* 3, Danby, p. 391. Cf. P. Winter, *On the Trial of Jesus*, pp. 67–74. It is significant that Stephen was stoned (Acts vii. 57–9), and also James, the Lord's brother (see below, pp. 115 ff.), whereas John the Baptist, who was clearly regarded by Herod Antipas as politically dangerous, was beheaded (Mark vi. 27; Jos. *Ant.* XVIII. 118–19). Cf. S.B. *Kommentar*, I, 706; J. Blinzler in *Z.N.T.W.* 52 (1961), p. 57, n. 14a.

[3] E.g. Acts xxviii. 23–8. Cf. *B.C.* II, 183–7 (the editors); Brandon, *Fall of Jerusalem*, pp. 208–9. ⁴ Cf. Acts v. 24–8.

[5] Acts xii. 4: βουλόμενος μετὰ τὸ πάσχα ἀναγαγεῖν αὐτὸν τῷ λαῷ. Cf. *B.C.* IV, 134 *in loc.* If Peter, a celebrated leader of the Christian Messianists, had been the unpopular head of an unpopular sect, Agrippa would surely have made a demonstration of his own orthodoxy by executing him when Jerusalem was packed with pilgrims.

That Agrippa should have singled out the Christians, or rather certain of them, for suppression on the grounds of their being dangerous to the maintenance of good Romano-Jewish relations,[1] is remarkable in view of the fact that no action against the Zealots is recorded. The most probable reason that suggests itself for this distinction could be of considerable significance for our assessment of the relation between the Zealots and the Jewish Christians. That nothing is heard of the Zealots during Agrippa's brief reign might well be explained by the fact that one of their chief sources of grievance no longer obtained, namely, the payment of tribute to Rome. But, even if the Jewish Christians had also been satisfied on this score, their fervent expectation of the imminent return of Jesus as the Messiah to 'restore the kingdom to Israel' would not have been lessened.[2] In view of the probability that the Markan Apocalypse preserves evidence of Jewish Christian agitation over the threat of Gaius, as we have seen, it is also likely that much had been heard of their *Parousia* hopes during the crisis and that the knowledge of it led Agrippa to regard those leaders who had been most vociferous as the most politically dangerous in his kingdom. The selection of James, the son of Zebedee, as the first victim would suggest that he had distinguished himself in some form of energetic advocacy of the Messiahship of Jesus, and such action recalls the violent disposition attributed to him in the Gospel tradition, together with his brother John, and their sobriquet of 'Sons of thunder'.[3]

---

[1] According to A. Momigliano, 'I motivi opposti della politica di Claudio verso gli Ebrei sono già evidenti da questi fatti. Essa è rispettosa dei loro diritti e pronta a tutelarli, ma d'altra parte è sospettosissima di ogni moto religioso e, come tale, incline a equiparare il Guidaismo al culto dei Druidi e a trattarlo, finchè sia possibile, con sistema uguale' (*L'Opera dell'Imperatore Claudio*, p. 71). Knowing this, Agrippa would have been intent on suppressing the dangerous Messianic movement that Christianity seemed to be at its source, i.e. in Jerusalem. Cf. Nock in *C.A.H.* x, 500–1.

[2] Cf. Acts i. 6. 'Eine nothwendige Consequenz seiner [Agrippa's] jüdischen Politik war es endlich, daß der sonst gemüthige König zum Verfolger der jungen Christengemeinde, insonderheit der Apostel wurde', Schürer, *G.J.V.* I, 557–8.

[3] Cf. Luke ix. 51–5; Mark x. 35–7; see also Mark iii. 17. G. Dalman, *Jesus-Jeshua* (London, 1929), p. 12, thought that Βοανηργές derived from the Aramaic *benē regēsh*, 'sons of rage'. Cf. Taylor, *St Mark*, pp. 231–2; *Th.Wb.* IV, 888. On the tradition that John was also martyred with James, cf. *B.C.* IV, 133–4; R. Eisler, *The Enigma of the Fourth Gospel* (London, 1938); Meyer, *Ursprung*, III, 174; Goguel, *La naissance du Christianisme*, pp. 126, 503, n. 3.

That Peter should also have been regarded as politically dangerous is not surprising in view of the strong and impetuous nature that finds expression in the Gospels and Acts, as well as the fact that he is represented as the first of the apostles to recognise Jesus as the Messiah.[1]

Agrippa's reign ended with his sudden death in A.D. 44, and with it was terminated also the chance that a fatal clash with Rome might be avoided or at least delayed. For Claudius passed over Agrippa's son on account of his youth, and placed the whole realm under procuratorial government.[2] And so, not only Judaea, but Galilee also now became subject to the rule, and too often the misrule, of the officials of heathen Rome. In retrospect, it would seem that the brief interlude of Agrippa's reign served only to make the Jews more bitterly conscious of the ignominy of their position as a subject people, and so to render more certain and more fatal their eventual revolt.[3]

After the death of Agrippa, Jewish history seems to take on the guise of a Greek tragedy as it moves inexorably to what appears to be the predestinated catastrophe of A.D. 70. Probably something of the sense of impending doom is due to Josephus, as he looked back from the ruin of his people and discerned in the preceding two decades the developing pattern of the ultimate disaster. There is, however, no reason for doubting the soundness of his interpretation; for the twin factors of Jewish religion and Roman government, or rather misgovernment, made conflict, radical and ruthless, inevitable.

Evidence of Jewish unrest soon reappears—Cuspius Fadus, the first procurator to be appointed by Claudius, found it necessary to clear Judaea of what Josephus calls brigands (*lēstai*), and he also caught and executed one Tholomaios, described as 'the arch-brigand' (ὁ ἀρχιληστής), who had been causing trouble on the borders of Nabataean Arabia and Idumaea.[4] How far these *lēstai* may be regarded as Jewish resistance fighters or Zealots is not certain, owing to Josephus' ambiguous use of the term; but it is surely significant that we hear of them again as soon as Judaea passes once more under direct Roman rule. Even more eloquent of the religious fanaticism

---

[1] Mark viii. 27–33; Matt. xvi. 13–23; Luke ix. 18–22.

[2] Jos. *Ant.* xix. 360–3; *War*, ii. 220. M. P. Charlesworth (in *C.A.H.* x, 681) thinks that Claudius' decision not to give the kingship to Agrippa's son was due to his wish to avoid a block of frontier-kingdoms united by marriage-ties and religion, which seemed to be resulting from the policy pursued by Agrippa I.

[3] Cf. E. Stapfer, *La Palestine au temps de Jésus-Christ* (Paris, 1885), p. 85.

[4] Jos. *Ant.* xx. 5. Cf. Hengel, *Die Zeloten*, p. 350, n. 5.

current among the Jews at this time is the episode of Theudas, which is recorded both by Josephus and in the Acts of the Apostles.[1] Theudas is described by Josephus as a magician (γόης τις), who claimed to be a prophet (προφήτης).[2] For some unspecified purpose, he persuaded a considerable body of Jews to follow him with their belongings to the river Jordan, which he promised to divide miraculously, thus to provide an easy passage to the country beyond. The procurator, evidently interpreting the movement as politically dangerous, prevented the demonstration by dispatching a force of cavalry. A number of Theudas' followers were killed and others taken prisoner: Theudas himself was captured and beheaded. Although neither Josephus nor Acts says anything of the teaching or aims of Theudas, the few details that are given are significant. It would seem that a kind of new Exodus had been proclaimed, with Theudas playing the role of a Moses *redivivus*, who would repeat at the Jordan the miracle of the Red Sea.[3] His followers had obviously been exhorted to abandon their homes, perhaps because they were in a land now under heathen control, and to cross the Jordan into the wilderness beyond, as their forefathers had once left Egypt for the desert. The traditional forty years which Israel had spent in the desert became in the prophetic imagination the golden age of Israel's communion with Yahweh.[4] In true prophetic tradition, as well as by practical necessity, the Zealots sought to maintain their liberty in the desert, and thither, as we have seen, the Jewish Christians were about to retire when the Temple was threatened with desecration. That Theudas also sought to lead his followers into the desert country of Trans-Jordan would suggest that he, too, was moved by such motives. Whether he was a Zealot or led

[1] Jos. *Ant.* xx. 97–9; Acts v. 36.
[2] Eisler (ΙΗΣΟΥΣ ΒΑΣΙΛΕΥΣ, II, 190) thinks that Josephus used the term γόητες with reference to a nomadic sect of healers called the *Beth-Refā* ('Sippe des Heilers'), who derived from the Rechabites. 'Diese Leute sind es, die Josephus im Auge hat, wenn er von den γόητες oder 'Zauberern' spricht, die das Volk mit ihren Wundertaten und Verheißungen in Aufregung halten, und die er für verschiedene Aufstände gegen die Römer verantwortlich macht'; cf. I, 54. 'γόης. Der Begriff hat für Josephus ausgesprochen den Sinn von Betrüger u. Volksverführer. Er verwendet ihn vor allem für die falschen Profeten', Hengel, *Die Zeloten*, p. 235, n. 4, see also pp. 235–9. See below, pp. 108–9, 112–13.
[3] Moses was expected to return as a 'forerunner' of the Messiah; cf. Mowinckel, *He That Cometh*, pp. 299–300; *R.G.G.*³, IV, 1154.
[4] Cf. Acts vii. 44 ff.; Brandon, *Time and Mankind*, p. 79 (see refs.); Hengel, *Die Zeloten*, pp. 255–9.

a kind of para-Zealot movement is unknown.[1] The fact that his movement took place when Judaea again came under direct control, which raised the question once more of the tribute to Rome, might be significant. Perhaps he sought to lead a migration of pious Israelites, who held the payment of tribute to be disloyalty to Yahweh, into the desert where they would be free from this hateful obligation to a heathen master, impiously proclaimed as divine. How the movement affected the Jewish Christians is unrecorded. The author of Acts, writing some fifty years later and intent on showing that the Roman government had been tolerant of Christianity, represents the rabbi Gamaliel as recalling Theudas and his fate, and linking the outcome of his movement with that of Judas of Galilee. That this association is to be interpreted as implying some knowledge of a connection between Judas and Theudas cannot, unfortunately, be affirmed, owing to the chronological confusion evident in the passage.[2] However, it is notable that the author of Acts was led to depict an eminent rabbi as seeking to evaluate Christianity in terms of the movements of Judas of Galilee, the founder of Zealotism, and Theudas. We can only wonder whether he was prompted to do this in the light of some tradition that did connect them together.

During the procuratorship of Cuspius Fadus another Roman action also contributed to the deepening of Jewish mistrust. For some unexplained reason, Claudius decided to cancel the privilege, conceded in A.D. 36 by the legate Vitellius, that the Jewish authorities should have possession of the vestments of the high priest. The order was now given that these sacred garments, symbolic of Israel's service to Yahweh, should be placed under Roman custody in the Antonia fortress. Jewish resistance to this decision was evidently expected, and Longinus, the legate of Syria, came to Jerusalem with a powerful army. The Jewish authorities asked permission to send a delegation to the emperor to petition him about the matter. In Rome their case was supported by Agrippa, the son of the late king, and Claudius was persuaded to revoke his order.[3] The whole transaction

---

[1] Cf. Hengel, *Die Zeloten*, p. 236: 'Als "zelotischer Profet" im eigentlichen Sinne kann Theudas nicht betrachtet werden, man wird in ihm vielmehr einen profetisch-messianischen Prätendenten eigener Prägung sehen dürfen'; cf. *ibid.* p. 238. The extant evidence does not permit of a decision either way.

[2] Acts v. 34–7. Cf. Schürer, *G.J.V.* I, 566, n. 6; *B.C.* IV, 60–1.

[3] Jos. *Ant.* xx. 6–15. At the same time as he confirmed the concession concerning the vestments, Claudius granted to Herod, the brother of Agrippa I,

appears strange. Claudius must surely have had some strong reason for changing the custom inaugurated by Vitellius, as a gesture, it would seem, to improve Romano-Jewish relations. The reinforcement of the Roman troops in Judaea indicates that the serious nature of the step was realised and precautions taken against a revolt.[1] Having antagonised the Jews by his order and show of force, it is strange that Claudius was persuaded to change his mind. From what we know of the matter from Josephus' account, it would seem that the Roman action was maladroit and unwise. Although they undoubtedly rejoiced at the restoration of their privilege, the Jews must also have been strengthened in their belief that resistance to Rome could be successful. The withdrawal of the Roman forces, after their ineffectual display of strength, was more likely to be attributed to divine providence than to the vacillation of Claudius. Thus the episode, like that of the sudden death of Gaius, would have gone to endorse the Zealot gospel, that Yahweh would surely bless Israel's faithfulness with success.

In reading Josephus' account of these happenings which took place during the procuratorship of Cuspius Fadus (c. A.D. 44–5), it is natural once more to wonder at the silence of Acts about such events. Did the Roman troop concentration at Jerusalem in no way affect the Jewish Christians there, especially when the presence of these troops was due to an issue of vital significance to the Temple cultus, at which they devoutly assisted? And what of the movement of Theudas? This is indeed mentioned, as we have noted, but in a chronological setting that implies that the author of Acts thought that

who was appointed ruler of Chalcis, authority over the Temple and its treasury, as well as the right to appoint to the high priesthood (τὴν ἐξουσίαν τοῦ νεὼ καὶ τῶν ἱερῶν χρημάτων καὶ τὴν τῶν ἀρχιερέων χειροτονίαν), Jos. *Ant.* xx. 15. The granting of such authority surely implies acceptance of Roman control over the Temple and its resources. Josephus makes no comment in recording this grant to Herod of Chalcis, yet he suggests that Pilate acted wrongly in using Temple funds for building the aqueduct.

[1] Schürer, *G.J.V.* I, 565, assumes that the procurator Fadus acted on his own initiative in taking charge of the vestments: this may, indeed, be fairly inferred from Josephus' explanation of the presence of Longinus and his army (φόβῳ τοῦ μὴ τὰ προστάγματα Φάδου τὸ πλῆθος τῶν Ἰουδαίων νεωτερίζειν ἀναγκάσῃ); however, the fact that Longinus and his troops were already in Jerusalem indicates that he was cooperating with Fadus in the matter. Moreover, these officers would surely never have permitted the sending of Jewish envoys to petition the emperor about the matter, if they had acted without his instructions.

it had happened long before the time, i.e. A.D. 44–5, to which Josephus dates it.[1] Such confusion can only be explained by the author's lack of concern to provide an accurate record of the life of the Jerusalem Church during this period. He undoubtedly drew upon Palestinian traditions; but what their original nature was and how he used them are matters beyond our ability to know. Consequently, the silence of Acts about such events as the attempt of Gaius to erect his image in the Temple, or the tension caused by the change of Roman policy about the high priest's vestments, cannot now be interpreted as indicative of the insulation of the Jerusalem Christians from the political tensions and strifes of the time.

Claudius replaced Cuspius Fadus by Tiberius Alexander (c. A.D. 46–8). This officer was the son of Alexander, the Jewish alabarch of Alexandria and a nephew of Philo. The emperor probably regarded him as peculiarly fitted to govern Judaea, since his Jewish origin and upbringing would enable him to understand the Jews with a native insight lacking to Romans. But this asset was offset by the fact that Tiberius Alexander had renounced his ancestral faith; for this reason he was likely to be more of a *persona non grata* to the Jews than a Roman would have been.[2] Josephus records one action only of Tiberius Alexander during his term of office, and that action is very significant. He caused the two sons of Judas of Galilee, Jacob and Simon, to be crucified.[3] No other details are given; but it is evident that these two descendants of the founder of the Zealots had distinguished themselves, either by the expression of their sentiments

---

[1] See p. 101, n. 2 above. The one chronological reference that the author of Acts makes for this period, namely, the famine during the reign of Claudius (xi. 28), raises more problems than it solves; cf. K. Lake in *B.C.* v, 453–5.

[2] Jos. *Ant.* xx. 100. Josephus is significantly laconic in his reference to the apostasy of Tiberius Alexander, having praised the piety of his father: τοῖς γὰρ πατρίοις οὐκ ἐνέμεινεν οὗτος ἔθεσιν. In the *War* (II. 220), he merely remarks that Tiberius Alexander preserved peace by refraining from interference with the customs of the country (τῶν ἐπιχωρίων ἐθῶν). According to E. R. Goodenough, Tiberius Alexander, as procurator in Judaea, 'seems to have been a severe but acceptable ruler' (*Politics of Philo Judaeus*, p. 65). Cf. G. Chalon, *L'Édit de Tiberius Julius Alexander* (Lausanne, 1964), p. 44, n. 6.

[3] Jos. *Ant.* xx. 102–3: οἱ παῖδες Ἰούδα τοῦ Γαλιλαίου ἀνήχθησαν...Ἰάκωβος καὶ Σίμων, οὓς ἀνασταυρῶσαι προσέταξεν Ἀλέξανδρος. 'Diese kurze Notiz zeigt deutlich, wie 40 Jahre nach Gründung der zelotischen Bewegung diese unter Führung der Familie des Gründers weiter ihren unterirdischen Kampf gegen die Römer führte' (Hengel, *Die Zeloten*, p. 353).

103

or by their actions, so as to incur this fate. It is legitimate to wonder whether they led a new outburst of Zealot activity against a Roman procurator who was also an apostate Jew—such a person would have been pre-eminently the target for the religious zeal of a Phinehas.[1] In turn, we may also wonder how the Jewish Christians regarded the martyrdoms of these two Jewish patriots, sons of that Judas who had also given his life, witnessing to his uncompromising loyalty to the prophetic ideal of Yahweh's sovereignty. Acts makes no reference to them; but it is difficult to believe that the followers of the crucified Jesus would have been unmoved by the crucifixion of these patriots at the hands of one who had denied his Jewish faith for the service and religion of heathen Rome.[2]

Tiberius Alexander was succeeded by Cumanus (A.D. 48–52), who was soon embroiled with the Jews, ultimately to his own detriment. Two incidents recorded by Josephus witness to the explosive atmosphere that now pervaded Romano-Jewish relations, and how easily it could be ignited by the inevitable friction arising from the presence of a coarse and brutal foreign soldiery among a people passionately attached to their own peculiar religion and seething with resentment against their foreign masters. The first incident occurred during a festival of the Passover, when one of the Roman soldiers on duty on the roof of the Temple portico made an obscene gesture to the Jews assembled for worship in the courts below. An uproar immediately resulted, and the Jews began to stone the troops. Cumanus, fearing that the situation would get out of hand, sent in reinforcements, and in the ensuing fracas multitudes of Jews were killed—Josephus gives an incredible figure of between twenty and thirty thousand.[3]

---

[1] See above, pp. 43–6.

[2] It is remarkable that the Slavonic version of Josephus records the revolutionary action of the followers of the Wonder Worker during the dual procuratorship of C. Fadus and T. Alexander: cf. *La prise de Jérusalem*, I, 156–9; see also below, pp. 364–8.

[3] Jos. *Ant.* xx. 105–13; *War* II. 224–7. Orosius, *Hist. adversus Paganos*, VII. 5 gives the more likely number of 3,000, but probably due to a misreading. It is probable that the offending soldier was one of the force, raised in Caesarea and Sebaste, who had violated the daughters of Agrippa I, after his death. According to Josephus, Claudius decided to send them on service in Pontus but was persuaded by a delegation to rescind his order. Josephus saw in these troops one of the causes of the Jewish disaster (οἱ καὶ τοῖς ἐπιοῦσι χρόνοις τῶν μεγίστων Ἰουδαίοις ἐγένετο συμφορῶν ἀρχὴ τοῦ κατὰ Φλῶρον πολέμου σπέρματα βαλόντες, *Ant.* XIX. 366). See above, p. 66, n. 4.

The second incident took place shortly after, and the two accounts which Josephus gives of it are especially revealing both of the growing activity of the Jewish resistance fighters and of the way in which Josephus describes them.[1] On the road leading up to Bethhoron an imperial servant (Καίσαρος δοῦλον) was attacked and robbed. In his earlier account in the *War*, Josephus describes the attackers as brigands (*lēstai*), and he calls the incident a 'brigand disturbance' (ληστρικὸς θόρυβος); but in the *Antiquities* the attack is made by 'certain of those disposed to revolt' (τῶν γὰρ ἀφεστώτων ἐπὶ νεωτερισμῷ), who operate as brigands (ληστεύσαντες). The equation is very revealing: rebels act as 'brigands' in attacking an important Roman official—such is the description given by the pro-Roman historian, writing for a Gentile public; it is not difficult to see what terms would have been used, if the record had been written by a Jewish patriot. Roman reaction took a form only too well known during the Second World War. The procurator sent troops to pillage the neighbouring villages and arrest the leading inhabitants, holding them responsible for not preventing the attack. During these punitive operations, a Roman soldier desecrated and burnt a copy of the sacred Torah. The insult to their religion immediately caused a widespread and vehement demand from the Jews that the perpetrator of the outrage should be punished. The situation grew so menacing that Cumanus decided to sacrifice the offending soldier and ordered his execution.[2]

These two incidents so directly touched Jewish religious susceptibilities that it would seem impossible that the Jewish Christians could have remained unmoved by them. On the earlier occasion many members of the Jerusalem Church must surely have been in the Temple at the Passover: would they not have burned with indignation, as did their compatriots, at the obscene insult offered in that holy place, and would not some of them have fallen victims to the violence of the Roman troops when they attacked the Jewish crowd? That Acts makes no reference to the incident does not, again, signify that it was viewed with unconcern by the Christian community of Jerusalem; indeed, rather to the contrary, such silence

---

[1] *Ant.* xx. 113–17; *War*, ii. 228–31. 'Die Zeloten fühlten sich schließlich so stark, daß sie den Versuch wagten, das ganze Volk zum Kampf gegen die römische Herrschaft mitzureißen' (Hengel, *Die Zeloten*, p. 353).

[2] By so doing, according to Josephus, Cumanus prevented a second revolt: ἔπαυσεν τὴν στάσιν ἐκ δευτέρου μέλλουσαν ἐξάπτεσθαι (*Ant.* xx. 117). In the earlier account in the *War* a less dangerous situation is depicted, and, after the execution, Ἰουδαῖοι μὲν ἀνεχώρουν (ii. 231).

about events of this kind, which so profoundly disturbed Jewish life, tends to excite suspicion as to its cause.

Acts is similarly silent about the events which finally brought the procuratorship of Cumanus to an abrupt end and almost amounted to a general revolt. The accounts of Josephus in the *War* and the *Antiquities* contain some notable differences, the later record making more clear the truly serious nature and extent of the disturbance.[1] The trouble originated from the killing of some Galilaeans *en route* for Jerusalem by the inhabitants of a Samaritan village. The Galilaeans appealed to Cumanus to avenge their murdered kinsfolk; but the procurator, bribed by the Samaritans, took no action. Infuriated by this Roman refusal to do justice, the Galilaeans called upon the Judaean Jews to take arms on their behalf. Their aim, according to Josephus in his later work, was 'to maintain their liberty' (τῆς ἐλευθερίας ἀντέχεσθαι), for the present outrage had rendered their servitude (δουλείαν) more bitter.[2] Despite the attempts of their magistrates to quieten them by promising to appeal to Cumanus for justice to be done, the Jews sprang to arms and sought the aid of an Eleazar, son of Deinaios, a brigand (*lēstēs*) who had long maintained himself in the mountains.[3] The Jewish action in this is very significant: it surely indicates that resort is made to a Zealot leader, experienced in conducting a long guerrilla warfare against the Romans and other enemies of Israel. Under Eleazar, the Jewish insurgents attacked and massacred the inhabitants of a number of Samaritan villages. Stirred at last to action, Cumanus intervened to crush the rebels, many of whom were either killed or captured. The Jewish authorities also succeeded in quietening others, and the Zealots (*lēstai*) withdrew to their strongholds (ἐπὶ τοὺς ἐχυροὺς τόπους). Josephus adds the significant comment, that from this time the whole of Judaea became full of 'brigands' (λῃστηρίων ἐπληρώθη),[4] a situation which is only intelligible if the word 'brigands' is understood as Josephus' usual opprobrious designation for 'Zealots'. Quite clearly the worsening of Romano-Jewish relations brought more of these patriotic resistance fighters into the open.

The uprising had further repercussions. The Samaritan leaders appealed to Quadratus, the legate of Syria, who came into Judaea to

---

[1] Jos. *Ant.* xx. 118–36; *War*, ii. 232–46.

[2] *Ant.* xx. 120.

[3] *Ant.* xx. 121; *War*, ii. 235 (which associates another leader, called Alexander, with Eleazar). Cf. Hengel, *Die Zeloten*, p. 354, n. 1.

[4] *Ant.* xx. 124; cf. *War*, ii. 238.

investigate the matter. He crucified the prisoners taken by Cumanus, executed other leading revolutionaries (νεωτερισταί), and sent the high priests Jonathan and Ananias, and Ananus the commander of the Temple, in fetters to Rome. Other Jewish and Samaritan leaders, together with Cumanus and a tribune named Celer, were ordered to appear before the emperor for judgement. Through the intercession of the Jewish prince Agrippa, the Jews obtained a favourable verdict: Cumanus was sent into exile, and Celer returned to Judaea for public execution in Jerusalem.[1]

The accounts which Josephus gives of these years tell only of Roman maladministration and the reaction, often violent, of the Jews. Moving in and out of this sorry tale are those whom he calls 'brigands', but who were in fact, as we have seen, patriots who conducted resistance operations from strongholds in the mountainous desert country. They undoubtedly stemmed from or were related, in varying ways, to the movement founded in A.D. 6 by Judas of Galilee. They probably called themselves, or were known to their compatriots as, Kannā'im or Zealots; some were actually led by descendants of Judas.[2] Josephus' concentration of attention on the steadily deteriorating relations of the Jews and their Roman masters does, indeed, give the impression that the conflict between the two dominated the whole of Jewish life in Palestine. But there is no obvious reason for thinking that this impression does not correspond to the real situation; for to the natural resentment of any subject people towards the unjust government of their foreign masters, there must be added the profound devotion of the Jews to their peculiar religion which logically envisaged Israel as a theocracy. From the standpoint of our own particular subject here, this evidence of a

---

[1] Tacitus (Ann. XII. 54) gives an account of the affair that differs on some essential points from the accounts of Josephus. Most notably he states that at this time Galilee only was governed by Cumanus, and that Samaria and Judaea were under Felix, the brother of the imperial favourite Pallas: 'Felix...iam pridem Iudaeae impositus—aemulo ad deterrima Ventidio Cumano, cui pars provinciae habebatur, ita divisae, ut huic Galilaeorum natio, Felici Samaritae parerent.' Such a division of the Roman government of Palestine is only attested here, and it appears *in se* improbable. Tacitus may have represented the situation thus in order to magnify the misdeeds of Felix, and so render Claudius' predisposition to favourites more reprehensible. Possibly Felix already occupied some minor office in Palestine, as is suggested by Tacitus' statement: 'Quadratus Felicem inter iudices ostentavit.' Cf. Schürer, G.J.V. I, 570, n. 14; Meyer, Ursprung, III, 46–8; Momigliano in C.A.H. x, 853; Hengel, Die Zeloten, p. 355, n. 1.
[2] See above, pp. 41 ff.

fundamental detestation of the Romans on the part of the Jews must mean that the Jewish Christians would have shared in it, unless there is clear proof to the contrary. The silence of Acts, as we have already had occasion to notice, cannot be interpreted as proof of this kind. Indeed, all that we do know of the Jewish Christians during this period suggests that they would inevitably have been involved in such clashes with the Romans, and, moreover, that they would have been at one with their compatriots in their resentment and resistance. To think of them as unmoved by such issues implies a degree of insulation from contemporary Judaean life which is not only unsupported by evidence, but is contrary to the logic of what evidence there is. As we have already had reason to believe, the silence of Acts is due to other causes than to what would have been an unnatural indifference towards, and non-involvement in, the social and political affairs of their nation on the part of the Jewish Christians.

This conclusion must also be valid for the remaining years before the outbreak of the fatal revolt in A.D. 66. The period is presented by Josephus as the penultimate act of ever-darkening menace to the final tragedy of Israel's doom.[1] It began with the appointment of Antonius Felix (A.D. 52–60). The choice was an unfortunate one; for Felix, although a favourite of Claudius, was a freedman, whereas the procurators of Judaea had heretofore been men of equestrian rank. But the social standing of Felix was the least of his defects: both Josephus and Tacitus agree in depicting him as vicious in disposition and action.[2] He quickly scandalised the Jews by seducing Drusilla, the sister of Agrippa, from her husband and marrying her, thus causing her 'to transgress the laws of her ancestors'.[3] However, Felix seems to have started his term of government effectively by taking vigorous action against the growing strength of the resistance movement. According to Josephus, the whole land was now full of 'brigands' (λῃστηρίων) and 'impostors' (γοήτων), who deceived (ἠπάτων) the people.[4] The association of these two categories is

---

[1] *Ant.* xx. 160: Τὰ δὲ κατὰ τὴν Ἰουδαίαν πράγματα πρὸς τὸ χεῖρον ἀεὶ τὴν ἐπίδοσιν ἐλάμβανεν· λῃστηρίων γὰρ ἡ χώρα πάλιν ἀνεπλήσθη καὶ γοήτων ἀνθρώπων, οἳ τὸν ὄχλον ἠπάτων.

[2] Jos. *Ant.* xx. 137, 162–4, 177–8, 182; *War*, ii. 247 (in this account Felix appears as an efficient, if ruthless, governor); Tacitus, *Hist.* v. 9 ('per omnem saevitiam ac libidinem ius regium servili ingenio exercuit'); cf. Suetonius, *Claudius*, 28; Acts xxiv. 25–7. Cf. Schürer, *G.J.V.* I, 571–3; B. W. Henderson, *The Life and Principate of the Emperor Nero* (London, 1903), pp. 363, 366.

[3] Jos. *Ant.* xx. 141–3; cf. Acts xxiv. 24.   [4] *Ant.* xx. 160.

significant: it means, translating Josephus' tendentious terminology, that the Zealots were connected with men who were reputed to be 'wonder workers'.[1] The nature of the wonders or miracles which these men claimed to work is evident, as we shall see, from some examples cited by Josephus in describing a later episode: they were signs portending divine intervention, clearly patterned on the miracles of God's providence for Israel during the Exodus and Conquest of Canaan. The leader of these Zealots was the same Eleazar who had led the Jewish insurgents in the time of Cumanus.[2] Felix was more successful than his predecessor: he succeeded in capturing Eleazar, whom he sent to Rome, and he crucified many of his Zealot followers (*lēstai*) and the ordinary folk, who had supported them.[3]

Josephus follows his accounts of this episode in his *War* and *Antiquities* with descriptions of a new form of Zealot activity, or, as he designates it, 'a new form of bandits' (ἕτερον εἶδος λῃστῶν).[4] His two accounts differ seriously, however, about the first and most notorious deed of these men. According to the earlier account in the *War*, which we noted in the previous chapter, this new form of Zealotism originated in Jerusalem, and its members were called Sicarii, a name obviously given to them by the Romans.[5] It would seem that they were formed to deal with certain persons, usually Jews, who were deemed to be pro-Roman or dangerous to the well-being of Israel, according to the Zealot ideal.[6] Their method was that of clandestine assassination, accomplished the more conve-

---

[1] See above, p. 100, n. 2.

[2] Jos. *Ant.* xx. 161; *War*, II. 253: ἀρχιλῃστὴν Ἐλεάζαρον ἔτεσιν εἴκοσι τὴν χώραν λῃσάμενον: according to *Ant.* xx. 121, he had lived during this period in the mountains. [3] Jos. *Ant.* xx. 161; *War*, II. 253.

[4] *War*, II. 254-7; cf. *Ant.* xx. 162-5. Cf. Schürer, *G.J.V.* I, 574, n. 31; Hengel, *Die Zeloten*, pp. 47-51.

[5] See above, pp. 39-40. Cf. *Der Jüdische Krieg*, hrg. O. Michel u. O. Bauernfeind, I, 444, n. 145.

[6] According to *Ant.* xx. 165, the Sicarii murdered both their enemies and those whom they were bribed to kill by others (ἀνήρουν μέν τινας ἑαυτῶν ἐχθρούς, οὓς δ' ἐπὶ χρήμασιν ἄλλοις ὑπηρετοῦντες). It would seem that the latter part of this statement is an innuendo deriving from the fact, according to Josephus (*ibid.*), that a Jew named Doras had bribed the Sicarii, on behalf of Felix, to assassinate the high priest Jonathan (see below). This Doras is, moreover, described as the most faithful (τὸν πιστότατον) of the friends of Jonathan. The whole episode, as related by Josephus, contains so many problems, due to the fact that it is either incorrectly reported or vital details are omitted, that the representation of the Sicarii as hired assassins must be regarded as at least improbable, if not tendentious.

niently, as well as more significantly, at religious festivals, when they suddenly stabbed their victims with daggers concealed in their clothing. The first to be murdered by them was Jonathan, the high priest. In the *War* no reason is given for his removal by these extremists; but in the later *Antiquities* the surprising statement is made that the assassination was actually contrived by Felix, who was annoyed by Jonathan's constant admonishing of him to rule justly. According to Josephus, the murder had been arranged with the Sicarii through a friend of the high priest, whom Felix had bribed.[1] The story appears improbable, and it is strange that no reference is made to it in the *War*. Whatever the degree of truth it may contain, it is significant that Josephus uses it to represent the Sicarii as violating the sanctity of the Temple by this and other murders, which profanation caused God to forsake it and decree its doom.[2] This is the first intimation of his thesis, already noted, that the Zealots caused the destruction of the Temple by their impiety, thus controverting their well-known devotion to it and their desire to free it from the pro-Roman sacerdotal aristocracy who controlled it.[3]

After dilating on the iniquities of the Sicarii, Josephus goes on to describe what he calls 'another body of villains' (στῖφος ἕτερον πονηρῶν), who were even more impious. He designates these as 'deceivers and impostors', who, claiming divine inspiration, aimed at revolutionary changes.[4] They, like Theudas before them, led another exodus out into the desert, believing that there God would perform miracles of deliverance (σημεῖα ἐλευθερίας). Felix saw the movement as the beginning of an insurrection, and he suppressed it by force, killing many.[5]

This disastrous expression of Jewish belief that God would deliver his people from their heathen oppressors was followed by yet another, attesting to the intensity and persistence of the conviction that God would raise up a leader to save them. This time it was an Egyptian Jew, who assembled a great following on the Mount of Olives, promising, like a second Joshua, that the city's walls would fall at his command and that he would lead his followers in to

---

[1] *Ant.* xx. 162–3; *War*, ii. 256 (nothing is said here of Felix's being involved). See p. 109, n. 6 above. Schürer, *G.J.V.* i, 574, thinks that the Sicarii hated Jonathan 'als Mann der Mitte'. Cf. Smallwood in *J.T.S.* xiii (1962), 24–5.   [2] *Ant.* xx. 166.

[3] See above, pp. 58–9. Cf. Hengel, *Die Zeloten*, pp. 188–90.

[4] *Ant.* xx. 167; *War*, ii. 258–9 (πλάνοι γὰρ ἄνθρωποι καὶ ἀπατεῶνες, [ὑπὸ] προσχήματι θειασμοῦ νεωτερισμοὺς καὶ μεταβολὰς πραγματευόμενοι).

[5] *Ant.* xx. 168; *War*, ii. 259–60.

slaughter the Roman garrison. Again, Felix was alert, and in the ensuing engagement many Jews were killed or taken prisoner, but the Egyptian succeeded in eluding capture.[1] Reference is made to the incident in the Acts of the Apostles, and in a context that suggests that it had happened shortly before Paul's arrest in the Temple, on the occasion of his last visit to Jerusalem.[2] The reference, moreover, which is attributed to the Roman centurion who arrested Paul, contains the interesting statement that the followers of the Egyptian were Sicarii, and numbered four thousand. Josephus says nothing about their being Sicarii; the reference in Acts appears to be independent of Josephus' record, so this detail may derive from some other source of information.[3] However, the reference raises the same question that the silence of Acts on other matters prompts, namely, why is no comment made on the reaction of the Christian community at Jerusalem to events of such a disturbing character? The question is not so serious here, since in this part of the narrative of Acts attention is concentrated on Paul, who had only recently arrived in Judaea.[4] However that may be, it is well that we should remember in what sort of atmosphere the Jerusalem Christians lived at this time, as Jewish aspirations for freedom grew ever more fervent and fanatical and were met by the fierce repressive action of Rome.[5]

[1] *Ant.* xx. 169–72; *War*, II. 261–3. In the *Ant.* Josephus refers to him as τις ἐξ Αἰγύπτου, and in the *War* as ὁ Αἰγύπτιος ψευδοπροφήτης. According to the *War* account, the Egyptian led his followers by a circuitous route from the desert to the Mount of Olives.

[2] Acts xxi. 38. The last visit of Paul to Jerusalem can be dated variously between 53 and 58; cf. *B.C.* v, 473.

[3] Hengel, *Die Zeloten*, p. 238, thinks that the Egyptian, like Theudas, was not strictly a Zealot, in the sense of belonging to the party founded by Judas of Galilee: 'Er gründete eine eigene Bewegung und erhob Herrschaftsansprüche für seine eigene Person.' He seeks to explain the fact that his followers are designated as Sicarii in Acts on the supposition 'daß für die Römer unter Felix alle bewaffneten Aufrührer als "sicarii" d. h. Mörder bezeichnet werden konnten'. This explanation implies that the author of Acts was here using a source that employed the terminology current in Roman circles during the procuratorship of Felix. Roth thinks that the 'Egyptian' split 'the *sicarii* body, and is possibly to be identified with the dissident leader of the Habakkuk *pešer*, who is called "the Preacher of Lies"' (in *J.S.S.* IV, 1959, 339). Cf. Feldman in Loeb ed. of Josephus, IX, 480, n. *a*.   [4] Cf. Acts xx. 8 ff.

[5] It is permissible to ask whether the forty Jews who 'bound themselves under a curse' to fast until they had killed Paul (Acts xxiii. 12–15, 21, 30) were Sicarii. Paul would have been a marked man for them, since it was believed that he was undermining the foundations of Judaism (Acts xxi. 21). See above, pp. 66 ff.

Josephus concludes his accounts of the disturbance caused by the Egyptian, who undoubtedly advanced Messianic claims, by further comments upon the growth of revolutionary activity. These comments are worth examining, since, as we have seen, Josephus is our only informant on Jewish affairs at this time and his treatment of the Zealots is very tendentious.

Since his comment in the *Antiquities* is the briefer we may take that first.[1] He states that the brigands (λησταί) continued to excite the people to war against the Romans, exhorting them to civil disobedience (μηδὲν ὑπακούειν αὐτοῖς), and punishing those who did not conform to their instructions by pillaging and burning their villages. The statement is particularly revealing for its gratuitous admission that those whom he denigrates as 'brigands' were actually patriots devoted to raising their compatriots to active resistance against the Romans, and who were prepared to coerce the fainthearted. In the *War*, the situation is summarised as one in which the 'impostors' (γόητες) and 'brigands' (ληστρικοί) unite in fomenting revolt. They urge their countrymen to assert their freedom, and threaten with death those who voluntarily accept servitude (τοὺς ἑκουσίως δουλεύειν προαιρουμένους). They operated in companies throughout the country against the wealthy, who were undoubtedly supporters of the *status quo*, and, therefore, regarded as pro-Roman. These unfortunates were murdered and their homes pillaged. Uncooperative villages were also burned.[2] This hostility towards the rich is significant: having sacrificed all for the cause of Israel's freedom, the Zealots naturally hated those who managed to prosper in the Roman-controlled state; their sympathy would instinctively be with the common people, from whom they doubtless drew many recruits and received economic support. The associating of impostors (γόητες) with the Zealots, which Josephus does here, is also significant. We have already noticed earlier uses of this designation (γόητες) in his writings, in connection with what were surely Messianic movements to secure Israel's freedom.[3] It would, accordingly, appear that Zealotism was closely linked with Messianic expectation, and that the accepted evidence of Messianic leadership was the ability to work miracles or the claim to be able to work them at some crucial moment.[4] The type of miracle, mentioned by

---

[1] *Ant.* xx. 172. [2] *War*, ii. 264–5. [3] See above, pp. 100, 108–9.

[4] See the list of signs cited to convince the disciples of John the Baptist of the Messianic authority of Jesus: Matt. xi. 2–5; Luke vii. 18–22. See also pp. 312–13, 353.

Josephus, clearly indicates the influence of the traditional Hebrew *Heilsgeschichte*, of which the essential pattern was the miraculous Exodus from bondage and settlement in the Promised Land. Such miracles were eschatological by nature, in that they were to achieve an ultimate state of deliverance and well-being. In practice, they necessarily found expression only in the promises of the Messianic pretenders who made them, and whose failure to accomplish them resulted usually in their own destruction and the collapse of their movement. It would seem probable, however, from the fact that Josephus calls such persons γόητες, which suggests thaumaturgic practices, that they each began by acquiring a reputation for supernatural powers by performing certain remarkable acts, perhaps of curing the sick or insane, which were naturally regarded as signs (σημεῖα) of divine authority.[1] The conclusion is of considerable importance for our future inquiry: it means that Messianic pretenders were regarded as γόητες by the unsympathetic, such as Josephus, because they were popularly reputed to be wonder-workers, and that they won followers by promising a final miracle of eschatological significance; that such claimants to Messiahship were Zealots or closely associated with Zealotism; that their Messianic reputations did not survive the failure of their attempts and their consequent deaths;[2] that the disastrous outcome of successive Messianic movements did not undermine the popular conviction that Yahweh would send his Anointed One to redeem Israel.

The high priests, who should have been the natural leaders of their people and the guardians of the priesthood which maintained the elaborate ritual of the Temple, now became so unpopular that they had both the populace of Jerusalem and the lower orders of the priesthood arrayed against them. Since the reign of Agrippa I, the high priests had not been the nominees of the Romans, but of Herodian princes:[3] the change, however, had evidently not improved the quality of those appointed or made them generally more acceptable to the Jews. Josephus does not make clear why the high

---

[1] Cf. Bauer, *Wörterbuch*[2], 1201–2. On Josephus' use of σημεῖον cf. K. H. Rengstorf in *Th.Wb.* VII, 222. See also above, p. 100, n. 2.

[2] It would seem that at this period Messiahship was confirmed by success and disproved by failure and death, cf. Luke xxiv. 21: hence the peculiarity of the Christian claim, namely, that the crucified Jesus was, and would be, the Messiah. See below, pp. 176–8.

[3] Herod of Chalcis had obtained the privilege of appointment from Claudius (see p. 101, n. 3 above); after his death, the privilege passed to Agrippa II. Cf. E. M. Smallwood in *J.T.S.* XIII (1962), 22.

priests now, i.e. *c*. A.D. 59, in particular, became so generally execrated. Indeed, his statement in the *Antiquities* is curiously ambiguous,
and it implies a situation about which he may perhaps have been
designedly reticent. He states that the high priests were embroiled
in strife (στάσις) with the priests (ἱερεῖς) and the leaders (πρώτους)
of the Jerusalem mob (πλήθους). Each faction commanded a body
of desperate and seditious (νεωτεριστῶν) men, who engaged in
mutual violence. The Roman authorities, for some unexplained
reason, did not intervene. The high priests were able to take effective
action against the lower clergy by depriving them of their tithes,
which constituted their only source of income.[1] The episode is
certainly a curious one, and Josephus' account of it, on analysis,
clearly indicates the existence of a situation at Jerusalem of profound
significance for our subject, especially in view of an event that
happened shortly after. The fact that Josephus speaks of high priests
(ἀρχιερεῖς) must mean that it was the sacerdotal aristocracy which
was involved, i.e. the group of related families from which the high
priests were chosen.[2] Who the leaders of the Jerusalem mob were is
not clear; but everything points to their being Zealots, for the
Sicarii had already given proof of their hostility towards the sacerdotal aristocracy.[3] The fact that the lower orders of the priesthood
had been antagonised, and had apparently joined forces with the
Zealots, is consistent with what we know of their attitude a few years
later when the final revolt took place.[4] Being very closely involved
with the cultic practice of Judaism by virtue of their vocation, the
priests were likely to be zealous for their faith and resentful of the
superior clergy, who not only exploited the economic advantages of
their office, but were nominees of the Herodian dynasts and inclined
to be pro-Roman.[5] Sentiment and interest operated, accordingly, to
align them with the Zealots.

Porcius Festus replaced Felix as procurator in A.D. 60, being
appointed by Nero, who also at this time settled a long-standing
dispute between the Jewish and Syrian inhabitants of Caesarea in
favour of the latter, thus unwittingly providing what was to prove

---

[1] *Ant.* xx. 180–1. E. M. Smallwood, in *J.T.S.* xiii (1962), 27, n. 2, thinks
that this episode and a similar one that happened a few years later (see
below, p. 126) may be duplicated versions of one single occurrence. It is
perhaps significant that no high priest is named here, but Ananus plays
the leading role later.

[2] Cf. Jeremias, *Jerusalem*, ii, 52–9.

[3] See p. 110. [4] See below, pp. 130–1.

[5] On the lower clergy of the Temple see Jeremias, *Jerusalem*, ii, 60–87.

the immediate cause of the fatal revolt in A.D. 66.[1] Festus found Judaea in a state of disorder, due to the operations of the Zealots. The Sicarii had grown in numbers, according to Josephus, and were now engaged in open activities, instead of restricting themselves to clandestine attacks.[2] The new procurator was soon obliged, like his predecessors, to suppress the followers (apparently Sicarii) of another so-called impostor (ἀνθρώπου γόητος), who promised salvation (σωτηρίαν) and an end of troubles (παῦλαν κακῶν) to those who followed him into the desert.[3] During the brief period that Festus was procurator (he died in A.D. 62), the Jews also clashed with Agrippa about a palace which he built overlooking the Temple. Although the Jews won their case on this occasion through the intervention of the empress Poppaea, the incident shows that this Agrippa was not so zealous for Judaism as had been his father, and so was unable to exercise a restraining influence upon the Jewish people as they moved towards ultimate disaster.[4]

Nero appointed L. Lucceius Albinus (A.D. 62–4) in the place of Festus; but before he reached Judaea an extraordinary episode occurred, which is of the greatest importance for our subject. According to Josephus, in the extant text of his *Antiquities*, King Agrippa had, just about this time, appointed Ananus, the son of a distinguished high priest, to this sacred office. This man, who was a Sadducee, and described as being of a bold and daring character, apparently seized the opportunity of the procuratorial interregnum to call a meeting of the Sanhedrin (συνέδριον κριτῶν), in order to try James, the brother of Jesus, 'the so-called Christ' (τοῦ λεγομένου Χριστοῦ), and others (τινας ἑτέρους). They were charged with breaking the Law (παρανομησάντων κατηγορίαν), condemned, and stoned (λευσθησομένους).[5] Josephus does not explain the exact

---

[1] Jos. *Ant.* xx. 182–4.
[2] *Ibid.* 185–6: οἱ σικάριοι δὲ καλούμενοι, λῃσταὶ δέ εἰσιν οὗτοι, τότε μάλιστα ἐπλήθυνον... Cf. *War*, ii. 271.   [3] Jos. *Ant.* xx. 188.
[4] *Ibid.* 189–95. It is significant that Agrippa's coinage, almost without exception, bore the name and image of the reigning emperor. Like his father, Agrippa I, he used the title φιλόκαισαρ. Cf. Madden, *Coins of the Jews*, pp. 144–5, 148–54, and *History of Jewish Coinage*, pp. 117–19; Schürer, *G.J.V.* i, 590–1; Derenbourg, *Essai*, pp. 252–4; Graetz, *History of the Jews*, ii, 237; Reifenberg, *Israel's History in Coins*, p. 28; Perowne, *The Later Herods*, pp. 103–4.
[5] *Ant.* xx. 197–200. The phrasing here is of interest: τὸν ἀδελφὸν Ἰησοῦ τοῦ λεγομένου Χριστοῦ, Ἰάκωβος ὄνομα αὐτῷ. It suggests, if the passage is genuine, that, for Josephus, James derived his significance from his relationship to Jesus.

nature of the charges; but his next statement suggests that they were unfounded. For he says that the most fair-minded (ἐπιεικέστατοι) of the citizens and the most diligent in their respect for the Law (τοὺς νόμους) were grieved at the matter, and they secretly informed Agrippa II (τὸν βασιλέα), begging him to restrain Ananus from further deeds of this kind. Others went to meet the new procurator, to tell him that Ananus had convoked the Sanhedrin without his consent (χωρὶς τῆς ἐκείνου γνώμης). Ananus was severely rebuked by Albinus, and removed from the high priesthood by Agrippa.[1]

This account, which has no parallel in the earlier record of the *War*, has been the subject of much debate among scholars; for it contains one of the two so-called *Testimonia Flaviana* to Jesus Christ to be found in the works of Josephus.[2] On a cursory reading, the account provides no obvious grounds for doubting its authenticity; many of its statements do indeed raise questions, but they are not *per se* fatal to its general credibility. However, the mention of Jesus necessarily implies that some account had already been given of him earlier in the narrative.[3] Such an account does in fact exist in the extant text of the eighteenth book of the *Antiquities*; but, as is well known, grave doubt exists as to whether it represents what Josephus originally wrote.[4] The passage concerned is of such importance for our evaluation of Jesus that it must be examined in detail later;[5] for our present purpose we may anticipate some of the conclusions which will there be argued at length. They are, briefly, that Josephus saw Jesus as a Messianic pretender (γόης) in a political sense, and that his account was so offensive to Christians that it was subsequently 'revised', probably towards the end of the third century.

If Josephus had, accordingly, regarded Jesus as one of the many 'impostors' (i.e. as a γόης) whose activities he describes and condemns, it is reasonable to think that he would not have been

---

[1] *Ant.* xx. 200–3.

[2] Cf. Schürer, *G.J.V.* i, 548–9, 581–2; Goguel, *La naissance du Christianisme*, pp. 144–8, 151–2; Förster, *Palestinian Judaism in New Testament Times*, p. 105, n. 9.

[3] τοῦ λεγομένου Χριστοῦ (or, in the quotation given by Eusebius, *Hist. eccl.* ii. xxii, τοῦ Χριστοῦ λεγομένου). The use of Χριστός here surely implies that its qualification by λεγομένου had already been explained. The Ἰησοῦν τὸν λεγόμενον Χριστόν of Matt. xxvii. 17 provides an interesting parallel (cf. A. H. McNeil, *The Gospel according to St Matthew*, London, 1915, p. 411). Cf. Schürer, *G.J.V.* i, 548.

[4] *Ant.* xviii. 63–4. See next note.   [5] See below, pp. 359–64.

favourably disposed to James, the brother of Jesus. From his account, as it stands, it is impossible to be certain of his attitude; he appears to be primarily concerned to relate how Ananus aroused the antagonism that led to his dismissal from office. As we have already noted, although he does not explicitly say whether James was guilty or not of transgressing the Law, his innocence seems to be implied in what he tells of the reaction to Ananus' action. However, even this implication is obscured by the curious vagueness of the description of this reaction. So far as sense can be made of the involved and imprecise terminology used by Josephus here, it would seem that certain fair-minded citizens of Jerusalem, who were particularly zealous in their observance of the Law, expressed their resentment of Ananus' action in two different ways. Some besought Agrippa, who had appointed him, to use his influence to prevent a repetition of such conduct; others complained to Albinus about his unauthorised summoning of the Sanhedrin.[1] Although their courses of action were different, both parties were moved by a common resentment over the high-handed nature of Ananus' conduct; but nothing is said about their sympathising with James and those who had suffered with him.

Our interest naturally fastens upon James, and the reason which Ananus had for executing him. On these issues Josephus is tantalisingly vague. That James was tried by the Sanhedrin for breaking the Law, and that he was stoned to death, suggest that his alleged offence was of a religious character. That certain persons, apparently not members of the Sanhedrin but zealous for the Law, were shocked by the action of the high priest, would seem to indicate that James was obviously not a notorious transgressor of the Torah. The question why Ananus proceeded against James in this manner consequently becomes the more puzzling. In seeking an answer, two pieces

[1] The implication here that the Sanhedrin could not meet without the procurator's permission seems to be attested only by this passage in Josephus' *Antiquities*. It is possible that such permission was needed only when a case involving a capital sentence was to be tried. J. Spencer Kennard seems to miss this point in discussing what he terms the 'Ethnic Assembly', cf. *Z.N.T.W.* 53 (1962), p. 44. Cf. Schürer, *G.J.V.* II, 210. According to P. Winter (*On the Trial of Jesus*, p. 18), 'The most probable explanation of the words used (here) by Josephus is that, on the arrival of a new procurator, the high-priest, in his capacity as Head of the Local Administration, was obliged to renew Roman authorization for the functioning of the Jewish senatorial assembly.' E. M. Smallwood thinks that Ananus offended by usurping 'the High Priests' former powers of independent jurisdiction' (in *J.T.S.* XIII, 1962, 26). See below, pp. 254 ff.

of evidence may possibly be relevant to the case. The first, which we have already noticed,[1] is the breach which had opened about this time between the sacerdotal aristocracy and the lower orders of the priests. It is, incidentally, significant that Josephus stresses that Ananus was one of a family whose members had often held the office of high priest, and that he was a Sadducee.[2] The other fact which may be pertinent here is that, according to the Acts of the Apostles, the Christian community at Jerusalem included many priests, as well as many who were noted for their zealous observance of the Torah (ζηλωταὶ τοῦ νόμου).[3] This being so, it would surely have been inevitable that the Church of Jerusalem would become involved in the strife between the Sadducean sacerdotal aristocracy and the ordinary priests. What might have been the extent of this involvement cannot be estimated; but it would be intelligible that, if the Christian community had strongly championed the cause of the priests, its leader, James, would have been regarded as dangerous by Ananus, especially since James was evidently a powerful personality.[4] To strike at him, during the procuratorial interregnum, by forcing an acquiescent Sanhedrin to condemn him, was an astute move by Ananus, but one that miscarried. Although he commanded the allegiance of the Sadducean party, the opposition of others, distinguished by their zeal for the Torah, accomplished his downfall.

On the identity of those who were offended by Ananus the account of Josephus is curiously vague, as we have noted. We may legitimately ask whether, in view of the connection between the priests and the Zealots,[5] the latter were among those who condemned the action of Ananus against James: as we have seen, the Zealots were distinguished by their zeal for the Torah. However, it is at this point that we must reckon with the possibility that this passage in the *Antiquities* of Josephus has been tampered with by Christian scribes. The

---

[1] See above, p. 114.

[2] *Ant.* xx. 197–9. Cf. Jeremias, *Jerusalem*, II, 55–6.

[3] Acts vi. 7 (πολύς τε ὄχλος τῶν ἱερέων ὑπήκουον τῇ πίστει), xxi. 20. On the MSS variants for vi. 7 cf. *B.C.* IV, 66. Cf. Brandon, *Fall of Jerusalem*, pp. 29, 81. Luke i. 5 ff. implies a primitive tradition deriving from a priestly source; cf. P. Winter, 'The Cultural Background of the Narrative in Luke I and II', *J.Q.R.* XLV (1954), 160–7.

[4] On his rise to leadership of the Christian movement, thereby displacing Peter, cf. Brandon, *Fall of Jerusalem*, pp. 5, 20, 27–8, 47–53, 97–8; K. L. Carroll in *B.J.R.L.* 44 (1961), pp. 50–5; A. A. T. Ehrhardt, *The Apostolic Succession* (London, 1953), pp. 28–30.

[5] See above, p. 114.

grounds for such a suspicion are of a complicated kind; but we must notice them in view of the importance of this *Testimonium Flavianum* for our subject.

The great Alexandrian scholar Origen, writing about the middle of the third century, asserts that Josephus had recognised the fall of Jerusalem in A.D. 70 as divine punishment on the Jews for killing the righteous James; he also complains that, whereas Josephus acknowledged the righteousness of James, he had refused to accept Jesus as the Messiah.[1] Now although, as we have noted, Josephus does not make clear his attitude to James, the passage concerned could fairly be interpreted as implying that he did recognise that James was righteous. However, in its extant form the passage contains nothing whatsoever that could possibly be construed as indicating a connection between the death of James and the fall of Jerusalem. Origen's statement has, accordingly, been explained by some scholars as due to his ascribing to Josephus a comment made by Hegesippus, connecting the death of James with the siege of Jerusalem.[2] Hegesippus, a second-century Palestinian Christian, whose account of the death of James we must presently consider, actually made James's death immediately antecedent to the Roman siege, which he erroneously attributes to Vespasian, not Titus (καὶ εὐθὺς Οὐεσπασιανὸς πολιορκεῖ αὐτούς).[3] Such an explanation, however, convicts Origen of a truly incredible blunder; for it would mean that on three occasions, in two different works, he confused Hegesippus with Josephus, and he did this despite rightly quoting the title and particular book of Josephus' *Antiquities* in which the

---

[1] Ὁ δ' αὐτὸς [Josephus]...ζητῶν τὴν αἰτίαν τῆς τῶν Ἱεροσολύμων πτώσεως καὶ τῆς τοῦ ναοῦ καθαιρέσεως...φησὶ ταῦτα συμβεβηκέναι τοῖς Ἰουδαίοις κατ' ἐκδίκησιν Ἰακώβου τοῦ δικαίου, ὃς ἦν ἀδελφὸς Ἰησοῦ τοῦ λεγομένου Χριστοῦ, ἐπειδήπερ δικαιότατον αὐτὸν ὄντα ἀπέκτειναν (*contra Celsum*, I. 47; cf. II. 13 *fin.*); καὶ τὸ θαυμαστόν ἐστιν, ὅτι τὸν Ἰησοῦν ἡμῶν οὐ καταδεξάμενος εἶναι Χριστόν, οὐδὲν ἧττον Ἰακώβῳ δικαιοσύνην ἐμαρτύρησε τοσαύτην (*Comm. in Matth.* x. 17, ed. Lommatzsch, III, 46); ὁ δ' αὐτὸς [Josephus] καίτοι γε ἀπιστῶν τῷ Ἰησοῦ ὡς Χριστῷ κ.τ.λ. (*contra Celsum*, I. 47). Cf. Schurer, *G.J.V.* I, 546, n. 2, 581, n. 45; Brandon, *Fall of Jerusalem*, pp. 111–12; also below, pp. 361–3.

[2] Cf. Thackeray, *Josephus: the Man and the Historian*, p. 135; W. E. Barnes, *The Testimony of Josephus to Jesus Christ* (London, 1920), p. 19; Ricciotti, *Flavio Giuseppe*, I, 175–6; Feldman in Loeb ed. of Josephus, IX, 497, n. *e*.

[3] *Apud* Euseb. *Hist. eccl.* II. xxiii. 18. Cf. Schürer, *G.J.V.* I, 582, n. 46; Eisler, ΙΗΣΟΥΣ ΒΑΣΙΛΕΥΣ, I, 148–50. It is to be noted that in *contra Celsum*, II. 13 *fin.*, Origen assigns the destruction of Jerusalem to Titus (Τίτος καθεῖλε τὴν Ἱερουσαλήμ).

relevant passage occurs.[1] And that would not be the full extent of his error. The very purpose of his citation of Josephus was to show that this Jewish writer had recognised the righteousness of James, while refusing to accept the Messiahship of Jesus. It would, of course, have been well known that Hegesippus was a Christian writer, who had lived only about one generation before Origen, so that his testimony would have had no value in this connection.[2]

If, then, it seems impossible that Origen could have made so egregious a blunder, we have to assume that, in his copy of the *Antiquities*, he had read something that would have justified his assertion that Josephus saw in the Jewish catastrophe of A.D. 70 divine retribution for the death of James. Now, as we shall presently see, there is reason for thinking that Origen's text of the *Antiquities* did not have the same account of Jesus as that in the extant Greek version, which can be traced back to the fourth century.[3] If the present text of the *Testimonium Flavianum* concerning Jesus is, therefore, a 'revised' version of what Josephus had originally written, it would be reasonable to suppose that the passage about James has been similarly 'revised'. In what way this might have been done is not so apparent as it is in the Jesus-passage. It is particularly difficult to imagine, from what we otherwise know of him, how Josephus would have interpreted the ruin of Israel as divine vengeance for the death of James, the brother of one whom he deemed to be a Messianic pretender. However, in our earlier analysis of the passage concerned we noticed a curious vagueness in Josephus' description of those who resented the action of Ananus.[4] It is conceivable that this may be due

---

[1] ἐπὶ τοσοῦτον δὲ διέλαμψεν οὗτος ὁ Ἰάκωβος ἐν τῷ λαῷ ἐπὶ δικαιοσύνῃ, ὡς Φλάβιον Ἰώσηπον, ἀναγράψαντα ἐν εἴκοσι βιβλίοις τὴν Ἰουδαϊκὴν ἀρχαιολογίαν, τὴν αἰτίαν παραστῆσαι βουλόμενον τοῦ τοσαῦτα πεπονθέναι τὸν λαόν, ὡς καὶ τὸν ναὸν κατασκαφῆναι... (*Comm. in Matth.* x. 17). Origen also makes careful reference to the testimony of Josephus in another connection: ἐν γὰρ τῷ ὀκτωκαιδεκάτῳ τῆς Ἰουδαϊκῆς ἀρχαιολογίας ὁ Ἰώσηπος μαρτυρεῖ τῷ Ἰωάννῃ ὡς βαπτιστῇ γεγενημένῳ... (*c. Celsum*, I. 47). Cf. Brandon, *Fall of Jerusalem*, p. 111.

[2] On Hegesippus see Eusebius, *Hist. eccl.* II. xxiii. 3, IV. viii. 1–2, xxii. 1–9. Cf. F. J. Hort, *Judaistic Christianity* (London, 1894), pp. 164–9; H. Lietzmann, *Gesch. d. alten Kirche*, I, 192; K. Lake in Loeb ed. of Eusebius, I, xlvi–xlvii; Brandon, *Fall of Jerusalem*, pp. 32–3, 53.

[3] Eusebius is the earliest witness to the account in its extant form in the Greek text of the *Antiquities*: the passage concerned is cited in *Hist. eccl.* I. xi. 7–8, and *Demonstr. evang.* III. 3. 105–6. Cf. Schürer, *G.J.V.* I, 546; Eisler, ΙΗΣΟΥΣ ΒΑΣΙΛΕΥΣ, I, 7. See below, pp. 361–3.

[4] See above, pp. 117 ff.

to some alteration of the original text by a Christian scribe, who found it in some way offensive to Christian taste. Our previous inquiry has shown that the high priest possibly took action against James because he was closely identified with the ordinary priests in their antagonism towards the sacerdotal aristocracy; these priests, moreover, were closely linked in their ideals and interests with the Zealots.[1] Accordingly, it is possible that Josephus had described this aspect of James's martyrdom, and that he had also shown that Ananus' attack had contributed to that worsening of class relations that ended in the nation's ruin.[2] In amending this account, some time during the period between Origen and Eusebius,[3] a Christian scribe may have removed some words of Josephus which Origen had interpreted as implying that the fall of Jerusalem was God's punishment of the Jews for the death of James. Such an explanation is essentially speculative, and it must be treated as such. It is, however, a hypothesis that reasonably explains an otherwise inexplicable situation of very great importance for our understanding of Christian Origins. James, the head of the Christian community of Jerusalem, was evidently done to death in circumstances concerning which the record of Josephus is curiously vague, and the statements of Origen suggest that the extant version of this record does not represent its original form.

The importance of James and the manner of his death is such that we must also consider the account given by Hegesippus, to which reference has already been made. This account, which was written about a century after that in the *Antiquities*, presents a completely different version of the cause and circumstances of James's death.[4] As a record, it shows evidence of much confusion of thought and it contains many patent improbabilities; yet it also exhibits certain

---

[1] See pp. 117–18.

[2] Eisler (*Messiah Jesus*, pp. 143–4) suggested a reconstruction of *Ant.* xx. 200–1, indicating the places where Josephus probably said something that was deemed derogatory to Christianity by later Christian censors. He did not, however, connect the death of James with the strife between Ananus and the lower clergy.

[3] The criticisms of Origen may have led to the emending of the text o Josephus' account of the death of James: cf. Brandon, *Fall of Jerusalem*, pp. 112–13. According to Meyer, 'Die Fälschung [of the passage concerning Jesus] ist also gegen Ende des dritten Jahrhunderts entstanden' (*Ursprung*, I, 206).

[4] In Eusebius, *Hist. eccl.* II. xxiii. 1–19; cf. Schürer, *G.J.V.* I, 582, n. 46; Goguel, *La naissance du Christianisme*, pp. 148–51; Brandon, *Fall of Jerusalem*, pp. 97–9.

original traits that seem to indicate a primitive tradition. It is, accordingly, significant for us as representing a tradition about James which was current in Christian circles in second-century Palestine, and which probably stems from an earlier period. Certain aspects of Hegesippus' account will occupy us later, when we attempt to evaluate the faith and practice of the Jerusalem Church;[1] here we must notice those points which relate James's death to the context of contemporary Jewish affairs.

According to Hegesippus, James was distinguished by his extra-ordinary zeal for the ritual practice of Judaism. He had taken the Rechabite and Nazarite vows, he was to be found constantly in the Temple, and he had the unique privilege of entering the sanctuary (τούτῳ μόνῳ ἐξῆν εἰς τὰ ἅγια εἰσιέναι). This last statement is remarkable, because, if true, it would imply that James must have had some priestly office.[2] His exceeding zeal for the Torah earned him such a reputation that he was called the 'Just' (δίκαιος) and 'Oblias' (ὠβλίας), which is interpreted to mean 'Rampart of the

---

[1] See below, pp. 188–9.

[2] Euseb. *Hist. eccl.* II. xxiii. 5–6. Hegesippus also states that James did not wear wool but linen (σινδόνας); the point is interesting, since, according to Jos. *Ant.* xx. 216, during the procuratorship of Florus, who succeeded Albinus, the Levites obtained permission to wear the priestly linen tunic (λινῆν στολήν). Epiphanius (*Haer.* xxix. 3–4, in *P.G.* t. 41, p. 396) makes a still more amazing statement that James exercised the privilege and wore the mitre of the high priest; it is not known whether his authority was Hegesippus: Ἔτι δὲ καὶ ἱερατεύσαντα αὐτὸν κατὰ τὴν παλαιὰν ἱερωσύνην εὕρομεν. Διὸ καὶ ἠφίετο αὐτῷ ἅπαξ τοῦ ἐνιαυτοῦ εἰς τὰ Ἅγια τῶν ἁγίων εἰσιέναι, ὡς τοῖς ἀρχιερεῦσιν ἐκέλευσεν ὁ νόμος, κατὰ τὸ γεγραμμένον. Οὕτω γὰρ ἱστόρησαν πολλὰ πρὸ ἡμῶν περὶ αὐτοῦ, Εὐσέβιός τε καὶ Κλήμης, καὶ ἄλλοι. Ἀλλὰ καὶ τὸ πέταλον ἐπὶ τῆς κεφαλῆς ἐξῆν αὐτῷ φέρειν, καθὼς οἱ προειρημένοι ἀξιόπιστοι ἄνδρες ἐν τοῖς ὑπ' αὐτῶν ὑπομνηματισμοῖς ἐμαρτύρησαν: cf. *Haer.* LXXVIII. 6–7, in *P.G.* t. 42, p. 721. Eisler used this statement to support his theory that the nationalist party maintained a rival high priesthood against that of the pro-Roman Sadducees (ΙΗΣΟΥΣ ΒΑΣΙΛΕΥΣ, II, 580–4, *Messiah Jesus*, pp. 540–3). This ascription to James of the status of high priest probably derives from the legends current in the church of Aelia Capitolina, which was founded on the site of ruined Jerusalem. It was natural for the members of this church, of whom Hegesippus was surely one, to seek to enhance its prestige by claiming that it descended from the original Church of Jerusalem, about which they doubtless had certain traditions. Cf. Meyer, *Ursprung*, III, 601; Brandon, *Fall of Jerusalem*, p. 53, n. 1; F. C. Burkitt, *Christian Beginnings* (London, 1924), pp. 60–1; W. Telfer, 'Was Hegesippus a Jew?', *H.Th.R.* LIII (1960), 143–53; P. Carrington, *The Early Christian Church* (Cambridge, 1957), I, 248–9.

people and righteousness'.[1] His influence with the people was so
great that the Jewish leaders (apparently the Sadducees) became
alarmed, because the whole people (πᾶς ὁ λαός) were in danger
(κινδυνεύει) of expecting Jesus to come as the Messiah.[2] To remove
this danger, the Jewish authorities apparently decided to interrogate James publicly about the matter. The decision was a strange
one; for they seem to have expected that James would assist

[1] Euseb. *Hist. eccl.* II. xxiii. 7. 'Ebenso kann das überlieferte ὠβλιας nur
ὠβλιαμ (Σ für M!) gelesen werden "ein Vater für das Volk *'abh lə'am*"
und hat mit aram. *'ubla* "korbartiges Geflecht" "Palisade" (so richtig
Hennecke NTL. Apokr.[2], S. 104) daher "περιοχὴ τοῦ λαοῦ" (Euseb. III,
7, 3, "ἕρκος ὥσπερ ὀχυρώτατον", Epiphan. haeres. 78. 7 "ἑρμηνευόμενον
τεῖχος" — also lauter Glossen von Lesern zu dem semitischen Ausdruck
des Hegesipp!) gar nichts zu tun' (Eisler, ΙΗΣΟΥΣ ΒΑΣΙΛΕΥΣ, II, 583,
n. 2). Cf. Klausner, *Jesus of Nazareth*, p. 41; H. J. Schoeps, *Theologie und
Geschichte des Judenchristentums* (Tübingen, 1949), p. 123, n. 1, and *Aus
frühchristlicher Zeit: religionsgeschichtliche Untersuchungen* (Tübingen, 1950),
pp. 120–5 (who interprets it as *scheliach sedeq*, making James 'der Apostel
in der ursprüngliche Bedeutung des Vertreters der Gemeinde vor Gott').
The identity of the Jewish leaders here is problematic. In the narrative
they are clearly described thrice as 'the Scribes and Pharisees', although
in the first mention these two groups are associated with the Jews: 'the
Jews and the Scribes and the Pharisees' (*Hist. eccl.* II. xxiii. 10)—thus,
curiously, differentiating the two Jewish groups from the Jews. However,
just before in the narrative, some members of what is called 'the seven
sects' (τῶν ἑπτὰ αἱρέσεων) are briefly described as putting to James the
question which is later put by the 'Scribes and Pharisees', namely, what
was 'the gate of Jesus'? (see p. 124, n. 2 below). A note is added that these
sectaries did not believe in resurrection or in a future judgement, conducted
presumably by the Messiah (*ibid.* 9). Such a description fits the Sadducees,
not the Pharisees, as both the Gospels and Josephus make clear (cf.
Brandon, *Man and his Destiny*, pp. 146–7). According to Hegesippus,
whom Eusebius quotes here *in extenso*, James's answer, that Jesus was 'the
Saviour' (see below, pp. 188–9), caused many of the rulers (τῶν ἀρχόντων)
to believe, and this resulted in a 'tumult' (θόρυβος) of the Jews and the
Scribes and Pharisees' (*Hist. eccl.* II. xxiii. 10). Nothing more is said of the
sectaries, and the 'Scribes and Pharisees' now become the interrogators
of James, and, ultimately, his murderers. This confusion may be simply
explained, as Ed. Schwartz suggested (*Z.N.T.W.* 4, 1903, pp. 50 ff.), by
assuming that the Sadducees were the slayers of James, being introduced
as the sectaries in *Hist. eccl.* II. xxiii. 9, and that reference is made to the
'Scribes and Pharisees' later in the account since, from their more
frequent appearance in the Gospels, they were a better-known grouping
of the opponents of Jesus. On Schoeps's interpretation of the death of
James (*Theologie*, pp. 381–4, 417, 431, 435, 446–7), and of Paul's part in
it, see below, p. 188, n. 2.
[2] Euseb. *Hist. eccl.* II. xxiii. 10: Ἰησοῦν τὸν Χριστὸν προσδοκᾶν.

them.[1] The only explanation that would seem to make sense of this part of Hegesippus' account is that the Sadducean leaders wanted to quieten a widespread popular belief that the *Parousia* of Jesus as the Messiah was imminent. This interpretation may also help to elucidate the strange question which, according to Hegesippus, these authorities put to Jesus: 'tell us, what is the gate of Jesus?'[2] James confounded them by publicly attesting his belief in the imminence of the *Parousia* of Jesus, which attestation was greeted by the crowd with the essentially political salutation, 'Hosanna to the Son of David'. In their chagrin and anger, the Jewish leaders assaulted James, throwing him down from the battlement of the Temple and causing him to be beaten to death. Hegesippus ends his account with the note that James was buried at the place where he died, the spot being marked by a stone (στήλη), and that straightway (εὐθύς) began the siege of Jerusalem.[3]

This tale, despite its many obvious problems, curiously accords with the situation which our analysis of Josephus' account appeared to indicate. Although what Hegesippus tells of the circumstances of the martyrdom of James contradicts the record of Josephus, Hegesippus supplies a number of details that seem to corroborate inferences which we were led to make from certain statements in the *Antiquities*. Thus, most notably, what he says about the sacerdotal privilege enjoyed by James and his attachment to the Temple accords remarkably with our inference from the Josephean account, namely, that

[1] Euseb. *Hist. eccl.* II. xxiii. 11: πεῖσον οὖν σὺ τὸν ὄχλον περὶ Ἰησοῦ μὴ πλανᾶσθαι· καὶ γὰρ πᾶς ὁ λαὸς καὶ πάντες πειθόμεθά σοι.

[2] *Ibid.* 12: ἀπάγγειλον ἡμῖν τίς ἡ θύρα τοῦ Ἰησοῦ (cf. *ibid.* 8, and previous note). This expression has never been satisfactorily explained; it is probably a corruption of some Aramaic expression. The explanation of K. Kohler, in *J.E.* VII, 68, has much to commend it, namely, that Hegesippus gave the original Jewish question: 'What is the gate of salvation?' (*sha'ar ha-yeshu 'ah*), which possibly contained a reference to Ps. cxviii. 20, and that this was later erroneously copied as *sha'ar Yeshua* (the 'gate of Jesus'). Cf. Eisler, *Messiah Jesus*, pp. 518–20, ΙΗΣΟΥΣ ΒΑΣΙΛΕΥΣ, II, 537–9; Burkitt, *Christian Beginnings*, p. 64; K. Lake, Loeb ed. Eusebius, I, 173; E. Lohmeyer, *Galiläa und Jerusalem* (Göttingen, 1936), p. 71; J. Weiss, *Earliest Christianity* (E.T.), II, 712, n. 7; Schoeps, *Theologie*, p. 414.

[3] Euseb. *Hist. eccl.* II. xxiii. 18. The killing of James by the club of a laundryman (εἷς τῶν γναφέων) completed the stoning of him (*ibid.* 17), which Josephus records. The stoning would have been the penalty pronounced by the Sanhedrin for a religious offence; cf. Sanhedrin, 7. 4, in Danby, *The Mishnah*, p. 391. See Eisler's ingenious interpretation of the στήλη (ΙΗΣΟΥΣ ΒΑΣΙΛΕΥΣ, II, 538–41).

James probably championed the cause of the priests and so was considered dangerous by the sacerdotal aristocracy of the Sadducees.[1] Then Hegesippus' representation of the death of James as resulting from his public proclamation of the imminent *Parousia* of Jesus as the Messiah, at a time of intense Messianic expectation, could well describe another aspect of Ananus' action—that James was not only the champion of the priests, and thereby closely associated with the Zealots; but he was also encouraging dangerous Messianic hopes centred on the imminent return of Jesus with full Messianic authority and power.[2] Nor is it without significance that, according to Josephus, as soon as the new procurator Albinus arrived in Judaea, he had to pacify (εἰρηνεύεσθαι) the land, which was disturbed by numerous bands of Sicarii.[3]

This long and involved discussion of the death of James has been fruitful, because, despite all the obscurities of the relevant material, there is strong reason for thinking that the procuratorial interregnum of A.D. 62 marked a crisis in Jewish Messianic expectation, and that James, the leader of the Jerusalem Church, and probably other members of it, became fatally involved in it. It has, moreover, indicated that the Jerusalem Christians were probably associated closely in sympathy and aspiration with both the lower orders of the

---

[1] Although the so-called Epistle of James is not, by the general consensus of expert opinion, to be regarded as written by James, the brother of Jesus, it is significant that a document showing such social consciousness should be ascribed to him: see e.g. i. 9–11, ii. 1–9, v. 1–6. It is to be noted also that Hegesippus records that James was recognised as one who did not respect persons (πρόσωπον οὐ λαμβάνεις), *apud* Euseb. *Hist. eccl.* ii. xxiii. 10. Cf. Moffatt, *Introduction to the New Testament*, p. 464; Grant, *Economic Background of the Gospels*, p. 122, n. 1; W. K. Lowther Clarke, *New Testament Problems* (London, 1929), p. 114.

[2] Cf. Euseb. *Hist. eccl.* ii. xxiii. 13–14. It is not without significance that Eusebius quotes Hegesippus as saying that James suffered martyrdom for the same reason as Jesus: καὶ μετὰ τὸ μαρτυρῆσαι ᾽Ιάκωβον τὸν δίκαιον, ὡς καὶ ὁ Κύριος, ἐπὶ τῷ αὐτῷ λόγῳ, . . . (*op. cit.* iv. xxi. 4). The only common factor in the two cases would seem to be that each was condemned for sedition, i.e. for threatening the established order. In his study of the accounts given by Hegesippus and Ps. Clem. *Rec.* i. 43–71 of the martyrdom of James ('Das Jakobusmartyrium und seine Verwandten in der frühchristlichen Literatur', *Z.N.T.W.* 56, 1965, pp. 149–78), K. Beyschlag poses the interesting question: 'Damit erscheint hinter Jakobus, Paulus und Stephanus die Gestalt Jesu selbst. War er der "Märtyrer"?' (p. 165). However, the significant parallels which he adduces do not challenge the historicity of Josephus' account; but they may well attest an original Jewish Christian evaluation of the death of Jesus as a martyrdom (see below, pp. 177 ff.).   [3] *Ant.* xx. 204.

hierarchy and the Zealots, and consequently opposed to the priestly aristocracy, as well as the heathen Romans who ruled them.

The ambiguity that invests Josephus' account of this episode also clothes what he records of the procuratorship of Albinus; it is in fact made worse by the disagreement that exists between the accounts given in the *Antiquities* and the *War*. In the *Antiquities*, which was written later, the two years concerned are dominated by the activities of Ananias, the high priest, and little is said of Albinus. In his record here, Josephus seems to be more concerned in tracing out the social disorder caused by the tyrannous action of the sacerdotal aristocracy, and what he says links up with his account of Ananus during the interregnum.[1] The Ananias who now plays the leading role is evidently the ex-high priest, the son of Nedabaios, who had held office about A.D. 47–59. A rich man and a powerful personage, Ananias dominated the Jerusalem scene, Albinus and the reigning high priest Jesus, son of Damnaios, both taking his bribes.[2] According to Josephus, he intensified the oppression of the lower clergy.[3] His activity, significantly, provoked bolder action from the Sicarii, who, during a festival, seized an important official of Eleazar, the commander of the Temple, who was also a son of Ananias.[4] The move was an exceedingly bold one; for they used their captive as a means of forcing Ananias to obtain from the procurator the release of ten Sicarii, who were his prisoners. Encouraged by their success, the Sicarii continued to use this means, i.e. holding servants of Ananias to ransom, for the surrender of other imprisoned members of their group.[5] These disorders begat others, and the whole situation

[1] *Ant.* xx. 205–7.
[2] *Ibid.* On Ananias, cf. Schürer, *G.J.V.* ii, 221–2; Jeremias, *Jerusalem*, ii, 57–9; Smallwood in *J.T.S.* xiii (1962), 27–31; Feldman in Loeb ed. of Josephus, ix, 444, n. *b*.   [3] *Ant.* xx. 206–7.
[4] *Ibid.* 208 (reading, with Loeb ed. of Josephus, ix, 498, n. 3, 'Ανανίου instead of 'Ανάνου). Josephus refers to Eleazar as τοῦ στρατηγοῦντος, and in *War*, ii. 409 as 'Ελεάζαρος υἱὸς 'Ανανία τοῦ ἀρχιερέως... στρατηγῶν τότε... The office of commander of the Temple (ὁ στρατηγὸς τοῦ ἱεροῦ or סגן) was of the highest importance in the Jewish state. According to Schürer, *G.J.V.* ii, 265, 'es begreift sich bei der Wichtigkeit dieser Stellung leicht, daß er als der im Rang dem Hohenpriester am nächsten stehende Priester angesehen wurde', cf. pp. 264–6; also Jeremias, *Jerusalem*, ii, 74–5.
[5] Jos. *Ant.* xx. 209–10: 'Man darf wohl aus solchen Vorkommnissen schließen, daß die Zeloten im offenen Lande die wahren Herren waren, und daß der Machtbereich der Römer sich weitgehend auf das hellenistische Gebiet und auf größere Orte mit römischer Besatzung beschränkte', Hengel, *Die Zeloten*, p. 361.

was further worsened by Albinus, who, at the end of his term of office, freed all the prisoners who paid him, executing only those who were the most notorious. Josephus comments that the emptying of the prisons filled the country with Zealots (*lēstai*).[1]

In the *Antiquities*, Josephus also records two other events symptomatic of the growing discord in Jerusalem at this time. The Levites, who managed the choral side of the Temple services, now demanded and obtained the right to wear the linen vestments of the priesthood. Josephus suggests no other motive for this demand than that of enhanced status, which seems somewhat curious in view of the oppression of the priests at this time by the sacerdotal aristocracy.[2] The final completion of the Temple now left a great number (more than eighteen thousand) workmen unemployed. As a temporary measure of relief, they were given the task of paving the city with white stone.[3] Their sense of economic insecurity must have made this large body of men discontented and fearful, and, therefore, a further dangerous element in the city.

In his earlier record of these times, i.e. the *War*, Josephus tells only of the misdeeds of Albinus, declaring that there was no form of villainy which he did not practise. His corruption encouraged the audacity of those intent on revolution (τῶν νεωτερίʒειν βουλομένων) in Jerusalem. The phrase is revealing, as is also the sequel, namely, that powerful men (οἱ δυνατοί) bribed the procurator to let them continue their seditious activities (τοῦ στασιάʒειν) unmolested.[4] The point of particular interest here to us is not so much the alleged venality of Albinus as the tacit admission that there were now in Jerusalem rebels, or men planning sedition, who were able to command sufficient money to buy the connivance of the procurator. As so often, Josephus does not supply explanatory details to an obviously important situation; however, since such revolutionaries must surely have been Zealots or some form of 'para-Zealot', it would appear that Zealotism was now firmly established in Jerusalem, with powerful supporters and a war-chest. Josephus does not explain what form their sedition took, but he goes on to describe their victimisation of moderate citizens (τῶν μετρίων).[5] It would, accordingly, appear that some three or four years before the actual

---

[1] *Ant.* xx. 215.
[2] *Ibid.* 216–18. Jeremias, *Jerusalem*, II, 76, thinks that Agrippa II granted the request of the Levites to spite the priests, to whom he was then antagonised.
[3] Jos. *Ant.* xx. 219–22.
[4] *War*, II. 273–4.   [5] *Ibid.* 275.

outbreak of rebellion in A.D. 66, the Zealots were coercing the peaceable and cautious elements in Jerusalem into cooperation or at least conformity with them.

Albinus was replaced by Gessius Florus (A.D. 64–6), whom Josephus holds responsible for the final acts of provocation that caused the fatal rebellion. Compared with Florus, the Jewish historian maintains that even the execrable Albinus appeared a paragon of virtue.[1] In the interests of his apologetic theme, Josephus undoubtedly exaggerates the vicious conduct of Florus; but that Florus did succeed in provoking the final explosion is attested, in a laconic statement, by the Roman historian Tacitus.[2] The long and involved account which Josephus gives of the enormities of Florus is designed to contrast with the truly amazing patience displayed by the Jews, led by their high priests and chief citizens, which he also describes at length.[3] The difference between this presentation of the Jewish situation and that which he gives for the situation existing under Albinus is, however, too great to be credible. It would seem that now Josephus had reached, in his *War*, the part of his narrative concerned with events in which he had himself been so fatefully, and so ambiguously, involved, he became increasingly dominated by his apologetic theme. It is, moreover, significant that no mention is made of the Zealots during these two years in which Florus so deliberately outraged Jewish feelings and sentiment; in the light of all that had gone before, it is beyond belief that these patriots remained quiescent under such extreme provocation. From Josephus' lengthy narrative four facts, however, seem to emerge which indicate a more intelligible situation. First, a serious clash between the Gentile and Jewish inhabitants of Caesarea, revolving around the religious susceptibilities of the latter, greatly incensed the Jews against Florus for his handling of the matter.[4] Next, Florus raided the Temple treasury, which led to a series of clashes between the Jews and the Roman forces: the Jews suffered heavy casualties; but Florus was forced to withdraw from Jerusalem and report to Cestius Gallus, the legate of Syria, that Judaea was in revolt.[5] A possible reason for Florus' raiding of the Temple treasury is the significant

[1] *War*, II. 227; cf. *Ant.* xx. 253.
[2] 'duravit tamen patientia Judaeis usque ad Gessium Florum; sub eo bellum ortum' (*Hist.* v. 10); cf. Jerome, trans. Euseb. *Chron.* col. 445a; Sulpicius Severus, II. 29. Cf. E. M. Smallwood in *History Today*, xv (1965), 319.
[3] *War*, II. 227 ff.; cf. *Ant.* xx. 253–8 (the record of the *Antiquities* ends here).
[4] *War*, II. 284–92.
[5] *Ibid.* 293–333.

fact that the Jews were in arrears with their payment of tribute.[1] The fourth fact, which may be reasonably inferred from Josephus' tendentious presentation, is that those elements in the Jewish state whose interests were bound up with the preservation of the existing order, which caused them to be pro-Roman in policy, if not in sentiment, now made strenuous efforts to save the situation from final collapse into armed revolt.[2] Three groups now tended to join forces: the sacerdotal authorities, certain lay magnates, whom Josephus calls οἱ δυνατοί,[3] and King Agrippa and those attached to the Herodian dynasty.[4]

Josephus describes Agrippa as endeavouring to win the people to a more peaceable attitude in a long speech. How far the speech given in the *War* was Agrippa's own or wholly the creation of Josephus cannot be determined; but it does provide a valuable indication of the views of those who counselled peace, and so opposed Zealotism.[5] The main argument employed in the speech is that of the hopelessness of successfully challenging the power of Rome—a detailed review is given of Roman might and its victorious assertion over many other peoples, far stronger and more populous than the Jews.[6] An appeal is even made to religion: it is argued that Rome could not have won world-empire without divine aid, and that to fight a war effectively would mean for the Jews the violation of the

---

[1] Josephus says that Florus took seventeen talents from the Temple treasury, σκηψάμενος εἰς τὰς Καίσαρος χρείας (*ibid.* 293). The χρεία of the emperor may well be the deficit in tribute to which reference is made in *ibid.* 404. Cf. Momigliano in *C.A.H.* x, 855; Hengel, *Die Zeloten*, p. 363.

[2] *War*, II. 301–4, 309–10, 315–25, 332, 333–4, 336–406.

[3] *Ibid.* 301: to them Josephus adds here the 'leading citizens' (τό τε γνωριμώτατον τῆς πόλεως).   [4] *Ibid.* 335 ff.

[5] *Ibid.* 345–404. Josephus, who had returned from Rome on the eve of the war, tells how he endeavoured 'to repress the promoters of sedition and persuade them to change their minds' (καταστέλλειν οὖν ἐπειρώμην τοὺς στασιώδεις καὶ μετανοεῖν ἔπειθον, *Life*, 17). His close association with Agrippa II would indicate a community of view on the situation.

[6] οὐ περισκέψεσθε τὴν Ῥωμαίων ἡγεμονίαν; οὐ μετρήσετε τὴν ἑαυτῶν ἀσθένειαν; (*War*, II. 362). The complete absence of any sharing in Zealot faith finds expression in the derisive question: τί τὸ πεποιθὸς ὑμᾶς κατὰ Ῥωμαίων ἐπαίρει; (*ibid.* 364). It is also significant that Agrippa is represented as referring contemptuously to the Jews' new passion for liberty (τό γε νῦν ἐλευθερίας ἐπιθυμεῖν), *ibid.* 355. On the question of the attitude of Babylonian Jewry and Parthian policy, which this speech raises, cf. J. Neusner, *History of the Jews in Babylonia* (Leiden, 1965), I, 64–7; *Life of Rabban Yohanan ben Zakkai* (Leiden, 1962), p. 173. Cf. B. Pin, *Jérusalem contre Rome* (*Un duel pour l'hégémonie en Méditerranée orientale*), Paris, 1938, p. 13.

sabbath, and inevitably lead to the destruction of the Temple.[1] The speech closes with an exhortation to pay the tribute (τελέσετε τὴν εἰσφοράν).[2] The whole composition is remarkable for its realistic appreciation of Roman strength and its complete omission of any reference to faith in Israel's unique destiny as the Elect People of God. It also represents a tacit repudiation of the Zealot ideal of Israel as a theocracy by endowing Rome's *imperium* with divine sanction, which meant that Israel's subjection to Rome was according to God's will.[3] Hence the payment of tribute to Caesar was a religious duty. Such a travesty of the doctrine of Israel's divine Election could come only from one who lacked the prophetic faith and was moved solely by a shrewd appraisal of the material resources of each side. The assessment was certainly Josephus', and it explains his subsequent defection to Rome; it probably represented also the view of Agrippa and those others with vested interests in the existing order. But it was vehemently rejected by the Jewish people, and those whose leadership they now followed, namely, the Zealots.[4]

Two events finally announced that the period of subversive activity and guerrilla tactics was ended, and that the resistance fighters had now gone over to open warfare against the Romans. In Jerusalem, by one of those renunciations of family loyalties that have often marked the young revolutionary, a son of the powerful high priest Ananias suddenly led his countrymen into what was a virtual declaration of war against Rome. The young man, Eleazar, who was commander of the Temple, persuaded the priests, despite the opposition of the higher clergy, to stop the daily sacrifice offered on behalf of the emperor and the Roman people. This cultic act was the accepted symbol of Jewish loyalty to Rome, and its cessation was tantamount to rebellion.[5] It is significant that it was the priests who took this

---

[1] *War*, II. 391-4, 397-401.   [2] *Ibid.* 404.

[3] Agrippa argues that the Romans could not build so great an empire without divine aid (δίχα γὰρ θεοῦ συστῆναι τηλικαύτην ἡγεμονίαν ἀδύνατον, *War*, II. 391).

[4] Josephus states that the people accepted Agrippa's advice, and that the tax arrears, amounting to forty talents, were soon collected. However, subsequently (αὖθις), when the king tried to induce them to submit to Florus, the people revolted and drove him out of Jerusalem (*ibid.* 405-7).

[5] *Ibid.* 409. On these sacrifices see chapter 2, p. 58, n. 2. It is significant that Josephus represents the high priests, together with the δυνατοί and leading Pharisees, as trying to have the sacrifices restored by arguing with the people that not only was the offering of sacrifice for Gentiles legal, but its rejection was tantamount to an act of impiety, for it meant putting the Romans and their emperor beyond the pale (περιορᾶν δ' ὅτε 'Ρωμαῖοι

decisive step; but Josephus, with that usual plethora of ambiguous terms which indicates his embarrassment, admits that they were supported by the most vigorous party of the revolutionaries (τὸ ἀκμαιότατον τῶν νεωτεριζόντων συνήργει).[1] Such cooperation is, of course, intelligible in the light of the earlier association between the lower clergy and the revolutionary party. The secession of Eleazar from the high-priestly party is interesting, and it would doubtless be illuminating, if his motives could be determined; whatever they were, his adherence to the priests now provided them with a natural leader, which they seem hitherto to have lacked.[2] Eleazar also became the leader of the other revolutionaries in Jerusalem, as the sequel shows.

About the same time, i.e. the summer of A.D. 66, what might be termed the dynastic party of Zealotism seized the fortress of Masada, near the Dead Sea, killing the Roman garrison. These Zealots were led by Menahem, a son of Judas of Galilee.[3] The move seems to have been strategically conceived; for not only did the armoury of the fortress provide an abundance of equipment, but the fortress itself provided an almost impregnable stronghold, where resistance could be continued in the event of misfortune elsewhere. Equipping himself and his followers from the armoury, and leaving a garrison, Menahem went to Jerusalem, evidently intending to enter on his father's heritage as the recognised leader of Zealotism.[4]

Meanwhile the capital was in a state of civil war. The sacerdotal

καὶ ὁ Καῖσαρ ἔκσπονδος γίνεται, *ibid.* 415). Cf. Ricciotti, *Flavio Giuseppe*, II, 320, n. on 414. Hengel (*Die Zeloten*, p. 111, n. 2) is surely right in thinking that the Zealots must have found it intolerable that sacrifice was offered in the Temple on behalf of a Gentile ruler who was worshipped by the Gentiles as a god; see also Hengel, pp. 365–8. Roth has shown from Talmudic evidence that Rabbinic opinion was not unanimous on the legality of sacrifices on behalf of Gentiles (*H.Th.R.* LIII, 1960, 93–7). On Eleazar and the significance of his office see above, p. 126, n. 4.

[1] *War*, II. 410.
[2] Josephus probably tries to tone down the seriousness of Eleazar's secession by calling him a νεανίας θρασύτατος (*ibid.* 409). 'Vielleicht hatte ihn [Eleazar] die Erkenntnis, daß der Einfluß des römerfreundlichen Priester-adels ständig zurückging, während der zelotische Geist in der Masse der Priesterschaft unaufhaltsam wuchs, zu diesem kühnen Schritt bewogen' (Hengel, *Die Zeloten*, p. 366).
[3] Jos. *War*, II. 408. See above, pp. 52, 61, n. 4. On the position and strength of Masada see Jos. *War*, VII. 280–303; cf. M. Avi-Yonah in *I.L.N.* 5 November 1955, pp. 784–7; *I.E.J.* VII (1957), 1–60.
[4] Jos. *War*, II. 433–4; τούτοις τε χρώμενος δορυφόροις, οἷα δὴ βασιλεὺς ἐπάνεισιν εἰς Ἱεροσόλυμα καὶ γενόμενος ἡγεμὼν τῆς στάσεως...

aristocracy, realising that they now had to fight for their existence, enlisted the aid of King Agrippa to suppress the revolt before it was too late.[1] The assistance of the royal troops was more than offset by strong reinforcements of Sicarii, who enabled Eleazar not only to hold the Temple but also to take the Upper City and the Antonia.[2] During these operations the rebels burnt the palaces of Agrippa and his sister, Bernice, and the house of Ananias, the high priest, and the public archives. These acts are significant of the social aspect of the revolt: although the Romans were the principal enemy, popular animus was strong against the Herodian dynasts and the sacerdotal aristocracy who were both pro-Roman and oppressive to the poor. As Josephus observes, the destruction of the money-lenders' bonds encouraged the poor to rise against the rich.[3]

When Menahem arrived in Jerusalem, he at once assumed the leadership of the revolt (γενόμενος ἡγεμὼν τῆς στάσεως).[4] This apparently automatic assumption of command eloquently testifies to the reverence in which Judas of Galilee and his sons were held, and it helps to explain the statement of Josephus that Menahem came to Jerusalem as a king (οἷα δὴ βασιλεύς).[5] For such a person as Menahem to be regarded as a king can only mean that his followers recognised him as the Messiah, and this conclusion seems to be supported by Rabbinic evidence.[6] His arrival seems to have inspired the rebels; they quickly forced Agrippa's troops to surrender and drove the remnant of the Roman garrison into the three Herodian towers. Ananias, the high priest, with his brother Ezekias, were also captured and executed.[7] Menahem's advent and exaltation were, however, resented by Eleazar, who caused him to be murdered while at his devotions in the Temple, arrayed in regal attire and with a Zealot

[1] Jos. *War*, II. 417–24.
[2] *Ibid.* 425–32. Josephus' account of how the Sicarii joined the rebel priests in the Temple is to be noted as an example of his vague and confused terminology when dealing with an embarrassing situation. He evidently found it repugnant to admit that the priests were quickly and effectively supported by the Sicarii in their revolt, and that they willingly accepted this support.
[3] *Ibid.* 426–7: τοῖς εὐπόροις ἐπαναστήσωσι τοὺς ἀπόρους. Cf. above, p. 56.
[4] See p. 131, n. 4 above.
[5] *Ibid.* 434. Cf. Hengel, *Die Zeloten*, pp. 369–70: 'Die Zeloten hatten ihr seit 2 Generationen erstrebtes Ziel erreicht: nahezu das ganze Volk war in den Heiligen Krieg mit Rom eingetreten' (p. 370).
[6] Cf. Roth, *Historical Background of Dead Sea Scrolls*, pp. 60–2; Hengel, *Die Zeloten*, pp. 299–302, 369–70; Eisler, ΙΗΣΟΥΣ ΒΑΣΙΛΕΥΣ, II, 602–3, 712.
[7] Jos. *War*, II. 433–41.

bodyguard.[1] Those of Menahem's party who survived the attack escaped to Masada, where they were commanded by a relative of Menahem, named Eleazar, thus preserving the dynastic succession.[2]

The death of Menahem deprived the Zealot movement of its hereditary head and charismatic leader. There is indeed a tragic irony in the fact that, having suffered so much in maintaining the cause of Israel's freedom for sixty years, the family of Judas of Galilee was thus robbed of the leadership when that cause was at last brought to the arbitration of war.[3] Without Menahem, the various Zealot groups throughout the country were left to the direction of their own local leaders. In Jerusalem, Eleazar once more assumed control of the revolt, and he was responsible for massacring the survivors of the Roman garrison, after they had surrendered on terms.[4]

[1] *Ibid.* 442-8. Josephus indicates his dislike of Menahem by the strength of the invective he uses when referring to him: success brutalises the Zealot leader (ἐτύφωσεν εἰς ὡμότητα), so that he becomes an 'intolerable tyrant' (ἀφόρητος ἦν τύραννος), and is described as a 'native executioner' (οἰκείῳ δημίῳ); but it is significant that Josephus also refers to him as τὸν σοφιστήν (*ibid.* 445), thus attesting to his rabbinic status (see above, pp. 37, 52). Josephus represents what he oddly calls 'the rest of the people' (ὅ τε λοιπὸς δῆμος) as joining in the killing of Menahem in the hope of thus crushing the whole revolt (διατρέψειν ὅλην τὴν στάσιν), cf. *ibid.* 449. It would appear that, though originally embarrassed by the fact that the Temple *sagan* had initiated the revolt, Josephus tends to excuse Eleazar in praising him for his murder of Menahem. On C. Roth's identification of Menahem with the Teacher of Righteousness of the Qumran Scrolls, see chapter 2, p. 61, n. 4. According to this interpretation, Eleazar fits the role of the Wicked Priest (*Historical Background of Dead Sea Scrolls*, pp. 10-14); Driver, *Judaean Scrolls*, pp. 266-84, 472-3. Ricciotti, *Flavio Giuseppe*, II, 325, n. on 441, raises the question whether Eleazar sought thus to avenge his father's death. Cf. Hengel, *Die Zeloten*, pp. 370-2: 'Vielleicht hatten Eleazar und Menahem ursprünglich an eine priesterlich-königliche Doppelherrschaft gedacht, wie wir sie bei den Essenern finden und wie sie später unter Bar Koseba angedeutet wird, doch ließen die militärischen Erfolge des Menahem dessen Streben nach uneingeschränkter Gesamtherrschaft immer unverhüllter hervortreten' (p. 371).

[2] Jos. *War*, II. 447. Eleazar ben Jair is described as προσήκων τῷ Μαναήμῳ κατὰ γένος. Roth, *Historical Background of Dead Sea Scrolls*, p. 10, thinks he was probably a nephew.

[3] The murder of Menahem and the retreat of his followers to Masada appear to have split the freedom movement, leaving it without a charismatic or dynastic head. 'Die folgende Zersplitterung in teilweise sich bekämpfende Gruppen gab Rom den Sieg in die Hand, bevor der Krieg richtig begonnen hatte' (Hengel, *Die Zeloten*, p. 373).

[4] Jos. *War*, II. 449-56. Since the massacre of the Roman garrison involved breaking an oath of safe conduct, and it took place on a sabbath, Josephus

It is not necessary to our purpose that we should trace out in detail the course of the Jewish war against Rome until the final disaster in A.D. 70. The very full and graphically presented record which Josephus gives in his *Jewish War* is clearly a tendentious account which requires detailed analysis; for it is particularly suspect in those parts which concern Josephus' own conduct or interests.[1] It will, however, meet the needs of our subject, if we summarise those aspects of the struggle which are relevant to our estimate of the involvement of the Jewish Christians in the fatal conflict of their nation with the avenging might of heathen Rome.

First, it is important to note that the raising of the standard of revolt in Jerusalem quickly had its repercussions throughout Palestine and for many Jewish communities of the Diaspora. News of the revolt, and especially of the slaughter of the Roman garrison at Jerusalem, proved fatal to the Jews of Caesarea, who were already involved in a bitter feud with the Gentile inhabitants of this city, which was also the headquarters of the Roman government. According to Josephus, twenty thousand were slaughtered and the rest reduced to slavery in the dockyards there.[2] This massacre provoked Jewish reprisals against the Gentile cities of Philadelphia, Heshbon, Gerasa, Pella, Scythopolis, Gadara, Hippos, Kedesa, Ptolemais, Gaba, Ascalon, Anthedon, and Gaza, and the district of Gaulonitis and the neighbouring Syrian villages.[3] What happened in Samaria is not clear: generally it would appear that the Samaritans were

sees in the crime a presage of his people's ruin ('Ιουδαίοις δὲ προοίμιον ἁλώσεως ἔδοξεν). In introducing this account, Josephus once more tries to represent the people (ὁ δῆμος) as being now deceived in their hopes of peace by the determination of Eleazar's party to continue the revolt. However, as Ricciotti observes, 'Ma qui Giuseppe è probabilmente vittima della sua tesi, secondo cui pochi turbolenti coinvolsero nella guerra contro Roma i moltissimi Giudei pacifisti (vedi §324); in realtà il popolo che *aveva cooperato a questi fatti* doveva essere il gruppo di Eleazaro, o almeno dei simpatizzanti per lui, ad ogni modo erano Zeloti anti-romani: vedi §441 (cfr. §443)' (*Flavio Giuseppe*, II, 326, n. on 449). Cf. *Der Jüdische Krieg*, hrg. Michel und Bauernfeind, I, 448, n. 203.

[1] Cf. B. Niese in *E.R.E.* VII, 571 *b*–572 *a*, 575 *b*; F. Jackson, *Josephus and the Jews*, pp. 7–19; Ricciotti, *Flavio Giuseppe*, I, 171–2.

[2] *War*, II. 457.

[3] *Ibid.* 458–60. It would appear, however, from *War*, III. 9–25 that Ascalon was not taken. Josephus also includes Caesarea in the list of places that suffered from Jewish reprisals (*War*, II. 459); but it is improbable that the city was actually taken, as it was the headquarters of the Roman government and there is evidence of cohorts there throughout the period: cf. Jos. *War*, III. 66. Cf. Ricciotti, *Flavio Giuseppe*, II, 328, n. on 458–60.

coerced into cooperation with the Jews, and the Roman garrison at Sebaste was destroyed.[1] In turn, for these attacks, the Jews resident in many places in Syria and in Alexandria in Egypt had to pay the penalty.[2]

Since the situation in Judaea had now got beyond the resources of the procurator Florus, it was the task of the legate of Syria, Cestius Gallus, to restore the Roman position and punish the rebels. This officer took some three months from the outbreak of the revolt to gather his forces for the punitive expedition.[3] Entering the country with a strong body of legionary and auxiliary troops, he advanced through Galilee and Samaria, encountering little opposition;[4] the rebels had evidently not had time to consolidate their position outside the capital. After a minor reverse at Beth-horon, Cestius Gallus laid siege to the insurgent city and pressed his attack successfully to the point of breaching the Temple walls.[5] Then, for some inexplicable reason, he suddenly ordered the assault to stop and withdrew his troops to Mount Scopus, on the northern side of the city. After spending the night there, the Roman army began to retire northwards, evidently breaking off the siege.[6] The beleaguered Jews could

[1] War, II. 459. Josephus does not make clear how far or in what way the Samaritans were involved in the revolt. The taking of Sebaste would imply the reduction of the Roman garrison there, although the fact is not recorded. Cf. I. E. H. Thomson, The Samaritans (Edinburgh, 1919), p. 39.

[2] Jos. War, II. 461–8, 477–83, 487–98.

[3] See the discussion of the dates involved in Brandon, The Fall of Jerusalem, p. 157, n. 5. The army of C. Gallus comprised the twelfth legion in full strength, two thousand other legionaries specially selected, six cohorts of other infantry and four squadrons of cavalry, and auxiliaries of various armies to the number of fourteen thousand; other auxiliaries were collected en route; cf. War, II. 500.

[4] Ibid. 499–527. G. A. Smith, Historical Geography of the Holy Land (London, 1907), p. 299, considers that Cestius was too precipitate in his advance on Jerusalem; however, according to Josephus (ibid. 507–12, 513–14), all opposition had been eliminated in Galilee, and it was unlikely that Samaria would give trouble.

[5] Ibid. 517–37. According to Josephus, the Jews believed the fall of the city to be imminent (ὡς ἁλωσομένης αὐτίκα, ibid. 538).

[6] Ibid. 538–42. The calling off of the assault on the Temple and the retreat of the Roman army have never been satisfactorily explained. According to Josephus, Cestius could have taken the city, if he had immediately attacked the Upper City after taking the district known as Bezetha; but his staff, bribed by the procurator Florus, had persuaded him against such action (ibid. 531). This extraordinary assertion would seem to be motivated by Josephus' presentation of Florus as responsible for goading

scarcely believe the evidence of their eyes; for they had been reduced to despair, expecting the seemingly invincible Romans to complete their success by finally breaking into the Temple and proclaiming their victory in the desecrated shrine of Yahweh. At first, undoubt-

the Jews into revolt (cf. *ibid.* 277–9, 333). Whatever truth there may be in the statement (cf. *ibid.* 558), it does not explain the calling off of the assault on the Temple when victory seemed assured. All that Josephus can say in explanation of the decision of Cestius then is that it must have been due to the divine will that the revolt should not so quickly be ended and the Temple saved (ἀλλ᾽ οἶμαι διὰ τοὺς πονηροὺς ἀπεστραμμένος ὁ θεὸς ἤδη καὶ τὰ ἅγια, τέλος λαβεῖν ἐπ᾽ ἐκείνης τῆς ἡμέρας ἐκώλυσεν τὸν πόλεμον, *ibid.* 539). The suggestion of Schürer, *G.J.V.* I, 605 (cf. Mommsen, *Das Weltreich der Caesaren*, p. 386; Noth, *History of Israel*, p. 437), that Cestius found his forces too small, seems to be based on the size of the army later used by Vespasian and Titus. However, by that time the revolt was well established; moreover, from all that Josephus says Cestius had been very successful and was at the point of final victory. That Cestius decided that the season was too late, as Graetz, *History of the Jews*, II, 263, thinks, is quite untenable, since the legate had already committed himself to the assault on the metropolis and success was within his grasp. Schlatter (*Gesch. Israels*), perhaps significantly, offers no explanation. Momigliano's solution is that Cestius feared an attack on his flanks (*C.A.H.* X, 856), but he does not indicate who would have mounted this. Zealot guerrillas undoubtedly constituted a danger to his communications; but Josephus says nothing of them, and Cestius' best policy in this respect would have been to finish off the centre of rebel resistance as soon as possible. Ricciotti, *Flavio Giuseppe*, II, 348, rightly stresses the obvious discrepancies in Josephus' account of the matter; but his suggestion that Cestius had initially underestimated his task is contradicted by his rapid success, i.e. if Josephus is to be trusted on this point. Hengel seems to suggest that lack of discipline on the part of the Syrian legionaries was the cause—'Auch wenn der rein militärische Erfolg gegen die wegen ihrer Disziplinlosigkeit berüchtigten syrischen Legionen nicht zu hoch eingeschätzt werden darf...' (p. 376). But any lack of efficiency on the part of these troops only became apparent during the retreat; until the assault on the Temple was called off, they had given a good account of themselves. Perowne (*The Later Herods*, p. 134) does not seem to be aware of the problem, although he discusses the campaign at some length. Cf. Brandon, *Fall of Jerusalem*, p. 159, n. 4. From the passage previously quoted it is evident that Josephus was at a loss to explain the action of Cestius. There seems to be no obvious reason why Josephus might have exaggerated the extent of the Romans' success before the assault was halted, although whether the people (ὁ δῆμος) looked upon Cestius as a benefactor (ὡς εὐεργέτην) and wished his success may be doubted—unless by ὁ δῆμος he means people like himself (cf. *Life*, 23). The only sound conclusion that can be drawn would seem to be that Josephus was genuinely puzzled about the reason for the Roman withdrawal, and that he does not supply enough data to enable us to discern what that reason may have been.

edly suspecting the Roman action, the Zealots hesitated; but when the retreat continued, their joy and relief were unbounded.[1] The mysterious discomfiture that Yahweh had once wrought on the army of Sennacherib now seemed to be repeated on the army of Caesar.[2] Doubtless the promise of Judas of Galilee was remembered, that God would succour them, if they made the venture of faith and withstood the heathen.[3] Exulting in this signal proof of divine providence, the Jews pursued the retreating Romans, harassing their march and cutting off stragglers. Disaster befell the army of Cestius Gallus as it descended through the narrow pass of the Beth-horons. Here the Jewish attack grew intense, inspired undoubtedly by memories of the glorious victories of their ancestors there—Joshua's defeat of the Amorites and the triumph of Judas Maccabaeus over the Seleucid army under Seron.[4] Only by sacrificing his rearguard did Cestius Gallus struggle free and continue his retreat, which became a veritable rout, to safety beyond the borders of Palestine.[5] The effect

[1] Jos. *War*, II. 540. Josephus, significantly, calls the defenders οἱ λῃσταί. He also says explicitly that Cestius had suffered no reverse (καταγνοὺς ἐπ' οὐδεμιᾷ πληγῇ τῶν ἐλπίδων).

[2] Cf. II Kings xviii. 17–xix. 36. It is interesting to note that Josephus, in his account of the calamity that befell the Assyrian army (*Ant.* x. 21–2), rationalises the record of II Kings by replacing 'the angel of the Lord went out and smote the camp of the Assyrians' by a reference to the effect of plague: cf. R. Marcus, Loeb ed. of Josephus, VI, 168, n. *c*. Farmer, in tracing out the influence of the fate of Sennacherib's army on the authors of I and II Maccabees, remarks that, 'if we had histories of the war of the Jews against Rome written by men sympathetic with the national resistance to heathen dominion, we should find that these Jews also—outnumbered as they were by the imperial armies of Rome with their nation and sanctuary imperilled—would have been portrayed in such histories as having been inspired by the story of the miraculous defeat of Sennacherib's overwhelming hosts, before the very gates of Jerusalem' (*Maccabees, Zealots and Josephus*, pp. 99–100). Cf. Y. Yadin, *Scroll of the War*, pp. 212–13.

[3] *Ant.* XVIII. 5: τὸ θεῖον οὐκ ἄλλως ἢ ἐπὶ συμπράξει τῶν βουλευμάτων εἰς τὸ κατορθοῦν συμπροθυμεῖσθαι μᾶλλον, ἂν μεγάλων ἐρασταὶ τῇ διανοίᾳ καθιστάμενοι μὴ ἐξαφίωνται πόνου τοῦ ἐπ' αὐτοῖς. See above, pp. 33, 51.

[4] Jos. *War*, II. 542–50. See also Josh. x. 10–11; I Macc. iii. 13–24. On the difficult nature of the road through the Beth-horons see Smith, *Historical Geography*, pp. 210–11; Lightfoot, *Horae Hebraicae*, I, 43–4; Ricciotti, *Flavio Giuseppe*, II, 349–50, nn. on 542, 546, p. 352 (ill.).

[5] Jos. *War*, II. 551–5. Josephus gives the Roman losses, including those of auxiliary troops, as 5,300 infantry and 480 cavalry. In addition they lost their baggage, including battering-rams, catapults and other siege weapons. Cf. Tacitus, *Hist.* v. 10; Suetonius, *Vespasian*, 4, who mentions a *rapta aquila*; Orosius, VIII. 9 (478).

of this spectacular, and unexpected, victory on the Jews was immense. They, a tiny nation, had challenged the might of imperial Rome, and God had blessed their act of faith and routed a Roman army as he had routed the armies of other heathen oppressors before. Opposition to the revolt now disappeared, and Josephus records that even the surviving pro-Romans (τοὺς . . . τῶν ἔτι ῥωμαϊзόντων) now joined in the national effort to meet the next Roman attack.[1] In this rallying of all parties to maintain the newly won freedom of Israel, certain of the sacerdotal aristocracy now emerged to lead the nation, chief among them being the (former) high priest Ananus.[2] An attempt was made to exclude the Zealot leader who had distinguished himself in the overthrow of Cestius Gallus. Josephus gives his name as Eleazar, son of Simon: there appears to be some discrepancy in Josephus' record here because this Eleazar is suddenly introduced without previous notice of his exploits, whereas the Eleazar, son of Ananias, who had played the leading role so far in the revolt, disappears without further mention.[3] However that may be,

[1] *War*, II. 562; cf. *Life*, 24. Cf. Hengel, *Die Zeloten*, pp. 290, 376.
[2] Jos. *War*, II. 563. Josephus' statement is rather confused here. He says that those 'who pursued Cestius', having obtained the allegiance, partly by force and partly by persuasion, of the pro-Roman party, appointed additional (πλείονας) generals. Joseph ben Gioron, together with Ananus ὁ ἀρχιερεύς, was elected (ἡρέθη) to supreme control (αὐτοκράτορες) of affairs in the city, with the special charge of heightening the walls. Since those who had led the pursuit of Cestius were the Zealots (λησταί), according to *ibid*. 541, the new situation seems rather inexplicable. Cf. Schürer, *G.J.V.* I, 606–7; Ricciotti, *Flavio Giuseppe*, II, 355, n. on 563.
[3] *War*, II. 564–5. According to Josephus, Eleazar ben Simon was passed over because of his 'despotic nature' (τυραννικόν), and his bodyguard of Zealots (τοὺς ὑπ' αὐτῷ зηλωτὰς δορυφόρων ἔθεσι χρωμένους); cf. Ricciotti, *Flavio Giuseppe*, II, 356 *in loco*. In *War*, II. 566 an 'Eleazar, son of the high priest Neus' is among the generals selected for the defence of Idumaea. Since no high priest called Neus is known, it would appear that Νέου should be corrected to 'Ανανίου, as Hudson does; cf. Thackeray, Loeb ed. of Josephus, II, 540, nn. 1 and *a*; Ricciotti, II, 356, n. on 566–8, who, commenting on the remarkable fact that such a leader of the revolt as Eleazar ben Hananiah should have been relegated to so unimportant a command, suggests that 'in questa prudenziale misura si può scorgere l'influenza di persone moderate, sul tipo di Anano (§563), che volevano allontanare gli intransigenti dalle zone più importanti per lasciare la possibilità di un accomodamento con i Romani'. In the *Life*, 28, Josephus says nothing about this, but says that the leading men (οἱ πρῶτοι), fearing the well-armed Zealots and other rebels, sought to equip themselves against them. He explains this policy as an introduction to his own mission to Galilee. Cf. Roth in *J.S.S.* IV (1959), 342. Eleazar ben

it would appear that the Zealots in Jerusalem, who included the lower clergy, and were led by Eleazar, were reluctant to accept the control of such erstwhile opponents as Ananus.[1] In the country, outside the capital, many groups of Zealots appear to have operated without a concerted plan or unified command. To control this situation, Ananus and his supporters sent out commissioners; among those appointed to Galilee was the future historian Josephus.[2] In his *Jewish War* and his *Life*, Josephus gives long and often conflicting accounts of his very involved and acrimonious dealings with these insurgent groups, his special *bête noir* being one of their leaders, John of Gischala.[3]

The anticipated Roman counter-attack came in A.D. 67, and it was commanded by the veteran general Vespasian, well inured to hard fighting from his campaigns in Britain.[4] A very different situation now confronted the Romans as they entered the country from the north. A series of fortified cities had to be subdued before Jerusalem, the centre of the revolt, could be assailed. The task was a long and difficult one, involving much fierce fighting; for, although they could not face the legions in the field, the Jews fought hard and skilfully in defending strongholds and cities. These operations occupied Vespasian until he left Palestine in the year 69.[5] In the meantime, Jerusalem had become the scene of internecine warfare, as various factions strove for supremacy. The defection of Josephus

Simon was of priestly descent (*War*, IV. 225, reading Σίμωνος for Γίωνος, cf. Thackeray, Loeb ed. of Josephus, III, 68, n. 1; Ricciotti, III, 160, n. on 225). Cf. Roth, 'The Constitution of the Jewish Republic of 66–70', *J.S.S.* IX (1964), 299–300.

[1] Jos. *War*, II. 565.

[2] *Ibid.* 566–8; cf. *Life*, 29, according to which Josephus was commissioned to disarm the rebels. On the discrepancies in the *War* and the *Life* concerning his activities in Galilee see F. Jackson, *Josephus and the Jews*, pp. 7–18.

[3] See preceding note. For Josephus' initial account of John of Gischala see *War*, II. 585–9, where he is described as a 'brigand' (λῃστής). Roth is rightly doubtful whether John of Gischala was originally a Zealot; Josephus is confusing in what he says in different parts of his narrative: cf. Roth in *J.S.S.* IV (1959), 343, 346–7; see also Hengel, *Die Zeloten*, p. 378, n. 3, on the respective relationship of Josephus and John to the Sadducean and Pharisaic parties. Driver, *Judaean Scrolls*, pp. 28–9, has suggested that John of Gischala is the 'Man of Falsehood' of the Qumrân Covenanters.

[4] Jos. *War*, III. 3–7. Cf. B. W. Henderson, *Life and Principate of the Emperor Nero*, p. 372; B. M. Bersanetti, *Vespasiano* (Rome, 1941), pp. 17–18.

[5] Cf. Brandon, *Fall of Jerusalem*, pp. 161–4, where relevant documentation is given.

to the Romans, after the fall of Jotapata, undoubtedly shook the prestige of the party he had represented;[1] but more serious was the increase of Zealot strength within the capital as bands of insurgents withdrew there from the Roman advance.[2] The priestly Zealots, led by Eleazar, finally rejected the control of Ananus, and entrenched themselves in the Temple. It would seem that by this time they had completely lost faith in the leadership of the sacerdotal aristocracy; they probably still suspected the sincerity of their intention to wage the holy war *à toute outrance* against the Romans, a suspicion which was not unfounded.[3] Their attitude now found significant expression by reviving the ancient custom of choosing the high priest by lot. By this means a simple country priest was appointed to represent Israel in the performance of the highest cultic acts of the liturgy. Josephus naturally regards this decision as outrageous, and he uses it to reinforce his apologetic thesis that the Zealots so polluted the Temple and its institutions that God forsook his sanctuary and gave it over to destruction.[4] He actually represents Ananus, the high priest, as exhorting the people to destroy these Zealots and not to wait for the Romans to deliver God's sanctuary.[5] In the succeeding struggle for mastery the Zealots finally prevailed, aided by insurgents from Idumaea, and Ananus, with his chief supporters, perished.[6]

[1] Jos. *War*, iii. 438–42.   [2] *Ibid.* 106, 121–7, 135–9.
[3] Jos. *War*, iv. 151–2, cf. 226–9, 320–1.
[4] *Ibid.* 147–50 (Josephus here uses the plural, thus implying that the Zealots appointed more than one high priest), 152–7. Cf. Roth in *J.S.S.* iv (1959), 343–4. In choosing by lot a high priest from the Eniachin clan (φυλή), the Zealots were actually reverting to the ancient Zadok line. Hence, as Hengel shows (*Die Zeloten*, pp. 224–5), Josephus, in representing their appointment of a new high priest as an act of impiety, is pursuing his policy of denigrating the Zealots by distorting their motives in seeking to reform appointment to the high priesthood, which had been so grossly exploited for some decades by certain powerful families. Cf. Jeremias, *Jerusalem*, ii, 12, 52–3. It is not without significance that the high priest who was elected in consequence of this Zealot reform was named Phanni, or Phinehas, according to Rabbinic tradition (T. Joma, i, 6. 180; cf. Derenbourg, *Essai*, pp. 268–9). Eisler, citing the *Midrash* that equates Phinehas with Elijah (see above, pp. 43–5), interprets it as applying to the Phinehas ben Samuel, of Aphthia, whom the Zealots made high priest: 'Dieser messianische Hochpriester Pinḥas kann nicht gut jemand ander gewesen sein, als jener Pinḥas...' (ΙΗΣΟΥΣ ΒΑΣΙΛΕΥΣ, ii, 159, n. 4, cf. 83, n. 1, *Messiah Jesus*, pp. 310–11). Cf. Roth in *J.S.S.* ix (1964), 315–16.
[5] Ῥωμαίους ἄρα περιμενεῖτε, ἵν' ἡμῶν βοηθήσωσι τοῖς ἁγίοις; (*War*, iv. 173).
[6] *Ibid.* 193–318. Josephus does not make clear why the Idumaeans played so large a part in Israel's struggle against Rome. That they should have

Josephus dated the downfall of the Jewish state from the day on which Ananus was killed, whom.he describes as 'the high priest and leader of their [the Jews'] salvation' (τὸν ἀρχιερέα καὶ ἡγεμόνα τῆς ἰδίας σωτηρίας), thereby revealing the role that he had hoped Ananus would play, if, by suppressing the Zealots, he had been able to lead the nation back to its allegiance to Rome.[1]

That such a struggle for leadership of the nation, at this critical juncture, would have happened, if Menahem had survived, is unlikely. The attempt of the sacerdotal aristocracy, led by Ananus, to seize control, though ostensibly to consolidate the situation after the defeat of Cestius Gallus, was surely motivated by the double aim of making terms with Rome and preserving their own position. The resistance of the Zealots, particularly those of the lower orders of the priesthood, was instinctively sound.[2] They saw in Ananus, despite his prestige as a high priest, one who would re-establish Israel's double yoke of servitude: to the heathen Romans and to the sacerdotal nobility. Their struggle against this menace, in the knowledge that Rome was concentrating its forces for revenge, was indeed suicidal, and it was Josephus' policy to present it as such, and to dilate on the atrocities committed by the Zealots. However, it is significant that, despite subsequent contests between rival rebel leaders, when the Roman siege of Jerusalem began in A.D. 70, all differences ceased and a united front was shown to the enemy.[3]

There is no need here to give a précis of Josephus' vivid narrative of the famous siege that followed. Despite the Jewish historian's

done so is remarkable, since they had been forcibly Judaised by John Hyrcanus (134–104 B.C.), and much of the hatred that the Jews felt for Herod the Great had originally stemmed from his Idumaean birth. Roth suggests, not very strongly, that the Idumaeans concerned in the revolt were Jewish inhabitants of the northern part of what had been Idumaea (*J.S.S.* IV, 1959, 345, n. 1). Whatever may have been their origin, the Idumaeans certainly regarded the Zealots as the true patriots, and not Ananus and his party; see the reply of Simon, one of the Idumaean leaders, to the representatives of Ananus: οὐκέτι θαυμάζειν ἔφη φρουρουμένων ἐν τῷ ἱερῷ τῶν προμάχων τῆς ἐλευθερίας... (*War*, IV. 272).

[1] *Ibid.* 318–25. Cf. Smallwood in *J.T.S.* XIII (1962), 29–30.

[2] See the anti-Zealot and temporising sentiments which Josephus attributes to Ananus in *War*, IV. 173–84, 320–1; even if they are the invention of the historian, he was surely justified in ascribing them to Ananus. See also *ibid.* 216 ff.

[3] *War*, V. 71, 277 ff.; cf. 248–57, where Josephus revealingly contrasts the iniquity of the Jerusalem factions with the justice of the Romans: καὶ τὸ μὲν σκυθρωπὸν τοῖς οἰκείοις, τὸ δίκαιον δ' ἄν τις εὐλόγως 'Ρωμαίοις προσγράφοι (*ibid.* 257).

tendentious denigration of the rebel forces, particularly the Zealots, it is clear that they fought with an inspired courage. The odds against them were hopeless, and they must have realised that they were so; yet they rejected all offers of terms and made no attempt to escape from the doomed city.[1] Significant of the faith that animated them was the reply made by the Zealot commander, John of Gischala, to a Roman offer of terms. The offer was made by Titus at what was evidently deemed a good psychological moment. The Jews had been reduced to such straits, by the rigours of the siege, that no more lambs were available for the daily sacrifice in the Temple. Profiting from their despondency, Titus commissioned Josephus to invite their surrender on terms. John, having upbraided the renegade who now made the Roman offer, ended by declaring that 'he never would fear (its) capture, since the city was God's'.[2]

But the city was captured: on 29 August, in the year 70, the Roman legionaries stormed the Temple and burnt it; their victory was completed by taking the Upper City a month later.[3] Jewish sufferings had been terrible and casualties enormous. According to Josephus, 1,100,000 perished during the siege: the figure is undoubtedly grossly exaggerated; but it must have been very large, because the siege was long, famine severe and the fighting fierce and at close quarters.[4] Josephus puts the number of prisoners taken during the whole war at 97,000.[5] The Temple, which had been the pride and glory of the Jewish people, became the death-place of thousands. Not only did its massive walls make it an excellent fortress which the Zealots defended with fanatical courage; but many sought its shelter in response to a prophecy that God would there work a miracle of deliverance (τὰ σημεῖα τῆς σωτηρίας).[6] Instead,

---

[1] Not only were the Zealots themselves resolved to fight to the end in Jerusalem, but they took savage measures to prevent others from leaving the city, although Josephus insinuates that the rich could bribe their way out (War, v. 377 ff.).

[2] War, VI. 98: ὡς οὐκ ἄν ποτε δείσειεν ἅλωσιν· θεοῦ γὰρ ὑπάρχειν τὴν πόλιν. Cf. Ricciotti, Flavio Giuseppe, IV, 150, n. on 98.

[3] Jos. War, VI. 249–87, 316–55, 358–408.

[4] Ibid. 420. Josephus notes that the greater number were pilgrims, who had come to Jerusalem for the passover and were unable to get away.

[5] Ibid. According to the compilation made by H. Milman (History of Jews, London, 1909, II, 100–1) from figures given by Josephus in various places in his work, the Jewish losses during the whole war amounted to 1,356,460. On the fate of the captives see War, VII. 23–5, 37–40, 118, 138.

[6] Ibid. 285. Josephus describes the prophecy as uttered by a false prophet (ψευδοπροφήτης). R. H. Charles suggested that Rev. xi. 1–3 may preserve

the Roman legionaries, burning with hate and elated by victory, slaughtered there the priests and people of the God of Israel, and then they erected their standards in the sacred courts and did sacrifice to them, acclaiming Titus, the emperor's son, as Imperator. Thus, once more, the 'abomination of desolation' stood where it ought not.[1]

The fall of Jerusalem marked the end of Jewish national resistance, and Titus returned to Rome, there to celebrate in the following year, with his father Vespasian, an elaborately staged triumph over prostrate Israel.[2] In Judaea groups of rebels still held out in various strongholds and were systematically eliminated.[3] The last stand of the Zealots, in the land for which they had fought and suffered so much, was at Masada. There, in A.D. 73, when, finally, Roman military science and fortitude had overcome the almost impregnable fortifications and Zealot valour, the Zealot commander, Eleazar, a descendant of Judas of Galilee, persuaded his companions to rob their enemies of complete victory by mass suicide. When the Romans broke into the fortress the dead bodies of the garrison, including those of their wives and children, witnessed to Zealot resolution not to submit to a heathen lord.[4] Josephus, following his usual custom,

a fragment of a Zealot prophecy concerning the inviolability of the Temple (*Revelation*, I.C.C. 1, 270 ff., 274 ff.). Cf. Streeter, *Four Gospels*, pp. 517–18. An echo of the prophecy occurs in the *Sibylline Oracles*, v. 401–2 (ed. Charles, *Apoc. and Pseudepig.* 1, 404). Cf. Hengel, *Die Zeloten*, pp. 246–9.

[1] Jos. *War*. VI. 316. Cf. Brandon, *Fall of Jerusalem*, pp. 165, 173–4, 245, and in *N.T.S.* VII (1960–1), 133–4; see below, pp. 231–3, 240.

[2] Jos. *War*, VII. 120–57. On the present Arch of Titus in the Forum Romanum two famous sculptured panels preserve a precious record of the triumph. The inscription on this Arch, which was erected after the death of Titus, does not refer to the Jewish War; it was, however, commemorated in the inscription of another Arch dedicated to Titus by the Senate and the Roman people, which stood in the Circus Maximus and was destroyed in the fourteenth or fifteenth century. Cf. Schürer, *G.J.V.* 1, 635, n. 128; Mommsen, *Das Weltreich der Caesaren*, p. 390 n.; Ricciotti, *Flavio Giuseppe*, IV, 246–52 and notes; G. Bendinelli, *Compendio di Storia dell'Arte etrusca e romana*, pp. 301–4; L. Curtius and A. Nawrath, *Das Antike Rom* (Wien, 1944), pp. 39–40, Bilder 40–4. It would appear that the new Flavian dynasty exploited the victory over rebel Judaea to enhance its own prestige. The propaganda value of the imperial coinage commemorating the subjugation of the Jews is illuminatingly discussed by H. St J. Hart, 'Judaea and Rome: the Official Commentary', *J.T.S.* III (1952), 172–98 and plates. Cf. Charlesworth in *C.A.H.* XI, 4–5; Bersanetti, *Vespasiano*, pp. 40–2; Reifenberg, *Israel's History in Coins*, pp. 32–3. See Plates X–XII.

[3] Jos. *War*, VII. 163–215.

[4] *Ibid.* 252–3, 275–406. It would appear that the Masada Zealots had controlled a wide area; cf. Roth in *J.S.S.* IV (1959), 348, see also pp. 352–4.

places a long speech in the mouth of Eleazar as he exhorts his followers to seek freedom in death. He uses the speech to make this rebel leader attest to his own thesis that the Roman victory was God-given.[1] However, he does, himself, therein attribute to Eleazar words that fittingly serve as an epitaph on the Zealots and their ideals: 'Long since, my brave men, we determined neither to serve the Romans nor any other save God, for He alone is man's true and righteous Lord; and now the time is come which bids us verify that resolution by our actions...For as we were the first of all to revolt, so are we the last in arms against them.'[2]

As an epilogue to that ultimate gesture of faith and defiance, we may notice the like spirit of unyielding loyalty to their ideals with which the Sicarii who escaped to Egypt met their end. Josephus does not tell how these rebels succeeded in eluding the Roman forces and making good their escape to Alexandria. There, instead of lying low, they endeavoured to rouse the great Jewish population of the city to revolt, using their same basic argument that Jews should only recognise God as their lord (θεὸν δὲ μόνον ἡγεῖσθαι δεσπότην).[3] That they still actively propagated their faith, after the tragedy in Judaea, witnesses to the absolute nature of their commitment to the ideal of Yahweh's sovereignty over Israel. The Jewish authorities in Alexandria, however, moved at once to suppress such dangerous fanaticism. Josephus is not clear as to how this action was

---

'Sogar der Selbstmord konnte im Judentum zu einer besonderen Form der Hingabe des Lebens für Gesetz und Volk werden' (Hengel, *Die Zeloten*, p. 268; see instances, pp. 268–71). Many bronze coins have been found at Masada; the significance of their inscriptions is rendered more poignant by their finding there: e.g. חרות ציון (Freedom of Zion), or לגאלת ציון (for the Redemption of Zion); see L. Kadman in *I.E.J.* 7 (1957), p. 61. A cache of seventeen silver shekels of the Revolt has also been found, three for the 'year five'. These silver coins are inscribed 'Jerusalem the Holy—Shekel of Israel': cf. Y. Yadin in *I.L.N.* 31 October 1964, fig. 1 and p. 696; *The Excavation of Masada, 1963/64*, pp. 80–1, Plate 19F–G. According to a recent report (*The Times*, 27 August 1965), Professor Yadin may have found at Masada the actual lots drawn by the last eleven Zealot survivors; cf. M. Livneh and Z. Meshel, *Masada*, p. 23: '11 ostraca were found, inscribed with names: one of them bears the name "Beniair" (Ben Yair, Zealot commandant of Masada), the others nicknames, possibly of Zealot officers.' See also above, p. 61, n. 4.

[1] *War*, VII. 329–33; however, he also uses the speech as an *apologia* for his people, ascribing the origin of the revolt to the iniquity of the anti-Semite population of Caesarea, *ibid.* 361–2.

[2] *Ibid.* 323–4; trans. Thackeray, Loeb ed. *Josephus*, III, 595, 596.

[3] Jos. *War*, VII. 409–10.

(a)   (b)

PLATE I

Roman coins offensive to Jewish religious scruples. (a) Silver *denarius* of
Tiberius. Reverse showing Livia, the emperor's mother, as Pax; inscribed
Pontif(ex) maxim(us). (b) Bronze coin of Pontius Pilate, showing a *lituus*
(augur's wand); inscribed *Tiberius Caesar*. NOTE: the obverse of the *denarius*
is shown on the Frontispiece. (*Enlarged reproduction, reproduced by courtesy of the
Manchester Museum.*)

PLATE II

Inscription of Pontius Pilate found at Caesarea in 1961, now in the Israel
Museum, Jerusalem. The undamaged part of the inscription reads

...]s TIBERIEVM
...PON]TIVS PILATVS
...PRAEF[ECTVS IVDA[E

(*Reproduced by courtesy of the Israel Department of Antiquities and Museums.*)

(a)   (b)

(c)   (d)

PLATE III

Coins of the Revolt (A.D. 66–70). (a) Silver shekel, inscribed 'Shekel of
Israel' and dated 'Year 3' (i.e. A.D. 68–9). The chalice may symbolise the
'cup of salvation'. (b) Reverse of silver shekel, inscribed: 'Jerusalem the
Holy'. The three pomegranates probably symbolise fertility. (c) Bronze
coin, inscribed: 'Year 2' (i.e. A.D. 67–8). The amphora probably represents
a ritual vessel. (d) Reverse of preceding coin, showing vine-leaf, and inscribed: 'Deliverance of Zion'. (*Enlarged reproductions, reproduced by courtesy of
the Manchester Museum.*)

(a)   (b)

(c)   (d)

PLATE IV

Coins of the Revolt (A.D. 66–70). (a) Bronze coin showing chalice, and inscribed: 'Redemption of Zion'. (b) Reverse of preceding coin, showing a *lulab* (a ritual plant arrangement), inscribed: 'Year 4' (i.e. A.D. 69–70). (c) Bronze coin showing palm-tree (symbol of Judaea), and inscribed 'Eleazar the Priest'. (d) Reverse of preceding coin, showing bunch of grapes, and inscribed 'First year of the Redemption of Israel'. (*Enlarged reproductions, reproduced by courtesy of the Manchester Museum.*)

(The second coin is usually assigned to the Second Revolt, A.D. 132–5. However, since no Eleazar the Priest is known as a leader during this Revolt, whereas Eleazar, the *sagan* of the Temple, played a leading role in the Revolt of 66 (see chapter 3), there is reason for assigning the coin to him.)

PLATE V

The Fortress of Masada. One of the Roman camps appears in the foreground. The ramp built by the Romans to reach the wall is visible in the centre of the photograph. (*Photo: The Masada Archaeological Expedition.*)

PLATE VI

PLATE VII

Masada: The Ritual Immersion Pool (*Miqveh*). (Cf. Y. Yadin, *The Excavation of Masada, 1963/64*, pp. 91–2 and Plate 16A.) Roman camps are visible below. (*Photo: The Masada Archaeological Expedition.*)

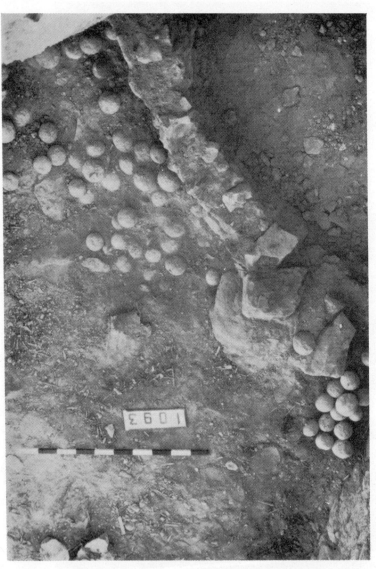

PLATE VIII

Masada: ballistae stones from the siege of A.D. 73. Near this place the scroll

PLATE IX

Masada: a pathetic relic of Zealot fortitude. The scalp and plaited hair of a Zealot woman who perished in A.D. 73. Nearby is a sandal. (Cf. Y. Yadin, *The Excavation of Masada, 1963/64*, pp. 16–17.) (*Photo: The Masada Archaeological Expedition.*)

(a)

(b)

(c)

(d)

PLATE X

Coins of the Roman Victory. (*a*) Bronze *sestertius* of Vespasian. Rome,
A.D. 71. (*b*) Reverse shows a symbolic palm-tree between the triumphant
emperor and the mourning Judaea. Inscribed: IVD(AEA) CAP(TA). (*c*) Bronze
sestertius of Titus. Rome, A.D. 80–1. (*d*) Reverse shows symbolic palm-tree
between mourning Judaea and a Jewish captive. Inscribed: IVD(AEA)
CAP(TA). (*Enlarged reproductions, reproduced by courtesy of the Manchester Museum.*)

PLATE XI

Sculptured scene on the Arch of Titus, Rome, depicting the triumphal procession of A.D. 71. The victorious legionaries bear the spoils of the Temple: the *Menorah*, the silver trumpets and the altar of shew-bread.

PLATE XII

Sculptured scene on the Arch of Titus, representing the triumphant Titus,

implemented. It would seem that the Jewish leaders denounced these unwelcome refugees to the Romans, who executed them after torture. According to Josephus, they were tortured for the sole object of making them acknowledge Caesar as lord (Καίσαρα δεσπότην ὁμολογήσωσιν). All remained resolute, even the young children among them. Their constancy apparently made a great impression, and even Josephus pays tribute to their courage.[1]

And so this tragic chapter in Israel's long history closes. The Zealots stood in true succession to the Yahwist prophets of old. They were, like Phinehas, zealous for the God of Israel. Their ideal was the ancient prophetic one of Israel as the Elect People of Yahweh. In their zeal to maintain that ideal they could be cruelly uncompromising and fanatical; but no more so than many of the revered heroes of their sacred tradition.[2] Their tragedy was that, unlike the Maccabees before them in their struggle with the ramshackle empire of the Seleucids, in Rome they had themselves to contend with the greatest power of the ancient world, and, for all their courage and zeal, that power was invincible to them.[3] But, if they could not win, they knew how to suffer for their faith. When Jesus of Nazareth called upon his disciples to take up their cross, he uttered a grim challenge that every Zealot had to face for himself.[4] The cross was the symbol of Zealot sacrifice before it was transformed into the sign of Christian salvation.

[1] *Ibid.* 411–19: τοσοῦτον ἄρα τῆς τῶν σωμάτων ἀσθενείας ἡ τῆς τόλμης ἰσχὺς ἐπεκράτει (*ibid.* 419). Commenting on the evidence of the Zealot readiness for martyrdom, Hengel observes: 'Man wird abschließend annehmen dürfen, daß die Zeloten eine ausgeprägte Märtyrer-tradition besaßen, die zugleich Ausdruck der festen Disziplin innerhalb der Sekte war…Denn durch die eschatologische Deutung erhielt das Martyrium auch bei den Zeloten seinen positiven Sinn: es war der rascheste und sicherste Weg, der Freuden des messianischen Reiches teilhaftig zu werden' (*Die Zeloten*, pp. 276–7, see also pp. 382–3). What Josephus calls the 'madness of the Sicarii' also caused trouble in Cyrene (*War*, VII. 437 ff.). Possibly the half-shekel of the second year of the revolt found at Cyrene in 1956 may be a relic of this: cf. J. F. Healy in *J.S.S.* II (1957), 377–9.

[2] E.g. Phinehas (Num. xxv. 7–8), and Mattathias (I Macc. ii. 23–6).

[3] Josephus makes Agrippa II attest to the invincibility of Rome (cf. *War*, II. 357–89), and he explicitly states that Ananus considers Rome's power irresistible (ἄμαχα γὰρ ᾔδει τὰ 'Ρωμαίων, *War*, IV. 320).

[4] Mark viii. 34; cf. Matt. x. 38. Cf. Hengel, *Die Zeloten*, p. 266: 'liegt doch die Vermutung nahe, daß Jesus hier eine zelotische Formel aus dem allgemeinen Sprachgebrauch übernommen hat.'

CHAPTER 4

THE JEWISH CHRISTIANS AND
THE ZEALOT IDEAL

It is natural for any subject people to hate their foreign rulers. But with the Jews, during the six decades preceding the revolt of A.D. 66, that instinctive hatred was profoundly deepened by their religious beliefs. As we have seen, hostility to the Romans pervaded the whole of Jewish society. Even the sacerdotal aristocracy, whose interests caused them to cooperate with the Roman government, and calculating individuals such as Josephus, who regarded Roman rule as inevitable, must have secretly hated the arrogant and corrupt officials and the brutal soldiery whose presence and actions constantly reminded them of Israel's servitude. To such men, too, despite their temporising attitude, the Romans were heathens; although their reason counselled submission and cooperation, their religious feelings must often have been uneasy about assisting a regime of which the very presence in their native land outraged their ancestral faith. But apart from the minority which managed, howbeit uncomfortably, to compromise between their vested interests and their religion, for the great majority of Jews the Roman rule was wholly abhorrent. Forced, as most were, by fear to acquiesce in that rule, their acquiescence was sullen, and they longed to be free of the heathen foreigners who oppressed them by a heavy taxation and other imposts, who often abused their persons and insulted their customs, and whose very presence so grievously contradicted their cherished belief that they were the Chosen People of God. Such men and women, of both the peasant and professional classes, must secretly have sympathised with those of their countrymen whose faith and patriotism led them to risk their lives in active resistance to the Romans. They were ready to give them what clandestine aid they could; indeed, the very continuance of Zealot activity from A.D. 6, as we have seen, confirms the fact, so well known in recent times, that a foreign occupying force can rarely be secure when its presence is resented by the native population. Always there is the hope of ultimate freedom to inspire the subjugated. For most peoples in this condition, it is accepted that this hope can only be achieved by their own efforts, aided perhaps by some friendly nation; but with the Jews, at this time, there was also the deeply rooted belief that Yahweh, their god, would eventually intervene, as he had so wonderfully done in the past of their nation to save them from their bondage to the heathen. The holding of this belief, as we have noted, did not result in a passive waiting for Yahweh to act. There were indeed some who thought that Israel had only to prepare itself spiritually for divine redemption;[1] but the present reality of the Roman rule, with its frequent acts of cruelty and injustice, and its abiding threat to the sanctity of the Temple and the Torah, made quiet submission difficult and unpopular. Moreover, not only did their sacred history afford the Jews many heroic examples of zealous action in defence of their faith, but Judas of Galilee had proclaimed uncompromisingly that subjection to Caesar was disloyalty to Yahweh. For the freedom of Israel Judas and many of his followers had died, adding their names to the revered company of martyrs who had suffered for that glorious cause; others of his followers survived to continue the struggle against the heathen oppressor and to exhort their countrymen to aid them in their resistance.

Such was the situation of tension, begotten of hatred, fear and apocalyptic expectation, in which Christianity was born and lived out its first formative years. It is our task to endeavour to evaluate the reaction of Jesus to that situation, which constituted an unavoidable challenge to every Jew. But, before we can approach that task, we have first to determine what was the attitude of the followers of Jesus, who formed the original church at Jerusalem, to the same issues. The need to do this arises from the fact that Jesus left no written record of his own views; the memory of those views was, however, preserved by his followers who formed, in Jerusalem, what was to be the Mother Church of Christianity. But the recollection of what Jesus taught and did was, naturally, an amalgam of what his

---

[1] The clearest description of a 'quietist' attitude among the Jews is given by Josephus, when he represents the people as replying to Petronius' question whether they intended to make war against the emperor (Gaius): 'We have no intention at all of fighting (οὐδαμῶς πολεμήσαιμεν), but we shall die rather than transgress our laws' (*Ant.* xviii. 271). This testimony cannot be taken at its face value, in view of Josephus' apologetic intention here (see p. 87); it is, moreover, significant that even he testifies to the readiness of the Jews to resist the emperor's command to the death. Cf. Schürer, *G.J.V.* ii, 395–6; Klausner, *Jesus of Nazareth*, pp. 171–3; Guignebert, *Le monde juif*, pp. 217–19; Herford, *The Pharisees*, pp. 51–2, 187–9; Förster, *Palestinian Judaism*, pp. 88–9, 108.

followers remembered of him and his teaching, of their interpretation of what they had seen and heard, and of their own ideas, and hopes and aspirations. Moreover, that amalgam, which constituted their faith, was not definitively fixed at some particular moment after the Crucifixion and Resurrection experiences; it was a living thing, subject to growth and adjustment according to current needs and concerns. Thus, the problem has to be faced that the tradition about Jesus which was held by his original Jewish disciples was essentially an interpretation of his teaching and career, and that it formed the faith of devout Jews, living through those tensions and stresses which inevitably led Israel into the fatal revolt against Rome in A.D. 66.

To evaluate the attitude of Jesus to his nation's cause against Rome, we have, accordingly, first to interrogate the tradition concerning him held by the original Jewish Christians. But, when we seek to do this, we at once find ourselves confronted by a problem of peculiar complexity. It is constituted by the fact that we have no direct access to that tradition. The reason for this is well known, although its significance seems rarely to be appreciated. It is that the Christian community at Jerusalem, which was the Mother Church of the faith, disappeared so completely after A.D. 70 that none of its documents survived.[1] The discovery of the Dead Sea Scrolls serves, by analogy, to remind us how great this loss must be for our knowledge of Christian Origins. Until the finding of the first of the Scrolls in 1947, nothing was known of the Jewish monastic community at Qumrân that once owned them. All that might have been deduced about its beliefs and institutions, if a connection had been perceived between the ruins at Qumrân and the Essenes, would have come from what Josephus tells of this sect, supplemented by the brief and enigmatic references of a few other writers.[2] When we reflect, therefore, on the revelation that has come from the discovery of this library of the Qumrân community, something of the magnitude of the loss of the records of the Jerusalem Church can be sensed. The parallel has a further significance. The Qumrân community hid its books before it was wiped out by a Roman punitive force in A.D. 68:[3]

[1] See below, pp. 208 ff.
[2] It is instructive to read what an authority such as E. Schürer wrote about the Essenes in 1898 (*G.J.V.* II, 556–84), in the light of the Qumrân evidence; see also Meyer, *Ursprung*, II, 393–402. Cf. Rowley, *The Zadokite Fragments and the Dead Sea Scrolls*, pp. 1–3.
[3] Cf. de Vaux, *L'Archéologie et les manuscrits de la Mer Morte*, pp. 75–84. The recent finding of scrolls at Masada similar to those at Qumrân may indicate that some members of the Qumrân sect brought their sacred

is the disappearance of the Mother Church of Christianity after A.D. 70 to be attributed similarly to Roman action? Before we can attempt to answer that important question, we have to determine what was the attitude of the members of that Church to the Romans and to the cause of Israel's freedom from the Roman yoke. But here we are faced again by the same *impasse* caused by the absence of any original records of that Church.

Such an *impasse* would be fatal to our inquiry, but for the fact that other sources of information, though indirect and problematic, do exist. The four Gospels are obviously based upon traditions that must ultimately derive from the original Jewish Christians of Palestine. The Acts of the Apostles also embodies traditions concerning the primitive Christian community in Jerusalem that must surely go back to some early source.[1] However, these traditions have been so worked into the narratives of the documents concerned that it is often difficult, and sometimes impossible, to discern their original form and context. Each of the Gospels, it must be remembered, was written for a Greek-speaking community, mainly Gentile in composition, and situated outside Palestine.[2] Moreover, Matthew and Luke follow the narrative structure and theme of Mark. This document, as we have already noticed briefly,[3] shows signs of deep embarrassment about the Roman condemnation of Jesus, and we shall find reason presently for concluding that it was written for the Christian community in Rome shortly after the Flavian triumph there in A.D. 71, and it is, consequently, inspired by a strong apologetical concern.[4] This means that the original Jewish Christian tradition, upon which the Markan Gospel is based, has been utilised to present an interpretation of Jesus which Mark deemed appropriate to the difficult situation in which the Roman Christians found themselves in consequence of the Jewish War. Since the interpretation thus established by Mark provided the pattern for Matthew and

writings to the Zealot stronghold for safety. Cf. Y. Yadin in *I.L.N.* 31 October 1964, pp. 696–7; *The Excavation of Masada, 1963/64*, pp. 81, 105–8.

[1] *B.C.* II, 130 ff.; W. L. Knox, *Acts of the Apostles* (Cambridge, 1948), pp. 16–39; F. F. Bruce, *Acts of the Apostles* (London, 1951), pp. 21–3.
[2] W. D. Davies (*The Setting of the Sermon on the Mount*) has recently argued that Matthew originated in Syria or Phoenicia, and that its *Sitz im Leben* was closely related to the Pharisaic revival at Jamnia after A.D. 70; for a critique of this thesis see Brandon in *The Modern Churchman*, VIII (1965), 152–61; see also pp. 287 ff. below.
[3] See above, pp. 4 ff.   [4] See below, pp. 224 ff.

Luke, their use of the primitive tradition has, in turn, been generally affected by the Markan evaluation, although other environmental factors operated to produce instructive variations, as we shall duly see.[1] Acts, which forms a sequel to the Lukan Gospel, is generally recognised as having an apologetical theme, namely, to show how the faith evoked by Jesus, though rejected by the Jews, became established, under divine guidance, in the chief cities of the Roman empire.[2] Consequently, this apologetic interest operated to exclude or tone down whatever was deemed in the early years of the Church to conflict with the major theme of the work: we have already had occasion to comment on the absence of any reference in Acts to the attempt of the emperor Gaius to desecrate the Temple,[3] and its silence about the conflict between Paul and the Jerusalem Apostles, to which Paul's epistles so vividly attest, is well known.[4]

We find ourselves, accordingly, in a difficult position when we turn, as we are indeed obliged to turn, to the Synoptic Gospels and Acts for information concerning the attitude of the original Jewish Christians towards their nation's cause against Rome. The Gospel of John, though standing apart from these documents, provides no better help. For, while it is not inspired with quite the same motives as the other writings in its use of Palestinian tradition, its interpretation is conditioned by its distinctive Christology.

All these writings, incorporating as they do traditions of primitive Jewish Christianity, are of post-A.D. 70 date,[5] and thus are representative of Christianity after the ruin of the Jewish state and the disappearance of the Mother Church of Jerusalem. But there remains for our consideration the supreme witness which Paul's writings bear to the Christian faith before that fateful convulsion of Jewish life which started with the revolt of A.D. 66.

The Epistles of Paul not only provide our earliest evidence of Christianity, but also raise the most profound questions concerning the original form of the faith. So far as our preliminary assessment of their testimony for our subject is concerned, we may notice here the remarkable absence of reference to Jesus as a

---

[1] See chapter 6.

[2] Cf. *B.C.* II, 177–86; Bruce, *Acts of the Apostles*, pp. 29–34.

[3] See pp. 92 ff.

[4] Cf. Brandon, *Fall of Jerusalem*, pp. 126–36, 208–10, and the documentation there given; G. Bornkamm, 'Paulus', *R.G.G.*[3], v (1961), 167.

[5] On a post-A.D. 70 date for Mark see below, pp. 224 ff.

historical person that is manifest in every letter.¹ This feature cannot
be accounted for by the fact that Paul, in each of the documents
concerned, was not writing a formal description of the faith. It is,
indeed, true that his letters deal primarily with specific issues, mostly
of a disciplinary kind, that had arisen in the various Christian communities to which they are addressed. However, granting the *ad hoc*
nature of the documents, it is still surprising that this great apostle
could write so much concerning the faith to his own converts, and
to the Christians in Rome, without mentioning the events of Jesus'
life, as they are recorded in the later Gospels, and also without
quoting his teaching. But this apparent lack of concern about the
historical Jesus is paralleled by an equally remarkable evaluation of
the death of Jesus which lifts the event completely out of its historical
setting. Indeed in Paul's most precise statement about the crucifixion,
the event is presented as the achievement of a divine plan which
caused the daemonic rulers of the present world-age (οἱ ἄρχοντες
τῶν τοῦ αἰῶνος), unwittingly and to their own detriment, to crucify
the pre-existent 'Lord of glory' (τὸν κύριον τῆς δόξης), whom Paul
evidently identified in some way with Jesus.² Nothing is said of the
location of the event in either time or space, and the agents were the
archontes, not the Roman soldiers carrying out the orders of Pilate and
the wishes of the Jewish leaders.³

This esoteric evaluation of Jesus and his death is the focal point of
what Paul calls his 'gospel', which he claims was revealed to him
directly by God, without any human mediation.⁴ Now, despite the

---

¹ Cf. Brandon, *History, Time and Deity*, pp. 150–1, 159–69, 172, and the
documentation given in the notes.
² I Cor. ii. 6–8; cf. Meyer, *Ursprung*, III, 350–1.
³ On the variety of concepts connoted by *aiōn* see H. Sasse in *R.A.C.* I, 193–
204; W. L. Knox, *St Paul and the Church of the Gentiles* (Cambridge, 1939),
pp. 94–5. On the *archontes* cf. Dibelius in *R.A.C.* I, 631–3; Festugière, *La
Révélation d'Hermès Trismégiste*, I, 89–96; Seznec, *La survivance des dieux
antiques*, pp. 35–46; Bultmann, *Urchristentum*, p. 219 (E.T. p. 233);
Schoeps, *Paulus*, p. 9 (E.T. p. 21); cf. Brandon, *Man and his Destiny*,
pp. 191–2, 213–16, and *History, Time and Deity*, pp. 166–9.
⁴ Gal. i. 11–12 (οὐκ ἔστιν κατὰ ἄνθρωπον· οὐδὲ γὰρ ἐγὼ παρὰ ἀνθρώπου
παρέλαβον αὐτό), cf. i. 15–17. 'Mit anderen Worten: Jesus Christus
selbst hat nach dem Urteil des Paulus kraft seiner Enthüllung die Botschaft
des Apostels gebildet, nicht aber wurzelt sie in anderer apostolischer
Überlieferung'; 'Die Offenbarung hat Paulus nicht der menschlichen
Diskussion ausgeliefert. Er hat sie aber auch zunächst nicht dem Urteil der
Jerusalemer Apostel unterworfen' (Schlier, *Der Brief an die Galater*,
pp. 48, 58, cf. pp. 43–58). Cf. Manson, *Studies*, p. 170, n. 1; Brandon, *Fall
of Jerusalem*, pp. 55–6, 58.

fact that Paul's writings provide our earliest evidence of Christianity, it is difficult to believe that such esoteric doctrine represented the faith of the original disciples of Jesus, if only because of the absence of reference to the historical context of his life and death and the un-Jewish concepts employed. Such doubts are confirmed when we look more closely into Paul's writings and certain incidents recorded in the Acts of the Apostles. In the first place, Paul himself provides ample evidence that his teaching and authority were being seriously challenged by powerful opponents. These opponents, as Paul warns his converts, were teaching a 'different gospel' from that which he taught, and they were presenting 'another Jesus'.[1] Such statements can only mean that Paul's interpretation of the nature of Jesus and the significance of his death was opposed by some other interpretation. The question of the identity of the exponents of this other 'gospel' is, accordingly, a matter of fundamental concern. Paul, curiously, despite his exceeding agitation over their activity, never names them. Whoever they were, they were obviously Christians of great authority or representative of leaders of great authority; for they were able to go among Paul's own converts and successfully present a rival interpretation of the faith.[2] Moreover, although he is so profoundly disturbed by their action, Paul never questions their authority as they did his.[3] These facts, taken together with Paul's

[1] Gal. i. 6–8; II Cor. xi. 3–4. On the meaning of εὐαγγέλιον ἕτερον and ἄλλον 'Ἰησοῦν see Brandon, *Man and his Destiny*, p. 196, n. 1. Cf. Schlier, *Der Brief an die Galater*, p. 38, n. 1; A. Menzies, *The Second Epistle to the Corinthians* (London, 1912), p. 78; Manson, *Studies*, p. 170; Bruce in *B.J.R.L.* 45 (1963), pp. 331–4.

[2] Gal. i. 6–9, ii. 11 ff., vi. 12–13; I Cor. i. 12, iii. 22, ix. 1 ff.; II Cor. iii. 1, x. 12–18, xi. 1–xii. 13. W. L. Knox, *St Paul and the Church of Jerusalem* (Cambridge, 1925), p. 229, n. 13, acutely suggests that εἰ μή τινές εἰσιν κ.τ.λ. of Gal. i. 7 should be rendered: 'only they who trouble you and would pervert the Gospel of Christ are somewhat' (i.e. are persons of some importance, τινές being used in the same contemptuous sense of persons regarded as important as τι in ii. 6 and τινα in Acts v. 36). Cf. F. Sieffert, *Der Brief an die Galater* (Göttingen, 1899), p. 18; Goguel, *La naissance du christianisme*, pp. 144, 174, n. 1, 340–1; Schlier, *Der Brief an die Galater*, pp. 38–43; Brandon, *Fall of Jerusalem*, pp. 138–9.

[3] See the revealing remark with which Paul follows his statement in II Cor. xi. 4 about the anonymous person who preaches 'another Jesus' and 'a different gospel': λογίζομαι γὰρ μηδὲν ὑστερηκέναι τῶν ὑπερλίαν ἀποστόλων (v. 5). 'He insists that he is no whit inferior to what he calls the "super-Apostles" (xi. 5; xii. 11); and it is clear from xi. 22–31 that these super-Apostles came from Palestine' (Manson, *Studies*, pp. 207, 215, cf. p. 163). Cf. Knox, *St Paul and the Church of Jerusalem*, p. 311, and *St Paul*

very evident embarrassment about his relations with the leading Apostles at Jerusalem,[1] point irresistibly to one conclusion only: that the 'other gospel', which opposed Paul's own, was the interpretation of the nature and mission of Jesus propounded by the Jerusalem Church, which comprised the original Apostles of Jesus and eye-witnesses of his life.[2] Paul, owing to the peculiar circumstances of his conversion, had conceived of a different interpretation, which he believed God had specially confided to him for the evangelisation of the Gentiles.[3] This very distinction, which Paul himself makes,

and the Church of the Gentiles, p. 129; A. D. Nock, *St Paul*, pp. 161, 168–70, 200–2; Brandon, *Fall of Jerusalem*, pp. 141–5; Schoeps, *Paulus*, p. 71 ('Diese korinthischen Eindringlinge hätten ja auch niemals sein Ansehen untergraben können, wenn sie sich nicht auf eine wirkliche, in christlichen Augen undiskutable Autorität berufen konnten, eben die Muttergemeinde'), E.T. p. 76. It is significant that W. Schmithals (*Paul and James*), who is concerned to claim that relations between Paul and the Jerusalem Church were excellent, does not discuss this passage in II Cor. xi. 4 ff.

[1] Gal. i. 17–19, ii. 1 ff.; I Cor. i. 12, iii. 22, ix. 1–5; II Cor. xi. 5, xii. 11–12.

[2] 'The Galatians are receiving another account of Christianity (ἕτερον εὐαγγέλιον) from missionaries who claim to be accredited from the Mother-Church in Jerusalem. They point out that Paul lacks these credentials'; 'The Galatian and Corinthian epistles are all of one piece: they all reflect the same situation of conflict between Paul and the Palestinian Church, caused, I think, by the attempts of the Jerusalem authorities, in defiance of the agreement made with Paul (Gal. ii. 9), to extend their power and influence into the churches of his foundation' (Manson, *Studies*, pp. 170, 216). Cf. Brandon, *Fall of Jerusalem*, ch. 4, pp. 136 ff., and *Man and his Destiny*, pp. 195–8; Nock, *St Paul*, pp. 110–11, 168–9; Lietzmann, *Gesch. der alten Kirche*, I, 108–9; A. Schweitzer, *The Mysticism of Paul* (London, 1931), pp. 155–8; Goguel, *La naissance du christianisme*, pp. 173–6, 320–49, and *Les premiers temps de l'Église* (Neuchâtel, 1949), pp. 103–9; Meyer, *Ursprung*, III, 432–45, 453–9; Simon, *Verus Israel*, pp. 310–11, and *Les premiers Chrétiens*, pp. 79–81; Schoeps, *Paulus*, pp. 71, 72 ('und den Galatern ein ἕτερον εὐαγγέλιον eingeredet, nämlich die Lehre des Judenchristentums'), 73–7 (E.T. pp. 76–82); Ehrhardt, *Framework of the New Testament Stories*, pp. 155–6. For a critique of the attempt of J. Munck (*Paulus und die Heilsgeschichte*; E.T., *Paul and the Salvation of Mankind*, London, 1959), to show that there was no real difference between Paul and the Church of Jerusalem, see Brandon, 'The Perennial Problem of Paul', *H.J.* LVIII (1960); see also W. D. Davies, *Christian Origins and Judaism* (London, 1962), pp. 179–98. Schmithals, faced with the embarrassing evidence of Gal. ii. 11 ff., tries to negate it by supposing that τοὺς ἐκ περιτομῆς refers to some hypothetical Jews, who threatened the Antiochean community, and not, as the logic of the statement clearly implies, to τινας ἀπὸ 'Ιακώβου (*Paul and James*, pp. 66–8).

[3] Gal. i. 15–16; cf. Schlier, p. 56. Cf. Brandon, *Fall of Jerusalem*, pp. 59–60, *Man and his Destiny*, p. 212.

namely, that his was the 'gospel of the uncircumcision', reveals that Paul recognised that his version of Christianity was designed to appeal to the Gentiles, which the 'gospel of the circumcision' evidently did not.[1]

According to Paul's own testimony, his 'gospel' was repudiated and his authority as apostle was rejected by his opponents.[2] This the leaders of the Jerusalem Church could effectively do, because Paul had never been an original disciple of Jesus, nor had he learned the faith from them.[3] However, the irony of the situation, from our point of view, is that it is Paul's 'gospel' that has survived and is known to us from his own writings, whereas the 'gospel' of the Jerusalem Christians can only be reconstructed from what may be inferred from Paul's references to it and what may be culled, also by inference, from the Gospels and Acts. This apparent triumph of Paul's version of the faith is surely to be traced to the Jewish overthrow in A.D. 70,[4] and it constitutes another aspect of the fundamental problem with which we are concerned here: namely, to discern the ideas and outlook of the original Jewish Christians through the writings of others, who either were antagonistic to them or utilised their knowledge thereof for their own particular ends.

It is patent, therefore, that we have no easy task in seeking to elicit, from such complex and tendentious material, some knowledge of the attitude of the original Jewish Christians to their nation's cause against Rome. It will, accordingly, be best to proceed by

---

[1] Gal. ii. 7–9. 'Es ist das "Heiden-Evangelium" gemeint, aber nicht als ein inhaltlich besonderes Evangelium, sondern als das Evangelium, das unter ihnen verkündet wird' (Schlier, *Der Brief an die Galater*, p. 76). But, even if the 'gospel of the uncircumcision' was not an 'inhaltlich besonderes Evangelium', surely the fact that Paul believed that God had specially selected him to preach Christ to the Gentiles means that he regarded God's intervention for this purpose as an act initiating something that had not hitherto existed? Consequently the distinction which Paul draws must have some greater significance than the mere fact that his preaching was directed to the Gentiles and Peter's to the Jews. Paul's own Hellenistic background would have made him particularly aware that the ethnic outlook implied in the 'Gospel of the circumcision' could have little relevance or appeal to Gentiles: the nature of his 'gospel' clearly shows how un-Jewish it was, and how effectively it was conceived in terms of current Graeco-Roman religious thought. Cf. Bultmann, *Theology of the New Testament*, I, 187–9.

[2] See p. 152, nn. 2 and 3, and p. 153, n. 2 above.   [3] Gal. i. 13–17.

[4] Cf. Brandon, *Fall of Jerusalem*, chh. VII–XI.

observing first the testimony of whatever information appears un-complicated by the many issues which we have noted. We may begin with certain incidental statements in Acts, which are illu-minating as to the general practice of these Jewish disciples, and which in turn indicate something of their outlook. Thus, it appears that the Temple at Jerusalem was their customary place of worship and that they were diligent in their attendance there.[1] This evidence of their attachment to the great shrine of their ancestral religion is confirmed by what may reasonably be considered a reminiscence of the primitive attitude to the Temple preserved in Matthew: 'He therefore that sweareth by the altar, sweareth by it, and all the things thereon. And he that sweareth by the temple (ἐν τῷ ναῷ), sweareth by it, and by him that dwelleth therein' (ἐν τῷ κατοικοῦντι αὐτόν).[2] The currency of such a saying among the original Jewish Christians must surely mean that they regarded the Temple, as did all loyal Jews, as the actual dwelling place of their national deity, whom they held, of course, to be the God of the universe. The saying also indicates a familiarity with the Temple cultus, and an accept-ance of its validity, which are borne out by many references in Acts and the Gospels.[3] Their continuous participation in the Temple cultus,

---

[1] Acts ii. 46, iii. 1 ff., v. 12, 20–1, 25, xxi. 23–4, 26; cf. Mark xii. 41–4.

[2] Matt. xxiii. 20–1. Cf. Lohmeyer and Schmauch, *Das Evangelium des Matthäus*, p. 344. It is interesting to note that, according to Josephus, some time before the destruction of the Temple (which he attributes to its desecration by the Zealots), God was heard departing from the sanctuary (μεταβαίνομεν ἐντεῦθεν), *War*, VI. 300; Tacitus, *Hist.* v. 13 also reports the happening.

[3] See the references in nn. 1 and 2 above. Whether Stephen's words in Acts vii. 47–50 imply an attack on the Temple and its cultus (cf. Acts vi. 13) or are part of his general attack upon the Jews, Stephen obviously did not represent the position of the apostles, cf. Acts viii. 1. Schoeps's thesis (*Theologie und Geschichte des Judenchristentums*, pp. 236–7, 441, 446), that Stephen's speech contains an original Jewish Christian polemic against the Temple cultus, both assumes that Acts vii. 47–50 is actually an attack on that cultus and overlooks all the other evidence, to which reference has been made, of the attachment of the *Urgemeinde* to the Temple and its cultus: M. Simon (*Les premiers Chrétiens*, p. 48, and *St Stephen and the Hellenists*, London, 1958, pp. 92–9) has maintained that, in condemning the Temple, Stephen stood nearer in thought to Jesus than did the original disciples. This judgement is based on the assumption that Jesus 'thought and foretold that the Temple would be destroyed'; on the validity of this assumption see below, pp. 234 ff. The anti-cultic attitude expressed in the Ebionite literature undoubtedly reflects the abhorrence felt for Paul's soteriological interpretation of the death of Jesus, as Schoeps shows

JESUS AND THE ZEALOTS

thus implying an orthodoxy in faith and practice, is not the only evidence that the members of the Jerusalem Church remained faithful to Judaism. They were also zealous in observing the dietary regulations of the Torah—indeed, to such a degree that Peter, who had once eaten with Gentiles at Antioch, had withdrawn when the impropriety of his action was pointed out by emissaries of James, the brother of Jesus, who, as we shall see, became the leader of the Jerusalem Church.[1] Their zeal for the observation of the Torah was not, however, limited to what may be regarded as the normal practice of an orthodox Jew. The record of Acts reveals that certain members of the Jerusalem Church took the Nazarite vow, performing the prescribed ritual in the Temple at the end of the period of the vow.[2] Indeed, in Acts, James, the head of the Jerusalem Christians, is represented as pointing out to Paul how numerous were the Jews who accepted the faith and that they were 'all zealous for the Torah' (πάντες ζηλωταὶ τοῦ νόμου ὑπάρχουσιν).[3]

To this evidence of their notable devotion to Judaism, which naturally included emphasis upon the necessity of circumcision,[4]

(p. 157); but it is clearly unsound to infer from this antipathy an original Jewish Christian antipathy, especially when the evidence of Paul, Acts and the Gospels attests not only an acceptance of the Temple cultus, but a genuine devotion to it. Cf. Brandon, *Fall of Jerusalem*, pp. 29, 84–6, 88–9, 263; Goguel, *La naissance du christianisme*, p. 122; J. Weiss, *Earliest Christianity*, I, 53–6; Guignebert, *Le Christ* (Paris, 1943), pp. 111–13; Ehrhardt, *Framework of the New Testament Stories*, p. 91. On the question whether Jesus claimed that he would destroy the Temple see below, pp. 233 ff. E. Preuschen, *Die Apostelgeschichte* (Tübingen, 1926), pp. 36–7, suggested that the conversion of so many priests provided the 'Motivierung für die Stephanusepisode'. Schmithals thinks that Luke has distorted the Stephen episode in the interests of his missionary thesis (*Paul and James*, pp. 35–6).

[1] Gal. ii. 11–12.

[2] Acts xxi. 23–4. Cf. *B.C.* IV, 272–3. Even Paul freely observed such ritual practices, as the discharge of a similar vow at Cenchreae attests, Acts xviii. 18; cf. Klausner, *From Jesus to Paul*, p. 382.

[3] Acts xxi. 20: 'the majority probably belonged to the Pharisaic party' (Bruce, *Acts of the Apostles*, p. 391). There is no evidence in the text for the suggestion of Schoeps (*Paulus*, p. 62, E.T. p. 68) that 'James and the elders' are expressly contrasted with the ζηλωταὶ τοῦ νόμου here. Neither is there any justification for regarding τῶν πεπιστευκότων as an interpolation, because it removes a difficulty, as do Weiss, *Earliest Christianity*, I, 370, and Munck, *Paul and the Salvation of Mankind*, pp. 240–1. Because the evidence of Acts here does not suit his theory, Schmithals also dismisses it (*Paul and James*, p. 88).

[4] E.g. Acts xv. 1, 5, xvi. 3, xxi. 21. Whatever Paul means in Gal. ii. 3–5, the passage attests to the importance of circumcision in the Jerusalem Church.

there are to be added two other significant items. According to Acts, among the members of the Church in Jerusalem were many priests (πολύς τε ὄχλος τῶν ἱερέων) and Pharisees.[1] Since these professional representatives of the cultic and legal aspects of Judaism are mentioned without explanation, and nothing is said of their renouncing their former vocation or profession, it must be concluded that nothing was found incompatible in being either a priest or a Pharisee and at the same time an adherent of Jewish Christianity.[2]

From this evidence, therefore, it would appear that those Jews who were originally disciples of Jesus, and those who subsequently joined them, saw nothing in their acceptance of Jesus that rendered it necessary for them to give up the practice of Judaism. Indeed, the evidence seems to suggest that the original Jewish Christians were so distinguished for their orthodox zeal that they attracted many priests and Pharisees into their ranks. This conclusion has some interesting implications. It means that the Jewish Christians, by their participation in the Temple cultus, continued to believe in the efficacy of the Deuteronomic sacrificial system, according to which atonement was made for the sins of Israel by offering the life of an animal. This inference remains valid, even if the episode of Stephen attests to the existence of an anti-cultic element in the primitive Christian community.[3] Indeed, it is confirmed by the fact, according to Acts, that, in the ensuing persecution, the Jewish authorities distinguished between the apostles and Stephen's followers.[4] Moreover, in the

---

[1] Acts vi. 7, xv. 5.

[2] The priests undoubtedly belonged to the lower orders of the priesthood; see pp. 118ff. It is interesting to note that Luke i. 5, 8, 21 shows a considerable familiarity with the priesthood and its service. Cf. P. Winter in *J.Q.R.* xlv (1954), 160–7.

[3] See p. 155, n. 3 above. It is significant that it is not until the Epistle to the Hebrews (cf. v. 1–10, vii. 22–x. 39) that the logic of Paul's soteriology produced a reasoned repudiation of the Temple cultus. Cf. Goguel, *La naissance du christianisme*, pp. 372–6; Weiss, *Earliest Christianity*, ii, 670–1; Bruce in *Peake's Commentary*², 880 ff.; Manson, *Studies*, pp. 251–8 (but on his ascription of the Epistle to Apollos see below, p. 195, n. 2); Meyer, *Ursprung*, iii, 591–4; J. Moffatt, *Introduction to the New Testament*, pp. 443–50.

[4] Acts viii. 1. It is interesting to note that Codex Bezae adds after ἀποστόλων the additional information οἱ ἔμειναν ἐν Ἱερουσαλήμ 'which is doubtless a correct interpretation' (*B.C.* iv, 87). Knox suggested that the Twelve went into hiding, 'refusing to desert their posts, for the Church had no existence outside the city...' (*St Paul and the Church of Jerusaem*, p. 45); but there is no warranty for this in the text, and the suggestion itself is clearly inspired by a reluctance to admit that Stephen was not representative of the views of the *Urgemeinde*. Cf. J. Weiss, *Urchristentum* (Göttingen,

speech attributed to Stephen before the Sanhedrin, an attack is made rather upon the Jewish people for having originally built a Temple than upon the cultus itself.[1] It is, accordingly, legitimate to conclude at this point that, however they may have interpreted the death of Jesus, the original Jewish Christians did not cease to believe that the covenanted means for atonement was that prescribed in the Torah and practised in the sacrificial cultus of the Temple.

From the writings of Paul and Acts we gain some incidental information about the organisation of the Church in Jerusalem which is of considerable importance for our subject. According to Paul, at Jerusalem there was a triumvirate, comprising James, the brother of Jesus, Cephas or Peter, and John, who were regarded as the 'pillars' (στῦλοι) of the Church.[2] Of this triumvirate, Paul names James first.

1914), p. 123; Burkitt, *Christian Beginnings*, pp. 104–5; L. W. Barnard, 'St Stephen and Early Alexandrian Christianity', *N.T.S.* VII (1960–1), 31–3, 34.

[1] This fact is usually overlooked by commentators concerned to see in Stephen's movement a primitive Christian polemic against the Temple cultus. However, in his résumé of Hebrew history, Stephen admits (Acts vii. 46) that David brought the 'tabernacle of the testimony' into Jerusalem and asked to find 'a tabernacle for the God of Jacob' there (reading τῷ θεῷ instead of τῷ οἴκῳ, with the R.V. and R.S.V., which alone makes sense in relation to the context): cf. *B.C.* III, 72, IV, 81; Bruce, *Acts of the Apostles*, p. 175. This, Stephen continues, was done by Solomon. The following quotation from Isa. xvi. 1, which can reasonably be interpreted as condemnatory, only makes a point that is admitted in Solomon's dedicatory prayer (I Kings viii. 27), a fact which Stephen would presumably have known. It may, therefore, be questioned whether Solomon's action in building the Temple is really intended to represent the most heinous offence committed by Israel. The real climax of the speech does not come here, but in the following *vv.* 51–3, and constitutes a condemnation of the Jewish people for the Crucifixion. The anti-Jewish polemic of this speech reflects the attitude of the author of Acts, and it reaches its culmination in xxviii. 24–8, where Paul is represented as finding in Isaiah a foretelling of the Jews' rejection of the Gospel. Cf. H. Windisch in *B.C.* II, 319–20; A. F. J. Klijn, 'Stephen's Speech—Acts vii. 2–53', *N.T.S.* IV (1957–8), 25–6.

[2] Gal. ii. 9. στῦλος is used as a metaphor for a person holding a key position, providing supporting strength, in Rev. iii. 12: ὁ νικῶν, ποιήσω αὐτὸν στῦλον ἐν τῷ τοῦ Θεοῦ μου: cf. I Tim. iii. 15. Rabbi Johanan ben Zakkai was called עמוד הימיני, i.e. 'the right pillar', with reference to I Kings vii. 21, in Berakhoth IV, ii (fol. 28b); cf. *Der babylonische Talmud* (ed. L. Goldschmidt), I, 124. Cf. J. B. Lightfoot, *The Epistle to the Galatians* (London, 1881), p. 109; Eisler, ΙΗΣΟΥΣ ΒΑΣΙΛΕΥΣ, II, 289, also p. 788, note on p. 39; R. H. Charles, *Revelation of St John*, I, 90–1; Brandon, *Fall of Jerusalem*, p. 20, n. 1; Schlier, *Der Brief an die Galater*, pp. 78–9.

This precedence of order would not seem to be accidental; for, shortly after in the narrative concerned, he tells how Peter, at Antioch, submitted to the orders brought by emissaries of James on the question of table-fellowship with Gentiles.[1] This precedence of James is attested to by the author of Acts in his account of Paul's last visit to Jerusalem. There James clearly presides, supported by the elders;[2] he receives Paul's report on his missionary activities and he instructs him on what he has to do to prove his Jewish orthodoxy, since this was being seriously questioned.[3] A similar eminence and authority are implied in the so-called council at Jerusalem recorded in Acts xv. On this occasion, after Peter and Paul had put their cases, James is described as setting forth a ruling on the question at issue, to which the assembly assented without demur.[4]

This precedence of James, in the Jerusalem Church, is surprising in the light of what the Gospels tell of both Peter and James during the lifetime of Jesus. According to the Gospel evidence, there had also been a triumvirate of Apostles who formed a kind of inner circle

[1] Gal. ii. 11–12. O. Cullmann (Petrus², p. 46), commenting upon textual variants in the order given in ii. 9, sagely remarks on the fact that the oldest MSS give 'James, Cephas, John': 'Das könnte Zufall sein. Aber in einem Text wie diesem, in dem die Autorität der Verhandlungspartner nicht unwichtig ist, hat die Reihenfolge doch etwas zu bedeuten. Das haben auch die alten Abschreiber richtig empfunden. Daher die Textvarianten, was gerade diese Reihenfolge betrifft. Der mit D bezeichnete Text stellt nämlich Petrus hier vor Jakobus. Nach dem Prinzip, daß die "schwierigere" Lesart die ältere ist, haben wir diese von D bezeugte Variante als sekundär anzusehen. Denn wir begreifen, daß man späterhin an der Voranstellung des Jakobus vor Petrus Anstoß nehmen konnte' (E.T. p. 42). On the Antioch episode see Manson, Studies, pp. 178–81.

[2] Acts xxi. 18: The words πρὸς Ἰάκωβον, πάντες τε παρεγένοντο οἱ πρεσβύτεροι depict a kind of monarchical pontiff, supported by his curia. Cf. Ehrhardt, The Apostolic Succession, pp. 23, 28–9, 82; B.C. IV, 270; Brandon, Fall of Jerusalem, pp. 27–8; Carroll in B.J.R.L. 44 (1961), pp. 54–5.   [3] Acts xxi. 18–24.

[4] Acts xv. 6–22. Note the imperative ἄνδρες ἀδελφοί, ἀκούσατέ μου with which James commands attention, after Peter, Paul and Barnabas have made their statements. It is significant also that, after James had given his verdict (διὸ ἐγὼ κρίνω), there was no further discussion and what James had decided 'seemed good' to the assembly. On the ἐγὼ κρίνω of v. 19 see B.C. IV, 177: '"I decree". In the context this seems the probable meaning. It is the definite sentence of a judge, and the ἐγὼ implies that he is acting by an authority which is personal.' Whatever be the degree of historicity in the Acts account of this Council, the fact that he depicts James acting in this manner indicates that, despite his evident reticence about James, the author of Acts was aware of James's supremacy in the Jerusalem Church.

around Jesus: they had been specially selected as witnesses of his Transfiguration.[1] Now, this apostolic triumvirate is made up, curiously, of three disciples having the same names as those of the Jerusalem triumvirate, according to Paul, i.e. Peter, James and John, invariably in this order. However, the James of the inner circle of Jesus' disciples was James, the son of Zebedee, who was later put to death by Agrippa I.[2] During the lifetime of Jesus, his brother James had not been one of his disciples: indeed, according to the Markan Gospel, he would presumably have been among the relatives of Jesus (οἱ παρ' αὐτοῦ) who tried to restrain him, thinking him to be mad.[3]

This Gospel evidence is, of course, later, in date of composition, than the evidence of Paul in the Galatian Epistle. There is, however, reason for believing that James, the brother of Jesus, was not originally a disciple of Jesus, or, at least, was not prominent as such. He is not included in any list of the Twelve Apostles of Jesus, and he is not even recorded as having been a candidate to make up the number of the Twelve after the defection and death of Judas Iscariot.[4] His rise to leadership must, however, have been very rapid after the Crucifixion. He is named, together with Peter, as a special recipient of an appearance of the Risen Jesus, in the list of otherwise anonymous Resurrection witnesses which Paul cites to the Corinthian Christians as a tradition which he had himself received, presumably from the Jerusalem Church.[5]

---

[1] Mark v. 37, ix. 2, xiii. 3, xiv. 33; Matt. xvii. 1, xxvi. 37; Luke viii. 5, ix. 28. Cf. Goguel, *Jesus*, pp. 342–3; V. Taylor, *St Mark*, p. 294.

[2] Acts xii. 2; cf. *B.C.* IV, 133. See pp. 93 ff.

[3] Mark iii. 21; cf. Taylor, *St Mark*, pp. 235–7: see also John vii. 5. Cf. Lietzmann, *Gesch. d. alten Kirche*, I, 58; Carroll in *B.J.R.L.* 44 (1961), pp. 51, 56–7; Brandon, *Fall of Jerusalem*, pp. 45–7.

[4] Acts i. 15–26. James was already a member of the Christian community according to Acts i. 14: καὶ Μαριὰμ τῇ μητρὶ [τοῦ] 'Ιησοῦ καὶ σὺν τοῖς ἀδελφοῖς αὐτοῦ. Cf. Lightfoot, *Galatians*, pp. 261–2; Bruce, *Acts of the Apostles*, p. 74; K. Lake, *B.C.* v, 40–1.

[5] I Cor. xv. 5, 7: ἔπειτα ὤφθη 'Ιακώβῳ. Cf. Lietzmann, *An die Korinther*, I–II, pp. 78–9. According to the fragment of the lost Gospel acc. to the Hebrews, cited by Jerome, *Vir. ill.* 2 (*Apocrypha II*, ed. E. Klostermann, pp. 6–7), James was converted by the vision of the Risen Jesus. P. Vielhauer comments interestingly on the exaltation of James in the Gospel acc. to the Hebrews, see *Neutestamentliche Apokryphen* (ed. Hennecke–Schneemelcher), I, 105. Goguel (*La naissance du christianisme*, p. 57) makes the interesting suggestion: 'Nous sommes en présence d'un récit créé dans le milieu du Christianisme dynastique *ad majorem Jacobi gloriam*, sur la base de la simple mention de l'épître aux Corinthiens.' Cf. Lightfoot, *Galatians*, pp.

The antecedents of James and his rapid rise to the leadership of the Church seem to have been a subject about which the author of Acts was strangely reticent. It would be natural to suppose that, in describing the origin of the Church and the critical years of its early life, he would have given special attention to recording how James, the brother of Jesus, came to lead the movement which Jesus had initiated. But this is not so. In his account of the early days of the Church, it is Peter who is obviously the leader and upon whose exploits attention is focused.[1] Nothing whatsoever is said of James, the Lord's brother, during this period, although presumably he was included among the brethren of Jesus, who, with his mother Mary, are briefly recorded as continuing 'steadfastly in prayer', together with the reconstituted Twelve.[2] The first mention of this James occurs in a very curious manner, so that his identity is a matter of inference only. After telling of the death of James, the son of Zebedee, and of Peter's miraculous escape from the prison of Agrippa I, the author of Acts goes on to describe Peter's instructions before departing to 'another place'. The disciples, in the house of John Mark's mother, are requested: 'Tell these things unto James, and to all the brethren', and then he left.[3] In this way it would appear that the author of Acts sought to introduce another James into his narrative, and it is, to say the least, so strange as to excite wonder, if not suspicion. Quite clearly Peter's message, as it is given here, implies that this James already held so unique a position in the Church that he had thus to be specially informed of the escape and departure of him who had apparently been the leading Apostle. The next time that this James appears in the narrative it is in the account of the so-called Council of Jerusalem, where, as we have already noticed, he presides and clearly holds a position superior to that of Peter.[4]

But who is this James? The author of Acts introduces him into his narrative as one having a unique status, yet he gives not one word of explanation about his identity or antecedents. The fact that he is

265, 274, 364; Knox, *St Paul and the Church of Jerusalem*, p. 80; Klausner, *From Jesus to Paul*, p. 215; Brandon, *Fall of Jerusalem*, pp. 20, 50; Ehrhardt, *Framework of the New Testament Stories*, pp. 29, n. 1, 175, n. 1. On the exaltation of James in the Gospel of Thomas, see below, p. 300.

[1] Acts i. 15–22, ii. 14–39, iii. 1, iv. 23, v. 3–33, viii. 14–24, ix. 32–xi. 18, xii. 3–19. Cf. Cullmann, *Petrus*[2], pp. 35–41 (E.T. pp. 33–9).

[2] Acts i. 14.   [3] Acts xii. 1–17.

[4] Acts xv. 6–22: see p. 159, n. 4 above. Cf. Weiss, *Earliest Christianity*, I, 51–2, 369, II, 724; Brandon, *Fall of Jerusalem*, pp. 5, 27–8, 46–7.

introduced after the death of James, the brother of John, prevents his being identified with that famous son of Zebedee, who was one of the inner circle of Jesus' Apostles. But why leave this other James, who was henceforth to figure in the narrative as the head of the Jerusalem Church, unidentified? If it were not for Paul's description of him as 'James, the brother of the Lord ('Ιάκωβον τὸν ἀδελφὸν τοῦ κυρίου)',[1] we should not know from any first-century source the very significant fact that the leadership of the Christian movement had passed to this brother of Jesus. Why the author of Acts does not inform us on a matter so important cannot but stir suspicion. Unless we are prepared to accept that a writer of considerable literary ability, as the author of Luke and Acts undoubtedly was,[2] could be so inept as to introduce a new major figure into his narrative without explanation, we must obviously look for some other cause. The two that appear most likely are interrelated.

In the first place it is obvious, if the tradition of Peter's precedence among the apostles of Jesus be sound, that James must have supplanted him some time after the Crucifixion. According to the testimony of Acts, Peter was the leader of the community until his imprisonment by Agrippa I, i.e. about A.D. 43–4. In other words, if the record of Acts is to be trusted here, Peter would have led the infant Church for about ten years after the Crucifixion. But what was James, the brother of Jesus, doing during this period? Paul met him in Jerusalem about A.D. 37–8, if his conversion is dated for A.D. 34.[3] On that occasion Paul went to Jerusalem to consult Peter (ἱστορῆσαι), and he mentions that he saw (εἶδον) James, but he apparently did not seek to consult (ἱστορῆσαι) him.[4] This brief statement is interesting. Although the purpose of his visit was to consult Peter, Paul evidently felt it worthwhile to mention that he had seen James,

---

[1] Gal. i. 19. Cf. Schlier, Der Brief an die Galater, pp. 60–1.

[2] Luke claims in the preface to his Gospel (i. 3–4) to be a careful writer. Cf. Meyer, Ursprung, I, 8–11, III, 7–10; J. M. Creed, St Luke, p. 2; Bruce, Acts of the Apostles, pp. 15–18.

[3] Cf. G. Ogg, 'The Chronology of the New Testament', Peake's Commentary[2], 637a. Commenting upon μετὰ τρία ἔτη of Gal. i. 18, Schlier, Der Brief an die Galater, pp. 59–60, remarks: 'Die Zeitangabe ist nicht in erster Linie in chronologischem Interesse hervorgehoben, sondern um auch durch sie die Unabhängigkeit des Apostels und seines Evangeliums zu betonen.'

[4] Gal. i. 18: 'Denn ἱστορῆσαι bezeichnet im hellenistischen Griechisch den Besuch zum Zwecke des Kennenlernens, sei es von Städten und Ländern oder, wie hier, von Personen' (Schlier, Der Brief an die Galater, p. 60). Cf. G. D. Kilpatrick, 'Galatians 1: 18, ἱστορῆσαι Κηφᾶν', New Testament Essays (ed. A. J. B. Higgins), pp. 144–9.

the Lord's brother. It would, accordingly, appear that at this time James was already a notable personage in the Church at Jerusalem; however, Paul seems to have preferred to consult Peter only. The reason for this preference is not apparent: it could be that Peter was then the more important figure of the two or that he had the information which Paul wanted; it could also be that Paul felt that Peter would be more sympathetic to his case, as indeed he seems to have been until the Antioch episode.[1] However that may be, when he visited Jerusalem fourteen years later, i.e. about A.D. 51, Paul seems to have recognised that James was the leading member of the three 'pillars', which is confirmed by Peter's subsequent submission to James's emissaries at Antioch.[2]

In the light of this Pauline evidence, we may ask whether the strange silence of Acts about the antecedents of James and the manner in which he came to displace Peter was deliberate. Was he reticent about these things because they were embarrassing? It would seem likely; but for what reason is unclear. The suggestion naturally occurs that some unedifying struggle had taken place between Peter and James for the leadership of the movement, which the author of Acts did not wish to record. Paul's evidence, however, gives no hint of any division among the Jerusalem leaders. According to his statement, the triumvirate of James, Peter and John appears completely united in attitude and policy; but he may provide a clue to the problem in another way. In the passage concerned in his Epistle to the Galatians, Paul is seeking to convince his converts that his 'gospel' is of divine origin and that his apostolic authority had been recognised by the leaders of the Jerusalem Church. To this end he represents them as recognising that he was entrusted, presumably by God, with what he calls the 'gospel of the uncircumcision' as Peter was entrusted with the 'gospel of the circumcision'.[3] Now the

---

[1] The author of Acts probably had some justification for representing Peter as, by implication, sympathetic to Paul's case at the so-called Council of Jerusalem (xv. 7–11). Cf. Cullmann, *Petrus*[2], pp. 56–7 (E.T. pp. 50–1).

[2] Gal. ii. 1, 9; cf. p. 158, n. 2 and p. 159, n. 1 above. E. Haenchen (*Z.N.T.W.* 54, 1963, p. 172) has argued that, 'wenn sich Paulus mit dem mächtigsten Mann auf der Gegenseite gleichstellt', then that person must be Peter; but he fails to appreciate that Paul is concerned here to compare himself with Peter in terms of missionary spheres, a fact which actually attests James's headship of the Church.

[3] Gal. ii. 7–9. J. B. Lightfoot was conscious of the seriousness of the distinction which Paul makes here between the two 'gospels', and he sought to lessen it by explaining that the 'gospel of the circumcision' 'denotes a

word 'gospel' (εὐαγγέλιον), as used by Paul in his Galatian Epistle, has a twofold meaning. Primarily it means teaching or doctrine about Jesus Christ; but it also connotes the propagation of this teaching or doctrine.[1] Accordingly, when he writes here about a 'gospel of the circumcision' and a 'gospel of the uncircumcision', Paul envisages two forms of teaching about Jesus, the one designed for propagation among Jews and the other for propagation among Gentiles. Whether the distinction which he draws here was actually accepted by the Jerusalem leaders is another matter; but it is probable that, in describing Peter as being entrusted with the 'gospel of the circumcision', Paul was referring to the fact that Peter had been given the task of propagating the faith among the Jews resident outside Palestine. There is evidence to support this view: Peter seems to have visited Corinth and Rome,[2] and possibly also Alexandria, as we shall see.[3] This commission would account for his absence from Jerusalem on the occasion of Paul's last visit there,

distinction of sphere and not a difference of type' (*Galatians*, p. 109). We have seen above, p. 154, n. 1, that the distinction which Paul makes certainly reflected his awareness that his 'gospel' differed from the 'other gospel', and he believed that this was due to divine revelation, made for the specific purpose of evangelising the Gentiles. However, it must be recognised that the distinction which Paul makes here was a theoretical, not an actual one; for, according to the evidence of Acts, which is supported, for example, by the Epistle to the Romans, Paul usually commenced his evangelisation by speaking in the local synagogue. It is also evident (see below) that Peter did not confine his missionary activity to the 'circumcision'. It is interesting to note that F. C. Bauer clearly perceived the significance of Paul's distinction here: 'Mit aller Selbstgewißheit seines Standpunkts stellt sich der Apostel dem Petrus gegenüber, so daß Mann gegen Mann, Lehrer gegen Lehrer, ein Evangelium gegen das andere, ein Apostelamt gegen das andere steht, und der Beweis, auf welchen der Apostel sich stützt, ist der bestimmte thatsächliche Erfolg, auf welchen er schon hinweisen kann [i.e. in *v.* 8]' (*Paulus*, p. 141). Cf. Brandon, *Fall of Jerusalem*, pp. 60–1; W. D. Davies, *Paul and Rabbinic Judaism*, p. 68.

[1] This is seen in Gal. i. 7, 11–12, 15–16, where Paul speaks of his 'gospel' both as 'doctrine' about Christ (τὸ εὐαγγέλιον τοῦ Χριστοῦ) and as the 'evangelising' of him (εὐαγγελίζωμαι αὐτόν); cf. Schlier, *Der Brief an die Galater*, p. 39.

[2] The existence of a 'Peter' party at Corinth (I Cor. i. 12) would suggest that Peter was known personally to the Christians there, as does the reference to Peter's wife (I Cor. ix. 5). The tradition concerning Peter's presence in Rome is very ancient, and there seems no reason for doubting its truth. Cf. Cullmann, *Petrus*[2], pp. 60–1, 80–148 (E.T. pp. 53–4, 71–131); Brandon, *Fall of Jerusalem*, pp. 20, 137–8, 139–40.

[3] See below, pp. 191, 196ff., 297–9.

as it would also explain the supreme position which James then held.[1]

If Peter's missionary commission was the cause of his apparent replacement by James as the leader of the Church, which Acts xii. 17 also seems to imply, why did the author of Acts not explain this? Two reasons suggest themselves, each being of considerable importance for our subject. The first is that the author of Acts did not wish to record Peter's missionary activities outside Palestine. This is a necessary conclusion; for it is surely incredible that, in an account of the propagation of Christianity, nothing should be said of the missionary labours of him who had been the leading Apostle of Jesus. The objection which the author of Acts felt to mentioning the matter must, consequently, have been a very strong one for him. Of its nature we can only surmise; but, undoubtedly, it would have concerned his theme, namely, to show how Christianity, rejected by the Jews, had been accepted by the Gentiles.[2] Presented in this manner, Christianity was a salvation-religion of universal validity, and the fact that Paul is represented as the missionary apostle *par excellence* means that the author of Acts was a Pauline Christian.[3] Peter's missionary activities must, therefore, have conflicted with Paul's presentation of Christianity so seriously that, looking back to them some two decades after the disappearance of the Jerusalem Church, the author of Acts found it wisest to remain silent about them. In what way Peter's 'gospel' and his propagation of it proved so objectionable constitutes a problem to which we must return. For the present we must consider the other reason why the author of Acts was so reticent about James, the brother of Jesus.

That James achieved such a position of supremacy in the Christian movement could only have been due, at least originally, to his relationship to Jesus.[4] Here we are reminded forcibly of the dynastic

---

[1] Cf. Cullmann, *Petrus*[2], pp. 62–72 (E.T. pp. 55–65).

[2] Acts xxviii. 23–8. Cf. *B.C.* II, 180–7; Bruce, *Acts of the Apostles*, pp. 30–2; Ehrhardt, *Framework of the New Testament Stories*, pp. 97–100.

[3] The author of Acts clearly states his evaluation of Paul in the divine attestation which Ananias received concerning the newly converted Paul: 'he is a chosen instrument of mine to carry my name before the Gentiles and kings and the sons of Israel' (ix. 15): it is, incidentally, significant that Acts does not recognise the limitation of Paul's activity to the Gentiles which Gal. ii. 7–9 defines (see p. 163, n. 3 above). On the Apollos episode as evidence of the Paulinism of Acts see below, pp. 191 ff. Cf. Bruce, *Acts of the Apostles*, pp. 34–40.

[4] The dynastic factor in the leadership of the primitive Christian movement has long been recognised. According to Eusebius, *Hist. eccl.* II. xxiii. 1,

succession among the Zealots. As we have seen, the sons of Judas of Galilee succeeded him in the leadership of the movement. The position immediately accorded to Menahem, when he arrived in Jerusalem at the outbreak of the revolt in 66, indicated recognition of a charismatic as well as dynastic right to leadership in the holy war.[1] On his murder, the leadership of the original party devolved on Eleazar, a relative of Menahem, undoubtedly the nearest surviving one, and it was he who led the last devoted stand against the Romans at Masada.[2] The fact that Jesus had no son meant that his eldest brother was his natural successor, and as such he was accepted by the community of Jesus' disciples. How James came, personally, to effect the transition, if indeed he had not been a follower of Jesus before his crucifixion, is beyond our comprehension. As we have seen, primitive tradition ascribed to him a special vision of the Risen Jesus, and it could be reasonably assumed that the experience wrought his conversion.[3] However, on psychological grounds it would seem that some predisposing factors must already have existed to render him susceptible to such an experience. But speculation about such matters is not useful, and a more fruitful line of inquiry is that of the significance of this dynastic succession in the primitive Christian movement.

The dynastic succession in Zealotism was undoubtedly a powerful factor in securing the continuity of the movement founded by Judas, and in preserving his teaching and ideals. His defeat and death at the hands of the Romans did not mean the end of his aims. Those of his followers who survived looked to his sons to lead the movement until its object was achieved, namely, the liberation of Israel from

the Apostles had allotted ὁ τῆς ἐπισκοπῆς θρόνος to James, 'the brother of the Lord', and, after his death, the Apostles, disciples and the 'family of the Lord' (γένους κατὰ σάρκα Κυρίου) unanimously decided that Symeon, 'a cousin of the Saviour' (ἀνεψιόν... γεγονότα τοῦ σωτῆρος), was the one worthy (ἄξιον) to be his successor (διαδοχῆς), *ibid.* III. xi. Eusebius appears to have got his information about the family of Jesus (*desposyni*) from the second-century Julius Africanus and Hegesippus (*ibid.* I. vii. 14; III. xii). Cf. J. Weiss, *Earliest Christianity*, II, 716–19; Meyer, *Ursprung*, III, 224–5; Harnack, *Die Mission und Ausbreitung des Christentums*, II, 77; Lohmeyer, *Galiläa und Jerusalem*, p. 53; B. H. Streeter, *The Primitive Church* (London, 1929), pp. 39–40, and in *C.A.H.* XI, 272; Eisler, ΙΗΣΟΥΣ ΒΑΣΙΛΕΥΣ, II, 541, n. 1; Goguel, *La naissance du Christianisme*, pp. 130–4; Brandon, *Fall of Jerusalem*, p. 50, n. 2; Schoeps, *Theologie und Geschichte des Judenchristentums*, p. 262; Manson, *Studies*, pp. 195–6.

[1] See above, pp. 132–3.   [2] See above, pp. 133, 143.
[3] See p. 160, n. 5 above.

the Roman yoke. Whether any Messianic role had originally been attributed to Judas is unknown; Josephus refers to him, curiously, as 'awesome' (δεινότατος), and the memory of him and his teaching certainly survived.[1] The prestige which Menahem enjoyed, and the state which he affected at Jerusalem, certainly suggest that he was regarded, if only temporarily, as the Messiah who had come to deliver Israel.[2] The question that naturally arises is, how far does all this afford an instructive parallel for evaluating James's position in the primitive Christian community?

There is a certain analogy in the pattern of facts connecting the succession of James with the death of Jesus. Jesus was crucified as a rebel by the Romans; his followers did not abandon his cause, but looked to his brother for leadership of the movement which he, Jesus, had founded. A difference seems to lie in the fact that it was believed that the crucified Jesus would return, with supernatural power, to complete his Messianic role, although this purpose was similar to the Zealot in being defined as restoring 'the kingdom to Israel'.[3] According to later tradition, on the death of James in A.D. 62, the leadership of the Church passed to another relative of Jesus, Symeon, who was doubtless the senior male representative of the founder's family.[4]

Concerning the outlook of James, the testimony of Paul and of Acts seem in accord. He was rigorous in maintaining strict observance of the Torah among the Jewish Christians.[5] If the later traditions, preserved by Hegesippus, are to be trusted, he enjoyed a high reputation among the Jews generally for his exceeding devotion to the practice of Judaism, a reputation that may possibly be confirmed by Josephus, as we have previously noticed.[6] In his dealings with Paul, during his last visit to Jerusalem, he appears to have been very astute. Paul's presence in the city was obviously an embarrassment to James, since rumours were rife of Paul's unorthodox views and

[1] See above, p. 53.   [2] See above, pp. 132–3.
[3] Acts i. 6. 'The disciples interpret the reappearance of Jesus as a sign of the restoration of the Messianic Davidic Kingdom,...' (B.C. IV, 8).
[4] See p. 165, n. 4 above.
[5] Gal. ii. 12; Acts xxi. 18–24. According to Schoeps (Theologie und Geschichte des Judenchristentums, p. 261), 'Jakobus war schwerlich ein judaistischer Extremist'. This attempt to represent James as a moderating influence lands him into the logical contradiction in his later book (Paulus, p. 62) of describing τινὲς ἀπὸ 'Ιακώβου of Gal. ii. 12 as 'Sendboten der Jerusalemer Extremisten, der ӡηλωταὶ τοῦ νόμου von Acta 15. 5...'. Cf. Goguel, La naissance du christianisme, pp. 333, 345–6; Weiss, Earliest Christianity, II, 707.
[6] See above, pp. 122 ff.

practice.[1] Under James, the reputation of the Jewish Christian community with the Pharisees and other zealous Jews seems to have been good, and he was intent on keeping it so.[2] He clearly perceived the weakness of Paul's position; for, while Paul professed to be an orthodox Jew, the whole logic of his teaching negated the peculiar spiritual status of Israel.[3] James, therefore, challenged him to give public proof of his orthodoxy by assisting a number of Jewish Christians to discharge their Nazarite vows in the Temple.[4] It was a shrewd move which placed Paul in the dilemma of either refusing to demonstrate his Jewish orthodoxy or compromising himself with his Gentile converts.[5] It also witnesses to the authority which James exercised; for Paul, despite all his former assertions of independence to his converts, submitted without protest.[6]

That such a zealous Jew was leader of the Jerusalem Church is of the greatest significance. It surely confirms the other evidence we have seen that the members of that Church saw themselves as an integral part of Israel. That they also formed a specific community within the state was due to their continuing belief that Jesus, whom the Romans had crucified, was the Messiah of Israel, and they prepared, accordingly, under the leadership of his brother, for the return of Jesus to 'restore the kingdom to Israel'. Hence it was for this reason, as well as that of James' connection with Peter's missionary commission as we have seen, that the author of Acts was so strangely reticent about the 'Lord's brother' who ruled the church during these fateful years as an essentially Jewish Messianic sect.

In this context also we must set the death of James in A.D. 62. As we have seen, James was condemned to death for breaking the Law by the high priest Ananus and died by stoning.[7] His execution aroused the indignation of certain Jews against Ananus, who was a leader of the Sadducean aristocracy and unpopular for his violence against

---

[1] Acts xxi. 20–2.

[2] See particularly the reason which James gives for requiring Paul to provide a public demonstration of his orthodoxy, Acts xxi: καὶ γνώσονται πάντες ὅτι ὧν κατήχηνται περὶ σοῦ οὐδέν ἐστιν, ἀλλὰ στοιχεῖς καὶ αὐτὸς φυλάσσων τὸν νόμον. See also above, pp. 117–18, 122 ff.

[3] Cf. Brandon, Fall of Jerusalem, pp. 134–5, 150–1.

[4] Acts xxi. 23–4, 26: see above, p. 156, n. 2. In his endeavour to minimise the seriousness of the clash between James and Paul, Schmithals describes James's demand as 'a very mild case of legal observance' (Paul and James, p. 92).

[5] Cf. B.C. IV, 273; Fall of Jerusalem, pp. 150–1.

[6] Acts xxi. 26.   [7] See above, pp. 115–16.

the lower orders of the priesthood. Since many of these lower priests were members of the Jerusalem Church, it is probable that James was sympathetic to their cause.[1] Moreover, as we also saw, the lower clergy of the Temple were infected with Zealot views, and it was their action in stopping the imperial sacrifices that sparked off the revolt in 66.[2] If Ananus struck at James because he was the leader of a group associated with the lower clergy, it is possible, as we noted, that James and the Jewish Christians were also in sympathy with the Zealots, who were hostile to the Sadducean sacerdotal aristocracy for their pro-Roman policy.[3]

Such connections and sympathies on the part of James would be wholly consistent with what we otherwise know of his character and outlook. Because he was the head of a sect of zealous Jews, who were distinguished for their belief that the crucified prophet of Nazareth would return to restore Israel's freedom from the Roman yoke, the Sadducean leaders would have regarded James as both politically and socially dangerous. In this connection, too, we may recall the communism of the primitive Christian community,[4] and the significance of the fact that the essentially Jewish writing known as the Epistle of James is characterised by its sympathy for the poor and its animus against the rich and influential.[5]

If the Jewish Christians were thus such zealous Jews and looked for the restoration of Israel's freedom and sovereignty, what was their attitude to those Gentiles who sought to join the Church? From what we have inferred so far, it would seem that they would have been instinctively hostile to the Gentiles and could never have envisaged Gentile participation in their movement, still less have welcomed it. Yet, as an abundance of evidence attests, Gentile churches were soon established throughout the eastern Mediterranean area, and Christianity was destined to become a Gentile religion.

A critical examination of the idealised picture of the development of Christianity in Acts quickly shows that the evangelisation of the Gentiles had no place in the policy of the original Jewish Chris-

---

[1] Pp. 118 ff.   [2] Pp. 130–1.   [3] Pp. 131–2.

[4] Acts iv. 32–5. Cf. Preuschen, *Apostelgeschichte*, pp. 27–8; Klausner, *From Jesus to Paul*, p. 277, n. 17. The social outlook of the Jerusalem Christians would have been close to that of the Zealots, as we have seen, pp. 58, 132.

[5] James ii. 1–9, v. 1–6. Cf. H. Windisch, *Die katholischen Briefe* (Tübingen, 1930), pp. 13–14, 28–9; Grant, *Economic Background of the Gospels*, pp. 122–5; Goguel, *La naissance*, pp. 405–9; S. E. Johnson in *The Scrolls and the New Testament* (ed. K. Stendahl), pp. 132–3.

tians. Its beginning is attributed to some of the followers of Stephen, who first began 'preaching the Lord Jesus' to the Gentile inhabitants of Antioch, having hitherto confined their missionary efforts outside Palestine to the Jews of the Diaspora.[1] Stephen and his movement, as we have already noted, constituted an aberration from the original form of the faith, the distinction being obvious to the Jewish authorities who suppressed Stephen. The author of Acts seems to have prepared for this new stage in his theme, namely, the evangelisation of the Gentiles, by recounting the story of the conversion of the centurion Cornelius, for which, in turn, Peter had to be prepared by a special divine revelation.[2]

Having thus, doubtless unintentionally, admitted that the evangelisation of the Gentiles was not due to the initiative of the Jerusalem Christians, the author of Acts is also obliged to record that, when faced with the *fait accompli* at Antioch, their first reaction was to require that these Gentiles be circumcised, i.e. made Jews.[3] This requirement, according to him, was discussed at a specially convoked council at Jerusalem. Peter is represented as an ardent advocate of the freedom of Gentile converts from the obligation of circumcision, maintaining in a thoroughly Pauline manner: 'We believe that we shall be saved through the grace of the Lord Jesus, in like manner as they.' James, too, is depicted as equally cooperative, and he ruled that the Gentile converts should only be required to observe certain moral and dietary regulations.[4]

There is much reason for suspecting the accuracy of the account of this so-called Council of Jerusalem in Acts.[5] But, even if it is to be accepted as an authentic record, it would only mean that the Jeru-

---

[1] Acts xi. 19–21.   [2] Acts x. 1–xi. 18.

[3] According to Acts xi. 22, the Jerusalem Church sent Barnabas to investigate the new situation at Antioch; but, instead of reporting back, he joined Paul and the two were commissioned by the Antiochean Christians for missionary work further afield (xi. 23–6, xiii. 1–3). It would appear from the interposition of chapter xii, dealing with Agrippa's persecution, that the author of Acts was manipulating different sources, in order to develop his thesis; cf. *B.C.* IV, 127, 132, 140–1. The concluding statement in xiv. 27, that God had 'opened a door of faith to the Gentiles', provides the cue for telling how the demand for circumcision was dealt with (xv. 1–21).

[4] Acts xv. 7–11, 13–21. 'Le premier [i.e. Peter], rappelant la conversion de Corneille, expose des idées qui sont la pure doctrine paulinienne de la justification par la foi (15. 6–11)', Goguel, *La naissance du christianisme*, p. 328. Cf. Brandon, *Fall of Jerusalem*, pp. 130–1.

[5] See note xvi by K. Lake in *B.C.* v.

salem Church made certain regulations for a *fait accompli*, namely, the conversion of Gentiles, in which they had had no part. Once the situation had been created, they were faced with a choice between repudiating it completely and trying to control it. Acts, unfortunately, gives no information as to the form of Christianity which the disciples of Stephen originally presented to the Gentiles. Of its Pauline form we are, of course, well informed; but we may legitimately wonder whether, at the beginning of Paul's missionary activity, the Jerusalem Christians had any exact idea of Paul's 'gospel'—indeed, it is very probable that at this stage Paul himself had not yet developed it as it appears in his Epistles. One fact does, however, appear significant in connection with the acceptance of Gentile members of the faith by the Jerusalem Church. On Paul's testimony, it would seem that considerable emphasis was laid upon the Gentile converts making a financial contribution to the support of the Jerusalem community.[1] It is not impossible that an astute leader, such as James undoubtedly was, perceived the value of the movement's having Gentile supporters throughout the empire, provided that the essential principles of the movement were not compromised —hence his concern when it became apparent that Paul was teaching these Gentiles a version of the faith which negated the peculiar spiritual status of Israel.[2]

Although they thus accepted the existence of Gentile adherents and legislated for it, the Jewish Christians remained firm in their conception of the Election of Israel as a nation.[3] The most illuminating evidence of their attitude to the Gentiles has been preserved in the story of Jesus and the Syro-Phoenician woman. This story, although recorded in the Markan Gospel,[4] must go back to the original Jewish Christians in Palestine, in view of its uncompli-

---

[1] Gal. i. 10; I Cor. xvi. 1-6; II Cor. ix. 1-15; Rom. xv. 25-7. Cf. Brandon, *Fall of Jerusalem*, pp. 21, 141, 142, 145, 146, 150.

[2] E.g. Rom. x. 12; I Cor. xii. 13; Gal. iii. 28, v. 6; Col. iii. 11.

[3] Even Paul, despite his advocacy of Gentile participation in the gospel, remained instinctively attached to the idea of Israel's Election, as his metaphor of the olive tree graphically shows, Rom. xi. 13-24. Despite the liberal attitude taken by other Hellenistic Jews towards the Gentiles, the Election-idea remained for them also basic and essential: P. Dalbert, *Die Theologie der hellenistisch-jüdischen Missions-Literatur unter Ausschluß von Philo und Josephus* (Hamburg, 1954), pp. 137-43.

[4] Mark vii. 24-30; cf. Matt. xv. 21-8: the episode is, significantly, omitted by Luke. Cf. Goguel, *Jesus*, pp. 321-2; V. Taylor, *The Formation of the Gospel Tradition* (London, 1945), pp. 75-6; Bultmann, *Gesch. d. synop. Tradition*, p. 38.

mentary attitude to the Gentiles. Jesus is represented as refusing the petition of this Gentile woman that he should heal her little daughter, giving as the reason for this cruel decision: 'Let the children first be fed, for it is not right to take the children's bread and throw it to the dogs.' Long familiarity with this story, together with the traditional picture of the gentleness of Jesus, tends to obscure the shocking intolerance of the saying. As the words are uttered by Jesus, a Jew, the 'children' to whom he refers are Jews, and their right to be 'fed' precedes all other needs and considerations. But this brutal assertion of Jewish privilege is not enough: the Gentiles are 'dogs' (κυνάρια), to whom it was unfitting to cast (βαλεῖν) the children's food.[1] Jesus is represented as relenting from this attitude of extreme racial intolerance only when the Gentile woman, humbly accepting for herself and her little daughter the designation of 'dogs', renews her request for 'the crumbs' of the children's food fallen under the table. That her request is finally granted does not reduce the significance of the contrast drawn between Jew and Gentile. The Jews have the inherent right of children to the ministration of Jesus; the Gentiles have no right, and are only grudgingly conceded the 'crumbs' which may fall to them.[2]

Whatever the origin of the story, i.e. whether it records an actual incident in the life of Jesus or not, the story obviously originated among the Jewish Christians, and its very currency proves that it represents the attitude taken towards Gentiles who sought to participate in the faith. That a story concerning Jesus, so replete with Jewish intolerance, should have been preserved in the Gospel of Mark, is certainly surprising; for this Gospel is addressed to a predominantly Gentile church, and, as we shall see, it has a distinct anti-Jewish bias.[3] For Mark to have included a story so uncomplimentary to Gentiles can only mean that it had a value that offset this aspect of it. An explanation which suggests itself, and reasonably accords with the situation of the Gentile converts vis-à-vis the Jewish Christians, is that the original purpose of the story had been transformed.

[1] Cf. S.B. *Kommentar*, I, 724–5; C. H. Turner in *New Comm. N.T.* p. 76a; Taylor, *St Mark*, p. 350.

[2] 'La réponse première de Jésus correspondait sans nul doute à son état d'esprit, ou du moins à celui que les Évangélistes lui supposaient avec vraisemblance et qu'ils n'auraient pas inventé pour s'en embarrasser à plaisir', Guignebert, *Jésus*, p. 384; cf. Klausner, *Jesus of Nazareth*, p. 364; Schmithals, *Paul and James*, p. 111.

[3] See ch. 5. It is possible that Mark added the attenuating πρῶτον in v. 27; Bultmann, *Gesch. d. synop. Tradition*, p. 38; Taylor, *St Mark*, p. 350.

Starting as a ruling on the relative status of Jews and Gentiles with regard to the faith, the story probably became established as sanctioning a carefully qualified recognition of Gentile discipleship. Thus it came to be valued by thè Gentile Christians as a Dominical endorsement of their membership of the Church, despite its harsh comparison of Jewish and Gentile worth.[1]

This story does not stand alone as evidence of the attitude of the original Jewish Christians. The Gospel of Matthew contains a passage in which Jesus is represented as sending out his twelve apostles to evangelise Palestine.[2] Their mission, however, is to be strictly limited to Jews; for Jesus begins his charge by warning them: 'go nowhere among the Gentiles (εἰς ὁδὸν ἐθνῶν), and enter no town of the Samaritans, but go rather to the lost sheep of the house of Israel'. Although this account of the commissioning of the apostles is clearly composed of diverse materials, the verse just cited, and that with which it ends, imply a situation prior to A.D. 70; for the apostles are told that they 'will not have gone through all the towns of Israel, before the Son of man comes'. In other words, it would seem that we have here a reminiscence of a primitive tradition that the original disciples concentrated their missionary work on their fellow-Jews in Palestine, believing that the time was short before the return of Jesus as the Messiah.[3]

The Matthaean version of the parable of the Wedding Feast contains an addition which can be reasonably interpreted as evidence of Jewish Christian concern about the fitness of the Gentiles for membership of the Church.[4] This addition to the Lukan form of the parable[5] tells how, after guests had been obtained to replace those originally invited to the Wedding Feast, one was found having no Wedding Garment and was cast out. In the context of the parable, it would seem that the Wedding Garment signifies some form of qualification, probably of a moral or ritual character, necessary for

[1] Cf. Brandon, *Fall of Jerusalem*, pp. 33–4.
[2] Matt. x. 5–6. The Matthaean account appears to be a conflation of Markan and Q material: cf. Streeter, *Four Gospels*, pp. 255 ff.; Moffatt, *Introduction to the New Testament*, pp. 246–7; T. W. Manson, *The Teaching of Jesus* (Cambridge, 1935), p. 222; Klostermann, *Matthäusevangelium*, pp. 86–7; S.B. *Kommentar*, 1, 538–60.
[3] Matt. x. 23. Cf. Klostermann, *Matthäusevangelium*, p. 89; Brandon, *Fall of Jerusalem*, pp. 35, 174–6.
[4] Matt. xxii. 1–14.
[5] Luke xiv. 16–24. Cf. F. W. Beare, *Earliest Records of Jesus* (Oxford, 1962), pp. 177, 210–11.

membership of the Church: this qualification an alien guest, i.e. a Gentile convert, might not have. However, although this part of the parable does seem to deal with the suitability of Gentile converts, it would appear more likely that both the parable of the Wedding Feast, and its addition concerning the Wedding Garment, reflect the outlook of the Matthaean author relative to the *Sitz im Leben* of the community for which he wrote a decade or more after the destruction of Jerusalem.[1] Whether another pertinent saying, attributed to Jesus, in Matthew preserves a primitive tradition is difficult to decide; but it has a certain significance. It is the admonition: 'Do not give dogs what is holy; and do not throw your pearls before swine, lest they trample them under foot and turn to attack you.'[2] In view of the fact that 'swine' is a term used in rabbinic literature for Rome or the non-Israelite world, and 'dogs', as we have seen, was a Jewish Christian appellation for Gentiles, the saying undoubtedly refers to the Gentiles.[3] Such a saying would well reflect the bitter experience of Jewish Christians who survived the catastrophe of A.D. 70; but it might well have expressed the instinctive caution of a member of the Jerusalem Church before that fatal event.

From the evidence we have surveyed, the existence of Gentile Christians is found in no wise to contradict the conclusion, which we had previously reached, that the Jewish Christians were profoundly attached to their national religion and that their faith in Jesus made them more zealous Jews. They saw the mission of Jesus as limited exclusively to Israel; indeed it only made sense in terms of the doctrine of Israel's election to be the People of God. The Gentiles were despised and hated as dogs or swine. The presentation of their faith to Gentiles was, therefore, by the very nature of that faith, excluded even from their contemplation, no less than from their aim or desire. Its presentation was the work of others, and was clearly unexpected. Faced with a *fait accompli*, the Jewish Christians, under the astute leadership of James, sought to control it and to exploit its economic possibilities. Consequently, when they began to realise that Paul was presenting to the Gentiles a version of the faith that not only conflicted with their own, but might also compromise

---

[1] Cf. Brandon, *Fall of Jerusalem*, pp. 36, 230–1.

[2] Matt. vii. 6.

[3] Cf. S.B. *Kommentar*, I, 449–50; Klostermann, *Matthäusevangelium*, pp. 66–7. On the question of the interpretation of τὸ ἅγιον and 'pearls' relative to the Torah, see M. Black, *An Aramaic Approach to the Gospels and Acts* (Oxford, 1946), pp. 146–8.

them dangerously with their own countrymen, they took action to repudiate him and bring his Gentile converts under their own authority.[1]

We now reach the point in our investigation when we must turn to inquire what was the 'gospel' of the Jerusalem Christians, i.e. their conception of the nature and mission of Jesus in relation to their ancestral faith. We have already noted, incidentally, some aspects of their belief; we must now endeavour to apprehend it as a whole. To this end, as we saw earlier, we have to face the very difficult task of deducing what was the faith of the Jerusalem Christians, not from documents of their own composition, but from the hostile witness of Paul and from what the Gospel writers chose to preserve of it for their own particular purposes. However, indirect though the evidence is and tortuous the process of its evaluation, the essential nature of the Jewish Christian 'gospel' can be discerned.

We may best begin by noting that which is most certain, namely, that the Jewish Christians believed Jesus to be the Messiah of Israel. So firmly established had the identification become within two decades of the Crucifixion that Paul, writing to his Gentile converts, uses, without explanation, the title *Christos* almost as a personal name for Jesus.[2] Since the concept of the Messiah at this period was so essentially bound up with the national destiny of Israel, we may well wonder what the Gentile converts made of it or how it was explained to them. In view of its essentially Jewish connotation, it would seem that the first Gentile converts must have come from those proselytes and 'God-fearers', attached to many Jewish communities of the Diaspora, who were disposed to associate themselves closely with the Jewish people.[3] Once a tradition was established for the Gentiles to use the Greek equivalent of *Messiah*, i.e. *Christos*, as a name for Jesus, its use in connection with non-Jewish concepts of Jesus, such as those introduced by Paul, would gradually have divested it of its original association with Jewish national hopes. However that may be, the fact that Paul could so easily refer to 'Jesus Christ' or 'Christ Jesus' attests an identification that must stem from the practice of the original Jewish Christians.

Whether this identification was made before the Crucifixion and

---

[1] Cf. Brandon, *Fall of Jerusalem*, pp. 136–51, and the references there given.
[2] E.g. if the Epistle to the Galatians is taken as the earliest surviving letter of Paul, note the alternation of personal name and title in ii. 16.
[3] Cf. Schürer, *G.J.V.* III, 122–35; Jeremias, *Jerusalem*, II, 191–207.

the Resurrection experiences of the disciples might be questioned. Such a statement as that attributed to Peter in his Pentecost speech, by the author of Acts, could be cited as evidence that the identification resulted from these events: 'Let all the house of Israel, therefore, know assuredly that God has made him both Lord and Christ, this Jesus whom you crucified.'[1] However, not only does such a crucial episode as that of Peter's Confession at Caesarea Philippi,[2] together with an abundance of other gospel evidence, indicate that Jesus was regarded as the Messiah before his death, but the identification is required by the logic of his career. To have caused such a movement among the Jews that the Jewish authorities regarded him as dangerous, and the Romans executed him for sedition, means that he was regarded as a significant figure by his fellow-countrymen. Since Messianic expectation was high at this time and there is a strong tradition that his followers held him to be the Messiah during his lifetime, the dating of the identification as pre-Crucifixion would seem beyond reasonable doubt. Whether Jesus claimed, himself, to be the Messiah is, however, another matter, and one which we shall have to consider at length later.[3]

If the disciples of Jesus had regarded him as the Messiah, it is obvious that his crucifixion by the Romans must have constituted a most serious objection to their continuing so to regard him. From all that we know of Jewish Messianic belief at this time, the Messiah was expected, on his coming, to accomplish the salvation of Israel from its servitude and oppression.[4] The failure of any claimant to achieve this automatically cancelled his claim, or those made by his followers on his behalf, to be the Messiah. As we have seen, during this period there were many who claimed, or were thought, to be

---

[1] Acts ii. 36. Cf. Bruce, *Acts of the Apostles*, p. 96; Bultmann, *Theology of the New Testament*, I, 27; *B.C.* I, 367 (the editors).

[2] Mark viii. 27–33; cf. Matt. xvi. 13–23; Luke ix. 18–22. Even if this is a 'Glauberslegende', as Bultmann supposes (*Gesch. d. synop. Tradition*, p. 276; cf. Ergänzungsheft, p. 36), it indicates, nevertheless, a belief that Jesus was recognised as Messiah by his disciples before the Crucifixion: however, see below, pp. 277–8.Cf. Taylor, *St Mark*, pp. 374–5; Guignebert, *Jésus*, pp. 342–5 ('Tout ce que prouverait la confession de Pierre, si elle était substantiellement authentique, c'est qu'à la veille de la montée à Jérusalem, les disciples croyaient que Jésus tiendrait la première place dans le Royaume qu'il annonçait', p. 345); Goguel, *Jesus*, pp. 378–85; Klausner, *Jesus of Nazareth*, pp. 299–303; Cullmann, *Petrus*², pp. 197–200 (E.T. pp. 171–4).

[3] See below, pp. 337 ff.

[4] Cf. Schürer, *G.J.V.* II, 525–44; Mowinckel, *He that Cometh*, pp. 311–21.

the Messiah who would deliver Israel; but their lack of success, usually resulting in their deaths, ended their Messianic reputations, their surviving followers were disillusioned, and their memory perished.[1] The death of Jesus, at the hands of the Romans, must, accordingly, have been taken as proof that he was not the Messiah,[2] and the gospels have preserved the memory of the disillusionment and despair that befell his followers at his execution. The words which the author of Luke puts in the mouth of Cleopas, when he answers the question of the Unknown Stranger on the way to Emmaus, are especially illuminating in this context.[3] Asked what concerned him and his companion that made them so sad as they talked, Cleopas replies: 'Concerning Jesus of Nazareth, who was a prophet mighty in deed and word before God and all the people, and how our chief priests and rulers delivered him up to be condemned to death, and crucified him. But we had hoped that he was the one to redeem Israel (ὁ μέλλων λυτροῦσθαι τὸν 'Ισραήλ).'[4]

In one sense, from the Jewish point of view, Jesus had died an honourable death. To perish at the hands of the hated Romans, who oppressed Israel, was to die as a martyr and join that venerated company of heroes who had sacrificed their lives for their ancestral faith.[5] But the death of Jesus was a problem to his followers, because they had seen in him the Messiah of Israel. Disillusioned and dispirited, their movement would undoubtedly have broken up and disappeared, like those which had centred on other Messianic

---

[1] See above, pp. 112–13.

[2] Paul eloquently shows how the idea of a 'crucified Messiah' (Χριστὸν ἐσταυρωμένον) was a *skandalon* to the Jews (I Cor. i. 22–3); he incidentally witnesses here to his consciousness that the presentation of a 'crucified Messiah' would be nonsense (μωρίαν) to Gentiles (see above, p. 13). Cf. A. Deissmann, *Paulus: eine kultur- und religionsgeschichtliche Skizze* (Tübingen, 1923), p. 155; Goguel, *Jesus*, p. 116; Klausner, *Jesus of Nazareth*, pp. 301–2.

[3] Luke xxiv. 13–36. 'Sie ist ihrem Gehalt nach die älteste der synoptischen Auferstehungsgeschichten...' (Bultmann, *Gesch. d. synop. Tradition*, p. 314).

[4] Luke xxiv. 21. 'Nur der Emmaus-Geschichte liegt noch das Wissen darum zugrunde, daß die Gewißheit der Auferstehung Jesu identisch ist mit der Gewißheit, ὅτι αὐτός ἐστιν ὁ μέλλων λυτροῦσθαι τὸν 'Ισραήλ (Lk. 24, 21)' (Bultmann, *ibid.*). Cf. Creed, *St Luke*, p. 296; A. Ehrhardt in *N.T.S.* x (1963–4), 188.

[5] Cf. Lohmeyer in *Congrès d'Histoire du Christianisme*, II, 121–37; T. W. Manson, 'Martyrs and Martyrdom', *B.J.R.L.* 39 (1957), pp. 463–78; C. K. Barrett in *New Testament Essays* (ed. A. J. B. Higgins), pp. 11–14.

pretenders who had perished.[1] That the movement which had centred on Jesus did not suffer this fate was due to a new belief which his disciples acquired: that he would return to fulfil his Messianic role, which had been interrupted by his death. Such a belief stemmed from their conviction that Jesus had been raised up from death by God. The origin of this extraordinary belief must remain unknown to us.[2] What is known is that certain of Jesus' disciples became so convinced that he had risen from the dead that they were able to communicate their conviction to others, who in turn felt that they, too, had had a corroborative experience.[3] But one feature of this belief, which is very important but often overlooked, is that Jesus was not thought to have been resurrected to resume his life on earth. The Gospels do contain evidence of belief in the resuscitation of the dead to continue their former lives, which presumably terminated later in death: Lazarus and the Widow of Nain's son are the most notable examples.[4] But the resurrection of Jesus was rather of the order of that ascribed to the ancient Egyptian mortuary god, Osiris. As the Egyptian texts show, the resurrection of Osiris was conceived very realistically; yet, despite the emphasis

[1] The Qumrân community may constitute an exception here, in that it has been maintained that the Teacher of Righteousness, who had been killed by his enemies, was the Messiah and would be resurrected and return to fulfil his Messianic role: cf. J. M. Allegro, *The Dead Sea Scrolls*, pp. 148–50; A. Dupont-Sommer, *Les Écrits esséniens*, pp. 330–3, 371–9. Cf. K. Stendahl in *The Scrolls and the New Testament* (ed. K. Stendahl), pp. 14–17; K. G. Kuhn, *ibid.* pp. 54–64; H. H. Rowley, 'The Teacher of Righteousness and the Dead Sea Scrolls', *B.J.R.L.* 44 (1961), pp. 122–9. Even if it were certain that the Qumrân sectaries conceived of their Teacher in this way, the question would still remain how they related this belief to their political outlook; and here we are faced with the same problem as that with which we are concerned regarding the fate of the Jerusalem Church: both the Christian and Qumrân communities disappeared during the war of A.D. 66–70.

[2] Goguel's comment upon the Resurrection-faith sums up a historian's evaluation of the issue: 'L'Église a exprimé et justifié cette foi dans un cycle de récits qui vont de la mort de Jésus à son ascension. La relation entre la foi et les récits est moins simple que la tradition ne l'a cru. Les récits ne sont pas seulement le fondement de la foi; ils en sont aussi le produit et l'expression et en même temps la défense' (*La naissance du christianisme*, p. 41).

[3] Paul's *traditio* in I Cor. xv. 3–7 is set forth in a chronological sequence which, in its first three initial stages, is a significant catena of an expanding body of witnesses: Cephas, the Twelve, five hundred brethren. Cf. Bultmann, *Gesch. d. synop. Tradition*, p. 312.

[4] Luke vii. 11–15; John xi. 1–44, xii. 2.

upon its actuality, Osiris did not resume his *pre-mortem* life, but became the ruler of the *duat*, the realm of the dead.[1] This *religions-geschichtliche* comparison is useful, since it provides an instructive parallel to the primitive Christian belief in the resurrection of Jesus. Although the intensity of the Resurrection experience inspired belief in the physical resuscitation of the crucified Jesus, no claim was made that he was continuing to live on earth.[2] The story of the Ascension in Acts undoubtedly witnesses to the conviction that, despite the reality of his Resurrection, the physical presence of Jesus had been withdrawn from this world.[3]

Whatever the nature of the experiences which convinced the disciples that Jesus had been resurrected, the problem of his death, if he were indeed the Messiah, still remained. His death had left his Messianic role unfulfilled. How was this shocking contradiction of all that was expected of God's Anointed One, who was to restore Israel, to be explained, if Jesus, being the Messiah, could have been killed by the Romans, the oppressors of Israel? The Crucifixion actually presented a twofold problem to the disciples of Jesus; for they, despite their Resurrection experiences, still had to explain to themselves why it had happened, and they had also to explain it to their fellow-countrymen, if they were to present Jesus to them as the Messiah with any hope of success.

We can fortunately trace in the New Testament documents the way in which an answer was found. A specially illuminating passage occurs in the story of the encounter of the two disciples with the Risen Jesus on the way to Emmaus, to which reference has already been made. After the disciples had told the Unknown Stranger why they were so sad, he is represented as replying in reproof and instruction: ' "O foolish men, and slow of heart to believe all that the prophets have spoken! Was it not necessary that the Christ should suffer these things and enter into his glory?" And beginning with Moses and all the prophets, he interpreted to them in all the scriptures the things concerning himself.'[4] In other words, the claim is made that the crucifixion of Jesus was certainly not an objection to his being the Messiah, for such suffering had actually been fore-told in the scriptures, if one had the insight to see it. The fact that

---

[1] Cf. Brandon, *Man and his Destiny*, pp. 36–7, and *History, Time and Deity*, pp. 23–4.

[2] Note the emphasis on the physical reality of the Risen Jesus in Luke xxiv. 36–43; John xx. 24–9.

[3] Cf. Acts i. 11. [4] Luke xxiv. 25–7: cf. Acts iii. 18.

it is the Risen Lord who has to show how the scriptures are to be interpreted to this end is significant. It indicates that the idea of the death of the Messiah had hitherto been unknown, and that scriptural attestation had been found only after the Crucifixion.[1]

It is patent, therefore, that the texts which have become in subsequent Christian tradition the classic oracles foretelling the passion and death of Christ, had first been interpreted in this manner by the early disciples, seeking to justify their faith in the Messiahship of the crucified Jesus. The Acts of the Apostles affords a very instructive example of the exegesis which achieved this end. It occurs in the story of the conversion of the Ethiopian Eunuch, whom the evangelist Philip encounters on his way from Jerusalem.[2] Philip finds the Eunuch perplexed about the meaning of the famous passage in Isaiah concerning the Suffering Servant of Yahweh. Philip's opening question and the Eunuch's reply clearly set the scene for the ensuing exegesis: 'Do you understand what you are reading?' 'How can I, unless some one guides me?' The passage of Isaiah to be explained is that in which the Servant is likened to 'a sheep led to the slaughter'. The Eunuch asks for the identity of the mysterious Sufferer: 'About whom, pray, does the prophet say this, about himself or about some one else?' The identification is made clear in the following verse: 'Then Philip opened his mouth, and beginning with this scripture he told the good news (εὐηγγελίσατο) of Jesus.'[3]

The removal of the objection that the death of Jesus negated his Messianic character, by such scriptural exegesis, did not, however, touch the problem that Jesus had not 'restored the kingdom to Israel' before his death and that he was now no longer on the earth. The only solution possible was taken: since Jesus was truly the Messiah, then he would return again to the world to complete his Messianic task. But, when he did return, it would be with supernatural power and on the clouds of heaven.[4] His return, too, was imminent; for the Roman yoke grew ever more unbearable and its abolition could not long be delayed.[5]

The idea of the return from the dead of some prophetic figure, to

[1] See Mark ix. 32; cf. Taylor, *St Mark*, p. 403.
[2] Acts viii. 26–39.
[3] Cf. Bruce, *Acts of the Apostles*, pp. 192–3.
[4] Mark xiii. 26 (cf. ix. 1); Matt. xxv. 31, xxvii. 64. Cf. T. F. Glasson, 'The Reply to Caiaphas (Mark xiv. 62)', *N.T.S.* VII (1960–1), 88–93.
[5] It is likely that the complaint of the martyred dead in Rev. vi. 10 goes back to a Jewish source: cf. Charles, *Revelation of St. John*, I, 175–6; E. Lohmeyer, *Die Offenbarung des Johannes* (Tübingen, 1926), pp. 60–1.

fulfil an eschatological mission, was not unknown at this time. The Gospels provide evidence of such current belief: Herod Antipas thought that Jesus was John the Baptist *redivivus*,[1] and the return of Elijah, to 'restore all things', was commonly expected[2]—this latter belief being transformed among the Zealots into an expectation of a Phinehas *redivivus*, as we have noted.[3] The Jewish Christian belief was distinctive, in that it conceived of a Messiah *redivivus* in the person of the Risen Jesus. He would return to 'restore the kingdom to Israel', which necessarily implied the overthrow of the Roman government.[4] To await and prepare for this glorious event was the treasured duty of his followers, under the leadership of James, who thus, during this period of waiting, acted as the vicegerent of his brother, whom Yahweh had chosen to be his Anointed One for the deliverance of Israel.[5]

To this presentation of Jesus the significance of his crucifixion was conveniently adapted. For Jews, the only problem that his death at the hands of the Romans caused was its apparent contradiction of his Messianic role. But when scriptural warranty had been found for the death of the Messiah, the fact itself could be interpreted to reinforce the case, which the Jewish Christians presented to their compatriots, for recognising Jesus as the Messiah. Jesus had died as a martyr for Israel and also for Israel's sins. He had come as the Messiah to save his people; but they had failed to respond, so that he had been betrayed to the pro-Roman aristocracy and the Roman procurator. A reminiscence of this interpretation is preserved in a speech to the Jews of Jerusalem, attributed by the author of Acts to Peter: 'But you denied the Holy and Righteous One, and asked for a murderer to be granted to you, and killed the Author of life, whom God raised from the dead. To this we are witnesses...And now, brethren, I know that you acted in ignorance, as did also your rulers. But what God foretold by the mouth of all the prophets, that his Christ should suffer, he thus fulfilled.'[6] Consequently, the tradi-

---

[1] Mark vi. 14. Cf. Taylor, *St Mark*, p. 309.

[2] Mark ix. 11–12. Cf. Klausner, *Jesus of Nazareth*, pp. 243–4.

[3] See pp. 44–5.

[4] Cf. Schürer, *G.J.V.* II, 532–6; Bruce, *Acts of the Apostles*, p. 70.

[5] Cf. Acts ii. 36: note especially the nationalist address: ἀσφαλῶς οὖν γινωσκέτω πᾶς οἶκος Ἰσραήλ... Cf. Bruce, *Acts of the Apostles*, p. 96.

[6] Acts iii. 14–18. It is significant that, in *vv.* 19–21, repentance will induce (ὅπως) God to send Jesus as the Messiah (ἀποστείλῃ τὸν προκεχειρισμένον ὑμῖν Χριστὸν Ἰησοῦν). Cf. *B.C.* IV, 37; C. H. Dodd, *The Apostolic Preaching and its Developments* (London, 1944), p. 23.

tion developed, as the *credo* in 1 Cor. xv attests, that 'Christ died for our sins in accordance with the scriptures (κατὰ τὰς γραφάς) '.[1]

Such an interpretation of Jesus and the significance of his death was made completely within terms of Jewish hopes and aspirations. Jesus had come the first time, 'a prophet mighty in deed and word', to 'redeem Israel'; but the nation had grievously frustrated his Messianic role through ignorance and sin, so that he had died, 'according to the scriptures', a martyr to Roman hate and Jewish blindness. Yet Yahweh would fulfil his promise of redemption, and vindicate his Messiah, by sending him back, with power and glory, to 'restore the kingdom' to a repentant Israel, for whose repentance and fitness it was the task of the Church of Jerusalem to prepare. Hence, both the Messianic vocation of Jesus and the meaning of his crucifixion concerned the destiny of Israel, seen in the context of its bondage to the impious power of heathen Rome. This interpretation, accordingly, constituted the 'gospel' of the Jerusalem Church, and as such it conflicted radically with the 'gospel' which Paul believed had been entrusted by God to him, for the evangelisation of the Gentiles.

In the 'gospel' of the Jerusalem Christians it is obvious that the Gentiles could have no part. Indeed, the end which that 'gospel' had in view, namely, the vindication of Israel, implied both the overthrow of Rome and the punishment of the Gentiles.[2] Jesus was the Messiah of Israel, who had been done to death by the Romans as a menace to their rule. His death was thus a martyrdom for Israel, witnessing to Yahweh's purpose for Israel as his holy and elect people against Roman oppression and Jewish obduracy. Paul had been scandalised, as other Jews were, before his conversion, with this Jewish Christian doctrine of a 'crucified Messiah', and he had taken practical action to suppress it.[3] His subsequent assertion, that his conversion was not due to the Jewish Christians and that he had received his 'gospel' directly from God, attests, together with an abundance of other evidence, that Paul recognised how profoundly his interpretation of Jesus differed from that of the original

---

[1] I Cor. xv. 3. Cf. Brandon, *Fall of Jerusalem*, p. 77, n. 3; Bultmann, *Theology of the New Testament*, I, 42, 82.

[2] It is significant that the Last Judgement in Matt. xxv. 31 ff. begins with the Gentiles assembled before the Messiah of Israel. Cf. Klostermann, *Matthäusevangelium*, p. 205; Brandon, *Man and his Destiny*, p. 210.

[3] Gal. i. 13, 23. Cf. Brandon, *Fall of Jerusalem*, pp. 69–70; see also p. 177, n. 2, above.

disciples of Jesus.[1] His depreciatory references to knowledge of Christ 'according to the flesh' (κατὰ σάρκα) clearly indicate his defensive repudiation of the 'gospel' of the Jerusalem Church, which was based upon 'eyewitness' knowledge, which Paul had not shared, of the historical Jesus, whom the Romans had crucified for sedition.[2]

When, as a result of mystical experience, Paul became convinced that the crucified Jesus, whose followers he had persecuted, was, in some transcendental manner, alive, he did not, however, accept those disciples' evaluation of their Master.[3] Believing that his conversion was due to the direct interposition of God, he tells us that he kept away from Jerusalem.[4] He gives no explanation why, at this moment of great spiritual crisis in his life, he deliberately refrained from seeking the help of the original disciples of Jesus. Evidently he had to interpret his new experience to himself, and it would seem that instinctively he sought to do this independently of 'those who were apostles before him'.[5] In this process of interpretation, Paul clearly found concepts, familiar to him through his Hellenistic culture, more meaningful than those of traditional Judaism. His attention concentrated on the significance of the Crucifixion. Starting from his former revolt against the idea of a 'crucified Messiah', he sought for some deeper meaning in the death of Jesus than its his-

[1] Gal. i. 11–17. See above, pp. 151–4; also Brandon, *Fall of Jerusalem*, chh. IV, V, VII; cf. H. G. Wood, 'The Conversion of St Paul: its Nature, Antecedents and Consequences', *N.T.S.* I (1954–5), 278–9.

[2] Cf. II Cor. v. 16. The expression κατὰ σάρκα Χριστόν has led to much debate, most of it apologetically inspired, concerning its interpretation: H. Windisch, *Der zweite Korintherbrief* (Göttingen, 1924), pp. 186–8, lists six different interpretations; see also W. Bauer, *Wörterbuch*[2], 1194–6, also 637–7a (under κατά). Cf. Lietzmann, *An die Korinther, I–II*, pp. 124–5; Nock, St Paul, p. 243; Klausner, *From Jesus to Paul*, pp. 313–15; A. Loisy, *Les mystères païens et le mystère chrétien* (Paris, 1914), pp. 242–3; Guignebert, *Jésus*, pp. 25–6, 35, 74; A. Schweitzer, *Paul and his Interpreters* (London, 1912), pp. 245–6; Goguel, *La naissance du christianisme*, pp. 254, 270–2; Schoeps, *Theologie*, pp. 425–6; Brandon, *Fall of Jerusalem*, pp. 56–7, and *History, Time and Deity*, pp. 159–72; Bultmann, *Theology of the New Testament*, I, 236–8; Manson, *Studies*, p. 224. W. Schmithals has rightly emphasised, in his recent (1962) study (*Z.N.T.W.* 53, pp. 156–8), that Paul's lack of concern about the historical Jesus is not unique but is reflected in Christian literature (apart, of course, from the Gospels) down to the time of Justin; however, he neglects to notice the significance of the fact that the 'gospel' of the Jerusalem Church incorporated the tradition of the historical Jesus and that Paul was hostile to it.

[3] See n. 1 above.   [4] Gal. i. 15–17.

[5] Gal. i. 17: πρὸς τοὺς πρὸ ἐμοῦ ἀποστόλους...

torical cause, namely, Roman action against a person deemed dangerous to their government. He found it in an esoteric imagery which endowed it with a transcendental significance. Turning from the Jewish concept of salvation as the redemption of Israel from heathen oppression, Paul conceived of mankind, as a whole, being in a state of perdition through its subjection to the daemonic powers which ruled the universe. Salvation, to him, was the rescue of all men, Jews and Gentiles, from this parlous condition; not the freeing of the Jewish nation from its bondage to Rome. This universal salvation, he believed, had been planned by God before the aeons, and it was accomplished by a pre-existent divine being's incarnation in the person of Jesus, in order to deceive the daemonic powers into exceeding their rights by crucifying him.[1] Thus, in Paul's 'gospel', Jesus was transformed from the Messiah of Israel into the divine Saviour of all mankind. The logic of this conception, moreover, deprived the Jews of their cherished spiritual status as the Elect People of God; for they, like the rest of mankind, were in a common state of perdition, needing the same redemption as the Gentiles.[2] The universalism of Paul's 'gospel' explains his claim that God had so revealed his Son to him, in order that he might present him in a manner intelligible to the Gentiles.[3] It also explains the action of the Jerusalem Church in seeking so strenuously to supplant Paul's 'gospel' with their own, and in repudiating Paul's claim to be an apostle.

To the Jewish Christians Paul's teaching outraged their deepest convictions. That the tragic death of their Master, the Messiah of Israel, at the hands of the hated Romans, should be presented as a divine act to save the Gentiles from the perdition they so richly deserved, was, in their eyes, tantamount to blasphemy.[4] Moreover, for such an interpretation to become known to their fellow-Jews, and for themselves to be regarded as responsible for it, was obviously

---

[1] I Cor. ii. 6–8; cf. Col. ii. 13–15, 20. Cf. Bultmann, *Urchristentum*, pp. 211–12, 219; Werner, *Die Entstehung des christlichen Dogmas*, p. 238 (E.T. p. 95); A. Grillmeier, *Christ in Christian Tradition from the Apostolic Age to Chalcedon* (London, 1965), p. 15; Brandon, *Time and Mankind*, pp. 213–14, and *History, Time and Deity*, pp. 166–9.

[2] Rom. iii. 9, 23–5. Cf. W. Sanday and A. C. Headlam, *The Epistle to the Romans* (Edinburgh, 1900), pp. 76, 84–6.

[3] Gal. i. 16, ii. 8; cf. Rom. xi. 13.

[4] Paul was obviously very acutely aware of what the logic of his doctrine meant to Jews, when writing to the Christian community at Rome, which seems to have been predominantly Jewish: cf. Rom. ix. 30–3, xi. 1, 11, 15, 17–36.

very dangerous for the Jerusalem Christians. From the Jewish point of view, such a presentation of the death of Jesus was not only theologically outrageous, it amounted to apostasy of a most shocking kind, involving both race and religion.[1] The fear that inspired the reaction of the Jerusalem leaders against Paul, and the action which they took to vindicate their own loyalty to Judaism, are significantly indicated in the following passage from Paul's Epistle to the Galatians:

> It is those who want to make a good showing in the flesh that would compel you to be circumcised, and only in order that they may not be persecuted for the Cross of Christ...But far be it from me to boast (καυχᾶσθαι), except in the cross of our Lord Jesus Christ, by which the world has been crucified to me, and I to the world. For neither circumcision counts for anything, nor uncircumcision, but a new creature (καινὴ κτίσις).[2]

Evidently, whatever truth there may be about the decision made at the so-called Council of Jerusalem,[3] the Jerusalem Christians were certainly, on Paul's evidence, demanding the circumcision of his Gentile converts, and their reason for so doing, according to Paul, was fear of persecution for the cross of Christ. Since the circumcision of Gentile converts was not likely to save the Jewish Christians from persecution by the Roman authorities, the action can only have had a Jewish reference.[4] No more effective demon-

---

[1] The accusation cited by James on the occasion of Paul's last visit to Jerusalem (Acts xxi. 21), though not strictly accurate regarding Paul's policy about circumcision, reveals an appreciation of the subversive nature of Paul's teaching from the Jewish point of view. It is significant also that Paul was accused of bringing Gentiles into the Temple (Acts xxi. 28). Cf. A. Deissmann, *Licht vom Osten* (Tübingen, 1923), pp. 62–3.

[2] Gal. vi. 12, 14–15. Cf. Schmithals, *Paul and James*, pp. 25, 37.

[3] Acts xv. 5–29.

[4] 'Die Propagierung der Beschneidung dagegen würde sie der Verfolgung durch die Juden entheben. Denn durch sie erwiesen sie sich ja als Juden, auch wenn sie daneben den gekreuzigten Jesus als Messias verkündeten' (Schlier, *Der Brief an die Galater*, p. 280). T.W. Manson suggested (*Studies*, p. 164, n. 1) that Gal. vi. 12 indicates that an attempt was being made to shelter behind Judaism, as a *religio licita*, by circumcising converts. This scarcely seems likely in view of the great abhorrence in which Jewish circumcision was held by Gentiles ('mutilare genitalia', according to Spartianus, *Hadrian*, 14): it had been one of the charges Apion had made against the Jews (Josephus, *contra Apionem*, II, 137, 141, 143–4). Indeed, to submit to circumcision would more probably have brought trouble on Gentile converts from the Roman government: Antoninus Pius forbade the circumcision of Gentile converts to Judaism ('in non ejusdem religionis qui hoc fecerit, castrantis poena irrogatur', *Digest*, xlviii. 8. 11 pr.), as did

stration of their loyalty to Judaism could have been given to their compatriots by the Jerusalem Christians than to require the circumcision of Paul's Gentile converts in addition to repudiating his authority and teaching.

There is cogent evidence that the Jewish Christian campaign against Paul was successful. Paul's position had evidently been made so untenable that he was moved, against the advice of the Holy Spirit according to Acts, to go to Jerusalem to seek some *modus vivendi* from James and the elders of the Church there.[1] James, astutely, demanded public proof of Paul's Jewish orthodoxy.[2] The sequel was disastrous for Paul, and it conveniently disembarrassed the Jerusalem community of his compromising presence. From the time of his arrest in the Temple, Paul was effectively removed from his pastoral and missionary activity.[3] What the outcome of his appeal to Caesar was is unknown; there is much reason for believing that it was not successful.[4] However that may be, the author of Acts,

also Septimius Severus (Spartianus, *Sept. Sev.* 17). It is unlikely that the attitude of the Roman authorities had notably changed in this matter between the first and second centuries A.D. It is not without significance in this connection that Metilius, the commander of the Roman garrison of the Antonia, saved his life by offering to the Jewish insurgents to be circumcised (Jos. *War*, II. 454). Cf. Schürer, *G.J.V.* III, 76, 418–19.

[1] Acts xx. 23, xxi. 9–12. Cf. Brandon, *Fall of Jerusalem*, pp. 133–4, 148–50.

[2] Acts xxi. 20–4. E. Haenchen ('Judentum und Christentum in der Apostelgeschichte', *Z.N.T.W.* 54, 1963, p. 181) raises an interesting point about the gift of money which Paul brought with him on this occasion: 'Konnten denn Jakobus und die Ältesten die große Geldspende annehmen, mit der Paulus erschienen war, ohne bei ihrer eigenen Gemeinde und den Juden den Eindruck zu erwecken, daß sie sich kaufen ließen?'

[3] Acts xxi. 33 ff. Cf. Brandon, *Fall of Jerusalem*, pp. 152, 214–15. 'Damit läßt Lukas den Vorhang vor der Urgemeinde fallen' (Haenchen, *Z.N.T.W.* 54, 1963, p. 181). Beyschlag (in *Z.N.T.W.* 56, 1965, pp. 159–62) sees behind Acts xxi a Jewish Christian tradition concerning James which the author of Acts has drastically revised to suit his own thesis.

[4] 'Readers of Acts would feel no surprise if after the gloomy predictions and close escapes it continued to carry Paul's case to a fatal outcome. Their surprise is that it leads to no outcome at all. And certainly no other evidence that we possess is authoritative enough to disprove that as a matter of fact the two years in Rome were followed by the Apostle's crown of martyrdom' (H. J. Cadbury in *B.C.* v, 338; see also his survey of the issue, pp. 319–38). Cf. *B.C.* IV, 349–50; Bruce, *Acts*, pp. 480–1, and 'St Paul in Rome', *B.J.R.L.* 46 (1964), pp. 342–5; Manson, *Studies*, pp. 66–7. The evidence of Paul's farewell speech to the elders of the Church at Ephesus seems conclusive: see below.

who did know what had happened, hints at the ruin of Paul's work after his arrest at Jerusalem. He does this in the farewell speech to the elders of the church at Ephesus, which he represents Paul as making when *en route* for his last visit to Jerusalem:

And now, behold, I am going to Jerusalem, bound in the Spirit, not knowing what shall befall me there; except that the Holy Spirit testifies to me in every city that imprisonment and affliction await me...And now, behold, I know that all you among whom I have gone about preaching the kingdom will see my face no more...Take heed to yourselves and to all the flock, in which the Holy Spirit has made you guardians, to feed the church of the Lord which he obtained with his own blood. I know that after my departure fierce wolves will come in among you, not sparing the flock; and from among your own selves will arise men speaking perverse things, to draw away the disciples after them.[1]

This passage surely reveals, from the viewpoint of a Pauline Christian, what had happened after Paul was removed from direct contact with his Gentile converts. The 'fierce wolves', which entered in among them, are undoubtedly the emissaries of the Jerusalem Church, which intensified its propaganda when Paul could no longer combat it personally. Those who rose up in the Gentile churches, 'speaking perverse things, to draw away the disciples after them', were probably those who notably supported the Jerusalem 'gospel' and spoke against Paul's teaching. Since the propagation of the Jerusalem version of the faith had made such progress as Paul's great perturbation over it testifies, its success must have been even greater when he was no longer present to oppose it. If it had continued, Paul's version of Christianity would surely have perished, and the movement which stemmed from Jesus of Nazareth would have remained a small sect, with a peculiar Messianic belief, within the body of Judaism. But it was not to be so; for the raising of the standard of revolt against Rome in A.D. 66 precipitated the ruin of the Jewish nation, in which the Jerusalem Church disappeared. How critical the future of Christianity was, during the decade from Paul's arrest until war ended the career of the Jerusalem Church, is significantly attested by the state of the *Corpus Paulinum*. For the evidence of loss and damage, which Paul's writings sustained until a definitive attempt was made to collect and preserve them, points

---

[1] Acts xx. 22–30. Note also the significance of *v.* 38, which tells of the Ephesian elders, 'sorrowing most of all for the word which he had spoken, that they should behold his face no more'. Surely the author of Acts could not have written this, if he had known that Paul had later visited Ephesus after being released in Rome.

to a period when his letters were not treasured as memorials of a revered apostle—a period that must surely have coincided with the eclipse of his reputation from the time of his imprisonment until his rehabilitation consequent on the destruction of Jerusalem in A.D. 70 and the disappearance of the Church there.[1]

To complete our survey of the evidence, such as it is, that bears upon the teaching and outlook of the primitive Christian community of Jerusalem, we must notice that which Hegesippus may provide. We have already examined his account of the death of James, evaluating it as evidence of the tradition current in second-century Palestine, and noting therein certain indications of an earlier tradition.[2] Whatever the sources of Hegesippus' information, it is certainly significant that he represents James as a highly venerated figure among the Jews of Jerusalem, and that, on the occasion which led to his death, he had actually been appealed to by the Jewish leaders to use his influence to restrain the people, 'because they were straying after Jesus as though he were the Messiah'.[3] That the help of James should have been sought in this way is so amazing, in the light of all that we otherwise know, that, unless we dismiss the account as a complete fabrication, we can only assume that Hegesippus gives a garbled version of a situation which he had not rightly understood. If the Jewish leaders (their identity is problematic)[4] did thus invoke the aid of James, knowing him to be the head of the Christian community, it could scarcely have been so that he might publicly refute the belief that Jesus was the Messiah. That belief was the very *raison d'être* of his position as leader of the Jerusalem

---

[1] Cf. Brandon, *Fall of Jerusalem*, chh. VII and XI.

[2] See above, pp. 121–4. The account of the death of James in the *Clementine Recognitions*, I. lxvi–lxx, is remarkably similar to that of Hegesippus on a number of points. The problem of the sources underlying the Pseudo-Clementine writings is still debated. If the view of H. J. Schoeps (*Theologie u. Geschichte des Judenchristentums*, pp. 381–4, 417, 431, 435, 441, 446–7) could be substantiated about a lost Ebionite *Acts of the Apostles*, Paul would be responsible, according to *Urgemeinde* tradition, for the 'Mordanschlag' on James: cf. Brandon, *Fall of Jerusalem*, pp. 99, 262–4. For a detailed comparison of the accounts of Ps. Clem. *Rec.* and Hegesippus see Beyschlag in *Z.N.T.W.* 56 (1965), pp. 150–5.

[3] Eusebius, *Hist. eccl.* II. xxiii. 10: ἐπεὶ ἐπλανήθη εἰς Ἰησοῦν, ὡς αὐτοῦ ὄντος τοῦ Χριστοῦ. Cf. Schoeps, *Theologie*, p. 414.

[4] Cf. Brandon, *Fall of Jerusalem*, pp. 97–9; see above, pp. 123–4; Telfer in *H.Th.R.* LIII (1960), 144, 153.

Christians, and it would be incredible for them to have thought that he would have been willing to repudiate this belief in public, to help them, as Hegesippus describes. If, however, as we earlier suggested, the need was to quieten the people, who had been stirred by some happening to a dangerous pitch of excitement, believing that the return of Jesus as the Messiah was imminent, an intelligible situation can be made out. It would not have been impossible for James's help to be sought in this way, if it were felt that he would recognise that the popular expectation, centring on Jesus, at that particular time was both unjustified and dangerous. The Gospels provide evidence that warnings had to be issued to the Christian community against a too fervent expectation of the imminence of the *Parousia*.[1] On this occasion, however, if Hegesippus is to be believed, James did not attempt to abate the people's excitement, but rather increased it by strongly testifying to the Messianic role of Jesus and the certainty of his *Parousia*. His declaration, significantly, evoked from the crowd the Messianic salutation, charged with political meaning: 'Hosanna to the Son of David.'[2]

If a real historical situation does underlie the patently inaccurate account of Hegesippus, it may be related to the dissension caused by the oppressive action of the high priest Ananus against the lower clergy, as we have seen.[3] During the procuratorial interregnum of A.D. 62, with Zealot activity growing throughout the country and infecting the lower priesthood, Messianic expectation, centring on Jesus, might well have been a factor, among others, which led Ananus to remove James, as being the chief leader of a movement which threatened the stability of the Jewish state and the position of those who held high office in it.

From this disparate evidence, indirect, circumstantial and problematic as much of it is, there emerges, nevertheless, a consistent and intelligible picture of the beliefs and outlook of those original Jewish disciples of Jesus who formed the Mother Church of Jerusalem. Drawing upon the twofold witness of Paul and Acts to the continuing and zealous attachment of these disciples to the faith and practice of Judaism, we have been able to reconstruct the lost 'gospel' of the Jerusalem Church in a form that makes sense of the tensions, apologetic and controversies that characterise Paul's

---

[1] E.g. Mark xiii. 5–6, 21–3, 32–3; cf. Acts i. 7.

[2] Eusebius, *Hist. eccl.* II. xxiii. 13–14.

[3] See above, pp. 118 ff.

Epistles and show beneath the idealised portrait of Acts. We have discerned a community of Jews who, recognising in Jesus the Messiah of Israel, surmounted the shock of his death at the hands of the Romans. Convinced that God had raised him from death, these disciples' faith in his Messiahship was intensified, taking the form of an urgent expectation that he would soon return, with supernatural power, to fulfil his Messianic task of 'restoring the kingdom to Israel'. In anticipation of that glorious event, they believed that it was their vocation to prepare their fellow-Jews by presenting Jesus to them as the Messiah, by urging them to repent of those sins which had caused him to die a martyr's death to Roman cruelty and Jewish obduracy, and by exhorting them to be worthy of divine redemption. When faced with the unexpected and unwelcomed fact of Gentile adherents to their movement, they required their conformation to certain Jewish laws, even seeking to have them circumcised as a guarantee against Paul's antinomianism. Thus they continued as zealous Jews, distinguished from their compatriots only by their expectation that Jesus would soon return to earth as the Messiah. Their movement was given both dynastic continuity and effective leadership by James, the brother of Jesus, and on his death, if later tradition is to be trusted, the succession passed to another relative, Symeon.[1] The reputation of the movement seems to have stood high in Jewish religious circles, and it attracted the allegiance of both priests and Pharisees, and its members merited the description of 'zealots of the Torah' (ζηλωταὶ τοῦ νόμου).[2]

Although the evangelisation of the Gentiles was initiated by others, as we have seen, there is evidence that the Jerusalem Christians sought to propagate their 'gospel' among the Jewish communities outside Palestine. Whether this represented originally a definite policy of missionary endeavour, or the adventitious outcome of interest caused by Jewish pilgrims, who brought the new faith back from Jerusalem to their own communities, is not known. What is certain, for example, is that a church was established in Rome before Paul went there, and that it appears to have been

---

[1] Eusebius, *Hist. eccl.* III, xi; cf. xxxii. See p. 165, n. 4, above.

[2] Acts xxi. 20. G. Hoennicke (*Das Judenchristentum im ersten und zweiten Jahrhundert*, Berlin, 1908, p. 175) maintained that at this period Gentile converts outnumbered Jewish converts in the Christian Church: there is no evidence that proves this, whereas Acts suggests that the number of Jewish converts was considerable: cf. Brandon, *Fall of Jerusalem*, p. 28, n. 3.

originally Jewish in character.[1] However such a movement may have started, it would seem that the Jerusalem leaders felt that their obligation to prepare Israel for the return of the Messiah Jesus involved their evangelising the Jews of the Diaspora. Peter seems to have taken a leading part in this: Acts records his going to 'another place',[2] and witnesses to his absence from Jerusalem on the occasion of Paul's last visit there;[3] in his First Epistle to the Corinthians, Paul seems to indicate that Peter had been in Corinth;[4] later tradition also records Peter's presence at Antioch and his martyrdom in Rome.[5]

In the early Christian records there is a strange absence of reference to the beginnings of Christianity in Alexandria or other places in Egypt. The record of Acts is particularly notable in this connection. It purports to describe the spread of Christianity from its tiny beginnings in Jerusalem until Paul presents it in Rome, the metropolis of the empire.[6] It traces out the movement as being exclusively one in a northerly direction from Palestine into Asia Minor, then westwards to Greece, and ultimately to Italy and Rome. Are we to conclude, therefore, that Christianity was not carried during this period to Alexandria and other places in Egypt? Such a conclusion would seem to be most improbable; for Alexandria was the second largest city in the Roman empire, with an immense Jewish population,[7] and cultural relations between Egypt

---

[1] Cf. Weiss, *Earliest Christianity*, I, 360–2; Sanday and Headlam, *Epistle to the Romans*, pp. xxv–xxxiv. The statement here is not affected if the Epistle to the Romans was not originally addressed to the church in Rome, as T. W. Manson has suggested (in *Peake's Commentary*[2], 815 c–e; *Studies*, pp. 227–30).

[2] Acts xii. 17: see below, pp. 196–8, 297–9.

[3] An obviously very different situation existed in the Jerusalem Church on the occasion of this visit from that depicted in the early chapters of Acts, where Peter was evidently the leader of the community. It is incredible that the author of Acts should have written as he does in xxi. 18 ff., if Peter had also been present.

[4] I Cor. i. 12: see p. 164, n. 2 above.

[5] Cf. Lietzmann, *Gesch. d. alten Kirche*, I, 109, 134; Cullmann, *Petrus*[2], pp. 59, 78–148 (E.T. pp. 52, 70–132). Paul records Peter's presence at Antioch (Gal. ii. 11).

[6] This is very clearly evident on maps of Paul's missionary journeys.

[7] Cf. H. I. Bell in *C.A.H.* x, 296–7; F. Oertel, *ibid.* pp. 398–400, 412. Philo estimated that there were not less than one million Jews living in Alexandria and other parts of Egypt (*In Flaccum*, 43). Cf. J. Juster, *Les Juifs dans l'Empire romain* (Paris, 1914), p. 209; Cary, *Geographical Background to Greek and Roman History*, p. 216; W. Schubart in *R.A.C.* I, 275, 277.

and Palestine had been long established and were very strong[1]—
moreover, in distance Alexandria was no farther from Jerusalem
than Antioch in Syria. Furthermore, although Acts says nothing of the
origins of Christianity in Alexandria, the fact that the faith was already
established there is incidentally admitted in a very curious context.
The author of Acts evidently thought it important to record how an
Alexandrian Jew, named Apollos, who was apparently a Christian,
had visited Ephesus and had preached in the synagogue there. Two
friends of Paul, Priscilla and Aquila, heard him and judged his
knowledge of Christianity to be defective. Consequently, 'they took
him and expounded to him the way of God more accurately (ἀκρι-
βέστερον αὐτῷ ἐξέθεντο)', after which correction and instruction
he went on to Achaia, with the commendation of Priscilla and
Aquila to the Christian communities there.[2] As a kind of sequel,
the narrative goes on to tell that, when he later visited Ephesus,
Paul found some disciples (τινας μαθητάς) there who had apparently
been converted by Apollos. When he inquired of them: 'Did you
receive the Holy Spirit when you believed?', they replied: 'No, we
have never even heard that there is a Holy Spirit.' On receiving this
disquieting answer, Paul asked a rather curious question: 'Into what,
then, were you baptized?' Their answer was: 'Into John's baptism.'
Paul proceeded to explain that John's baptism was one of repentance, and that he directed the people to believe in 'the one who
was to come after him, that is, Jesus'. The men were, accordingly,
'baptized in the name of the Lord Jesus', and after the imposition
of Paul's hands, the Holy Spirit came upon them.[3]

The whole episode, as recounted in Acts, is most extraordinary

[1] About one-third of Alexandria was in Jewish hands, and the Jewish
population of the city was wealthy and flourishing, possessing many
synagogues and enjoying many peculiar privileges: cf. H. I. Bell, *Juden und
Griechen im römischen Alexandreia* (Leipzig, 1926), pp. 10–14, and *Jews and
Christians in Egypt*, pp. 11 ff.; H. Box, *Philonis Alexandrini in Flaccum*,
pp. xx ff.; Smallwood, *Leg. ad Gaium*, pp. 4–14; Schürer, *G.J.V.* III,
20–5; W. O. E. Oesterley, 'Egypt and Israel', *The Legacy of Egypt*
(ed. S. R. K. Glanville), pp. 234–8; H. I. Bell, *Cults and Creeds in Graeco-
Roman Egypt*, pp. 25–49; R. Kasser, 'Les origines du christianisme
égyptien', *R.Th.P.* XI (1962), 11–14.
[2] Acts xviii. 24–8.
[3] xix. 1–7. Although they are only referred to as μαθητάς, the twelve men
were evidently converts of Apollos: cf. *B.C.* IV, 237; Bruce, *Acts of the
Apostles*, p. 353; G. W. H. Lampe in *Peake's Commentary*², 796 f.; Ehrhardt,
Framework of the New Testament Stories, pp. 159–60; Manson, *Studies*,
pp. 254–6.

and raises many very obvious questions. First, the introduction of the episode at this point of the narrative of Acts disrupts the sequence of attention which has been on Paul's activities, a concentration of attention that is quickly resumed again.[1] It is understandable that the author of Acts should mention Apollos, who was obviously an important personage in the Christian movement at this time, as Paul's references to him testify.[2] But in Acts Apollos makes only a brief appearance, and nothing further is said of him in the rest of the narrative. It would seem, accordingly, that the author of Acts had some special reason for thus introducing Apollos, and pointing out the strange defects in his knowledge of Christianity.

These defects are, indeed, strange and merit examination. Apollos is described as 'an eloquent man, well versed in the scriptures (δυνατὸς ὢν ἐν ταῖς γραφαῖς)'. Such a description is commendatory, as is that which follows: 'He had been instructed in the way of the Lord...'[3] Such an expression would seem to denote a properly instructed Christian, because in Acts 'the Way' (ἡ ὁδός) is an accepted term for Christian faith and practice.[4] It is surprising, therefore, when this introductory description of Apollos goes on to say that, although he was 'fervent in spirit' and 'spoke and taught accurately the things concerning Jesus', Apollos 'knew only the Baptism of John' (ἐπιστάμενος μόνον τὸ βάπτισμα 'Ιωάννου).[5] If the twelve

---

[1] Acts xviii. 23 seems to be a summary of Paul's activities given in preparation for the Apollos episode in xviii. 24–8; xix. 1 appears to be designed to take up the story of Paul again.

[2] I Cor. i. 12, iii. 4–9, 22. Although he is intent on maintaining concord between himself and Apollos, Paul was evidently not wholly happy in his relations with him, and he admits that the Corinthians saw him and Apollos as rivals.

[3] Acts xviii. 25: οὗτος ἦν κατηχημένος τὴν ὁδὸν τοῦ Κυρίου.

[4] Cf. Acts ix. 2, xvi. 17, xviii. 26, xix. 9, 23, xxii. 4, xxiv. 14, 22; also John xiv. 4–6. The reading τὸν λόγον for τὴν ὁδὸν in Codex Bezae 'is clearly an attempt to make a hard word easier', according to J. H. Ropes, B.C. III, 178 (26). The suggestion made in B.C. IV, 233 that κατηχημένος means 'hearsay' knowledge, thereby implying an understandable degree of imperfection, is not justified in view of its use in Luke i. 4; Rom. ii. 18; I Cor. xiv. 19; Gal. vi. 6. It is, of course, most probable that κατηχημένος means 'oral instruction', as Bruce says (Acts, p. 351); however, all instruction at this period must have been oral. Cf. Guignebert, Le Christ, p. 290; Brandon, Fall of Jerusalem, p. 24, n. 3; H. J. Cadbury in B.C. II, 508–9.

[5] Acts xviii. 25. Lietzmann (Gesch. d. alten Kirche, I, 56) pertinently comments upon a significant illogicality in the Acts account here: Apollos, 'der auch nur die johanneische Taufe empfangen hat, aber doch bereits vom Geist

disciples, whom Paul met later at Ephesus, were converts of Apollos, as indeed they seem to have been, then his teaching contained nothing about the Holy Spirit, the reception of which Paul regarded as so important.[1] But now we must ask, with legitimate wonder, how Apollos could have been 'instructed in the way of the Lord' and have been able to speak and teach 'accurately the things concerning Jesus' (ἀκριβῶς τὰ περὶ τοῦ 'Ιησοῦ), and yet 'know only the Baptism of John', into which he baptised his converts.[2]

Such a description of one who was apparently a Christian is so strange, together with the fact that Paul's friends had to expound the faith more accurately to him before he could be commended to other Pauline communities, that one conclusion only is possible, namely, that the author of Acts wished to show that the Christianity of Apollos was so seriously defective from the Pauline point of view that it went no further than the baptism of John. To impute a Christianity so limited can, however, only be adjudged a denigration of the faith of a non-Pauline Christian.[3] But what kind of Christianity would the author of Acts have chosen to represent in this way? Apollos is described in the *textus receptus* of Acts as 'an Alexandrian by race' ('Αλεξανδρεὺς τῷ γένει), and the Codex Bezae adds the reading ὃς ἦν κατηχημένος ἐν τῇ πατρίδι τὸν λόγον τοῦ Κυρίου, thus preserving a tradition that he had learned his Christianity in Alexandria, which would be a natural inference from the fact that he was a native of that city.[4] The author of Acts, therefore, is writing in this manner about an Alexandrian Christian. What he says, moreover, about the deficiency of Apollos' knowledge of the faith is not to be explained by any personal dullness, because he praises the Alexandrian's learning and ability.[5] The conclusion is, accordingly, inescapable: the author of Acts took this opportunity, in introducing

getrieben als christlicher Missionar auftritt'. Cf. Guignebert, *Le Christ*, p. 293; Klausner, *From Jesus to Paul*, p. 387; W. Manson, *Jesus the Messiah* (London, 1943), p. 166.

[1] ἀλλ' οὐδ' εἰ πνεῦμα ἅγιον ἔστιν ἠκούσαμεν, xix. 2. Cf. *B.C.* IV, 237; Bruce, *Acts of the Apostles*, p. 354; Preuschen, *Apostelgeschichte*, p. 115.

[2] Acts xviii. 25. It is instructive to note the use of ἀκριβῶς in Luke i. 3; see also the use of the comparative in Acts xviii. 26, xxiii. 15, 20, xxiv. 22. Cf. *B.C.* IV, 233–4; Bauer, *Wörterbuch*[2], 50.

[3] '"the baptism of John" was a Christian term, describing the heretical baptism in Apostolic times' (Ehrhardt, *Framework of the New Testament Stories*, p. 44, n. 4).

[4] Acts xviii. 25 (Codex Bezae): in *B.C.* III, 179.

[5] ἀνὴρ λόγιος...δυνατὸς ὢν ἐν ταῖς γραφαῖς (xviii. 25).

Apollos into his narrative, to make clear to his readers the defective nature of the Christianity taught at Alexandria.[1]

According to Acts, from the Pauline standpoint, Alexandrian Christianity was defective in two ways. In its interpretation of Jesus, it went only as far as the Baptism of John. This curious evaluation must surely mean that Jesus was regarded as the Messiah only, and not as the divine Saviour of Paul's 'gospel'; for 'to teach accurately the things concerning Jesus, knowing only the Baptism of John' must, in the light of the Lukan account of John's activity, denote the Baptist's attestation of the Messianic character of Jesus, when the people were wondering whether he, John, were the Messiah.[2] That the converts of Apollos knew nothing of (a) Holy Spirit doubtless indicates that Alexandrian Christianity did not lay emphasis upon the inspiration of the Holy Spirit, which to Paul was the means *par excellence* of understanding divine truth.[3]

This denigration of Alexandrian Christianity by a Pauline Christian, together with the fact that Paul is never recorded to have visited Alexandria, surely attests to two facts of the greatest significance for our understanding of Primitive Christianity. The first is that Christianity was established at a very early date in this great city, and by missionaries other than Paul and his associates. Secondly,

[1] Cf. Brandon, *Fall of Jerusalem*, pp. 24–6, 224–5; H. C. Snape, 'The Fourth Gospel, Ephesus and Alexandria', *H.Th.R.* XLVII (1954), 4–6, 7.

[2] Luke iii. 15–17: cf. Creed, *St Luke*, pp. 53–4. The suggestion (e.g. of Meyer, *Ursprung*, III, 112) that Apollos was a member of a Johannine baptist sect cannot be seriously entertained in view of the fact that he had been 'instructed in the way of the Lord' and 'taught carefully the things concerning Jesus' (Acts xviii. 25); such language can only describe a Christian, howbeit a defective one from the Pauline standpoint. Cf. Guignebert, *Le Christ*, p. 293. T. W. Manson (*Studies*, pp. 254–7) put forward the interesting theory that Apollos was the author of the Epistle to the Hebrews. However, his attempt to represent Apollos, before his meeting with Priscilla and Aquila, as 'a Jewish revivalist' (he does not explain what such a description means), and not as a Christian, lands him into very evident difficulties when he tries to account for the curious language of Acts (*ibid.* pp. 255–6).

[3] It is not without significance that, even after his 're-education' by Paul's friends, Apollos is particularly described as 'confuting the Jews' by showing 'by the scriptures that Jesus was the Christ' (Acts xviii. 28). One can only wonder what his teaching could have been about previously, when he 'taught carefully the things concerning Jesus, knowing only the Baptism of John'. As Guignebert pertinently remarked about Apollos: 'C'est que, sans doute, il a, lui aussi, *son Évangile*, qui n'est pas tout à fait celui de Paul, ou qu'il pense autrement que lui sur la conduite à tenir à l'égard des judaïsants. Nous ne savons pas' (*Le Christ*, p. 292).

the form of Christianity current there was regarded by the Pauline Christians as so seriously defective that, before any Alexandrian Christian could be accepted among them, he had to be properly instructed, and possibly rebaptised.

Now, in view of the fact that the only other version of the faith with which Paul was in antagonism was that of the Church of Jerusalem, it seems necessary to conclude that the Christianity current at Alexandria was the same as that of Jerusalem, and that it had been established there by missionaries from the Mother Church. It is natural to wonder who might have brought the faith there from Jerusalem. In the first instance it probably came with returning pilgrims; for there is much evidence of close ties between Jerusalem and the Alexandrian Jews.[1] There is some reason also for thinking that Peter went there, either to preach or to consolidate work already established. As we have noted earlier, the author of Acts is curiously vague as to the destination of Peter, after he had escaped from the Herodian captivity. He merely says that Peter went 'to another place' (εἰς ἕτερον τόπον).[2] Since he ends his account of Peter's activity, which had formed the chief theme hitherto of his narrative, with these words, we may legitimately feel puzzled about their vagueness. From this point on, in his record of the progress of the faith, Peter no longer plays the leading role at Jerusalem, and the extant evidence points to his absence from Palestine on certain occasions.[3] It might, accordingly, be expected that, in finishing his account of this leading apostle, the author of Acts would have given some better indication of where he went than is contained in the words 'to another place'. Indeed, such vagueness in such a context excites the suspicion that the author of Acts preferred not to say where Peter went.

There are three places to which Peter might have gone, which would, understandably, have been embarrassing for the author of Acts to mention in this connection. They are Alexandria, Corinth and Rome.[4] If the Acts account is correct in representing Peter's

---

[1] As Acts vi. 9 shows, there was a synagogue of Alexandrians in Jerusalem. It is, moreover, significant that it was with these Jews particularly that Stephen, whose version of the faith obviously differed from that of the apostles, clashed. Cf. *B.C.* iv, 68; Bruce, *Acts of the Apostles*, p. 156.

[2] Acts xii. 17.   [3] See above, p. 164.

[4] Antioch was a possible destination; but if it had been the actual one, why does not Acts record the fact, since it clearly draws upon Antiochene traditions? Cf. Bruce, *Acts of the Apostles*, pp. 23–4; Cullmann, *Petrus*², pp. 41, 59 (E.T. pp. 38, 53).

departure from Jerusalem as caused by the repressive action taken by Agrippa I, it is unlikely that the apostle would have fled in the first instance to either Corinth or Rome.[1] Alexandria was nearer, and more easy of access from Judaea; it was, moreover, the traditional place of retreat for Jewish refugees.[2] If a Christian community were already established in the city, Peter's presence would undoubtedly have greatly reinforced it. Thus, the church in Alexandria would have been a daughter church of Jerusalem, its ties being greatly strengthened by Peter's sojourn there.[3] If, as we shall see, there are reasons for believing that the Gospel of Matthew originated in Alexandria, the unique status accorded therein to Peter is intelligible: in this most Jewish of the Gospels, Peter is the apostle upon whom the Church is founded by Christ.[4] The form of the faith taught there would naturally have been that of the Jerusalem Church, which, as we have seen, regarded Jesus as essentially the Messiah, who would soon return to restore the kingdom to Israel. This would mean that the Alexandrian Christians, like those of Jerusalem, would have zealously maintained the validity of Judaism, into which they integrated their new faith in the Messiahship of Jesus. It is, accordingly, understandable that, as Paul insinuated that the Jerusalem Christians taught 'another gospel', which concerned 'another Jesus' and involved a 'different Spirit',[5] so a Pauline Christian could describe a member of the church of Alexandria as knowing the faith only as far as the Baptism of

---

[1] To reach either of these places from Jerusalem would have meant a sea passage from a Palestinian port or a long land journey, traversing first the whole of Agrippa's kingdom, northwards, with its attendant dangers of arrest.

[2] On the significance of the Flight of the Holy Family to Egypt (Matt. ii. 13 ff.) see below, pp. 295 ff.

[3] Cf. Brandon, *Fall of Jerusalem*, pp. 210–12, 224–5. W. D. Davies (*The Setting of the Sermon on the Mount*, p. 318), desiring to prove that Matthew originated in 'Syria, at Antioch, or in Phoenicia' (p. 293), summarily dismisses the case set forth in *Fall of Jerusalem*, ch. XII, for the Alexandrian origin of Matthew by referring to the review of the book by C. F. D. Moule in *J.T.S.* (new series), III, 106–8; but in this review the Alexandrian attribution is merely described as 'a quite amazing suggestion' (p. 107), without any reason being given for this opinion or any refutation of the attribution being made. For an extended critique of Dr Davies's book see the present writer's article 'Matthaean Christianity' in *The Modern Churchman*, VIII (1965), 152–61. See below, pp. 288 ff.

[4] Cf. Brandon, *Fall of Jerusalem*, pp. 232–6. See below, pp. 297 ff.

[5] See pp. 151 ff.

John.[1] It explains also why Paul never visited Alexandria, but worked far away from it on the other side of the Mediterranean Sea.

The establishment of Christianity among the great Jewish population of Alexandria was a natural undertaking for the Jerusalem Christians, intent as they were on preparing Israel for the *Parousia* of the Messiah Jesus. The propagation of the faith in this city, in which there was strong anti-Semite feeling, may well have provoked those disturbances to which the emperor Claudius refers in his celebrated Letter to the Alexandrians.[2] Nor is it without significance that Peter's influence at Corinth led to the formation of both a 'Peter' and a 'Christ' party in opposition to Paul,[3] and that Claudius had to expel the Jews from Rome owing to Messianic disturbances there.[4] Accordingly, it would not be too speculative, in the light of our knowledge of Jewish Christianity, to think that Peter's preaching in Alexandria, Corinth and Rome stirred Messianic excitement in those places, provoking in turn anti-Semitic reaction among the Gentile populations, which was a matter of some concern to the imperial government.

The picture that finally emerges of Jewish Christianity, from our examination of this diverse and complex material, is that of a body of zealous Jews, who were distinguished from their compatriots by their belief that Jesus of Nazareth, whom the Romans had crucified, would shortly return, with supernatural power, as the Messiah of Israel. They regarded it as their duty, under the leadership of the brother of Jesus, to prepare their fellow-Jews, both in Judaea and elsewhere, for this supreme event. Such being their belief and out-

[1] See above, p. 192. Cf. H. C. Snape in *H.Th.R.* XLVII, 4–6, 7, and 'The Composition of the Lukan Writings: a Re-assessment', *H.Th.R.* LIII, 44–5; J. Daniélou and H. Marrou, *The Christian Centuries*, E.T. (London, 1964), I, 45.

[2] Cf. *Select Papyri*, II (ed. A. S. Hunt and C. C. Edgar), 86, 87; see above, pp. 96 ff.

[3] See above, p. 197. The formation of a 'Christ' party in the Corinthian church was probably due to the emphasis upon the Messiahship of Jesus, in the Jewish Christian propaganda there, with which Peter was associated. Those Corinthians who were especially impressed by this new emphasis styled themselves 'Christ's' ('Ἐγὼ δὲ Χριστοῦ), I Cor. i. 12. Cf. Brandon, *Fall of Jerusalem*, pp. 140, 142.

[4] Suetonius, *Claudius*, 25; Acts xviii. 2; Dio Cassius, LX. 6: cf. Momigliano, *L'Opera dell'Imperatore Claudio*, p. 76; V. M. Scramuzza in *B.C.* v, 295–6; Bruce in *B.J.R.L.* 44 (1962), pp. 315–18.

look, we now have to face the question of what was their attitude to the Romans who ruled their nation, and to those who organised resistance to the Roman rule as the duty of all loyal Jews. Only by some satisfactory answer to this question shall we be in a position to evaluate the tradition which the Jerusalem Christians preserved of Jesus, and upon which the Evangelists later drew.

From our investigation so far one conclusion, of basic importance, clearly emerges. It is that there was nothing, either by way of instinct or principle, that should have caused these Jewish Christians to have liked the Romans, or to have approved of their rule over Israel. Indeed, from all our knowledge of them, it would seem that their attitude towards the Romans would scarcely have differed from that of the Zealots. Both stressed the absolute sovereignty of God, and looked for divine aid to restore the kingdom to Israel.[1] To each, the Romans were heathens, who worshipped a man, the emperor, as a god. To each, the Torah and the Temple were the cherished institutions of their ancestral religion, so that each party was surely shocked at the frequent insults which the Romans offered to these objects of their devotion, and each would have feared the ever-present menace of the repetition of such an outrage as that planned by the emperor Gaius. For both parties the tribute to Caesar must have been intolerable; for it meant giving of the resources of Yahweh's Holy Land to the upkeep of the heathen rule of Caesar.[2] The founders of both movements had died at the hands of the Romans, and to Christian and Zealot alike the prospect of suffering on a Roman cross was a real and constant threat.[3] Both had cause, also, to hate the pro-Roman sacerdotal aristocracy, and both drew their adherents from the 'people of the land' and instinctively shared their hostility to the rich and powerful.[4] Both undoubtedly shared the same eschatology, which finds graphic expression in the Mat-

---

[1] The petitions of the Lord's Prayer are significant in this connection: ἐλθάτω ἡ βασιλεία σου· γενηθήτω τὸ θέλημά σου, ὡς ἐν οὐρανῷ καὶ ἐπὶ γῆς (Matt. vi. 10; cf. Luke xi. 2; *Didache*, viii. 2). Cf. K. Stendahl in *Peake's Commentary*[2], 680 d; G. D. Kilpatrick, *Origins of Gospel of Matthew*, p. 21.

[2] The test question 'Is it lawful to give tribute unto Caesar or not?' (Mark xii. 14), which Mark attributes to the Pharisees and Herodians, was obviously well known in Jewish Christian circles and represented an issue of very great concern. On Mark's reapplication of this question, in the interest of his apologetical theme, see chapter 5; see also pp. 271, 345–9.

[3] See above, pp. 57, 145.

[4] E.g. on the Christian attitude see Mark x. 24–5; Luke vi. 24; Acts ii. 44–5, iv. 32, 34–v. 11; James ii. 2–6, v. 1–6. On the Zealot attitude see above, pp. 56, 132.

thaean Gospel, where the Messiah is represented as judging the assembled Gentiles (τὰ ἔθνη);[1] and both would surely have equated Gentiles with tax collectors and sinners.[2]

Seeing, then, that there is no reason why the Jewish Christians should have differed in their attitude to the Roman rule from that taken by the Zealots, we should expect that a certain sympathy would have existed between them, in view of their identity of outlook on a number of basic issues. The fact, then, that Jesus included a Zealot among his twelve disciples,[3] and the fact that he is never recorded to have condemned the Zealots or their principles, constitute evidence of the greatest importance. It is perhaps well to insist that the testimony of the latter fact is not to be reduced on the ground that it is really an *argumentum ex silentio*. For the silence here about the Zealots must be matched with the explicit condemnation pronounced by Jesus on the Pharisees and Sadducees, and even by implication on the Herodians.[4] If the primitive Jewish Christian tradition, on which the Evangelists drew, had contained a similar condemnation of the Zealots, why was it not recorded by them as carefully as the condemnations of the other parties?[5] Indeed, there

[1] Matt. xxv. 31, 32: see above, pp. 48 ff., 60.
[2] Matt. xviii. 17: ἔστω σοι ὥσπερ ὁ ἐθνικὸς καὶ ὁ τελώνης (cf. v. 46–7). Cf. McNeil, *St Matthew*, pp. 72, 266–7; Kilpatrick, *Origins of Gospel of Matthew*, p. 117.
[3] Mark iii. 18; Matt. x. 4; Luke vi. 15; Acts i. 13. See pp. 16, 316.
[4] E.g. Mark iii. 6, vii. 1–8, viii. 15, xii. 18–27, xiii. 13; cf. Matt. xxiii. 1–39. The references to the Herodians in these condemnatory contexts are interesting; for the Herodians were a political, not a religious, party: cf. H. H. Rowley, 'The Herodians', *J.T.S.* xli (1940), 14–27; *B.C.* i, 119–20. Supporters of the Herodian dynasty were probably known in Rome in the years immediately following the fall of Jerusalem, owing to Titus' liaison with Berenice, the sister of Agrippa II; cf. Brandon in *N.T.S.* vii (1960–1), 139, n. 3; see also below, p. 271, n. 4.
[5] Even if the βιασταί of Matt. xi. 12 were Zealots (cf. A. von Gall, ΒΑΣΙΛΕΙΑ ΤΟΥ ΘΕΟΥ, Heidelberg, 1926, p. 353), it is not clear whether they are commended or condemned: cf. Klostermann, *Matthäusevangelium*, pp. 98–9. Moreover, if Zealots are meant, why are they not clearly named? Cf. *Th.Wb.* i, 612–13 (G. Schrenk), ii, 888 (A. Stumpf); Hengel, *Die Zeloten*, p. 345. There is a similarly curious silence about the Qumrân sectaries: was this due to closeness of association or complete opposition? It could not have been due to ignorance. Davies, *Setting of the Sermon on the Mount*, p. 235, has argued that 'the Sermon reveals an awareness of the Sect and perhaps a polemic against it'. Cf. Rowley in *B.J.R.L.* 44 (1961), p. 130. The silence of the New Testament documents about the Qumrân sectaries is a fact that all students of Christian Origins should very carefully consider. It is a chastening thought, in view of the present great

would have been the most cogent reason for them to do so, particularly Mark, as we shall see.[1] To be able to record that Jesus had denounced the Zealots as vehemently as he had denounced the Pharisees would surely have been of the greatest value to the Christian cause, when it was known that the Zealots had been responsible for the terrible war of A.D. 66–70.[2]

Such inferences, which are not only legitimate but compelling, authorise our regarding the Jewish Christians as a party closely allied by sympathy and outlook with the Zealots. Their chief difference was that they believed that the restoration of the kingdom to Israel would be effected by the return of Jesus as the Messiah. They would thus have constituted a kind of para-Zealot movement: possibly many of their adherents such as Simon the Zealot, and the priests, as we have seen,[3] were also members of the Zealot party or moved freely in both groups, without any sense of that incompatibility of profession which, for example, a tax collector is reported to have felt on his conversion.[4]

Such community in sympathy and outlook inevitably raises the question whether the Jewish Christians also shared the Zealot belief

concern of New Testament scholars with the Qumrân writings, that until 1947 all this evidence was unknown. Whatever may have been the relations of the primitive Christian movement with the Qumrân community, one thing is certain: the complete absence of reference to the sect in the Christian documents attests the fact that these documents do not provide a complete picture of the origins of Christianity. If C. Roth (*Historical Background of Dead Sea Scrolls*, pp. 22 ff.) and G. R. Driver (*Judaean Scrolls*, pp. 236, 239–42, 244 ff.) are correct in identifying the Qumrân Covenanters with the Zealots, the silence of the Gospels about both becomes a single problem.   [1] See chapter 5.

[2] This issue seems to be consistently overlooked by those who categorically declare that Jesus, and his disciples, absolutely repudiated Zealotism.

[3] See above, pp. 118 ff.

[4] Cf. Luke xix. 1–10: Zacchaeus was an ἀρχιτελώνης. See also the case of Levi or Matthew, Mark ii. 14; Matt. ix. 9; Luke v. 27–8. Quite obviously the primitive tradition preserved no record of Simon's having definitively repudiated his Zealot principles and connections on becoming an apostle. Moreover, the fact that the tradition knew him as the 'Cananaean' or 'Zealot' indicates that he continued to be distinguished by his attachment to Zealotism. It would surely have been both uncomplimentary and compromising to continue to call Simon 'the Zealot', if he had repudiated his former profession, and especially so, if the primitive Christian community was a pacifist body and opposed to Zealotism. To use a modern parallel: it would have been tantamount to a convert's being still called 'the communist' by his co-religionists after leaving Communism for the Roman Catholic Church.

in active resistance to Rome. The surviving tradition gives no clear indication in either direction. There are, however, certain observations which may be usefully made. The first is that Zealotism, so far as the evidence of Josephus shows, had its strongholds at first in the country areas outside Jerusalem;[1] it was only about the year 63 that the Sicarii began to operate in the capital.[2] It is, moreover, probable, on the analogy of resistance movements in more recent times, that, in addition to the dedicated members who lived a nomadic existence, many Zealot supporters and sympathisers lived normal lives in towns and villages, operating clandestinely when the opportunity arose. Jesus and his original disciples lived a nomadic existence;[3] but after the Resurrection experiences the headquarters of the movement were established in Jerusalem, and remained there until the catastrophe of A.D. 70. In terms of this comparison, therefore, the Christian community in the city could scarcely have engaged, if it had been so disposed, in active opposition to the Romans or their Jewish cooperators. However, this situation does not preclude undercover support of the resistance movement, which probably became more openly practised as the situation deteriorated in Jerusalem from the time of the procurator Felix on to the revolt in 66.[4]

The mere idea that the Jewish Christians might have countenanced violent resistance to the Romans provokes an instinctive rejection in the minds of most people today, inured as they are to a long-established tradition that the original disciples must have been quiet and peaceable men, if not actually pacifists. But, on analysis, that tradition is based upon no clear and irrefutable New Testament evidence. It is true that many texts can be cited counselling the 'turning of the other cheek' and 'not resisting evil';[5] but a parallel series can also be produced indicating an opposite attitude, such as 'I have not come to bring peace but a sword'[6] or Peter's

---

[1] See above, pp. 54–5.   [2] See pp. 39–40.

[3] Matt. viii. 20: cf. Klostermann, *Matthäusevangelium*, p. 77.

[4] See above, pp. 114 ff. There were, of course, Christian communities elsewhere in the country.

[5] See Matt. v. 38–44. Cf. W. P. Paterson in *E.R.E.* xii, 678a. Commenting upon the likelihood that v. 41 refers to the right of Roman troops to require non-Roman subjects to carry equipment, K. Stendahl remarks: 'Hence the anti-zealotic note in the Sermon on the Mount is apparent' (*Peake's Commentary*², 679i). On the origin of this pacifist attitude see below, pp. 283 ff.

[6] Matt. x. 34: cf. Klostermann, *Matthäusevangelium*, p. 92; Bultmann, *Gesch. d. syn. Trad.* pp. 166, 176. Cf. P. Martinetti, *Jésus Christ et le Christianisme* (Paris, 1942), pp. 172–3; Klausner, *Jesus of Nazareth*, pp. 315, 364.

baleful words to Sapphira.[1] Moreover, as we shall see, it became prudent, after the shock of the Jewish War of A.D. 66–70, to emphasise the pacific nature of Christianity and represent the beginnings of the faith as insulated from the violence of Jewish life during the first decades of the first century.[2]

There are, besides, some other factors for consideration which, if they do not prove a bellicose attitude on the part of the Jewish Christians, do at least indicate that militant or violent action was not inherently impossible for them. The fact that some, at least, of the disciples of Jesus were accustomed to go about with concealed weapons, after the manner of the Sicarii, is attested by Luke xxii. 38,[3] and all four Gospels record that armed resistance was offered in Gethsemane to the arrest of Jesus.[4] The witness of these facts cannot be lightly set aside. If some of the disciples were accustomed to bear arms, and if Jesus on a critical occasion ensured that they were armed,[5] the idea that the primitive Christian movement was pacific cannot be sustained. Further, if the custom of being armed had existed before the Crucifixion, there is no reason for assuming that it ceased after that event. Then, there are the indications that certain disciples were of a violent disposition. The title 'Boanerges', given to James and John, the sons of Zebedee, suggests a reputation which is significantly attested by their desire to resort to violence against a village of uncooperative Samaritans.[6] Both the name of Judas

---

[1] Acts v. 9. 'in both cases [of Ananias and Sapphira] the author probably means it to be understood that power went forth from Peter as an apostle inspired by the Holy Spirit and slew the offenders, just as the same power blinded Elymas and threatened damnation to Simon Magus' (*B.C.* IV, 51).

[2] See below, pp. 224 ff., 283 ff.

[3] The fact that Jesus had to make sure that the disciples were armed on this occasion (see *vv.* 36, 38) indicates that their weapons were concealed in their garments in Sicarii-fashion (see above, pp. 39–40).

[4] Mark xiv. 47; Matt. xxvi. 51; Luke xxii. 38, 49–50; John xviii. 10–11. The statements about re-sheathing the drawn sword in Matt. xxvi. 52 (ἀπόστρεψον τὴν μάχαιράν σου εἰς τὸν τόπον αὐτῆς) and John xviii. 11 (βάλε τὴν μάχαιραν εἰς τὴν θήκην) imply a significant familiarity with the idea of a disciple's wearing a sword and scabbard. Cf. Cullmann, *The State in the New Testament*, p. 16.

[5] Cf. Brandon, *Fall of Jerusalem*, pp. 102–3: see below, pp. 340–2, for a discussion of the significance of these passages for evaluating the attitude of Jesus.

[6] Mark iii. 17; Luke ix. 54. From the many attempts to explain the original Hebrew or Aramaic sobriquet that lies behind Mark's transliteration, it at least seems clear that the expression was meant to characterise 'wrath' or 'fierceness' (could one say 'the zeal of a Phinehas'?). Mark's translation

Iscariot and his role of the betrayer suggest a person to whom the dangers and tensions of a politico-religious situation were known and attractive.[1] The epithet 'Barjona' given to Peter in Matt. xvi. 17 could reasonably be taken to mean 'outlaw' or 'rebel'.[2] And the

of the expression as 'Sons of Thunder' has its own significance (see below, pp. 243–4). Cf. Taylor, *St Mark*, pp. 231–2; Klausner, *Jesus of Nazareth*, p. 260; G. Dalman, *Jesus-Jeshua* (London, 1929), p. 12; Olmstead, *Jesus in the Light of History*, p. 110; Eisler, *The Enigma of the Fourth Gospel*, pp. 86–9.

[1] Mark iii. 19. The meaning of Ἰσκαριώθ (ὁ Ἰσκαριώτης, Matt. x. 4) still remains a puzzle, despite the numerous efforts to explain the name. Cf. Dalman, *Jesus-Jeshua*, pp. 28–9; Taylor, *St Mark*, p. 234; Klausner, *Jesus of Nazareth*, p. 285; McNeil, *St Matthew*, p. 133; Eisler, ΙΗΣΟΥΣ ΒΑΣΙΛΕΥΣ, ιι, 528, n. 5. The idea put forward in 1917 by F. Schulthess (*Das Problem der Sprache Jesu*, pp. 41, 54–5), and restated recently by Cullmann (*The State in the New Testament*, pp. 15–16), that ὁ Ἰσκαριώτης was a corruption of ὁ σικάριος, thus making Judas a member of the Sicarii, should not be dismissed so peremptorily as it usually is, particularly in view of the fact that Mark, for apologetical purposes, kept from his Gentile readers the embarrassing fact that another of Jesus' disciples was a Zealot (see pp. 243–5). Hengel (*Die Zeloten*, p. 49) briefly dismisses the possibility that Judas was a member of the Sicarii on grounds of date ('Ein früheres Auftreten des Begriffs läßt sich nicht nachweisen'). However, he overlooks the possibility that, if Acts (xxi. 38) uses the term proleptically, this might also have happened in the tradition concerning Judas. According to Josephus, the Sicarii first appeared during the procuratorship of Felix, i.e. A.D. 52–60 (see pp. 39–40); but the name *sicarius*, perhaps because of its opprobrious nature, could easily have been later assigned to Judas, if he were a Zealot. There is, incidentally, a variant reading of Σκαριωτης for Matt. x. 4 (see *Novum Test. Graece*, ed. E. Nestle[19], p. 23). It is also interesting to note the variant reading 'Judas Zelotes' in some Old Latin MSS (cf. Nestle, *ibid.*).
'Diese *Barjonim*, sing. hebr. *barjon* aram. *barjonā*' kommen auch sonst selten vor... Die *Barjonim* sind somit die "Draußenstehenden", die *externi*, ja der Bildung des Wortes nach geradezu die "zu äußerst stehenden", die "Extremisten", wobei der Ausdruck naturgemäß im Munde der Gegner leicht die pejorative Bedeutung von englisch *outsider, outcast, outlaw*, deutsch "Auswurf" (der Gesellschaft), "Ausgestoßene", "Geächtete", italienisch "bandito" annimmt und überdies diejenigen kennzeichnet, die dem Druck der Fremdherrschaft durch die Flucht in die unzugänglichen Berge, Wälder und Wüsten ausweichen' (Eisler, ΙΗΣΟΥΣ ΒΑΣΙΛΕΥΣ, ιι, 67–8). 'Ob eine andere, auf ein jüdisches Lexikon sich berufende Erklärung richtig ist, muß fraglich bleiben. Nach ihr hätte das aramäische barjona nichts mit Johannes zu tun, sondern würde soviel bedeuten wie "Terrorist". Dann hätte Petrus der Partie der entschiedenen Römerfeinde, der sogenannten "Zeloten", angehört, wie Simon der "Zelot" (Luk. 6, 15, Apg. 1, 13) und vielleicht Judas Iskarioth' (Cullmann, *Petrus*[2], pp. 23–4, E.T. p. 22, *The State in the New Testament*, pp. 16–17). Commenting on the

significance of Simon the Zealot's membership of the apostolic band needs no further emphasis.[1]

All this evidence builds up into a picture of the Jewish Christians as a sect of zealous Jews who believed that Jesus of Nazareth, whom the Romans had executed as a rebel, would shortly return as the Messiah, endowed with supernatural power and glory, to restore the kingdom to Israel—an achievement which would necessarily involve the overthrow of the Roman government. Under the leadership of James, the brother of the Messiah Jesus, the movement included men accustomed to bear arms and ready to use them, and one at least was a Zealot. They believed that they had been commissioned to prepare Israel for the coming of their Master, the Messiah, and that his advent would mark the end of the existing world-order, manifest in the empire of Rome, and the judgement of the Gentiles.[2] Although closely allied to the Zealots in sympathy and outlook, their residence in Jerusalem would have precluded the Jewish Christians from taking part in the guerrilla warfare against the Romans which the Zealots maintained in the country areas. Whether the Jewish Christian communities which existed in those areas participated in such activity is not known, the extant evidence being almost exclusively concerned with the Jerusalem community.[3] Such general conclusions, however, do not rule out the

reference to the Barjonim and their leader Abba Sikara in the Babylonian Talmud (Git. 56a), Hengel says: 'Man könnte daraus schließen, daß "Barjone" (בַּרְיוֹנֵי) Pl. von בַּרְיוֹנָא bzw. בִּירְיוֹנָא; hebr. בַּרְיוֹן Pl. בַּרְיוֹנִים) eine feste, ursprüngliche Bezeichnung für die Zeloten war' (Die Zeloten, p. 55). He also cites some interesting Rabbinic references to the Barjonim destroying images of the Roman emperor (ibid. p. 57). He is, however, of the opinion that the 'Barjona' of Matt. xvi. 17 is to be understood in terms of John i. 42 and xxi. 15 as 'son of Joannes': on Hengel's attitude to the question of the relations between Christianity and Zealotism see below, pp. 204, n. 1, 209, n. 1, 345, n. 3.

[1] See pp. 243–5.
[2] See above, pp. 178–82.
[3] E. Lohmeyer has suggested that for Mark 'Galilee is the holy land of the Gospel, the place of its eschatological fulfilment', while 'Jerusalem is the city of deadly enmity to Jesus, of sin, and of death' (Galiläa und Jerusalem, pp. 29, 34); cf. R. H. Lightfoot, Locality and Doctrine in the Gospels (London, 1938), pp. 62–5, 111, 123–4. This antithesis probably results from Mark's apologetic: see chapter 5. There is, however, evidence of a strong independent Galilaean Christianity in the fact that a tradition was current which located the Resurrection Visions in Galilee, in opposition to the Jerusalem location recorded in the Lukan writings: cf. Brandon, Fall of Jerusalem, pp. 41–3; L. E. Elliot-Binns, Galilean Christianity, pp. 43–53.

possibility that the Jerusalem Christians were involved in those clashes with the Roman forces which we noticed in the preceding chapter. It will, indeed, be well briefly to recall our former observations on these episodes, before seeking to assess what was the attitude and what the ultimate fate of the Jerusalem Christians once the revolt broke out in the year 66.

The crucifixion of Jesus occurred in a context of unrest and strife caused by Pilate's various attempts to assert Roman sovereignty against Jewish religious intolerance. And it was in such an atmosphere, and under the impact of the Roman execution of their Master, that the Christian church was founded in Jerusalem.[1] Within some nine years of the Crucifixion the Christians in Jerusalem were faced, as were all other Jews, with the awful prospect of the Temple's desecration by the image of Zeus which Gaius planned to instal therein. As we have seen, the whole Jewish nation was convulsed by this terrible threat to their ancestral faith, and only the sudden death of the emperor prevented a revolt.[2] The episode, however, goes unrecorded in Acts. But it is impossible to believe that the Jewish Christians remained wholly undisturbed and insulated from the fears and passions which agitated their compatriots. Doubts about this silence of Acts concerning the attempt of Gaius are strengthened by the possibility, which we have noted, that the Markan Apocalypse contains a fragment of an oracle, of either Jewish Christian or Zealot origin, that refers to the threatened sacrilege.[3] To what extent the Jewish Christians had been seriously involved in the agitation against the Roman design is not known; but we noticed the significance of the fact that Agrippa I, who succeeded to the government of Judaea immediately after the death of Gaius and who was concerned about future Romano-Jewish relations, struck at two leading members of the Jerusalem Church.[4]

The growing tension, marked by increasing Zealot activity, under the succeeding procurators, which Josephus records, can scarcely have left the Jewish Christians unaffected. The outbreaks of violence during the governorship of Cumanus (A.D. 48–52), caused as they were by Roman insults to the Temple and the Torah and resulting in bloodshed in Jerusalem, must surely have involved zealous Jews such as were the Christian community in the city, who worshipped regularly in the Temple and were distinguished by their devotion

[1] See above, pp. 68 ff.   [2] Pp. 84 ff.
[3] Pp. 88 ff.   [4] Pp. 93 ff.

to the Torah.[1] The increasing fanaticism of the Jews, exasperated
by such acts and fearful of worse outrages, found expression in many
Messianic movements, led by wonder-workers and prophets, claiming supernatural authority and power to redeem Israel.[2] Such
movements evidently caused much excitement among the Jewish
Christians, looking, as they were, for the return of the Messiah. The
warnings uttered by their leaders against false hopes and precipitate
action have been preserved in the apocalyptic discourses ascribed
to Jesus: 'Then if any one says to you, "Lo, here is the Christ!"
or "there he is!" do not believe it. For false Christs and false prophets will arise and show great signs and wonders, so as to lead
astray, if possible, even the elect. Lo, I have told you beforehand.
So, if they say to you, "Lo, he is in the wilderness", do not go out;
if they say "Lo, he is in the inner rooms" do not believe it.'[3]

The action taken against James by Ananus, the high priest,
resulting in his execution, we have found reason for interpreting as
motivated by the fear felt by this leader of the sacerdotal aristocracy
for the head of a movement, closely allied with the lower clergy and
the Zealots, which threatened the stability of the existing social and
political order.[4] The fact that the Jewish Christians immediately
replaced James by another relative of the Messiah Jesus indicates
that they were not cowed by the attack, and their resentment against
these pro-Roman aristocrats, who had been partly responsible for
the death of Jesus, was surely increased by their murder of his
brother.[5]

Such would have been the temper of the Jerusalem Christians
who had next to endure, with their compatriots, the injustice and
provocation of the last and worst of the procurators, Gessius Florus.[6]
There can be little doubt, therefore, where their sympathies would
have lain when the lower priests, many of them members of the
Church, refused any more to offer the daily sacrifices in the Temple
for the well-being of the emperor and the Roman people. This act,
which was both a proclamation of Israel's freedom and a repudiation
of a heathen overlord, signified both an act of national repentance
for having so long accepted another master than Yahweh and an act

---

[1] See pp. 104 ff.   [2] See pp. 108 ff.

[3] Matt. xxiv. 23–6; cf. Mark xiii. 21–2.

[4] See pp. 115 ff.

[5] Whatever its place of origin, the Epistle of James appears particularly
apposite in this connection: cf. v. 1–6. Cf. L. E. Elliott-Binns in *Peake's
Commentary*[2], 896 f.; Grant, *Economic Background of the Gospels*, pp. 122–4.

[6] See pp. 128 ff.

of faith in divine providence.[1] It was a practical endorsement of the teaching of Judas of Galilee, which would surely have evoked the wholehearted approval of the Jewish Christians as it did of the Zealots.

How the Jewish Christians reacted to the struggle for the leadership of the revolt, which resulted from the murder of Menahem, the Zealot leader, we have no means of knowing. Whatever their attitude, they were soon involved in the turmoil of the siege of Jerusalem by the Roman army under Cestius Gallus in the autumn of 66. With their compatriots, they were doubtless plunged in an agony of despair when the Roman assault seemed at the very point of breaching the last defences of the Temple. With them, too, they would have been astounded when the enemy suddenly desisted and then withdrew. Like them, they would surely have seen the hand of God in this strange withdrawal of the Romans at the very moment of apparent victory—and, need we ask, would they then, in the face of such a miracle of deliverance, have refrained from joining their fellow-Jews in pursuing the retreating foe, thus so signally humiliated and overthrown by the God of Israel?[2]

As we have seen, so marvellous a victory confirmed the Jewish people in their revolt against Rome. From all that we have been able to glean heretofore of their outlook and beliefs, there is no reason to think that it was otherwise with the Jewish Christians, namely, that they might have withdrawn from their nation's cause at this moment of exultation and commitment. Indeed, even to raise the question of the possibility that they might have done so, in the face of evidence surveyed and the logic of the fact that after A.D. 70 the Church of Jerusalem completely disappears, would seem absurd but for a long-established tradition that the Jewish Christians fled from Jerusalem to Pella before the end in A.D. 70. Evidence of this tradition dates back to the fourth century, when it first appears in the *Ecclesiastical History* of Eusebius of Caesarea;[3] it is repeated, with some variations, in the following century by Epiphanius.[4] There are grave reasons for doubting the authority of this

---

[1] See above, pp. 130 ff.　　　　[2] See pp. 135 ff.　　　　[3] III. v. 2–3.

[4] *adv. Haer.* xxix. 7 (*P.G.*, ed. Migne, t. xli), cf. xxx. 2. 2; *de Mens. et Pond.* xv (*P.G.*, ed. Migne, t. xliii). The statements of Epiphanius are both brief and vague, a fact which is overlooked by those scholars who confidently cite them as conclusive evidence (see the following note). The relevant passages are as follows: ἐκεῖθεν γὰρ ἡ ἀρχὴ [of the Nazoraean heresy] γέγονε μετὰ τὴν ἀπὸ Ἰεροσολύμων μετάστασιν πάντων τῶν μαθητῶν ἐν Πέλλῃ ῴκηκότων, Χριστοῦ φήσαντος καταλεῖψαι τὰ Ἰεροσό-

tradition, quite apart from its inherent improbability in the light of the evidence already noticed.[1]

λυμα καὶ ἀναχωρῆσαι δι' ἣν ἤμελλε πάσχειν πολιορκίαν, καὶ ἐκ τῆς τοιαύτης ὑποθέσεως τὴν Περαίαν οἰκήσαντες ἐκεῖσε ὡς ἔφην διέτριβον (adv. Haer. XXIX. 7); ἐπειδὴ γὰρ πάντες οἱ εἰς Χριστὸν πεπιστευκότες τὴν Περαίαν κατ' ἐκεῖνο καιροῦ κατῴκησαν, τὸ πλεῖστον ἐν Πέλλη... (adv. Haer. XXX. 2); ἡνίκα γὰρ ἔμελλεν ἡ πόλις ἁλίσκεσθαι ὑπὸ τῶν Ῥωμαίων καὶ ἐρημοῦσθαι προεχρηματίσθησαν ὑπὸ ἀγγέλου πάντες οἱ μαθηταὶ μεταστῆναι ἀπὸ τῆς πόλεως μελλούσης ἄρδην ἀπόλλυσθαι, οἵτινες μετανάσται γενόμενοι ᾤκησαν ἐν Πέλλη... (de Mens. et Pond. xv). It is evident, from these passages, that Epiphanius was primarily concerned with explaining the origin of the Jewish Christian sect of the Nazoraeans, and he repeats, with no especial care, the obviously vague knowledge which he had about a flight of the original Jerusalem Christians to Pella. He is clearly not recording historical fact, but making incidental reference to some tradition, probably known only by hearsay; for, if its source had been known, he would undoubtedly have noted it.

[1] In 1951 the present writer made a critical examination of this Pella-flight tradition, and concluded that it was in origin a second-century 'foundation legend', probably designed to justify the claim of the church later established in Aelia Capitolina, to be a lineal descendant of the original Church of Jerusalem (Brandon, Fall of Jerusalem, pp. 168–73, 263–4). Since that time, many scholars have recognised the strength of the case against the authenticity of the legend (e.g. Farmer, Maccabees, Zealots and Josephus, p. 125, n. 2; G. Strecker, Das Judenchristentum in den Pseudo-klementinen, pp. 229–31; J. Munck, 'Jewish Christianity in Post-Apostolic Times', N.T.S. VI (1959–60), 103–4); but many others have continued to cite it, without attempting to prove its assumed historicity: e.g. W. D. Davies in Peake's Commentary², 761 d; P. Carrington, The Early Christian Church, I, 227–8, 250, 437–8; Hengel, Die Zeloten, pp. 306–7; F. V. Filson, A New Testament History (London, 1965), pp. 297, 302, 329, 331; W. G. Kümmel in R.G.G.³, III, 969, who refers to Elliott-Binns's Galilean Christianity for his authority. Elliott-Binns (op. cit. pp. 67–9) starts his short discussion of the question with an erroneous assertion that the present writer, in rejecting the accuracy of the Pella tradition, was following Robert Eisler: but Eisler actually accepts the tradition without question (ΙΗΣΟΥΣ ΒΑΣΙΛΕΥΣ, II, 601–2, 764). The chief argument advanced by Elliott-Binns, in support of the truth of the legend, is that the Jerusalem Christians would have fled from the persecution of the Zealots as did Johanan ben Zakkai. The comparison is an unfortunate one for his case. So vigilant were the defenders of beleaguered Jerusalem that the rabbi only managed to escape by hiding in a coffin (see below, p. 215). How, then, if the Pella legend be accepted, can it be explained that a whole community, including women and children and the aged, succeeded in escaping? In his review of The Fall of Jerusalem in The Journal of Ecclesiastical History, III (1952), H. J. Schoeps was especially concerned to rebut the criticism made therein (pp. 263–4) of his assumption of the historicity of the Pella legend in his Theologie und Geschichte des Judenchristentums (Tübingen, 1949), p. 267,

The tradition has been long accepted for two reasons: there was no other to contradict it and cause it to be questioned, and it has been generally assumed that the tradition was derived from Hegesippus, a second-century Palestinian Christian. It will be better to consider the second reason first. The assumption that Eusebius and Epiphanius derived the tradition from Hegesippus was a natural one to make, since these writers draw upon Hegesippus for other information about primitive Jewish Christianity.[1] However, though natural, the assumption may fairly be questioned, since Eusebius appears to have made a point of mentioning Hegesippus when drawing from him,[2] but he does not do so here. The accuracy of the

see also p. 47, nn. 1 and 2. In answer to the detailed consideration of the chronology of such an assumed flight relative to the military situation of Pella during the years 66–70 (Brandon, *Fall of Jerusalem*, pp. 170–2), Schoeps, in his review (p. 102), dates the flight for 'probably not until 67', assuming also that Pella had been completely abandoned by its Gentile inhabitants after the Jewish attack in 66 (Jos. *War*, II. 458). But, on this dating, he overlooks the fact that the Jewish Christians would have been occupying the ravaged Gentile city when Vespasian's punitive expedition took place in that area in 68 (Jos. *War*, IV. 413–39)—it would surely have been unlikely that the Roman troops would then spare a body of Jews who had apparently taken possession of a Gentile city which had been sacked by Jews. M. Simon defended the Pella legend in his review of *The Fall of Jerusalem* in *The Modern Churchman*, XLII (1952), 51. In the first place he assumed uncritically that the story came from Hegesippus (see below, p. 210). Then he assumed, without discussion, that the Jewish Christians would have sought to escape from Jerusalem because they did not agree with their nation's struggle for freedom from Rome. He thought that 'no more suitable date can be postulated for their migration than the period of the great Jewish War'; but he neglects the very serious problem of dating such a migration relative to the military situation of Pella during 66–70. Cf. H. B. Kossen, *Op Zoek naar de Historische Jezus* (Universiteit van Amsterdam, 1960), pp. 210–11; also note on L. E. Keck, p. 384 below.

In view of the fact that the Pella-flight legend has been a major factor in encouraging the belief that the Jerusalem Christians refused to be involved in Israel's struggle for freedom, in the following pages the Pella story and its implications have been reconsidered, but without repeating the inquiry into the dating difficulties, which were set forth in detail in *The Fall of Jerusalem*, pp. 170–2, and which no scholar has since attempted to answer when advocating the Pella thesis.

[1] Cf. H. J. Lawlor, *Eusebiana* (Oxford, 1912), pp. 28–34; H. J. Lawlor and J. E. L. Oulton, *Eusebius: Hist. eccl.* II, 82; Hort, *Judaistic Christianity*, p. 175; A. von Harnack, *Die Mission und Ausbreitung des Christentums in den ersten drei Jahrhunderten* (Leipzig, 1906), II, 78 (he also suggested Julius Africanus as an alternative source). 'Was in den primären Quellen gestanden hat, wissen wir nicht mehr' (Schoeps, *Theologie*, p. 265).

[2] E.g. *Hist. eccl.* II. xxiii; III. xx, xxii; IV. viii, xxii.

tradition would not, however, be put beyond doubt, if it were certain that it came from Hegesippus. It would only mean that a tradition was current among the Greek-speaking Christians of Palestine, in the second century, that the original Christian community in Jerusalem had escaped from the city before its destruction and taken refuge in Pella, a Hellenistic city in Transjordan. Whether this tradition, if it were preserved by Hegesippus, would have derived from an original Jewish source, thus guaranteeing its authority, would, however, be uncertain; for it is doubtful whether Hegesippus himself was a Jew or used other than Hellenised sources.[1]

In addition to the question of the original source of the tradition, recorded by Eusebius and Epiphanius, being thus so problematical, the tradition itself is found to have no inherent probability when critically examined. According to Eusebius,

when the people of the church in Jerusalem, having been commanded by an oracle (κατά τινα χρησμόν), given by revelation to men approved before the war, to depart from the city and to dwell in a certain city of Peraea, namely, Pella, (and) when those who believed on Christ had migrated thither from Jerusalem, so that the royal city of the Jews and the whole land of Judaea had been utterly forsaken by holy men, the judgement of God finally overtook those who had abused Christ and his apostles and completely wiped out that generation from among men.[2]

The impression which this statement conveys is that the Jerusalem Christians were wholly insulated from their fellow-Jews, who were thoroughly vicious and deserving of the disaster that befell them in A.D. 70. But this account of how the Jerusalem Christians escaped from the doomed city forms part of Eusebius' philosophy of Jewish history; its theme being that the ruin of the Jewish nation in A.D. 70 was divine punishment for the crucifixion of Jesus, the killing of Stephen, James the son of Zebedee, and James the brother of Jesus, and the expulsion of the other Apostles from Judaea.[3] In answer to the obvious question why God did not immediately punish the Jews for the crime of the Crucifixion, but allowed forty years to elapse, Eusebius explains that the residence of the Apostles in Jerusalem 'afforded, as it were, a strong protection to the city', and God was patient.[4] To illustrate his thesis, Eusebius proceeds to quote from Josephus' account of the portents foretelling the destruc-

---

[1] Cf. W. Telfer in *H.Th.R.* LIII (1960), 143–53.
[2] *Hist. eccl.* III. v. 3.   [3] *Ibid.* iv. 2 ff.
[4] *Ibid.* vii. 8–9: καὶ ἐπ' αὐτῆς τῆς Ἱεροσολύμων πόλεως τὰς διατριβὰς ποιούμενοι, ἔρκος ὥσπερ ὀχυρώτατον παρέμενον τῷ τόπῳ, τῆς θείας ἐπισκοπῆς εἰς ἔτι τότε μακροθυμούσης...

tion of Jerusalem and its Temple, which he interprets as further evidence of God's efforts to induce the Jews to repent, so that they might be spared the sufferings which befell them, the horrors of which Eusebius also illustrates by quotations from Josephus' *Jewish War*.[1]

On analysis, then, what Eusebius tells of the Jewish Christians and their escape from doomed Jerusalem is part of his interpretation of the Jewish catastrophe of A.D. 70 which he has constructed from New Testament material and from Josephus.[2] Looking back from the triumph of the Church under Constantine, Eusebius was only concerned to evaluate the events of the first century in terms of the divine providence which had led the Church from its humble beginnings, through great tribulation, to the proud position it now enjoyed under imperial patronage.[3] His knowledge of the first decades of the Church's life was derived primarily from the New Testament and Josephus.[4] From these sources, only too easily could an interpretation of the ruin of the Jewish nation in A.D. 70 as divine punishment for the crucifixion of Christ and the persecution of his Apostles be made out. The Jewish Christians, in accordance with this interpretation, would naturally be presented as a community of holy men, wholly unconnected with and uncontaminated by the passions and deeds that led to the fatal revolt against Rome.

The actual statement that the Jerusalem Christians escaped from Jerusalem, in response to an oracle, and found refuge in Pella, is only notable for the mention of Pella. That the Christians of Jerusalem could not have been involved, with their guilty compatriots, in the horrors of the siege, was itself an inevitable concomitant of all that Eusebius thought about primitive Christianity *vis-à-vis* the Jews, as we have seen. That they would have fled from the doomed city in response to an oracle was also naturally suggested by such a warning as that attributed to Jesus in the Matthaean apocalypse: 'So when you see the desolating sacrilege spoken of by the prophet Daniel, standing in the holy place (let the reader understand), then let those who are in Judaea flee to the mountains.'[5] But, granting

---

[1] *Hist. eccl.* III. vii. 9 ff.

[2] He draws upon the Pseudo-Clement and Hegesippus for his account of the death of James, the Lord's brother (II. xxiii. 3 f.); see above, pp. 122 ff.

[3] Cf. Brandon, *History, Time and Deity*, pp. 193–4.

[4] Cf. K. Lake, Loeb. ed. of Eusebius, I, xxxv.

[5] Matt. xxiv. 15. Eusebius uses the expression κατά τινα χρησμὸν τοῖς αὐτόθι δοκίμοις δι' ἀποκαλύψεως ἐκδοθέντα πρὸ τοῦ πολέμου, which suggests some prophetic utterance from a member of the Jerusalem Church

all this, what are we to make of so precise a statement concerning their place of refuge? Does not the mention of Pella indicate a basis of historical fact?

A double problem is actually involved here. The first is that the naming of Pella certainly points to a tradition that some Jewish Christians took refuge there, and that they were identified with the members of the Mother Church of Jerusalem. But to accept this does not necessarily mean that the tradition, which may be sound as to the fact that some Jewish Christians did settle at Pella, is also to be trusted in its claim that these persons actually composed the Christian community from Jerusalem. Even if the assumption be made (and there is little justification for doing so, as we have seen) that the tradition comes from Hegesippus, it can only be traced back to the second century. But between that time and the fall of Jerusalem in A.D. 70 much had happened in Palestine. The Roman city, named Aelia Capitolina, which the emperor Hadrian had constructed in 130 on the ruined site of Jerusalem, contained a Christian community which, according to Eusebius, was wholly Gentile (ἐξ ἐθνῶν συγκροτηθείσης).[1] These Gentile Christians must have moved into the new city from somewhere, and it could have been from Pella, a city of the Decapolis, where a Christian community might well have grown up from the refugees from various war-devastated areas of Galilee and Samaria. If this were so, it would have been natural for such a community, settled now on such a hallowed site, to claim that it descended from the original Mother Church, especially if this community preserved the memory that it had originated from Jewish Christian refugees from the war of A.D. 66–70.[2]

such as that of Agabus recorded in Acts xxi. 10–11. Epiphanius, however, says that Christ himself gave the warning (Χριστοῦ φήσαντος), adv. Haer. xxix. 7, and in de Mens. et Pond. xv, that it was given by an angel (προεχρηματίσθησαν ὑπὸ ἀγγέλου).

[1] Hist. eccl. iv. vi. 4; v. xii. 1. Cf. W. Weber in C.A.H. xi, 313.

[2] A review of Eusebius' various statements about the Jerusalem Church during the period concerned shows how vague, and often contradictory, were the traditions he records. Despite his statement in iii. v. 3 that the Jerusalem Christians had migrated to Pella before the destruction of the city, he describes the Urgemeinde as still continuing in Jerusalem. Thus in iii. xi. 1, Symeon is elected bishop after the fall of the city, and he is still functioning there as bishop at the accession of Trajan in A.D. 98 (iii. xxii). Symeon, still bishop of Jerusalem at the age of 102 years, is martyred in the time of Trajan: Hegesippus is cited for this information (iii. xxxii. 1–7). A Jew named Justus succeeds Symeon as bishop (τῆς

This conclusion brings us to the other, related, problem which we noted above. This problem arises from the fact that Pella would have been a most unlikely destination for refugees from Jerusalem. It was a Hellenistic city in origin and tradition, and it lay some sixty miles north-eastward from Jerusalem, and to reach it from there meant crossing the river Jordan at some point.[1] But even more serious than these objections is that which concerns the time when such a mass migration of the Christian community of Jerusalem, which would have included women, children and aged folk, might have taken place. Eusebius gives no clear indication of the date,[2] while Epiphanius says that it occurred just before the siege of the city, which presumably means the final siege by Titus in A.D. 70 and not the abortive one of 66 by Cestius Gallus.[3] The possibility of such a flight taking place at any time between 66 and the start of the siege in 70, relative to the current situation in both Jerusalem and Pella and the course of the Roman punitive campaign, has been investigated at length elsewhere.[4] The conclusion reached was that at no time, during these years, did a combination of circumstances permit a large body of defenceless and slow-moving persons either to escape the vigilance of Jewish defence forces in Jerusalem, or to pass in safety through Roman-held territory, or to settle and remain unmolested in Pella. The fact that a body of the Sicarii did succeed in getting away from Jerusalem, after the collapse of resistance there, and reach Egypt cannot be cited as a parallel.[5] They appear to have got away in the confusion of the last days of the capture of the city, and they were desperate men, armed and ready

ἐν Ἱεροσολύμοις ἐπισκοπῆς τὸν θρόνον), III. xxxv. In IV. v. 1–4 a list of fifteen Jewish bishops of Jerusalem is given, μέχρι τῆς κατὰ Ἀδριανὸν Ἰουδαίων πολιορκίας. Eusebius' description of them implies an uninterrupted succession in Jerusalem (τοσοῦτοι καὶ οἱ ἐπὶ τῆς Ἱεροσολύμων πόλεως ἐπίσκοποι...οἱ πάντες ἐκ περιτομῆς). No explanation is given of why the church in the new Aelia Capitolina should suddenly have become completely Gentile, with a Gentile bishop (IV. vi. 4). It seems quite evident, therefore, that there was no continuity between the original Mother Church of Jerusalem and the church of Aelia Capitolina.

[1] Cf. Schürer, *G.J.V.* II, 137–40; G. A. Smith, *Historical Geography of the Holy Land*, pp. 593, 597–8, 602; Schoeps, *Theologie*, p. 267.

[2] πρὸ τοῦ πολέμου (*Hist. eccl.* III. v. 3).

[3] ἡνίκα γὰρ ἔμελλεν ἡ πόλις ἀλίσκεσθαι ὑπὸ τῶν Ῥωμαίων (*de Mens. et Pond.* xv).

[4] Brandon, *Fall of Jerusalem*, pp. 170–2.

[5] Jos. *War*, VII. 410: τοῖς γὰρ ἐκ τῆς στάσεως τῶν σικαρίων ἐκεῖ διαφυγεῖν δυνηθεῖσιν...

to fight. They fled, moreover, away from the war zone, to a land with a large Jewish population; but even there they were rooted out and exterminated.[1] Jewish tradition relates also how the famous rabbi Johanan ben Zakkai escaped from beleaguered Jerusalem; but his feat only serves to show how impossible the undertaking would have been for a large and diverse party such as were the Jerusalem Christians—he escaped in a coffin.[2]

The apparent physical impossibility of such a flight to Pella during the period concerned goes to reinforce all the other objections against the truth of the tradition. However, there still remains the fact that Pella is specifically named as the place of asylum, which suggests some basis of historical fact. That suggestion may indeed be accepted as valid; but Pella would have been a more convenient place of retreat for other Jewish Christian communities than that of Jerusalem. There were doubtless communities in Galilee and Samaria which might have escaped across the Jordan from the Roman army, as it moved southwards, and settled finally in Pella.[3] In process of time the descendants of such refugees, perhaps having intermarried with Gentile Christians, migrated from Pella to the city of Aelia, which Hadrian founded on the site of Jerusalem. Established there, these Gentile Christians might well have claimed, as we have already noted, that they represented the original Church of Jerusalem, justifying that claim by appealing to their descent from Jewish Christians who had sought refuge in Pella, it being then easily assumed that they had come from Jerusalem.[4] This interpretation of the Pella tradition is confirmed by the very significant fact that,

---

[1] *War*, VII. 410–19: it must be noted that these Sicarii tried, unsuccessfully, to incite the Egyptian Jews to revolt; see below, pp. 291 ff.

[2] Midrash, Ekah, x. i. 5: cf. Oesterley, *History of Israel*, II, 456.

[3] It is significant that Pella was never recognised as an ancient Christian settlement, although Eusebius states that there was a strong church there (*Demonstr. Ev.* III. 5. 108): the existence of a bishop there dates only from the fifth century; cf. Schürer, *G.J.V.* II, 140. It would seem likely that Aristo, a second-century Christian apologist, was a member of the church of Pella: his works have not survived; he could well have been the source from which Eusebius drew his story of the Pella-flight, since he recorded Hadrian's building of Aelia on the site of Jerusalem, and probably also the establishment of the Christian church there (*Hist. eccl.* IV. vi. 4). Cf. Schürer, I, 63–5; K. Lake, Loeb ed. of Eusebius, I, xlviii–xlix; Simon, *Verus Israel*, pp. 287–8; C.-H. Hunzinger in *R.G.G.*³, V, 207–8.

[4] Epiphanius records the return of the supposed descendants of the *Urgemeinde* (τοὺς μαθητὰς τῶν μαθητῶν ἀποστόλων): ἦσαν γὰρ ὑποστρέψαντες ἀπὸ Πέλλης τῆς πόλεως εἰς Ἱερουσαλήμ (*de Mens. et Pond.* xv).

despite this claim of descent from the original Mother Church, the later Church of Jerusalem never enjoyed the prestige that should rightfully have belonged to it, if that claim had been so indubitable that other churches had been obliged to treat it seriously.[1]

It has been necessary to discuss this tradition about the flight of the Jerusalem Christians to Pella at some length, because it has generally been accepted, without question, as true. It has been customary, moreover, to cite it as evidence that the Jerusalem Christians kept themselves carefully aloof from the political aspirations and actions of their fellow-countrymen.[2] That the tradition is found, on examination, to lack validity as a record of the events of A.D. 70 is not surprising not only in the light of all that we can glean of the character and outlook of the Jerusalem Church, but also in view of the indisputable fact that this Church disappeared entirely after A.D. 70. Before that time, as the writings of Paul and Acts clearly attest, the Mother Church of Jerusalem was the unchallenged source of faith and authority for Christianity.[3] If that Church had survived the ruin of the Jewish nation by moving elsewhere, its power and prestige would surely have continued undiminished, and the fact would be plain in the records of the Apostolic and Sub-apostolic Ages.[4] But the veil of silence is complete: the Mother Church of Christianity is heard of no more, and the control and

[1] Until the fifth century the see of Jerusalem was suffragan to that of Caesarea: *Oxford Dictionary of the Christian Church* (ed. F. L. Cross), p. 721 a; J. R. Palanque *et alii*, *The Church in the Christian Roman Empire* (London, 1952), II, 623–4; Harnack, *Mission* (ed. 1902), pp. 418–19.

[2] E.g. Weiss, *Earliest Christianity*, II, 713–16; Meyer, *Ursprung*, III, 584; Schoeps, *Theologie*, pp. 266–7; Filson, *New Testament History*, pp. 302–3.

[3] Cf. Brandon, *Fall of Jerusalem*, pp. 19, 26–7, and the references there given.

[4] Filson, *New Testament History*, p. 331, who accepts the Pella-flight tradition, tries to explain the disappearance of the Jerusalem Church as the centre of authority in faith and practice as resulting from its losing touch at Pella with Gentile Christianity. But Pella was a Gentile city of Decapolis; moreover, if the Mother Church had migrated to Pella, surely its supposed return to Jerusalem (i.e. Aelia Capitolina), in the time of Hadrian, would not have gone uncommemorated in Christian literature, and its unique prestige would have been enhanced by its tribulations. It should be noticed also, by way of comparison, that the rabbinical teachers, under Johanan ben Zakkai, quickly established a school of great repute at Jabneh (Jamnia) after the fall of Jerusalem; a different location did not reduce their prestige: cf. Oesterley, *History of Israel*, II, 456; W. O. E. Oesterley and G. H. Box, *A Short Survey of the Literature of Rabbinical and Mediaeval Judaism* (London, 1920), p. 20. The vague and confused statements of Eusebius about the Church of Jerusalem are eloquent in this connection; see p. 213, n. 2.

direction of the faith lay henceforth with the churches of the great cities of the empire, with Rome, Antioch and Alexandria.

The surviving remnants of Jewish Christianity in Palestine and Syria sank into obscurity, and in time were despised and rejected by Gentile Christians as heretics.[1] The faith of these Ebionite sects, so far as it can be reconstructed from the problematic Clementine literature and the hostile references of Catholic writers, reveals a continuity of Christological belief with that of the original Jerusalem Christians. By Catholic standards, which derived from Paul's doctrine, Ebionite Christology was wholly 'Adoptionist', the Baptism and Resurrection being the two events that definitively determined the status and role of Jesus.[2] The Crucifixion had no soteriological significance,[3] and Ebionite repudiation of Paul's 'gospel' was so profound that Paul himself was identified with the notorious Simon Magus, the arch-enemy of true religion.[4] And so the miserable remnants of the original form of Christianity, transformed by the catastrophe of A.D. 70 into despised and dying sects, continued to maintain the faith once expounded by Peter and James, the brother of the Lord. The 'gospel' of Paul, so signally rescued from oblivion by the Jewish overthrow, became the source of Catholic Christianity, in which the Messiah Jesus was metamorphosed into the Divine Saviour God of all mankind.[5]

---

[1] 'Wie die Zerstörung Jerusalems die große Schicksalswende für das Judentum bedeutet, so gilt das gleiche für Judenchristentums... So ist wenig später schon diese Urzelle der Christenheit, die Nachkommenschaft der ersten Jünger Jesu, der sich ausformenden Großkirche καθ' ὅλην γῆν — welch weltgeschichtliches Paradoxon! — als Häresie erschienen' (Schoeps, *Theologie*, pp. 269–70; cf. Brandon, *Fall of Jerusalem*, p. 264). Cf. Simon, *Verus Israel*, pp. 277–314; O. Cullmann, *Le problème littéraire et historique du Roman Pseudo-Clémentin* (Paris, 1930), pp. 258–60; J. Daniélou, *Théologie du Judéo-christianisme* (Tournai, 1958), pp. 68–81.

[2] Cf. Schoeps, *Theologie*, pp. 71–8, *Urgemeinde, Judenchristentum, Gnosis* (Tübingen, 1956), pp. 23–5. See also Werner, *Die Entstehung des christlichen Dogmas*, pp. 331–2 (E.T. pp. 133–4); Daniélou, *Théologie*, pp. 169–71.

[3] Cf. Schoeps, *Theologie*, pp. 76, 157, *Urgemeinde*, pp. 26–9.

[4] Cf. Schoeps, *Theologie*, pp. 128 ff., 257, 420–7, 448–50, *Urgemeinde*, pp. 17–19; Cullmann, *Le Problème*, pp. 243–50.

[5] Cf. Brandon, *Fall of Jerusalem*, pp. 180–4, 200–1, 208–16, 231–7, 249–51. J. Munck regards the fall of Jerusalem as so definitive that he declares: 'After primitive Jewish Christianity perished with the destruction of Jerusalem in A.D. 70, all later Jewish Christianity has its origin in the Gentile-Christian Church of the post-apostolic period' (in *N.T.S.* VI, 1959–60, 114). It is of interest to note that J. Daniélou (*Théologie*, pp. 80–1) has discerned a continuance of a 'Zélotisme chrétien', stem-

From our lengthy investigation of data so complex and problematical, we have been able to distinguish certain traits and aspects of Jewish Christian belief and action which are of the greatest significance for our subject. First, it has emerged, clearly and without doubt, that the original disciples of Jesus did not regard their faith in Jesus as something that inevitably set them apart from their own nation and national religion. Although their identification of Jesus with the promised Messiah was truly distinctive, they saw themselves, like other Jewish sects, as an integral part of Israel and were especially zealous in their observance of the legal and cultic requirements of Judaism. Secondly, and as a corollary to their fundamental attachment to Judaism, we saw that in identifying Jesus as the Messiah, the *Weltanschauung* of the Jewish Christians was still essentially that of all Jews, namely, the destiny of Israel as the Elect People of God. Owing to Israel's subjugation to Rome, the achievement of this destiny necessarily involved the overthrow of the Roman rule and the restoration of 'the kingdom to Israel'. Since their belief was concentrated on the return of the resurrected Jesus, with supernatural power, to accomplish this restoration, the Jewish Christians were as fervently concerned as the Zealots for the salvation of Israel, which would end the domination of heathen Rome. They differed from them, primarily, in believing that a prophet, who had died a martyr's death at the hands of the Romans, had been raised from the dead by God and would return as the Messiah to redeem Israel. They had found scriptural warranty for this peculiar belief; but they did not emphasise the significance of the death of Jesus beyond maintaining that he had died as a martyr for Israel, owing to the people's blindness and obduracy to his message. The crucifixion of Jesus by the Romans was no more embarrassing to the Jewish Christians than were the Roman executions of Judas of Galilee and his sons to the Zealots. Death at the hands of hated oppressors of Israel was honourable; the only problem which the crucifixion of Jesus raised for his followers was that it seemed to negate his Messianic character, but that difficulty was satisfactorily explained, as we have seen, by skilful exegesis of the scriptures.

ming from primitive Jewish Christianity, in the teaching of Cerinthus, who 'croyait à la restauration matérielle du Temple de Jérusalem et des sacrifices. Tout ceci est dans le prolongement d'un judaïsme politique, d'un messianisme temporel, teinté seulement de christianisme. Le judaïsme de Cérinthe apparaît d'ailleurs au fait qu'il maintient la circoncision et le sabbat et ne reconnaît que l'Évangile de Matthieu' (p. 81). See also Daniélou and Marrou, *The Christian Centuries*, I, 18–19.

We may take, as the third significant aspect of the Jerusalem Church, its organisation, which embodied its aims. After the Resurrection experiences, the disciples of Jesus did not think that they only had passively to await their Master's return. They believed that they were commissioned to prepare Israel for its coming redemption by winning their fellow-Jews to accept Jesus as the Messiah, and to exhort them so to order their lives that they would be ready for his *Parousia* and all that it would signify. To this end, they organised themselves by pooling their economic resources and by placing themselves under the leadership of James, the brother of Jesus. Their missionary efforts were extended to the Diaspora, probably under the direction of Peter, and converts were won in many places, most notably in Rome and Alexandria. The presentation of the faith to the Gentiles was essentially and originally no part of their policy. It was first done by the followers of Stephen, and Paul soon became identified with the undertaking. The Jerusalem leaders accepted the *fait accompli*, and arranged to profit financially from it. When they learned that Paul was teaching his own 'gospel', which logically negated the peculiar status and destiny of Israel, they were quick to repudiate him and persuade his converts to accept their own teaching and discipline.

Organised thus to prepare their compatriots for the restoration of the kingdom to Israel, which was to be achieved by the return of the Risen Jesus as Messiah, the Jewish Christians were closely allied to the Zealots in sympathy and purpose; indeed some of their adherents were probably also professed adherents of Zealotism. When the Roman yoke was finally repudiated in A.D. 66, and this act of faith seemed so signally to be blessed by God in the defeat of Cestius Gallus, there is every reason for supposing that the Jerusalem Christians wholly identified themselves with their people in this fateful struggle for the freedom of Israel—doubtless they expected, as did their fellow-Jews, that now the Messiah would come, and for them he would be the Risen Jesus, invested with divine power and glory.

What happened to them in the fierce and bitter struggle to defend their holy city and Yahweh's chosen shrine from the relentless assault of the heathen can well be surmised. As Josephus has so graphically recorded, the whole population was involved in the suffering and the slaughter, women and children as well as the fighting men. As the community at Qumrân was wiped out by a Roman force in A.D. 68, so the Christian community perished without trace in the holocaust at Jerusalem two years later. Perhaps many Christians were among those who, in response to a prophetic command, had gone to the Temple, 'to receive there the tokens of salvation (τὰ σημεῖα τῆς σωτηρίας)', on the very day of the final assault, and who died there at the hands of the savage legionaries.[1]

If such, then, were the character and outlook of the original disciples of Jesus, and if such was their fate, their beliefs and actions must reflect the influence which their Master had exercised upon them. The 'gospel' of the Jerusalem Church was essentially the evaluation which those disciples formed from their personal experience of Jesus, from what they remembered and understood of his teaching, and from their conviction that he had been raised by God from death. Consequently, because we have no personal record of what Jesus thought and taught, and no documents of the Jerusalem Church have reached us, we have to evaluate the interpretations of the Gospels, which date from after the fall of Jerusalem, in the light of what we have thus been able to discover of the original Christian community that perished in A.D. 70.[2] In other words, the fact that their sense of loyalty to Jesus, as the Messiah who would return to restore the kingdom to Israel, made Jerusalem Christians so zealous in their devotion to Judaism and led them to identify themselves with their compatriots in rejecting the rule of Rome, surely indicates what was the attitude of Jesus to his nation's cause against Rome. A later presentation of Jesus, which shows his attitude as cooperative towards the Roman government in Judaea or as studiously neutral to the political issue, must, accordingly, be treated as suspect and its motives must be very carefully evaluated. Since the Gospel of Mark is the key document in this connection, it will now be our task to investigate its interpretation of Jesus both in the light of what we know of primitive Jewish Christianity and relative to the Gospel's own *Sitz im Leben*.

[1] Jos. *War*, VI. 285.   [2] See above, pp. 146ff.

CHAPTER 5

THE MARKAN GOSPEL: AN
APOLOGIA AD CHRISTIANOS ROMANOS

The uniqueness of the Gospel of Mark became apparent as soon as its chronological priority in relation to the other Gospels was established; for it was recognised that not only was it prior to them in time, but it also provided the pattern for the Gospels of Matthew and Luke.[1] Although efforts have subsequently been made to reduce this unique character of Mark,[2] its position as the first of the Christian Gospels remains as an established datum for New Testament scholarship. It may, however, be questioned whether proper attention has ever been given to the cause of its production. If the composition of such a document represents an innovation in current Christian practice, there must surely have been some 'sufficient cause' for its having happened when it did and where it did. In other words, the Gospel of Mark must be the product of some specific situation in the Christian Church; it must have a *Sitz im Leben* that explains why it came to be written at all.

To explain the *raison d'être* of the Markan Gospel necessitates, accordingly, the determining first of the date and the place of its composition. The latter can, fortunately, be done with little trouble. An ancient tradition, which scholars have never found serious reason to question, associates Mark with Rome;[3] this tradition is, moreover, supported by the occurrence of Latinisms in the text which suggest an environment where Latin was commonly known.[4] To these weighty reasons for accepting a Roman origin may be added the consideration that each of the Gospels probably

---

[1] Cf. Streeter, *Four Gospels*, ch. vii; Beare, *The Earliest Records of Jesus*, pp. 13–15; Williams in *Peake's Commentary*[2], 653a–d; G. Bornkamm in *R.G.G.*[3], ii, 754–5.

[2] Notably by Dom B. C. Butler, *The Originality of St Matthew* (1951); cf. Williams in *Peake's Commentary*[2], 653d.

[3] Cf. B. W. Bacon, *Is Mark a Roman Gospel?* (Harvard University Press, 1919), *passim*; Streeter, *Four Gospels*, p. 12; Taylor, *St Mark*, p. 32; R. McL. Wilson, 'Mark', *Peake's Commentary*[2], 696b; Manson, *Studies*, pp. 7, 38–40; Guignebert, *Jésus*, p. 31; Goguel, *Life of Jesus*, p. 141.

[4] Cf. Bacon, *Is Mark a Roman Gospel?*, pp. 53–4; Taylor, *St Mark*, p. 45.

originated in some important centre of early Christianity and Mark is the only Gospel linked with Rome;[1] further, in view of the fact that Mark, because of its brevity, compared unfavourably with the other Gospels, its preservation and canonical status were probably due to its original association with some powerful Church, which that at Rome certainly was from the earliest times.[2]

The question of the date of Mark, however, is far more obscure, and its elucidation involves a long and complicated inquiry. The general consensus of expert opinion dates its composition and publication for the period A.D. 60 to 75.[3] Now, these fifteen years cover the period of the Jewish War against Rome, i.e. 66–70, which includes that great climacteric event, the destruction of Jerusalem in the year 70. On *a priori* grounds, therefore, it would seem that the production of the first Christian Gospel might be in some way related to these tremendous happenings which resulted in the ruin of the Jewish state and its metropolis, where the Mother Church of Christianity was situated. The Gospel of Mark, however, contains no reference or allusion to these events which is so obvious as to constitute definitive proof that its author was writing after their occurrence. But, it must be asked, is it reasonable to expect that Mark should have referred or alluded very clearly to such events? The assumption has certainly been made by some New Testament scholars, particularly British scholars; and, because such obvious evidence is not to be found, they have concluded that the Markan Gospel must have been written before A.D. 70.[4] The validity of this

---

[1] Cf. Bacon, *Is Mark a Roman Gospel?*, pp. 7–33; Streeter, *Four Gospels*, pp. 9–15, and *The Primitive Church*, pp. 62, 229.

[2] Cf. C. H. Turner, in *New Comm. N.T.* p. 46a; Streeter, *Four Gospels*, pp. 340–1.

[3] Cf. Taylor, *St Mark*, pp. 31–2.

[4] E.g. Turner in *New Comm. N.T.* p. 42; Streeter in *C.A.H.* XI, 259; J. Moffatt, *Introduction to New Testament*, p. 212; Taylor, *St Mark*, p. 32; McL. Wilson in *Peake's Commentary*[2], 696b. G. R. Beasley-Murray in his *Jesus and the Future* and *A Commentary on Mark Thirteen* (London, 1957) has argued for a pre-A.D. 70 date on his interpretation of Mark xiii. The former work was reviewed at some length by the present writer in *The Modern Churchman*, XLIV (1954), 315–23: see also *Fall of Jerusalem*[2], Add. Note III. See below, pp. 230ff. Scholars of other nationalities tend to date Mark for post-A.D. 70: cf. H. Lietzmann, *Gesch. der Alten Kirche*, I, 35; Guignebert, *Jésus*, p. 31; Goguel, *Life of Jesus*, p. 141, and *Les premiers temps de l'Église*, p. 28; H. Conzelmann, 'Geschichte und Eschaton nach Mc 13', *Z.N.T.W.* 50 (1959), p. 215, n. 27. See also G. Bornkamm in *R.G.G.*[3], II, 761; P. Winter, 'The Marcan Account of Jesus' Trial by the Sanhedrin', *J.T.S.* XIV, n.s. (1963), 101.

assumption must, however, be questioned. In the first place, it must be remembered that the author of Mark was concerned to give an account of Jesus, who had died some forty years before the destruction of Jerusalem. Accordingly, his theme did not require that he should allude explicitly to events contemporary with his own time of writing, any more than the authors of Matthew and Luke should have related their accounts of Jesus to current events of their time. This comparison with Matthew and Luke does, in fact, raise a further, related, question of considerable significance. It has been argued that Luke shows evidence of having had the destruction of Jerusalem in mind at certain points when he wrote,[1] and that, if Mark had been writing after A.D. 70, he would also have given similar indication. But it must not be overlooked, in drawing such an inference, that we naturally expect that Luke would have made reference to the fall of Jerusalem, because we accept that he was writing after A.D. 70; without this predisposition of mind, it is possible that his reference would not be deemed so explicit.[2] However that may be, Luke's reference is of a detached academic kind such as a Christian writer might well make some fifteen years after the event, in the immediate consequences of which he had not been personally involved. The same would seem to be the case with Matthew, whose apparent references also date from about A.D. 80 to 85.[3]

But there is a more serious objection to such a comparison, for it seems to be based upon a fallacious assumption. Thus, it is assumed that, if he had written just after the fall of Jerusalem, Mark would have made more explicit reference to the event than Luke or Matthew, since he was closer to it; that he makes no obvious reference proves, therefore, that he must have written before it happened. Such reasoning, however, by assuming that Mark, in writing about Jesus, would have related his account to contemporary events in Judaea, thereby presupposes a degree of personal detachment from these events at least equal to that of the other Evangelists when writing a decade later: but such an argument neglects to consider

---

[1] See Luke xix. 43, xxi. 24. Cf. Creed, *St Luke*, pp. xxii, 253–4; V. Taylor, *Behind the Third Gospel* (Oxford, 1926), pp. 118–24.

[2] See Streeter's argument against Harnack's contention that neither Luke xix. 41 ff. nor xxi. 20 ff. refers to the destruction of Jerusalem (*Four Gospels*, p. 540). Streeter assigned Luke xix. 43, with its apparent allusion to the Roman circumvallation of Jerusalem in A.D. 70, to his Proto-Luke (*ibid.* p. 222); cf. Taylor, *Behind the Third Gospel*, pp. 118–24.

[3] Cf. Brandon, *Fall of Jerusalem*, pp. 227 ff.; see below, pp. 300 ff.

the possibility that Mark was so close and so involved in the consequences of those events that such detachment was impossible for
him—in fact, so close and so involved that his very writing of the
Gospel was occasioned by those events.

That this was indeed the reason for the lack of conscious and explicit reference to the fall of Jerusalem in the Markan Gospel soon
becomes evident on consideration of a number of facts, which are
also found to provide clear indications of the date of the book's
composition. We will consider first a fact, the significance of which
can be quickly appreciated. It is constituted by the very obvious
concern shown in Mark about the attitude of Jesus on the subject of
the Jewish payment of tribute to Rome. Jesus is represented as
having been questioned about the matter, with evil intent, by
members of two Jewish parties, the Pharisees and the Herodians.[1]
Now, since the payment of tribute was a normal obligation of all
subject peoples in the Roman empire, and to refuse to pay it was
abnormal and signified rebellion, to raise the question of the Jewish
payment at all clearly implied that the issue was one of topical
interest. Indeed, the author of Mark would surely have never
bothered otherwise to record the incident in his short account of
Jesus, addressed to the Christians of Rome; for the incident had no
particular spiritual significance, and the answer which Jesus gave
merely endorsed what all Romans would have taken for granted,
namely, the obligation of the Jews, as a subject people, to pay tribute.
These considerations, accordingly, raise a very pertinent question:
when were the Christians of Rome likely to have been so interested
in the subject of Jewish payment of tribute to Rome, and in the
attitude of Jesus about it?

The period of time under consideration here is A.D. 60–75, i.e. the
period within which it is generally thought that Mark was written.
So we can narrow our inquiry by asking when, during these fifteen

---

[1] Mark xii. 13–17. Cf. Brandon in *N.T.S.* vii (1960–1), 139–40. It is to be
noted that in A.D. 71 Vespasian ordered that all Jews, wheresoever
resident, must pay a poll-tax (φόρον) of two drachmas annually into the
Capitol in lieu of the contribution to the Temple (Jos. *War*, vii. 218;
Dio Cassius, lxvi. 7). Cf. Schürer, *G.J.V.* ii, 259–60. It is likely that the
Christian community in Rome would have known of this new tax, and it
may have increased their interest in the question of the Jewish obligation
to pay tribute to Rome. However, it is evident that the tribute with
which Mark xii. 13–17 is concerned was that which had troubled the Jews
from the time of its imposition in A.D. 6. Cf. H. Montefiore in *N.T.S.* xi
(1964), 63 ff,

years, it was likely that the issue of the Jewish payment of tribute would have been a topic of such vital concern to the Roman Christians. The years before 66, when the Jewish revolt started, are improbable: Jewish reluctance about the tribute was perhaps sometimes discussed in official circles in Rome, but it is very unlikely that it was known to the Christians there or that it stirred their interest. One of the factors in the revolt of 66 was the payment of tribute, as we have seen; however, it is improbable that it became a matter of immediate concern to the Christians living in Rome. Without the modern means of news-broadcasting, information about events in a far-off and insignificant country such as Judaea would have been slow in reaching the ordinary inhabitants of Rome, from which the Christian community drew its members. Moreover, during the years 68–70 events in the capital, following the death of Nero, would have dominated the attention of its people. But in the year 71 popular interest in Jewish affairs was powerfully stimulated in Rome by the magnificent triumph with which the new emperor Vespasian and his son Titus celebrated their conquest of rebel Judaea.[1] The new dynasty was intent on impressing the populace of Rome by the magnitude of their victory. Consequently, as Josephus records, special efforts were made to present to the inhabitants of the capital, who watched the triumphal procession on its way through the streets to the Capitol, a graphic record of the Jewish War. To this end, a number of movable scaffolds (*pegmata*) were included in the procession, on which were staged scenes from the campaign, all designed to emphasise the fierceness of the struggle

---

[1] The two sculptured scenes on the present Arch of Titus in the Forum Romanum graphically record the impressive character of the triumphal procession: cf. Curtius and Nawrath, *Das Antike Rom*, pp. 39–40, Bilder 40–4. The short dedicatory inscription on this arch does not refer to the Jewish War. This arch was erected after the death of Titus in A.D. 81. There was another arch in the Circus Maximus, destroyed in the fourteenth or fifteenth century, which, somewhat mendaciously, commemorated the event: *Senatus populusque Romanus imp. Tito Caesari divi Vespasiani f. Vespasiano Augusto...quod praeceptis patri(is) consiliisque et auspiciis gentem Judaeorum domuit et urbem Hierusolymam omnibus ante se ducibus regibus gentibus aut frustra petitam aut omnino intemptatam delevit* (in Schürer, *G.J.V.* I, 636, n. 128). Cf. Mommsen, *Das Weltreich der Caesaren*, p. 390, n.; G. Ricciotti, *Flavio Giuseppe*, IV, 246–52 and notes; H. St J. Hart, 'Judaea and Rome: the Official Commentary', *J.T.S.* III, n.s., 180–1; M. R. Scherer, *Marvels of Ancient Rome* (New York–London, 1956), pp. 75–6, plates 119–23. See also Charlesworth in *C.A.H.* XI, 4–6; Bersanetti, *Vespasiano*, pp. 40–2. The scenes appear on Plates XI and XII.

and the greatness of the Flavian victory.[1] Coins were also issued, commemorating the event: inscribed IVDAEA CAPTA, the humiliated figure of Judaea was shown, seated beneath a symbolic palm-tree.[2] Thus, to the people of Rome the Jewish revolt and its bloody suppression were made dramatically real. And this spectacle of Jewish fanaticism and intransigence, together with reports of Jewish atrocities, also helped to inflame the anti-Semitism already current in Graeco-Roman society.[3]

To the Christian community in Rome this vivid presentation of the Jewish revolt and its consequences must have been profoundly disturbing. They could not view it with the same detached interest as the rest of the population; for they were uncomfortably conscious that their religion had originated in Judaea and that their Lord had been crucified as a Jewish rebel. Such knowledge, moreover, was not only personally embarrassing: the fact that their faith was of Jewish origin was known to others, so that there was a real danger that they might be viewed with suspicion as 'fellow-travellers' with Jewish nationalism and disposed to sedition.[4] Consequently, the

---

[1] Jos. *War*, VII. 116–62. Josephus emphasises the realistic nature of the tableaux: ἡ τέχνη δὲ καὶ τῶν κατασκευασμάτων ἡ μεγαλουργία τοῖς οὐκ ἰδοῦσι γινόμενα τότ' ἐδείκνυεν ὡς παροῦσι (*ibid.* 146).

[2] Cf. Reifenberg, *Israel's History in Coins*, pp. 32–3; Hart in *J.T.S.* III, n.s., 172–98 and plates, who discusses the propaganda value of the imperial coinage commemorating the subjugation of Judaea. See Plate x (*a*), (*b*).

[3] Josephus refers to accounts of the Jewish War which were inspired by hatred of the Jews (μίσει τῷ πρὸς 'Ιουδαίους, *War*, I. 2): his tractate *Against Apion* was a defence against the anti-Semitism of the Alexandrian grammarian Apion. The scurrilous account which Tacitus (*Hist.* v. 4–5) gives of the Jews and their customs clearly reflects the popular feeling against them at this period. Cf. A. Piganiol, *Histoire de Rome*, p. 281; J. Carcopino, *La vie quotidienne à Rome à l'apogée de l'Empire* (Paris, 1939), p. 163; Mommsen, *Das Weltreich der Caesaren*, pp. 390–1; Simon, *Verus Israel*, pp. 239–45; J. Leipoldt in *R.A.C.* I, 469–73.

[4] Tacitus undoubtedly reflects contemporary suspicion of Christianity on account of its Jewish origin, in his celebrated statement about Christian origins: 'Auctor nominis eius Christus Tiberio imperitante per procuratorem Pontium Pilatum supplicio adfectus erat; repressaque in praesens exitiabilis superstitio rursum erumpebat, non modo per Judaeam, originem eius mali, sed per urbem etiam quo cuncta undique atrocia aut pudenda confluunt celebranturque' (*Annales*, xv. 44). Juvenal appears to confuse Jews and Christians (cf. *Sat.* xiv. 96–105). Epictetus' opprobrious allusion to the Galilaeans (IV. vii. 6) could apply equally to Christians or Zealots. Cf. Hengel, *Die Zeloten*, p. 60; Fuchs in *V.C.* I (1950), 82–8; W. H. C. Frend, *Martyrdom and Persecution in the Early Church* (Oxford, 1965), pp. 162–3, 210–11.

subject of the Jewish payment of tribute to Rome, and what had been the attitude of Jesus to the issue, became a topic of urgent interest and concern. And it would have been reassuring, therefore, to learn that Jesus had dealt authoritatively with the question, endorsing the obligation of the Jews to render tribute unto Caesar.[1]

How far the Markan episode concerning the tribute money accurately portrays the attitude of Jesus must be carefully investigated later.[2] For our present purpose, it is important to note that this preoccupation with the question of the Jewish payment of tribute points indubitably to the date of the composition of Mark, namely, to a time shortly after A.D. 71, when the Flavian triumph in Rome had presented the late Jewish War vividly to the inhabitants of the city.

Another indication of the Gospel's date, which is also linked with the Flavian triumph, occurs in Mark xv. 38, where it is recorded that, at the moment of Jesus' death, 'the curtain of the temple was torn in two, from top to bottom'.[3] The incident is evidently regarded by Mark as a *theologoumenon*, proclaiming that the sacrificial death of the Son of God marked the end of the Temple cultus, decreed under the Old Covenant with Israel.[4] However, for his record of the

---

[1] Whatever the reply of Jesus in xii. 17 originally meant (see below, pp. 345–9), there can be no doubt that Mark's account of the episode was intended to show that Jesus endorsed the Jewish obligation to pay tribute to Rome. Cf. Taylor, *St Mark*, pp. 479–80; L. Goppelt, 'The Freedom to Pay the Imperial Tax (Mark 12, 17)', *Studia Evangelica*, II, 185–7; E. Klostermann, *Das Markusevangelium* (Tübingen, 1950), pp. 124–5; Turner in *New Commentary*, *N.T.* pp. 97–8; R. McL. Wilson in *Peake's Commentary*, 708 c; H. Loewe, '*Render unto Caesar*': *Religious and Political Loyalty in Palestine* (Cambridge, 1940), pp. 107 ff. It is significant that Mark says nothing of the accusation, recorded by Luke xxiii. 2, that Jesus urged the people not to pay tribute to Caesar.

[2] See below, pp. 270–1, 345–9.

[3] Mark's statement has caused much trouble for commentators, and even a conservative critic like Dr V. Taylor has observed: 'The reference to the rending of the Temple veil appears to be a legendary addition doctrinal in origin' (*St Mark*, p. 596). Cf. Bultmann, *Gesch. d. syn. Trad.* pp. 305–6; T. A. Burkill, *Mysterious Revelation: an Examination of the Philosophy of St Mark's Gospel* (New York, 1963), pp. 246–8.

[4] In view of the devotion of the Jewish Christians to the Temple, it is unlikely that they would have either invented or cherished a tradition which signified the abrogation of the Temple cultus, in which they so zealously participated. The Gospel according to the Hebrews (in M. R. James, *The Apocryphal New Testament*, p. 5) recorded that the death of Jesus was marked by the fall of one of the great lintels of the Temple, not by the rending of the Temple Veil. The difference is significant. The

incident to have had any meaning for his readers, it is evident that they must have been familiar with the fact that the Jerusalem Temple had a veil or curtain (τὸ καταπέτασμα τοῦ ναοῦ), and they must have had some knowledge of its significance, since Mark did not find it necessary to explain it to them as he does other Jewish customs and institutions. We may ask, accordingly, how it came to be that Christians in Rome, for the most part undoubtedly poorly educated persons, knew that the Temple in far-off Jerusalem had such a curtain, and were informed about its function.[1]

The answer is surely to be found in Josephus' account of the Flavian triumph. For he tells that there were carried in procession through the streets of Rome on that day in the year 71, among the other spoils of victory, the purple curtains of the Temple (τὰ πορφυρᾶ τοῦ σηκοῦ καταπετάσματα), and that Vespasian afterwards ordered them to be deposited in the imperial palace, together with the cere-monial copy of the Torah which had been used in the Temple.[2]

rending of the Veil signified the end of God's presence in the sanctuary, whereas the falling lintel was a portent, in Jewish idiom, symbolising the death of a great teacher: the death of R. Jassi was attended by the shaking of the lintels of seventy Galilaean houses (G. Dalman, *Jesus-Jeshua*, p. 220). Cf. Klostermann, *Markusevangelium*, p. 167. The ingenious interpretation of D. Daube (*The New Testament and Rabbinic Judaism*, London, 1956, pp. 23-6) is beside the point, because it disregards the essential fact that the portent is recorded in a writing addressed to Gentile readers. A Hellenistic parallel is cited by C. Clemen, *Religions-geschichtliche Erklärung des Neuen Testaments* (Giessen, 1924), p. 257. It is significant that, when later Ebionite thought came to reckon with the now established tradition of the Rending of the Veil, it was explained: 'velum templi scissum est, velut lamentans excidium loco imminens' (*Clem. Rec.* I, xli). Cf. Schoeps, *Theologie*, p. 241; Daniélou, *Théologie*, pp. 196-8; H. Montefiore, *Josephus and the New Testament* (London, 1962), pp. 16-18.

[1] It would seem unlikely that, at this early stage in the development of Christianity, the members of a Gentile church such as that at Rome would have been familiar with the LXX account of the two veils of the Holy Place and the Holy of Holies in Exod. xxvi. 31-7; or, if they were, that they would have identified the Tabernacle of Exodus with the Temple at Jerusalem. The theological significance attached to the Temple veils in Heb. vi. 19, ix. 3, x. 10, presupposes a Jewish Christian *milieu*, in which theological speculation had been developed concerning the cultic institu-tions of Judaism. Such a *milieu* is patently far removed from that indicated in Mark.

[2] *War*, VII. 162. According to Josephus (*War*, VI. 387-91), many of the treasures of the sanctuary (ναός), including the curtains and material for repairing them (πορφύραν τε πολλὴν καὶ κόκκον), had somehow escaped destruction when the Temple was burnt and were handed over to the

Josephus does not inform us how these curtains and the other Temple treasures were displayed and their meaning explained to the people during the triumph; but, from the great care which was given to providing full publicity for the Flavian achievement on this occasion, it may safely be inferred that the significance of the Temple veil was made known to the populace of Rome.[1] It is not fanciful to conclude, therefore, that many Roman Christians stood in the streets of the city that day to watch the triumphal procession, and that they were impressed by the sight of the curtains that had veiled the inner sanctuary of Judaism, signifying, as their presence did among the spoils of the Roman victory, the catastrophic end of that cultus which was the exclusive privilege of the Jewish people and which gave them their sense of spiritual superiority over other nations.[2]

But to one Roman Christian, as he meditated upon this evidence of the supersession of Jewish religion, it must have seemed that what the Roman victory had then achieved was surely but the practical completion of what the Apostle Paul had taught of the death of Jesus: 'Christ redeemed us from the curse of the Torah, having become a curse for us—for it is written, "Cursed be every one who hangs on a tree".'[3] Hence, the death of Jesus had already, some

Romans by two Temple officials prior to the Roman attack on the Upper City, the last centre of Jewish resistance in Jerusalem. On the subsequent fate of the Temple spoils cf. Schürer, *G.J.V.* I, 637, n. 133.

[1] There were two veils or curtains in the Temple, according to Jos. *War*, v. 209–19. Before the golden doors of the first (open) chamber (οἶκος) hung one curtain, which Josephus describes at length: it was of Babylonian tapestry, with embroidered symbols in various colours. The other curtain, which he does not describe, screened the inner chamber, which ἄβατον καὶ ἀθέατον ἦν πᾶσιν, ἁγίου δὲ ἅγιον ἐκαλεῖτο. Cf. Jeremias, *Jerusalem*, II, 27–8. According to S.B. *Kommentar*, I, 1044, 'Aus dem Ausdruck καταπέτασμα ergibt sich also keine bestimmte Antwort auf die Frage, ob Mt. 27, 57; Mk. 15, 58 u. Lk. 23, 45 der Vorhang vor dem Heiligen oder vor dem Allerheiligsten gemeint ist.' However, for Mark, concerned only with the symbolism of the portent, there was no need to discriminate between these two curtains, and it was enough for his Gentile readers to know that the καταπέτασμα τοῦ ναοῦ had been rent at the moment of Jesus' death.

[2] It is well to reflect on the fact that, at this primitive period, Gentile Christians must have felt themselves to be much inferior to the Jewish Christians in knowledge of the Jewish scriptures and religious institutions which formed the background of their new faith. They must surely have looked very curiously at the cult objects of the Temple, such as the *Menorah* and altar of shew-bread, and have been impressed by the fact that all these essential appurtenances of Judaism were now in the hands of the Romans.   [3] Gal. iii. 13.

forty years before, made the Torah obsolete, thus anticipating in essence what the Roman destruction of the Temple had now completed in fact. And so he was inspired to tell his fellow-Christians in Rome that, when Jesus died on Golgotha, the Temple veil had been rent by divine agency—indeed, perhaps the very curtain that they had seen in the triumphal procession of Vespasian and his son Titus.[1]

The interest stirred among Roman Christians by the spoils of the Temple not only explains Mark's otherwise enigmatic statement about the rending of the Temple veil at the Crucifixion, but it also throws light on the puzzling parenthetic comment in the apocalyptic discourse about the Abomination of Desolation in xiii. 14: 'But when ye see the abomination of desolation standing where he ought not (let him that readeth understand)...'[2] These words are part of the long discourse concerning the events heralding the *Parousia* of the Son of Man, which is attributed to Jesus, but which is generally regarded by New Testament scholars as a composition of Mark, embodying diverse material.[3] Indeed, as we have already noted, there is reason for believing that the passage concerning the Abomination of Desolation was probably taken from a Zealot or Jewish Christian apocalypse relating to the attempt of the emperor Gaius in A.D. 39–40 to set up his image in the Temple.[4] Now, as we shall presently see, there is evidence in the introduction to this apocalyptic discourse (i.e. xiii. 1–4) that Mark was especially concerned to show that Jesus had foretold the destruction of the Temple, a concern which is understandable in view of the interest of the Christian community in Rome resulting from the Flavian triumph in 71.[5] But what of the Abomination of Desolation and the curious parenthetic admonition?

If Mark was here using traditional Palestinian material relating

---

[1] The rending of the Temple veil may actually have been suggested by rents that were seen in those exhibited in the triumphal procession; for it is possible that these curtains had been damaged during their violent removal. Jewish legend does in fact tell how Titus himself had slit the Temple veil with his sword (Gittin, 56*b*, in S.B. *Kommentar*, I, 1044; cf. pp. 946 ff.). Cf. Eisler, ΙΗΣΟΥΣ ΒΑΣΙΛΕΥΣ, I, 161–2 and notes. In this connection see also Testament of Levi xv and Testament of Benjamin ix.

[2] Ὅταν δὲ ἴδητε τὸ βδέλυγμα τῆς ἐρημώσεως ἑστηκότα ὅπου οὐ δεῖ, ὁ ἀναγινώσκων νοείτω... 'Die Parenthese ἀναγινώσκων νοείτω (nur Mc Mt) ist im Munde Jesu selbst undenkbar' (Klostermann, *Markusevangelium*, p. 135). Cf. Brandon in *N.T.S.* vii, 133 ff.

[3] Cf. Taylor, *St Mark*, pp. 498–9; Klostermann, *Markusevangelium*, pp. 131–2.

[4] See above, pp. 88 ff. [5] See below, pp. 233 ff.

to a threatened violation of the sanctity of the Jerusalem Temple by the erection of an image of a pagan god or divinised man, it is obvious that the strange expression 'the Abomination of Desolation' (τὸ βδέλυγμα τῆς ἐρημώσεως) must already have been explained to his readers, i.e. the Roman Christians. This means that already in Rome an essentially Jewish oracle relating to the Temple was being interpreted in the Church there in terms of what had recently happened during the Roman destruction of the Temple. But what had actually happened then that seemed to fulfil the earlier prophecy about 'the Abomination of Desolation' profaning the Jewish sanctuary? Quite obviously it could not have been the Roman act of destruction itself. There are, however, two incidents, recorded by Josephus as happening during the short period between the Roman seizure of the Temple and its destruction by fire, which might well have been seen by a Christian as the fulfilment of the 'Abomination of Desolation' prophecy.

The first incident, in the order in which Josephus records them, occurred when Titus realised that it was impossible to control the fire that had been started during the assault on the Temple. The Roman leader then entered the inner sanctuary, the famous 'Holy of Holies' (τοῦ ναοῦ τὸ ἅγιον), with his staff, and inspected its contents.[1] To the Jewish mind (and the author of Mark was probably a Jew)[2] this act constituted a double sacrilege: for not only did Titus, being a Gentile, violate the sanctity of Yahweh's shrine by entering where only the high priest could rightly go, but he was also the son of the Roman Emperor who was regarded as divine. In other words, the son of one blasphemously worshipped as a god stood 'where he ought not', namely, in the innermost sanctuary of the God of Israel.[3]

The other incident must have happened shortly after. While the sanctuary and the adjacent buildings were still burning, the vic-

---

[1] Jos. *War*, vi. 260.

[2] Cf. Taylor, *St Mark*, pp. 55–66; Black, *An Aramaic Approach to the Gospels and Acts*, pp. 153–62.

[3] On the significant use of the masculine participle ἑστηκότα to qualify the neuter noun βδέλυγμα see below, p. 232, n. 3. Pompey, accompanied by his staff, had entered the Holy Place (εἰς τὸν ναόν), after his conquest of Jerusalem in 63 B.C. Josephus records that the Jews had been more deeply affected by this sacrilege than by all the other calamities which then befell them (*War*, I. 152). Herod had been careful to preserve the Temple from profanation when he captured it, with the help of Roman forces, in 37 B.C.: cf. Jos. *War*, I. 354.

torious Roman troops assembled in the Temple court, and, erecting their standards opposite the eastern gate, sacrificed to them and hailed Titus as 'Imperator'.[1] As a violation of the sanctity of the Temple, these acts were perhaps even more shocking than the earlier one. The legionaries' standards were sacred objects to the Romans, and they were adorned with medallions bearing the image of the emperor.[2] Thus, in a very real sense the erection of these standards and the consequent act of worship achieved in A.D. 70 what the emperor Gaius had intended to do in A.D. 39, and what to the Jewish mind was the setting up of the 'Abomination of Desolation'. The association of Titus with this act of heathen worship in the Temple is also significant; for, in the Markan text, the βδέλυγμα τῆς ἐρημώσεως was clearly regarded as having been manifested in a human person, since the masculine participle ἑστηκότα is deliberately used to qualify the neuter noun βδέλυγμα. This fact surely provides the clue to the otherwise puzzling parenthetic admonition that follows the statement in v. 14: '...the Abomination of Desolation, standing (ἑστηκότα) where he ought not (let the reader understand)'.[3] If the fulfilment of the 'Abomination' prophecy had been explained orally in the Christ-

---

[1] Jos. *War*, VI. 316: 'Ρωμαῖοι δὲ...κομίσαντες τὰς σημαίας εἰς τὸ ἱερὸν καὶ θέμενοι τῆς ἀνατολικῆς πύλης ἄντικρυς ἔθυσάν τε αὐταῖς αὐτόθι καὶ τὸν Τίτον μετὰ μεγίστων εὐφημιῶν ἀπέφηναν αὐτοκράτορα. On the significance of the title Imperator, cf. *O.C.D.* p. 450.

[2] Cf. Tertullian, *Apol.* XVI. 7–8: 'Sed et Victorias adoratis...Religio Romanorum tota castrensis signa veneratur, signa iurat, signa omnibus deis praeponit.' The Qumrân *Habakkuk Commentary*, VI. 1 (in Dupont-Sommer, *Les écrits esséniens*, p. 274), notes that the Kittim (Romans?) sacrifice to their standards: cf. Yadin, *The Scroll of the War of the Sons of Light against the Sons of Darkness*, pp. 63–4, 245. See Eisler, ΙΗΣΟΥΣ ΒΑΣΙΛΕΥΣ, II, 167 and n. 2, I, Tafel xxxiv; *O.C.D.* p. 857 b. It is significant that, in his attempt to prove that Mark xiii was written before A.D. 70, G. R. Beasley-Murray, *A Commentary on Mark Thirteen*, pp. 63, 72, ignores the fact that Josephus records this cultic act of the legionaries in the Temple and their salutation of Titus as Imperator, and that he seeks instead to relate the prophecy to Pilate's introduction of military standards into Jerusalem (not the Temple): cf. Jos. *Ant.* XVIII. 55; *War*, II. 169–70; see also below, pp. 236–7.

[3] 'the masc. participle ἑστηκότα...suggests a personal agent rather than a statue'...'The intentional change from the neuter τὸ βδέλυγμα to the masc. ἑστηκότα, the vague local statement ὅπου οὐ δεῖ, the warning ὁ ἀναγινώσκων νοείτω, and the general atmosphere of reserve that marks the passage, must all be taken into account', Taylor, *St Mark*, p. 511. Cf. C. H. Dodd, 'The Fall of Jerusalem and the "Abomination of Desolation"', *J.R.S.* XXXVII (1947), 53–4; Daube, *New Testament*, pp. 422–36.

ian community in terms of these incidents, especially the second, in which Titus had played the leading role, it is understandable that more discretion had to be observed in writing about it. Accordingly, Mark, writing shortly after the Flavian triumph, when the recent destruction of the Jerusalem Temple had been so graphically presented to the Roman Christians, sought to show how an earlier prophecy, which he attributed to Jesus, had thus been fulfilled; but he discreetly left to his readers the identification of the 'Abomination', who had stood 'where he ought not' in the Temple at Jerusalem.[1]

The clue which the 'Abomination' passage affords to the date of the Markan Gospel is further strengthened when other aspects of the apocalyptic discourse in chapter xiii are considered in relation to the position of the Roman Christians at the time of the Flavian triumph. This quickly becomes apparent in recalling that, in the introductory verses (1–3) to the discourse, Jesus is represented as foretelling the destruction of the Temple, while in the next chapter, in the account of the trial before the Sanhedrin, those who accuse Jesus of threatening to destroy the Temple are described as bearing false witness against him (ἐψευδομαρτύρουν κατ' αὐτοῦ).[2] This implicit denial that Jesus had spoken against the Temple is repeated later in the narrative, when the bystanders at the Crucifixion are depicted as slandering (ἐβλασφήμουν) Jesus by the mocking taunt: 'Ha! thou that destroyest the temple (τὸν ναόν) and buildest it in three days...'[3] It will be our task presently to investigate this charge about threatening to destroy the Temple, which was evi-

---

[1] The need for caution in making this reference to Titus would have been even greater, if there had been the danger that the Roman government might have seen some connection between Christianity and the Temple. Such a connection was actually seen according to the fifth-century writer Sulpicius Severus. Thus, in recording the Roman council of war before the attack on the Temple, he states: 'At contra alii, et Titus ipse, evertendum templum in primis censebant, quo plenius Judaeorum et Christianorum religio tolleretur, quippe has religiones, licet contrarias sibi, iisdem tamen auctoribus profectas; Christianos ex Judaeis exstitisse; radice sublata stirpem facile perituram' (*Chronica*, Lib. II, c. xxx, in *P.L.*, ed. Migne, t. xx). The possibility that Sulpicius Severus derived this account from the lost portion of the *Historiae* of Tacitus has been long debated, inevitably without decision either way: cf. Schürer, *G.J.V.* I, 631, n. 115; Thackeray, *Josephus*, p. 37, in the Loeb *Josephus*, II, xxv; Mommsen, *Das Weltreich der Caesaren*, p. 391, note; A. Momigliano in *C.A.H.* x, 862, n. 1; Streeter in *C.A.H.* XI, 254–5; Eisler, ΙΗΣΟΥΣ ΒΑΣΙΛΕΥΣ, II, 600–3; Ricciotti, *Flavio Giuseppe*, I, 86–8; H. Montefiore, 'Sulpicius Severus and Titus' Council of War', *Historia*, XI (1962), 156–70.

[2] Mark xiv. 56–9. [3] Mark xv. 29.

dently brought against Jesus; but for the moment what especially concerns us here is the apparent discrepancy between the record of Jesus' prophecy of the coming destruction of the Temple in xiii. 1–3 and the later repudiation of the charge that he would destroy the sacred edifice as a lying calumny.

The rejection of the charge, in the account of the Sanhedrin trial, as 'false witness' must surely represent a tradition which Mark had derived from the Jerusalem Christians; for the fact that they were so devotedly attached to the Temple and its cultus, as we have seen,[1] means that they must have denied any suggestion that Jesus had condemned this covenanted institution of Israel or threatened that he would destroy it—indeed, they treasured the memory that he called it the 'house of God' and sought to cleanse it of the abuses for which the pro-Roman sacerdotal aristocracy was responsible.[2] Now, since Mark was obviously aware of this, for he actually records the rejection of the charge about destroying the Temple as false witness, how was it that he also represents Jesus as foretelling the destruction of the Temple? Surely such a prophecy could be construed as a threat or at least as indicating a hostile attitude to the Temple, thus seemingly to contradict the representation of the charge at the trial as false. That he must have realised that his narrative might thereby give the impression of containing contradictory statements seems to be indicated by the fact that, while he represents Jesus as prophesying the destruction of the Temple, he is careful not to suggest that he would himself destroy it.[3] The distinction is not merely academic; for both the Gospel of John and Acts attest the currency of a tradition that Jesus would destroy the Temple, thus indicating that the charge brought against him at the Sanhedrin trial was not entirely 'false witness'.[4] It would appear, therefore, that Mark was concerned to follow a tradition, which must have derived from the Jerusalem Christians, that Jesus was innocent of threatening to destroy the Temple, and yet he took the risk of being misunderstood by depicting Jesus as prophesying its

---

[1] 'It is not clear why Mark represents the testimony as false...It is more probable that Mark reflects the uneasiness of primitive Christianity regarding the saying on the part of those who continued to observe the Temple worship' (Taylor, St Mark, p. 566).   [2] Mark xi. 17.

[3] xiii. 2. Note the impersonal nature of the statement: οὐ μὴ ἀφεθῇ ὧδε λίθος ἐπὶ λίθον ὃς οὐ μὴ καταλυθῇ. Cf. Goguel, Jesus, pp. 412–20.

[4] John ii. 18–19; Acts vi. 14. Cf. Klostermann, Markusevangelium, p. 155; Bultmann, Gesch. d. syn. Trad. pp. 126–7, Ergänzungsheft, pp. 17–18; Simon, Recherches d'histoire judéo-chrétienne, pp. 11–12.

catastrophic ruin, that 'there will not be left here one stone upon another, that will not be thrown down'.[1] It thus seems that Mark was especially intent on informing his readers that Jesus had foretold the destruction of the Temple, and we may reasonably ask why this should have been.

When the verses that introduce the prophecy are considered, the impression is given that a definite *mise en scène* has been carefully composed by the author of Mark. It is well to cite the passage concerned *in extenso*:

And as he came out of the temple, one of his disciples said to him, 'Look, Teacher, what wonderful stones and what wonderful buildings!' And Jesus said to him, 'Do you see these great buildings? There will not be left here one stone upon another, that will not be thrown down.' And as he sat on the Mount of Olives opposite the temple, Peter and James and John and Andrew asked him privately (κατ' ἰδίαν), 'Tell us, when this will be, and what will be the sign when these things are all to be accomplished?' And Jesus began to say to them, 'Take heed that no one leads you astray. Many will come in my name, saying, "I am he!" and they will lead many astray.'[2]

In writing thus for his fellow-Christians in Rome, the author of Mark was clearly concerned to tell them two things: that Jesus had foretold the destruction of the Temple at Jerusalem, but that he had warned his disciples against being misled, when the event happened, by pretenders, who would claim, 'in the name of Jesus', to be some significant personage, cryptically designated by the words ἐγώ εἰμι, whose identity the Roman Christians evidently knew.[3] Then follows, as being uttered by Jesus, a series of oracles

---

[1] Mark xiii. 2. On the parallel case of Jesus, son of Ananias, and his prophecies, as recorded by Jos. *War*, VI. 300–9, see below, p. 331, n. 2.

[2] xiii. 1–6 (R.S.V.). The contention that the prophecy in *v.* 2 is not a *vaticinium ex eventu*, because the Temple was actually destroyed by fire (cf. Taylor, *St Mark*, p. 501), overlooks the fact that Josephus says that Titus ordered the whole city and the Temple to be razed to the ground (τήν τε πόλιν ἅπασαν καὶ τὸν νεὼν κατασκάπτειν), leaving only the three towers to witness to the former strength of the city (*War*, VII. 1–3). Very probably one of the tableaux in the triumphal procession depicted this utter destruction of the city and its Temple. On other Messianic claimants see pp. 108–9, 110, 112–13.

[3] This enigmatic reference, presupposing the ability of the Roman Christians to understand it, would be intelligible if it concerns Vespasian, whom Josephus (*War*, VI. 312–15) recognised as the prophesied world-ruler (i.e. Messiah): cf. Tacitus, *Hist.* v. 13; Suetonius, *Vesp.* 4, 5. The Roman Christians had undoubtedly heard of the 'signs and wonders' which Vespasian was reputed to have performed at Alexandria; cf. Tac. *Hist.* IV. 81–2; Suet. *Vesp.* 7.

concerned both to intimate that the end of the world and the coming of the mysterious Son of Man were imminent, and also to warn against precipitate identification of the arrival of the Last Day (τὸ τέλος).[1] It will be our task presently to evaluate the significance of this apocalyptic discourse as a whole in terms of the *Sitz im Leben* of Mark; but for the present we must consider the evidence of the introductory verses (1–3).

As we have suggested, the *mise en scène* presented in these verses creates an impression of artificiality of composition. A disciple is represented as specially drawing the attention of Jesus to the size or quality of the stones (ποταποὶ λίθοι) of which the Temple was constructed, and the magnificence of the buildings (ποταπαὶ οἰκοδομαί). Now, considering that most Palestinian Jews, even those living in Galilee, would have been familiar with the Temple from childhood, since it was the custom to go there for the greater festivals, as Luke ii. 41 ff. graphically shows, it is patently naïve to think of a disciple pointing out to Jesus the splendour of the Temple as though they were seeing it for the first time.[2] However, this emphasis upon the grandeur and beauty of the Jerusalem Temple would be intelligible in Mark, when writing for the Christians of Rome, who had just seen representations of the Temple and its magnificent treasures, the Menorah, the golden table of shew-bread and the trumpets, paraded through the streets of the city by the victorious legionaries of Titus.[3] The Jerusalem Temple was 'in the news' for them, and they had been impressed by the evidence of its greatness and splendour, and also by its catastrophic destruction. Now Mark told them that this signal disaster which had befallen the Jewish nation had been foretold by their divine Lord, Jesus, and that it was one of the signs that heralded his Second Coming and the end of the present world-order.[4]

---

[1] xiii. 7: δεῖ γενέσθαι, ἀλλ' οὔπω τὸ τέλος ('das Ende des gegenwärtigen Äons und damit zugleich der Anbruch der zukünftigen Welt', Klostermann, *Markusevangelium*, p. 133). Cf. H. Conzelmann in *Z.N.T.W.* 50 (1959), pp. 214–15.

[2] G. R. Beasley-Murray (*Commentary on Mark Thirteen*, pp. 19–20) endeavours to meet this objection by arguing that Josephus gives a long account of the splendours of the Temple; but he forgets that Josephus is writing for Gentile readers who had not seen the Temple—as, indeed, Mark was doing. [3] See Plate XI.

[4] 'für die Weissagung der Tempelzerstörung Mk 13, 2 besteht mindestens die Möglichkeit, daß sie [die Worte] erst von der Gemeinde Jesus in den Mund gelegt worden sind' (Bultmann, *Gesch. d. syn. Trad.* p. 132).

This preoccupation with the Temple, in a writing addressed to the Christian community in Rome, is thus consistent with the other evidence, already noticed, in pointing to a date just after the Flavian triumph in A.D. 71. But, before we go on to consider the testimony of the apocalyptic discourse that follows the significant *mise en scène* of xiii. 1–3, it will be helpful to notice another aspect of Mark's interest in the Temple. In his account of the Cleansing of the Temple, the author of Mark depicts Jesus as saying, in explanation of his attack upon the trading establishment there, 'Is it not written, "My house shall be called a house of prayer for all the nations"? But you have made it a den of thieves' (σπήλαιον λῃστῶν).[1] Now, this saying combines the LXX text of Isa. xlvi. 7 and an adaptation of Jer. vii. 11, and it is evidently an *ad hoc* composition of Mark's, inspired by his own evaluation of the Temple and the fate which had befallen it.[2] Thus he sets forth his view of God's intention for the Temple by quoting, in notable distinction from Matthew and Luke at this place, the whole of Isa. xlvi. 7, which represents God as proclaiming that the Temple was not to be the exclusive possession of the Jews, but a house of prayer for all the Gentiles.[3] This is truly a remarkable declaration, considering Mark's *Sitz im Leben*; for it means that the author of Mark would have his Roman readers believe that God had intended that they and other non-Jewish peoples should worship in his great sanctuary at Jerusalem, and that its use was not the peculiar privilege of the Jews.[4] But that is not

[1] xi. 17.

[2] 'καὶ ἐδίδασκεν καὶ ἔλεγεν erweckt den Eindruck, als ob Handlung und Wort nicht ursprünglich zusammengehörten...Also dürfte V. 17 eine nachträgliche Deutung — wenn man will, ein "Predigtspruch" — der altüberlieferten Szene V. 15 f. sein, wie Joh 2, 17 eine weitere solche Deutung hinzugekommen ist' (Bultmann, *Gesch. d. syn. Trad.* p. 36).

[3] πᾶσιν τοῖς ἔθνεσιν. Cf. Matt. xxi. 13; Luke xix. 46; E. Schweizer, 'Mark's Contribution to the Quest of the Historical Jesus', *N.T.S.* x (1963–4), 429.

[4] In this connection it is important to recall that Gentiles were debarred from the inner courts of the Temple, where the cultus was performed, by a stone balustrade, on which inscriptions, in Greek and Latin, threatened death to any who transgressed this boundary. See Jos. *War*, v. 193, *Ant.* xv. 417: cf. Loeb ed. of Josephus, III, 258, n. *c*. One of these inscriptions was found in 1871: see illustration in Ricciotti, *Flavio Giuseppe*, IV, 44: cf. Eisler, ΙΗΣΟΥΣ ΒΑΣΙΛΕΥΣ, I, Tafel L (29), II, 535–6. Is it too fanciful to suppose that one of these inscriptions had been brought to Rome and displayed in the triumphal procession as evidence of Jewish religious intolerance? On the attitude towards Gentiles which these inscriptions

all: when he wrote, that sanctuary had been destroyed in consequence of the Jewish revolt against Rome. Moreover, during the siege, the Temple had been the chief citadel of Jewish resistance and it had been held by Zealots, who in Roman eyes were ληϲταί ('brigands').[1] Josephus, in his *Jewish War*, published *c.* 75–9, attributed the burning of the Temple to God's desire to purge it from the iniquities which the Zealots had perpetrated there.[2] Mark evidently thought the same: invoking what must have seemed to him the inspired utterance of Jeremiah, he represents Jesus as condemning the Jews for making (πεποιήκατε) the Temple a σπήλαιον ληϲτῶν, which might well have been a current Roman expression for the Zealot-held Temple.[3] In other words, as part of his anti-Jewish polemic which we have yet to study, Mark explains the destruction of the Temple to his Roman readers as due to the wickedness of the Jews, who made God's sanctuary at Jerusalem into a 'den of brigands, *sc.* Zealots', instead of a 'house of prayer for all the nations'.

The Temple, then, was 'in the news' at Rome, when the Gospel of Mark was written; its destruction, however, had not only to be explained in terms of the past for the Roman Christians, it had also to be interpreted to them relative to the future. So signal a catastrophe had clearly excited the eschatological hopes of the Christian community; it was being related to other recent events, and regarded as an indubitable portent that the end of the existing world-order was imminent and the return of Christ at hand.[4] The author of Mark clearly shared in these views; but it is evident that he realised that such expectation could be dangerous for the life and well-being of the community, if it became too fervent and prompted indiscreet utterance or action. His handling of the situation in the apocalyptic discourse which he attributes to Jesus as he sits on the Mount of Olives, contemplating the ill-fated Temple, is a masterly balance of recognition that the 'signs of the times' did indeed point to the imminence of the end, and of wise caution concerned to control

expressed see E. J. Bickerman, 'The Warning Inscription of Herod's Temple', *J.Q.R.* xxxvii (1946–7), 390, and S. Zeitlin, 'The Warning Inscription of the Temple', xxxviii, 116.

[1] See above, pp. 132, 137, n. 1, 140 ff.   [2] Jos. *War*, iv. 201, 323–4.

[3] It is significant that Mark calls the two men crucified with Jesus ληϲταί (xv. 27); since they appear to have been connected with the insurrection in the city, they were probably Zealots. Cf. Hengel, *Die Zeloten*, p. 30; also below, p. 351, n. 1.

[4] Mark xiii. 4. See below, p. 240.

excessive excitement that might arouse the suspicion of the pagan neighbours of the Roman Christians and provoke persecution.

The pertinence of the apocalyptic discourse to the situation created by the destruction of the Temple is clearly revealed in xiii. 4. Prompted by the prophecy of Jesus, his disciples are represented as immediately asking: 'Tell us, when shall these things (ταῦτα) be? and what shall be the sign (σημεῖον) when these things are all (ταῦτα...πάντα) about to be accomplished?' Both the use of the plural forms here and the future reference are significant. Jesus had foretold one event only, namely, the destruction of the Temple.[1] This presumably should have led the disciples to inquire about the date of its occurrence and how it would happen, because great stone-built temples are not normally subject to such sudden catastrophic destruction.[2] But the fact that the question put in the mouth of the disciples by Mark is concerned with the accomplishment of a number of things, and that some 'sign' was expected of the imminence of this accomplishment, surely indicates that in the mind of the author, and doubtless of his readers, the destruction of the Temple, already a *fait accompli*, was linked with the evaluation of other contemporary events which seemed to have an eschatological significance.[3] If the composition of Mark is dated for some time shortly after A.D. 71, as the body of evidence so far surveyed suggests, then the catena of events to which the apocalyptic discourse makes reference can be convincingly identified and the existent situation in the Roman church, indicated by that discourse, becomes intelligible.[4]

Thus, starting from Jesus' prophecy concerning the fate of the Temple, the actual accomplishment of which had evidently excited the eschatological expectations of the Roman Christians, the apocalyptic discourse proper opens cautiously with a Dominical warning against deception and an assurance calculated to reduce the tension which recent events had evidently caused in the Roman community:

[1] Cf. Klostermann, *Markusevangelium*, p. 133; Taylor, *St Mark*, p. 502.

[2] The completeness of the Roman destruction of the Temple was clearly extraordinary, as Josephus shows: see p. 235, n. 2 above.

[3] Note the demonstrative ταῦτα (πάντα). It is also significant that the revelation here is represented as having been originally given privately (κατ' ἰδίαν) to three disciples only.

[4] Conversely, the assumption of a pre-A.D. 70 date for Mark necessitates a more convincing series of identifications with earlier events and their relation to the situation of the Christian community in Rome about A.D. 60.

'And when you hear of wars and rumours of wars, do not be alarmed; this must take place; but the end is not yet. For nation will rise against nation, and kingdom against kingdom; there will be earthquakes in various places, there will be famines; this is but the beginning of the sufferings.'[1] In the year A.D. 71 the inhabitants of Rome could look back on many 'wars and rumours of wars'; for there had been the internal struggles, following on the death of Nero in 68, in which Galba, Otho, Vitellius and Vespasian had successively contended for the imperial power,[2] while the external security of the empire had been threatened by dangerous revolts in Gaul in 68, in Moesia and on the Rhine in 69, and in Judaea from 66 to 70.[3] There had been earthquakes at Laodicea in 60 and at Pompeii in 63,[4] and with these upheavals there was undoubtedly much economic and social distress. The discourse goes on to tell of persecution (*vv.* 9–13), which would poignantly remind the Roman Christians of their own sufferings under Nero in 64.[5]

The author of Mark, accordingly, leads his readers through a survey of recent events and experience, showing their eschatological significance in terms of the 'birth-pangs of the Messiah'.[6] Thus he approaches the signal event which had provided the impetus to all this eschatological excitement. In *v.* 14 he introduces the apocalyptic oracle which had originated from the attempt of Gaius to desecrate the Temple in 39, and, by his discreet parenthetic comment, he reminds his readers how this oracle had been fulfilled by the actions of Titus and the Roman legionaries at the taking of the Temple, as we have also seen.[7] The warnings contained in this

---

[1] xiii. 7–8 (R.S.V.). S.B. *Kommentar*, I, 950, see in ἀρχὴ ὠδίνων ταῦτα the Rabbinical concept of 'the birth-pangs of the Messiah', thereby assuming its currency at this period. Cf. Klausner, *Jesus of Nazareth*, p. 199; Klostermann, *Markusevangelium*, p. 133.

[2] Josephus gives a summary description of the critical state of the Roman world at the time of the Jewish revolt, *War*, I. 4–5. Cf. *C.A.H.* x, chh. xxiv, xxv; A. Peretti, *La Sibilla babilonese*, pp. 18–20.

[3] See the Chronological Table in *C.A.H.* x.

[4] Tacitus, *Ann.* XIV. 27, XV. 22. Cf. Peretti, *La Sibilla babilonese*, p. 470. It is significant that the Jews interpreted the famous eruption of Vesuvius in A.D. 79 as divine punishment upon the Romans for their treatment of Israel (*Sib. Orac.* IV. 130).

[5] Cf. Taylor, *St Mark*, pp. 88, 509–10.

[6] See above, n. 1.

[7] See above, pp. 143, 231–3. It is significant that Beasley-Murray, in his attempt to date the Markan Apocalypse before A.D. 70, seeks to emend the text of xiii. 14, despite its being attested by the best MSS (cf. *Jesus and the Future*, pp. 255–7).

'Little Apocalypse' about 'false Christs' and 'false prophets' enable him to reinforce the warning already given in *vv.* 5 and 6, and to bring this first section of the discourse, dealing with the events of the recent past, to a close with a suitable Dominical admonition: 'But take heed; I have told you all things beforehand.'[1]

Having thus shown his fellow-Christians in Rome the relevance of these recent happenings, culminating in the desecration and destruction of the Temple at Jerusalem, the author of Mark turns to deal with the current situation and what it portended for the future. Quite clearly eschatological excitement was running high in the Christian community at Rome; the author of Mark shared in it, seeing in recent events, as did his fellow-believers, signs of the imminence of the *Parousia* and the end of the world. But it would seem that, when he wrote, there was a sense of anti-climax. The series of events culminating in the fall of Jerusalem and the destruction of the Temple had naturally led to the conviction that such a catastrophe was surely immediately antecedent to the final catastrophe and the longed-for appearance of their Lord.[2] But now there was a pause; nothing seemed to happen, and the faithful began to be puzzled. The Markan author deals adroitly with the situation: he wanted to encourage hope, without stimulating excitement, but at the same time he was cautious. Already in *v.* 10 he had made a convenient qualification, as it were, concerning the future; for he represents Jesus as saying 'the gospel must first (πρῶτον) be preached to all nations'. What this saying implied exactly is uncertain, since it is not clear what Mark envisaged as 'all nations' (πάντα τὰ ἔθνη), or how intensively the gospel should 'first' be preached (κηρυχθῆναι) to what is logically the whole of mankind.[3] However, in making this qualification, a convenient lien was taken on the future, and provision made for any continuance of the seeming present delay. The note of caution thus adumbrated in *v.* 10 finds more extended expression after the section (*vv.* 24–7) describing the cosmic cataclysm which will precede the actual *Parousia* of the Son of Man. The disciples are admonished to learn from the burgeoning of the fig-tree, that as the appearance of its leaves heralds

[1] xiii. 21–3. See above, pp. 235–6.
[2] See above, p. 236. The disciples' question in xiii. 4 clearly indicates that the destruction of the Temple had an eschatological significance. The Matthaean parallel (xxiv. 3) shows that more than a decade later the ruin of the Temple was still regarded as the prelude to the *Parousia*.
[3] 'This verse [i.e. 10] is widely regarded as an insertion made by Mark (or, less probably, a redactor) in his source' (Taylor, *St Mark*, p. 507).

the approach of summer, so recent events announced the imminence of the Second Advent.[1] But, having thus reaffirmed his belief that the End was near by another Dominical confirmation of its proximity,[2] the author of Mark goes on to warn his readers against attempting to forecast the time: 'But of that day or that hour no one knows, not even the angels in heaven, nor the Son, but only the Father. Take heed, watch; for you do not know when the time will be.'[3] Reinforcing this admonition with a corresponding parable, he brings the apocalyptic discourse to a close with a final exhortation, so worded that the Roman Christians should not mistake that the divine words applied to them: 'And what I say to you I say to all: Watch.'[4]

The cumulative witness of all this evidence is unmistakable. It points indubitably to a *Sitz im Leben* for the Markan Gospel which corresponds exactly to that of the Christian community at Rome in the years immediately following the Flavian triumph of A.D. 71 over insurgent Judaea. The graphic ocular proof which the Roman Christians had then received of the Jewish overthrow affected them profoundly in two closely related ways, besides stimulating their eschatological expectations. It brought, disturbingly, to their

[1] xiii. 28–9. Meyer (*Ursprung*, I, 127) is right in seeing that the eschatology of this passage is universal in its reference: 'Es handelt sich ja auch garnicht um eine Katastrophe, sondern um das Weltende.' However, in concluding that it indicates a pre-A.D. 70 date, he falls into the fallacy of expecting from Mark the same degree of detachment from the events of A.D. 70 of which Luke was capable when writing more than a decade later: he fails to take account of the possibility that Mark was too closely involved in those events to write as Luke does in xxi. 20, 23 f. See above, pp. 222 ff. According to Taylor, *St Mark*, p. 520, 'The reference to ἐπὶ θύραις is also obscure, for it is not clear whether a person or an event, or even a series of events, is meant. These ambiguities strongly suggest that the parable is used by the compiler for a purpose for which it was not originally intended.'

[2] xiii. 30–1. The assurance given in the words οὐ μὴ παρέλθῃ ἡ γενεὰ αὕτη μέχρις οὗ ταῦτα πάντα γένηται would only be intelligible to a Christian community at a period when many of its members had died and doubt was beginning to form as to whether its surviving members would witness the *Parousia*. 'A genuine saying has been adapted in the interests of contemporary apocalyptic' (Taylor, *St Mark*, p. 521). Cf. Bultmann, *Gesch. d. syn. Trad.* pp. 130, 132; Klostermann, *Markusevangelium*, p. 138.

[3] xiii. 32–3. 'V. 33 ist zweifellos eine redaktionelle Bildung des Mk.' (Bultmann, *Gesch. d. syn. Trad.* pp. 187–8). Cf. Taylor, *St Mark*, pp. 522–3.

[4] xiii. 34–7. Cf. Klostermann, *Markusevangelium*, p. 139.

attention the fact that their faith stemmed from this Jewish people who had so fiercely revolted against Roman rule, and it faced them also with the serious possibility that they might be regarded by their pagan neighbours and the Roman authorities as being themselves infected with Jewish revolutionary ideas. This danger was indeed a very real one; for the embarrassing fact could not be concealed that the founder of their faith had been executed, some years before, by a Roman procurator of Judaea as a rebel against the Roman government of that country.[1]

As we shall see, the author of Mark was profoundly concerned with the problem which the crucifixion of Jesus thus constituted; but his Gospel also reveals his embarrassment about another matter, and his manner of dealing with it is particularly illuminating with regard to the motive that informs his account of the Roman trial and execution of Jesus. The matter concerned, to which reference has already been made, is Mark's handling of the fact that one of the Twelve Apostles of Jesus was a Zealot. In giving a list of the Twelve, whom Jesus appointed 'that they might be with him, and that he might send them out to preach the Gospel (κηρύσσειν), and to have authority to cast out demons', one, Simon, is given the title 'the Kananaios' (τὸν Καναναῖον).[2] No explanation is provided of this strange title, which must have been quite incomprehensible to the Greek-speaking Christians of Rome.[3] This omission is the more

---

[1] Cf. p. 226, n. 4 above. The *graffito* traced on the wall of a room in the imperial palace on the Palatine, representing a crucified man, with the head of an ass, adored by a young man, accompanied by the caption 'Alexander worships his god', raises an interesting question in this connection. It appears to date from about the end of the second century and to be a blasphemous caricature of Christian worship. It may indicate that, still at this period in Rome, Christianity in the popular mind was associated with Judaism: for Tacitus had asserted that the Jews worshipped the figure of an ass in the Temple (*Hist.* v. 3–4). The *graffito* would suggest the currency of a popular belief concerning Christianity, which embodied the twin facts of the crucifixion of the founder and its Jewish origin. Cf. H. Leclercq, *La vie chrétienne primitive* (Paris, 1928), p. 85, plate XLIX. On the continuing identification of Christianity as a form of Judaism cf. Frend, *Martyrdom and Persecution*, pp. 163–4.

[2] iii. 18. It is of some interest to note that certain Old Latin MSS give *iudas zelotes* for Θαδδαῖος in *v.* 18: cf. Taylor, *St Mark*, p. 233.

[3] The article would have informed Mark's readers that *Kananaios* was a title, and must, therefore, have some significance. In the previous *v.* 17 the strange title *Boanērges* had been explained to them, although Υἱοὶ Βροντῆς may be a euphemistic interpretation of the enigmatic original which was perhaps more compromising.

remarkable, for it is the custom of the author of Mark to explain all
Hebrew or Aramaic words and Jewish customs to his readers.[1]
The fact that he does not do so here with the Hebrew title assigned
to Simon cannot be due to an oversight, because he had, just before,
explained the sobriquet 'Boanerges' given to the brothers James
and John.[2] Now, as we have seen, the word Καναναῖος is a Greek
transliteration of the Aramaic קַנְאָנָא, meaning 'Zealot'.[3] That Simon
was known as 'the Zealot' (ὁ Ζηλωτής) is confirmed by the Lukan
writer in his lists, twice given, of the Twelve.[4] But he wrote some
fifteen years or more after the Jewish revolt and the destruction of
Jerusalem, when the passions excited by those events, in which the
Zealots had played so notorious a part, had subsided and it was
a matter of historical interest only that one of Jesus' Apostles had
been a Zealot. When the Gospel of Mark was written, the name
'Zealot' had an ugly and dangerous sound in Roman ears; accordingly, its author deemed it unwise to record the fact, for a Roman
public, that one of the Twelve had actually been a member of this
execrable sect of Jewish fanatics who had been responsible for the
Jewish revolt. He departed, therefore, from his usual practice of
explaining Jewish names and customs to his Gentile readers, and left
the strange expression τὸν Καναναῖον to conceal its dangerous secret.[5]

His act has a twofold significance. The fact that, when Mark was

---

[1] Cf. iii. 17, v. 41, vii. 3–4, 34, xv. 22, 34. Cf. Bacon, *Is Mark a Roman
Gospel?*, pp. 55–9.

[2] See p. 243, n. 3 above. Cf. Bacon, *Is Mark a Roman Gospel?*, p. 56; Taylor,
St Mark, pp. 231–2.

[3] See above, pp. 42–4. 'Es ist nicht ein כְּנַעֲנִי, das wäre Χαναναῖος, auch nicht
einer *de uico Chana Galilaeae, ubi aquam dominus uertit in uinum* Hieronymus —
das wäre Καναῖος, sondern ein קַנְאָנָא, d. h. ein (ehemaliger) Angehöriger
der Zeloten-partei unter den Pharisäern' (Klostermann, *Markusevangelium*,
p. 35). Cf. Schürer, *G.J.V.* 1, 486, n. 138; Dalman, *Jesus-Jeshua*, p. 12;
Eisler, ΙΗΣΟΥΣ ΒΑΣΙΛΕΥΣ, 11, 68; Klausner, *Jesus of Nazareth*, p. 254;
S.B. *Kommentar*, 1, 537; Taylor, *St Mark*, p. 234; Hengel, *Die Zeloten*,
pp. 72–3.

[4] Luke vi. 15; Acts i. 13. Cf. J. M. Creed, *St Luke*, p. 88; F. F. Bruce, *Acts of
the Apostles*, p. 73.

[5] That Matthew (x. 4) also describes Simon only as ὁ Καναναῖος is susceptible of two (complementary) explanations. Since his Gospel is addressed
to a predominantly Jewish-Christian community, the meaning of ὁ
Καναναῖος would need no explanation; if Matthew was written in Alexandria (see below, pp. 289 ff.), it would also have been expedient there, as in
Rome, not to give the term its Greek equivalent, i.e. ὁ Ζηλωτής, because
the Sicarii had caused great trouble there after A.D. 70 (cf. Jos. *War*, vii.
409 ff.).

written, the name 'Zealot' was so much 'in the news' at Rome, surely points unmistakably to those years when Jewish affairs had so urgently intruded themselves upon the attention of the Christian community in the capital. No other time can be found, within the limits of the period during which Mark could conceivably have been written, when the name 'Zealot' might have been charged with such meaning for the Roman Christians that it was deemed safer to leave it, in this record of Jesus, in its original, but unintelligible, Aramaic form. This evidence of the contemporary significance of 'Zealot', however, has further meaning. That the author of Mark thought it necessary thus to disguise the fact that an Apostle of Jesus had been a Zealot, surely indicates that he was aware of an aspect of the career of Jesus which it was dangerous to make plain to his Roman readers at this critical time. In other words, the fact that Jesus had chosen a Zealot as one of the inner band of his disciples had to be concealed, because it could not be denied. And this, in turn, can only mean that, in the interests of the portrait which he wished to present of Jesus, the author of Mark could not afford to let it be known that the profession of Zealotism had evidently been compatible with a close association with Jesus.

This masking of the fact that one of the Twelve had been a Zealot indicates that the author of Mark was not concerned to present an accurate historical record of the career of Jesus, but that he was moved by a definite apologetical motive. What that motive was is clear. In his presentation of Jesus he did not want it to be known that Jesus had had a connection with Zealotism which might fairly be interpreted as sympathetic. If he thus sought to suppress the evidence of such sympathy, it is legitimate to infer that his purpose in writing was closely related to the potentially dangerous situation in which the Christian community at Rome found itself, as a result of the Jewish War and the vivid reminder of it that the Flavian triumph had produced. Mark's action over the delicate matter of Simon's Zealotism further suggests that he was aware of certain politically compromising factors in the career of Jesus. Now if, as is likely, the Roman execution of Jesus involved factors of this kind, we may reasonably expect that Mark's apologetic concern would be especially manifest in his account of the trial which led to Jesus' condemnation by Pilate. To this basic issue we must now turn our attention.

It is obvious, in view of the situation of the Roman Christians about A.D. 71, that the knowledge that their Lord had been executed for sedition, as many Jewish rebels had been, was both disturbing and embarrassing. Whether they had originally felt it to be so, when they had been converted to Christianity, is an interesting question which, unfortunately, we have not the means of answering. We do not know who was responsible for the founding of a church in Rome, and how the faith had been presented and developed before the writing of the Markan Gospel.[1] It is reasonable to think that the Christian community there was originally a Jewish foundation, and, if the tradition of Peter's sojourn there be sound, it would seem that the form of the faith first taught there was that of the Mother Church of Jerusalem.[2] This would mean, in the light of what we know of this primitive Jewish Christianity, that Jesus was presented as the Messiah who would shortly return with supernatural power to 'restore the kingdom to Israel'. In this Jerusalem 'gospel', the Crucifixion would have been interpreted as a martyrdom, at the hands of the heathen, for Israel. To the Jewish mind, as we have seen, no embarrassment would have been felt that Jesus had been executed by the Romans as a rebel against their government in the Holy Land; indeed, on the contrary, it would have been deemed an honourable death.[3] It is probable, moreover, that this original Jewish Christianity in Rome, with its strong Messianic emphasis, caused those riots concerning 'Chrestus', which Suetonius records, and which led the emperor Claudius to expel the Jews from the city.[4]

If Paul's Epistle to the Romans was indeed addressed to the Christian community there, then many Jews must have soon found their way back again to Rome.[5] However, if the record of Acts

---

[1] Cf. Sanday and Headlam, *Epistle to the Romans*, pp. xxv–xxxi; Weiss, *Earliest Christianity*, ii, 837 ff.; Cullmann, *Petrus*, pp. 78–178; Frend, *Martyrdom and Persecution*, pp. 160 ff.

[2] Cf. Sanday and Headlam, *Epistle to the Romans*, p. xxvi; Bruce in *B.J.R.L.* 44 (1962), pp. 317–18; Brandon, *Fall of Jerusalem*, pp. 145 ff.

[3] See above, pp. 177 ff.

[4] Suet. *Claudius*, 25. 4; Acts xviii. 2. Cf. P. de Labriolle, *La réaction païenne*, pp. 42–3; V. M. Scramuzza in *B.C.* v, 295–6; Bruce in *B.J.R.L.* 44 (1962), pp. 315–18.

[5] Whether the Epistle to the Romans, in its extant form, was originally addressed to the Christian community in Rome or not (cf. T. W. Manson, *Studies*, pp. 227 ff.), it was evidently sent to Rome and envisages Jewish-Christian readers. According to V. M. Scramuzza, 'The practical difficulty of expelling all the Jews, which Dio points out, suggests that Suetonius's statement should be interpreted in the sense that only those individuals were expelled who took actual part in the disorders' (in *B.C.* v, 296).

is to be trusted, when Paul came to Rome, the Jewish community there spoke as though they had no first-hand knowledge of Christianity, and the impression is given that Paul began to form a community there, presumably of Gentiles.[1] If this were so, then it would be reasonable to suppose that Paul's 'gospel' formed the faith of this newly established Church, so that his interpretation of the Crucifixion as the divinely planned means of mankind's salvation was current there; and this interpretation, as we have seen, paid scant regard to the historical circumstances of Jesus' death.[2] This Pauline evaluation of the Crucifixion had possibly suffered a temporary eclipse, if the Roman Christians had been subjected to a period of intensive Jerusalem propaganda after Paul's death, for which there is certain evidence.[3] Accordingly, by the time of the fall of Jerusalem, it is likely that the Christians in Rome were aware both of the fact that Jesus had been executed by the Romans as a rebel and that his death had a saving efficacy for all mankind who would accept him as Lord. In their minds these two traditions were, doubtless, but vaguely related until the Jewish catastrophe of A.D. 70 and its repercussions in Rome. Then the fact of the Roman execution of Jesus for sedition became a problem, with disquieting possibilities: how came it that Jesus had been condemned to this kind of death? What to Jewish Christians had appeared an honourable death for Israel was not seen in this way by Gentile Christians, living in Rome, who were now acutely conscious that many thousands of Jewish rebels had died similar deaths for contesting Rome's right to dominion over their land. The problem was an urgent and disturbing one: if Jesus had indeed been crucified as a rebel, how could his death be regarded as a divine act of salvation?

A most pressing need, then, existed in the Christian community in Rome at this time for an explanation of Pilate's condemnation and execution of Jesus as a revolutionary against Rome's suzerainty over Judaea. Such an explanation the author of Mark undertakes to supply, and the effect of his explanation has been incalculable for all subsequent Christian thinking. So far as we know, his was a pioneer attempt, and it set the pattern for the other Gospels. That

---

[1] Acts xxviii. 17–30. Cf. G. W. H. Lampe in *Peake's Commentary*², 803*d*; Preuschen, *Apostelgeschichte*, p. 158. See also Bruce in *B.J.R.L.* 46 (1964), pp. 342–5.

[2] See above, pp. 183 ff.; cf. Brandon, *Fall of Jerusalem*, ch. iv, and *History, Time and Deity*, pp. 150–1, 159–69.

[3] Cf. Brandon, *Fall of Jerusalem*, pp. 152–3, 199–200.

some connected narrative of the events leading to the Crucifixion was already in existence, and that it derived from the Church of Jerusalem, is most probable,[1] and we shall presently consider whether some of its lineaments can be discerned beneath the Markan story; but our task now is to try to evaluate the motive that underlies the Passion Narrative as it now stands in Mark.

Briefly, Mark's account of the trial of Jesus may be said to show that, although the verdict of death for sedition was actually given by the Roman procurator, the responsibility really lay with the Jewish authorities, who, intent on destroying Jesus, forced the reluctant Pilate to do their will. Such an explanation is not incredible *per se*, and history provides many other examples of the unjust and illegal condemnation of innocent persons. But, on a cursory consideration, it must certainly be adjudged remarkable that the native authorities of a small subject people, as were the Judaean Jews, could have compelled a Roman magistrate, against his better will and judgement, to do what they wanted. Such initial doubt, moreover, quickly deepens when one begins to examine the Markan account critically; for not only is it found to be vague and imprecise on many important points, besides presupposing the existence of an otherwise unknown and unlikely custom, but it is also self-contradictory on grounds of internal logic.

The author of Mark carefully prepares his readers for the decisive part which the Jewish leaders play, according to his account, in the Roman condemnation of Jesus. Thus, in the early days of Jesus' ministry in Galilee, we are told that, angered that Jesus should have healed a man with a withered hand on the sabbath, 'the Pharisees immediately took counsel with the Herodians against him, in order to destroy him (ὅπως αὐτὸν ἀπολέσωσιν)'.[2] The statement reveals more of the mind of Mark than it does of the event described. For, in the first place, it seems incredible that, after only their fourth encounter with Jesus over fairly trivial issues, the Pharisees become so hostile that they plan to destroy him. The statement is undoubtedly proleptic, being designed to prepare the way for the

---

[1] Cf. Bultmann, *Gesch. d. syn. Trad.* pp. 297–308, Ergänzungsheft, p. 42; Taylor, *Formation of the Gospel Tradition*, pp. 44–59.

[2] iii. 6. T. A. Burkill, in interpreting iii. 1–5 as a Christian defence for 'la pratique de la guérison le jour du sabbat', is obliged to describe *v.* 6 as 'la note de l'éditeur', which 'pointe réellement vers le résultat final du conflit qui sera décrit en détail dans le récit de la passion' ('L'antisémitisme dans l'évangile selon saint Marc', *R.H.R.* 154, 1958, pp. 24–6). Cf. P. Winter, *On the Trial of Jesus*, pp. 111 ff.

ultimate presentation of the Jewish leaders as responsible for the Crucifixion. The fact that the Pharisees, with the Herodians, first appear in Mark's narrative as the Jewish authorities who plan to destroy Jesus, is interesting; because, in the end, it is not they, but the 'chief priests' (οἱ ἀρχιερεῖς), who are represented as having forced Pilate to give the fatal sentence.[1] The explanation would seem to be, as Mark vii. 3 indicates, that to the Gentile Christians of Rome the Pharisees represented the typical Jewish religious leaders;[2] for them οἱ ἀρχιερεῖς would not have denoted persons distinctively Jewish. In Mark the Pharisees appear as the exponents of all that the Gentiles found strange and objectionable in Judaism, as well as being the enemies of Jesus.[3] Hence, at the beginning of his Gospel, the author of Mark presents these type-figures as plotting the death of Jesus. The association of the Pharisees with the Herodians in this design to destroy Jesus also has its significance. The two groups appear again, in the narrative, united in evil intent, namely, to trap Jesus into making a disloyal pronouncement about the Jewish payment of tribute to Caesar.[4] As we have seen, the Herodians were supporters of the native pro-Roman dynasty, whose head, Agrippa II, and his sister Berenice were well known in Rome after A.D. 70—in fact, they would have formed a little foreign coterie there who were in ill-repute with the Romans, owing to the infatuation of Titus for Berenice.[5] Thus, the author of Mark associates with the Pharisees, in their intent to kill Jesus, this Jewish group, whom the Roman Christians would have been predisposed to dislike. Accordingly, in setting the stage for his *apologia* concerning the Roman execution of Jesus, the Markan writer gives his readers an early clue to the problem by making known to them the malignant design of these two detestable Jewish parties.

Having thus made clear the theme of his *apologia*, the author of Mark makes equally clear who were responsible for the sequence of events that finally, in Jerusalem, resulted in the crucifixion of Jesus by the Romans. He relates how, during the last days, having been challenged by 'the chief priests and the scribes and the elders' to reveal his authority for his teaching and actions, Jesus replied

---

[1] xv. 10–11.

[2] οἱ γὰρ Φαρισαῖοι καὶ πάντες οἱ ᾽Ιουδαῖοι. Cf. Taylor, *St Mark*, p. 335.

[3] See Klostermann's pertinent question: 'denkt Mc an die Diasporajuden des Westens, die überwiegend Pharisäer waren?' (*Markusevangelium*, p. 67). Cf. Bacon, *Is Mark a Roman Gospel?*, p. 72.   [4] xii. 13.

[5] See above, p. 129. See also Suetonius, *Titus*, 7; Jones, *The Herods of Judaea*, pp. 257–8.

(αὐτοῖς...λαλεῖν) by telling the Parable of the Wicked Husband-men.[1] This Parable is evidently an allegory, designed by the author to explain the recent Jewish overthrow as divine punishment for the death of Jesus.[2] In terms of the Parable, the Jews had appropriated to themselves what God had entrusted to them for his own purpose. The messengers, whom he had sent to remind them of their obliga-tions, they had variously ill-treated or killed. Finally, they had murdered his beloved Son (υἱὸν ἀγαπητόν),[3] and so drew upon themselves destruction (ἐλεύσεται καὶ ἀπολέσει τοὺς γεωργούς). The 'vineyard' of God, which the Jews had thus so signally failed to cultivate for him, is then given to others (δώσει τὸν ἀμπελῶνα ἄλλοις)—the identity of these 'others', to whom the divine heritage was now committed, would have been readily, and gratefully, recognised by Mark's Gentile readers. According to Mark, the point of the Parable was not lost on the Jewish leaders, and their reaction was hostile: 'And they tried to arrest him, but feared the multitude, for they perceived that he had told the parable against them; so they left him and went away.'[4]

Accordingly, Mark provides by his own interpretation of the Jewish catastrophe of A.D. 70, which he attributes to Jesus, the cause for the resentment of the Jewish leaders and their desire to arrest him. The fact that they were then frustrated in their intention, because of Jesus' position with the multitude, is a matter which we must examine later. What we have to notice now is that, after this episode, the narrative goes on to tell how Jesus countered the efforts of various influential groups, namely, the Pharisees, the Herodians and the Sadducees, to discredit him, thus providing further cause for their hostility.[5] The opportunity to give practical effect to their hatred of Jesus soon came to the Jewish leaders, according to Mark,

[1] xi. 27 ff.
[2] xii. 9. Commenting upon *v.* 9, with reference to the destruction of Jeru-salem, Klostermann remarks (*Markusevangelium*, p. 122): 'Die Drohrede ist mit V. 9 völlig abgeschlossen.'
[3] xii. 6. A maturity of Christological thinking is implied in this term which is consistent with the Roman community and Paul's connection with it. Cf. E. Hoskyns and N. Davey, *The Riddle of the New Testament* (London, 1931), p. 148; Bacon, *Is Mark a Roman Gospel?*, p. 88; Taylor, p. 162.
[4] xii. 12. Cf. Taylor, *Formation of Gospel Tradition*, pp. 179–80.
[5] xii. 13–27. If ἀποστέλλουσιν in *v.* 13 is an impersonal plural, as Taylor suggests (*St Mark*, p. 478), it is indicative of Mark's attitude, namely, of setting Jesus over against a hostile collective 'they', comprising various groups, representative of Judaism, on both its national and religious

through the defection of Judas Iscariot, who offered to betray his master to the chief priests.[1]

Having thus explained how Jesus came to be arrested, through the malice of the Jewish leaders and the treachery of a disciple, Mark at once makes it clear that the subsequent trial was but a legal sham, for the destruction of Jesus was already agreed upon: 'Now the chief priests and the whole council sought testimony against Jesus to put him to death (εἰς τὸ θανατῶσαι αὐτόν).'[2]

It would appear that, in the ensuing account of the Jewish trial, the author of Mark was drawing upon a tradition which must have come from the Jerusalem Christians; for, as we have already noticed, he describes the chief charge brought against Jesus, namely, that he would destroy the Temple, as due to the testimony of false witnesses, whereas he had just before claimed that Jesus had prophesied the Temple's destruction.[3] The fact is important, since it provides a valuable clue to what had probably happened at the trial of Jesus before the Sanhedrin. The Jerusalem Christians, who were distinguished for their attachment to the Temple, must have composed an *apologia* concerning Jesus' condemnation by the Sanhedrin, which especially refuted an accusation that Jesus had in some way threatened the Temple. That the accusation should have been made at all, and indeed, as it seems, constituted the chief charge against Jesus, suggests that it could not have been completely groundless.[4]

sides. So far as an analysis of the sequence of Mark's narrative shows, ἀποστέλλουσιν should refer back through xii. 12 (ἐζήτουν) to xi. 27 (οἱ ἀρχιερεῖς καὶ οἱ γραμματεῖς καὶ οἱ πρεσβύτεροι).

[1] xiv. 10–11. See below, pp. 334 ff. The opportunity which this act of betrayal provided is anticipated to his readers by Mark in xiv. 1–2. The assumption of knowledge of the motives and deliberations of 'the chief priests and the scribes' is very revealing and attests the care with which Mark planned the presentation of his apologetical thesis. Cf. Bultmann, *Gesch. d. syn. Trad.* pp. 282, 300; Taylor, *St Mark*, p. 528.

[2] xiv. 55.

[3] xiv. 57–8. See above, pp. 233 ff. Cf. A. Jaubert, 'Les séances du Sanhédrin et les récits de la Passion', *R.H.R.* 166 (1964), p. 160: 'le passage de Marc cherche à justifier Jésus par rapport à *des juifs* qui pouvaient se scandaliser de cette parole. Il a été composé en fonction d'un auditoire très judaïsant.'

[4] Matthew's interesting variant version of the charge (xxvi. 61) suggests that some utterance against the Temple was made the chief charge against Jesus. The fact that it did not succeed, apparently due to a conflict of statements among the witnesses, together with the tradition preserved by John ii. 19 and Acts vi. 14, would indicate that Jesus had made some pronouncement about the Temple which gave the impression of being a threat but which could not be formulated and attested with

However, in view of the attachment of the original community of Jesus' disciples to the Temple, it is unlikely that Jesus, who himself frequented the Temple, declared that he would destroy it. What is more probable is that, during his so-called Cleansing of the Temple, when Jesus had attacked the trading system, which was highly profitable to the priestly aristocracy, he had spoken in condemnation of the control of Yahweh's sanctuary by these rapacious pro-Roman magnates and had threatened to destroy their control, as indeed the Zealots actually did in the year 66.[1] Such denunciation, coming from a popular leader, would naturally have been taken as dangerously subversive by the authorities, both Jewish and Roman, and it could easily have been presented at his trial as a threat to destroy the supreme religious institution of Israel and replace it by some revolutionary form of his own.[2]

This accusation the Jerusalem Christians had vigorously repudiated as a calumny on their master made by 'false witnesses'.

sufficient preciseness to enable it to be pressed against him in the Sanhedrin trial. Cf. J. Blinzler, *The Trial of Jesus* (Cork, 1959), pp. 99–101; G. D. Kilpatrick, *The Trial of Jesus*, pp. 10–14 (who does not take account of the fact that the charge was not pressed); T. A. Burkill, 'Trial of Jesus', *V.C.* xii, 6–8; Taylor, *St Mark*, pp. 566–7; Bultmann, *Gesch. d. syn. Trad.* pp. 126–7; Goguel, *Jesus*, pp. 504–9; C. H. Dodd, *Historical Tradition in the Fourth Gospel*, pp. 90–1, who observes that an oral tradition existed, connecting Jesus with the destruction of the Temple, and that it 'was something of an embarrassment to the Church'; P. Winter in *J.T.S.* xiv, n.s. (1963), 99.

[1] See above, pp. 140 ff. It is not without significance that the Zealots, who were so deeply concerned for the Temple and its cultus, are accused by the hostile Josephus of causing its destruction, and that Jesus, who was similarly concerned, was also accused by his enemies of threatening the Temple's ruin.

[2] It would be interesting to know whether the idea of a Temple χειροποίητος and another ἀχειροποίητος was in Mark's source, or whether it was his own invention. Eisler, ΙΗΣΟΥΣ ΒΑΣΙΛΕΥΣ, ii, 501, regards it as an interpolation ('Das ist natürlich der ἀχειροποίητος ναός des Interpolators von Mk. 14. 58'). In the light of the suggestion made above, namely, that Mark blamed the Jews for making the Temple a 'den of thieves', which caused its destruction (see p. 237), it is possible that the contrast implied in χειροποίητος and ἀχειροποίητος was his own, and that he saw Christ as having established a spiritual Temple in the place of that destroyed in A.D. 70. Mark may have initiated a conception which finds expression in Rev. xxi. 22, where God and the Lamb constitute the Temple in the Heavenly Jerusalem, and in Heb. ix. 11, 24, where the Heavenly Tabernacle is 'made without hands'. Cf. C. Clemen, *Religionsgeschichtliche Erklärung*, pp. 225–6; Burkill, *Mysterious Revelation*, pp. 286–7.

The repudiation had probably been embodied in an *apologia*, which went on to show how Jesus, as the Messiah of Israel, had not only been thus slanderously accused by the unpopular pro-Roman priestly aristocrats, who themselves abused their high office and exploited their control of the Temple, but also been condemned by them for claiming to be the Messiah and acting in accordance with that claim.[1] This account the author of Mark had inherited, and it served his purpose to reproduce it; for it presented the Jewish religious leaders as responsible for arresting and condemning Jesus to death. But now the question arises: how did the original Jewish Christian account go on from here? If the high priest and the Sanhedrin had condemned Jesus to death for blasphemy, why did they not proceed to carry out the sentence according to the Jewish Law, which would have meant death by stoning?[2]

The indisputable fact is that Jesus was put to death by the Romans, and by crucifixion, as guilty of sedition against their government. Consequently, if Jesus had originally been arrested at the orders of the high priest and had been condemned for his claims and actions as being those of a Messianic pretender, there must have been some reason for his subsequent condemnation as a rebel against Rome and his execution by the Romans. But the author of Mark does not supply this reason. Instead, without explanation, he relates that the Jewish sacerdotal authorities delivered Jesus, bound, the next morning to the Roman procurator Pontius Pilate.[3] In doing so, they

---

[1] xiv. 60–4. The affirmative reply ascribed to Jesus, followed by the thoroughly Jewish concept of the glorious manifestation of the Messiah, clearly expresses, as we have seen, the eschatological hopes of the Jerusalem Christians, and provides a logical sequel to the repudiation of the 'Temple destruction' charge in a Jewish Christian apologetic concerning the condemnation of Jesus by the Sanhedrin. Cf. Meyer, *Ursprung*, I, 194; Klausner, *Jesus of Nazareth*, pp. 341–3; Manson, *Teaching of Jesus*, pp. 134, 214, 266, 278 ff.; Taylor, *St Mark*, pp. 567–9; Bultmann, *Gesch. d. syn. Trad.* pp. 291–2; Blinzler, *Trial of Jesus*, pp. 101–4.

[2] As, for example, in the case of Stephen, Acts vii. 56–8; see also Sanhedrin, 6. 4–5 (in Danby, *Mishnah*, pp. 391–2). For a discussion of death penalties according to Rabbinic law cf. Winter, *On the Trial of Jesus*, pp. 67–74; see also Klausner, *Jesus of Nazareth*, pp. 344–5; Taylor, *St Mark*, p. 645.

[3] xv. 1. Mark appears to summarise his source here by mentioning that the Jewish authorities consulted together, without stating the subject of their consultation or its outcome. Presumably they met to prepare the charge to be laid before Pilate. Cf. Taylor, *St Mark*, p. 578. 'Accusations are duly made by *delatores*, the chief priests and the elders of the people acting as such' (A. N. Sherwin-White, *Roman Society and Roman Law in the New Testament*, Oxford, 1963, p. 24).

must also have preferred a charge of sedition, based upon his Messianic claim, because Pilate is recorded as immediately asking him, 'Are you the King of the Jews?'[1]

Now, it has become the tradition to explain this delivery of Jesus by the Jewish authorities to the Roman governor as due to the fact that the Jews had not the power at this time to execute on a criminal charge.[2] This explanation is based upon the statement in the Gospel of John (xviii. 31) that the Jews told Pilate, in handing over Jesus: 'It is not lawful for us to put any man to death.' The statement has led to much expert debate as to whether the Jewish authorities could then execute a person of their own race who was guilty of a capital offence according to Jewish Law. The most reasonable conclusion seems to be that they had first to obtain the Roman governor's consent before proceeding with such an execution.[3] Whether this was the point that the Johannine writer wished to make may be doubted; for it seems more likely, in view of his next statement, that he was really concerned to explain how Jesus' own words (surely a *vaticinium ex eventu*) came true, namely, that he would be crucified—crucifixion being a Roman penalty.[4] However all that may be, what

---

[1] xv. 2. καὶ κατηγόρουν αὐτοῦ οἱ ἀρχιερεῖς πολλά comes as a kind of *arrière pensée*. The chief priests must obviously have stated the charge against Jesus, unless Jesus was already so well known to Pilate that he at once, unbriefed, asked him whether he was the 'king of the Jews'. The significance of Pilate's question, as recorded by Mark, must be fully appreciated. To hear of their Lord being called ὁ βασιλεὺς τῶν 'Ιουδαίων, and condemned as such, must surely have been very distasteful to Gentile Christians, so that Mark must have been constrained here by a tradition too strong to gloss over or avoid. The implications of such a title are obvious and very serious—to be regarded as a claimant to that title in Roman Judaea was tantamount to sedition. Cf. J. Spencer Kennard in *Z.N.T.W.* 53 (1962), pp. 50–1; Burkill in *V.C.* xii, pp. 16–18.

[2] E.g. Taylor, *St Mark*, p. 646; Klostermann, *Markusevangelium*, p. 158; Klausner, *Jesus of Nazareth*, p. 345; Blinzler, *Trial of Jesus*, pp. 188–9.

[3] Cf. Sherwin-White, *Roman Society and Roman Law in the New Testament*, pp. 32–43: this writer, however, in accepting what he calls 'the old solution' as not improbable (p. 46), fails to appreciate the intricate issues that lie behind the various Evangelists' accounts of the Trial. His neglect to deal with the Barabbas episode is also a serious defect in his study of the trial of Jesus. It is to be noted that P. Winter admits in effect (*On the Trial of Jesus*, pp. 87–8) that death sentences passed by the Sanhedrin had to be approved by the Roman authorities. Cf. S. Zeitlin, 'The Crucifixion of Jesus Re-examined', *J.Q.R.* xxxi, 344–5, and *Who Crucified Jesus?* (New York, 1942), p. 81; Jaubert in *R.H.R.* 167 (1965), pp. 3–9.

[4] John xviii. 32. Cf. Dodd, *Interpretation of the Fourth Gospel*, pp. 427, 433–4.

is essential to note, in terms of our inquiry, is that the author of Mark gives no explanation whatever for the fact that, according to his narrative, the Jewish authorities handed Jesus over to Pilate, charged with sedition.[1]

If Mark had drawn upon a Jewish Christian account of the San-hedrin trial, as we have seen reason to believe, such a record would not have been apologetically concerned about the fact that Jesus had thus been put to death by the Romans. Such a death, at the hands of these heathen oppressors, would have been deemed a noble death in Jewish eyes, and Jesus would have been, as we have seen, a martyr for the freedom of Israel.[2] What the Jewish Christian record was concerned to repudiate was the accusation, made at the Sanhedrin trial, that Jesus had spoken against the Temple. Accordingly, if the Jewish authorities had originally arrested Jesus, undoubtedly because of his attack on the Temple trading system and what appeared to be other revolutionary activi-ties, they would have proceeded to examine him about these things. After this examination, by which they established, to their own satisfaction, that he was a Messianic pretender who was dangerous to the existing political and social order, it was their duty to hand him over to the Romans.[3] Consequently, the record would have gone on to describe how Pilate, on the evidence laid before him by the Jewish authorities, which probably confirmed his own informa-tion,[4] condemned Jesus to death for sedition. Thus, in Mark's source

[1] It is very necessary that this point should be properly appreciated; for the issue here concerns what Mark chose to present to his readers in Rome, not what may be learned by reference to the accounts of the later Gospels.

[2] See above, pp. 177 ff.

[3] Mark makes it quite clear that the arrest of Jesus was effected by an armed force sent by the Jewish authorities (xiv. 43). By describing this force as ὄχλος, Mark undoubtedly intends to give the impression that the Jewish authorities employed an armed mob ('a hired rabble', Taylor, *St Mark*, p. 558). It is most unlikely that these authorities would have resorted to such an undisciplined body when they possessed an efficient military body in the Temple police (cf. Jeremias, *Jerusalem*, II, 39, 72–5). Winter (*On the Trial of Jesus*, pp. 44–8) thinks, on the strength of the Johannine account, that the arrest was effected by the Romans, and that Mark suppressed the fact. He sees in Jesus' words ὡς ἐπὶ λῃστὴν ἐξήλθατε... (xiv. 48) the original reason for his arrest (pp. 49–50). On the arrest of Jesus see further below, pp. 306, 340 ff.

[4] It is unlikely that the Romans were unaware of the Triumphal Entry and the fracas in the Temple: the Roman commander in the Antonia had been quickly informed of the riot occasioned by Paul's presence in the Temple (Acts xxi. 31 ff.). Cf. O. Betz, 'Jesu Heiliger Krieg', *N.T.* II, 133.

there would have been no explanation of why, having been condemned for blasphemy as a Messianic pretender by the Sanhedrin, Jesus had been handed over to the Romans, who executed him as a rebel.[1] Such an account, however, would have shown, even if hostilely orientated, that Pilate proceeded, in an orderly and intelligible way, to execute one whom the Jewish authorities had found to be guilty of subversive action that threatened the stability of the Roman rule, which it was his duty to maintain, with the cooperation of the native leaders.[2] But such a presentation would have been fatal to the Markan writer's apologetical thesis, namely, to show that Jesus had endorsed the Roman government of Judaea.[3]

Having followed his Jewish Christian source so far, because it served his cause of representing the death of Jesus as essentially due to Jewish malice, the author of Mark was now faced with the task of explaining how it was that, in the end, the Romans executed Jesus as a revolutionary. His attempts to do this are so awkward and naïve that it is manifest that his was a pioneer effort, and that he had not the benefit of improving upon an earlier tradition.

In the passage (xv. 1–15) dealing with Pilate's condemnation of Jesus, the Markan writer is concerned to show two things, namely, that Pilate, recognising the innocence of Jesus, tried to save him, and that he was forced by the Jewish leaders to order his execution. Now, as we have noted, such a situation would not, *per se*, be an impossible one; but it would be a remarkable one, and we should

[1] It must be remembered that, though the condemnation for blasphemy may be regarded as theologically motivated, the Jewish authorities were more concerned with the social and political consequences of the Messianic role of Jesus. See John xi. 47–8.

[2] John seems to have been aware of this aspect of the action of the Jewish authorities (see xi. 47–8, xviii. 19, 29–30, 35, xix. 12). Cf. Brandon, *Fall of Jerusalem*, pp. 124–5; Dodd, *Historical Tradition in the Fourth Gospel*, pp. 24, 95, 97–8. Mlle Jaubert (*R.H.R.* 167, 1965, p. 11) makes an interesting comment on the Sanhedrin trial: 'Du point de vue des autorités juives, ce jugement était nécessaire pour éclairer le peuple qui se fourvoyaient et pour désarçonner les partisans de Jésus. Livrer directement Jésus à Pilate, cela ne tranchait pas le conflit religieux et pouvait déclencher l'agitation... On peut ajouter que selon toute vraisemblance une condamnation juive était importante même par rapport à Pilate.'

[3] Having shown Jesus as approving of Roman sovereignty in Judaea in terms of the payment of tribute (xii. 13–17), Mark obviously had a difficult task in accounting for the Roman execution of Jesus as a rebel a few days later. Jewish leaders had, accordingly, to be shown as relentlessly pursuing their purpose to destroy Jesus because he threatened their religious authority.

naturally ask whether Pontius Pilate was a likely person to submit to the Jewish leaders in this way. However, that is an issue that we can consider later.[1] The important point now is the credibility of Mark's account of how it came about that Pilate did sentence Jesus.

If we are right in thinking that Mark had followed, up to this point, a Jewish Christian account, telling how Jesus had been falsely accused of threatening to destroy the Temple by the Jewish leaders, and that they had handed him over to Pilate as a dangerous Messianic pretender, it would be reasonable to expect that the procurator would have been satisfied that he was guilty. The situation in Jerusalem at this time was a very tense one; for already, as Mark himself informs us, there had been an insurrection (στάσις), in which the rebels had caused fatal casualties, doubtless among the Roman garrison.[2] Pilate would not, therefore, have been surprised by the accusation which was brought against Jesus. The accusation was naturally formulated in detail by the Jewish authorities; for Mark records that they 'accused him of many things' (κατηγόρουν αὐτοῦ ...πολλά).[3] What these things were is significantly indicated in Pilate's first question to Jesus: 'Are you the King of the Jews?'[4] It is obvious from what Mark himself records, namely, the triumphal entry of Jesus into Jerusalem, his attack on the Temple trading system, and the armed resistance in Gethsemane, that a good *prima facie* case for seditious activity could be made out against Jesus. Yet, despite all this apparent evidence, Mark suggests that Pilate was reluctant to proceed against him.

The suggestion of reluctance is given in the statement that, when Jesus did not answer his question, Pilate wondered (ὥστε θαυμάζειν).[5] No reason is offered by Mark for this unexpected reaction by the procurator towards a prisoner against whom a formidable case of seditious behaviour had been made out. However, Mark's statement here has an evasive air about it which excites suspicion. It may fairly be asked: if Mark had evidence that Pilate had refused to accept the accusations of the Jewish authorities against Jesus, why did he not unequivocally say so? Indeed, to be able to produce such evidence would most powerfully have assisted his case that the Roman execution was really due to the implacable hatred of the

---

[1] See pp. 261 ff. [2] xv. 7.
[3] xv. 3. [4] See p. 254, n. 1 above.
[5] xv. 5. It is uncertain what Mark intends to convey by ὥστε θαυμάζειν τὸν Πειλᾶτον: whether the governor was impressed by the bearing of Jesus or whether his silence in the face of the accusations puzzled him.

Jewish leaders.[1] But he does not do so; instead, after this vague suggestion that Pilate was favourably disposed to Jesus, he suddenly breaks off to recount the strange episode concerning Barabbas.[2]

In the context of Mark's narrative this Barabbas episode is clearly intended to show that Pilate sought to save Jesus, having perceived his innocence, but that he was forced by the Jewish leaders to order his crucifixion. Taken at its face value, therefore, the story provides final and dramatic evidence of the thesis, already adumbrated many times in the Gospel, that the Jewish leaders were essentially responsible for the Roman crucifixion of Jesus. To those Gentile Christians who read Mark's narrative in the anxious days following the Flavian triumph in 71, the story provided great relief; for it constituted a seemingly convincing explanation of a very embarrassing fact, namely, that the founder of their faith had been executed as a Jewish revolutionary. The story, it is important to remember, was written for humble and poorly educated people, living in Rome, who would have had very little knowledge of Roman administration in Judaea some forty years before and no incentive to question the truth of so dramatic an episode that solved what had been a very awkward problem for them, both personally and *vis-à-vis* their pagan neighbours.[3]

The Barabbas episode has long been a crux for New Testament scholarship on historical grounds. The problem involved therein is twofold. First, there is no other evidence than that of the Gospels that, during the Roman administration of Judaea, it was the custom that the Roman governor should release periodically whatever prisoner the people, i.e. the population of Jerusalem, should ask of him. The fact that there is no other evidence confirming such a practice does not necessarily mean that Mark's account of it, and those in the other Gospels which derive from it, are necessarily fabrications. However, there is one powerful argument against the

[1] This omission to state clearly that Pilate was convinced of the innocence of Jesus is even more significant when Mark asserts in xv. 10 that Pilate knew that the chief priests had delivered up Jesus 'through envy'. What Mark does, in effect, is to suggest that Pilate privately recognised the innocence of Jesus (this is also implied in xv. 14); but he is careful not to assert that Pilate publicly recognised this—to have done so might have raised certain obvious and awkward questions.

[2] xv. 6 ff.

[3] Christian apologists such as Justin Martyr and Tertullian made similar preposterous claims, probably knowing that their readers were not likely to question their veracity: cf. Brandon, *History, Time and Deity*, pp. 198–9.

authenticity of Mark's statement. The Jewish historian Josephus was specially intent on recording all the privileges which the Roman government at various times had accorded to the Jews. It is, therefore, passing strange that he should have neglected to mention so notable a privilege as this, if it had indeed existed.[1]

The other objection is equally serious. The practice of such a custom would so dangerously hamper effective government in a country seething with revolt as was Judaea that it is inconceivable that the Romans would ever have tolerated it. For example, if the Markan story is true, it would mean that on this particular occasion Pilate had to release a desperate patriotic leader, probably a Zealot, who had just been involved in a revolt against the Roman rule.[2] Consequently, in view of the intrinsic improbability of such a custom ever existing, together with the very serious objection that Josephus' silence constitutes, the Markan story cannot be accepted as authentic. Moreover, if it is argued that the author of Mark would never have made an assertion that could so easily have been refuted, it must be remembered, as we have already noted, that he was writing for a public which was unlikely to have the knowledge or inclination to check his story. There is also ground for reflection in the fact that Tertullian, in an *apologia* for Christianity actually addressed to the Roman magistrates, later had the temerity to assert that Tiberius had been convinced by a report from Pilate of Christ's divinity: *consulite commentarios vestros* was his audacious challenge.[3]

It has been necessary to notice the force of these historical objections to accepting the Barabbas story as a record of fact; however, for our purpose, it is even more important to note that Mark's use of this improbable story reveals the desperate straits to which he was reduced in trying to prove that Pilate recognised the innocence of Jesus.

Mark, as we have already observed, suddenly introduces the Barabbas episode after his elusive suggestion that Pilate had perceived that Jesus was guiltless of the charge preferred against him.

---

[1] Even if he had by chance forgotten to mention so extraordinary a privilege, it is strange that throughout his long circumstantial narrative Josephus never records an instance of the release of a prisoner on such grounds.   [2] xv. 7. Cf. Hengel, *Die Zeloten*, p. 347.

[3] *Apol.* v. 3; see p. 258, n. 3 above. The attempts made to find parallels to the custom elsewhere are pathetic for the paucity and irrelevance of the supposed instances: cf. A. Deissmann, *Licht vom Osten* (Tübingen, 1923), pp. 229–31; Taylor, *St Mark*, pp. 580–1; Goguel, *Jesus*, p. 519; Guignebert, *Jésus*, pp. 573–4; Blinzler, *Trial of Jesus*, pp. 205–8, 218–21; Winter, *On the Trial of Jesus*, pp. 92–4; Stauffer, *Jesus and His Story*, p. 107.

He begins with a brief statement about the custom: 'Now at the feast he used to release for them one prisoner whom they asked.'[1] The statement is significantly vague; for Mark evidently concluded that his readers would not be inquisitive about so extraordinary a custom. The statement was a necessary introduction to the scene that is mounted in the following verses: 'And among the rebels (τῶν στασιαστῶν) in prison, who had committed murder in the insurrection (τῇ στάσει), there was a man called Barabbas. And the crowd (ὁ ὄχλος) came up and began to ask (αἰτεῖσθαι) Pilate to do as he was wont to do for them.'[2] The impression which these introductory verses give, in the context of Mark's narrative, is that, Pilate's interrogation of Jesus having left him favourably disposed towards Jesus, the proceedings are suddenly interrupted by the intervention (ἀναβάς) of the crowd, demanding their customary privilege. However, it would be unwise to draw such an inference; for Mark is obviously not writing here with strict attention to time-sequence. He is concerned only with the presentation of a scene designed to explain away Pilate's responsibility for the Crucifixion and to fix that responsibility on the Jewish leaders. Indeed, so eager is he to do this that he represents the procurator as immediately responding to the crowd's unspecified demand for a prisoner's release, by offering to release Jesus, whom he significantly calls 'the King of the Jews'.[3] The revealing comment is then added, since Mark wanted to make the reason for Pilate's action absolutely plain to his readers: 'For he perceived that it was out of envy that the chief priests had delivered him up.'[4]

Having thus made quite clear the murderous intent of the chief

[1] xv. 6. It may well be asked whether the imperfect tense of ἀπέλυεν is meant to imply that this was Pilate's own peculiar custom. This seems to be the meaning of καθὼς ἐποίει αὐτοῖς in v. 8. The vagueness of the statement is significant. The more precise statements of Matt. xxvii. 15 and John xviii. 39 are undoubtedly improvements on the original Markan account.

[2] xv. 7–8.

[3] xv. 10. Cf. Goguel, Life of Jesus, pp. 518–19; Burkill, Mysterious Revelation, p. 294; Klostermann, Markusevangelium, p. 159: 'Die Barabbasepisode dient dazu, die Römer zu entschuldigen und die Juden zu belasten.' It is surprising that Sherwin-White ('The Trial of Christ', Historicity and Chronology in the New Testament, p. 115) should not see that it was fear that motivated Mark to transfer the responsibility for the execution from the Romans to the Jews. In seeking to evaluate the Gospel accounts of the Trial of Jesus, at their face value, as a specialist on Roman law, he fails to appreciate the unique character of the Markan Gospel. His failure to deal with the Barabbas episode has a similar significance.

[4] xv. 10: see p. 258, n. 1 above.

priests, Mark proceeds to tell how Pilate's plan to save Jesus was frustrated. What had apparently been a spontaneous and unformulated request of the crowd is now changed by the chief priests into a specific demand for the release of Barabbas.[1] We can only wonder at the speed and efficiency with which these priestly aristocrats acted, on the spur of the moment, thus to influence the crowd to demand the death of Jesus, when that crowd had so enthusiastically supported him against themselves only a few days before.[2] Mark, however, does not bother to explain such details to his readers, who were unlikely to scrutinise the implications of his statements as a modern historian does; nor was he concerned with the implications of his account of Pilate's behaviour in all this. For, in effect, he would have his readers believe that a Roman magistrate, who was, as we know from Philo and Josephus, a remarkably tough character and notorious for his contempt of the Jews,[3] acted as a veritable weakling, devoid alike of dignity, efficiency and spirit. Convinced that Jesus was the innocent victim of the malice of the chief priests, Pilate, instead of acting with the dignity and firmness that became a Roman magistrate, backed by military strength, and dismissing the charge against Jesus, is depicted as resorting to subterfuge. Thus, he is represented as clutching at the opportunity afforded by the custom as a means of saving Jesus, when he had himself the authority and the power to dismiss the charge. But that is not all. When the chief priests counter his subterfuge by causing the crowd to demand the release of Barabbas, he is reduced to asking weakly of the crowd, 'Then what shall I do with this man whom you call the King of the Jews?'[4] It is well to appreciate fully the incredible situation that Mark's statements imply. Here was a Roman governor, supported by an efficient military force, who, convinced of the innocence of a prisoner, accused of sedition by the Jewish authorities, resorted to an otherwise unknown custom in order to do what he knew was right, i.e. release him. His subterfuge being frustrated, he then asks the crowd, which is apparently controlled by the chief priests, what he is to do with the prisoner, who has been formally accused by the proper authorities of his people of sedition, and whom he himself has adjudged innocent.

Mark's story becomes even more impossible in the sequel. First, we must note that, if he had indeed resorted to the alleged custom to save Jesus, then Pilate must have been not only incredibly weak,

[1] xv. 11.
[2] Cf. xi. 32, xiv. 1–2.
[3] See above, pp. 68 ff.
[4] xv. 14.

but also unbelievably stupid. For, if Jesus was the pro-Roman pacifist that Mark makes him out to be,[1] surely Pilate must have realised what the decision would be, were the crowd given the choice between Jesus and a patriotic leader such as Barabbas, who had struck at their Roman oppressors. And then there is the question of the release of Barabbas. According to Mark, the outcome of Pilate's amazing conduct was that he condemned to death one whom he knew to be innocent, and released a popular resistance fighter, probably a Zealot, who had just proved how dangerous he could be. We may well ask how Pilate would have justified his conduct both to his Roman officers and officials, and, even more important, in his report to the emperor Tiberius.[2]

Such, then, is the way in which the author of Mark sought to explain to the Christian community in Rome how Jesus came to be crucified as a Jewish revolutionary. On analysis, as we have seen, the story is incredible both on historical grounds and because of its intrinsic impossibility. However, for simple-minded readers it served its purpose. It showed, in a dramatic narrative, calculated to hold the attention by its vigorous action, that the Jewish leaders were essentially responsible for the Roman execution of Jesus. The Roman governor, Pontius Pilate, had perceived his innocence of the charge of sedition; but his efforts to save Jesus had been frustrated by the Jewish authorities, who had been determined from the beginning to destroy him. Accordingly, having already represented Jesus as endorsing the Roman rule in Judaea by recognising the Jewish obligation to pay tribute to Caesar, Mark adroitly explained away the obvious problem of Jesus' execution for sedition against Rome. That explanation was doubtless received with much gratitude and relief by the Christians in Rome, worried as they were by the evidence of the Jewish rebellion which they had recently witnessed in the imperial triumphal procession.

We have been concerned to evaluate the Barabbas episode in the

---

[1] See below, p. 271. The expression 'pro-Roman pacifist' is justified. Mark's presentation of the Tribute Money episode shows Jesus as endorsing the Roman rule in Judaea, while the contrast he suggests between the warlike Barabbas and the guiltless Jesus serves to portray Jesus as pacifist. However, Mark does not stress the pacifism of Jesus as Matthew and Luke do: see pp. 305 ff.

[2] This aspect of the matter is always overlooked by those scholars who accept the traditional view that Pilate condemned Jesus because he feared an uprising of the people, or, alternatively, on the strength of John xix. 12, that Pilate feared that the matter would be reported to the emperor, if he freed Jesus.

context of Mark's apologetic; but, before we leave the subject, we may briefly consider what might have been the origin of the story. Although Mark had used the story to transfer responsibility for the Crucifixion from Pilate to the Jewish leaders, it seems unlikely that the whole episode was invented by him for this purpose. It would appear more probable that, in the last days at Jerusalem, Jesus had been connected in some way with a popular resistance leader who had been involved in a rising against the Romans. The name 'Barabbas' is puzzling. Mark's expression 'who was called Barabbas' (ὁ λεγόμενος Βαραββᾶς) suggests that it was a title that should be preceded by a personal name, and there is Rabbinic evidence for the use of 'Son of the father' (*Bar Abba*) in this manner.[1] The variant reading in some MSS of 'Jesus Barabbas' in Matt. xxvii. 16, 17, could well indicate the original name of this leader, who was probably a Zealot: 'Ἰησοῦς, ὁ λεγόμενος Βαραββᾶς would make a significant parallel to 'Ἰησοῦς, ὁ λεγόμενος Χριστός.[2] If a historical basis does underlie the story, it would seem reasonable to draw two conclusions, both of considerable significance for our subject. The first is that Jesus had become associated in some way with an insurgent leader during the last fateful days in Jerusalem. The second is that this association gave rise to some tradition that Jesus had been crucified by the Romans instead of this leader Barabbas.[3] How this came about it is impossible to say; for we have seen that the case against Mark's version is overwhelming, and that it was clearly inspired by his apologetical purpose. That an insurrection had taken place at this time in Jerusalem, which Mark incidentally

---

[1] xv. 7. Cf. S.B. *Kommentar*, I, 1031; Klostermann, *Markusevangelium*, p. 160.

[2] Cf. *Novum Testamentum Graece*, 19th ed. E. Nestle, p. 78; Klostermann, *Matthäusevangelium*, pp. 218, 220–1; Taylor, *St Mark*, p. 581; Winter, *On the Trial of Jesus*, pp. 98–9; Eisler, ΙΗΣΟΥΣ ΒΑΣΙΛΕΥΣ, II, 463–9, *Messiah Jesus*, pp. 473–6.

[3] It is tempting to wonder whether the idea found in the Qumrân *Manual of Discipline* (serek ha-yahad) of two Messiahs, the one priestly and the other political, might be reflected in the tradition that, so puzzlingly, links Jesus and Barabbas: that Jesus, as the priestly Messiah, led the attack on the impious sacerdotal aristocracy in the Temple, while the political Messiah Barabbas attacked the Romans in the city. However, the extant evidence does not justify the development of such a theory; we know only that in some inexplicable way the fate of Jesus was linked with the revolutionary action of Barabbas. Cf. K. G. Kuhn, 'The Two Messiahs of Aaron and Israel', in *The Scrolls and the New Testament*, ed. K. Stendahl, pp. 54–64; Dupont-Sommer, *Les écrits esséniens découverts près de la Mer Morte*, pp. 87, 123–7.

attests, is a fact of key importance. It must surely be adjudged remarkable that Jesus should have been acting in ways likely to be regarded as subversive by the authorities, both Jewish and Roman, when such a rising was taking place. It is natural to wonder whether there could have been any connection between his triumphal entry into the city and his attack on the Temple trading system and the insurrection in which Barabbas had been involved. However, consideration of this issue must be reserved for the chapter on the attitude of Jesus to Israel's cause against Rome. For the present, it is enough to have noted the probability that, behind Mark's tendentious use of the Barabbas episode, there lies some significant connection between the fate of Jesus and the insurrection with which Barabbas was concerned.

Returning to the subject of Mark's *Apologia ad Christianos Romanos*, it will be well to summarise our findings to this point. We have seen a catena of evidence attesting a preoccupation with Jewish political affairs, which is only intelligible in terms of the *Sitz im Leben* of the Christian community of Rome at the time of the Flavian triumph in A.D. 71. We have found the author of Mark concerned to show that Jesus endorsed the Jewish obligation to pay tribute to Caesar. He was also seen to be concerned with the significance of the Temple veil, with the profanation and destruction of the Temple by the Romans in A.D. 70, and with the relation of those events to the *Parousia*. Further, he suppresses the information that one of Jesus' Apostles had been a Zealot. This last fact also indicated that there were aspects of the original tradition concerning Jesus that Mark was intent on hiding from his Gentile readers in Rome. This clue led us on to consider evidence which pointed to a carefully calculated presentation of the Jewish leaders as responsible for the death of Jesus. Finally, we saw that the Barabbas episode was utilised to explain how the long-standing intention of the Jewish leaders to destroy Jesus actually took the form of the Roman execution for sedition. Thus, by shifting the responsibility for the Crucifixion from the Roman governor to the Jewish leaders, the most embarrassing problem of all for the Christians of Rome at this time was adroitly answered. In this manner, the most urgent need of the Roman Christians was provided for; however, there is reason for thinking that the author of Mark also utilised his Gospel to deal with certain other difficulties which the Jewish War and its disastrous outcome had raised for his fellow-Christians.

The events of A.D. 66–70 were not only politically embarrassing for the Christians of Rome, they also greatly increased the antipathy already widely felt towards the Jews.[1] Consequently, as the famous jibe of Tacitus about Christianity's Jewish origin would suggest, Gentile Christians must often have felt very sensitive that their faith had stemmed from a race so disliked and despised, and, even worse, that their Lord was born a member of this race.[2] It is likely also that Gentile Christians, such as those at Rome, had often been made acutely aware of the spiritual superiority assumed by the Jewish Christians with whom they had contact—even Paul, the great champion of Gentile rights, had referred to Gentile Christians as a 'wild olive shoot', 'grafted contrary to nature', into the 'cultivated olive tree', which was Israel.[3] Now it would seem that the author of Mark was conscious of Gentile feeling in this connection, and he sought to alleviate it in his Gospel, which afforded a very suitable means for so doing.

Accordingly, besides his theme of the responsibility of the Jewish leaders for the Crucifixion, Mark also develops the thesis that Jesus, though born a Jew, was never properly appreciated by Jews, and that, in turn, he implicitly repudiated his racial relationship with the Jews. The thesis is worked out by recording how Jesus was rejected or misunderstood by various representative Jewish groups, whom he in turn rejected or from whom he dissociated himself.[4] The first, and the most obvious, group that Mark is concerned to set in an emphatic contradistinction to Jesus comprises the Jewish religious leaders and experts on the Torah. Not only are these men cast for the role of the murderers of Jesus, but, since they were the official representatives of Judaism, Mark deemed it necessary to show that Jesus accepted neither their authority nor their doctrine. An indication is given right at the beginning of Jesus' ministry of the fundamental difference that existed between him and the traditional exponents of Judaism. At Capernaum the congregation in the synagogue at once notices that Jesus taught as 'one who had authority, and not as the scribes'.[5] The first clash comes shortly after, also at Capernaum. Prefacing his healing of a paralytic man

---

[1] Josephus speaks of those who through hatred of the Jews (μίσει τῷ πρὸς Ἰουδαίους) misrepresented the facts of the Jewish War (*War*, I. 2). Cf. Frend, *Martyrdom and Persecution*, pp. 210–11. See above, p. 226.

[2] See p. 226, n. 4, and p. 237, n. 4, above.   [3] Rom. xi. 17 ff.

[4] Cf. Brandon in *Studia Evangelica*, II, 42 ff.

[5] i. 22: cf. Taylor, *St Mark*, p. 173. On the significance of the scribes in Mark see below, pp. 271–2.

by an absolution of his sins, Jesus provokes the scribes, who are present, into accusing him of blasphemy.[1] Next, having censured 'the scribes of the Pharisees' for objecting to his eating with 'sinners and tax collectors', and having explained why his disciples did not fast like 'John's disciples and the disciples of the Pharisees', Jesus is represented as pronouncing on the obsolescence of Judaism, of which these scribes and Pharisees were the accepted exponents. This is done in terms of the metaphor of the uselessness of repairing an old garment with new material or putting new wine into old wine skins.[2] The application of this Dominical oracle would have been plain to Mark's readers: recent events had clearly shown that Judaism was obsolete, and that the attempt made by the Jewish Christians to adapt Christianity to Judaism was hopeless—new wine cannot be held in old wine skins. The ruin of the Temple had ended the compromise which the Jerusalem Christians had sought to maintain, and now Christianity was free of its Judaistic swaddling bands.[3]

The next encounter is with the Pharisees over the observance of the sabbath.[4] It is probable that the Jewish Christians had insisted on the strict observance of the Jewish sabbath, which must have been difficult and irksome for the Gentile Christians in Rome, immersed as they were in a completely pagan environment, where cessation of work on the seventh day was not provided for.[5] Hence the Dominical pronouncement 'The sabbath was made for man, not man for the sabbath; so the Son of man is lord even of the sabbath' was both a welcome dispensation for the Roman Christians and further evidence of the detachment of Jesus from Jewish customs.[6] To illustrate this difference still further, Mark follows the

[1] ii. 6–7.
[2] ii. 21, 22: cf. Klostermann, *Markusevangelium*, p. 28: 'Man kann das alte Kleid des Judentums nicht mit neuen Flicken konservieren, und man kann den neuen Wein des Christentums nicht in alten Schläuchen konservieren.'
[3] The significance of this parable depends on the events of A.D. 70, a fact which escapes the notice of those who put Mark before this date.
[4] ii. 23–8.
[5] Considerable hostility is shown towards the Jewish Sabbath by certain Greek and Latin writers. If it was difficult for Jews in the Diaspora to observe the Sabbatical rest, it must have been infinitely harder, and more dangerous, for Gentile Christians: cf. I. Abrahams in *E.R.E.* x, 892*a*; H. Riesenfeld, 'Sabbat et Jour du Seigneur', *New Testament Essays* (ed. A. J. B. Higgins), pp. 210–17.
[6] Taylor, *St Mark*, p. 220, thinks that Mark found *v*. 27 'supplemented by a Christian comment expressing the conviction that Jesus is the Lord of all

ruling on the sabbath with an account of a healing performed by Jesus on that day to the chagrin of the Pharisees.[1] The occasion is further used to give the first intimation of the murderous intent of these Jewish leaders; for it is recorded that 'the Pharisees went out, and immediately held counsel with the Herodians against him, how to destroy him'.[2]

Even more spiritually significant perhaps is the next clash with the exponents of Judaism, this time described as 'scribes who came down from Jerusalem'.[3] These authorities attribute the miraculous power of Jesus to his being possessed by Beelzebul, the prince of demons. This accusation constitutes, according to Jesus, 'an eternal sin', that has no forgiveness (οὐκ ἔχει ἄφεσιν εἰς τὸν αἰῶνα, ἀλλὰ ἔνοχός ἐστιν αἰωνίου ἁμαρτήματος).[4] It would seem that such an offence had already achieved, in the understanding of the Roman Christians, a specific identity and status: it is described as blasphemy against the Holy Spirit.[5] Thus the author of Mark, in pursuit of his thesis of denigrating the leaders of Judaism, presents them as guilty of what his readers had been taught to regard as the most heinous of sins; and he drives the lesson home in a revealing editorial comment: 'for they had said, "He has an unclean spirit"'.[6]

The opportunity is next taken of ridiculing and condemning certain Jewish customs of ritual lavations, of which the Pharisees and the Jerusalem scribes are presented as the exponents. It would appear that these customs were not well known to the Roman Christians, since Mark explains them at length.[7] Replying to the protest of these authorities about the non-observance of the customs by his disciples, Jesus is depicted as severely censuring them for their hypocrisy, quoting as applicable to them a passage of Isaiah, which is surely designed to condemn both Judaism and the exponents of it: 'This people honours me with their lips, but their heart is far from

---

that belongs to man, including the Sabbath'. Such a view could certainly not have arisen in the Jerusalem Church, which was distinguished for its zeal for the Torah.

[1] iii. 1–6.   [2] iii. 6: see above, pp. 248–9.
[3] iii. 22.   [4] iii. 22–9.
[5] Bultmann (*Gesch. d. syn. Trad.* p. 138, n. 1) cites A. Friedrichsen: 'Die Mk-Form...identifiziert Jesus und den Geist und polemisiert gegen den heidnischen Vorwurf, Jesus sei ein Magier gewesen.'
[6] iii. 30. 'Erklärlicher wäre dieser redaktionelle Schluß zu V. 28–30, wenn das Stück einst nicht mit V. 22–27 zusammengehangen hätte' (Klostermann, *Markusevangelium*, p. 38).
[7] vii. 1–4. Cf. Bacon, *Is Mark a Roman Gospel?*, pp. 58–9; Taylor, *St Mark*, p. 335.

me; in vain do they worship me, teaching as doctrines the precepts of men.'[1]

Another encounter with the Pharisees soon follows, when they came and began to argue with him, seeking from him a sign from heaven, to test him (πειράζοντες αὐτόν).[2] What the Pharisees sought here is obscure; very probably the sign (σημεῖον) was some demonstration of miraculous power attesting the Messianic claim of Jesus such as Theudas and others performed, as we have seen.[3] Whatever its nature, for us Mark's editorial comment is significant, emphasising the evil intent (πειράζοντες αὐτόν) of these Jewish religious leaders. This encounter is followed by the puzzling account of the dialogue that ensues between Jesus and his disciples, when it is discovered that they had forgotten to take sufficient bread for their voyage across the lake. The discovery draws forth the enigmatic admonition from Jesus: 'Take heed, beware of the leaven of the Pharisees and the leaven of Herod.'[4] The saying has challenged the ingenuity of scholars who have sought to interpret it, and some have argued that its incomprehensibility attests its primitive authenticity. So far as it concerns us, we can reasonably conclude that, since no explanation is given, Mark evidently felt that the meaning was clear to his readers in Rome. Accordingly, in view of the fact that leaven (ζύμη) is generally used metaphorically in a bad sense, its use here in connection with the Pharisees continues Mark's policy of denigrating them, either by direct statement or by innuendo, in relation to Jesus.[5] The opprobrious reference to Herod would have seemed appropriate to Mark's readers, who had just previously, in the narrative, learned of Herod's wickedness in connection with John the Baptist.[6]

---

[1] vii. 6–7. On the possibility of Pauline influence here see Bacon, *Is Mark a Roman Gospel?*, pp. 66, 69, 70–1, 72. Cf. Taylor, *St Mark*, pp. 337–8.

[2] viii. 11.

[3] See above, pp. 110–13. 'Die Pharisäer stellen Jesus vor die Entscheidung, indem sie über seine bisherigen Taten hinaus eine Beglaubigung seiner Messiantät durch ein außerordentliches Zeichen, nämlich ein *Zeichen vom Himmel* (S.B. *Kommentar*, I, 726 f.) verlangen' (Klostermann, *Markusevangelium*, p. 76).

[4] viii. 15.

[5] Cf. Taylor, *St Mark*, p. 365; Klausner, *Jesus of Nazareth*, p. 297; Klostermann, *Markusevangelium*, p. 77.

[6] vi. 14–29. The inclusion in Mark's short Gospel of the comparatively long story of the occasion which led to the death of the Baptist is puzzling. The story is certainly colourful, but it has little religious value. Perhaps the fact that it contains a Latinism (σπεκουλάτορα, vi. 27: cf. Taylor, *St Mark*,

After Peter's acknowledgement of the Messiahship of Jesus at Caesarea Philippi, the significance of which we must consider later,[1] Jesus is represented as foretelling the manner of his death. The author of Mark clearly uses the statement to warn his readers, in detail, of the identity of those responsible for the Crucifixion, as well as of the fact that these persons would also reject (ἀποδοκιμασθῆναι) Jesus: 'And he began to teach them that the Son of man must suffer many things, and be rejected by the elders and the chief priests, and the scribes, and be killed, and after three days rise again.'[2] We may note also that, after recording Peter's protest and the rebuke he incurred, the narrative goes on to tell how Jesus indicated what form his death would take: 'If any man would come after me, let him deny himself and take up his cross and follow me.'[3] This reference to crucifixion, in this context, is particularly significant. To anticipate the responsibility of the Jewish leaders for the death of Jesus would naturally suggest that he would have been executed according to Jewish law; but Mark obviously felt that it was also necessary at this juncture to prepare his readers for the fact that Jesus suffered the Roman death of crucifixion. As we have seen, the idea that discipleship involved the risk of crucifixion was probably of Zealot origin: the occurrence of the idea here is, therefore, not without significance for us.[4]

pp. 316–17) indicates that it circulated in Rome. This hostility towards the Herodian dynasty and its supporters, which characterises Mark, would be understandable, as we have noted (pp. 248–9), in Rome, where Agrippa II and Berenice held court and the latter's liaison with Titus was a cause of scandal. Bacon (*Is Mark a Roman Gospel?*) did not apparently take account of this last factor in his comments on pp. 64–5.

[1] Pp. 277 ff.

[2] viii. 31. This saying has been the subject of much debate, since conservative scholars have been intent on defending it, or parts of it, as an authentic utterance of Jesus: cf. Taylor, *St Mark*, pp. 377–9; Klostermann, *Markusevangelium*, pp. 80–2; Bultmann, *Gesch. d. syn. Trad.* pp. 163, 357; Manson, *Teaching of Jesus*, p. 226. However, what concerns us here is beyond dispute, namely, that Mark wrote this saying, containing its clear ascription of the death of Jesus to the Jewish authorities, in his Gospel for the Christians at Rome.

[3] viii. 34: it is to be noted that the idea of 'cross-bearing' is not found in the older Rabbinic literature (cf. S.B. *Kommentar*, 1, 587; Klausner, *Jesus of Nazareth*, p. 302).

[4] See above, pp. 57 ff. The comment of T. W. Manson is interesting in this connection: 'The implication of the words is that Jesus is aware of an irreconcilable hostility between the Kingdom for which He stands and the Empire represented by Pontius Pilate' (*The Sayings of Jesus*, p. 131).

This anticipation of the culpability of the Jewish leaders is renewed, shortly after, when Jesus begins what was to prove to be his last fatal visit to Jerusalem. The fact that once again the statement is placed in the mouth of Jesus also implies a clear recognition on his side of the difference between them. The prophecy is even more explicit than the preceding one, and it includes a definite preparation for the part of the Gentiles (i.e. the Romans) in it: 'Behold, we are going up to Jerusalem; and the Son of man will be delivered up to the chief priests and the scribes, and they will condemn him to death, and deliver him to the Gentiles; and they will mock him, and spit upon him, and scourge him, and kill him; and after three days he will rise.'[1] Quite evidently the author of Mark was taking every care that his readers in Rome should fully understand that it was the Jewish leaders who engineered the crucifixion of Jesus by the Romans.

The tragedy for which Mark had thus prepared his readers quickly begins to move towards its accomplishment after Jesus' attack on the Temple trading system. As we have already noted, after being challenged by 'the chief priests and the scribes and the elders' about his authority to act in this manner, Jesus replies by telling, against them, the Parable of the Wicked Husbandmen. The Parable is, in fact, an allegorical explanation of the catastrophe of A.D. 70 as divine punishment for the Jews' rejection and killing of Jesus. According to Mark, the Jewish leaders take it as aimed against themselves, and they attempt, unsuccessfully, to seize Jesus.[2]

This incident is followed in Mark by the hostile encounter with the Pharisees and Herodians over the tribute and with the Sadducees about the resurrection of the dead.[3] In the sequence of Mark's narrative, these incidents really constitute a kind of anticlimax to the preceding one, since that had ended with a practical declaration by the Jewish authorities of their intention to destroy Jesus. However that may be, what specially concerns us here is Mark's explanatory comments on the Tribute Money episode. He begins his

The saying may well have been uttered by Jesus, and preserved in Jewish Christian tradition; however, in using it here, Mark sought to show that Jesus foretold that the Jewish leaders would cause him to be executed by the Romans, thus preparing his readers for the strange transaction that his account of the trial before Pilate constitutes.

[1] x. 33. Even Taylor admits that 'in its precision [x. 33]...is a *vaticinium ex eventu*' (*St Mark*, p. 437, cf. p. 438). Cf. Bultmann, *Gesch. d. syn. Trad.* pp. 23, 163.

[2] xi. 27–xii. 12: see above, pp. 249–50.   [3] xii. 13–27.

account by connecting the question about the payment of the tribute with the preceding incident. The Jewish leaders, frustrated in their attempt to arrest Jesus, because of his popularity with the crowd, 'leaving him [apparently in his immunity], went away'.[1] Then, Mark seems to imply, 'they sent (ἀποστέλλουσιν) to him some of the Pharisees and some of the Herodians, to entrap him in his talk' (ἵνα αὐτὸν ἀγρεύσωσιν λόγῳ). This indication of their evil intent is supplemented by the comment that Jesus perceived their hypocrisy (ὁ δὲ εἰδὼς αὐτῶν τὴν ὑπόκρισιν).[2] We have already considered the significance of Mark's concern to tell his readers in Rome what was Jesus' attitude towards the Jewish payment of tribute, and we have later to attempt to discover what was the original form of this Tribute Money episode;[3] but here we must estimate the meaning of Mark's account of it *vis-à-vis* his presentation of the Jewish leaders. That meaning is quite clear. Mark obviously intended his Roman readers to know that the Jewish leaders had definitely tried to compromise Jesus on this burning issue of Jewish politics, and that they had not succeeded. From the Roman point of view, the Jews had the same obligation as all other subject peoples to pay tribute; to question this obligation was seditious, and the actual refusal to pay was a declaration of revolt. Thus to Mark's readers the attitude of Jesus to the issue was of profound importance. Mark not only reassures them that the attitude of Jesus, from the Roman standpoint, was impeccable, but he also represents the Jewish leaders as trying to entrap him into making a compromising statement about the tribute. It is not unreasonable to ask whether Mark had any special reason for doing this, beyond the general one of denigrating the Jewish authorities. It could well be that such a presentation was designed to rebut an accusation, possibly made by members of the Herodian clique in Rome, that Jesus had, like Judas of Galilee, forbidden the payment of tribute.[4]

Shortly after this account, Mark relates how Jesus, while teaching in the Temple, had asked his audience what appears to be a rhetorical question: 'How can the scribes say (πῶς λέγουσιν οἱ γραμματεῖς) that the Christ is the son of David?' He follows this question with a quotation from Psalm cx, which is designed to constitute a *reductio*

---

[1] xii. 12: καὶ ἀφέντες αὐτὸν ἀπῆλθον.
[2] xii. 12, 15.   [3] See pp. 271, 345–9.
[4] On the possibility that Mark's many hostile references to the Herodians are inspired by an antipathy to the followers of Agrippa II and Berenice in Rome, see above, pp. 248–9 and p. 268, n. 6.

ad absurdum of this scribal doctrine.[1] Such a presentation raises serious problems for Christian exegesis, since the Davidic descent of Jesus was clearly a well-established belief in primitive Christian circles.[2] It is, moreover, particularly surprising that Mark should thus present the Davidic descent of the Messiah in this derisory manner, as a doctrine of the Jewish scribes, of whom he also so manifestly disapproves; for Paul's Epistle to the Romans actually provides the only pre-Markan attestation of the Davidic descent of Jesus, κατὰ σάρκα.[3] Now, if this Epistle was indeed originally addressed to the Christian community in Rome, Paul's mention of the Davidic descent in his salutation would suggest that he knew the relationship was highly valued there. Such an evaluation would be consistent with the probability which we have noticed, that, in its first phase, the Christianity at Rome was Jewish Christian, having close relations with the Church of Jerusalem.[4] If this were so, it would be natural that Jesus should have been presented as the Messiah of Israel, with emphasis upon his Davidic descent.[5] Paul's subsequent influence and the Jewish revolt would have rendered this aspect of the primitive form of the faith suspect. It would, accordingly, make Mark's strange defamation of the Davidic descent of Christ intelligible, if he felt that the doctrine was now an undesirable one and that it would be convenient to represent Jesus as dismissing it as a self-contradictory fancy of the Jewish scribes.[6]

After the apocalyptic discourse, Mark begins to describe the events immediately preceding the arrest and trial of Jesus. He prefaces his account with a statement, undoubtedly designed to connect up with the earlier abortive attempt to arrest Jesus, which also re-emphasises the enmity of the Jewish leaders and their resolve to destroy Jesus: 'And the chief priests and the scribes were seeking

---

[1] xii. 35–7. Cf. Brandon, *Fall of Jerusalem*, pp. 189–91; Bultmann, *Gesch. d. syn. Trad.* pp. 144–6, Ergänzungsheft, p. 21.

[2] E.g. Matt. (genealogy) i. 1, 6–16, ix. 27, xii. 23, xv. 22, xx. 30, 31, xxi. 9, 15; Luke (genealogy) iii. 23–31, xviii. 38, 39; Rom. i. 3. Cf. Taylor, *St Mark*, p. 491; Klostermann, *Markusevangelium*, pp. 128–9.

[3] Rom. i. 3.

[4] See pp. 246–7.

[5] If the 'Chrestus' of Suetonius, *Claudius*, 25, is meant for 'Christus', thus indicating the existence of Messianic disturbances among the Jews of Rome (see pp. 96, 246), emphasis on the Davidic descent by the Jewish Christians could have been a potent cause of the troubles.

[6] It is likely that the term γραμματεῖς was well known to the Roman Christians as a designation for the official exponents of Judaism in Rome: cf. Brandon, *Fall of Jerusalem*, p. 190.

how to arrest him by stealth, and kill him; for they said, "Not during the feast, lest there be a tumult of the people"'[1]—the last remark, incidentally, revealing the doubtful nature of Mark's later picture of their influence over the crowd in the Barabbas episode.[2]

Mark's depiction of the murderous intent of the Jewish leaders at the Sanhedrin trial, and the way in which they compelled Pilate to do their will, we have already discussed at length.[3] It only remains now to note how Mark completes this damning picture of these leaders of the Jewish state and its religion. As the victim of their jealousy and malice hangs dying on the Roman cross, they are shown taunting him as a Messianic impostor: 'He saved others; he cannot save himself. Let the Christ, the King of Israel, come down now from the cross, that we may see and believe.'[4]

And so the author of Mark rounds off his portrait of the Jewish authorities: they are seen, from the very beginning of his ministry, as hostile to Jesus, attributing his power to demonic inspiration, and finally accomplishing his death, even against the will of the Roman governor. In turn, Jesus rejects and condemns these leaders of his people, thus giving proof of his essential independence of Judaism as it found expression in the official exponents of its cultic and legal requirements.

The author of Mark was not content with thus showing how Jesus had been rejected and foully done to death by the leaders of his nation: he evidently felt it desirable to show his Gentile readers that the Jewish people as a whole failed to understand and in the end demanded his death; in turn Jesus is represented as setting aside any claim that his Jewish nationality might have had on him. Thus Jesus remains unimpressed by the numbers that are attracted to him in Galilee, and he teaches them in parables, particularly that of the Sower and the Seed, which is incomprehensible without an explanation.[5] This explanation he only gives to his Twelve Apostles in private, telling them that the 'mystery of the kingdom of God' is to be communicated 'to those outside (ἐκείνοις δὲ τοῖς ἔξω)' only in parables, so that 'they may indeed see but not perceive, and

---

[1] xiv. 1–2. [2] See above, p. 261.

[3] Pp. 251 ff.

[4] xv. 31–2. 'The railing of the chief priests and scribes raises difficulties. Their presence at the crucifixion, while not impossible, excites surprise, and looks like an attempt to find room for the traditional opponents of Jesus' (Taylor, *St Mark*, p. 591; cf. Klostermann, *Markusevangelium*, p. 165).

[5] iv. 1 ff.

may indeed hear but not understand; lest they should turn again, and be forgiven'.[1]

When Jesus visits his own homeland (τὴν πατρίδα αὐτοῦ) and teaches there, the reaction of the people towards the 'local boy', whose family they know, is distinctly adverse (ἐσκανδαλίζοντο ἐν αὐτῷ), and their attitude draws forth from Jesus the bitter comment: 'A prophet is not without honour, except in his own country, and among his own people, and in his own house.' And he is represented as marvelling at their unbelief.[2] Next, the Jewish people, as a whole, are linked with the Pharisees in the condemnatory citation from Isa. xxix. 13, because of their observation of ritual lustrations, as we have previously noted.[3] Finally, at Jerusalem, although the crowd at first enthusiastically welcomes and supports Jesus, in the Barabbas episode it is depicted as demanding, at the instigation of the chief priests, his crucifixion, and, as he hangs on the cross, the bystanders deride him about his threat to destroy and rebuild the Temple.[4]

Accordingly, the reader of the Markan Gospel is led to see Jesus as both rejected by, and in turn rejecting, his fellow-Jews. The impression is thus created of the complete severance, on both sides, of the natural ties that bound Jesus to Judaism. But that is not all: the Jews, or at least the Jerusalem crowd, actually appear as the willing instruments of the hatred of the chief priests and press on the reluctant Pilate their demand for Jesus' crucifixion.

This Markan denigration of the Jewish people implies that Jesus was rejected also by his own family and relations; for, in the words attributed to Jesus after his hostile reception in his homeland, the prophet is not honoured 'among his own people and in his own house'.[5] Any doubt there might be about the soundness of seeing

---

[1] iv. 10–12. Cf. Black, *Aramaic Approach to the Gospels and Acts*, pp. 153–8; Taylor, *St Mark*, pp. 256–8.

[2] vi. 1–6. The phrase ὁ υἱὸς τῆς Μαρίας (v. 3) occurs nowhere else in the Gospels and Epistles; if it represents the original text (cf. Taylor, *St Mark*, pp. 299–300; Klostermann, *Markusevangelium*, p. 55), it raises an interesting possibility. It could be that Mark purposely places in the mouth of these Jews of Nazareth a calumny concerning the parentage of Jesus which circulated among the Jews of Rome. It would not be impossible that some version of the later Talmudic legends about Ben Pandera was already current: cf. Klausner, *Jesus of Nazareth*, pp. 48–9; Stauffer, *Jesus and His Story*, pp. 23–5.

[3] vii. 6–8.   [4] xv. 11 ff., 29–30.

[5] ἐν τοῖς συγγενεῦσιν αὐτοῦ καὶ ἐν τῇ οἰκίᾳ αὐτοῦ (vi. 4). Cf. Taylor, *St Mark*, p. 301; R. H. Lightfoot, *Locality and Doctrine in the Gospels*, pp. 145–6.

such an implication in these words is removed by the remarkable statement in iii. 21 that, on a certain occasion, members of Jesus' family (οἱ παρ' αὐτοῦ) believed him to be insane and tried to restrain him.[1] The incident is connected in Mark's narrative with that of the scribes' imputation that Jesus was possessed by Beelzebul and derived his miraculous power from the prince of the demons. This imputation causes Jesus to condemn them for committing the 'Unforgivable Sin'.[2] The juxtaposition of the action of the relatives of Jesus and the imputation of the scribes in Mark's narrative is certainly amazing; at the least it creates a truly shocking impression of these members of the family of Jesus. Even more surprising is the sequel. For Mark follows Jesus' denunciation of the 'Unforgivable Sin' with a pericope concerning his attitude to his mother and brothers: 'And his mother and his brothers came; and standing outside they sent to him and called him.' Informed by the attendant crowd of their message, Jesus is represented as replying: 'Who are my mother and my brothers?' And looking around on those who sat about him, he said, 'Here are my mother and my brothers! Whoever does the will of God is my brother, and sister, and mother.'[3]

So categorical a repudiation of the blood-relationship and its replacing by disciple-relationship is truly amazing, when it is recalled what the prestige of blood-relationship to Jesus meant in the Jerusalem Church. As we have seen, this was the cause of the sudden emergence of James, the brother of Jesus, to leadership of the movement, and, after his death, it ensured the election of Symeon, another close relative, as his successor.[4] This negating of blood-relationship to Jesus, moreover, follows immediately on the bad impression given of the family of Jesus by the record of their attempt to restrain him on grounds of insanity. Accordingly, we cannot but recognise that the author of Mark is not only concerned to inform his Gentile readers that blood-relationship to Jesus has no value and that they can be as closely related to Jesus as were his mother and brethren,

---

[1] 'οἱ παρ' αὐτοῦ...entspricht hebr. בֵּיתוֹ (Prov. 11. 29) und bedeutet geradezu "die Familie"' (Klostermann, *Markusevangelium*, p. 36). 'The family at Nazareth, and not merely "His friends" (RV) are indicated' (Taylor, *St Mark*, p. 236).

[2] iii. 20–30. Cf. J. Coutts, 'Those Outside (Mark 4, 10–12)', *Studia Evangelica*, II, 155–7; Burkill, *Mysterious Revelation*, pp. 136–7; E. Schweizer in *N.T.S.* x (1963–4), 425.

[3] iii. 31–5. Goguel, *La naissance du Christianisme*, pp. 130–3, interprets these passages as expressive of an early anti-dynastic polemic, but he does not connect this specifically with Mark. [4] Pp. 165–7.

but he also shows a certain animus towards these members of the family of Jesus. In other words, we find here in Mark what amounts to a silent, but a very effective, polemic against that dynastic control of the faith which was exemplified in James's position at Jerusalem. The origins of such an attitude doubtless lie back in those decades when the Mother Church of Jerusalem was predominant, tightly controlling daughter-churches such as that at Rome would have been. The dynastic prestige of James was undoubtedly felt and resented by many others besides Paul; but in those years it could not be questioned. However, when Mark was written that control had been broken since the year 66, when the Jewish revolt cut all normal communication with the Mother Church. The destruction of Jerusalem had ended that control for ever, and with it the unique status and prestige of the family of Jesus.[1] But the memory of that status and prestige would still have been fresh in the minds of the Roman Christians, so that the author of Mark felt obliged to exorcise it. And this he does with considerable skill in the passages under consideration. By his presentation here, he assures his Gentile readers that communion with Jesus depends upon the commitment of discipleship, and not on being a Jew closely related by birth to Jesus. But he does more than this: by the innuendo contained in iii. 21, he succeeds in conveying a truly shocking impression of the family of Jesus.

This defamation of the family of Jesus is paralleled by a derogatory presentation of his Apostles, who formed the essential nucleus of the Jerusalem Church. Although Jesus is described as specially choosing these twelve men, 'to be with him, and to be sent out to preach and to have authority to cast out demons',[2] they show themselves, according to Mark, as signally failing to justify their selection. They generally fail to understand their Master's true nature and mission, and they lack his miraculous power.[3] They quarrel among themselves over precedence and their future rewards,[4] one of them finally betrays him,[5] and, when he is arrested, they all desert him and seek their own safety.[6] It is indeed a most depressing picture of spiritual insensitivity, ambition, greed, and moral cowardice, and

---

[1] See above, pp. 208 ff. The traditions recorded by Eusebius of the status of the Lord's family in the time of Domitian (*Hist. eccl.* III. xix–xx) and his list of bishops of Jerusalem (*ibid.* IV. v) are eloquent in this connection.

[2] iii. 14.

[3] ix. 6, 10, 18, x. 13–16, 28–31, 32. Cf. Bacon, *Jesus and Paul*, pp. 149–50.

[4] ix. 34, x. 35–45. [5] xiv. 10, 11, 20, 21, 43–5.

[6] xiv. 50.

it is unrelieved by any final rehabilitating act of courage or faithfulness. Particularly instructive is the presentation of Peter, who is clearly depicted as the leading Apostle and spokesman for the rest. He is the first to recognise Jesus as the Messiah; yet, in the famous episode at Caesarea Philippi, he immediately incurs the terrible rebuke of being called 'Satan' for failing to appreciate the soteriological necessity of Jesus' coming death.[1] Shortly after this, when witnessing the Transfiguration of Jesus, he fails to understand its spiritual import and is concerned only to provide accommodation for Jesus and the two representatives of Judaism, Moses and Elijah, who appear and converse with him.[2] It is significant that Mark chose also to include in his relatively short Gospel the long detailed account of Peter's denial that he knew Jesus;[3] for, since it contains no rehabilitating factor, it completes a very uncomplimentary picture of this leading Apostle, who possibly was associated with the original Jewish Christian phase of Christianity in Rome.[4]

It seems likely that the Caesarea Philippi episode provides the best clue to understanding this derogatory presentation of the Twelve Apostles, and particularly of Peter, by the author of Mark. On analysis, the episode witnesses to two related facts which were

[1] viii. 33.

[2] ix. 5–7. It is difficult to understand the purpose of the Transfiguration in the structure of the Markan Gospel. It is, in effect, one of the divine attestations of the Divine Sonship of Jesus, the other being at his baptism (i. 11). On that occasion the divine voice was heard by Jesus only ('The subject of εἶδεν is Jesus', Taylor, *St Mark*, p. 160). At the Transfiguration the living witnesses were the three leading disciples, but they did not understand. As we shall see, the first human being who recognises the Divine Sonship is the Roman centurion on Calvary (xv. 39). There is much reason for agreeing with H. Baltensweiler in his monograph on the Transfiguration (*Die Verklärung Jesu: historisches Ereignis und synoptische Berichte*, Zürich, 1959, p. 115): 'Markus hat also deutlich einen Gegensatz herausgestellt. Auf der einen Seite stehen die Gestalten der drei "unwissenden und sich fürchtenden" Jünger, die gerade dadurch in ihrem Unglauben und in ihrer Verhärtung gezeichnet. Auf der andern Seite aber steht umso höher und überlegener die Gestalt des Messias als des "Sohnes Gottes".'It would, accordingly, appear that the episode has its place in Mark's apologetical theme, namely, that the Jewish disciples recognised Jesus as the Messiah but failed to comprehend his divinity. See below, pp. 278ff. Cf. Burkill, *Mysterious Revelation*, pp. 168–72.

[3] xiv. 66–72 (cf. *vv.* 29–31). Goguel thought that the story of Peter's denial is not historical, but grew out of the dialogue recorded in xiv. 29–30. In the context of our subject what is important is that Mark chose to include this derogatory story about Peter.

[4] Cf. Cullmann, *Petrus*², pp. 78–178 (E.T. pp. 70–152).

undoubtedly of crucial significance to the author. These facts find expression in Peter's recognition of the Messiahship of Jesus, and his subsequent failure to appreciate the soteriological role of his Master, when Jesus speaks of his coming death.[1] To appreciate the full significance of what the author of Mark does here, it must carefully be borne in mind that his was the first written account of the ministry of Jesus, and that the Christians in Rome, for whom he wrote, were unlikely to possess any other comparable sources of information. This means that they were purposely being given to understand that the original Apostles, and pre-eminently Peter, had regarded Jesus only as the Messiah of Israel, and that they had been unable to grasp, even when Jesus told them, that he, as the Messiah, must suffer many things and be killed. That, in Mark's mind, this utterance was not just a foretelling by Jesus of his death, but that the death would have a divinely decreed soteriological efficacy, is proved by his connecting the death of Jesus with his subsequent resurrection.[2] Accordingly, we find the author of Mark, in effect, declaring here that the original disciples of Jesus, who formed the nucleus of the Jerusalem Church, conceived of Jesus as the Jewish Messiah, but they balked at accepting him as the divine Saviour of mankind. In other words, this first of the apologists writes from the Pauline viewpoint, and he is concerned here to inform his readers of the limitations of the Christology of the Jerusalem Christians.[3]

All this evidence of intent to diminish, and even to controvert, the authority and prestige of the original disciples, must also be seen in conjunction with the Markan presentation of the family of Jesus. Thus, although he does not actually mention James, the brother of Jesus, the author of Mark represents, either by direct statement or by implication, the two outstanding members of the Jerusalem Church, namely, James and Peter, as men who failed to understand the true nature and mission of Jesus.

---

[1] viii. 29, 31–2.

[2] viii. 31: καὶ μετὰ τρεῖς ἡμέρας ἀναστῆναι. Cf. Bultmann, *Gesch. d. syn. Trad.* p. 163, n. 2.

[3] 'Car au moment même où Pierre a fait la déclaration "tu es le Messie", il devait, d'après le récit de Marc, déjà avoir la *conception diabolique* du rôle du Messie, celle que la majorité des Juifs partageaient et qui excluait sa souffrance' (O. Cullmann, 'L'apôtre Pierre instrument du diable et instrument de Dieu: la place de Matt. 16: 16–19 dans la tradition primitive', *New Testament Essays*, ed. A. J. B. Higgins, p. 96). See above, pp. 246–7.

There can, accordingly, be traced throughout the Markan Gospel a consistent denigration of the Jewish leaders and people, and of the family of Jesus and his original Apostles, which adds up to a truly damning indictment of the Jews for their treatment of Jesus. The Jewish leaders and people are responsible for his death, his family regard him as insane, and his Apostles fail to understand him and finally desert him. In turn, Jesus is shown as rejecting those of his nation who reject him, as making the serving of God, not blood-relationship, the basis of communion with himself, and as vehemently rebuking his chief Apostle's obsession with a nationalistic conception of his own status and mission. Consequently, in Mark, despite the lively depiction of his essentially Jewish environment, Jesus is portrayed as essentially independent of his Jewish origin and relationships.

This fundamentally anti-Jewish thesis of the author of Mark reaches its climax in the recording of an incident which is virtually the climax of the Gospel. Having shown throughout his narrative how the Jewish leaders and people, how his family and his Apostles, had failed to realise the divinity of Jesus, Mark represents the Roman centurion in charge of the Crucifixion as the first human being to perceive the truth.[1] As Jesus hangs dying on the cross, derided by the Jews who had brought him to his death, it is this Gentile, a soldier of Rome, who has the faith and courage to exclaim: 'Truly this man was the Son of God.'[2] This confession does in fact represent the fulfilment of the author's intention adumbrated in his opening statement: 'The beginning of the Gospel of Jesus

---

[1] Demoniacs are represented as being aware of the divine nature of Jesus: Mark i. 24, 34 (οὐκ ἤφιεν λαλεῖν τὰ δαιμόνια, ὅτι ᾔδεισαν αὐτόν), iii. 11–12, v. 7. The insane were regarded in contemporary society as possessed of supernatural knowledge, through the indwelling demon. Cf. Clemen, *Religionsgeschichtliche Erklärung*, pp. 218–19.

[2] xv. 39: 'Ἀληθῶς οὗτος ὁ ἄνθρωπος υἱὸς θεοῦ ἦν. The absence of the article before υἱός has no significance in this context, and υἱὸς θεοῦ here clearly corresponds to i. 1: 'Ἀρχὴ τοῦ εὐαγγελίου 'Ἰησοῦ Χριστοῦ υἱοῦ τοῦ θεοῦ. 'υἱὸς θεοῦ müßte indeterminiert sein und nur *ein Gottessohn* bedeuten, wenn eine wirkliche Äußerung eines Heiden berichtet würde. Mc aber will doch wohl Jesus als den Gottessohn sogar durch einen Heiden anerkennen lassen, der dann als Muster für die Heidenchristen dasteht' (Klostermann, *Markusevangelium*, p. 167). It is of interest to note that Mark uses a transliteration of the Latin *centurio*—κεντυρίων, whereas Matthew and Luke in their records use ἑκατόνταρχος. ὁ κεντυρίων would surely have been better appreciated in Rome. Cf. E. Schweizer in *N.T.S.* x (1963–4), 430.

Christ, the Son of God.'[1] It would surely have been a revelation, reassuring and inspiring, to Mark's Gentile readers in Rome, thus to learn that a Roman centurion, a Gentile like themselves, had had the insight, which even the Jewish disciples lacked, to perceive the divinity of Jesus at the very moment of his redeeming death. Here, in a very true sense, Mark's *Apologia ad Christianos Romanos* completed its task. Jesus died, with the centurion's confession presaging Gentile acceptance of his saving divinity, while the rending of the Temple veil signified Judaism's supersession by a nobler faith.

The Markan achievement was immense. Produced to meet the urgent needs of the Christian community in Rome in the early years of the eighth decade, it decided the pattern in which the primitive tradition concerning Jesus was henceforth to be presented. Faced by the need to explain the Roman execution of Jesus, the author of Mark replaced the original Jewish Christian story of the martyr's death, at the hands of the heathen Romans and their Jewish collaborators, by that of the long-intentioned murder of the Son of God by the Jewish leaders, supported by their people. Seeking to remove any suggestion that Jesus had been implicated in the Jewish freedom movement, Mark presents him as serenely insulated from contemporary political interests and concerns, except that he is shown as endorsing the payment of tribute to Rome. The fact that he chose a Zealot for an Apostle is discreetly suppressed.

This abstraction of Jesus from the political life of his time meant also the representing of him as essentially detached from his racial origins and heritage; for, since Judaism is fundamentally an ethnic religion, faith and politics were inextricably one for the Jew of that period, and it was necessary to show that in this Jesus was different. Mark, accordingly, initiated a kind of ambivalent conception of the life of Jesus which decisively shaped subsequent Christian thinking. On the one hand, by his use of the primitive tradition, he set Jesus firmly in the context of Palestinian life in the third decade of the first century; on the other hand, this Palestinian environment seems strangely unaffected by all those disturbances which were caused by Pilate's government or misgovernment according to the testimony of Philo and Josephus. In other words, although Mark's narrative gives a vivid impression of Palestinian society at this time, that society seems strangely unconcerned by those stresses and tensions, caused by the Roman rule, that led eventually to the explosion

[1] i. 1: see preceding note.

of A.D. 66. However, despite this apparent absence of political agitation, the incidental mention in Mark xv. 7 of insurrection in Jerusalem indicates the existence of a situation more consistent with that which might be expected from the writings of Philo and Josephus. And the complete absence of any reference to Zealotism reveals also a significant silence about one of the most dynamic factors in Jewish life at that time.

Although, in the interests of his apologetical theme, the author of Mark thus represented Jesus as unconcerned with politics, except for endorsing the Roman tribute, in this first Gospel there is no attempt to portray what may be termed a 'pacific Christ'. For example, Mark did not use the Temptation of Jesus for this purpose as did the later Evangelists, as we shall see.[1] However, by seeking to show that Jesus was innocent of sedition against Rome, Mark provided the impetus to a transcendental conception of Christ, which put him beyond concern for contemporary Jewish politics.

How far the author of the Markan Gospel was influenced by Paul's teaching has often been discussed by New Testament scholars.[2] This discussion seems frequently to have suffered from the tendency to seek in Mark clear indications of ideas that are known to us through Paul's Epistles. But it is improbable, in view of the state of the *Corpus Paulinum*, that many of these writings would have been available in Rome at this time.[3] The more likely situation would be that Paul's sojourn in the city would have made his main ideas known to the Christians there.[4] These would have been that Jesus was a divine being, incarnated to fulfil God's plan for mankind's salvation, and that this salvation had been accomplished by his crucifixion. The manner of this soteriological transaction involved much esoteric thought, as we have seen,[5] and it is probable that it was not clearly understood by the Christians of Rome. But what was important is that they had learned from Paul to see in Jesus a divine being who had saved them from spiritual perdition, and not

---

[1] Pp. 310 ff.

[2] Cf. Bacon, *Jesus and Paul*, pp. 16, 143–54; Moffatt, *Introduction to the New Testament*, pp. 235–6; M. Werner, *Der Einfluß paulinischer Theologie im Markusevangelium* (*passim*); Taylor, *St Mark*, pp. 16–17, 125–9; Burkill, *Mysterious Revelation*, pp. 173–4.

[3] Cf. Brandon, *Fall of Jerusalem*, pp. 213 ff.; G. Zuntz, *The Text of the Epistles* (London, 1953), pp. 217–20, 225–6.

[4] Whatever may have been the fate of Paul, according to Acts xxviii. 30–1 he spent at least two full years (διετίαν ὅλην) teaching in Rome.

[5] Pp. 151 ff.

the Messiah who would return to restore the kingdom to Israel. It is of such a divine being that the author of Mark writes: he announces his theme in the opening sentence as that of 'the gospel of Jesus Christ, the Son of God', and its *epiphaneia* is the centurion's confession, 'Truly this man was the Son of God.' The obsolescence of Judaism, which the logic of Paul's teaching implied, even if he did not formally recognise it, is symbolised by Mark in the Rending of the Temple Veil, consequent on the death of Jesus.

As an *Apologia ad Christianos Romanos*, the Markan Gospel was a very able work. For it did provide the Christians in Rome (who were not highly critical historians) with a convincing explanation of why Jesus had been crucified by the Roman governor for sedition. They were further reassured about Jesus' loyalty to Rome by his endorsement of the Jewish obligation to pay tribute to the Roman emperor. And they were encouraged by the knowledge that, though he was born a Jew, Jesus was essentially detached from his race, and that it was the Jews who had rejected and killed him. Finally, they would have learned with much natural satisfaction that, whereas the Jewish disciples could only see in Jesus the Messiah of Israel, his divinity had been perceived first by a Gentile soldier.

The success of the Markan *apologia*, however, had very far-reaching consequences. It obscured the real cause of the Crucifixion by explaining away the fundamental fact that Jesus had been executed by the Romans for sedition. Accordingly, instead of attention being focused on the relations of Jesus with the Roman government of Judaea, it has been the relations of Jesus with the official representatives of Judaism upon which study has been concentrated. Thus the crucifixion of Jesus has become a theological, not a political problem. But the fact remains that Jesus was executed as a rebel against Rome, and not as a heretic against Judaism.

We have shown that the transference of responsibility for the Crucifixion from the Roman to the Jewish authorities was motivated by the apologetical purpose of the Markan Gospel. The problem constituted by the Roman execution still remains, however, for our investigation. But, before undertaking that task, we must consider whether the other three Gospels reveal any evidence of the original situation which is independent of the Markan version.

CHAPTER 6

THE CONCEPT OF THE PACIFIC CHRIST: ITS ORIGIN AND DEVELOPMENT

The author of the Markan Gospel, seeking, as we have seen, to explain the Roman execution of Jesus, presented Jesus as the victim of the hatred of the Jewish leaders. Ancillary to this presentation was the depiction of Jesus as endorsing the Jewish payment of tribute to Rome. Further, in pursuance of this apologetical theme, Jesus is represented as moving in a society untroubled by political issues, all reference to the Zealots and the disturbances caused by Pilate's government being discreetly suppressed. The only hint of a more sinister situation is given in the episode of Barabbas; but this occurs in the course of representing Jesus as insulated from current political affairs, of which he becomes the victim. The militant Barabbas, who had been involved in a bloody insurrection against the Romans, is set over against the peaceable Jesus, who had counselled the Jews to pay their tribute to Rome.[1]

This Markan portrait was designed, as we noted, to meet the needs of the Christian community in Rome, involved as it was in the aftermath of the Jewish War. It was an *ad hoc* presentation, being primarily concerned with showing that Jesus had been loyal to the Roman government in Judaea. Since this was the first literary portrait of Jesus, and it was set in a vivid narrative of great dramatic quality, its influence became definitive for all subsequent portrayal. Unchallenged, owing to the disappearance of the Jerusalem Church in the catastrophe of A.D. 70, by the original Jewish Christian concept of Jesus as the Messiah who would 'restore the kingdom to Israel', this Markan portrait provided the pattern respectively for the writers of the Gospels of Matthew and of Luke when they sought to provide accounts of Jesus for their own respective Churches.[2]

When these Gospels were published, some ten to fifteen years had

[1] Pp. 258 ff.
[2] Cf. Streeter, *Four Gospels*, pp. 157–79; Williams in *Peake's Commentary*[2], 653 b–654 b.

passed since Mark was written for the Roman Christians.[1] Accordingly, the crisis which prompted the composition of Mark did not face the authors of Matthew and Luke. The immediate passions caused by the Jewish War had subsided, and two decades of independence from the control of the Mother Church of Jerusalem had removed the need for Mark's preoccupation with the status of the original Jewish Christians.[2] However, although they did not write under the immediate impact of the events of A.D. 70, the authors of Matthew and Luke were still sufficiently close to be concerned with the lessons which the Jewish catastrophe had for Christianity. The fate of the Jerusalem Church was a warning of what implication in political Messianism could mean. After A.D. 70 it was, of course, unlikely that Christians might become directly involved in Jewish nationalism; however, the revolutionary aspect of Jewish Messianism was calculated to make Roman officials suspicious of a movement which had stemmed from Judaea and was centred upon one recognised as the Messiah, whom the procurator of Judaea in the reign of Tiberius had been obliged to execute for sedition.[3] Accordingly, Mark's presentation of Jesus as guiltless of the charge on which he was crucified, and as the innocent victim of Jewish malice, was accepted and used as the basis upon which each Evangelist built his own account. These accounts were, however, conceived by their respective authors to meet the needs of the particular Christian communities for which they wrote. Therefore, the Matthaean and Lukan Gospels, although modelled on the Markan thesis, constitute two distinctive developments of Mark's presentation of the life and teaching of Jesus. For our purpose, of evaluating the attitude of Jesus to Israel's cause against Rome, these Gospels have a threefold importance: their authors utilised traditions not included in Mark;[4] they were not immediately involved with the consequences of the

---

[1] Critical opinion generally concurs in dating Matthew for about A.D. 80–5; cf. McNeil, *St Matthew*, pp. xxvi–xxviii; Streeter, *Four Gospels*, pp. 523–4; Goguel, *Life of Jesus*, p. 142; G. Bornkamm in *R.G.G.*[3], II, 763. G. D. Kilpatrick (*Origins of the Gospel of St Matthew*, pp. 6–7, 127–31) favours a date after A.D. 90, whereas K. Stendahl (*Peake's Commentary*[2], 673k) seems inclined to date it before A.D. 80.

[2] See pp. 274–9.

[3] Cf. P. de Labriolle, *La réaction païenne*, pp. 38–49. The Roman government took some time in distinguishing Christians from Jews: cf. Simon, *Verus Israel*, pp. 127–8; Frend, *Martyrdom and Persecution*, pp. 164–5, 186, 213.

[4] Cf. Meyer, *Ursprung*, I, 212–38; Streeter, *Four Gospels*, pp. 182–91, 227 ff.; Williams in *Peake's Commentary*[2], 654b–658a.

Jewish War and so were not obliged to be so circumspect as the Markan writer;[1] and they elaborated the Markan portrait of Jesus into that of the pacific Christ, which became the established tradition of Christianity. However, as a prerequisite to appreciating the significance of their work and the factors which influenced its achievement, we must understand the communities for which these authors wrote, which necessarily means trying to identify their location.

There is, fortunately, one fact that provides what might be called a key to the spatial relationship of the Matthaean and Lukan Gospels. It is that Matthew locates the appearance of the Risen Lord to the disciples in Galilee, whither they had been expressly commanded to go from Jerusalem.[2] According to the Lukan writer, however, the post-Resurrection appearances took place in and around Jerusalem, the disciples being ordered not to leave the city, and the Ascension was made from the Mount of Olives.[3] Now such a divergence of tradition on a matter of such basic importance as the place where the Risen Lord had appeared to the disciples and ascended into heaven is very revealing. It must surely mean that Matthew and Luke were written at places so far distant from each other that the author of each shows no awareness of the fact that the accuracy of his account was thus challenged by a rival version.[4] We

---

[1] Matthew followed Mark in withholding from his Greek-speaking readers the fact that one of Jesus' disciples had been a Zealot; however, Matthew's reason for so doing differed from that of Mark (see pp. 243 ff.).

[2] Matt. xxviii. 7, 10, 16 ff. Mark xiv. 28, xvi. 7, clearly indicates an exclusive Galilaean location for the Resurrection appearances to the disciples. Cf. Meyer, *Ursprung*, I, 13–15; Streeter, *Four Gospels*, p. 343; Kilpatrick, *Origins of the Gospel of St Matthew*, p. 49; R. H. Lightfoot, *Locality and Doctrine in the Gospels*, pp. 52 ff., 89; Taylor, *St Mark*, p. 549.

[3] Luke xxiv. 49 (ὑμεῖς δὲ καθίσατε ἐν τῇ πόλει...); Acts i. 4 (παρήγγειλεν αὐτοῖς ἀπὸ Ἰεροσολύμων μὴ χωρίζεσθαι).

[4] Even if E. Lohmeyer (*Galiläa und Jerusalem*, pp. 29, 34, 316) is right in thinking that Markan tradition, on doctrinal grounds, regarded Galilee as 'das gelobte Land', contrasting it with Jerusalem as the city of sin and death, the significance of the divergence of the Resurrection traditions in Matthew and Luke still remains: cf. Lightfoot, *Locality and Doctrine in the Gospels*, pp. 62–5, 111, 123, 124. John evidently felt the seriousness of this divergence and endeavoured to reconcile the conflicting testimony of the two traditions (John xx–xxi). Cf. Streeter, *Four Gospels*, pp. 351 f.; Guignebert, *Jésus*, pp. 615–17; Goguel, *La naissance du Christianisme*, p. 74; P. Gardner Smith, *Narratives of the Resurrection* (London, 1926), pp. 87–9; Burkitt, *Christian Beginnings*, pp. 79 ff.; L. E. Elliott-Binns, *Galilean Christianity*, pp. 39–42.

may, therefore, reasonably conclude that the places in which the Matthaean and Lukan Gospels were respectively produced, whatever their exact locations, were situated at a very considerable distance from each other.[1]

There has been much speculation about the places of origin of both the Gospels of Matthew and Luke. It has been generally accepted that each document must have been written for an important Christian centre, although no common agreement has been reached as to where these centres were situated. There are, however, certain aspects of the Lukan Gospel which would be generally allowed as being indicative of its area of origin. The early tradition that connects Luke with Achaea is consistent also with its being the most Hellenistic of the four Gospels.[2] Moreover, since it forms the first part of an account of Christian Origins which is continued in the Acts of the Apostles,[3] it follows that its author held that derogatory opinion of Alexandrian Christianity, expressed in Acts xviii. 24–xix. 7, which we have already noted.[4] Consequently, we may reasonably infer that the Lukan Gospel was not written in Alexandria, which was indeed an important centre of Hellenistic life, and that its traditional location in Achaea would agree with the very evident fact that its author was a Pauline Christian, who was keenly aware of the difference between Paul's version of the faith and that taught at Alexandria in Egypt.[5]

Now, in view of the fact that the conflicting locations given by these two Gospels for the post-Resurrection appearances of Jesus imply that they originated at a considerable distance from each other, the siting of Luke in Achaea means that we must look far to the south for Matthew's place of origin. Moreover, since Matthew is the most Jewish of the Gospels, we must also seek a strong centre of Jewish life.[6]

---

[1] The accounts of the end of Judas Iscariot in Matt. xxvii. 3–10 and Acts i. 16–20 are evidently derived from different traditions: cf. B. W. Bacon, *Studies in Matthew*, p. 252. The Matthaean and Lukan Birth and Infancy narratives show a similar divergence.

[2] Cf. Streeter, *Four Gospels*, p. 12; Creed, *St Luke*, p. xxi; Manson, *Studies*, pp. 48–9.

[3] Cf. H. J. Cadbury in *B.C.* II, 491 ff.   [4] Pp. 191 ff.

[5] According to Acts xviii. 26, Paul's friends had to expound 'the way of God more carefully' to the Alexandrian Apollos before he could be commended to other Pauline churches. See above, pp. 192 ff.

[6] Cf. Meyer, *Ursprung*, I, 239–41; Stendahl in *Peake's Commentary*², 673*f*–*g*; W. D. Davies, *Paul and Rabbinic Judaism* (London, 1948), p. 137 ('Mat-

THE CONCEPT OF THE PACIFIC CHRIST

The two places or areas which naturally suggest themselves as fulfilling these requirements are Syria (including Phoenicia and Palestine) and Alexandria in Egypt. A Syrian location has often been suggested, without the presentation of any strongly argued case;[1] but recently an impressive interpretation of Matthew has been published which is based upon the supposition that the document was composed in the near vicinity of Jamnia in Palestine. Professor W. D. Davies, believing that the author of the Matthaean Gospel turned an original polemic uttered by Jesus against the Essenes of Qumrân into a denunciation of the Pharisees, explains this remarkable undertaking as due to the *Sitz im Leben* of the community for which the Gospel was written.[2] He argues that Rabbi Johanan ben Zakkai, who escaped from Jerusalem in A.D. 70, established at Jamnia a centre of Pharisaic study and practice, which challenged the Jewish Christian community of which Matthew was a member.[3]

thew, the Gospel of Christian Rabbinism'); R. Hummel, *Die Auseinandersetzung zwischen Kirche und Judentum im Matthäusevangelium* (München, 1963), pp. 26–8.

[1] Streeter argued strongly in favour of an Antiochene origin for Matthew (*Four Gospels*, pp. 12, 500–26; *C.A.H.* XI, 260–1; *Primitive Church*, pp. 58–60). According to him, a party of Jewish Christians fled to Antioch from Jerusalem after the death of James in A.D. 62, bringing with them Jerusalem traditions peculiar to Matthew. Unfortunately he did not support his thesis with any demonstration of when and how such a flight *en masse* could have been successfully effected, relative to the political and military situation in Palestine and Antioch in the decade from A.D. 62; cf. Brandon, *Fall of Jerusalem*, pp. 217–19. On the situation of the Jewish community in Antioch after A.D. 70 see below, p. 288. Bacon (*Studies in Matthew*, pp. 19–22) argued that Matthew originated among the Greek-speaking Jewish Christian communities of northern and north-eastern Syria, and was later brought to Antioch (cf. F. W. Green, *The Gospel according to St Matthew*, pp. 19–22); but the language of the Jews in this area was Aramaic according to Josephus, *War*, Preface, 1–2. McNeil, *St Matthew*, p. xxviii, places Matthew in Syria, 'where the Christians were not in close touch with Jerusalem'. On the other hand, Meyer, *Ursprung*, I, 241, maintained that 'das Matthaeusevangelium aus den judenchristlichen Kreisen Palaestinas stammt'. Among other scholars who located the Gospel in Antioch or Syria, without a detailed discussion of the issue, are Weiss, *Earliest Christianity*, II, 752–3; E. J. Goodspeed, *Introduction to the New Testament* (Chicago, 1937), pp. 175–6; F. Jackson and K. Lake in *B.C.* I, 330; Manson, *Studies in Gospels and Epistles*, p. 87; G. Bornkamm in *R.G.G.*[3], II, 763; Stendahl in *Peake's Commentary*[2], 673 b; H. Ljungmann, 'Matthäusevangelium', *B.-h. H.-Wb.* II, 1172; C. W. F. Smith in *J.B.L.* LXXXII (1963), 167–8.

[2] Davies, *Sermon on the Mount*, pp. 255, 315.   [3] *Ibid.* pp. 256 ff.

287

This assumption necessarily involved the location of this community sufficiently close to Jamnia to make the challenge which its Pharisaic school allegedly constituted, so urgently felt that Matthew was induced to meet it by writing his Gospel. Consequently Professor Davies locates the Matthaean community 'in Syria, at Antioch, or in Phoenicia'.[1]

It is surprising to find Antioch regarded as being sufficiently close in this way to Jamnia. The suspicion arises that Professor Davies, wishing to find a Syrian location, was induced to suggest Antioch since it had already been proposed as the birthplace of Matthew.[2] However that may be, Antioch scarcely fulfils the conditions presupposed by the ethos and contents of the Matthaean Gospel. The Jewish population of the city suffered severely in consequence of the Jewish War, and its survivors were in a pitiful condition after A.D. 70.[3] The Church there, moreover, was distinguished by its Hellenistic character;[4] it had been the scene of Paul's famous dispute with Peter over the status of Gentile converts *vis-à-vis* Jewish Christians, and it had also notably supported Paul's missionary work and policy.[5] Further, the fact that Matthew must have been published in some centre far removed from that for which Luke was written, in view of the divergence of their locations of the post-Resurrection appearances, rules out Antioch as a likely place of origin; and to this consideration must be added that of the probability that the author of Luke had connections with the Syrian metropolis.[6]

[1] Davies, *Sermon on the Mount*, p. 293.   [2] See p. 287, n. 1 above.

[3] Josephus, *War*, VII. 41, 54–62, 100–11. Josephus refers to the Jews of Antioch after A.D. 70 as τοῖς ἐν ᾿Αντιοχείᾳ τῶν ᾿Ιουδαίων ὑπολειπομένοις (*ibid*. 41). And he reports Titus as replying, significantly, to the request of the Antiochenes that the remaining Jews should be expelled from the city: ἀλλ᾿ ἥ γε πατρὶς αὐτῶν, εἰς ἣν ἐκβαλεῖν ἐχρῆν ὄντας ᾿Ιουδαίους, ἀνῄρηται, καὶ δέξαιτ᾿ ἂν οὐδεὶς αὐτοὺς ἔτι τόπος (*ibid*. 109). The miserable situation of this remnant scarcely provides the setting of a flourishing Jewish community presupposed by Matthew.

[4] οἵτινες ἐλθόντες εἰς ᾿Αντιόχειαν ἐλάλουν καὶ πρὸς τοὺς ῾Ελληνιστάς, Acts xi. 20: on ῾Ελληνισταί here see *B.C.* III, 106, IV, 128, V, 66. χρηματίσαι τε πρώτως ἐν ᾿Αντιοχείᾳ τοὺς μαθητὰς Χριστιανούς, Acts xi. 26. Cf. J. Kollwitz in *R.A.C.* I, 463–4.

[5] Gal. ii. 11 ff.; Acts xiii. 1 ff., xiv. 26–7, xv. 35 ff. See above, pp. 156ff.

[6] According to Eusebius (*Hist. eccl.* III. iv. 6), Luke was a native of Antioch: Λουκᾶς δὲ τὸ μὲν γένος ὢν τῶν ἀπ᾿ ᾿Αντιοχείας. It is also interesting to note that the Codex Bezae reading for Acts xi. 28 starts the 'we' passages at Antioch: cf. J. H. Ropes in *B.C.* III, 109 and note; see also *B.C.* II, 158 ff., IV, 130. Cf. Streeter, *Four Gospels*, p. 554; Manson, *Studies*, pp. 48–9.

Professor Davies's alternative location for the Matthaean Gospel, namely, Phoenicia, is vague. Presumably, the Gospel would have been addressed to an urban church, and the most likely place for such a church would be Tyre, Sidon, Berytos or Byblos. However, none of these cities is known as a strong centre of Christian life in this early period, and it is significant that Professor Davies was not prepared to name any of them.[1] Then, to all these objections concerning the locations which he proposes there must also be added that of the fact that there is no certain evidence that Jamnia itself was such a centre of Pharisaic revival as to constitute the challenge to which he assumes Matthew to be the Christian response.[2]

Professor Davies's case for the location of the Matthaean Gospel at Antioch or in Phoenicia has been examined at some length, because it represents the most recent and elaborate attempt to locate the document at some place other than that which will be proposed here. The proposition now about to be made is, in fact, a restatement and an elaboration of an argument originally set forth in *The Fall of Jerusalem and the Christian Church*.[3] The devotion of so much attention to the question of the origin of the Matthaean Gospel is necessary, since upon the proper solution of this question the interpretation of the document, as evidence of a vital phase in the beginnings of Christianity, absolutely depends.

We have already noted in the Acts of the Apostles signs of a hostile or critical attitude towards the Christianity current in Alexandria.[4]

[1] Kilpatrick locates Matthew in Phoenicia, because of its alterations of the Markan story of the Syro-Phoenician woman (pp. 132–3): see below, p. 295.

[2] Professor Davies, *Sermon on the Mount*, frankly admits this on p. 292, n. 2; however, he is justified in assuming that Jamnia 'was a centre for Jewry', although whether it was at that time, i.e. *c.* A.D. 80, is perhaps questionable. Cf. Schürer, *G.J.V.* II, 98–9.

[3] Ch. 12. In order to establish his thesis that Matthew was written in reaction to the revived Pharisaism at Jamnia, Dr Davies felt obliged to attack the present writer's location of Matthew at Alexandria and his interpretation of the effect of the fall of Jerusalem (*op. cit.* pp. 317–20, 321, n. 1, 322–6, 332 ff., 336; see also his *Christian Origins and Judaism*, p. 83, n. 65, and in *Peake's Commentary*[2], 768 a). The points made by Dr Davies are answered in *The Modern Churchman*, VIII, n.s. (1965), 152–61. Agreement with the present writer's thesis that Alexandrian Christianity was derived from Jerusalem has recently (1964) been expressed by J. Daniélou and H. Marrou in *The Christian Church* (E.T.), I, 45: 'With the Judaeo-Christian Church of Jerusalem is linked the origin of the Church in Egypt.' Cf. H. C. Snape in *H.Th.R.* XLVII (1954), 2 ff., LIII (1960), 33 ff.

[4] See pp. 191 ff.

This attitude, in a writing of one who was evidently a Pauline Christian, is consistent with the fact that Paul himself never attempted to preach his 'gospel' in the great Egyptian metropolis, and it also helps to explain the otherwise strange silence about the origins of Christianity in Alexandria or other places in Egypt. We also found reason for believing that Alexandria had been evangelised by the Jerusalem Christians, that a strong link existed between the Mother Church and the church in Alexandria, and that it was likely that Peter had played an important part in establishing the church there.[1]

In seeking a likely location for the Gospel of Matthew, it is obvious that a strong a priori case, at least, exists for Alexandria and deserves consideration. Thus, if Mark originated in Rome and Luke in Achaea, what other centre of primitive Christianity, it may be asked, would seem a more likely home of Matthew? We have noted the objections to Antioch's fulfilling this role, and Ephesus can be ruled out as being too near to the Lukan centre, besides being an unlikely location for the most Jewish of the Gospels.[2] By this process of elimination we are, inevitably, left with Alexandria, which is sufficiently far removed from Luke's place of origin to account for the currency of a tradition concerning the post-Resurrection appearances of Christ that so strikingly contradicts the Lukan tradition. Moreover, besides being the second greatest city in the Roman empire, Alexandria had the biggest Jewish population outside Palestine.[3] Accordingly, in view of these considerations, and since there is no other more likely place in this area, the case for an Alexandrian origin of Matthew certainly has a presumptive justification. The matter, however, has not to be left there, for to these a priori considerations there is to be added the testimony of a number of points indicative of an Alexandrian or Egyptian origin which are evident on examination of the Gospel itself.

[1] Pp. 164, 191, 189–8.
[2] Both Paul and, according to later tradition, John were associated with Ephesus: cf. B.-h. H.-Wb. I, 419.
[3] Cf. H. I. Bell in C.A.H. x, 296–7, F. Oertel, ibid. pp. 398–400, 412. Philo (in Flaccum, 43) estimated the Jewish population of Egypt, including Alexandria, at not less than one million. Cf. Bell, Juden und Griechen im römischen Alexandreia, pp. 10–14, and Jews and Christians in Egypt, pp. 11 ff.; H. Box, Philonis Alexandrini In Flaccum, pp. xx ff.; Schürer, G.J.V. III, 21 ff.; E. M. Smallwood, Philonis Alexandrini Legatio ad Gaium, pp. 4 ff.; J. Juster, Les Juifs dans l'Empire romain, p. 209; W. Schubart in R.A.C. I, 276–7.

Before we consider this internal evidence, it will be useful to notice what information we have of the situation of the Jewish population of Alexandria in the years immediately following the fall of Jerusalem in A.D. 70. With the commencement of the Jewish War in 66, it would appear that rioting broke out in Alexandria between the Jews and Greeks. From Josephus' account it is not clear which side took the initiative; there was much bloodshed on both sides, and it would seem that the Jews suffered the heavier casualties in the end.[1] Again, Josephus' record is vague as to whether the conflict was directly connected with the revolt in Judaea; presumably it was, since what he tells of the troubles in Alexandria follows in the course of his recital of the clashes which occurred between Jews and Greeks in Syria and elsewhere in consequence of the events in Judaea.[2] However that may be, the Alexandrian Jews appear, after this, to have remained quiet during the war, probably chastened by their earlier experiences and being wisely controlled by the Roman governor, Tiberius Alexander, who, though an apostate Jew, doubtless knew best how to guide his compatriots through these critical years.[3] It would certainly seem that the Jews in Egypt were warned by the disasters which befell their compatriots in Judaea; for when a force of the Sicarii, which succeeded in escaping destruction when Jerusalem fell, came into Egypt and tried to persuade them to revolt, they caused them to be rounded up and handed over to the Roman authorities for execution.[4] Josephus states that the

[1] Josephus, *War*, II. 490–8.
[2] *War*, II. 477 ff. There seems to be no justification for the view of J. G. Milne (*History of Egypt under Roman Rule*, London, 1898, p. 35), that the disturbance 'was provoked by the expedition of a large body of Egyptian Jews to Palestine, with the object of setting Jerusalem free from Roman rule'.
[3] When the Alexandrian Jews attempted to burn their Greek neighbours assembled in the amphitheatre, Tiberius Alexander 'curbed (ἀνέκοψεν) their fury'. Having failed to reason (σωφρονίζειν) them out of armed violence, he used troops to teach them a sharp, but carefully controlled, lesson (*War*, II. 492–8). On Tiberius Alexander see above, pp. 103 ff.; he later secured Alexandria for Vespasian (*War*, IV. 616–17).
[4] Jos. *War*, VII. 410–19. It would seem that these Sicarii had actually caused trouble, including the murder of certain influential Jews who had opposed them, before the Jewish leaders in Alexandria (οἱ πρωτεύοντες τῆς γερουσίας) took effective action against them. It is interesting to note that, according to Josephus, the Romans were then regarding the profession of Zealotism as a capital offence (γνωσθέντας γὰρ ὑπὸ Ῥωμαίων εὐθὺς ἀπολεῖσθαι, *ibid*. 413). These Sicarii must have numbered well over the six hundred who were arrested in Alexandria, since others were

leaders of the Alexandrian Jews counselled their people to take this action, in order 'to make their peace with the Romans'.[1]

This practical demonstration of their peaceable intention does not seem, however, to have allayed Roman suspicion of the danger of seditious activity among the Jewish population of Egypt. According to Josephus, about the year 73 Vespasian, 'suspicious of the interminable tendency of the Jews to revolution', ordered Lupus, the governor of Egypt, to demolish the Jewish temple at Leontopolis.[2] This edifice, which Josephus denominates both ναός and ἱερόν, had been built in 170 B.C. by Onias, one of the chief priests, who had sought refuge in Egypt from the Seleucid monarch Antiochus Epiphanes.[3] In view of the Deuteronomic laws, ordaining a single sanctuary at Jerusalem only, it is strange that the contravention which this temple of Onias constituted was not condemned in Jewish literature.[4] The temple was furnished on the model of the

rounded up in other parts of Egypt. Cf. V. A. Tcherikover, 'The Decline of the Jewish Diaspora in Egypt in the Roman Period', *J.J.S.* xiv (1963), 27.

[1] παρεκάλουν καὶ περὶ αὐτῶν πρὸς Ῥωμαίους ἀπολογήσασθαι τῇ τούτων παραδόσει (*War*, vii. 414).

[2] *Ibid.* 420–1, 433–6. Cf. Eisler, ΙΗΣΟΥΣ ΒΑΣΙΛΕΥΣ, i, 254–5. In his interesting discussion of the use of the Temple site after A.D. 70, K. W. Clark ('Worship in the Jerusalem Temple after A.D. 70', *N.T.S.* vi, 280) does not see the significance of the Roman closing of the Leontopolis temple in this connection.

[3] *War*, vii. 422–32: cf. H. St J. Thackeray's note *b* on p. 623 of the Loeb edition of Josephus, vol. iii.

[4] *War*, vii. 428–9. Josephus here (*ibid.* 427) corrects his former statement that the temple of Onias resembled that at Jerusalem in architectural form: cf. *War*, i. 33 (also *Ant.* xii. 388, xiii. 63, xx. 236). The site of Onias' temple was excavated in 1906 by W. M. Flinders Petrie, who published his report in *Hyksos and Israelite Cities*, pp. 19–27. According to Petrie, 'The plan of the whole hill [on which the temple stood] is strikingly modelled on that of Jerusalem: the temple had inner and outer courts, like that of Zion; but it was smaller and poorer in size; and while the hill of Jerusalem was natural, and the temple was built on the top of the rock, here the artificial hill had to be revetted with a great stone wall, which made the temple like a tower 60 cubits high' (*ibid.* pp. 21, 27). Sacrifices were evidently offered there, being attested by a great mass of burnt bones of calf and lamb (*ibid.* pp. 26, 27). The validity of offerings made in the temple of Onias is discussed, in a surprisingly mild manner, in the *Mishnah*, Menahoth, 13. 10 (Danby, *The Mishnah*, pp. 512–13). R. Simeon is recorded as ruling that such an offering was not to be accounted a 'Whole-offering', and that 'if priests have ministered in the House of Onias they may not minister in the Temple in Jerusalem'. There seems to have been no uncompromising denunciation such as might be expected

Jerusalem Temple, which indicates that the same cultus was performed there.[1] The decision to destroy it, taken by Vespasian, would
suggest that some fear was felt that the temple at Leontopolis might
replace the ruined Temple at Jerusalem as the cultic centre of the
Jewish national faith, which had been so powerful a factor in the
Jewish revolt.[2] The Egyptian Jews seem meekly to have accepted
the Roman decision.[3]

This information which Josephus provides of the situation of the
Jewish inhabitants of Alexandria and other parts of Egypt is of the
greatest significance for our subject. It means that the Jewish Christian community in Alexandria, whose members doubtless shared in
the experiences of their compatriots during this critical period, were
warned, as they were, by the catastrophe in Judaea, to repudiate all
resort to violent action to hasten the restoration of the kingdom to
Israel. It would indeed also be interesting to know what was their
attitude to the temple at Leontopolis, both before and after A.D. 70;
whatever it was, that temple's destruction in 73 was probably seen
as an additional confirmation of the logic of the more signal destruction of the Jerusalem Temple, namely, that Yahweh had thus
punished Israel for its rejection of Jesus.[4] As Jews, however, they

from the prophetic tradition. Cf. Schürer, *G.J.V.* III, 99: 'Von den
Gelehrten Palästina's wurde dieser Cultus freilich niemals als berechtigt
und die dort dargebrachten Opfer nur in sehr beschränktem Maße als
gültig anerkannt'; see also *ibid.* pp. 97–100.

[1] Josephus, *War*, VII. 428.

[2] The Jew who wrote *vv.* 501–2 of the *Sibylline Oracles*, V, seems to suggest
that Onias' temple then had such a significance: cf. F. Blass in *Apok.
u. Pseudepig.* (ed. E. Kautzsch), II, 183, 216. According to Driver, *Judaean
Scrolls*, p. 234, the Sicarii made for 'the old headquarters of the Zadokite
movement', i.e. the temple at Leontopolis.

[3] Their bitterness seems to have found expression in the *Sibylline Oracles*, V.
507–10: 'For they will destroy the great temple of the land of Egypt; and
God shall rain down on them upon the earth the furiousness of His anger,
destroying all that evil and lawless people, and there shall be no sparing
in that land, because they kept not that which God had delivered to them'
(trans. by H. N. Bate, *The Sibylline Oracles*, London, 1918, p. 117: cf. *Apok.
u. Pseudepig.* II, 216; Schürer, *G.J.V.* III, 443).

[4] Josephus, himself a Jerusalem priest, regarded Onias' founding of the
temple as a transgression of the Torah. Thus, in his comment upon the
permission granted to Onias by King Ptolemy Philometer and his wife
Cleopatra for the foundation: τὴν γὰρ ἁμαρτίαν καὶ τὴν τοῦ νόμου
παράβασιν εἰς τὴν 'Ονίου κεφαλὴν ἀνέθεσαν (*Ant.* XIII. 69). Eisler explains
Josephus' statement (*War*, VII. 436) that the temple of Onias lasted for
three hundred and forty-three years as being a specially devised period of
7³ years or seven jubilees, inspired by his interpretation of the destruction

would also have had to interpret their own belief in the Messiah-ship of Jesus in terms of this terrible outcome of the Zealot endeavour to restore the kingdom to Israel by armed revolt against Rome. Accordingly, it might be expected that any account of Jesus which might have been produced in the Christian community at Alexandria at this time, would reflect the need to interpret the disaster of A.D. 70.

There is another important inference about the Church in Alexandria at this time which may legitimately be made from what Josephus tells of the situation of the Jews there after A.D. 70. That a large body of the Sicarii should have sought refuge in Egypt, after the Roman conquest of Jerusalem, is not surprising. Egypt was the traditional place of asylum for Jews whose safety was threatened in their own land; it was relatively easy of access from Judaea, and it contained long-established Jewish communities.[1] In A.D. 70 it was also logical for refugees to flee southwards from Judaea, since the Roman army had entered the country from the north and gradually closed in on Jerusalem.[2] The Sicarii sought both refuge in Egypt, and the opportunity of continuing their holy war against Rome by stirring the Alexandrian Jews to revolt. But other Jews also undoubtedly fled to Egypt for safety from Roman vengeance in conquered Judaea. Among them, it would be reasonable to think, there might have been Jewish Christians, possibly some survivors of the Jerusalem Church.[3] If this had indeed been so, we might

of both Jewish sanctuaries at this time as the judgement of God: 'läßt diese mystische Rechnung klar erkennen, daß Josephus in der Zerstörung der beiden Tempel der Juden — in Heliopolis und in Jerusalem — das Gottesgericht dafür sah, daß die entzweite Hochpriesterschaft in frevelhafter Übertretung des deuteronomischen Gesetzes zwei Heiligtümer an Stelle des einen, von Gott selbst gewählten gesetzt hatte' (ΙΗΣΟΥΣ ΒΑΣΙΛΕΥΣ, I, 251). Cf. Thackeray, Loeb ed. of Josephus, III, 627, n. c. See below, pp. 302 ff.

[1] Cf. Schürer, G.J.V. III, 19–26; E. Bevan, History of Egypt under the Ptolemaic Dynasty (London, 1927), pp. 111–14; R. Kasser in R.Th.P. XI (1962), 13–14. See pp. 191 ff.

[2] Cf. Brandon, Fall of Jerusalem, pp. 218–19.

[3] That there were possibly some survivors of the Jerusalem Church does not contradict the view taken above (pp. 208 ff.) that the Jerusalem Church disappeared in the catastrophe of A.D. 70. Such survivors would undoubtedly have been few in number and relatively unimportant; otherwise the authority and prestige of the Mother Church would have continued wherever its members had settled, if they had migrated en masse. Refugees from the other Judaean churches, mentioned by Paul (Gal. i. 22), would doubtless have found their way to Egypt.

fairly expect to find some reflection of the memory of this flight in the literature of the Alexandrian Christians.

It will be well to pause at this point and summarise the result of our inquiry so far. We have noted that *a priori* considerations indicate a strong possibility that the Gospel of Matthew originated in Alexandria. We have also seen something of the probable situation and attitude of the Christian community there in the critical period following the Jewish disaster in A.D. 70. Consequently, we are in a position to evaluate whatever evidence there may be in the Gospel of Matthew of what we may reasonably suppose the *Sitz im Leben* of the Alexandrian Christians to have been at this time, i.e. during the decade that is commonly thought to have elapsed from the destruction of Jerusalem to the composition of Matthew.

There is one unique feature of the Gospel of Matthew that immediately commands our attention, if we contemplate the possibility that the Gospel was produced in Alexandria. It is the fact that Matthew, alone among the Evangelists, records that Jesus as a child was taken by his parents for shelter to Egypt, and that he remained there for some time.[1] Now not only is this story of the Flight into Egypt peculiar to Matthew, but it also constitutes a kind of contradiction to the Jewish exclusiveness which characterises the document. This is particularly evident if we examine Matthew's version of the episode of the Syro-Phoenician woman, which he evidently derived from the Markan Gospel.[2] Matthew carefully corrects the impression given by Mark's account that Jesus had crossed over the border into the district of Tyre and Sidon and had entered a

---

[1] Matt. ii. 13–21. The story of the Magi and that of the Flight into Egypt appear to have no essential connection with each other: cf. Bultmann, *Gesch. d. syn. Trad.* p. 317; Klostermann, *Matthäusevangelium*, p. 11. On Jewish traditions about Jesus' sojourn in Egypt see S.B. *Kommentar*, 1, 84–5. 'Aber daß man zu dieser Identifizierung gerade auf Ägypten Bezug genommen hat, zeigt wiederum, daß der Aufenthalt Jesu in Ägypten eine innerhalb der Synagoge verbreitete Überlieferung gewesen ist' (*ibid.* p. 85). Origen (*contra Celsum*, 1. 66) also knew of such a Jewish tradition. Klostermann (p. 12) rightly asks: 'Aber sind diese jüdischen Nachrichten nicht gerade Verzerrung von Mt. 11?' If Matthew had used some already existing tradition of a sojourn of Jesus in Egypt, Luke's silence about it would be consistent with his silence about the beginnings of Christianity there and his antipathy to Alexandrian Christianity. Cf. Bultmann, p. 319.

[2] Matt. xv. 21–5: Mark vii. 24–30: see above, pp. 171 ff.

Gentile house.[1] He, accordingly, makes it quite clear in his version that it was the Gentile woman who came over the border (ἀπὸ τῶν ὁρίων ἐκείνων), into Palestine, to solicit Jesus to heal her child.[2] Matthew's motive in making this correction is plain: Jesus, the Messiah of Israel, could not have left the Holy Land of Israel and sojourned among Gentiles.[3] Yet, despite his meticulous emendation of the Markan narrative in this matter, it is Matthew who alone records the Flight into Egypt. It is, however, to be noted that the Flight of the Holy Family into Egypt is not depicted as a sudden spontaneous retreat to the nearest place of refuge. Matthew presents it as a divinely directed journey. The angel of the Lord commands Joseph: 'Rise, take the child and his mother, and flee to Egypt, and remain there till I tell you...'[4] Moreover, according to Matthew, the flight and the sojourn in the land of the Nile were divinely ordained, in order to fulfil an ancient prophecy: 'Out of Egypt have I called my son.'[5]

The Matthaean Gospel, therefore, represents Egypt as the land selected by God to shelter the infant Messiah of Israel from those who, in his own land, sought to kill him.[6] This evaluation of Egypt

[1] 'Jesus hat selbst das heidnische Gebiet nicht betreten; das war aber nicht die Meinung des Mc' (Klostermann, *Matthäusevangelium*, p. 134); cf. B. Weiss, *Das Matthäus-Evangelium*, p. 283; Lohmeyer and Schmauch, *Das Evangelium des Matthäus*, p. 252; Taylor, *St Mark*, pp. 348–9.

[2] Cf. McNeil, *St Matthew*, p. 230.

[3] Cf. Matt. x. 5, εἰς ὁδὸν ἐθνῶν μὴ ἀπέλθετε,...

[4] Matt. ii. 13: cf. Lohmeyer and Schmauch, *Das Evangelium des Matthäus*, p. 27.

[5] ii. 14–15. 'Der Heranziehung von Hos 11, 1 liegt der Gedanke zugrunde, daß die Erlösung Israels aus Ägypten ein Typus der messian. Erlösung sei, ein Gedanke, der...wie kein anderer neben ihm die Ausgestaltung des Lehrstücks von der Enderlösung schon frühzeitig in umfassendster Weise bestimmt hat' (S.B. *Kommentar*, 1, 85: cf. Klostermann, *Matthäusevangelium*, p. 17). Davies, *Sermon on the Mount*, pp. 78 ff., sees in Matt. i, ii the presentation of Jesus as a Second Moses. Whether such typology informs the Flight into Egypt story or not, the important point here is that this most Jewish of Gospels alone records a sojourn of Jesus in Egypt. It might be asked with equal reason whether it is Matthew's interest in Egypt that has initiated the typology. Lohmeyer and Schmauch (*Das Evangelium des Matthäus*, p. 28) pertinently remark, commenting upon possible Biblical motifs: 'Wohl ist der [*sc.* Gedanke der Flucht] dem Messiasmythus nicht fremd; Apk 12 führt ihn in grandiosen Zügen aus, und mancherlei außerbiblische Parallelen lassen sich beibringen, aber dem Erzähler ist das Verweilen in Ägypten wichtiger als die Tatsache der Flucht.'

[6] The twice-occurring phrase τὸ παιδίον καὶ τὴν μητέρα αὐτοῦ (ii. 13–14) suggests a familiarity with the idea of a holy mother and child, of which

is truly both remarkable and significant; for no other Gentile land could claim so unique a privilege. It is well to reflect that, if some other Gentile country had been accorded a comparable status by one of the Gospel writers, the fact would surely have been interpreted as indicating a close connection between that Gospel and the country concerned. This predilection which Matthew thus shows for Egypt is, therefore, rightly to be interpreted as attesting some special relationship, and it provides a remarkable confirmation of the *a priori* case for Matthew's being the Gospel of the Church of Alexandria.

But the story of the Flight into Egypt may also fairly be seen as bearing witness to another likely happening which affected the life of the Alexandrian Church at this time. We have noted the probability that the flight of a body of the Sicarii into Egypt, which Josephus records, was not an isolated phenomenon, and that many other Jews were likely also to have sought refuge in Egypt from war-devastated Judaea.[1] If among these refugees there had been survivors of the Jerusalem Church or of other Judaean churches, the story of the Flight into Egypt acquires a great poignancy. For such a tradition, that their Lord, when a child, had found refuge in Egypt from his enemies, would surely have been treasured by refugees who had also been forced to flee hither for shelter from the furious heathen.

This evidence of the Egyptian, or rather the Alexandrian,[2] origin of the Gospel of Matthew is reinforced by other testimony. The most notable of this is constituted by the remarkable exaltation of Peter which characterises the writing. In the list of the apostles he

Egyptian religion provides the most notable example in Isis and her son Horus. Jews resident in Egypt would have been very familiar with representations of the Holy Mother suckling her *Wunderkind*, whose birth had been miraculous. They would also have known of the legend of Isis' flight, with her child, into the Delta from the evil Set who sought his life. Nowhere else than in Egypt could such a combination of suggestive themes, stemming from prophetic tradition and cultural environment, have stimulated a Jewish Christian writing for a community containing refugees from heathen vengeance in Judaea: cf. C. Clemen, *Religionsgeschichtliche Erklärung*, pp. 119–20; W. K. L. Clarke, *New Testament Problems*, pp. 2–3; A. Erman, *Die Religion der Ägypter* (Berlin–Leipzig, 1934), pp. 74, 390–2; J. Leipoldt in *Bilderatlas zur Religionsgeschichte* (ed. H. Haas), 9.–11. Lieferung, Abb. 37–9.   [1] P. 294.

[2] As there were Jewish communities in other parts of Egypt, there were undoubtedly Jewish Christian communities outside Alexandria in the first century; however, Alexandria would surely have been the chief Christian centre as it was of Jewry. Cf. Kasser in *R.Th.P.* xi, 14 ff.

is definitively denominated the 'primus' (πρῶτος),[1] and his unique status is clearly proclaimed in Matthew's significant emendation and elaboration of the Markan version of the Caesarea Philippi incident.[2] Whereas Mark, as we have seen,[3] used the incident to denigrate Peter, by representing him as failing to perceive the true nature and role of his Master, Matthew disguises this by softening the harshness of Jesus' condemnation.[4] And in the previous part of the passage he ascribes to Peter the very insight which he lacked according to Mark. Thus, not only is Peter represented as recognising in Jesus the Messiah, but he also perceives his divinity: 'You are the Christ, the Son of the living God.'[5] And in the place of Mark's silence about the reaction of Jesus to Peter's recognition of his Messiahship only, Jesus is made to testify to Peter's divinely inspired vision: 'Blessed are you, Simon Bar-Jona! For flesh and blood has not revealed this to you, but my Father who is in heaven.'[6] But even this is not enough, and these gracious words are followed in Matthew's version by the famous declaration that confers on Peter a status and authority which are unique and of fundamental significance: 'And I tell you, you are Peter, and on this rock I will build my church, and the powers of death shall not prevail against it. I will give you the keys of the kingdom of heaven, and whatever you bind on earth shall be bound in heaven, and whatever you loose on earth shall be loosed in heaven.'[7]

---

[1] Matt. x. 2. Cf. Cullmann, *Petrus*[2], pp. 26, 27 (E.T. pp. 24, 26).

[2] Matt. xvi. 17-19. Cf. Cullmann, *Petrus*[2], pp. 183-243 (E.T. pp. 158 ff.).

[3] Pp. 277 ff.

[4] The addition of σκάνδαλον εἶ ἐμοῦ qualifies the condemnation in *v.* 23: according to Klostermann, *Matthäusevangelium*, p. 141, it 'erklärt den Ausdruck σατανᾶ'.

[5] xvi. 16: Σὺ εἶ ὁ Χριστὸς ὁ υἱὸς τοῦ θεοῦ τοῦ ζῶντος. Cf. McNeil, *St Matthew*, pp. 239-40. Matthew assigns to Peter priority in recognising Jesus' divinity, which Mark attributed to the Gentile centurion (xv. 39); see above, pp. 279 ff. Cullmann, *Petrus*[2], pp. 201-2, rightly points out that the disciples' recognition of Jesus' divinity in Matt. xiv. 33 robs Peter's confession in xvi. 16 of its uniqueness; however, it is evident that Matthew intends to make Peter's confession of superlative significance: the addition of τοῦ ζῶντος confirms this, as does the drama of the situation. Cf. Cullmann in *New Testament Essays* (ed. A. J. B. Higgins), pp. 102-4.

[6] xvi. 17: cf. Klostermann, *Matthäusevangelium*, p. 139: 'nur durch des Vaters Offenbarung ist solche Erkenntnis möglich'.

[7] xvi. 18-19. After his long detailed study of this passage, Cullmann concludes that Matt. xvi. 17 ff. is a genuine saying of Jesus (*Petrus*[2], p. 243, E.T. p. 211). If this conclusion is right, it is the more remarkable that it is given by Matthew, and not by Mark. Such suppression on Mark's part

In other words, the author of the Matthaean Gospel presents Peter to those for whom he wrote as the 'foundation apostle' of the Church, whose divine commission extended beyond this world. In view of Peter's traditional association with the See of Rome, it is indeed surprising that this stupendous claim does not appear in Mark, which was the Gospel of the primitive Christian community at Rome,[1] nor in a Gospel that can be reasonably located at Antioch which later claimed Peter as its first bishop.[2] That this presentation of Peter as the 'foundation apostle' should have been made in a Gospel which we have found reason for locating at Alexandria is, however, not surprising. For it is consistent with Peter's role as the Apostle of 'the circumcision', which Paul recognised,[3] and it is in accord both with the evidence which we have noted of a close association between the Mother Church of Jerusalem and the Church in Alexandria and with the probability that Alexandria was the 'other place', to which Peter went and about which the author of Acts is so strangely reticent.[4]

To this internal evidence, attesting the Alexandrian origin of the Matthaean Gospel, may be added the testimony of the fact that two early documents which seem to be of Alexandrian origin, namely, the Epistle of Barnabas and the so-called Second Epistle of Clement, appear to quote from Matthew as being the Gospel best known to them,[5] while the evidence of papyri-finds appears to indicate that

would be intelligible if Peter was the founder of the Alexandrian Church, which was not favourably regarded by Pauline Christians. However that might be, the passage must mean that Peter was regarded as the founder of the Church by that community for which Matthew wrote. On the nature of the power and authority given to Peter see S.B. *Kommentar*, I, 736–47. Cf. J. Allegro, *The Dead Sea Scrolls*, pp. 142–4; Klostermann, *Matthäusevangelium*, pp. 139–41; J. Weiss, *Earliest Christianity*, II, 752.

[1] See the preceding note, also above, pp. 277 ff.
[2] This Antiochene claim is late, and is expressive of ecclesiastical pretension rather than historical fact. It is significant that Ignatius of Antioch shows very little interest in Peter, mentioning him twice only (*Romans*, iv. 3; *Smyrnaeans*, iii. 2), while Eusebius names Evodius as the first bishop of Antioch: cf. E. Merrill, *Essays in Early Christian History* (London, 1924), p. 277; C. Schmidt, *Studien zu den Pseudo-Clementinen nebst einem Anhange* (Leipzig, 1930), pp. 368–9. For the improbability of Antioch being the birth-place of the Gospel of Matthew, see above, pp. 287–8.
[3] Gal. ii. 7–8.   [4] See pp. 164, 191, 196–8.
[5] Barn. iv. 14 (Matt. xxii. 14), Barn. v. 9 (Matt. ix. 13), Barn. v. 12 (Matt. xxvi. 31), Barn. vi. 13 (Matt. xx. 16), Barn. xii. 10 (Matt. xxii. 44), Barn. xii. 11 (Matt. xxii. 45). On II Clement see detailed references given in Brandon, *Fall of Jerusalem*, p. 242, n. 2; see also pp. 240–3.

more copies of Matthew circulated in Egypt than of any other Gospel.[1] And the Gospel of Thomas, found recently at Nag-Hamâdi in Upper Egypt, which probably dates in its original form from the second century, also reveals a close knowledge of the Matthaean Gospel.[2] In this connection, too, we may notice that the Gospel of Thomas, which evidently circulated in Egypt, emanated from a Jewish Christian community which preserved the memory of the leadership of James, the Lord's brother, attributing his pre-eminence in the Church to the command of Jesus.[3] The memory of James would doubtless have been reverenced in the Church of Alexandria, the daughter church of Jerusalem.

If Matthew is thus to be seen as the Gospel of the Church of Alexandria, having been written somewhere about A.D. 80–5, it constitutes a document of the highest importance for evaluating the reaction of an essentially Jewish Christian community, in fact a daughter church of the Church of Jerusalem, to the disaster that befell Israel in A.D. 70, and in which the Mother Church had been involved. In seeking to understand this reaction, we have also to bear in mind that these Alexandrian Christians were part of the Jewish population of Alexandria and doubtless shared in the dangers and anxieties that distressed that community during the critical decade that followed the destruction of Jerusalem. The desire of that community to keep itself uninvolved in Zealotism, taking warning from the catastrophe which had overwhelmed their brethren in Judaea, found practical expression, as Josephus records, in their rejection of the Sicarii refugees who sought to continue the struggle against Rome in Egypt.[4] If, in turn, we are right in interpreting Matthew's story of the Flight into Egypt as evidence of the presence of refugees from Judaea in the Alexandrian Church, we may assume that these unfortunates had been accepted and succoured by the Christians of Alexandria because they sought shelter only and not a further endeavour to restore the kingdom to Israel, as did the Sicarii.[5]

[1] C. H. Roberts in *J.T.S.* L (1949), 164, gives the following numbers: 9 texts of Matthew, 7 of John, 5 of Mark, and 4 of Luke. He remarks, but draws no conclusion: 'the preference for Matthew is surprising'.

[2] Logia 76 and 109 are derived from parables peculiar to Matthew: cf. *The Gospel according to Thomas* (ed. A. Guillaumont et alii), pp. 42–3, 54–5.

[3] Logion 12, *ibid.* pp. 8, 9. Cf. B. Gärtner, *The Theology of the Gospel of Thomas* (London, 1961), pp. 56–7; W. C. Van Unnik, *Evangelien aus dem Nilsand* (Frankfurt-am-Main, 1960), pp. 65–6. [4] See above, p. 291.

[5] It is possible that a memory of the Sicarii is preserved in Matt. xi. 12: ἀπὸ δὲ τῶν ἡμερῶν Ἰωάνου τοῦ βαπτιστοῦ ἕως ἄρτι ἡ βασιλεία τῶν

It would be helpful if we could determine the occasion of the writing of the Matthaean Gospel. That it was produced in response to some need of the community of which the author was a member is a safe inference to make; and, if that community is to be located at Alexandria, it was designed, therefore, to assist the Alexandrian Christians in some specific way during the period concerned. Now, since these Christians were mostly of Jewish birth, it would be reasonable to conclude that the aftermath of A.D. 70 would have faced them with some different problems from those which confronted the Gentile Christians of Rome, for whom Mark wrote his Gospel. Some clue to the general nature of those problems would seem to be provided by the fact that Matthew knows the Markan Gospel and follows the framework of the Markan narrative. Did Mark, then, provide the stimulus for the composition of Matthew? It would seem reasonable to suppose that Mark did at least provide the author of Matthew with the idea of a Gospel, i.e. a narrative account of the career of Jesus which would embody its author's interpretation of Jesus in relation to the *Sitz im Leben* of the Christian community whose life he shared and for whose members he wrote. But, if Mark provided the idea, the fact that Matthew felt moved to amend and elaborate the Markan record proves that he was not wholly content with it. We have already noted how he changed Mark's account of the Caesarea Philippi episode, so that, from being a derogatory evaluation of Peter, it became a categorical proclamation of Peter's unique status and authority in the Church. This

οὐρανῶν βιάζεται, καὶ βιασταὶ ἁρπάζουσιν αὐτήν. The saying, which is peculiar to Matthew, is set in an eschatological context relative to the Baptist's movement, and the question in xi. 7 (τί ἐξήλθατε εἰς τὴν ἔρημον θεάσασθαι;) is significant in view of the association of Zealotism and other Messianic movements with the desert (cf. Hengel, *Die Zeloten*, pp. 259–61). On the identification of the βιασταί with the Zealots cf. A. von Gall, ΒΑΣΙΛΕΙΑ ΤΟΥ ΘΕΟΥ, p. 353; H. Windisch, *Der messianische Krieg und das Urchristentum*, pp. 35 ff.; Klausner, *Jesus of Nazareth*, p. 206; Eisler, ΙΗΣΟΥΣ ΒΑΣΙΛΕΥΣ, II, 88; Cullmann, *The State in the New Testament*, pp. 20–2; Stendahl in *Peake's Commentary*[2], 684e. On the ambiguous meaning of Matt. xi. 12–15 see Klostermann, *Matthäusevangelium*, p. 99. Cf. S.B. *Kommentar*, I, 598–601. O. Betz would identify the βιασταί with the 'feindliche Geistermächte als auch irdische Machthaber' who oppose Jesus (in *N.T.* II, 1958, 125–9); it seems unlikely that every reference to violence and opposition in the Gospels is to be seen as having an ultimate demoniacal reference, even though demonology was a potent factor. F. C. Grant draws attention to the atmosphere of political tension in the Matthaean Gospel (*The Gospels: their Origin and Growth*, London, 1965, pp. 136–40).

exaltation of Peter can be reasonably interpreted as designed to offset the growing reputation of Paul, in consequence of the obsolescence of Judaism which the ruin of Israel in A.D. 70 seemed to demonstrate.[1] However that may be, what is of importance for our subject is that Matthew amends the Markan record in a variety of ways that appear to reflect his preoccupation with the significance of the catastrophe of A.D. 70 for his own community in Alexandria.

What is perhaps the most notable addition that Matthew makes, in this context, to the Markan record occurs in his account of the Trial before Pilate. As we saw, Mark was concerned to explain away the problem of the Roman execution of Jesus by showing that the Jewish leaders forced Pilate into condemning Jesus to death.[2] Matthew, although he had not the same interest as Mark had, who lived in Rome, in explaining the Roman condemnation of Jesus, obviously would not have deemed it politic to emphasise that Pilate was responsible for ordering Jesus' execution as a rebel against Rome. However, in dealing with the supremely significant issue of the Crucifixion, he was clearly motivated to interpret the terrible catastrophe that had befallen the Jewish people in A.D. 70 as punishment for their rejection and slaying of the Messiah; for, in contrast to Mark, it is the responsibility of the Jewish people, not primarily of their leaders, with which he is concerned.[3] Accordingly, he adds to the Markan account two passages which have the effect of underlining the innocence of Jesus and emphasising Jewish guilt. Thus, having followed Mark to the point at which Pilate offers the Jews a choice between Barabbas and Jesus, 'for he knew that it was out of envy that they had delivered him up',[4] Matthew introduces Pilate's wife to testify to Jesus' innocence. She warns her husband, 'Have nothing to do with that righteous man (τῷ δικαίῳ ἐκείνῳ), for I

---

[1] Cf. Brandon, *Fall of Jerusalem*, pp. 231–6. W. D. Davies (*Sermon on the Mount*, pp. 316 ff.) endeavours to answer the case presented there mainly by seeking to belittle Paul's significance. See the present writer's reply to this part of Dr Davies's thesis in *The Modern Churchman*, VIII, n.s. (1965), 155–6.

[2] Pp. 256 ff.

[3] This is understandable when Matthew wrote; for the reign of the high-priesthood and the sacerdotal aristocracy had ended with the destruction of the Jewish national state and the Temple cultus, but the Jewish people survived. In view of their situation in Alexandria, now probably the largest Jewish centre in the Roman empire, it was the meaning of A.D. 70 for the nation that mattered to Matthew and his fellow Jewish Christians.

[4] Mark xv. 10: Matt. xxvii. 18.

have suffered much over him today in a dream.'[1] Then, he adds to Mark's brief statement of Pilate's final acquiescence in the Jewish demand that Jesus should be crucified, the story of Pilate's symbolic act of ablution, thus disavowing all responsibility for the death of Jesus: 'I am innocent (ἀθῷος) of this man's blood; see to it yourselves.' To which all the people (πᾶς ὁ λαός) readily reply with the fateful words: 'His blood be on us and on our children!'[2]

That such a terrible avowal of responsibility for the Crucifixion should have been attributed to the Jewish people by a Jewish Christian author, writing for Jewish Christians, is only credible in terms of the situation in the Alexandrian Church in the aftermath of A.D. 70. What Matthew does, in effect, is to assert that the Romans could not be blamed for the Crucifixion. Since he is writing for Christians who were Jews by race, his insertion into the Markan record of Pilate's symbolic repudiation of responsibility was obviously not designed to quieten Roman consciences; it was evidently directed against a view that did regard the Romans as responsible for the execution of Jesus. Now such a view, as we have already seen, was held by the original Jewish Christians of Judaea;[3] to them Jesus had died as a martyr for Israel at the hands of the heathen power which oppressed the people of God. Mark, for his own apologetical purpose, had shifted the responsibility from the Romans to the Jewish leaders. For Matthew this was evidently not enough. Writing for the Jewish Christian community in Alexandria, containing now many refugees from Judaea, he felt it necessary to refute what had been the view of the Jerusalem Christians by in-

---

[1] Matt. xxvii. 19. It would appear that this episode is closely linked with that related in vv. 24–5 (cf. Klostermann, *Matthäusevangelium*, p. 221). 'Hinter der knappen Angabe steckt offenbar eine ausführliche Legende', (Bultmann, *Gesch. d. syn. Trad.* p. 305, n. 2). 'Daher braucht die Botschaft an sich nicht zu verwundern, aber die Art der Schilderung charakterisiert mehr den Erzähler als die Sache. Er stellt Gottes Willen und Rat — denn ein Traum ist von Gott gesandt, wie die Kindheitsgeschichten — gegen den Willen und Rat des Synedriums...' (Lohmeyer and Schmauch, *Das Evangelium des Matthäus*, p. 384). Cf. S.B. *Kommentar*, I, 1032; Kilpatrick, *Origins of St Matthw*, p. 46.

[2] Matt. xxvii. 24–5. 'Der Erzähler fährt ruhig und gemessen fort: "Und alles Volk erwiderte und sprach", und gerade diese Verhaltenheit läßt das unermeßliche Gewicht dieser Worte ahnen, auf welches das Wörtchen "alles" und das seltene Wort λαός schon hinweisen' (Lohmeyer and Schmauch, *Das Evangelium des Matthäus*, p. 386; cf. Klostermann, *Matthäusevangelium*, p. 221; McNeil, *St Matthew*, p. 412). Cf. S.B. *Kommentar*, I, 1032–3. On the textual significance of ἀθῷος cf. Brandon, *Fall of Jerusalem*, p. 246. [3] P. 177.

serting into his account of the trial of Jesus the story of this dramatic act of repudiation of responsibility by the Roman governor in the presence of the Jewish people; and he represents the Jewish people as not hesitating to accept that awful responsibility. The fateful words[1] which Matthew places in the mouths of those Jews, presumably the inhabitants of Jerusalem, who rejected Jesus, were surely intended to have a chastening significance for his readers in Alexandria—he little realised for how many centuries, and in what manner, his people were to suffer for those words: 'His blood be on us and on our children!'[2]

This ominous interpretation of the disaster of A.D. 70 as divine retribution, which the Jewish people had knowingly brought upon themselves in demanding the crucifixion of their Messiah, finds expression elsewhere in the Matthaean Gospel. The most notable instance occurs in Matthew's rendering of the Markan parable of the Wicked Husbandmen.[3] In Mark, as we saw,[4] the parable served to develop the Gospel's apologetical theme, namely, that the Jewish leaders planned and accomplished the death of Jesus. The author of Matthew, in adopting the parable into his Gospel, was clearly at pains to underline its application to the catastrophe of A.D. 70. Accordingly, in the *dénouement* of the parable, he emphasises the criminal character of the husbandmen by changing Mark's τοὺς γεωργούς to κακούς,[5] and he makes clear that the destruction of Jerusalem was retribution by rendering Mark's restrained comment 'He [the owner] will come and destroy (ἀπολέσει) the tenants...' as 'He will put those wretches to a miserable death (κακοὺς κακῶς ἀπολέσει).'[6] And he drives the lesson home by adding to the Markan version a verse which succinctly states a further aspect of his evaluation of recent Jewish history: 'Therefore I tell you, the kingdom of God will be taken away from you and given to a nation

---

[1] τὸ αἷμα αὐτοῦ ἐφ' ἡμᾶς καὶ ἐπὶ τὰ τέκνα ἡμῶν (Matt. xxvii. 25).

[2] The fact that the exoneration of subsequent generations of Jews from responsibility for the murder of Christ provoked opposition in the recent session (1965) of the Vatican Council is eloquent of the fatal influence of Matthew's record.

[3] Matt. xxi. 33–46. Cf. Beare, *Earliest Records of Jesus*, pp. 208–9; J. Weiss, *Urchristentum*, p. 522; Lohmeyer and Schmauch, *Das Evangelium des Matthäus*, pp. 312–15.

[4] Pp. 249 ff.

[5] xxi. 41: Mark xii. 9 (cf. Huck, *Synopse*, p. 166).

[6] xxi. 41: cf. Klostermann, *Matthäusevangelium*, p. 172; R. Hummel, *Die Auseinandersetzung*, pp. 83–5.

(ἔθνει) producing the fruits of it.'[1] Again, a cherished aim of the Jerusalem Christians is, in effect, repudiated, although the eschatological hope it embodied is retained and reinterpreted. The restoration of the kingdom to Israel by the Risen Jesus, returning on the clouds of heaven and with supernatural power, can no longer be envisaged. The ruin of Israel as a national state was accepted as definitive, and interpreted as divine judgement for the nation's rejection and murder of the Messiah. Hence, taught by the logic of events, Matthew takes the step adumbrated by Paul on different grounds, namely, of distinguishing between ethnic Israel and those Jews who did accept Jesus.[2] These latter fulfilled the prophetic concept of the 'godly remnant', and so constituted the true Israel. How far Matthew was prepared to see Gentile converts as members of this spiritual Israel, as Paul had done, is uncertain: the parable of the 'Guest without the Wedding Garment' would seem to be a grudging admission that Gentiles were inevitably taking the place of the proper guests, who had proved themselves unworthy; but grave doubt is implied about whether Gentiles could really qualify for this high privilege.[3]

The author of the Matthaean Gospel did not see in the catastrophe of A.D. 70 only the judgement of God on the Jewish people for killing their Messiah; like other Alexandrian Jews he saw the events of A.D. 66–70 as a warning. The rounding up of Sicarii, and the handing of them over to the Romans, was an effective, though grim,

---

[1] xxi. 43. Lohmeyer and Schmauch, *Das Evangelium des Matthäus*, p. 314, would connect the 'andere Volk' of *v.* 43 with the two different groups symbolised by the 'two sons' in the preceding parable (xxi. 28–32), which is peculiar to Matthew. This parable, however, seems to be aimed at the Jewish leaders and their attitude to John the Baptist (xxi. 23–7, 32). The son who repents and obeys his father symbolises the τελῶναι and the πόρναι, who, by their response to John, precede the Jewish leaders into the kingdom of God (*vv.* 31–2). This parable, accordingly, seems to be primarily concerned with the social status of those who responded to the Baptist mission, and it is especially significant in view of the social aspect of Zealotism (see pp. 56 ff.): on its bearing on the mission of Jesus see below, pp. 308 ff. Verse 43 in the parable of the Wicked Husbandmen indicates that a different, and a more coherent body, is envisaged under the term ἔθνος. Cf. Klostermann, *Matthäusevangelium*, pp. 170–1, 173; McNeil, *St Matthew*, pp. 307–8, 312; Kilpatrick, *Origins of St Matthew*, pp. 30, 118; Davies, *Sermon on the Mount*, pp. 328–9; S.B. *Kommentar*, 1, 866, 876.

[2] I Cor. x. 18 (βλέπετε τὸν 'Ισραὴλ κατὰ σάρκα); Rom. xi. 1 ff.; see also I Pet. ii. 9. Cf. Simon, *Verus Israel*, pp. 100 ff.

[3] Matt. xxii. 11–14; cf. Brandon, *Fall of Jerusalem*, pp. 230–1.

demonstration on the part of the leaders of the Jewish community in Alexandria that they recognised both the futility and danger of revolt against Rome. Matthew evidently shared in this sentiment, and he took the opportunity of warning his fellow-Christians against entertaining any further hopes that the kingdom might be restored to Israel by force of arms. Judas of Galilee had proclaimed that God would succour those who risked their lives in active resistance to the Roman rule,[1] and his followers had fought a holy war to the bitter end, preferring, in defeat, suicide to recognising Caesar as Lord.[2] To refute this doctrine, to which the Sicarii refugees had sought to win the Alexandrian Jews, Matthew developed the Markan portrait of a Jesus who endorsed the Roman rule in Judaea into that of a Christ who eschewed all resort to arms. The most notable instance of this presentation of what might fairly be termed the 'pacific Christ' occurs in the additions made to Mark's account of the arrest of Jesus in Gethsemane. Thus, he interpolates an utterance of Jesus in response to the action of that disciple who resorted to arms to prevent the arrest: 'Put your sword back into its place; for all who take the sword will perish by the sword. Do you think that I cannot appeal to my Father, and he will at once send me more than twelve legions of angels? But how then should the scriptures be fulfilled, that it must be so?'[3]

The significance of this saying, which Matthew thus attributes to Jesus on this critical occasion, is immense. We have yet to investigate the meaning of the armed resistance offered in Gethsemane in relation to the plans of Jesus during the last fatal days in Jerusalem.[4] That Mark records that armed resistance was offered indicates that the fact was so well established in the tradition which he was following, that he felt constrained to mention it, although it could raise awkward questions for his apologetical thesis.[5] However, he quickly

---

[1] See above, pp. 33 ff.

[2] The Sicarii who had been seized in Egypt were tortured, in vain, ὅπως αὐτῶν Καίσαρα δεσπότην ὁμολογήσωσιν (Jos. *War*, VII. 418).

[3] Matt. xxvi. 52–4. Klostermann, *Matthäusevangelium*, p. 213, makes the interesting comment: 'Die Frage, weshalb es zu keinem ernstlichen Kampfe kam, haben Mt und Lc (dieser trotz Lc 22 36. 38) durch eine Desavouierung des "schlagfertigen" Jüngers zu beantworten gesucht.' Cf. Davies, *Sermon on the Mount*, p. 202.　　　　　　　　　　[4] Pp. 340 ff.

[5] Mark disguises the fact that at least one disciple resisted by the vague statement: εἷς δέ τις τῶν παρεστηκότων σπασάμενος τὴν μάχαιραν ἔπαισεν τὸν δοῦλον τοῦ ἀρχιερέως (xiv. 47); cf. Taylor, *St Mark*, p. 559: it is 'possible that the name was withheld for prudential reasons'.

passes from his brief mention of it to emphasise to his readers the evil intent of the Jewish leaders in sending such an armed force to arrest Jesus secretly.[1] Matthew, undoubtedly knowing that the armed resistance put up to Jesus' arrest was a serious affair, felt constrained to explain the attitude of Jesus to his Alexandrian readers, to whom the issue involved would obviously have been of very great importance at this time. Consequently, he not only represents Jesus as stopping this armed action on his behalf, but also attributes to him words which had a poignant meaning in the years immediately following A.D. 70. 'All who take the sword will perish by the sword'—the relevance of these words would have been clear to the Alexandrian Christians.[2] They are presented as the verdict pronounced by Christ on the action of a disciple who sought to further his cause by resort to arms. But herein we surely have evidence of the fate of many Jewish Christians in the holy war against Rome. As we have already seen on other grounds, many Christians in Judaea, particularly those in Jerusalem, probably made common cause with their fellow-Jews in the struggle to redeem Israel from its servitude to the heathen.[3] They made the venture of faith to which Judas of Galilee had called his countrymen, believing undoubtedly that they would hasten the *Parousia* of their Lord; they took the sword, but they had perished by the sword.

Matthew knew that the awful logic of what had happened to the Jerusalem Church would prove to his readers the truth of the saying he assigned to Christ in Gethsemane. However, he evidently felt that he should make clear that the pacifism of Jesus was not due to

[1] Mark xiv. 48–9.
[2] Besides what they knew of the slaughter in Judaea, the recent extermination of the Sicarii in Egypt would doubtless have been much in the mind of the Alexandrian Christians. F. C. Grant (*The Gospels*, p. 138) sees Matt. xxvi. 52 as deriving 'from the tradition of a time when the temptation to resort to violence was pressed upon the Christian Jews by some at least of their Jewish neighbours. Such a time was clearly that of the uprising under Bar Kochba'. This interpretation means dating the Matthaean Gospel to the early decades of the second century, which Grant recognises as difficult. If he had located the Gospel in Alexandria instead of northern Palestine (*op. cit.* p. 140), he would surely have found the situation he was seeking. It is possible that some memory of the primitive Jewish Christians' involvement in the revolt of A.D. 66–70 is preserved in the *Didache* III. 2: μὴ γίνου...μηδὲ ζηλωτὴς μηδὲ ἐριστικὸς μηδὲ θυμικός· ἐκ γὰρ τούτων ἁπάντων φόνοι γεννῶνται: in J. B. Lightfoot, *The Apostolic Fathers* (London, 1891), p. 218. Cf. Bo Reicke, *Diakonie, Festfreude und Zelos in Verbindung mit der altchristlichen Agapenfeier* (Uppsala–Wiesbaden, 1952), p. 383.   [3] Pp. 208ff.

lack of power. He therefore represents Jesus as assuring the disciple who drew the sword in his defence, that he had at his own disposal all the supernatural power that Jewish apocalyptic ascribed to the Messiah.[1] Against the legions of Caesar, that terrible military machine that had now destroyed Israel, Christ could summon, if he so chose, twelve legions of angels.[2] But Christ, according to Matthew, had not chosen to invoke force then, nor should his disciples have resorted to its use later—the consequences had been fatal: those who had taken the sword had indeed perished by it.

Thus, motivated by the *Sitz im Leben* of the Christian community in Alexandria in the critical years following the fall of Jerusalem, Matthew was led to develop the Markan thesis, that Jesus had been innocent of sedition against Rome, into one more suited to the needs of his own church, namely, that of the pacific Christ who renounced all resort to armed force, whether human or angelic.

This portrait of the pacific Christ, which is most dramatically presented in Matthew's account of the arrest in Gethsemane, is anticipated in the Beatitudes, which form part of the Sermon on the Mount. Whatever the origin of the material drawn upon here, Matthew has clearly formulated his own version of the teaching which he ascribes to Jesus.[3] Most significant are the pronouncements that open this Dominical discourse, in which Jesus appears as the New Moses delivering the New Law to the New Israel: 'Blessed are the poor in spirit, for theirs is the kingdom of heaven'. . . 'Blessed are the meek, for they shall inherit the earth'. . . 'Blessed are the peacemakers, for they shall be called sons of God.'[4] The relevance of these statements to the situation in the Christian community at Alexandria in the decade following the catastrophe of A.D. 70 is manifest. For these Jewish Christians, shocked by the disaster in Judaea and fearful of an outbreak of Zealot fanaticism in Egypt, the need to counter that in-

---

[1] Cf. S.B. *Kommentar*, I, 997; J. Michl in *R.A.C.* v, 75–6, 79–80; Lohmeyer and Schmauch, *Das Evangelium des Matthäus*, p. 365, n. 2. See also the Qumrân *War Scroll*, VII. 6; cf. Yadin, *Scroll of the War*, pp. 230, 231; Farmer, *Maccabees, Zealots, and Josephus*, pp. 181–2.

[2] Josephus, undoubtedly like other Jews, was impressed by the disciplined might of the Roman legions (cf. *War*, III. 93 ff.). Lohmeyer and Schmauch, *Das Evangelium des Matthäus*, p. 365: 'Die Zahl der Engel ist unvorstellbar groß; ...und reizvoll ist es, daß ihre unvorstellbare Macht durch das lateinische Lehnwort Legion anschaulich gemalt wird.' Cf. Kilpatrick, *Origins of St Matthew*, p. 44.

[3] Cf. Beare, *Earliest Records of Jesus*, pp. 52–4; Davies, *Sermon on the Mount*, pp. 5 ff., 304 ff.

[4] Matt. v. 3, 5, 9. Cf. Davies, *Sermon on the Mount*, pp. 25 ff.

transigent spirit that the Sicarii had shown, even in defeat and under torture, was paramount.[1] Hence Jesus, as the true Messiah of Israel, is portrayed as blessing those who exhibit a contrary spirit, in being πτωχοὶ τῷ πνεύματι and πραεῖς.[2] And, instead of martial zeal, a peaceable disposition is commended—the followers of the pacific Christ become 'sons of God' by being εἰρηνοποιοί.[3] The situation in Alexandria at this time is also reflected in other Beatitudes. The refugees, bereft of home and many of families, are remembered in 'Blessed are those who mourn, for they shall be comforted.'[4] And resentment against the Roman military is checked, in a practical manner, by representing Jesus as commanding his disciples to render more service than the statutory requirement,[5] while the Levitical injunction that Israelites were to hate foreigners (τὸν ἐχθρόν σου) is changed into a command: 'Love your enemies (τοὺς

[1] Even after their suppression in Egypt, remnants of the Sicarii caused trouble in Cyrene (Jos. *War*, VII. 437 ff.).

[2] The 'poor in spirit' (עֲנֵי רוּחַ) appears in the Qumrân *War Scroll* (XIV. 7) in a militant context: 'Through the poor in spirit [there shall be gnaw]ed a hard heart, and through them that are upright in the way shall all wicked nations come to an end, and their mighty men shall not be able to resist' (trans. Y. Yadin, *Scroll of the War*, pp. 326, 327; cf. A. Dupont-Sommer, *Les écrits esséniens*, p. 205). Davies, *Sermon on the Mount*, p. 251, in stating his disagreement with K. Schubert's interpretation (in *The Scrolls and the New Testament*, ed. K. Stendahl, p. 122), does not see, contrary to his own thesis, 'a confrontation with the Sect' in this Matthaean Beatitude. Surely in placing the 'poor in spirit' together with the 'meek' and the 'peacemakers', Matthew was reinterpreting a well-known militaristic term. Cf. S.B. *Kommentar*, I, 197 ff.: 'Das Lob der Sanftmut ertönt nicht selten in der rabbin. Literatur.' See also Stendahl in *Peake's Commentary*[2], 678*f*.

[3] Lohmeyer and Schmauch, *Das Evangelium des Matthäus*, p. 92, referring to the fact that Caesars often bore the title of 'Friedenstifter der Welt', comment upon *v.* 9: 'Es bleibt freilich auch dann die tiefsinnige Fügung daß mit den gleichen Worten Jünger Jesu und die Kaiser des römischen Imperiums benannt werden.' Stendahl (in *Peake's Commentary*[2], 678) interprets 'peacemakers' as referring 'to the non-militant character of the true disciples of the Kingdom'. Cf. Klostermann, *Matthäusevangelium*, pp. 37–8; S.B. *Kommentar*, I, 215–20.

[4] Matt. v. 4: 'Neue Anregung erhielt das Trauern über Israels elende Gegenwart...durch die Ereignisse des Jahres 70 n. Chr. Kleinere Kreise schlossen sich zusammen, ihrer Trauer über Jerusalems Fall auch äußerlich in gewissen asketischen Bußübungen Ausdruck zu geben' (S.B. *Kommentar*, I, 195).

[5] Matt. v. 41: καὶ ὅστις σε ἀγγαρεύσει μίλιον ἕν, ὕπαγε μετ' αὐτοῦ δύο. Cf. Klostermann, *Matthäusevangelium*, p. 49; Lohmeyer and Schmauch, *Das Evangelium des Matthäus*, pp. 140–1.

ἐχθροὺς ὑμῶν) and pray for those who persecute you...'[1] Thus, Matthew, moved by the dangers which threatened the Church in Alexandria during these difficult years, not only presented Jesus to his fellow-Christians as the Messiah who rejected armed violence to promote his cause, but he represents him as commanding his followers to show themselves similarly pacific in their conduct. Those who had taken the sword in Judaea had perished by the sword: hence, Zealot virtues and Zealot action must be repudiated and replaced by the idea of the 'poor in spirit', the 'meek', and the 'peacemaker'.

The Matthaean Gospel, like the Lukan, elaborates Mark's passing reference to the Temptation of Jesus by Satan, after his baptism, into a dramatic episode that includes what appears to be a definitive renunciation of world-empire by Jesus.[2] Such a presentation, at the beginning of his account of the ministry of Jesus, might be interpreted as an announcement by Matthew of his theme of the peaceable nature and intent of Jesus, who was the true Messiah of Israel. However, the fact that Matthew's version does not differ significantly from that of Luke suggests that the story of the Temptation was derived by these writers from a common source, possibly Q.[3] If this be so, the question naturally follows whether we have, therefore, evidence that, prior to the writing of Matthew and Luke, and perhaps Mark, there already existed a tradition of Jesus as the Messiah who did not seek an earthly kingdom and its acquisition by force of arms.

Such a possibility appears unlikely on examination of the passages concerned. For it must be recognised in the first place that it is

---

[1] Matt. v. 43–4: 'Nirgends handelt es sich um einen persönlichen Gegner, sondern immer um den Gegner des Volkes...' (Lohmeyer and Schmauch, *Das Evangelium des Matthäus*, p. 143). Gentile belief that the Jews hated all foreigners finds classical expression in Tacitus, *Hist.* v. 5: 'apud ipsos fides obstinata, misericordia in promptu, sed adversus omnes alios hostile odium'. Cf. S.B. *Kommentar*, I, 353–71.

[2] Matt. iv. 1–11: Luke iv. 1–13; cf. Mark i. 12–13. Cf. Beare, *Earliest Records of Jesus*, pp. 42–3. On the third temptation as meaning world-power achieved by force see, e.g., P. P. Levertoff and H. L. Goudge in *New Commentary, N.T.* p. 136a; Klausner, *Jesus of Nazareth*, p. 253; A. T. Olmstead, *Jesus: in the Light of History*, p. 60; A. Köberle in *R.G.G.*[3], VI, 1386; McNeil, *St Matthew*, p. 41; J. W. Bowman in *Peake's Commentary*[2], 640f; C. J. Cadoux, *Historic Mission of Jesus*, pp. 169–70.

[3] Cf. Streeter, *Four Gospels*, pp. 182 ff., 273; McNeil, *St Matthew*, p. 37; Stendahl in *Peake's Commentary*[2], 677a–b; Bultmann, *Gesch. d. syn. Trad.* pp. 272, 275.

'all the kingdoms of the world and the glory of them', not lordship over Israel only, that Satan is represented as offering to Jesus.[1] Then, to suggest that acceptance of this offer was meant to signify resort to war, and that this was the Satanic temptation, is to assume that a considerable degree of sophistication underlies the Temptation tradition in its original form. Moreover, it must not be overlooked that Jesus is not described as refusing dominion over the world as such; what he vehemently repudiates is the Devil's suggestion that he should worship him.[2] However, the real nature of the Temptation story is not likely to be understood by considering one part of it only; it includes three acts of temptation, so that the story must be evaluated as a whole, for the three forms of temptation are undoubtedly related to each other in some way.

It is reasonable to suppose that a tradition, carefully articulated in structure and clearly constituting an apologetical theme such as the Temptation story embodies, was composed to meet some specific need in the primitive Jewish Christian community in Judaea.[3] Further, the fact that the story amounts to an assertion that Jesus rejected three specific actions as being demonically inspired suggests that it had been found necessary thus to refute corresponding charges that he had been guilty of such actions.[4] Now, the three temptations which Jesus is described as resisting are significant; for they can each be identified with some aspect of current Messianic belief and the practice of Messianic claimants. The idea of turning stones into bread would surely derive from those thaumaturgic acts which the 'wonder-workers' (γόητες), of whom Josephus writes, claimed to perform as evidence of their Messianic powers.[5] The temptation to

---

[1] iv. 8: πάσας τὰς βασιλείας τοῦ κόσμου καὶ τὴν δόξαν αὐτῶν = Luke iv. 5 ...πάσας τὰς βασιλείας τῆς οἰκουμένης... Cf. Lohmeyer and Schmauch, *Das Evangelium des Matthäus*, p. 59. On the current Jewish idea of Satan as κοσμοκράτωρ see S.B. *Kommentar*, I, 153.   [2] iv. 8 = Luke iv. 8.

[3] 'Die Bildung scheint also aus der Polemik und Apologetik zu stammen. Aber was wird verteidigt?' (Bultmann, *Gesch. d. syn. Trad.* p. 272).

[4] It would be unlikely that the original Jewish Christians should have conceived, *in vacuo*, the idea that Jesus was tempted in the three specific ways concerned. Even if Davies (*Sermon on the Mount*, pp. 45–8) is right in seeing Mosaic elements in the Temptation story, the three temptations are so distinctive that they inevitably predicate three equally distinctive stimuli, on the old adage that 'there is no smoke without a fire'.

[5] See above, pp. 108ff. Bultmann, curiously, overlooks this Josephean evidence when he declares that the first two temptations do not concern Messianic issues (*Gesch. d. syn. Trad.* p. 272). Cf. O. Betz in *N.T.* II, 132–3; G. Delling, 'Josephus und das Wunderbare', *N.T.* II, 297, n. 1.

force God's intervention by precipitating a dangerous situation is reminiscent of the conduct of that Messianic pretender who gathered a crowd of followers on the Mount of Olives, promising to cause the walls of Jerusalem to fall and to slaughter the Roman garrison.[1] The temptation to strive for world-dominion recalls the ancient oracle concerning the coming of a world-ruler from Israel, which Josephus adroitly interpreted as being fulfilled by Vespasian's election to the imperial power while resident in Palestine.[2]

That Jesus should have repudiated the course of action that each of these temptations represents would seem consistent with what has become the traditional view of his nature and character. However, on reflection it has to be recognised that the first temptation, namely, to turn stones into bread, is very similar to many miracles that are ascribed to Jesus by the Evangelists.[3] Further, it could be reasonably argued that such an act as Jesus' attack on the Temple trading system was calculated to produce the situation implied by the second temptation, namely, by provoking enemies to take action against him, thus deliberately to place himself in great jeopardy.[4]

In the light of these considerations it would appear, therefore, that the Temptation story was not composed to deny that Jesus did

---

[1] iv. 6–7. See above, p. 110. Cf. S.B. *Kommentar*, I, 152–3.

[2] Jos. *War*, VI. 312–13. As one of the contributive causes of the Jewish revolt, Josephus tells of an ambiguous oracle (χρησμὸς ἀμφίβολος), contained in the Jewish scriptures, that κατὰ τὸν καιρὸν ἐκεῖνον ἀπὸ τῆς χώρας αὐτῶν τις ἄρξει τῆς οἰκουμένης. Tacitus (*Hist.* v. 13) and Suetonius (*Vesp.* 4) mention such a belief. Cf. Eisler, ΙΗΣΟΥΣ ΒΑΣΙΛΕΥΣ, II, 591–9, *Messiah Jesus*, pp. 554–61; Ricciotti, *La guerra giudaica*, IV, 189, on 312–13; Brandon, *Fall of Jerusalem*, pp. 113–14; and above, p. 59. Tacitus and Suetonius describe the prophecy as being current in the Levant ('Oriente toto'); it would doubtless have been well known in Alexandria, and it may well have inspired Vespasian's fear that the Egyptian Jews would revolt (ὁ δὲ τῶν 'Ιουδαίων τὴν ἀκατάπαυστον ὑφορώμενος νεωτεροποιίαν καὶ δείσας..., Jos. *War*, VII. 421).

[3] E.g. the Multiplication of the Loaves and Fishes (Mark vi. 35–44 and parallels), and the Transformation of Water into Wine (John ii. 1–11). 'Jesus, who is at the same time Messiah and New Moses, is here tempted by Satan to reproduce the miracle of the giving of the manna by turning stones to bread' (Davies, *Sermon on the Mount*, p. 45).

[4] According to Mark (xi. 18), the 'chief priests and the scribes' were only prevented from seizing Jesus through fear of the crowd which supported him. The fact that Mark records immediately after this (xi. 19) that Jesus left the city each evening suggests that he realised the peril in which his action had placed him—it was moreover an action of which the consequences could obviously have been anticipated. See below, pp. 331 ff.

perform miracles or claim world-dominion; what it was intended to refute was the accusation that such action was inspired by the Devil. This conclusion is consistent with other evidence, and it throws light upon an interesting development of Jewish Christian apologetic. As we have seen, the performance of miracles was regarded as evidence of Messianic character and authority: Josephus tells of many γόητες or Messianic pretenders who were credited with miraculous power.[1] The miracles of Jesus were similarly regarded as 'signs' attesting his Messiahship, and they were cited by his followers in their teaching and apologetic as they sought to win their compatriots to acceptance of Jesus as the promised Messiah or to meet the objections of opponents.[2] Now, as the Beelzebul accusation shows, those who refused to accept the Messiahship of Jesus did not deny his ability to perform miracles; instead, they controverted the testimony of his miracles by attributing them to demonic agency.[3] The Temptation story, accordingly, represents a piece of traditional apologetic directed against such accusations concerning what were evidently considered three major aspects of Jesus' Messianic activity. The three issues involved are significant: performance of miracles; the precipitation of a crisis; ambition for world-dominion.

The identity of those who made such accusations is clearly a matter of considerable concern for our evaluation of the issue involved here. According to Mark, it was scribes from Jerusalem who accused Jesus of casting out demons by the aid of Beelzebul;[4] but

[1] Pp. 108–11.
[2] The miraculous acts of Jesus are cited as evidence of his Messianic character in answer to the Baptist's question: σὺ εἶ ὁ ἐρχόμενος, ἢ ἕτερον προσδοκῶμεν; (Matt. xi. 2–6; cf. Luke vii. 18–23.) Cf. Bultmann, Gesch. d. syn. Trad. p. 22; Klostermann, Matthäusevangelium, p. 94. See also the question of the Jewish authorities, as reported by John (xi. 47): τί ποιοῦμεν, ὅτι οὗτος ὁ ἄνθρωπος πολλὰ ποιεῖ σημεῖα; Cf. C. H. Dodd, Historical Tradition in the Fourth Gospel, p. 24. That there was much controversy between the original Jewish Christians and their fellow-Jews about 'signs' attesting the Messiahship of Jesus is also evident from such passages as Mark viii. 11–12; Matt. xi. 29–32, xii. 38–42, xvi. 1, 2, 4; Luke xi. 29–32. Cf. Taylor, St Mark, p. 362; Bultmann, Gesch. d. syn. Trad. p. 54.
[3] Mark iii. 22 ff.; cf. Taylor, St Mark, p. 238. The Matthaean version of this episode (xii. 22 ff.) significantly connects the crowd's acknowledgement of Jesus' Messiahship (μήτι οὗτός ἐστιν ὁ υἱὸς Δαυείδ;), when he heals one blind and dumb, δαιμονιζόμενος, with the Pharisees' accusation that the miracle is achieved by Satan's help. Cf. E. Best, The Temptation and the Passion: the Markan Soteriology (Cambridge, 1965), pp. 10 ff., and p. 314, n. 3 below.
[4] Mark iii. 22: Taylor, St Mark, p. 238, regards this verse as 'an editorial passage' of Mark.

Matthew imputes the charge to the Pharisees.[1] Now, if the Pharisees, in controversy with Jesus' disciples, had also maintained that Jesus, inspired by the Devil, had deliberately precipitated a crisis by his attack on the Temple banking system, we arrive at an interesting conclusion. The Pharisees who made such an accusation would undoubtedly have been members of that section of the party which pursued a policy of abstention from political affairs and issues.[2] The probability that such men countered the propagation of the Messianic claims of Jesus with the charge that Jesus had been inspired by Satan to seek world-empire and had caused a political crisis in Jerusalem, which resulted in his death, is of the greatest significance. For it explains why the Jewish Christians, in their turn, had sought to rebut such an accusation by asserting that Jesus had rigorously repudiated any demonic promptings in the pursuit of his Messianic mission. This refutation was, characteristically, presented in the form of a dramatic narrative, which Matthew and Luke have incorporated into their Gospels. Consequently, it would appear that the Temptation story does not connote an earlier tradition of the pacific character of Jesus; but, on the contrary, that it was originally designed to meet the charges of pacifist Pharisees against actions of Jesus deemed politically provocative. Moreover, the fact that Mark evidently knew of a Temptation tradition, but merely makes a passing reference to it,[3] suggests that he was aware that it stemmed from a situation which it was best to ignore in the interests of his own apologetical theme.

When Matthew and Luke wrote, the connection of Jesus with the role of world-ruler had not the dangerous implications that it had for Mark in Rome about A.D. 71. Consequently, they incorporated the Temptation story into their narratives at a point where it serves well to introduce their theme of the pacific Christ; for they would have had no reason for fearing that the origin and inner logic of the story would be closely scrutinised by their readers.

A somewhat similar problem attaches to Jesus' Lament over

[1] Matt. xii. 24.
[2] Cf. Schürer, *G.J.V.* II, 395–6; R. Travers Herford, *The Pharisees*, pp. 51–2, 186 ff., and *Society of Hebraic Studies*, no. 2, pp. 10–12; W. Förster, *Palestinian Judaism in New Testament Times*, pp. 88–9.
[3] Mark i. 12–13; cf. Taylor, *St Mark*, pp. 162–3. E. Best, *The Temptation and the Passion*, p. 15, would interpret Mark i. 12 ff. in the light of iii. 22–30, seeing in the Temptation 'a contest between Jesus and Satan'—'Satan is overcome; the demonic exorcism of the remainder of the ministry represents the making real of a victory already accomplished'.

Jerusalem. The passage, since it appears in Matthew and Luke in almost identical language, was obviously already well established in Jewish Christian tradition;[1] but its origin is obscure. Scholars have reasonably felt that it can scarcely be regarded as a verbatim report of an actual utterance of Jesus, in view of the implication of the words 'how often (ποσάκις) have I sought to gather thy children together'; for the Gospels give no indication that Jesus frequently proclaimed his message in Jerusalem.[2] The concluding statement, that the inhabitants of Jerusalem would not see him again until they welcomed him at his Triumphal Entry, seems to be a later comment on that event.[3] It would, accordingly, appear that, in its extant form, the pericope circulated in Christian circles as a prophecy *ex eventu*, explaining the significance of the destruction of Jerusalem or its Temple. That it presents Jesus as the gentle Messiah, seeking patiently, but in vain, to win the allegiance of the wicked and bloodstained people of Jerusalem, is incidental to its purpose of accounting for the catastrophe of A.D. 70 as punishment for the obduracy of the Jews to the message of Jesus.[4]

The Lukan writer, although moved by different motives from those that influenced Matthew, was equally interested to emphasise the pacific character of Jesus. As his Acts of the Apostles shows, he

[1] Matt. xxiii. 37–9: Luke xiii. 34–5. Cf. Streeter, *Four Gospels*, p. 254; McNeil, *St Matthew*, p. 341.

[2] Cf. Bultmann, *Gesch. d. syn. Trad.* p. 120.

[3] Cf. *ibid.* pp. 120–1; Klostermann, *Matthäusevangelium*, p. 191.

[4] The preceding two verses (xxiii. 35–6) concerning 'all the righteous blood shed upon earth from the blood of Abel the righteous to the blood of Zacharias, son of Barachias', for which retribution would be paid by the present generation (ἥξει ταῦτα πάντα ἐπὶ τὴν γενεὰν ταύτην), derive from a source common to Matthew and Luke (xi. 50–1). Although they follow on the denunciations of the Pharisees (Matt. xxiii. 1 ff.; Luke xi. 39 ff.), these verses by their reference to 'this generation' clearly envisage the contemporary generation of Jews, and not just the Pharisees. It is possible that the section Matt. xxiii. 32–6 was originally a separate pericope containing a prophecy of doom similar to that of Jesus ben Ananias which Josephus records (*War*, VI. 300–9). As Bultmann remarks (*Gesch. d. syn. Trad.* p. 120): 'Charakteristisch ist, daß ein jüdisches Prophetenwort von der christlichen Tradition angeeignet ist.' Cf. Klostermann, *Matthäusevangelium*, pp. 188–90; S.B. *Kommentar*, I, 939–44. The denunciations of the Pharisees, as well as the recognition of their authority (xxiii. 1–3), are easily intelligible in an Alexandrian *milieu*, where the largest Jewish population resided after the devastation of Judaea in A.D. 70.

was concerned to present Christianity as a faith which the Gentiles welcomed and Roman magistrates protected from Jewish malignity.[1] Consequently, it was important for him to portray Jesus as peaceable in disposition and action, and uninvolved in Jewish nationalist politics. Writing some fifteen or twenty years after Mark, he could view the events of A.D. 66–70 with more detachment, and unlike Matthew he did not write for a Jewish Christianity faced with the perils which beset the community in Alexandria. Accordingly, he was not prevented by their fears from recording that one of Jesus' disciples was a Zealot,[2] and that Jesus ordered his disciples to arm themselves before going to Gethsemane.[3] However, from the very start of his Gospel, Luke sounds a note of peace in his record of the angels' song that heralds the birth of Jesus: 'Glory to God in the highest, and on earth peace among men with whom He is pleased!'[4]

Luke's portrait of Jesus as the pacific Christ is not achieved by such overt touches as Matthew's additions to the Markan account of the arrest in Gethsemane. It is a more subtle delineation that continues the eirenical suggestion of the Birth story by making Jesus the author of noble parables such as the Good Samaritan and the Prodigal Son. It is reflected in Jesus' rebuke to his fierce disciples who wish to call down fire from heaven to consume certain uncooperative Samaritans,[5] and in his warning against the consequences of violence when told of Pilate's slaughter of some Galilaeans and those killed by the fall of the tower in Siloam.[6] It is subtly suggested by adding to the note of political Messianism in the crowd's saluta-

---

[1] Cf. F. J. Foakes Jackson and K. Lake in *B.C.* II, 177 ff.

[2] Luke vi. 15: Σίμωνα τὸν καλούμενον Ζηλωτήν; Acts i. 13: Σίμων ὁ Ζηλωτής. As we have seen (p. 244, n. 5), Matthew evidently found it more politic to describe Simon as ὁ Καναναῖος.

[3] xxii. 36–8: cf. Brandon, *Fall of Jerusalem*, p. 207, and below, pp. 340–2.

[4] ii. 14.

[5] ix. 52–6. 'The incident provides a practical illustration of the teaching of non-resistance to evil (vi. 29)', Creed, *St Luke*, p. 141.

[6] xiii. 3: οὐχί, λέγω ὑμῖν, ἀλλ' ἐὰν μὴ μετανοῆτε πάντες ὁμοίως ἀπολεῖσθε. The comment of Jesus on the fate of those killed by the falling tower (*v.* 5) differs only by the substitution of ὡσαύτως for ὁμοίως. Since this passage (xiii. 1–5) is followed by the parable of the Unfruitful Fig-tree (xiii. 6–9), which obviously refers to the destiny of Israel, it would appear that Luke intended the comment of Jesus in *vv.* 3 and 5 to be a warning to the Jews of the consequences of their bellicose spirit. However, since the political aspect of both incidents (xiii. 1, 4) is not evident, it is impossible to evaluate the comment of Jesus, if the passage is to be regarded as based upon an authentic tradition: cf. Bultmann, *Gesch. d. syn. Trad.* p. 21; see also above, p. 78.

tion to Jesus, as he entered triumphantly into Jerusalem, the dis-arming words: 'Peace in heaven and glory in the highest!'[1] And the suggestion is taken up again in the words of Jesus' subsequent lament over Jerusalem's coming fate: 'Would that, even today you knew the things that make for peace!'[2]

Although he reveals the very significant fact that Jesus saw that his disciples were armed before they went to Gethsemane,[3] Luke represents Jesus as intervening to stop the resistance offered to his arrest.[4] Then, by including the trial of Jesus before Herod Antipas in his Passion narrative, he makes both the Jewish ruler of Galilee and the Roman governor of Judaea witness to the innocence of Jesus.[5] The words of forgiveness which he assigns to Jesus as he is crucified,[6] together with his alteration of Mark's version of the cen-turion's testimony so that it testifies to the innocence of Jesus,[7] com-plete the picture of the career of one born to bring peace to men and who prayed for those who brought him to his death. This theme is carried over into Acts and is epitomised in Peter's speech, in which he is represented as castigating the Jews for their rejection of Jesus: 'the God of our fathers glorified His servant Jesus, whom you delivered up and denied in the presence of Pilate, when he had decided to release him. But you denied the Holy and Righteous One, and asked for a murderer to be granted to you, and killed the Author of life, whom God raised from the dead' (R.S.V.).[8]

Luke's interpretation of the Jewish catastrophe of A.D. 70 is closely integrated with his portrait of Jesus. Together with Matthew, as we saw, he incorporated into his Gospel an existing oracle con-cerning the destruction of Jerusalem which circulated as a Domini-cal prophecy of the event.[9] But he supplemented this with two other

---

[1] xix. 38b: ἐν οὐρανῷ εἰρήνη καὶ δόξα ἐν ὑψίστοις. Cf. Eisler, ΙΗΣΟΥΣ ΒΑΣΙΛΕΥΣ, ιι, 474.　　[2] xix. 42: cf. Creed, St Luke, p. 242.
[3] It is to be noted that, although he does record the arming, Luke attempts to explain it in terms of the fulfilment of a prophecy (xxii. 37). See below, pp. 340 ff.
[4] xxii. 51: 'Εᾶτε ἕως τούτου. The exact meaning of the words is obscure. They are probably Luke's invention and are intended to abate the implication of Jesus' arming of his disciples (xxii. 36–8). See below, p. 342.
[5] xxiii. 6–15. The trial before Herod seems to be an invention of Luke. Creed (St Luke, p. 280) suggests that 'Luke was perhaps glad to transfer the outrage from the soldiery of Rome to the soldiery of the local tetrarch'. Cf. Bultmann, Gesch. d. syn. Trad. p. 294.
[6] xxiii. 34: on the question of the authenticity of the saying cf. Creed, St Luke, pp. 286–7.　　[7] xxiii. 47: ὄντως ὁ ἄνθρωπος οὗτος δίκαιος ἦν.
[8] Acts iii. 13–15.　　[9] Luke xiii. 34–5; see above, p. 315.

passages, drawn from his own particular source-material, in which Jesus is represented as grieving over the disaster that he knows will overtake the people of Jerusalem. The first of these passages is designed to offset the enthusiastic welcome which Jesus had received on his entry into the city. The scene changes swiftly from that of triumph to one of dark foreboding: 'And when he drew near and saw the city he wept over it, saying, "Would that even today you knew the things that make for peace! But now they are hid from your eyes."'[1] Then comes the prophecy of doom, which by its mention of the circumvallation of the city seems to make reference to a notable feature of the actual siege by the Roman forces under Titus.[2] After certain additions to the Markan apocalypse, evidently inspired by the historic event,[3] Luke again depicts Jesus as concerned, when on the way to Calvary, with the fate that is to befall the inhabitants of the city, or rather a particular section of them: 'Daughters of Jerusalem, do not weep for me, but weep for yourselves and for your children. For behold, the days are coming when they will say, "Blessed are the barren, and the wombs that never bore, and the breasts that never gave suck!"'[4]

In the Fourth Gospel this emerging concept of the pacific Christ is given definitive endorsement by a Dominical pronouncement. John, who seems acutely aware of the political aspect of the career of Jesus,[5] attributes to Jesus a significantly formal repudiation of political ambition. Thus, in further answer to Pilate's question 'Are you the King of the Jews?', Jesus replies: 'My kingship (ἡ βασιλεία ἡ ἐμή) is not of this world; if my kingship were of this world, my servants would fight (οἱ ὑπηρέται ἂν οἱ ἐμοὶ ἠγωνίζοντο), that I might not be handed over to the Jews; but my kingship is not from the world (οὐκ ἔστιν ἐντεῦθεν).'[6] Instead, therefore, of Matthew's picture, inspired by Jewish apocalyptic, of the Messiah who had at his command more than twelve legions of angels, but

---

[1] xix. 41–2.
[2] xix. 43–4. On the circumvallation of Jerusalem see Jos. *War*, v. 491–510: cf. Brandon, *Fall of Jerusalem*, p. 207.
[3] Cf. Creed, *St Luke*, pp. 252–4.
[4] xxiii. 28–31: cf. Creed, *St Luke*, pp. 285–6; S.B. *Kommentar*, II, 263. Bultmann describes the passage as 'eine Jesus in den Mund gelegte christliche Prophetie' (*Gesch. d. syn. Trad.* p. 121, cf. p. 37).
[5] Cf. Brandon, *Fall of Jerusalem*, pp. 124–5; Dodd, *Interpretation of the Fourth Gospel*, p. 451, n. 1, and *Historical Tradition in the Fourth Gospel*, pp. 24, 95, 100–1.   [6] John xviii. 36–7.

who would not use them, John depicts Jesus, the incarnate Logos, as explaining carefully to the Roman governor that his kingship constituted no challenge to Rome, for it was an extra-mundane kingship,[1] and hence far removed from the primitive apocalyptic conception of restoring 'the kingdom to Israel'.[2] John, moreover, reveals the anti-Jewish orientation of his thought here by representing Jesus as assuring Pilate that, if his intentions had been political, his 'servants' would have fought to prevent his being handed over 'to the Jews'.[3] John was evidently concerned, as Mark was, but in a different way, to show his readers that the Jews were really responsible for the Roman execution of Jesus.[4] Accordingly, Jesus is made to explain by a carefully formulated argument to Pilate that the Jewish accusation, namely, that he claimed to be the 'King of the Jews', did not mean that he claimed an earthly kingdom, thereby challenging the sovereignty of Rome.[5] The evidence which Jesus is described as citing to prove his pacific intent is naïve in the extreme, but it is also very revealing: 'if my kingship were of this world, my servants would fight, that I might not be handed over to the Jews'. Owing to his anti-Jewish attitude, John has momentarily forgotten that it was the Romans who executed Jesus; instead he portrays Jesus as a leader disposing of sufficient forces that would have enabled him, had he chosen, to repulse the action which had led to what is curiously described as his being 'handed over' (παραδοθῶ) to the Jews—not, it is to be noted, to the Jewish leaders.[6] However

---

[1] ἡ βασιλεία ἡ ἐμὴ οὐκ ἔστιν ἐκ τοῦ κόσμου τούτου. Cf. Dodd, *Interpretation of the Fourth Gospel*, pp. 229, 427.

[2] Cf. Acts i. 6; see above, pp. 176 ff.

[3] The anti-Jewish attitude of John has its quintessential expression in viii. 44: ὑμεῖς ἐκ τοῦ πατρὸς τοῦ διαβόλου... Cf. J. Moffatt, *Introduction to the New Testament*, p. 531; Dodd, *Interpretation of the Fourth Gospel*, p. 159.

[4] The Jews are represented as the offspring of the Devil who seek to kill Jesus because he has told them God's truth (viii. 39 ff.). Caiaphas decides that it is expedient that 'one man should die for the people, and that the whole nation should not perish' (xi. 49–50). Cf. Dodd, *Interpretation of the Fourth Gospel*, pp. 345 ff.

[5] Whereas the Synoptic writers represent Jesus as either silent or very reticent before Pilate, John presents him as discoursing freely and at some length.

[6] John seems to suggest that Jesus had been handed over by some non-Jewish group to the Jews. This suggestion is consistent with the fact that John represents the Romans as arresting Jesus (xviii. 3, 12), which conflicts with the Synoptic record and militates against the consistency of John's own record of the Trial. Cf. P. Winter, *On the Trial of Jesus*, pp. 44 ff. The use of the word ὑπηρέται in *v.* 36 for the 'servants' of Jesus

that may be, what concerns us particularly now is that, in the interests of his own peculiar apologetic theme, John completed the portrait of the pacific Christ, which the earlier Evangelists had adumbrated, by representing Jesus as categorically avowing that his kingship was not ἐκ τοῦ κόσμου τούτου, and as specifically repudiating the armed support of his followers in achieving that kingship.

We see, then, that the authors of Matthew, Luke and John, each in his own way and for his own purpose, elaborated the Markan portrait of Jesus, as one innocent of sedition against Rome, into that of the pacific Christ, who taught his followers to love their enemies and rejected all resort to armed violence. This conception, once presented, had its own obvious appeal to Christians, who were intent on dissociating themselves from any imputation of Jewish nationalism and on assuring the Roman government that their disposition was essentially pacific. Hence the impetus was given to a conception which was soon to be reinforced by theological considerations. For the development of the doctrine of the divinity of Christ, and his role of the saviour of all mankind, made it impossible to contemplate that he could have involved himself in Jewish national affairs, especially of a revolutionary kind.[1] Accordingly, the representation of him as living aloof or insulated from the political realities of first-century Judaea, which the Evangelists fabricated for their own particular apologetic needs, confirmed and sanctioned an evaluation that became doctrinally imperative. However, it is well to remember that Christian tradition has preserved, in the Apocalypse of John, the memory of another, and doubtless more primitive, conception of Christ—of the terrible Rider on the White Horse, whose 'eyes are like a flame of fire...He is clad in a robe dipped in blood, and the name by which he is called is The Word of God...From his mouth issues a sharp sword with which to smite the nations, and he will rule them with a rod of iron; he will tread the wine press of the fury of the wrath of God the Almighty. On his robe and on his thigh he has a name inscribed, King of kings and Lord of lords.'[2]

is significant; John uses it in the sense of 'armed retainers' (e.g. xviii. 3, 12, 22).

[1] Cf. Brandon, *History, Time and Deity*, pp. 189–90.

[2] Rev. xix. 12 ff. 'Here there is no question as to the personality of the present Rider. He is the Messiah—"the Word of God"' (R. H. Charles, *Revela-*

tion of St John, II, 131; cf. E. Lohmeyer, *Die Offenbarung des Johannes*, pp. 155–6; O. Betz in *N.T.* II, 130). Matt. x. 34 and Luke xii. 51 preserve, incidentally, a reminiscence of this other aspect of Jesus in the 'I' pronouncement: 'Think not that I came to bring (βαλεῖν) peace on the earth: I came not to bring peace, but a sword' (Matt.). Verses 35 ff. (Luke xii. 52 ff.) appear to be an attenuating explanation of the original Messianic pronouncement ('ist offenbar sekundäre Umsetzung', Bultmann, *Gesch. d. syn. Trad.* p. 166). Since the pronouncement is recorded (in slightly differing forms) by Matthew and Luke, it would seem probable that it was originally in Q. It is possible that the explanation was inspired by the primitive community's experience of what discipleship of Jesus meant in human relations, for that experience seemed to fulfil what Jesus had originally said about the purpose of his mission. Cf. S.B. *Kommentar*, I, 585–6; Bultmann, pp. 164–6, 176; Klostermann, *Matthäusevangelium*, pp. 91–2.

CHAPTER 7

JESUS AND THE ZEALOTS

The long and involved investigation with which we have been occupied constitutes an essential preparation to serious consideration of the actual problem of Jesus and the Zealots. That it has been so tortuous and involved is due to a complex of causes: on the one hand, the Christian sources, for a variety of reasons, give a tendentious presentation of the events which led to the Roman execution of Jesus; on the other hand, Josephus, our chief informant of Jewish affairs during the period concerned, has, for his own special reasons, misrepresented the Zealot movement. Then, in addition to these difficulties, there is the fact that the records of the original Jewish Christian community at Jerusalem did not survive that community's disappearance in the catastrophe of A.D. 70, which has meant a tedious attempt to reconstruct its views from a variety of other sources. However, out of this investigation certain conclusions have emerged that appear reasonable and help to elucidate what may justly be described as the most fundamental problem of Christian Origins. It is our task now to coordinate these conclusions, and evaluate their joint witness.

The position of the Markan Gospel in relation to this problem is pivotal, as we have seen.[1] Since it provided the first written account of the career and death of Jesus, Mark established an interpretation which the other Evangelists, with certain minor variations, followed. But that interpretation was decisively shaped by the needs of the community for which the Markan Gospel was written. It was, as we saw, the embarrassing and potentially dangerous position in which the Christians of Rome found themselves about the time of the Flavian triumph in the year 71 that caused the writer whom we know as Mark to provide for his community, and any pagan who might be interested, an explanation of how Jesus came to be executed by the Romans for sedition against their government in Judaea.[2] To this end he represented Jesus as the victim of the Jewish leaders, who plotted, out of envy, to destroy him. To show how their evil intent was achieved, not by their executing Jesus under Jewish

[1] Pp. 280 ff.   [2] Pp. 224 ff.

law, but by his execution as a rebel against the Roman rule, Mark was obliged to represent the Jewish leaders as forcing a reluctant Roman governor to condemn one whom he knew to be innocent.[1] But this was not all. Feeling, doubtless, that the fact of the Roman execution might still arouse suspicion about Jesus' loyalty to Rome, Mark specifically depicts Jesus as having endorsed the Jews' duty to pay tribute to Caesar—an issue which was one of the most decisive for Roman-Jewish relations at this time.[2]

Accordingly, in developing his apologetical theme, Mark presents Jesus as the incarnate Son of God who was done to death by the *odium theologicum* of the Jewish leaders, backed by the Jerusalem mob, after being misunderstood by his own family and disciples, betrayed by one of his disciples and deserted by the rest.[3] Pursuing his mission curiously insulated from current political events, except for the occasion when he pronounced upon the justice of the Roman tribute, Jesus ends his career, surprisingly, by being executed for sedition on the order of Pontius Pilate; but this is explained as a tragic mistake, due to the perfidious behaviour of the Jews, both leaders and people. Mark rounds off his presentation by recording two incidents, cleverly juxtaposed for both apologetical and theological significance: the Roman centurion recognises the divinity of the dying Jesus, while the rending of the Temple Veil proclaims the end of the Old Covenant, which the events of A.D. 70 had made a practical reality.[4]

This interpretation of the death of Jesus was so vividly presented, and it was so essentially congenial to the Christian outlook after A.D. 70, that it was accepted, without serious emendation, by the other Evangelists. As we have seen, Matthew, Luke and John, each for his own particular needs, developed Mark's portrait of Jesus, as the innocent victim of the malice of the Jewish leaders, into that of the pacific Christ who not only definitively repudiated armed force, but also counselled meek acceptance of injury at the hands of others.[5] Such a conception of Jesus quickly became the established tradition, particularly since it was required theologically: the incarnated Son of God, who died to save mankind, obviously could not have involved himself in contemporary Jewish politics, which no later Christian theologian understood or had the slightest interest in understanding.[6]

[1] Pp. 256 ff.   [2] Pp. 270 ff.   [3] Pp. 264 ff.
[4] Pp. 279 ff.   [5] Pp. 283 ff.
[6] Cf. Brandon, *History, Time and Deity*, pp. 189 ff.

Hence, the Christian Gospels, taken on their own testimony, have established an interpretation of the career and death of Jesus of Nazareth, designed originally to meet the needs of Roman Christians about A.D. 71, as the orthodox belief of the Christian Church. However, behind this presentation, as soon as its credentials are interrogated, there are discerned the lineaments of a very different situation. We have noted that Mark found it expedient to conceal from his readers that one of the disciples of Jesus was a Zealot.[1] His account of the trial of Jesus, when critically examined, reveals such inherent inconsistencies that it becomes patent that he was concerned, even at the cost of logic, to transfer the responsibility for the Crucifixion from Pilate to the Jewish leaders.[2] The obvious conclusion therefrom, namely, that Pilate sentenced Jesus because he was convinced that he was politically dangerous, is confirmed by other evidence unintentionally given by Mark. Thus, Jesus is recorded to have initiated actions, namely, his Triumphal Entry into Jerusalem and the so-called Cleansing of the Temple, which were obviously calculated to cause the authorities, both Jewish and Roman, to view him and his movement as subversive.[3] Further, Mark admits, though he clearly plays down its seriousness, that armed resistance was offered in Gethsemane to the arrest of Jesus;[4] and Luke, writing some time later and with less circumspection, actually states that Jesus checked on the fact that his disciples were armed on that fatal night.[5]

These indications which the Gospels inadvertently provide of a different situation from that which they were intended to represent, fit in with other evidence that the views of the original Jewish Christians about Jesus were also significantly different. We have found that these disciples, who included the apostles and eyewitnesses of the career of Jesus, continued to live as devout Jews zealously observing the ritual and legal demands of Judaism, and looking for the 'restoration of the kingdom to Israel'[6]. They recognised Jesus as the Messiah of their people. The unexpected interruption of his Messianic career, which his crucifixion constituted, had been both a shock and a problem to them; but they had surmounted these obstacles, inspired by the personality of their crucified Master and by skilful biblical exegesis.[7] They saw in the Roman execution of

---

[1] Pp. 243 ff.   [2] Pp. 256 ff.   [3] See below, pp. 331 ff., 349 ff.
[4] Mark xiv. 47 leaves the identity of the person who struck the blow intentionally vague (εἷς δέ [τις] τῶν παρεστηκότων). See above, p. 306, n. 5.
[5] See pp. 317, 340 ff.   [6] Pp. 155 ff.   [7] Pp. 176 ff.

Jesus martyrdom for Israel, which many other Jewish leaders had suffered from the glorious days of the Maccabees to the recent deaths of Judas of Galilee and many of his Zealot followers.[1] Scriptural warranty being found for such sufferings of the Messiah, they looked forward to the imminent return of Jesus, with supernatural power, to complete his Messianic role. The achievement of this role meant the restoration of sovereignty to Israel, which necessarily involved the overthrow of the Roman government which then ruled in the Holy Land.[2]

That those who were the original disciples of Jesus should have viewed him in this way is profoundly significant. For it must surely follow that their conception of Jesus after his crucifixion must have stemmed from what they knew and understood of him and his actions and teaching before that tragic event. Other features of their life and beliefs bear a similar witness. They appear quickly to have organised themselves under the leadership of the senior male relative of Jesus, namely, his brother James, thus conforming to that dynastic principle which also found expression in Zealotism.[3] Like the Zealots, too, they appear to have had a close sympathy for the poor and unprivileged, and a corresponding antipathy towards the rich Jews whose wealth and social position made them pro-Roman.[4] This attitude doubtless led them to take the part of the lower orders of the priesthood, many of whom were Christians, against the sacerdotal aristocracy, and this alliance may have resulted in the murder of James.[5] From our point of view, such an alliance would be particularly significant, because the lower clergy were infected with Zealotism and actually started the revolt in 66 by refusing to offer the daily sacrifices in the Temple for the wellbeing of the emperor and Roman people—an institution which the sacerdotal aristocracy had inaugurated and was intent on maintaining as a public token of loyalty to Rome.[6]

The Jewish Christians must, accordingly, have been very close to the Zealots in sympathy and outlook; their most notable difference being their belief that Jesus was the Messiah *redivivus*, who would shortly return to restore the kingdom to Israel.[7] They repudiated Paul's teaching when they became aware of its implied equation of Jew and Gentile in the economy of God's providence, and they required him to give proof of his Jewish orthodoxy; moreover, they abandoned him to those so zealously orthodox that some of

---

[1] Pp. 181 ff. [2] Pp. 180-1. [3] Pp. 161 ff. [4] Pp. 199 ff.
[5] Pp. 118 ff. [6] Pp. 130 ff. [7] Pp. 180-1, 205.

their number, Sicarii-like, sought to murder him.[1] Although they were not themselves professed members of Zealotism, the fact that at least one professed Zealot was of their company indicates that no insurmountable barrier existed to prevent a Zealot from recognising the Messiahship of Jesus and from participating in membership of the Church.[2] When the final revolt came in 66, there seems to have been no compelling reason that would have kept the Jewish Christians from making common cause with their brethren in this supreme act of faith to free Israel from its heathen yoke, and the fact that the Church of Jerusalem disappeared after A.D. 70 suggests that most of its members shared the common fate of Jewish patriots.[3]

Christianity emerged among a people whose cherished ideal was that of being the Elect People of God, devoted wholly to his service in the Holy Land which he had given to their forefathers. But that ideal was rudely shattered in A.D. 6, when the Roman emperor Augustus incorporated their Holy Land into his empire and sent his officers to rule it and to take of its resources for tribute. Reaction had been immediate, and from it stemmed a resistance movement known as Zealotism.[4] Although Josephus, our chief informant of Jewish affairs during the period, purposely denigrates this movement and misrepresents its activities, it has become evident, in the light of recent research, that Zealotism was essentially religious in its inspiration and purpose.[5] It found practical expression in armed action, even including assassination; but in this it was wholly in line with Jewish tradition, most notably with the Maccabees, who had attacked both the heathen enemy and their Jewish collaborators in their struggle for Israel's liberty.[6] The basic principle of Zealotism, as enunciated by its founder, Judas of Galilee, was that of the absolute sovereignty of Yahweh over Israel, which meant accepting no human being, especially one who was a heathen, as lord, and the refusal to give any of the resources of Yahweh's Holy Land as tribute to a foreign ruler who claimed such lordship.[7] Resistance inevitably involved suffering; but the Zealot was ready to take up his cross and die a martyr's death in the belief that his sacrifice would not be in vain and that God would ultimately intervene to save Israel.[8]

Jesus must have known of the Zealot ideal, and of Zealot exploits

---

[1] Acts xxiii. 12–15. Cf. Goguel, *La naissance du Christianisme*, p. 346. See above, p. 111, n. 5.

[2] Pp. 205 ff.   [3] Pp. 208 ff.   [4] Pp. 29 ff.   [5] Pp. 31 ff.

[6] Pp. 47 ff.   [7] Pp. 31 ff.   [8] Pp. 57 ff.

and martyrdom, from boyhood. Because he was a Jew, nurtured in the traditions of his people and believing in the absolute sovereignty of God, both his religious instincts and his sense of patriotism must have been affronted by the presence of the heathen Romans, who dominated his people by force of arms and demanded tribute to support their ungodly rule. It is, accordingly, difficult to see on *a priori* grounds why he should not have sympathised with the Zealots and felt hostile towards the Romans and those Jews who, for worldly gain, cooperated with them. The possibility that he was so disposed is, moreover, confirmed by the fact that he chose a Zealot to be one of his inner band of disciples. It is also reinforced by the absence of any record of his condemnation of the Zealots. As we have seen, the argument from silence is certainly valid here, because Mark, followed by the other Evangelists, has recorded the condemnatory attitude of Jesus to other Jewish parties, namely, the Pharisees, the Sadducees and the Herodians. We may, therefore, reasonably conclude that, if Jesus' attitude to the Zealots had also been condemnatory, the fact would certainly have been recorded, particularly by Mark.[1] The Gospels' silence about the Zealots, like that concerning the Essenes,[2] must thus surely be indicative of a relationship between Jesus and these patriots which the Evangelists preferred not to disclose.

The convergent witness of these diverse considerations is unmistakable. It is that the original narrative account of the career and death of Jesus, namely the Gospel of Mark, was designed to explain away the embarrassing fact of the Roman execution of Jesus as a rebel. But that explanation, on analysis, is found to be not only demonstrably unsound, but also suggestive of its author's awareness of other embarrassing facts which he endeavoured to disguise. His successors, in their Gospels, not having to be so circumspect as he,

---

[1] Pp. 200–1, 243–5, 280–1.

[2] It is remarkable that, despite the very great attention devoted to the question of the relations between the Qumrân sectaries and the primitive Christians, little attention has been given to explaining the total lack of explicit reference to the sect in the Christian sources. W. D. Davies, *Sermon on the Mount*, pp. 235 ff., 255, seems to suggest that relations were so close and polemical that formal reference to the Covenanters in the Christian sources would have been unnecessary. If G. R. Driver is right in identifying the Covenanters with the Zealots (*Judaean Scrolls*, pp. 236, 239–42, 244 ff.), then the silence about the Covenanters (Essenes?) would be explained by the same reason as that about Jesus' relations with the Zealots (see above, p. 61, n. 4).

let drop certain information, such as that about the arming of disciples and the Zealot profession of the apostle Simon, which indicates something of the nature of those facts about which Mark was reticent or evasive. However, despite such clues, the situation remains essentially problematic. For, even though the Evangelists' accounts cannot be accepted at their face value, and, on examination, are found to indicate the existence of other factors in the career of Jesus suggestive of some degree of political involvement, what that involvement was is neither apparent nor easily to be discerned. To reach any understanding of it at all, we can only move, with the greatest care, from the signposts of the known in the direction they indicate towards the unknown; in so doing we must be ever mindful that we are seeking to understand the life and death of one from whom a great religion has stemmed, which still inspires and comforts countless persons and has powerfully affected the culture and history of mankind.

The known, from which all inquiry concerning the historical Jesus must start, is the fact of his execution by the Romans for sedition. The Romans could have executed Jesus on one or more of a number of other charges; but the fact that all four Evangelists agree that he was condemned for sedition, and that the *titulus* on his cross read 'The King of the Jews', must be accepted as authentic;[1] for, in view of its embarrassing character, Christians would never have gratuitously invented such a condemnation. Now, execution on such a charge was not a unique occurrence during this period in Judaea; many Jewish patriots met such an end, including some Messianic pretenders. That the Romans executed Jesus for sedition would naturally suggest, therefore, that they regarded him as dan-

---

[1] καὶ ἦν ἡ ἐπιγραφὴ τῆς αἰτίας αὐτοῦ ἐπιγεγραμμένη Ο ΒΑΣΙΛΕΥΣ ΤῶΝ ΙΟΥΔΑΙῶΝ, Mark xv. 26: cf. Matt. xxvii. 37; Luke xxiii. 38; John xix. 19–22. See Eisler, ΙΗΣΟΥΣ ΒΑΣΙΛΕΥΣ, II, 530–2, and particularly his comment upon the request of the Jewish chief priests, which John (*ibid.*) records: 'Schließlich war die αἰτία ein amtlicher Auszug aus dem gefällten Urteil, und eine Abänderung auf Grund des Einspruchs der Hierarchen — von deren Loyalität Pilatus sicher nicht sehr überzeugt war, und von denen er wohl nicht ohne Grund annehmen durfte, daß sie sich wahrscheinlich auf die Seite der Unabhängigkeitspartei geschlagen haben würden, wenn die Römer besiegt worden wären — konnte für ihn überhaupt nicht in Betracht kommen' (p. 532); also *Messiah Jesus*, pp. 514–15. Cf. Klostermann, *Markusevangelium*, pp. 164–5; S.B. *Kommentar*, I, 1038; Guignebert, *Jésus*, p. 591; P. Winter, 'Zum Prozeß Jesu', *Das Altertum*, 9 (1963), p. 162; W. C. Van Unnik, 'Jesus the Christ', *N.T.S.* VIII (1961–2), 111.

gerous to their government in Judaea, and that they had proof of this from his actions. These obvious inferences would, in turn, suggest that the Romans had arrested him either at the time of his seditious action, or, if he had escaped, subsequently, as happened with many Jewish resistance fighters and Messianic pretenders of whom Josephus writes.[1] However, according to the Synoptic Gospels, Jesus was arrested by the Jewish authorities and handed over by them to Pilate.[2] John seems to attribute his arrest to the Romans; but since this raises difficulties about the Jewish trial of Jesus, which preceded his trial by Pilate, the general consensus of opinion has been to regard John as inaccurate on this point.[3]

All four Evangelists agree that Jesus was subjected to some form of examination or trial by the Jewish authorities before being handed over by these authorities to the Roman governor. Such a procedure would be intelligible if the Jewish authorities had a responsibility for maintaining law and order among their own people, but had not the authority to execute on a capital charge of this kind.[4] John suggests that this was so, and that the Jewish leaders had felt obliged to anticipate Roman action in suppressing Jesus.[5] If the Jewish authorities had thus arrested Jesus, it would be logical, therefore, that they should have examined him first, in order to prepare their case for handing him over to Pilate as guilty of sedition. Unfortunately, however, the nature of the Jewish trial and the charges preferred

---

[1] See pp. 110 ff.

[2] Mark xiv. 43–53, xv. 1; Matt. xxvi. 47–57, xxvii. 2; Luke xxii. 47–54, xxiii. 1. Cf. Beare, *Earliest Records of Jesus*, pp. 230–3; Eisler, ΙΗΣΟΥΣ ΒΑΣΙΛΕΥΣ, I, 468, n. 2.

[3] John xviii. 3, 12: ἡ σπεῖρα and ὁ χιλίαρχος are technical terms denoting a cohort and a tribune respectively of a Roman legion. Cf. Dodd, *Historical Tradition in the Fourth Gospel*, p. 118, n. 2; Blinzler, *Trial of Jesus*, pp. 62–72. Some scholars have seen in John's account indications of an earlier tradition, according to which the Jewish authorities and the Romans combined in arresting and executing Jesus: cf. Goguel, *Jesus*, pp. 468–9; O. Cullmann, *The State in the New Testament*, pp. 44–5; Winter, *On the Trial of Jesus*, pp. 44–50.

[4] The question whether the Jewish authorities had the power to execute on a capital charge has been much debated; the probable answer seems to be that they had to obtain the procurator's confirmation of their sentence. Cf. Schürer, *G.J.V.* I, 466–73; Klausner, *Jesus of Nazareth*, p. 160; Winter, *On the Trial of Jesus*, pp. 75–90; Förster, *Palestinian Judaism in New Testament Times*, pp. 97–8, 121–4; Sherwin-White, *Roman Society and Roman Law in the New Testament*, pp. 35–43; Jaubert, *R.H.R.* 167 (1965), pp. 3–9. See above, p. 254.

[5] John xi. 47–51, xviii. 14, 31; see pp. 16–17, 254, 318.

against Jesus are obscured, owing to the Evangelists' desire to depict the Jewish leaders as really responsible for the execution of Jesus.

It is now important to observe that since, as we have seen, Mark originally, for apologetical purposes, sought to exonerate Pilate from responsibility for the Crucifixion and represent the Jewish leaders as plotting to destroy Jesus from the very beginning of his ministry, we have no real reason for supposing that Pilate did actually regard Jesus as innocent and was forced to condemn him. If the Jewish leaders had in fact arrested Jesus, examined him and then handed him over to Pilate, charged with sedition, his subsequent execution by the Romans naturally suggests that the evidence which they produced was considered by Pilate to substantiate the charge and justify the death penalty. It is likely, also, that the Romans would already have had some knowledge of Jesus and his activities; for the Roman guard in the Antonia fortress, which overlooked the Temple, must have observed the fracas caused by Jesus' so-called 'Cleansing of the Temple', and probably some report of his Triumphal Entry had reached the Roman security officers. We may, accordingly, conclude that the undisputed fact that Pilate did sentence Jesus to death for sedition was because he was convinced that Jesus was guilty of conduct subversive to the maintenance of Roman rule in Judaea.

If we accept the Gospel record that the Jewish leaders arrested Jesus, examined him and handed him over to Pilate, accused of sedition, and that Pilate acted on their evidence and sentenced him, we have next to consider the reason for the Jewish leaders' action. That they should have handed over one of their own nationals to the occupying power, charged with seditious action against that power, is not surprising in itself; for the extant evidence indicates that the Jewish sacerdotal authorities were responsible to the Roman governor for what might be termed 'native affairs', an arrangement for which many historical parallels could be cited.[1] But the question still remains of the cause which induced the Jewish authorities to take this action against Jesus.

Although the mechanism of their action is intelligible, the fact that the Jewish leaders did take this action implies that they must have been moved by some very powerful motive. Josephus does not

---

[1] μετὰ δὲ τὴν τούτων [i.e. Herod and Archelaus] τελευτὴν ἀριστοκρατία μὲν ἦν ἡ πολιτεία, τὴν δὲ προστασίαν τοῦ ἔθνους οἱ ἀρχιερεῖς ἐπεπίστευντο (Jos. *Ant.* xx. 251). Cf. Jeremias, *Jerusalem*, ii, 17, 59; see p. 329, n. 4 above.

describe any similar action against a Messianic pretender, and from his record it would appear that it was always the Romans who initiated action against the leaders of subversive movements.[1] Moreover, according to the Christian records, the Jewish authorities only beat and imprison Peter and John for conduct prejudicial to their reputation and authority, and Stephen is stoned to death for blasphemy according to Jewish Law.[2] Consequently, if they did hand Jesus over to the Roman governor, charging him with sedition, the Jewish leaders must have regarded him as too dangerous to themselves, and the public peace, to be left to continue his activity until the Romans took action against him.[3] For what reason these leaders so regarded him is unfortunately not to be discerned from the Gospel accounts of the Jewish trial, owing to their incoherent nature, which was probably due both to ignorance of what really happened in an exclusive conclave and to apologetical concern. However, the Gospels do record an event which, despite their obvious misrepresentation of it, must surely have constituted a very serious threat to the authority of the sacerdotal aristocracy and been likely to affect its position with the Roman government.

In his so-called 'Cleansing of the Temple', Jesus was in effect attacking the sacerdotal aristocracy; for the money-changers and other traders could have operated there only under licence from the higher clergy who controlled the Temple.[4] The organisation and maintenance of the Temple and its cultus were an immense undertaking, involving enormous economic resources and the employment of a great body of officials and servants, control of which was lucrative and conferred great power and influence.[5] Moreover,

[1] See pp. 108 ff.
[2] Acts iv. 21, v. 28, 40, vii. 54 ff. It is significant that the only recorded execution of an apostle is that of James, on the order of King Agrippa I (Acts xii. 1–2). It is also notable that Jesus ben Ananias, who predicted the fall of Jerusalem four years before the war, although arrested by the magistrates (οἱ ἄρχοντες) and brought before the Roman governor, was set free after a severe scourging, and allowed to continue his prophesying (Jos. *War*, VI. 300–9).
[3] See John xi. 47–51. Cf. Brandon, *Fall of Jerusalem*, pp. 124–5; Dodd, *Historical Tradition in the Fourth Gospel*, p. 24; and below, pp. 342–3, cf. 16–17.
[4] Cf. Jeremias, *Jerusalem*, I, 54–5; S.B. *Kommentar*, I, 850–2; Winter, *On the Trial of Jesus*, p. 143; V. Eppstein in *Z.N.T.W.* 55 (1964), pp. 43, 45–6.
[5] The Temple was also a place of safe-deposit for the money and treasure of private persons. Cf. Schürer, *G.J.V.* II, 266–71; Driver, *Judaean Scrolls*, pp. 32–3; Eisler, ΙΗΣΟΥΣ ΒΑΣΙΛΕΥΣ, II, 491–9, *Messiah Jesus*, pp. 489–93; N. Q. Hamilton, 'Temple Cleansing and Temple Bank', *J.B.L.* LXXXVIII (1964), 369–70.

the money-exchange there and the selling of sacrificial animals were necessary provisions for the worshippers who came to make their offerings in obedience to the sacred Torah—indeed, Jesus must himself have used these resources when, as a Jew, he performed his religious duties there.[1] Hence, Jesus' attack on this trading system could scarcely have been an act of simple-minded indignation against the petty persons who were actually employed in what was, after all, a necessary, if not an elegant, business transaction. The attack must surely have been aimed at the high priest and other magnates who controlled the Temple and profited from its operations. That this was so appears to be recognised by Mark, when he represents 'the chief priests and the scribes and the elders' as asking Jesus in the Temple: 'By what authority are you doing these things, or who gave you this authority to do them?'[2]

This attack on the Temple trading system constituted, therefore, a most radical challenge to the authority of the sacerdotal aristocracy, and it was also a truly revolutionary act, for the high priest held his office and authority from the Romans, and was thus an essential factor of the Roman government in Judaea.[3] To challenge the rule of the high priest was thus, in effect, to challenge the Roman rule.

The Evangelists depict Jesus as making this attack alone, and as driving out the crowd of money-changers and traders, thus upsetting their business and involving them in loss of their goods, quite

[1] The payment of the annual Temple tax, which was incumbent on all male Jews, had to be converted from Roman currency into the Biblical shekel. The money-changers were there for this necessary transaction. The tradition preserved in Matt. xvii. 24–6, whatever its origin and purpose, represents Jesus as paying this Temple tax: cf. H. Montefiore in *N.T.S.* XI (1964), 60–71. According to Luke ii. 22–8, a sacrifice of two turtle-doves or pigeons was made on behalf of the infant Jesus, and the Passover lamb consumed at the Last Supper had probably been purchased and slaughtered in the Temple. Cf. Eppstein in *Z.N.T.W.* 55 (1964), pp. 43, 45.

[2] Mark xi. 27–8. 'Denn eines ist über jeden Zweifel hinaus sicher: die Hochpriester mußten aus den Vorgängen den Eindruck gewinnen, daß die lebenswichtigsten Einnahmequellen durch den Angriff auf die Tempelbanken und auf die Viehhändler aufs schwerste bedroht seien' (Eisler, ΙΗΣΟΥΣ ΒΑΣΙΛΕΥΣ, II, 499). Cf. Klausner, *Jesus of Nazareth*, pp. 313–15; Eppstein in *Z.N.T.W.* 55 (1964), pp. 56–8, who connects Jesus' attack with a dispute between the sacerdotal aristocracy and the Sanhedrin. On the Zealots' 'Cleansing of the Temple' see Hengel, *Die Zeloten*, pp. 223–6. Cf. O. Betz in *N.T.* II (1958), 134, with reference to Qumrân policy in this connection. See above, p. 249.

[3] See above, p. 330, n. 1.

unaided—indeed the Johannine writer describes him as driving out, with a whip of cords, sheep and oxen as well.[1] It takes very little reflection, however, to realise that such a depiction can scarcely approximate to the truth. Surely no man, no matter how dynamic his personality, could have succeeded unaided in driving from their place of legitimate business a company of traders when engaged with their customers, who needed their services to fulfil their religious duties. Moreover, there were Temple police, whose duty it would have been to deal promptly with such an act, calculated alike to disturb the public peace and interrupt the normal running of the Temple business.[2] But Jesus was not alone in Jerusalem. If the chronology of the Synoptic Gospels be accepted, his 'Cleansing of the Temple' took place either on the same day as, or the next day after, his Triumphal Entry into the city.[3] At this time, as the Gospels clearly show, Jesus was accompanied by his disciples and powerfully supported by the crowd. Accordingly, it is improbable that his action in the Temple was unsupported; indeed, far on the contrary, it is likely that it was achieved by the aid of an excited crowd of his supporters and was attended by violence and pillage.[4] That no mention is made in the Gospel record of the intervention of the Temple police may well be due to the fact that that record

[1] Mark xi. 15–18; Matt. xxi. 12–13; Luke xix. 45–6; John ii. 14–16.

[2] Cf. Jeremias, *Jerusalem*, II, 72–5; Eppstein in *Z.N.T.W.* 55 (1964), pp. 46–7.

[3] According to Mark xi. 11, on the day of the Triumphal Entry, Jesus entered the Temple, and, περιβλεψάμενος πάντα (reconnoitring?), left, to spend the night at Bethany. The 'Cleansing' took place on the next day (xii. 12, 15). Matthew and Luke describe the 'Cleansing' as following immediately on the Triumphal Entry. John's placing of the event at the very beginning of Jesus' ministry (ii. 13 ff.) has caused unending discussion among New Testament scholars, since it is linked with John's chronological scheme, which many prefer to the Synoptic version. However that may be, the logic of events points to the Cleansing of the Temple as constituting the decisive event which precipitated the final tragedy in Jerusalem. Cf. Klostermann, *Markusevangelium*, pp. 128–30; Dodd, *Historical Tradition in the Fourth Gospel*, pp. 300–3; Montefiore, *Josephus and the New Testament*, pp. 22–9. According to E. Trocmé ('Jésus Christ et le Temple: éloge d'un naïf', *R.H.P.R.* 44, 1964, p. 249), 'La vigoureuse intervention de Jésus dans le Temple aura valu à celui qui n'était jusque-là qu'un obscur prédicateur et guérisseur galiléen formé à l'école de Jean-Baptiste une grande notoriété à travers toute la Palestine; elle aura attiré vers lui des Zélotes et des sympathisants de ceux-ci, dont l'adhésion serait inexplicable sans un recours de Jésus à l'action directe.'

[4] It is likely that some of the money from the overturned tables would have been purloined in the excitement and confusion of the attack. Cf. Klausner, *Jesus of Nazareth*, p. 315.

has been carefully edited, as we have seen; it could, however, also indicate that the action of Jesus was so powerfully supported by his followers that the Temple police either dared not intervene or were swept aside. It is curious, too, that the Roman troops in the Antonia, who must have observed the fracas, did not intervene to restore order, as they did when Paul was being lynched in the Temple courts.[1] The fact that Mark and Luke mention, in another connection, that there was an insurrection in the city about this time, which involved bloodshed,[2] makes it legitimate to wonder whether this attack by Jesus on the Temple trading system, which was tantamount to an attack on the sacerdotal aristocracy, was a far more serious affair than the Gospels show and whether it caused those authorities to plan his arrest, and thus forestall Roman action.

If the revolutionary action initiated by Jesus in the Temple thus caused the Jewish leaders to seize him, which they were apparently enabled to do only by the defection of one of his disciples,[3] certain aspects of his subsequent examination before the high priest become intelligible. As we have seen, Mark states that the chief evidence laid against Jesus was that he had declared that he would destroy the Temple and in three days build another 'made without hands'.[4] Mark describes these witnesses as 'false', and says that their testimony failed through lack of mutual corroboration.[5] Now, as we also found reason for believing, Mark was here drawing upon a tradition of the Jerusalem Church which repudiated as 'false witness' an accusation that Jesus had threatened to destroy the Temple.[6] However, the accusation had not been completely without foundation, and it had probably arisen out of some utterance of Jesus, made on the occasion of his attack on the Temple trading system, which had been misunderstood by those who heard it and who were produced as witnesses at his trial.[7]

That Jesus was thus accused of uttering some such threat against

[1] Acts xxi. 31 ff.

[2] Mark xv. 7, ἦν δὲ ὁ λεγόμενος Βαραββᾶς μετὰ τῶν στασιαστῶν δεδεμένος, οἵτινες ἐν τῇ στάσει φόνον πεποιήκεισαν; Luke xxiii. 19, 25. Cf. Taylor, St Mark, p. 581: 'Mark speaks of the circumstances as if they were well known ("the insurrection")...' According to Matt. xxi. 10, as a result of Jesus' Triumphal Entry, ἐσείσθη πᾶσα ἡ πόλις...

[3] Mark xiv. 10–11. The statement καὶ ἐζήτει πῶς αὐτὸν εὐκαίρως παραδοῖ confirms the impression that Jesus was too powerfully supported to be arrested publicly.

[4] Mark xiv. 56–8.

[5] xiv. 59.

[6] Pp. 234 ff.

[7] See pp. 251–3.

the Temple, and that it was the initial charge when he was examined by the high priest, are understandable in the light of his action in the Temple and what we also know of Zealot policy. By attacking the system which the sacerdotal aristocracy authorised and from which it drew a considerable revenue, and by making some pronouncement of his intention to destroy the present ordering of the Temple and replace it by another more pure and holy, Jesus anticipated what the Zealots achieved in A.D. 66.[1] For, when they then gained control of the Temple, these patriots appointed a new high priest by the ancient method of drawing lots instead of appointment by the secular power, whether Roman or Herodian.[2] In this connection we may also wonder what was the attitude of Jesus towards the sacrifices which were offered daily in the Temple for the well-being of the Roman emperor and the Roman people. According to Josephus, the sacerdotal aristocracy were greatly concerned with the maintenance of this pledge of loyalty to Rome,[3] but the lower priests, who were infected by Zealotism, finally refused, in A.D. 66, to offer these sacrifices as being offensive to the God of Israel.[4] We may fairly ask whether Jesus would have endorsed these sacrifices which betokened Israel's subjection to the heathen power of Rome, or whether, in attacking the sacerdotal aristocracy, like the Zealots, he also condemned as impious their use of the Temple cultus to recommend them to their Roman patrons.

If we are right in thinking that the 'Cleansing of the Temple' led to Jesus' arrest by the Jewish authorities, and that his action had this revolutionary significance, we can understand the otherwise puzzling fact that, whereas his trial before the Sanhedrin appears to have been concerned with Jewish issues, he was delivered to Pilate charged with sedition against Rome. According to Mark and Matthew, besides his alleged threat to destroy the Temple, Jesus was also interrogated on his Messianic claims or those made about him by his followers.[5] John also supplies an illuminating detail: that the high priest questioned Jesus about his disciples and his teaching.[6] Accordingly, tendentious and unreliable as the Gospel

---

[1] 'Auch die Tempelreinigung Jesu ist, wie schon die spätere Interpretation durch Ps. 69, 10 zeigt, als eine solche Tat des Eifers für das Heiligtum zu verstehen' (Hengel, *Die Zeloten*, p. 221, cf. pp. 222–6). 'Er [Jesus] tritt als ein priesterlicher Eiferer, ein Pinehas, auf, den der Eifer um das Haus Gottes gefressen hat' (Betz in *N.T.* II, 134).

[2] See above, pp. 58, 140. [3] See p. 130, n. 5.

[4] See pp. 130 ff. [5] Mark xiv. 61; Matt. xxvi. 63.

[6] John xviii. 19.

accounts of the Jewish trial are, they indicate an intelligible sequence of events when considered in connection with the 'Cleansing of the Temple'. Alarmed by Jesus' action in the Temple, and probably unable to proceed against him openly owing to the popular support he enjoyed, the Jewish authorities, when they succeeded in capturing him, were concerned to discover the exact nature of his aims and the identity of his main supporters. From what they learned, they were able to prepare a charge of sedition and hand him over to Pilate, thus discharging their obligation to cooperate in the maintenance of the Roman government in their land, as well as removing a threat to themselves.[1]

It would appear, therefore, that Jesus' execution by the Romans resulted not from any overt and direct revolutionary act against them, but from his attack on the authority of the Jewish sacerdotal aristocracy, which was construed as dangerous to the structure of government on which Roman rule was built in Judaea. This conclusion now faces us with a twofold question: why did Jesus thus attack the Jewish hierarchy, and what was his attitude to the Roman power that lay behind the rule of the Jewish hierarchy?

To seek an answer to the first of these questions leads us back inevitably to facing the profounder issue of what was Jesus' aim that it eventually induced him to attack the sacerdotal aristocracy which governed Israel, under the aegis of Rome. Here we meet an apparent impasse, well known to New Testament scholars, that we have no certain record of Jesus' teaching, preserved in his own words and accurately describing the context in which it was given.[2] We have to content ourselves with what appears to be a reliable concise summary statement of Jesus' message in the Markan Gospel. There it is recorded that, after his baptism and the arrest of John the Baptist, Jesus came into Galilee, preaching the gospel of God, and saying, 'The time is fulfilled, and the kingdom of God is at hand; repent, and believe in the gospel.'[3] Since Mark omits to say what 'the gospel of God' (τὸ εὐαγγέλιον τοῦ θεοῦ) was, the statements 'preaching the gospel of God' and 'believe in the gospel' may reasonably be regarded as editorial, leaving the terse, but pregnant, announcement: 'The time is fulfilled, and the kingdom of God is at

---

[1] Cf. S. Zeitlin in *J.Q.R.* xxxi (1940–1), 345, 361, 362; Jaubert in *R.H.R.* 167 (1965), p. 13.

[2] Cf. Brandon, 'The Logic of New Testament Criticism', *H.J.* xlvii (1948–9), 146–7.

[3] Mark i. 15; cf. Matt. iv. 17. Cf. Guignebert, *Jésus*, pp. 394–5; Goguel, *Jesus*, pp. 311–12.

hand; repent!'[1] The statement has an authentic ring, and it is intelligible in terms of current Jewish apocalyptic.[2] The meaning of the 'kingdom of God' is admittedly undefined, and it is capable of some variety of interpretation in view of the fluidity of contemporary eschatological expectation.[3] However, if the saying was indeed addressed by Jesus to a Jewish audience, it must have involved the destiny of Israel. In other words, the coming of the kingdom of God must have meant the achievement of the prophetic tradition of Israel as the Holy People of Yahweh, vindicated for its faithfulness before the nations of the world, and freed from all mundane hindrance to devote itself wholly to the service of its God.[4] Whether the achievement of this ideal state was located in this world or implied some cosmic cataclysm is not clear; but it would certainly involve a complete change of the existing world-order, whereby Israel was in bondage to the heathen power of Rome.

The action which Jesus is represented as urging on his hearers, namely, repentance, is also understandable in terms of contemporary apocalyptic belief. It was held by many Jewish teachers at this time that Israel's state of servitude to the heathen was due to unfaithfulness, and that repentance of evil and zealous observance of the sacred Torah would prepare the way for God's deliverance.[5] The aim of Jesus, therefore, would seem to have been that of bringing his fellow-Jews to a state of moral and spiritual readiness for the near advent of the kingdom of God. How he conceived of his own role in this is not clear. An interminable discussion revolves around the meaning of the expression 'Son of man' and Jesus' use of it, and no certain answer can be given to the question whether he considered himself to be the Messiah;[6] that his followers so regarded him is, however, beyond serious doubt.[7]

Whatever may have been Jesus' conception of his own status and office, it is evident that, in pursuit of his mission to prepare Israel

---

[1] Cf. Taylor, *St Mark*, p. 167; Bultmann, *Gesch. d. syn. Trad.* p. 124.

[2] *Ibid.* p. 134; Taylor, *St Mark*, pp. 166–7.

[3] Cf. Guignebert, *Jésus*, pp. 395–428; Goguel, *Jesus*, pp. 312–13; *B.C.* I, 269–82; Manson, *Teaching of Jesus*, pp. 118–41; Taylor, *St Mark*, pp. 114–15, 166–7.

[4] Förster, *Palestinian Judaism in New Testament Times*, pp. 193–8; Schürer, *G.J.V.* II, 533–44.

[5] Cf. S.B. *Kommentar*, I, 162–5.

[6] Cf. S. Mowinckel, *He That Cometh*, pp. 346–450; Goguel, *Jesus*, pp. 572–8; Guignebert, *Jésus*, pp. 323–57; H. Conzelmann in *R.G.G.*[3], III, 629–33.

[7] See pp. 175 ff.

for the coming of the kingdom of God, he would have seen the leaders of his people, in particular the higher ranks of the hierarchy who controlled the Temple and the Sanhedrin, as constituting the major impediment to a reformed people, deserving of God's salvation.[1] To him, a man of the people and a native of provincial Galilee, the sacerdotal aristocracy, living in their great and luxurious houses in Jerusalem, must have appeared as a corrupt and worldly society who waxed fat from their control of Yahweh's Temple and their cooperation with the heathen Roman who enslaved Yahweh's people.[2] Clearly, while they ruled Israel for Caesar and to their own advantage, the nation could never be made ready for God's kingdom.

In this attitude Jesus would have been very close to the Zealots, sharing with them also their hostility to the rich and sympathy for the poor.[3] But, so far as our evidence goes, he appears to have anticipated the Zealots in attacking the sacerdotal aristocracy; for the assassination of the high priest Jonathan and other magnates by the Sicarii, during the procuratorship of Felix (52–60), seems to have marked the commencement of Zealot activity against Roman collaborators,[4] which culminated in 66 in their seizure of the Temple and the election of a new high priest. The action of Jesus in 'Cleansing the Temple' appears to have been of a more symbolic character, in that it was an assault on an aspect of the sacerdotal government, and not a personal attack on members of the higher hierarchy.[5] However, we must remember that our sources have purposely presented the matter in an idealistic manner, and that the real event must have been very different, inevitably involving violence and pillage. The Gospel account is, moreover, unsatisfactory in that no indication is given of how Jesus intended to follow up his action.[6]

---

[1] Cf. Klausner, *Jesus of Nazareth*, pp. 313–15.

[2] See the view attributed to Jesus in Luke vii. 25: ἰδοὺ οἱ ἐν ἱματισμῷ ἐνδόξῳ καὶ τρυφῇ ὑπάρχοντες ἐν τοῖς βασιλείοις εἰσίν (cf. Matt. xi. 8). On the sacerdotal aristocracy cf. Jeremias, *Jerusalem zur Zeit Jesu*, II, 40–59.

[3] See pp. 56, 199.   [4] See p. 109.

[5] See pp. 331 ff. N. Q. Hamilton (in *J.B.L.* LXXXVIII, 372) and C. Roth (in *N.T.* IV, 1960, 175–6) think that Jesus' Cleansing of the Temple was an eschatological act, inspired by Zech. xiv. 21.

[6] Mark (xi. 18–19) follows his account of the incident with a note that the chief priests sought to destroy Jesus, because they feared him (ἐφοβοῦντο γὰρ αὐτόν), for the people were astonished (ἐξεπλήσσετο) at his teaching. On the ambiguous use of the particle γάρ here see Klostermann, *Markusevangelium*, p. 118. Then follows (*v.* 19) the inconsequential note that each evening Jesus left the city—'wie ein großer Teil der Festpilger' (Kloster-

Quite obviously a protest-demonstration of this nature was not likely to change the situation; for the money-changers and other vendors would surely have returned, after their expulsion, to carry on what they were licensed to do by the high priest and his ministers. We are, accordingly, faced with the question whether Jesus intended to go on, with his supporters, to seize the rest of the Temple, especially the treasury, the control of which was one of the greatest sources of sacerdotal power. For to induce the sacerdotal aristocracy to reform its ways, so that Israel might indeed be spiritually prepared for the coming of God's kingdom, would clearly have required more than the isolated act of 'Cleansing the Temple'. As we have seen, the Gospel evidence seems to indicate that Jesus' action in the Temple coincided with an insurrection in the city, in which Zealots appear to have been involved.[1] Whether the two events were connected, that evidence does not allow us to know; but it would be reasonable to suppose that they were, although in what manner can be a matter for speculation only. The most that our sources permit us to deduce is that the Jewish authorities were unable immediately to arrest Jesus, and that they only succeeded in doing so clandestinely on the information laid by Judas Iscariot;[2] further, that the Romans had apparently put down the insurrection, after bloodshed, and had captured some of the insurgents, including one named Barabbas.[3]

That the 'Cleansing of the Temple' had only a temporary success, and that it was taken by the sacerdotal aristocracy as a declaration of war against them by Jesus, seem evident from the Gospel narrative. It appears also that Jesus feared that he might be seized by his enemies when he was without the support of the crowd or the

mann, *ibid.*). On the probable 'telescoping' of the events which led to the arrest of Jesus see M. Black, 'The Arrest and Trial of Jesus and the Date of the Last Supper', *New Testament Essays* (ed. A. J. B. Higgins), pp. 19 ff.

[1] See p. 334, n. 2. There is much reason for thinking that Barabbas, and the λησταί who were crucified with Jesus, were Zealots: cf. Hengel, *Die Zeloten*, pp. 30, 347–8; Cullmann, *The State in the New Testament*, pp. 47–8; Stendahl in *Peake's Commentary*[2], 694 k; Klausner, *Jesus of Nazareth*, p. 347; Driver, *Judaean Scrolls*, p. 246; see below, p. 351. Although Mark xv. 7 does not state a coincidence, it would seem that the insurrection was of very recent occurrence.   [2] Mark xi. 18, 27–32, xii. 12, xiv. 10–11.

[3] Mark xv. 6–7. Eisler believed that Jesus and his followers did seize the Temple and were eventually expelled by the Romans (ΙΗΣΟΥΣ ΒΑΣΙΛΕΥΣ, II, 476–515, *Messiah Jesus*, pp. 480–506). He relates the curious passage in Luke xiii. 1, concerning the Galilaeans whose blood Pilate mingled with their sacrifices, to this operation.

main body of his supporters; for he left the city at nightfall.[1] For some unexplained reason, if we accept the Gospel chronology, he continued to stay on at Jerusalem after what seems to have been an abortive coup in the Temple.[2] By the time of the Passover, Jesus appears to have been conscious that his position was becoming very critical, and he was filled with foreboding.[3] It is difficult to interpret the pattern of events which led from the Last Supper to the arrest in Gethsemane. If the Gospel narrative is to be trusted, for some unexplained and not obvious reason, after the Supper within the city, Jesus and a number of his disciples passed out in the dark through one of the gates into the country beyond.[4] The movement must have been prearranged, since Judas Iscariot knew of it and was able to inform the Jewish leaders in time to allow their organisation of an arresting force.[5] What the intention of Jesus was in going to Gethsemane and remaining there is unknown.[6] The fact that he made sure that his disciples were armed is significant. Luke, who records this fact, endeavours to reduce its significance by saying that Jesus did so in order to fulfil a prophecy, and that he considered two swords enough for this purpose.[7] The ascription of such an

[1] Mark xi. 19.
[2] The incidents related in Mark xi. 20–31 come as an anticlimax to the 'Cleansing of the Temple': see p. 338, n. 6.
[3] Mark xiv. 18 ff.
[4] 'Das Hinausgehen an den Ölberg in der Passahnacht war kein Verstoß gegen die Halakha' (S.B. Kommentar, I, 992).
[5] Cf. Mark xiv. 10–11, 43. On the question of Judas' motive, cf. Guignebert, Jésus, pp. 549–58.
[6] There is some ground for asking whether the saying in Mark xiv. 27–8, about the general consternation caused by the smiting of the shepherd and the scattering of the sheep (πάντες σκανδαλισθήσεσθε), and the prophecy that Jesus would lead (προάξω) the disciples into Galilee, may not preserve some memory of Jesus' intention of withdrawing to the desert places of Galilee after the failure of his coup in Jerusalem, thus following the Zealot pattern. 'Aber besagt hier eine unerfüllt gebliebene Weissagung: der Hirt wird an der Spitze der Schafe siegreich nach Galiläa ziehen (vgl. Jo. 10. 4), um dort das Gottesreich aufzurichten (J. Weiss, Hauck vgl. Lohmeyer, Galiläa und Jerusalem 1936)?' (Klostermann, Markusevangelium, p. 149). Cf. Lightfoot, Locality and Doctrine in the Gospels, pp. 52 ff.; Taylor, St Mark, pp. 548–9; Elliott-Binns, Galilean Christianity, pp. 35, 41. C. F. Evans, 'I will go before you into Galilee', J.T.S. v, n.s. (1954), 13–15, thinks that the saying has reference to the evangelisation of the Gentiles; but he is not clear as to whether he attributes the idea to Jesus or Mark.
[7] Luke xxii. 35–8. This record of Jesus' arming of his disciples, or rather his checking on their armament, has greatly troubled commentators. It is

artificial fulfilment of an obscure passage of Isaiah to Jesus on such an occasion does no credit to Jesus and lowers our estimation of the sensibility of Luke. With how many swords the disciples were armed is immaterial; it is scarcely likely that it was only two, and the armament of the party sent to arrest Jesus suggests that Judas had given warning that the disciples were well armed and that armed resistance was to be expected.[1]

illuminating to give some examples of the variety of views. Creed (*St Luke*, p. 270), after discussing the difficulties inherent in the passage, concluded, rather lamely, that *v.* 36 is to be interpreted as a warning of coming disaster. Klostermann, *Das Lukasevangelium* (Tübingen, 1929), p. 214, recognised that 'schwerlich sind hier μάχαιραι dolchartige Messer zur Schlachtung des Pascha-lammes, trotz Chrysostomus, Hofmann, Zahn'. 'It is Luke who records the enigmatic conversation about the swords, which, whatever else it means, certainly presupposes bitter hostility between the Disciples and their fellow-countrymen' (Manson, *Studies*, p. 60). 'Their [the disciples'] previous instructions are cancelled, and they are told to safeguard their lives by worldly means in view of the crisis of the arrest of Jesus. It is not probable that Jesus wanted swords to be carried to prevent a private assassination, or to identify himself and his followers with revolutionary "transgressors"' (G. W. H. Lampe in *Peake's Commentary*[2], 733*e*). P. Martinetti, *Jésus Christ et le Christianisme*, p. 207, thought that Jesus did not intend to lead an armed revolt, 'mais se défendre d'une embûche que les prêtres du Temple pourraient lui tendre'. 'He [Jesus] seemed to imagine that he needed *armed* protection against his enemies' (Klausner, *Jesus of Nazareth*, p. 331). 'Das Wort gehört also in eine ganz andere Periode, in der Jesus seine Jünger — gewisse geraume Zeit nach der ersten Aussendung —, für eine längere Wanderung ausgerüstet und bewaffnet zu sehen wünscht' (Eisler, ΙΗΣΟΥΣ ΒΑΣΙΛΕΥΣ, II, 267, see pp. 267–70, *Messiah Jesus*, pp. 368–70). 'There is much to be said for the suggestion that some stray Zealot phrases have somehow intruded their way into the Gospel record' (Beare, *Earliest Records of Jesus*, p. 229). Cf. Windisch, *Der messianische Krieg*, pp. 47–9; Meyer, *Ursprung*, I, 182–3; Cullmann, *The State in the New Testament*, pp. 31–4.

[1] According to Eisler, the disciples had two swords each, one probably being a *sica*: 'Die Jünger haben bezeichnenderweise die Aufforderung Jesu nicht abgewartet. Sie antworten, indem sie ihm, — jeder von ihnen natürlich! — zwei Schwerter vorweisen' (ΙΗΣΟΥΣ ΒΑΣΙΛΕΥΣ, II, 268 and n. 2, cf. *Messiah Jesus*, p. 369; *Flavius Josephus-Studien*, I, n. 104 to p. 45). On Jewish swords or daggers at this time, cf. Driver, *Judaean Scrolls*, pp. 183–7. For a survey of the various interpretations advanced by commentators of ἱκανόν ἐστιν see Klostermann, *Lukasevangelium*, pp. 214–15. Note the significance of Jesus' recorded question to his captors: 'Ὡς ἐπὶ λῃστὴν [Zealot?] ἐξήλθατε μετὰ μαχαιρῶν καὶ ξύλων συλλαβεῖν με; (Mark xiv. 48.) Cf. Winter, *On the Trial of Jesus*, p. 49; Klausner, *Jesus of Nazareth*, pp. 336–7; Bultmann, *Gesch. d. syn. Trad.* p. 305.

What, then, we must ask, was the intention of Jesus that night, accompanied as he was by armed followers? It would be natural to presume that he intended to resist arrest, if an attempt should then be made. If this were so, it would suggest the view that Jesus felt safe in the daytime, when supported by the crowd, and that he still had some hope of achieving his purpose, whatever it was, in Jerusalem. Alternatively, it could be that he had realised that the tide of events was turning against him, and that he was hesitating whether to give up and withdraw to Galilee.[1] Whatever his intention was during those dark hours in Gethsemane, it is certain that armed resistance was offered to the force sent to arrest him. But what the extent of this resistance was, it is impossible to know. The Evangelists depict it as one isolated act of a sword-stroke, and say that Jesus intervened to stop any further action.[2] They may well be right: except for one of their number who reacted quickly, the disciples may have been confounded by a sudden and determined assault, and Jesus, realising that resistance was hopeless, surrendered himself. The possibility must be allowed, however, in view of the apologetical concern of the Gospel writers, which we have noted, that the resistance was of a more serious nature, even though it proved ineffective.[3]

The evidence at our disposal points, therefore, to the execution of Jesus as having its original cause in the reaction provoked by his attack on the sacerdotal aristocracy, whose chief members were responsible to the Romans for native affairs. This attack was motivated by Jesus' desire to prepare Israel spiritually for the advent of the kingdom of God. The Jewish aristocracy, through their cooperation with the Roman occupying power, appeared to him as the chief obstacle to the achievement of his mission. With popular support, he had ultimately challenged its leaders by attacking the Temple trading system, from which they derived a considerable revenue.

---

[1] See p. 340, n. 6. The account of the Agony in Gethsemane seems to preserve the memory that Jesus was then faced with a grievous decision about his future action (Mark xiv. 34–6). Cf. Klostermann, *Markusevangelium*, pp. 150–1.

[2] See above, pp. 306, 317.

[3] See above, p. 306. 'Auch sind hier und dort kleinere Züge in apologetischem Interesse angefügt: so Mk. 14, 48 f., der Vorwurf der nächtlichen Verhaftung, Mt. 26, 52–54 das Verbot des bewaffneten Widerstandes und die Betonung der Freiwilligkeit der Hingabe Jesu (ein Motiv, das bei Joh 10, 18; 18, 7; 19, 11 noch stärker hervortritt)' (Bultmann, *Gesch. d. syn. Trad.* p. 305).

Successful for the moment, he fell a victim to the counter-attack of these leaders, who understandably regarded him as endangering the social and political structure of the state, and, consequently, had no compunction in handing him over to Pilate as guilty of sedition. In all this Jesus was primarily concerned with those who were the religious leaders of his own people; for, in his estimation, they should have been foremost in preparing the nation for Yahweh's saving intervention. But now we must ask, what was Jesus' attitude to the Roman power which stood behind these Jewish leaders and demanded their cooperation in the subjection of Israel?

The Gospels record no contact of Jesus with the Romans until he was brought before Pilate charged with sedition against Rome. While he lived in Galilee, he might indeed have had no dealings with Roman officials or soldiers, since the country was governed by Herod Antipas.[1] However, as a pious Jew, he must often have visited Jerusalem, where he could not have failed to notice evidence of Roman rule that affronted his patriotic instincts, such as, for example, the presence of Roman troops watching Jewish worship in the Temple from the walls of the Antonia fortress.[2] Nor could he have avoided using Roman coins, stamped with the effigy of the emperor and bearing various pagan emblems.[3] Moreover, as we have already noted, in his boyhood he must have heard of Judas of Galilee who had suffered martyrdom in A.D. 6 for opposing the payment of tribute to Rome because it meant acknowledging a heathen prince as lord of Israel instead of Yahweh. As a child, he had probably also seen the damage done by the Romans to the Temple in the disturbances of 4 B.C.[4] As a man, he must have been well acquainted with the brutal realities of Roman rule; Luke tells of his being informed of those Galilaeans 'whose blood Pilate had mingled with their sacrifices',[5] and he could not have been ignorant

[1] Cf. Schürer, *G.J.V.* I, 431–49.
[2] Cf. Jos. *War*, v. 238–45: 'a Roman cohort was permanently quartered there, and at the festivals took up positions in arms around the porticoes to watch the people and repress any insurrectionary movement' (trans. H. St J. Thackeray, Loeb *Josephus*, III, 277).
[3] καὶ λέγει αὐτοῖς· τίνος ἡ εἰκὼν αὕτη καὶ ἡ ἐπιγραφή; οἱ δὲ εἶπαν αὐτῷ· Καίσαρος (Mark xii. 16). 'Man sieht, solch ein Denar ist Machtsymbol und Kultsymbol zugleich' (Stauffer, *Christus und die Caesaren*, p. 136). On coinage in circulation in Palestine at this period cf. Schürer, *G.J.V.* II, 53–5; for examples see Reifenberg, *Israel's History in Coins*, pp. 24, 29; Frontispiece and Plate I. Cf. B. Kanael, 'Ancient Jewish Coins and their Historical Importance', *B.A.* XXVI (1963), 54–5.
[4] See p. 29. [5] Luke xiii. 1–2: see above, pp. 65, 78.

of Pilate's other offensive acts, nor unconcerned by their affront to his ancestral religion.[1] Finally, his inclusion of a Zealot among his Apostles has its own unmistakable witness, as we have seen.

In seeking more explicit evidence of Jesus' attitude to the Romans, we must begin by noticing the significance of two facts. The first is that the Synoptic Gospels agree in representing Jesus as announcing that the kingdom of God was at hand, and as regarding himself as having a crucial role in preparing for its advent.[2] Now, whatever may have been his exact conception of the kingdom of God and the mode of its establishment, there can be no doubt that Jesus looked forward to the achievement of an apocalyptic situation that necessarily involved the elimination of the Roman government in Judaea. Further, even though he directed his attack against the Jewish leaders, since he saw these men as impeding Israel's spiritual preparation for the kingdom of God, behind them, and the authority they wielded, he must have known lay the power of Rome. Accordingly, it would seem inevitable that Jesus must have reckoned with the fact that his mission would ultimately bring him into conflict with the Roman government in Judaea. That he did foresee this seems to be attested by the second fact alluded to above for our consideration. It is the ascription to Jesus of a saying which was probably of Zealot origin, as we have seen: 'If any man would come after me, let him deny himself and take up his cross and follow me.'[3] Crucifixion was a Roman punishment, and, as the records of Josephus show, hundreds of Jewish patriots suffered the penalty during the period A.D. 6–70.[4] Unless this saying is a prophecy *ex eventu*, which the Evangelists have assigned to Jesus, it means that

---

[1] See above, pp. 77–8.

[2] Cf. Goguel, *Jesus*, pp. 310 ff.; Guignebert, *Jésus*, pp. 394 ff.; Klausner, *Jesus of Nazareth*, pp. 398 ff.; Conzelmann in *R.G.G.*[3], III, 641–5.

[3] Mark viii. 34: see above, p. 57. There is no justification for Stauffer's assertion, making reference to Jer. xxvii. 6 ff., 'so verkündet Jesus im Zeitalter der römischen Fremdherrschaft: Der Kampf gegen den Kaiser ist ein frevelhafter und aussichtsloser Kampf gegen den Gott, der ihn berufen hat, ist Theomachie!' (*Christus und die Caesaren*, Hamburg, 1952, p. 116.) The only piece of evidence he cites in support of his view is the parable given in Luke xix. 11–27, which he interprets as being based on Augustus' confirmation of Archelaus' claim to lordship over Judaea. He argues therefrom that it represents Jesus' view that 'der Kaiser von Gottes Gnaden ist die letzte geschichtliche Quelle aller politischen Legitimität'. It is passing strange that one who held such a view of the Roman emperor should have been regarded by Jews as the Messiah of Israel and executed by Pilate as a rebel against Rome!

[4] See above, p. 1.

Jesus foresaw that his mission was such that it could, or would, embroil him with the Romans and result in his dying the death which they inflicted on rebels.

The witness of these facts leads us on to consider what constitutes the most obvious passage in the Synoptic Gospels concerning the attitude of Jesus to the supreme issue of Roman-Jewish relations at that time, namely, the payment of tribute. As we have seen, the episode concerned first appears in the Markan Gospel, where it plays an essential part in that document's apologetical theme by representing Jesus as endorsing the Jewish obligation to pay tribute to Rome.[1] According to Mark, the question 'Is it lawful to pay tribute to Caesar, or not? Should we pay, or should we not?' was put to Jesus by certain of the Pharisees and the Herodians, 'to entrap him in his talk' (ἵνα αὐτὸν ἀγρεύσωσιν λόγῳ).[2] The implication of Mark's explanatory comment here is that, if Jesus had expressed himself as being in any way opposed to the payment of tribute, his enemies would have denounced him as teaching sedition. Since Mark's purpose was to present Jesus as innocent of the charge of sedition on which he was condemned, the answer he represents Jesus as making is evidently intended to be understood as refuting such a charge; in other words, the answer of Jesus is meant to prove that he agreed that the Jews should pay the Roman tribute. The attempt made by some scholars to represent Jesus' answer as a piece of justified sophistry, namely, that, if the Jews were prepared to benefit by the use of Caesar's coinage in trade, they should pay for it by contributing to the support of the government that made it possible, does credit neither to Jesus nor to the realities of the historical situation.[3] If Jesus had made such an answer, surely his

[1] Pp. 224, 270–1.

[2] Mark xii. 13: cf. Klostermann, *Markusevangelium*, p. 123. Luke (xx. 20) is more explicit about the political aspect of the incident: spies (ἐγκαθέτους) are sent to trap him, ὥστε παραδοῦναι αὐτὸν τῇ ἀρχῇ καὶ τῇ ἐξουσίᾳ τοῦ ἡγεμόνος. Cf. Creed, *St Luke*, p. 247.

[3] Cf. Eisler, ΙΗΣΟΥΣ ΒΑΣΙΛΕΥΣ, ΙΙ, 199–201, *Messiah Jesus*, pp. 334–5; Taylor, *St Mark*, p. 480; Manson, *Jesus and the Non-Jews* (University of London, 1955), p. 9; Filson, *New Testament History*, pp. 131–2; Stauffer, *Christus und die Caesaren*, p. 142. Besides this line of interpretation, two others have been put forward by those scholars who take the episode in its extant form as authentic: (i) that Jesus did on this occasion endorse the Jews' obligation to pay tribute to Rome, and that his ruling lost him popular support; cf. Klausner, *Jesus of Nazareth*, p. 318; Olmstead, *Jesus: in the Light of History*, pp. 214–15; Stauffer, p. 143: 'Das ist keine kleinbürgerliche Loyalitätsverpflichtung auf die nächste beste Obrigkeit...

questioners would have been quick to point out that he was evading the issue, and that all Jews, himself included, were obliged to use Roman coins, bearing the emperor's image, to purchase the common necessities of life. Moreover, the answer 'Render to Caesar the things that are Caesar's, and to God the things that are God's' would not have had, in Jewish ears, the *double entendre* that has sometimes been suggested. The devout Jew of that time had no doubt what were the things of God; and, conversely, what were not the things of Caesar: pre-eminent among these things would have been the Holy Land of Israel and its resources. Indeed, the very essence of the Zealot case against the payment of tribute was that it meant giving to Caesar what belonged to God.[1]

Accordingly, we may legitimately ask whether, behind Mark's apologetical use of the Tribute Money episode, there may not be a traditional saying of Jesus concerning the issue which originally had quite a different meaning from that which it is intended to have in its Markan setting. For, on reflection, it is quite obvious that Jesus could not have exercised his public ministry of preparing Israel for the coming of God's kingdom without having to make clear his attitude to the payment of the Roman tribute.[2] Moreover, it is also

Das ist das weltpolitische Ja zum Imperium Romanum, zum Imperium des fremden Herrschervolkes mit dem polytheistischen Imperator an der Spitze, ein ebenso unromantisches wie undialektisches Ja im Geiste der prophetischen und apokalyptischen Geschichtstheologie'; (ii) that Jesus, faced with a maliciously devised dilemma, cleverly avoided impaling himself on either of its horns—'Jesus entzieht sich trotz seines Mutes und seiner doch wohl antirömischer Gesinnung dem Dilemma mit einer Antwort, die sich gleich weit von der relativen Staatsfreundlichkeit des römischen Bürgers Paulus, wie von revolutionärem Zelotentum hält' (Klostermann, *Markusevangelium*, p. 124). The attempt, sometimes made, to argue that Jesus asked to see a coin because he would not carry an image-bearing object, is adequately answered by Goguel, 'Jésus et le Messianisme politique: Examen de la théorie de M. Robert Eisler', *Revue historique*, CLXII (1929), 42–3. H. Loewe in his 'Render unto Caesar', while rightly stressing that 'the question of tribute-paying was regarded as a religious and not as a political one' (p. 66), misses, despite the interesting material he reviews, the real issue, since he neglects to consider the passage in its original context, i.e. the Markan Gospel. Hengel (*Die Zeloten*, p. 346), although he recognises that 'man wollte Jesus als politischen Revolutionär festlegen', does not appreciate the complexity of the problem underlying Mark's account of the incident. Cf. Sherwin-White, *Roman Society and Roman Law in the New Testament*, pp. 176–7.

[1] See above, pp. 33 ff.
[2] This consideration constitutes a fatal objection to the argument of those scholars who maintain that, from the time that he gave his ruling on the

necessary to conclude that he would never have been popularly regarded as the Messiah, if he had ruled that the Jews had rightly to pay tribute to Rome. Consequently, there is much reason for seeing in the words 'Render to Caesar the things that are Caesar's, and to God the things that are God's' an authentic pronouncement of Jesus on this fundamental issue of Jewish religious and political life.[1] It was, indeed, a saying of which any Zealot would have approved, because, as we have seen, for the Zealot there was no doubt that God owned the land of Israel, not Caesar. When this saying of Jesus is laid alongside even the prejudiced report which Josephus gives of the teaching of Judas of Galilee, the founder of Zealotism, the similarity of outlook is striking. According to Josephus, Judas upbraided his countrymen 'as cowards for consenting to pay tribute to Rome and tolerating mortal masters, after having God for their lord'.[2] The only notable difference is that Josephus reports that Judas also urged his countrymen to revolt.[3] But here we have to face the unavoidable question: did Jesus, in seeking to fulfil his

Tribute, Jesus lost his popularity with the crowd (see p. 345, n. 3). For such a contention implies that Jesus had never before been questioned on this most burning issue of contemporary Jewish life.

[1] According to Bultmann (*Gesch. d. syn. Trad.* p. 25), 'Vielmehr liegt ein einheitlich konzipiertes und ausgezeichnet geformtes Apophthegma vor, bei dem man nur in V. 13 mit der redaktionellen Arbeit des Mk. zu rechnen hat. An Gemeindebildung zu denken, liegt m. E. kein Grund vor.' If Bultmann is right in thinking that *vv.* 14–17 constitute an authentic whole, the significance of the passage becomes even greater; for it would mean that Mark deliberately added *v.* 13 in order to make an authentic tradition conform to his own apologetical theme at this point, namely, of representing Jesus as endorsing the Jewish obligation to pay tribute to Rome. It does not appear that the fragment of the unknown gospel, preserved on the Egerton Papyrus 2, contains a more authentic version of the Tribute Money episode. In the passage concerned, those who 'tempt' Jesus ask: λέγε οὖν ἡμῖν· ἔξὸν τοῖς βασιλεῦσιν [ἀποδοῦ]ναι τὰ ἀνήκοντα τῇ ἀρχῇ; ἀπ[οδῶμεν αὐ]τοῖς ἢ μή; This question seems to be a more generalised form of Mark xii. 14. The answer of Jesus (ἐμβρειμησάμενος), quoting Isa. xxix. 13, is equally lacking in pertinency. Cf. H. Idris Bell and T. C. Skeat, *Fragments of an Unknown Gospel and Other Early Christian Papyri* (British Museum, 1935), pp. 10–13, 20–3, 26–7.

[2] See above, p. 31. 'Weit entfernt davon, die Zinsbarkeit gegenüber dem Cäsar zu billigen, steht Jesus ganz auf seiten Judah's des Galiläers: aber er geht weit über ihn hinaus, indem er von seinen Jüngern, von den Bürgern des kommenden Gottesreiches verlangt, daß sie sich nicht nur von der Knechtschaft des Cäsar, sondern vor allem auch von der Knechtschaft des Mammon lossagen' (Eisler, ΙΗΣΟΥΣ ΒΑΣΙΛΕΥΣ, II, 201; cf. *Messiah Jesus*, p. 335). [3] See p. 31.

mission, ever make any hostile reference to, or recommend any hostile action against, the Roman power which treated Yahweh's Holy Land as its own possession?

In view of the apologetical concern of each of the Evangelists, varying though their individual motives were, it is not surprising that no mention should be made by them of any anti-Roman utterance or action of Jesus, if indeed any such had occurred. However, Luke, who, as we have noted, was not so circumspect as Mark, does specify the charges preferred by the Jewish leaders against Jesus, and they are very significant. He states that these leaders informed Pilate, saying, 'We found this man perverting our nation (διαστρέφοντα τὸ ἔθνος ἡμῶν), and forbidding us to give tribute to Caesar (κωλύοντα φόρους Καίσαρι διδόναι), and saying that he himself is Christ a king.' Later they assert: 'He stirs up the people (ἀνασείει τὸν λαόν) teaching throughout all Judea, from Galilee even to this place.'[1] Luke, of course, intends his readers to understand that these accusations were malicious; but they have an air of verisimilitude, and they are logically interrelated. Thus, the first accusation concerns the general effect of Jesus and his teaching, namely, that it was revolutionary. The next two charges specify the two chief ways in which 'he stirs up the people': he denounces the tribute and claims a Messianic role that is political in character. Now, the significant thing about these two charges is that they were evidently not without some apparent grounds of justification. As we have just seen, it is probable that Jesus did pronounce on the vital issue of the tribute in the saying 'Render to Caesar the things that are Caesar's, and to God the things that are God's', and that this saying was naturally taken, as doubtless it was intended, to rule that the payment of tribute to Caesar was an act of disloyalty to Yahweh. The accusation

---

[1] Luke xxiii. 2, 5. We may justly wonder how Luke, after emphasising in xx. 20 (see p. 345, n. 2) that Jesus' opponents specifically sought to embroil him with the Romans on the Tribute issue and that Jesus had publicly endorsed the payment, did not see the problem involved in attributing such an accusation to the Jewish leaders in xxiii. 2. The explanation undoubtedly is that, in an endeavour to improve on Mark's apologetic by further demonstrating Jesus' loyalty to Rome and the malignity of the Jews, he did not notice the mutual illogicality of these statements. The nature of the charges brought against Jesus, according to Luke, is especially significant in the light of Mark's reticence about them (xv. 3): see above, pp. 257 ff. Cf. Manson, *Studies*, p. 62; G. W. H. Lampe in *Peake's Commentary*[2], 733*i* ('Lk. alone, either by inference from the Marcan narrative as a whole, or from a non-Marcan source, records the actual charge').

that Jesus claimed to be the Messiah, and that this was understood as embodying a claim to royalty, clearly had enough apparent justification to give point to the *titulus* placed on the cross: 'The King of the Jews.'[1]

It is natural to seek in the Gospels some indication, at least, of apparent justification for this accusation of political Messianism that was thus brought against Jesus. One notable possibility at once suggests itself, namely, the Triumphal Entry into Jerusalem. The Synoptic Gospels, in a truly surprising way, describe Jesus as purposely planning an entry into the Holy City which would fulfil a prophecy concerning the entry of a Messianic King.[2] If the tradition

---

[1] See above, p. 254.

[2] Mark xi. 1–7; Matt. xxi. 1–7; Luke xix. 29–35. Cf. Taylor, *St Mark*, pp. 451–3; Klostermann, *Markusevangelium*, p. 126 ('Der Einzug Jesu in Jerusalem erscheint als eine messianische Demonstration auf Grund der Weissagung Zach 9.9... So hätte nicht nur das Volk in Jesu Einzug in Jerusalem die Proklamierung zum Messias gesehen, sondern auch Jesus selbst mindestens den Anlaß... dazu gegeben, indem er auf dem Esel der messianischen Weissagung vom Oelberg her einzieht'); Meyer, *Ursprung*, I, 163 ('Offenbar hoffte er [*sc.* Jesus], durch eine große Demonstration seiner Anhänger die Massen in der Stadt, in die ja die Kunde von seiner Wirksamkeit schon früher gelangt war (2, 8. 22. 7. 1), mit sich fortzureißen und hier die leitende Stellung zu gewinnen'); S.B. *Kommentar*, I, 842–4; Klausner, *Jesus of Nazareth*, pp. 309–10; Eisler, ΙΗΣΟΥΣ ΒΑΣΙΛΕΥΣ, II, 459–63, *Messiah Jesus*, pp. 471–3; H. P. Kingdom, 'Messiahship and the Crucifixion', *Studia Evangelica*, III, 83; Beare, *Earliest Records of Jesus*, pp. 204–5. The attempt of some scholars to lessen the significance of the incident by stressing that an ass is a humble mount, and, therefore, that Jesus had arranged the matter as a demonstration of his humility and mild intention, is beside the point: the prophecy of Zech. ix. 9 foretold the coming of the Messianic King; the provision of the ass was necessary, if the fulfilment of the prophecy was to be acted out. 'Auf Grund von Sach 9. 9 war schon bei den Tannaiten der Esel zu dem Messiastier geworden' (H.-W. Kuhn, 'Das Reittier Jesu in der Einzugsgeschichte des Mc-Evangeliums', *Z.N.T.W.* 50, 1959, p. 88; cf. S.B. *Kommentar*, I, 842–4; Mowinckel, *He That Cometh*, pp. 63, 94, 171, 177, 179, 336 (for a later rabbinic tradition that the Messiah would come riding on an ass, and not on the clouds of heaven, if Israel were unworthy)). If the tradition just mentioned was current in the time of Jesus, his action could also be interpreted as a protest against the unworthiness of Israel's leaders, whom he had come to challenge. F. F. Bruce has made the interesting suggestion ('The Book of Zechariah and the Passion Narrative', *B.J.R.L.* 43, 1961, p. 347) that Jesus sought in this manner to present himself in Jerusalem 'not as a warrior-Messiah but as a peaceful prince—more precisely, as Israel's shepherd-king'. But, if this were so, Jesus took a grave risk of being misunderstood—as indeed he was by the crowd.

upon which they drew was authentic, this means that Jesus' entry into Jerusalem, riding on an ass, accompanied by his disciples, was not an ordinary happening that unexpectedly evoked the spontaneous enthusiasm of the crowd, which hailed him as the Messiah; but that it was a carefully planned demonstration by Jesus of his assumption of Messiahship. As such, his action must have been calculated to challenge both the Jewish leaders and the Romans; for, in the current ideology, Messiahship had an essentially political connotation, of which Jesus would surely have been aware. The demonstration, moreover, was followed, according to the Synoptic record, by the 'Cleansing of the Temple',[1] which constituted, as we have seen, an attack on the sacerdotal aristocracy, whose members were responsible to the Roman governor for the conduct of native affairs.

Our inquiry so far seems to have led us to certain reasonably based conclusions of considerable significance concerning the chain of events that led to Jesus' execution by the Romans, and it would be well now to recapitulate them. Believing that the kingdom of God was at hand, Jesus sought to prepare his fellow-Jews morally and spiritually for membership of this kingdom, whose advent would achieve Israel's destiny as the Elect People of God. Two great obstacles stood in the way of the fulfilment of his mission: the Jewish sacerdotal aristocracy and the Roman government. Jesus seems to have been more concerned with the former, probably because its members were Jews and the traditional leaders of Israel. Consequently, he saw their mode of life and abuse of power as constituting a scandalous contradiction of his ideal of a holy people, ready and prepared for the coming of God's kingdom. Their power, therefore, had to be challenged, and perhaps broken. How long Jesus took in coming to this conclusion is not clear;[2] but our sources point to his finally making a decision to go to Jerusalem at the Passover, for action that he believed would be fateful. He carefully planned an entry into the city, which was designed to demonstrate his Messianic role. This challenging action was quickly followed by his attack on the Temple trading system. The Gospels do not permit us to know whether this 'Cleansing of the Temple' was intended to be the pre-

[1] See above, p. 333.
[2] It may be significant that Mark places the first prophecy of Jesus' rejection and destruction by the Jewish leaders immediately after the Caesarea Philippi Confession (viii. 31), and the next (x. 33–4) in the foreboding account of the journey to Jerusalem (x. 32), which is clearly intended to convey a sense of crisis.

lude to further action against the hierarchy, although this would seem to be its logical implication. So far as our evidence shows, the 'Cleansing of the Temple' was not followed by measures designed to prevent the traffic from restarting; yet it appears that the Jewish leaders did not then feel strong enough to arrest Jesus publicly. The operation in the Temple apparently took place about the same time as an insurrection elsewhere in the city, which the Romans suppressed. This rising was undoubtedly instigated by the Zealots, and it is difficult to believe that it was quite unconnected with Jesus' action in the Temple, although the Gospels mention no connection. The Gospel record gives the impression that the action which Jesus had initiated by coming to Jerusalem proved in some way abortive, and that, by the time of the Passover, Jesus had to take precautions against a surprise attack by the Jewish authorities.

What plans Jesus had, when he was arrested, are unknown. The fact that he was taken by night, after his rendezvous had been betrayed to the Jewish leaders by Judas, suggests that he had no intention of surrendering himself voluntarily, as a kind of sacrificial victim, to his enemies. The latter, whose authority had been gravely challenged by him, proceeded, as we have seen, in a manner that is intelligible in terms of their responsibility to the Roman government for Jewish affairs. After his arrest, they examined him to obtain all possible information about his intentions, and probably the identity and strength of his followers, preparatory to delivering him to Pilate as guilty of subversive views and actions. That Pilate sentenced him to death for sedition was the logical sequel to the case submitted by the Jewish authorities—that he also ordered him to be crucified between two λῃσταί, who were probably Zealots, suggests that he connected Jesus with the insurrection that had coincided with Jesus' activities in Jerusalem.[1]

---

[1] Mark xv. 27; Matt. xxvii. 38. Luke xxiii. 32, 39 calls them κακοῦργοι, not λῃσταί, as do the other two Evangelists. It would seem unwise to see any particular significance in the words of the so-called 'Penitent Thief', ὅτι ἐν τῷ αὐτῷ κρίματι εἶ (xxiii. 40), because his subsequent words are clearly designed by Luke to make him attest Jesus' innocence and lead on to the promise, with its curious eschatology, in *v.* 43. Cf. Goguel, *Jesus*, p. 539. John's καὶ μετ' αὐτοῦ ἄλλους δύο ἐντεῦθεν καὶ ἐντεῦθεν, μέσον δὲ τὸν Ἰησοῦν (xix. 18, cf. xix. 32) is interesting: does the silence about their being λῃσταί here point to the author's perfunctory inclusion of an incident related in the Synoptic record, or could it indicate that he knew that these two crucified with Jesus were his followers? Cf. Eisler, ΙΗΣΟΥΣ ΒΑΣΙΛΕΥΣ, II, 525–6, *Messiah Jesus*, pp. 510–11; Klostermann, *Markusevangelium*, p.

In seeking to trace out, from the tendentious material at our disposal, the probable course of events which ended with Jesus' execution as a rebel against the Roman government in Judaea, we have not yet reckoned with the factor of popular reaction to the personality and teaching of Jesus. For it is obvious on reflection that Jesus may not have been able to control the response of either his disciples or the masses to his message. If he had taken over the mission of John the Baptist, being regarded as his charismatic successor, in preparing Israel for the coming of the kingdom of God,[1] and if, further, he had acquired the reputation of a 'wonder-worker' (γόης),[2] the enthusiasm and expectancy of his disciples and the populace must soon have begun to provide an impetus to his movement which he would have found difficult to resist, even if he had so wished. The Gospels seem, despite their apologetic concern, to preserve some memory of a gathering Messianic crisis, which has recently been described as the 'revolt in the desert'.[3] It appears to

165; Cullmann, *The State in the New Testament*, pp. 47–8; Hengel, *Die Zeloten*, pp. 265, n. 4, 347; Driver, *Judaean Scrolls*, p. 246. 'Was unterscheidet Jesus von diesen Messiasprätendenten und seinen heiligen Krieg von den Unternehmungen, die sie in Szene setzten? Daß die Römer zumindest ihn ähnlich beurteilt haben wie diese Aufrührer, zeigt sein Kreuzestod' (Betz in *N.T.* II, 133). It is legitimate to wonder whether the bystanders' mistaking of Jesus' cry of Ἐλωί Ἐλωί for an invocation of Elijah (Ἴδε Ἠλείαν φωνεῖ, Mark xv. 34–5), if authentic, might indicate that they regarded him as a Zealot, invoking the aid of the Zealot Messiah, i.e. Elijah-Phinehas, according to the Zealot conception: cf. Hengel, pp. 167–72; above, pp. 44–5.

[1] See Mark i. 14–15. Cf. Klausner, *Jesus of Nazareth*, p. 254; Goguel, *Jesus*, pp. 264–79; Meyer, *Ursprung*, I, 82–94; T. W. Manson in *B.J.R.L.* 36 (1954), pp. 398 ff.   [2] See pp. 108–10.

[3] H. W. Montefiore, 'Revolt in the Desert?', *N.T.S.* VIII (1961–2), 135–41. Montefiore concentrates his attention on the Markan account of the Feeding of the Five Thousand (Mark vi. 30 ff.). He notices (p. 136) that the phrase 'sheep without a shepherd' means, according to Old Testament usage, 'an army without a general', and that 'possibly Jesus went out into the desert precisely because he was as yet undecided whether or not to associate himself with this Messianic movement'. He sees in the Markan note that the *men* sat down in companies of fifty and a hundred 'not so much catering convenience as a military operation' (p. 137), and that 'five thousand men did not follow their leader into the wilderness without good cause. It is hard to see a sufficient reason other than that they wished to initiate a revolt' (p. 138). However, he concludes that, by sending away his disciples and dismissing the people, Jesus 'resisted a deliberate attempt to make him into a political and military Messiah' (p. 138). Commenting upon the Evangelists' handling of the incident, he

have been connected with the miracle of the Feeding of the Five Thousand. According to the Johannine version, the crowd's eschatological expectations were so aroused by what Jesus had done, which they saw as a Messianic 'sign' (σημεῖον), that they tried to 'take him by force to make him king'.[1] John goes on to tell that, perceiving their intention, Jesus withdrew himself into the hills.[2]

The traditional exegesis of the incident has naturally accepted John's explanation of how this crisis ended, since it is consistent with the concept of the pacific Christ, who kept himself insulated from current political interests and movements. But it takes very little imagination to see that a crisis of this nature was not likely to be resolved by the temporary withdrawal of Jesus. On his taking up his public ministry again, popular excitement would quickly have flared up once more, perhaps even more strongly, for his temporary disappearance would have been likely to enhance his numinous prestige.[3] Moreover, if, as is often suggested, Jesus publicly repudiated the Messianic role which popular enthusiasm attributed to him, it is difficult to account for his arranging his entry into Jerusalem as a Messianic demonstration.[4] Then, in addition to these considerations, it is surely strange that a quietist, who had carefully avoided all political involvement and vigorously rejected any suggestion that he should lead a nationalist movement against the Romans, should have been executed by them on a charge of stirring up the people, forbidding the payment of tribute, and claiming to be Christ, a king.

What were likely to have been the realities of the situation appear to be otherwise on reflection, and a sequence of events may be discerned that corresponds more with the final outcome. Presenting

thinks that 'either their [the events'] full significance has escaped the synoptic evangelists, or they have preferred to keep from their readers in the Roman Empire Jesus' involvement in an abortive attempt to revolt' (p. 140).

[1] John vi. 15: ἁρπάҙειν αὐτὸν ἵνα ποιήσωσιν βασιλέα... Cf. Winter, On the Trial of Jesus, p. 139; Goguel, Jesus, pp. 369 ff.

[2] John vi. 15. J. Blinzler ('Die Niedermetzelung von Galiläern durch Pilatus', N.T. II, 44–9) has suggested that the Galilaean crowd, after Jesus' withdrawal, went on to keep the Passover at Jerusalem, where their Messianic zeal alarmed Pilate and caused him to suppress them: Luke xiii. 1 records Jesus' reaction when he learned of their slaughter. Referring to John vi–vii. 2, he argues that Jesus refrained from going to Jerusalem, foreseeing 'messiaspolitische Demonstrationen'.

[3] This seems to be implied in John vi. 22 ff.

[4] See above, pp. 349–50.

himself to his compatriots in a Messianic role and urging them to prepare themselves for the imminent coming of the kingdom of God, Jesus evoked from his hearers a response that was politically dangerous. Whatever careful distinctions or reservations he may have made for the implementation of his mission, the character of that mission was inevitably affected by the passions and expectations of his followers. In turn, the reaction of the authorities, both Jewish and Roman, had to be reckoned with. These authorities would not have known, nor would they have been interested to discover, what unique spiritual ideal may have inspired Jesus' conception of himself, or his mission; they would have judged his significance from the reports of his public teaching and from his general effect upon his followers and the people. And what they heard and saw certainly provided legitimate cause for fear that Jesus was dangerous, politically and socially, especially from the time of his Triumphal Entry into Jerusalem and assault on the Temple trading system. How far Jesus became an unwilling victim of his followers' Messianic enthusiasm and revolutionary action, and of the inevitable reaction of the authorities, cannot be assessed. History provides many examples of popular leaders who were forced by the fervour and expectation of their followers into declarations and actions which did not represent their original aims. This could have happened to Jesus, and some scholars have sought to explain the Roman execution of Jesus along these lines.[1] That Jesus was thus wholly the victim of a situation that he could not control seems, however, to be contradicted by a number of considerations. It will suffice to mention two only. As we have seen, the evidence of the Synoptic Gospels suggests that Jesus personally arranged for the Messianic demonstration that marked his entry into Jerusalem, and that he initiated the action in the Temple. The other objection resides in the impression which the Gospels convey of the personality of Jesus. He appears in them as a dynamic leader, and not as a visionary who was swept along by forces which he had unleashed but could not hold in check. Accordingly, it is difficult not to see his execution for sedition, at the hands of the Romans, as the penalty paid for failure to accomplish aims which, in his estimation, should have saved Israel and ended the world-order embodied in the Roman empire.

How far the career of Jesus, which brought him to his tragic end on Calvary, is to be regarded as an episode in that resistance move-

---

[1] E.g. Eisler, ΙΗΣΟΥΣ ΒΑΣΙΛΕΥΣ, ΙΙ, 508 ff., *Messiah Jesus*, pp. 500 ff.; Winter, *On the Trial of Jesus*, pp. 138 ff.

ment to Roman suzerainty which was started by Judas of Galilee in
A.D. 6, and which ended in A.D. 73 with the resolute refusal of the
tortured Sicarii to acknowledge Caesar as lord, is not easily to be
estimated. Zealotism produced 'a long roll of martyrs for Israel's
freedom, and there are some aspects of Jesus' career that would seem
to entitle him to a place among them.[1] However, the fact that tradition preserved the memory that one of his Apostles was distinguished
as 'the Zealot' has an ambivalent significance in this connection. In
the first place, it seems logically to indicate that this Apostle, Simon,
was specifically known as 'the Zealot' because he was thereby
distinguished from the rest of the Apostles whom Jesus had chosen.[2]
This indication would, in turn, suggest that Jesus himself was not
a recognised Zealot leader, and that his selection of a professed
Zealot as one of his inner band of disciples was thus distinctively
notable. Therefore, the inclusion of Simon the Zealot in the apostolic
band actually points to the probability that Jesus was not a Zealot,
and that his movement was not an integral part of the Zealot resistance against Rome. However, the presence of a Zealot among
his disciples has also another significance: it means that Jesus deliberately chose a professed Zealot for an Apostle, which, in turn,
indicates that the profession of Zealot principles and aims was not
incompatible with intimate participation in the mission of Jesus.

This conclusion is not a surprising one; for there seems to be
nothing in the principles of Zealotism, as enunciated by Judas of
Galilee, that we have definite evidence for knowing that Jesus would
have repudiated.[3] The supreme emphasis upon the sovereignty of
God, with its corollary that the Israelite should recognise no other

---

[1] Χριστοῦ 'Ιησοῦ τοῦ μαρτυρήσαντος ἐπὶ Ποντίου Πιλάτου τὴν καλὴν
ὁμολογίαν... (I Tim. vi. 13). Cf. E. Lohmeyer in *Congrès d'Histoire du
Christianisme*, II, 130–4; C. K. Barrett in *New Testament Essays* (ed. A. J. B.
Higgins), pp. 11–15; Frend, *Martyrdom and Persecution*, pp. 81–2. 'Jesus is
a martyr *against* his nation, not for it. The fact that the Romans are
nowhere denounced for their part in Jesus' murder is no doubt due to this;
and also possibly to the editing of Mark and Luke, though this is purely
hypothetical' (J. Downing, 'Jesus and Martyrdom', *J.T.S.* XIV, n.s., 1963,
290). The situation is rather that, to the original Jewish Christians,
Jesus was a martyr *for* Israel; but Mark and the other Evangelists, as we
have seen, represent him as martyred *by* Israel.

[2] See above, p. 201.

[3] The one obvious objection that would be made to this statement by
conservative scholars, namely, that Jesus would not have resorted to
violence, cannot be maintained in the face of the evidence of Jesus' arming
of his disciples and his attack in the Temple.

lord, was wholly consistent with the attitude of Jesus.[1] Likewise Judas' exhortation to his followers that, in refusing to give the things of God to Caesar, they should be prepared for martyrdom, trusting that God would finally vindicate their cause,[2] is not far from the attitude of Jesus as set forth in the words ascribed to him: 'If any man would come after me, let him deny himself and take up his cross and follow me. For whoever would save his life will lose it; and whoever loses his life for my sake and the Gospel's will save it.'[3] Where Jesus seems to have differed from Zealot policy was in the fact that he was more immediately concerned to attack the Jewish sacerdotal aristocracy than to embroil himself with the Romans. But this difference, as we have seen, doubtless resulted from his immediate aim of preparing Israel for the coming of the kingdom of God. The Jewish leaders appeared to be the chief obstacle to the achievement of this aim, so he directed his attack primarily against them. However, he agreed with the Zealot view about the payment of tribute,[4] and he was conscious that his mission might result in his execution by the Romans;[5] but it would seem that his conviction about the imminence of God's kingdom, which would mean the end of Rome's sovereignty, caused him to be less concerned than the Zealots with the immediate prosecution of resistance to Rome. In the end, it would seem that the movement of Jesus and that of the Zealots converged in revolutionary action in Jerusalem. For Jesus' assault on the authority of the hierarchy in the Temple appears to have coincided with a Zealot uprising in the city.[6] Whatever may have been the relation between the two attacks, on Calvary Jesus was crucified between two λῃσταί, who were probably Zealots, his companions in paying that last penalty for revolt against Rome.

Recent research has revealed that Jesus and his movement did not constitute an isolated phenomenon in Judaea during the six fateful decades that followed the imposition of Roman rule in A.D. 6. A connection between the movement of John the Baptist and that of Jesus had, of course, long been recognised, although its evaluation remained essentially enigmatic.[7] If our interpretation of the significance of Luke's denigration of Alexandrian Christianity as 'knowing only the baptism of John' is correct,[8] it is possible that

---

[1] Cf. Mark xii. 28–30: see pp. 48–9.
[2] See pp. 33, 54, 56 ff.
[3] Mark viii. 34–5: see pp. 57, 145.
[4] See pp. 346 ff.
[5] Pp. 57, 269.
[6] See above, p. 263, n. 3, p. 351.
[7] See p. 352, n. 1.
[8] Pp. 191 ff.

a Pauline Christian would have regarded primitive Jewish Christianity, both as it had existed in the Mother Church of Jerusalem and as it was then existing in Alexandria, as a faith that had not essentially developed beyond the form it originally had when it stemmed from the Baptist's movement. But denigratory though this view was, it was probably closer to the facts than its author realised. For in a very real sense, as we have seen, Jesus was primarily concerned to carry on the mission inaugurated by John, of preparing Israel for the coming of the kingdom of God; his own essential contribution to his predecessor's programme being that of his personality and the conception of his own role in this Messianic prelude.

The documents discovered at Qumrân, although their interpretation will long be a matter for specialist research and discussion, have clearly shown that reformist ideas were current elsewhere in Judaea at this time. Dissatisfaction with the ordering of things in Jerusalem, particularly in the Temple cultus, was felt among the sectaries at Qumrân.[1] Moreover, they treasured a memory, which curiously anticipated the fate of Jesus, of a Teacher of Righteousness who was slain by a Wicked Priest.[2] The Qumrân community evidently preferred to pursue its ideals in the isolation of the desert than preach them through the countryside; but its members looked forward to, and prepared themselves for, a final Armageddon between the Sons of Light and the Sons of Darkness, of whom the protagonists would be the Romans.[3] The destruction of the Qumrân settlement by Vespasian's punitive expedition in A.D. 68 attests the fatal outcome of the Covenanters' resistance to the army of the *Kittim*, and it affords a significant parallel to the fate of the Mother Church of Jerusalem.[4]

Of the Zealot movement and its relation to that which Jesus

---

[1] Cf. Driver, *Judaean Scrolls*, pp. 234–6; Roth, *Historical Background of Dead Sea Scrolls*, pp. 70–2; Rowley in *B.J.R.L.* 44 (1961), pp. 126–7, 132.

[2] Cf. A. Dupont-Sommer, *Les écrits esséniens*, pp. 369–79; Allegro, *Dead Sea Scrolls*, pp. 142, 152 ff.; Rowley in *B.J.R.L.* 44 (1961), pp. 127–9; Roth, *Historical Background of Dead Sea Scrolls*, pp. 70 ff.; Driver, *Judaean Scrolls*, pp. 257–8 (who prefers to render the title 'the Rightful Teacher'), 266–84.

[3] See above, pp. 60–1.

[4] See pp. 61, 208 ff. The conclusion of Y. Yadin, commenting upon the archaeological evidence of a connection between the Zealots of Masada and the Qumrân Covenanters, is significant in this connection: 'Many sects of Jewry took part in the Great Revolt' ('The Exploration of Masada—1963/64. Preliminary Report', *I.E.J.* xv, 1965, 108).

founded we need say no more. Suffice it to note that, as a connection existed between the Zealots and the sectaries of Qumrân,[1] so a bond of common sympathy surely united Jesus and his followers with those who sought to maintain the ideals of Judas of Galilee. But sympathy, stemming from similar values and sufferings, finding expression sometimes in active cooperation, did not mean identity. Perhaps the reply which Jesus is recorded to have made to his disciples about one who cast out demons in his name, but did not belong to their company, could have applied to the Zealots: 'He who is not against us is for us.'[2] However that may be, Jesus met at the hands of the Romans the same fate suffered by Judas of Galilee and his two sons, and on either side of the cross that bore his title 'The King of the Jews' was crucified a ληστής, as the Romans contemptuously called Israel's resistance fighters, the Zealots.

[1] See p. 61, n. 4.   [2] Mark ix. 40: cf. Taylor, *St Mark*, pp. 406–8.

JOSEPHUS ON JESUS

It has been thought well not to introduce into the main discussion the complex problem of whether Josephus wrote about Jesus, and, if he did so, what he wrote. However, the subject cannot be left unnoticed; for, whatever might be the answer to the two related questions involved, that answer must necessarily have a considerable significance for our study. Thus, if this Jewish historian, who was concerned to record Jewish affairs during the first seven decades of the present era, did not mention Jesus, the fact itself would require explanation. If, on the other hand, he did mention him, it is obviously important to know what exactly he wrote.

The possibility that Josephus might not have written about Jesus is worth considering for a moment. Such silence would seem to have only two possible explanations. One would be that Jesus and his movement appeared to be too insignificant to Josephus, so that he did not feel it worth while to mention them. This explanation, when examined, does not appear convincing. For Josephus does record, howbeit sometimes very briefly and anonymously, the careers of persons who affected Jewish life during this period by conduct or action of a Messianic character.[1] Further, in view of the fact that Christianity was known in Rome, where Josephus wrote his works after the Jewish War, it seems incredible that he should not have mentioned Jesus in some of them because he regarded Jesus as less significant than those ephemeral Messianic pretenders whom he does mention. The fact that Christianity was known in Rome, and that it was in ill repute there,[2] brings us to the second possible explanation for Josephus' not mentioning Jesus, if indeed he did not mention him. For it could be argued that, since his writing was motivated by apologetical concern, Josephus might have deemed it prudent not to remind his Roman readers that Judaea had produced Christianity in addition to all the other ills with which it had

---

[1] See above, pp. 110–11, 113, 132–3.
[2] Cf. P. de Labriolle, *La réaction païenne*, pp. 36–45; H. B. Mattingly, 'The Origin of the Name *Christiani*', *J.T.S.* ix, n.s. (1958), 33–7; F. F. Bruce in *B.J.R.L.* 44 (1962), pp. 315–21; Frend, *Martyrdom and Persecution*, pp. 163–7.

recently afflicted the Roman empire. Such an explanation, however, does not appear feasible on further consideration. The references of Tacitus and Suetonius show that the Jewish origin of Christianity was too well known in Rome to have permitted Josephus thus to remain silent about it in a historical account of his people during this period.[1] Indeed, the very notoriety of Christianity should have impelled him to mention it. And he could have made good apologetical capital by doing so. For he could have shown how the Jewish leaders, recognising the pernicious influence of Jesus, had arrested him and delivered him to the Roman governor for execution. In other words, as he represented the Jewish ruling class, of which he was himself a member, as striving to suppress Zealotism, which had caused Rome so much trouble, so could he have made out a good case of their attempt to suppress Christianity at its beginning.

It would appear, therefore, on *a priori* grounds, that Josephus must have mentioned Jesus, and that what he recorded of him would have been of a condemnatory character; for there are no grounds for supposing that Josephus was a Christian, and would, consequently, have written approvingly.

These considerations form a useful *prolegomenon* to our examination of the famous passage concerning Jesus which stands in the present Greek text of Josephus' *Antiquities of the Jews*.[2] This so-called *Testimonium Flavianum* can be traced back to the fourth century, for it was known to Eusebius of Caesarea, who cites it *in extenso* in his *Historia Ecclesiastica* (I. xi. 7–8) and *Demonstratio Evangelica* (III. 3. 105–6). The passage follows immediately after the account, in the *Antiquities*, of Pilate's suppression of the disturbance caused by his using Temple funds for building a new aqueduct to Jerusalem.[3] The concluding words of this account are significant: 'and thus the insurrection ended' (καὶ οὕτω παύεται ἡ στάσις). Then comes the passage about Jesus:

About this time arose (γίνεται) Jesus, a wise man (σοφὸς ἀνήρ) [if indeed it is proper to call him a man]; for he was a doer of marvellous works (παραδόξων ἔργων ποιητής), a teacher of men who received the truth with

---

[1] Tacitus, *Ann.* xv. 44; Suetonius, *Claudius*, 25. See preceding note.

[2] *Ant.* XVIII. 63–4. For text and translation cf. L. H. Feldman, Loeb *Josephus*, IX, 48–51; Eisler, ΙΗΣΟΥΣ ΒΑΣΙΛΕΥΣ, I, 84–7, *Messiah Jesus*, pp. 58–62; *Flavii Josephi Opera*, ed. B. Niese, IV, 151–2 (text); G. Mathieu and L. Herrmann, *Œuvres complètes de Flavius Josephus* (ed. T. Reinach), IV, 145–6 (trans.); G. Ricciotti, *Flavio Giuseppe*, I, 174 (trans.).

[3] *Ant.* XVIII. 60–2: see above, pp. 75 ff.

pleasure, and he led after him many Jews, and many also of the Greek population. [This was the Christ (ὁ Χριστὸς οὗτος ἦν).] And, when Pilate had inflicted on him the punishment of the cross, on the indictment of our chief men (ἐνδείξει τῶν πρώτων ἀνδρῶν παρ' ἡμῖν), those who first loved him did not desist; [for he appeared to them on the third day, being alive again, the divine prophets having told of these and innumerable other wonders concerning him]. And up till now the race (φῦλον) of the Christians, being named after him, has not died out.

If the passage, in its extant form, had been written by Josephus, it would be necessary to conclude that he was himself a Christian; for the suggestion that Jesus was more than a man, and the assertions that he was the Christ and had risen from the dead on the third day, could surely not have been made by one who did not share in the Christian faith. However, as we have noted, we have no evidence that Josephus was a Christian; indeed, what evidence is relevant to the issue points indubitably the other way. Consequently, many scholars who have concerned themselves with the passage have agreed in regarding the statements placed in the square brackets above as later Christian interpolations.[1]

However, it seems unlikely that the original text of the passage is to be restored by simply extracting the statements thus marked. For not only would the resulting text contain no indication of a reason for Jesus' execution, but it would not explain why Origen, writing about a century before Eusebius, declares that Josephus did not accept Jesus as the Christ. From Origen's remarks in this connection, it would seem that Josephus did not just fail to mention that Jesus was the Christ, but that he had definitively stated that he was not.[2] Accordingly, it appears that between the time of Origen and that when Eusebius recorded the passage concerned, the original text of Josephus at this point had been more radically altered by excising some statement which rejected the Messianic character of Jesus and by its replacement with the present affirmation. It is possible that the complaints of Origen had moved some

[1] E.g. Guignebert, *Jésus*, pp. 19–20; Klausner, *Life of Jesus*, pp. 55–6; Eisler, ΙΗΣΟΥΣ ΒΑΣΙΛΕΥΣ, I, 87–8, see pp. 48–86, *Messiah Jesus*, pp. 61–2, see also pp. 49–58; P. Carrington, *The Early Christian Church*, I, 189–90: cf. Schürer, *G.J.V.* I, 544–9; B. Niese and L. H. Gray in *E.R.E.* VII, 577b–578b.

[2] καὶ τὸ θαυμαστόν ἐστιν, ὅτι τὸν Ἰησοῦν ἡμῶν οὐ καταδεξάμενος εἶναι Χριστόν (*Comm. in Matt.* x. 17); Ὁ δ' αὐτὸς [Josephus] καίτοι γε ἀπιστῶν τῷ Ἰησοῦ ὡς Χριστῷ (*c. Celsum*, I. 47). Cf. Ricciotti, *Flavio Giuseppe*, I, 175; Feldman, Loeb *Josephus*, IX, 49, n. *b*.

Christian scribes to make these emendations, so that Josephus became thereby a witness to the Christian evaluation of Jesus.[1]

If it is reasonable, therefore, to conclude that Josephus must originally have written something derogatory about Jesus, is it possible to gain any idea of it? In attempting an answer, it is useful first to recall that Josephus apparently chose to introduce his description of Jesus at a point in his narrative where it would follow on his account of the ills that befell the Jews during the governorship of Pontius Pilate.[2] Next, it is to be noted that, after dealing with Jesus, he goes on to record the troubles which happened to the Jews in Rome about the same time (καὶ ὑπὸ τοὺς αὐτοὺς χρόνους ἕτερόν τι δεινὸν ἐθορύβει τοὺς ᾿Ιουδαίους).[3] However, instead of proceeding with this account, he relates first a long story concerning the seduction of a Roman matron through the connivance of the priests of the temple of Isis in Rome: these priests, on the discovery of the matter, were crucified by the order of Tiberius (ἐξετάσει τῶν ἱερέων ἐκείνους τε ἀνεσταύρωσεν...).[4] Now, we may reasonably ask whether the interposition of the passage concerning Jesus between the account of the Jewish sufferings under Pilate and that of an unedifying piece of religious charlatanism, which resulted in the crucifixion of some of those involved, was accidental, or whether what Josephus did write about Jesus fitted aptly into such a context.

Another consideration which seems to offer a clue to what Josephus might have said of Jesus is that of the historian's attitude towards the Messianic hope of his people. As we have seen, one of the causes to which he assigns the Jews' fatal resistance to Rome was their belief in an ambiguous oracle (χρησμὸς ἀμφίβολος), concerning a world-ruler who would come forth from Palestine. Josephus held that the prophecy had been fulfilled in the person of Vespasian, who had been proclaimed emperor while campaigning in Palestine.[5] Now, in view of this politic, if sycophantic, interpretation of the Messianic hope, it is certain that he would have viewed the Messianic claims of Jesus with extreme distaste and disapproval. It is, moreover, unlikely that he would have spoken of 'the Christ' (ὁ Χριστός), even in rebutting the claims of Jesus, because to use the term would have meant explaining to his Gentile readers a

---

[1] Cf. Brandon, *Fall of Jerusalem*, pp. 110–12.
[2] *Ant.* XVIII. 55–62: see pp. 69 ff.
[3] *Ibid.* 65 ff.   [4] *Ibid.* 79.
[5] *War*, VI. 312–15: see above, pp. 59 ff.

Jewish belief which he obviously found embarrassing. Consequently, if Josephus did say something derogatory about the Messianic claim or status of Jesus, as Origen suggests, it was doubtless by way of describing him as a wonder-working charlatan (γόης), after the manner in which he treats other Messianic pretenders (γόητες), as we have seen.[1] It is possible, also, that the expression σοφὸς ἀνήρ, in the extant text, might be a Christian emendation of σοφιστής, which Josephus also uses for Judas of Galilee and Menahem.[2]

If we may, therefore, reasonably suppose that Josephus described Jesus as a σοφιστής and a γόης, it would undoubtedly mean that this pro-Roman Jewish historian equated Jesus with the many other Zealot leaders and Messianic pretenders, whose activity he deplores as leading the Jewish people into their fatal contest with Rome. Such a conclusion might well be expected, in view of what we know of Josephus and his outlook. However, from the point of view of our special concern with the Roman execution of Jesus, our attention is demanded rather by the statement, in the extant text of the passage, that Pilate executed Jesus 'on the indictment (ἐνδείξει) of our chief men'. In view of its terseness, it would seem that the statement must represent the original version of what Josephus wrote; for a Christian interpolator could surely not have left it at that, but would have added some phrase to make clear the malice of the Jewish leaders in securing the condemnation of Jesus. This being so, the expression ἔνδειξις is significant; for, in this context, ἔνδειξις is a straightforward legal term denoting the laying of information against a person, or a writ of indictment.[3] The fact that Josephus uses it here, without any explanatory comment, indicates that the action of the Jewish leaders in indicting Jesus, followed by Pilate's sentence of crucifixion, was a perfectly normal procedure that he could expect his readers to understand.

---

[1] See pp. 109–11, 113.

[2] *War*, II. 118, 433. 'It is a title which he [Josephus] applies elsewhere to persons learned in the Jewish law, perhaps Rabbis' (Roth, *Historical Background of Dead Sea Scrolls*, p. 7). Cf. Driver, *Judaean Scrolls*, pp. 251, 472–3. Eisler thinks that the terms used by ancient writers hostile to Christianity 'die Annahme sehr nahe legen, daß Jesus bei Josephus σοφιστὴς καὶ γόης ἀνήρ genannt war' (ΙΗΣΟΥΣ ΒΑΣΙΛΕΥΣ, I, 54, cf. *Messiah Jesus*, p. 52).

[3] Cf. Liddell and Scott, *Greek–English Lexicon*[9], I, 558 (ἔνδειξις). 'Auf eine Anzeige der Ersten bei uns' (Eisler, ΙΗΣΟΥΣ ΒΑΣΙΛΕΥΣ, I, 88); 'sur la dénonciation de nos premiers citoyens' (Mathieu and Herrmann, *Œuvres complètes de Flavius Josephus*, IV, 146); 'per denunzia degli uomini principali fra noi' (Ricciotti, *Flavio Giuseppe*, I, 174).

In other words, Josephus confirms what we have deduced from the Gospels, namely, that the Jewish authorities presented Pilate with evidence against Jesus, on the strength of which Pilate ordered his execution. And the nature of this evidence is clearly to be inferred from the terms σοφιστής and γόης, which it seems that Josephus employed in his description of Jesus, implying thereby that he was a Messianic pretender, with revolutionary aims, in accordance with his accustomed terminology in this connection.

Such an evaluation of Jesus would, of course, be consistent with all that we know of Josephus and his outlook. Moreover, his statement concerning the execution of Jesus would have been calculated to further his apologetical theme. For he would thereby have been informing his Gentile readers that the 'tribe of the Christians',[1] which they disliked, had indeed originated in Judaea, but the Jewish authorities, realising its pernicious nature, had dealt promptly with its founder, by providing the local Roman governor with the necessary evidence of his guilt to justify his execution.

The subject of Josephus' attitude to Jesus cannot be left without some consideration of the problem constituted by the passage concerning the *Wonder-worker* in the Old Russian or Slavonic version of his work. The origin of this version still remains a mystery. Robert Eisler in his massive work entitled ΙΗΣΟΥΣ ΒΑΣΙΛΕΥΣ ΟΥ ΒΑΣΙΛΕΥΣΑΣ, published in 1929–30, put forward the theory that this Slavonic version derived from either an Aramaic or a Greek prototype of the extant Greek version of Josephus' *Jewish War*.[2] Eisler called this hypothetical original the *Halôsis* or *Fall of Jerusalem*.[3] Eisler's interpretation was vigorously repudiated at the time by many scholars.[4] The opposition which it met was undoubtedly

---

[1] τῶν Χριστιανῶν... τὸ φῦλον (*Ant.* xviii. 64). On the question whether this expression could have been used by Josephus see Eisler, ΙΗΣΟΥΣ ΒΑΣΙ-ΛΕΥΣ, 1, 67, 80–1; H. St J. Thackeray, *Josephus: the Man and the Historian*, p. 148; Ricciotti, *Flavio Giuseppe*, 1, 182.

[2] The subtitle of the work reads: *Die messianische Unabhängigkeitsbewegung vom Auftreten Johannes des Täufers bis zum Untergang Jakobs des Gerechten nach der neuerschlossenen Eroberung von Jerusalem des Flavius Josephus und den christlichen Quellen.*

[3] ΙΗΣΟΥΣ ΒΑΣΙΛΕΥΣ, 1, 231, *Messiah Jesus*, p. 116. Cf. Shutt, *Studies in Josephus*, pp. 24–5.

[4] Most notably by M. Goguel in *Revue historique*, CLXII (1929); J. M. Creed, 'The Slavonic Version of Josephus' History of the Jewish War', *H.Th.R.* xxv (1932); J. W. Jack, *The Historic Christ: an Examination of Dr Robert Eisler's Theory according to the Slavonic Version of Josephus and Other Sources*

due very largely to the fact that Eisler used the Slavonic version as the basis for an account of Jesus and the beginnings of Christianity which shocked orthodox belief. Eisler's theory was, however, accepted or considered significant by certain distinguished scholars, including Dr St John Thackeray, the original editor and translator of the Loeb edition of Josephus, and one of the greatest authorities on the author and his works.[1] Since the controversy that marked the publication of Eisler's work, little attention has been given to the problem which the Slavonic version constitutes, although a critical edition of the text, and a French translation of it, were published, in 1934 and 1938 respectively, by the Institut d'Études slaves, in Paris.[2] The most significant study since that time has been an article by Mr A. Rubinstein in the *Journal of Semitic Studies* of 1957, who concluded: 'While there is nothing in the O.R. [Old Russian] version of the *Wars* to lead one to conclude that it is a translation of Josephus' original semitic version or of a short Greek version intermediate between the semitic and the standard version, there is some evidence in the O.R. version of its ultimate dependence on a

(London, 1933); W. Bienert, *Der älteste nichtchristliche Jesusbericht. Josephus über Jesus. Unter besonderer Berücksichtigung des altrussischen Josephus* (*Theol. Arbeiten z. Bibel-, Kirchen- und Geistesgeschichte*, hrg. v. D. Ernst Barnikol, Nr. IX, Akad. Verlag, Halle, 1936). Eisler answered this last monograph, with reference also to the objections of other scholars, in a privately circulated brochure entitled *Flavius Josephus-Studien. I. Das Testimonium Flavianum, Eine Antwort an Dr. Walter Bienert* (London, 1938). An obituary of Dr Eisler appeared in *The Times*, 20 December 1949. He informed the present writer privately in 1948 that he was preparing a supplement to his ΙΗΣΟΥΣ ΒΑΣΙΛΕΥΣ, designed to answer the criticisms made by scholars of various nationalities since its publication. The last contribution, known to the present writer, of Dr Eisler in this field of studies was a letter entitled 'Hebrew Scrolls: Further Evidence for their pre-Christian Date', *The Modern Churchman*, XXXIX (1949), 284–7. Dr Eisler was a man of vast erudition and a stimulating imagination: in the opinion of the present writer, his ΙΗΣΟΥΣ ΒΑΣΙΛΕΥΣ was not based upon a sufficiently close interrogation of the Christian sources; but its value as a treasury of learning and much acute thinking abides.

[1] Thackeray printed translations of the Slavonic version in his edition of Josephus for the Loeb Classical Library, vol. III, app. iii; cf. his book, *Josephus: the Man and the Historian*, p. 34. Cf. S. Reinach, *Orpheus* (London, 1931), pp. 247 ff.; B. S. Easton, *Christ and the Gospels* (New York, 1930), pp. 78–81; F. J. Foakes Jackson, *Josephus and the Jews*, pp. 280–3.

[2] *La Prise de Jérusalem de Josèphe le Juif.* Texte vieux-russe publié intégralement par V. Istrin. Imprimé sous la direction de A. Vaillant; traduit en français par P. Pascal, 2 tomes, Paris, Institut d'Études slaves, 1934, 1938.

fuller Greek text.'[1] The present writer made a critical survey of the controversy in 1951, in his *Fall of Jerusalem and the Christian Church*, and he now sees no reason to depart from the opinion which he then expressed:[2] that the Slavonic version cannot be accounted for either as the work of some anonymous person, perhaps of Judaising tendency, attempting to controvert Christianity,[3] or as a product of the Orthodox Church to combat heresy[4]—indeed these rival theories, in thus cancelling each other out, testify thereby to the extraordinarily ambivalent nature of the passage concerning the *Wonderworker*, which was evidently a designation for Jesus.

Whatever the truth about its origin, it will be useful to give the passage as it appears in M. Pascal's translation:

Alors parut un homme, s'il est permis de l'appeler homme. Sa nature et son extérieur étaient d'un homme, mais son apparence plus qu'humaine; et ses œuvres divines: il accomplissait des miracles étonnants et puissants. Aussi ne puis-je l'appeler homme; d'autre part, en considérant la commune nature, je ne l'appellerai pas non plus ange. Et tout ce qu'il faisait, par une certaine force invisible, il le faisait par la parole et le commandement. Les uns disaient de lui: 'C'est notre premier législateur qui est ressuscité des morts et qui fait paraître beaucoup de guérisons et de preuves de son savoir'. D'autres le croyaient envoyé de Dieu, mais il s'opposait en bien des choses à la Loi et n'observait pas le sabbat selon la coutume des ancêtres; cependant il ne faisait rien d'impur ni aucun ouvrage manuel, mais disposait tout seulement par la parole. Et beaucoup d'entre la foule suivaient à sa suite et écoutaient ses enseignements; et beaucoup d'âmes s'agitaient pensant que c'était par lui que les tribus d'Israël se libéreraient des bras des Romains. Il avait coutume de se tenir de préférence devant la cité, sur le mont des Oliviers; c'est là qu'il dispensait les guérisons au peuple. Et auprès de lui se rassemblèrent cent cinquante serviteurs, et d'entre le peuple un grand nombre. Voyant sa puissance, et qu'il accomplissait tout ce qu'il voulait par sa parole, ils lui demandaient d'entrer dans la ville, de massacrer les troupes romaines et Pilate et de régner sur eux. Mais il n'en eut cure. Plus tard, les chefs des Juifs en eurent connaissance, ils se réunirent avec le grand-prêtre

---

[1] 'Observations on the Old Russian Version of Josephus' *Wars*', *J.S.S.* II (1957), 329–48.

[2] *Fall of Jerusalem*, pp. 114–18. Cf. R. Dunkerley, 'The Riddles of Josephus', *H.J.* LIII (1954–5), 131–4; *Der Jüdische Krieg* (hrg. O. Michel und O. Bauernfeind), I, xxxiv–xxxv.

[3] Cf. Goguel in *Revue historique*, CLXII, 51–2: 'L'auteur du fragment a voulu insinuer sur Jésus des choses qu'il n'osait pas dire directement, parce qu'il ne voulait pas ou n'osait pas contredire ouvertement la tradition chrétienne. C'est donc qu'il la connaissait et voulait la combattre.'

[4] Cf. Jack, *Historic Christ*, pp. 50–67, 75, 77–9; Creed in *H.Th.R.* xxv, 318–19; S. Zeitlin, 'The Hoax of the "Slavonic Josephus"', *J.Q.R.* xxxix (1948–9), 177, 180. See also G. A. Williamson, *The World of Josephus* (London, 1964), pp. 309–10.

et dirent: 'Nous sommes impuissants et faibles pour résister aux Romains, comme un arc détendu. Allons annoncer à Pilate ce que nous avons entendu, et nous n'aurons pas d'ennuis: si jamais il l'apprend par d'autres, nous serons privés de nos biens, nous serons taillés en pièces nous-mêmes et nos enfants dispersés en exil'. Ils allèrent le dire à Pilate. Celui-ci envoya des hommes, en tua beaucoup parmi le peuple et ramena ce faiseur de miracles. Il enquêta sur lui, et il connut qu'il faisait le bien et non le mal, qu'il n'était ni révolté ni avide du pouvoir royal, et le relâcha. Car il avait guéri sa femme qui se mourait. Et, venu au lieu accoutumé, il faisait les œuvres accoutumées. Et de nouveau, comme un plus grand nombre de gens se rassemblaient autour de lui, il était renommé pour ses œuvres par-dessus tous. Les docteurs de la Loi furent blessés d'envie, et ils donnèrent trente talents à Pilate pour qu'il le tuât. Celui-ci les prit et leur donna licence d'exécuter eux-mêmes leur désir. Ils le saisirent et le crucifièrent, en dépit de la loi des ancêtres.[1]

The non-committal attitude towards the *Wonder-worker*, which is clearly evident in the passage, is certainly remarkable. It is impossible to tell whether its author approved or disapproved of him.[2] Equally puzzling is the elusive statement describing the response of the *Wonder-worker* to the invitation that he should lead an attack against the Roman forces, including Pilate, in Jerusalem, and establish himself there as king: 'Mais il n'en eut cure.'[3] Whatever the meaning of this statement may be, it must surely be adjudged very remarkable that this Old Russian translation of Josephus' *Jewish War*, which diverges so strangely from the extant Greek text,[4] should tell of an anonymous *Wonder-worker*, seemingly very much like Jesus, who was associated with a projected attack on the Romans in Jerusalem, which the latter anticipated and bloodily

[1] *La Prise de Jérusalem de Josèphe le Juif*, I, 149–50. An English translation, from the German version of the Slavonic text made by A. Berendts and K. Grass in their *Flavius Josephus vom Jüdischen Kriege, Buch I–IV, nach der slavischen Übersetzung* (Dorpat, 1926–7), is given by Thackeray in the Loeb *Josephus*, III, 648–50. Eisler provides an English translation in his *Messiah Jesus*, pp. 383–5; his German translation, with the Slavonic text, appears on pp. 296–300 of his ΙΗΣΟΥΣ ΒΑΣΙΛΕΥΣ, II.

[2] His infringement of certain matters of the Law is the only point mentioned for condemnation, and this condemnation seems to be qualified. The rest of the account is distinctly favourable.

[3] It is ironical that there are variant readings in the MSS concerned for this crucial verse. Three are given, in German translations, in Brandon, *The Fall of Jerusalem*, pp. 122–3.

[4] Thackery prints twenty of these divergent passages, together with a list of omissions in the Slavonic version from the extant Greek text, on pp. 635–60 in the Loeb *Josephus*, III. Cf. Eisler, ΙΗΣΟΥΣ ΒΑΣΙΛΕΥΣ, I, 241 ff., *Messiah Jesus*, pp. 170 ff.

suppressed. If it does not reflect what Josephus originally wrote, we can only wonder at the identity and purpose of him who wrote the account.[1]

[1] Attention should be drawn also to the passage in the Slavonic version concerning the followers of the *Wonder-worker*. These are described as telling the people, after their Master's death, that 'he will free you from your bondage' ('et il vous libérera de la servitude', *La Prise de Jérusalem*, I, 157). Since they won over many of the poorer people, the procurators, Cuspius Fadus and Tiberius Alexander (curiously serving in office together, contrary to the Greek text), took measures to suppress the movement. The account of the teaching of these followers of the *Wonder-worker* accords remarkably with what we have been led to infer concerning the teaching of the Jewish Christians (see pp. 177–81). For other accounts of the passage see Berendts and Grass, *Flavius Josephus vom Jüdischen Kriege, Buch I–IV*, p. 279; Eisler, ΙΗΣΟΥΣ ΒΑΣΙΛΕΥΣ, II, 561–79, *Messiah Jesus*, pp. 527–40; Thackeray, Loeb *Josephus*, III, 651–2.

BIBLIOGRAPHY

I. ANCIENT LITERARY SOURCES

Assumption of Moses (C. Clemen) in *Die Apokryphen und Pseudepigraphen*, hrg. E. Kautzsch, II. Band. Tübingen, 1900.

CLAUDIUS, IMPERATOR

Letter to the Alexandrians in *Select Papyri*, ed. and trans. A. S. Hunt and C. C. Edgar, Loeb Classical Library, vol. II. London, 1934.

Didache in *The Apostolic Fathers*, ed. and trans. J. B. Lightfoot. London, 1891.

DIO CASSIUS

Roman History, text and translation, E. Cary, Loeb Classical Library, vol. VII. London, 1924.

EPIPHANIUS

Adversus (Octoginta) Haereses, ed. J. Migne, *Patrologia Graeca*, tomes XLI, XLII. Paris, 1858.

De Mensuris et Ponderibus, ed. J. Migne, *Patrologia Graeca*, tome XLIII. Paris, 1864.

EUSEBIUS

Ecclesiastical History, text and translation, K. Lake, Loeb Classical Library, 2 vols. London, 1926. Trans. H. J. Lawlor and J. E. L. Oulton: vol. I (trans.), 1927; vol. II (notes), 1928. London.

Demonstratio Evangelica, ed. Dindorf, vol. III. Leipzig, 1867.

Gospel according to the Hebrews, ap. Jerome, *Vir. ill.* 2 in *Apocrypha* II, ed. E. Klostermann, Cambridge, 1904, and *Neutestamentliche Apokryphen*, hrg. E. Hennecke und W. Schneemelcher, I. Band, Tübingen, 1959.

Gospel according to Thomas, text and translation, A. Guillaumont *et alii*. London, 1959.

HIPPOLYTUS

Refutatio omnium haeresium, ed. L. Dunker and F. G. Schneidewin. Göttingen, 1859.

JOSEPHUS

The Jewish War; *Life*; *Against Apion*, text and translation, H. St John Thackeray in Loeb Classical Library, 3 vols. London, 1926–8. Italian translation, with notes, G. Ricciotti, *La guerra giudaica*, vols. II–IV, Turin, 1937 (*see* Ricciotti, G., *in* Bibliography II). German translation: *De Bello Judaico: Der Jüdische Krieg*, hrg. O. Michel und O. Bauernfeind, I. Band, Bad Homburg, 1960.

Jewish Antiquities, text and translation of Books XV–XVII, R. Marcus and A. Wikgren, vol. VIII; Books XVIII–XX, L. H. Feldman, vol. IX (in the Loeb Classical Library), London–Cambridge (Mass.), 1963, 1965. Text, B. Niese, *Flavii Josephi Opera*, vol. IV (*Ant.* XVI–XX and *Vita*),

Berlin, 1890. French annotated translation, G. Mathieu and L. Hermann in *Œuvres complètes de Flavius Josèphe* (sous la direction de Th. Reinach), tome IV, Paris, 1929.

Slavonic version of Josephus: *La Prise de Jérusalem de Josèphe le Juif*, texte vieux-russe publié intégralement par V. Istrin; imprimé sous la direction de A. Vaillant; traduit en français par P. Pascal; 2 tomes, Paris, Institut d'Études slaves, 1934, 1938. Berendts, A. und Grass, K., *Flavius Josephus vom Jüdischen Krieg, Buch I–IV, nach der slavischen Übersetzung*, Dorpat, 1926–7.

IV Maccabees (A. Deissmann), in *Die Apokryphen und Pseudepigraphen*, hrg. E. Kautzsch, II. Band. Tübingen, 1900.

New Testament

Novum Testamentum Graece, hrg. E. Nestle, 19. Aufl. Stuttgart, 1949.

(Gospels) A. Huck, *Synopse der drei Evangelien*. Tübingen, 1928.

ORIGEN

contra Celsum, I, 47. *Commentarium in Evangelium Mattheum*, ed. C. H. E. Lommatzsch. Berlin, 1834.

OROSIUS

Historia adversus Paganos, ed. J. Migne, *Patrologia Latina*, tome XXXI. Paris, 1846.

PHILO

Philonis Alexandrini in Flaccum, ed. H. Box. Oxford, 1939.

Philonis Alexandrini Legatio ad Gaium, ed. and trans. E. M. Smallwood. Leiden, 1961.

Biblical Antiquities, ed. G. Kisch, *Pseudo-Philo's Liber Antiquitatum Biblicarum*, University of Notre Dame, Indiana, 1949. Ed. and trans. M. R. James, *The Biblical Antiquities of Philo*, London, 1917.

Qumrân literature—*see* Bibliography II *under* Allegro, J., Burrows, M., Dupont-Sommer, A., Yadin, Y.

Rabbinical Literature

Der babylonische Talmud, German translation, L. Goldschmidt, I. Band. Berlin, 1930.

The Mishnah, trans. H. Danby. Oxford, 1933.

Strack, H. und Billerbeck, P. *Kommentar zum Neuen Testament aus Talmud und Midrasch*, 4 Bände. Munich, 1922–8.

Recognitiones S. Clementis, ed. J. Migne, *Patrologia Graeca*, tome I. Paris, 1865.

Sibylline Oracles in *Apocrypha and Pseudepigrapha*, ed. R. H. Charles, vol. II, Oxford, 1913. *Die Apokryphen und Pseudepigraphen*, hrg. E. Kautzsch, übersetz. F. Blass, II. Band, Tübingen, 1900.

SUETONIUS

Lives of the Caesars, ed. C. L. Roth. Leipzig, 1891.

SULPICIUS SEVERUS

Chronica, or *Historia Sacra*, ed. J. Migne, *Patrologia Latina*, tome XX. Paris, 1845.

BIBLIOGRAPHY: ANCIENT SOURCES

TACITUS
Annales; *Historiae*, ed. C. Halm, 2 vols. Leipzig, 1891.
The Annals of Tacitus, ed. H. Furneaux, 2nd ed. Oxford, 1934.
TERTULLIAN
Apology, Loeb Classical Library, ed. and trans. T. R. Glover. London, 1960.

II. MODERN WORKS

ALBRIGHT, W. F. *The Archaeology of Palestine*. Penguin Books, Harmondsworth, 1949.
ALLEGRO, J. *The Dead Sea Scrolls*. Penguin Books, Harmondsworth, 1956.
—— *The Treasure of the Copper Scroll*. New York, 1960.
ANGUS, S. 'Zealots', *E.R.E.* XII (1921).
AVI-YONAH, M. 'Where 960 Zealots committed suicide sooner than submit to a Roman army of 15,000', *I.L.N.* (5 November 1955), pp. 784–7.
AVI-YONAH, M. *et alii*. 'The Archaeological Survey of Masada', *I.E.J.* VII (1957).

BACON, B. W. *Is Mark a Roman Gospel?* Harvard University Press, 1919.
—— *Jesus and Paul*. London, 1921.
BALSDON, J. P. V. D. *The Emperor Gaius (Caligula)*. Oxford, 1934.
BALTENSWEILER, H. *Die Verklärung Jesu: historisches Ereignis und synoptische Berichte*. Zürich, 1959.
BARCLAY, W. *Jesus as They Saw Him*. London, 1962.
BARNARD, L. W. 'Saint Stephen and Early Alexandrian Christianity', *N.T.S.* VII (1960–1).
BARNES, W. E. *The Testimony of Josephus to Jesus Christ*. London, 1920.
BARRETT, C. K. 'The Background of Mark 10: 45', *New Testament Essays*, ed. A. J. B. Higgins. Manchester, 1959.
—— 'John', *Peake's Commentary*, 2nd ed.
BATE, H. N. *The Sibylline Oracles*. London, 1918.
BAUER, F. C. *Paulus, der Apostel Jesu Christi. Sein Leben und Wirken, seine Briefe und seine Lehre*, 2. Aufl. Leipzig, 1866.
BEARE, F. W. *The Earliest Records of Jesus*. Blackwell, Oxford, 1962.
BEASLEY-MURRAY, G. R. *Jesus and the Future*. London, 1954.
—— *A Commentary on Mark Thirteen*. London, 1957.
Beginnings of Christianity, The, ed. F. J. Foakes Jackson and Kirsopp Lake, 5 vols. London, 1920–33.
BELL, H. IDRIS. *Jews and Christians in Egypt*. London, 1924.
—— *Juden und Griechen im römischen Alexandreia (eine historische Skizze des alexandrinischen Antisemitismus)*. Leipzig, 1926.
—— 'Evidences of Christianity in Egypt during the Roman Period', *H.Th.R.* XXXVII (1944).
—— *Cults and Creeds in Graeco-Roman Egypt*. Liverpool, 1953.

BELL, H. IDRIS and SKEAT, T. C. *Fragments of an Unknown Gospel and other Early Christian Papyri.* British Museum, 1935.

BERSANETTI, B. M. *Vespasiano.* Rome, 1941.

BEST, E. *The Temptation and the Passion: the Markan Soteriology.* Cambridge, 1965.

BETZ, O. 'Jesu Heiliger Krieg', *N.T.* II (1958).

BEVAN, E. *A History of Egypt under the Ptolemaic Dynasty.* London, 1927.

BEYSCHLAG, K. 'Das Jakobusmartyrium und seine Verwandten in der frühchristlichen Literatur', *Z.N.T.W.* 56 (1965).

BICKERMAN, E. J. 'The Warning Inscription of Herod's Temple', *J.Q.R.* XXXVII (1946–7).

BIENERT, W. *Der älteste nichtchristliche Jesusbericht. Josephus über Jesus. Unter besonderer Berücksichtigung des altrussischen Josephus (Theol. Arbeiten z. Bibel-, Kirchen- und Geistesgeschichte,* hrg. v. D. Ernst Barnikol, Nr. IX. Akad. Verlag, Halle, 1936).

Bilderatlas zur Religionsgeschichte, hrg. H. Haas, 9.–11. Lieferung: J. Leipoldt, *Die Religionen in der Umwelt des Urchristentums.* Leipzig–Erlangen, 1926.

BLACK, M. *An Aramaic Approach to the Gospels and Acts.* Oxford, 1946.

—— 'The Arrest and Trial of Jesus and the Date of the Last Supper', *New Testament Essays,* ed. A. J. B. Higgins. Manchester, 1959.

—— *The Scrolls and Christian Origins.* London–Edinburgh, 1961.

BLINZLER, J. *The Trial of Jesus,* E. T. Cork, 1959.

—— 'Die Niedermetzelung von Galiläern durch Pilatus', *N.T.* II (1958).

—— 'Das Synedrium von Jerusalem und die Strafprozeßordnung der Mischna', *Z.N.T.W.* 52 (1961).

DEN BOER, W. 'Claudius', *R.A.C.* III (1957), 180–1.

BO REICKE. *Diakonie, Festfreude und Zelos in Verbindung mit der altchristlichen Agapenfeier* (Uppsala Universitets Årsskrift, 1951). Uppsala–Wiesbaden, 1952.

BORNKAMM, G. 'Paulus', *R.G.G.*[3], V (1961), 166–90.

BRANDON, S. G. F. 'The Logic of New Testament Criticism', *H.J.* XLVII (1949).

—— *The Fall of Jerusalem and the Christian Church.* London, 1951, 2nd ed. 1957.

—— *Time and Mankind.* London, 1951.

—— 'Tübingen Vindicated?', *H.J.* XLIX (1951).

—— 'The Markan Apocalypse', *The Modern Churchman,* XLIV (1954). Oxford.

—— 'Josephus: Renegade or Patriot?', *History Today,* VIII (1958). London.

—— 'Recent Study of the Sources for the Life of Jesus', *The Modern Churchman,* II, n.s. (1958–9). Oxford.

—— 'The Perennial Problem of Paul', *H.J.* LVIII (1960).

—— 'The Date of the Markan Gospel', *N.T.S.* VII (1960–1).

—— *Man and his Destiny in the Great Religions.* Manchester University Press, 1962.

—— 'The Jesus of History', *History Today,* XII (1962). London.

—— 'The Apologetical Factor in the Markan Gospel', *Studia Evangelica*, II, ed. F. L. Cross. Berlin, 1964.

—— 'Matthaean Christianity', *The Modern Churchman*, VIII, n.s. (1965). Oxford.

—— 'The Zealots: the Jewish Resistance against Rome, A.D. 6–73', *History Today*, XV (1965). London.

—— *History, Time and Deity*. Manchester University Press, 1965.

—— 'The Trial of Jesus', *History Today*, XVI (1966). London.

BRIERRE-NARBONNE, J. *Le Messie souffrant dans la littérature rabbinique*. Paris, 1940.

BRUCE, F. F. *The Acts of the Apostles*. London, 1951.

—— *Second Thoughts on the Dead Sea Scrolls*. London, 1956.

—— 'The Dead Sea Habakkuk Scroll', *A.L.U.O.S.* I (1958–9).

—— 'The Book of Zechariah and the Passion Narrative', *B.J.R.L.* 43 (1961).

—— 'Hebrews', *Peake's Commentary*, 2nd ed.

—— 'Christianity under Claudius', *B.J.R.L.* 44 (1962).

—— 'When is a Gospel not a Gospel?', *B.J.R.L.* 45 (1963).

—— 'St Paul in Rome', *B.J.R.L.* 46 (1964).

BULTMANN, R. *Urchristentum im Rahmen der antiken Religionen*. Zürich, 1949.

—— *Die Geschichte der synoptischen Tradition*, 3. Aufl., Göttingen, 1957; Ergänzungsheft, Göttingen, 1958.

—— *Theology of the New Testament*, vol. I, E.T. London, 1959.

BURKILL, T. A. 'L'antisémitisme dans l'évangile selon saint Marc', *R.H.R.* 154 (1958).

—— 'The Trial of Jesus', *V.C.* XII (1958).

—— *Mysterious Revelation: an Examination of the Philosophy of St Mark's Gospel*. Cornell University Press, New York, 1963.

BURKITT, F. C. *Christian Beginnings*. London, 1924.

BURROWS, M. *The Dead Sea Scrolls*. London, 1956.

CADOUX, C. J. *The Historic Mission of Jesus*. London, 1941.

CARCOPINO, J. *La vie quotidienne à Rome à l'apogée de l'Empire*. Paris, 1939.

CARRINGTON, P. *The Early Christian Church*, 2 vols. Cambridge, 1957.

CARROLL, K. L. 'The Place of James in the Early Church', *B.J.R.L.* 44 (1961).

CARY, M. *The Geographic Background of Greek and Roman History*. Oxford, 1949.

CHALON, G. *L'Édit de Tiberius Julius Alexander*. Lausanne, 1964.

CHARLES, R. H. *A Critical History of the Doctrine of a Future Life*, or *Hebrew, Jewish and Christian Eschatology*, 2nd ed. rev. London, 1913.

—— *The Revelation of St John*, 2 vols. International Critical Commentary. Edinburgh, 1920.

CHARLESWORTH, M. P. 'Gaius and Claudius', ch. XX, *C.A.H.* X (1934).

CLARK, K. W. 'Worship in the Jerusalem Temple after A.D. 70', *N.T.S.* VI (1959–60).

CLARKE, W. K. L. *New Testament Problems*. London, 1929.

CLEMEN, C. *Religionsgeschichtliche Erklärung des Neuen Testaments*. Giessen, 1924.

CONZELMANN, H. 'Jesus Christus', *R.G.G.*[3], III (1959), 619–53.

—— 'Geschichte und Eschaton nach Mc 13', *Z.N.T.W.* 50 (1959).

COUTTS, J. 'Those Outside (Mark 4, 10–12)', *Studia Evangelica*, vol. 2, II, ed. F. L. Cross. Berlin, 1964.

CREED, J. M. *Gospel according to St Luke*. London, 1929.

—— 'The Slavonic Version of Josephus' History of the Jewish War', *H.Th.R.* XXV (1932).

CULLMANN, O. *Le problème littéraire et historique du Roman Pseudo-Clémentin*. Paris, 1930.

—— *The State in the New Testament*, E.T. London, 1957.

—— 'L'opposition contre le Temple de Jérusalem; motif commun de théologie johannique et du monde ambiant', *N.T.S.* V (1958–9).

—— 'L'apôtre Pierre instrument du diable et instrument de Dieu: la place de Matt. 16: 16–19 dans la tradition primitive', *New Testament Essays*, ed. A. J. B. Higgins. Manchester, 1959.

—— *Petrus: Jünger-Apostel-Märtyrer*, 2. Aufl. Zürich–Stuttgart, 1960. E. T. *Peter: Disciple-Apostle-Martyr*. London, 1953.

CURTIUS, L. and NAWRATH, A. *Das Antike Rom*. Wien, 1944.

DALBERT, P. *Die Theologie der hellenistisch-jüdischen Missions-Literatur unter Ausschluß von Philo und Josephus*. Hamburg, 1954.

DALMAN, G. *Jesus-Jeshua*, E.T. London, 1929.

DANIÉLOU, J. *Théologie du Judéo-Christianisme*. Tournai, 1958.

DANIÉLOU, J. and MARROU, H. *The Christian Centuries*, vol. I, E.T. London, 1964.

DAUBE, D. *The New Testament and Rabbinic Judaism*. London, 1956.

DAVIES, W. D. *Paul and Rabbinic Judaism*. London, 1948.

—— *Christian Origins and Judaism*. London, 1962.

—— *The Setting of the Sermon on the Mount*. Cambridge, 1964.

DEISSMANN, A. *Licht vom Osten*, 4. Aufl. Tübingen, 1923.

—— *Paulus: eine kultur- und religionsgeschichtliche Skizze*, 2. Aufl. Tübingen, 1925.

DELLING, G. 'Josephus und das Wunderbare', *N.T.* II (1958).

DERENBOURG, J. *Essai sur l'histoire et la géographie de la Palestine (d'après les Thalmuds et les autres sources rabbiniques)*. Paris, 1857.

DIBELIUS, M. 'Archonten', *R.A.C.* I (1950), 631–3.

DODD, C. H. *The Apostolic Preaching and its Developments*. London, 1944.

—— 'The Fall of Jerusalem and the "Abomination of Desolation"', *J.R.S.* XXXVII (1953–4).

—— *The Fourth Gospel*. Cambridge, 1954.

—— *Historical Tradition in the Fourth Gospel*. Cambridge, 1963.

DOWNING, J. 'Jesus and Martyrdom', *J.T.S.* XIV, n.s. (1963).

DOYLE, A. D. 'Pilate's Career and the Date of the Crucifixion', *J.T.S.* XLII (1941).

DRIVER, G. R. *The Judaean Scrolls*. Blackwell, Oxford, 1965.

DUNKERLEY, R. 'The Riddles of Josephus', *H.J.* LIII (1954–5).

DUPONT-SOMMER, A. *Les écrits esséniens découverts près de la Mer Morte.* Paris, 1959.

EASTON, B. S. *Christ and the Gospels.* New York, 1930.

EHRHARDT, A. A. T. *The Apostolic Succession.* London, 1953.

—— *The Framework of the New Testament Stories.* Manchester University Press, 1961.

—— 'The Disciples of Emmaus', *N.T.S.* x (1964).

EISLER, R. ΙΗΣΟΥΣ ΒΑΣΙΛΕΥΣ ΟΥ ΒΑΣΙΛΕΥΣΑΣ (*Die messianische Unabhängigkeitsbewegung vom Auftreten Johannes des Täufers bis zum Untergang Jakobs des Gerechten. Nach der neuerschlossenen Eroberung von Jerusalem des Flavius Josephus und den christlichen Quellen*), 2 Bände, Heidelberg, 1929–30. *The Messiah Jesus and John the Baptist* (*According to Flavius Josephus' recently discovered 'Capture of Jerusalem' and other Jewish and Christian sources*), English edition by A. H. Krappe, London, 1931.

—— *Flavius Josephus-Studien.* I, *Das Testimonium Flavianum, Eine Antwort an Dr. Walter Bienert.* London, 1938.

—— *The Enigma of the Fourth Gospel.* London, 1938.

ELLIOTT-BINNS, L. E. *Galilean Christianity.* London, 1956.

EPPSTEIN, V. 'The Historicity of the Gospel Account of the Cleansing of the Temple', *Z.N.T.W.* 55 (1964).

ERMAN, A. *Die Religion der Ägypter.* Berlin–Leipzig, 1934.

EVANS, C. F. 'I will go before you into Galilee', *J.T.S.* v, n.s. (1954).

FARMER, W. R. *Maccabees, Zealots and Josephus.* Columbia University Press, New York, 1957.

FESTUGIÈRE, A.-J. *La Révélation d'Hermès Trismégiste*, 4 tomes. Paris, 1950–4.

FILSON, F. V. *A New Testament History.* London, 1965.

FISCHER, J. B. 'The Term ΔΕΣΠΟΤΗΣ in Josephus', *J.Q.R.* XLIX (1958–9).

FOAKES JACKSON, F. J. *Josephus and the Jews.* London, 1930.

FÖRSTER, W. *Palestinian Judaism in New Testament Times*, E.T. Edinburgh, 1964.

FREND, W. H. C. *Martyrdom and Persecution in the Early Church.* Blackwell, Oxford, 1965.

FUCHS, H. 'Tacitus über die Christen', *V.C.* I (1950).

GALL, A. VON. ΒΑΣΙΛΕΙΑ ΤΟΥ ΘΕΟΥ. Heidelberg, 1926.

GÄRTNER, B. *The Theology of the Gospel of Thomas*, E.T. by E. J. Sharpe. London, 1961.

GASTER, M. *The Samaritans* (Schweich Lectures, 1923). London, 1925.

GLASSON, T. F. 'The Reply to Caiaphas (Mark xiv. 62)', *N.T.S.* VII (1960–1).

GOGUEL, M. 'Jésus et le Messianisme politique: Examen de la théorie de M. Robert Eisler', *Revue historique*, CLXII (1929). Paris.

—— *The Life of Jesus*, E.T. London, 1933.

—— *La naissance du christianisme*. Paris, 1946.

—— *Les premiers temps de l'Église*. Neuchâtel, 1949.

GOODENOUGH, E. R. *The Politics of Philo Judaeus*, with a general bibliography of Philo, by H. L. Goodhart and E. R. Goodenough. Yale University Press, 1938.

GOODSPEED, E. J. *Introduction to the New Testament*. Chicago, 1937.

GOPPELT, L. 'The Freedom to Pay the Imperial Tax (Mark 12, 17)', *Studia Evangelica*, II, ed. F. L. Cross. Berlin, 1964.

GRAETZ, H. *History of the Jews*, E.T. vol. II. London, 1891.

GRANT, F. C. *The Economic Background of the Gospels*. Oxford, 1926.

—— *The Gospels: their Origin and their Growth*. London, 1965 (1957).

GRAY, L. H. 'Josephus' (additional note to article on Josephus by B. Niese), *E.R.E.* VII (1914).

GREEN, F. W. *The Gospel according to St Matthew*. Oxford, 1936.

GRILLMEIER, A. *Christ in Christian Tradition from the Apostolic Age to Chalcedon (451)*, E.T. London, 1965.

GUIGNEBERT, CH. *Le monde juif vers le temps de Jésus*. Paris, 1935.

—— *Jésus*, Paris, 1947 (1933); E.T. *Jesus*, by S. H. Hooke, London, 1935.

—— *Le Christ*. Paris, 1943.

HAENCHEN, E. 'Apostelgeschichte', *R.G.G.*³, I (1957), 501–7.

—— 'Judentum und Christentum in der Apostelgeschichte', *Z.N.T.W.* 54 (1963).

HAMILTON, N. Q. 'Temple Cleansing and Temple Bank', *J.B.L.* LXXXVIII (1964).

HARNACK, A. VON. *Die Mission und Ausbreitung des Christentums in den ersten drei Jahrhunderten*, 2 Bände. Leipzig, 1906.

HART, H. ST J. 'Judaea and Rome: the Official Commentary', *J.T.S.* III, n.s. (1952).

HEADLAM, A. C., see SANDAY, W. and HEADLAM, A. C.

HEALY, J. F. 'The Cyrene Half-Shekel', *J.S.S.* II (1957).

HENDERSON, B. W. *The Life and Principate of the Emperor Nero*. London, 1903.

HENGEL, M. *Die Zeloten*. Leiden, 1961.

HERFORD, R. TRAVERS. 'The Effect of the Fall of Jerusalem upon the Character of the Pharisees', *Society of Hebraic Studies*, no. 2. London, 1917.

—— *The Pharisees*. Boston, U.S.A., 1962 (1924).

HILGENFELD, A. *Die Ketzergeschichte des Urchristentums*. Hildesheim, 1963 (Leipzig, 1884).

HOENNICKE, G. *Das Judenchristentum im ersten und zweiten Jahrhundert*. Berlin, 1908.

HOHLWEIN, H. 'Reimarus', *R.G.G.*³, V (1961), 937–8.

HORT, F. J. *Judaistic Christianity*. London, 1894.

HOSKYNS, E. and DAVEY, N. *The Riddle of the New Testament*. London, 1931.

HUMMEL, R. *Die Auseinandersetzung zwischen Kirche und Judentum im Matthäusevangelium*. München, 1963.

JACK, J. W. *The Historic Christ: an Examination of Dr Robert Eisler's Theory according to the Slavonic Version of Josephus and Other Sources*. London, 1933.

JAUBERT, A. 'Jésus et le calendrier de Qumrân', *N.T.S.* VII (1960–1).

—— 'Les séances du Sanhédrin et les récits de la Passion', *R.H.R.* 166 (1964), 167 (1965).

JEREMIAS, J. *Jerusalem zur Zeit Jesu*, I, II. Teil, 2. Aufl. Göttingen, 1958.

JOHNSON, S. E. 'The Dead Sea Manual of Discipline and the Jerusalem Church of Acts', in *The Scrolls and the New Testament*, ed. K. Stendahl. London, 1958.

JONES, A. H. M. *The Herods of Judaea*. Oxford, 1938.

JUSTER, J. *Les Juifs dans l'Empire romain*. Paris, 1914.

KANAEL, B. 'Ancient Jewish Coins and their Historical Importance', *B.A.* XXVI (1963).

KASSER, R. 'Les origines du christianisme égyptien', *R.Th.P.* XI (1962).

KAUTSKY, K. *The Foundations of Christianity*, E.T. London, 1929.

KELLY, J. N. D. *Early Christian Creeds*. London, 1950.

KENNARD, J. SPENCER. *Politique et religion chez les Juifs au temps de Jésus et dans l'Église primitive*. Paris, 1927.

—— 'Judas of Galilee and his Clan', *J.Q.R.* XXXVI (1945–6).

—— 'The Jewish Provincial Assembly', *Z.N.T.W.* 53 (1962).

KILPATRICK, G. D. *The Origins of the Gospel of St Matthew*. Oxford, 1946.

—— *The Trial of Jesus*, published by the Friends of Dr Williams' Library. London, 1953.

—— 'Galatians 1:18, ἱστορῆσαι Κηφᾶν', *New Testament Essays*, ed. A. J. B. Higgins. Manchester, 1959.

KINGDOM, H. P. 'Messiahship and the Crucifixion', *Studia Evangelica*, III, ed. F. L. Cross. Berlin, 1964.

KLAUSNER, J. *Jesus of Nazareth*, E.T. London, 1929.

—— *From Jesus to Paul*, E.T. London, 1942.

KLIJN, A. F. J. 'Stephen's Speech—Acts vii. 2–53', *N.T.S.* IV (1957–8).

KLOSTERMANN, E. *Das Matthäusevangelium*, 2. Aufl. Tübingen, 1927.

—— *Das Lukasevangelium*. Tübingen, 1929.

—— *Das Markusevangelium*, 4. Aufl. Tübingen, 1950.

KNOX, W. L. *St Paul and the Church of Jerusalem*. Cambridge, 1925.

—— *St Paul and the Church of the Gentiles*. Cambridge, 1939.

—— *The Acts of the Apostles*. Cambridge, 1948.

KOHLER, K. 'Zealots', *J.E.* XII (1906).

KOSSEN, H. P. *Op Zoek naar de Historische Jezus*. Academisch Proefschrift, Universiteit van Amsterdam, 1960.

KRAELING, C. H. 'The Episode of the Roman Standards at Jerusalem', *H.Th.R.* xxxv (1942).

KUHN, H.-W. 'Das Reittier Jesu in der Einzugsgeschichte des Mc-Evangeliums', *Z.N.T.W.* 50 (1959).

KUHN, K. G. 'The Two Messiahs of Aaron and Israel', in *The Scrolls and the New Testament*, ed. K. Stendahl. London, 1958.

DE LABRIOLLE, P. *La réaction païenne: étude sur la polémique antichrétienne du Ier au VIe siècle.* Paris, 1942 (1934).

LAMPE, G. W. H. 'Luke', *Peake's Commentary*, 2nd ed.

LAWLOR, H. J. *Eusebiana.* Oxford, 1912.

LECLERCQ, H. *La vie chrétienne primitive.* Paris, 1928.

LIETZMANN, H. *An die Korinther, I–II*, 2. Aufl. Tübingen, 1923.

—— *An die Galater*, 2. Aufl. Tübingen, 1923.

—— *Geschichte der alten Kirche*, 1. Band, *Die Anfänge.* Berlin–Leipzig, 1937.

LIGHTFOOT, J. *Horae Hebraicae et Talmudicae*, ed. R. Gandell. Oxford, 1859.

LIGHTFOOT, J. B. *The Epistle to the Galatians.* London, 1881.

LIGHTFOOT, R. H. *Locality and Doctrine in the Gospels.* London, 1938.

LIVNEH, M. and MESHEL, Z. *Masada.* Tel Aviv, 1966.

LJUNGMANN, H. 'Matthäusevangelium', *B.-h. H.-Wb.* II, 1172.

LOEWE, H. *'Render Unto Caesar': Religious and Political Loyalty in Palestine.* Cambridge, 1940.

LOHMEYER, E. *Die Offenbarung des Johannes* (Handbuch zum Neuen Testament). Tübingen, 1926.

—— 'L'idée du martyre dans le Judaïsme et dans le Christianisme primitif', *Congrès d'Histoire du Christianisme*, ed. P.-L. Couchoud, vol. II. Paris, 1928.

—— *Galiläa und Jerusalem.* Göttingen, 1936.

LOHMEYER, E. and SCHMAUCH, W. *Das Evangelium des Matthäus.* Göttingen, 1958.

LOISY, A. *Les mystères païens et le mystère chrétien.* Paris, 1914.

MCNEIL, A. H. *The Gospel according to St Matthew.* London, 1952 (1915).

MADDEN, F. W. *History of Jewish Coinage.* London, 1864.

—— *Coins of the Jews.* London, 1881.

MANSON, T. W. *The Teaching of Jesus.* Cambridge, 1935.

—— 'John the Baptist', *B.J.R.L.* 36 (1954).

—— *Jesus and the Non-Jews.* University of London (Athlone Press), 1955.

—— 'Martyrs and Martyrdom', *B.J.R.L.* 39 (1957).

—— 'Romans', *Peake's Commentary*, 2nd ed.

—— *Studies in the Gospels and the Epistles.* Manchester University Press, 1962.

MANSON, W. *Jesus the Messiah.* London, 1943.

MARTINETTI, P. *Jésus Christ et le Christianisme.* Paris, 1942.

MATTINGLY, H. B. 'The Origin of the Name *Christiani*', *J.T.S.* IX, n.s. (1958).

MENZIES, A. *The Second Epistle to the Corinthians*. London, 1912.

MERRILL, E. *Essays in Earliest Christianity*. London, 1924.

MESHEL, Z., *see* LIVNEH, M. and MESHEL, Z.

MEYER, ED. *Ursprung und Anfänge des Christentums*, 3 vols. Stuttgart–Berlin, 1921–3.

MILIK, J. T. *Dix ans de découvertes dans le désert de Juda*. Paris, 1957.

MILMAN, H. *History of the Jews*, 2 vols. Everyman Library, London, 1909.

MILNE, J. G. *A History of Egypt under Roman Rule*. London, 1898.

MOFFATT, J. *Introduction to the Literature of the New Testament*. Edinburgh, 1933 (3rd ed. revised, 1918).

MOMIGLIANO, A. *L'Opera dell'Imperatore Claudio*. Florence, 1932.

—— 'Rebellion within the Empire', ch. xxv, *C.A.H.* x (1934).

MOMMSEN, T. *Das Weltreich der Caesaren*. Wien–Leipzig, 1933.

MONTEFIORE, H. W. 'Revolt in the Desert?', *N.T.S.* VIII (1961–2).

—— *Josephus and the New Testament*. London, 1962.

—— 'Sulpicius Severus and Titus' Council of War', *Historia*, XI (1962). Wiesbaden.

—— 'Jesus and the Temple Tax', *N.T.S.* XI (1964).

MOORE, G. F. *Judaism*, 3 vols. Cambridge, Mass., 1927.

MORRISON, W. D. *The Jews under Roman Rule*. London, 1890.

MOULTON, W. J. 'Samaritans', *E.R.E.* XI (1920).

MOWINCKEL, S. *He That Cometh*, E.T. Oxford, 1958.

MUNCK, J. *Paul and the Salvation of Mankind*, E.T. London, 1959.

—— 'Jewish Christianity in Post-Apostolic Times', *N.T.S.* VI (1959–60).

NEUSNER, J. *Life of Rabban Yohanan ben Zakkai*. Leiden, 1962.

—— *A History of the Jews in Babylonia*, I. Leiden, 1965.

A New Commentary of Holy Scripture, ed. C. Gore, H. L. Goudge, H. Guillaume. London, 1929.

New Testament Essays (*Studies in memory of T. W. Manson*), ed. A. J. B. Higgins. Manchester University Press, 1959.

NIESE, B. 'Josephus', *E.R.E.* VII (1914).

NOCK, A. D. 'Religious Developments from the Close of the Republic to the Death of Nero', ch. xv, *C.A.H.* x (1934).

—— *St Paul*. London, 1938.

NOTH, M. *A History of Israel*, E.T. London, 1960.

OESTERLEY, W. O. E. *History of Israel*, II. Oxford, 1932.

—— 'Egypt and Israel', *The Legacy of Egypt*, ed. S. R. K. Glanville. Oxford, 1942.

OESTERLEY, W. O. E. and BOX, G. H. *A Short Survey of the Literature of Rabbinical and Mediaeval Judaism*. London, 1920.

OGG, G. 'The Chronology of the New Testament', *Peake's Commentary*, 2nd ed.

OLMSTEAD, A. J. *Jesus: in the Light of History*. New York, 1942.

PALANQUE, J. R. *et alii*. *The Church in the Christian Roman Empire*, II, E.T. London, 1952.

Peake's Commentary on the Bible, 2nd ed., M. Black and H. H. Rowley. London-Edinburgh, 1962.

PERETTI, A. *La Sibilla babilonese nella Propaganda ellenistica*. Florence, 1943.

PEROWNE, S. *The Later Herods*. London, 1958.

PETRIE, W. M. FLINDERS and DUNCAN, J. GARROW. *Hyksos and Israelite Cities* (British School of Archaeology in Egypt). London, 1906.

PFEIFFER, R. H. *A History of New Testament Times, with an Introduction to the Apocrypha*. New York, 1949.

PIGANIOL, A. *Histoire de Rome*, 3rd ed. Paris, 1949.

PIN, B. *Jérusalem contre Rome (Un duel pour l'hégémonie en Mediterranée orientale)*. Paris, 1938.

PREUSCHEN, E. *Die Apostelgeschichte* (Handbuch zum Neuen Testament, IV. Band). Tübingen, 1926.

REIFENBERG, A. *Israel's History in Coins*. London, 1953.

REINACH, S. *Orpheus*, E.T. London, 1931.

RENGSTORF, K. H. 'ληστής', *Th.Wb.* IV, 262–7.

RICCIOTTI, G. *Flavio Giuseppe. Lo Storico giudeo-romano*. Turin, 1937 (*see* Bibliography I *under* Josephus).

RIESENFELD, H. 'Sabbat et Jour du Seigneur', *New Testament Essays*, ed. A. J. B. Higgins. Manchester, 1959.

ROBERTS, C. H. 'The Christian Book and the Greek Papyri', *J.T.S.* L (1949).

ROTH, C. *The Historical Background of the Dead Sea Scrolls*. Blackwell, Oxford, 1958.

—— 'The Zealots—a Jewish Religious Sect', *Judaism*, VIII (1959). New York.

—— 'The Zealots in the War of 66–73', *J.S.S.* IV (1959).

—— 'The Debate on the Loyal Sacrifices, A.D. 66', *H.Th.R.* LII (1960).

—— 'The Cleansing of the Temple and Zechariah xiv. 21', *N.T.* IV (1960).

—— 'Melekh ha-'olam: Zealot influence in the Liturgy', *J.J.S.* XI (1960).

—— 'The Historian and the Dead Sea Scrolls', *History Today*, XI (1961). London.

—— 'The Pharisees in the Jewish Revolution of 66–73', *J.S.S.* VII (1962).

—— 'The Constitution of the Jewish Republic of 66–70', *J.S.S.* IX (1964).

ROWLEY, H. H. 'The Herodians', *J.T.S.* XLI (1940).

—— *The Zadokite Fragments and the Dead Sea Scrolls*. Blackwell, Oxford, 1952.

—— 'The Teacher of Righteousness and the Dead Sea Scrolls', *B.J.R.L.* 40 (1957).

—— 'The Qumran Sectaries and the Zealots: an examination of a recent theory', *V.T.* IX (1959).

—— 'The Qumran Sect and Christian Origins', *B.J.R.L.* 44 (1961).

RUBINSTEIN, A. 'Observations on the Old Russian Version of Josephus', *J.S.S.* II (1957).

SALOMONSEN, B. 'Some Remarks on the Zealots, with Special Regard to the Term "Qannaim" in Rabbinic Literature', *N.T.S.* XII (1966).

SANDAY, W. and HEADLAM, A. C. *The Epistle to the Romans*, International Critical Commentary. Edinburgh, 1900.

SASSE, H. 'Aion', article in *R.A.C.* I (1950), 193–204.

SCHERER, M. R. *Marvels of Ancient Rome*. New York–London, 1956.

SCHLATTER, D. A. *Die Geschichte Israels von Alexander dem Großen bis Hadrian*. Stuttgart, 1925.

SCHLIER, H. *Der Brief an die Galater*. Göttingen, 1962.

SCHMAUCH, W., *see* LOHMEYER, E. and SCHMAUCH, W.

SCHMIDT, C. *Studien zu den Pseudo-Clementinen, nebst einem Anhange: die älteste römische Bischofsliste und die Pseudo-Clementinen* (in *Texte und Untersuchungen*, hrg. A. von Harnack und C. Schmidt, XLVI. Band, 1. Heft. Leipzig, 1930).

SCHMIDTKE, F. 'Chronologie', *R.A.C.* III (1957), 49–50.

SCHMITHALS, W. 'Paul und der historische Jesus', *Z.N.T.W.* 53 (1962).

—— *Paul and James*, E.T. London, 1965.

SCHOEPS, H. J. *Theologie und Geschichte des Judenchristentums*. Tübingen, 1949.

—— *Aus frühchristlicher Zeit: religionsgeschichtliche Untersuchungen*. Tübingen, 1950.

—— *Urgemeinde, Judenchristentum, Gnosis*. Tübingen, 1956.

—— *Paulus: die Theologie des Apostels im Lichte der jüdischen Religionsgeschichte*. Tübingen, 1959.

—— *Paul: the Theology of the Apostle in the Light of Jewish Religious History*, trans. H. Knight. London, 1961.

SCHÜRER, E. *Geschichte des jüdischen Volkes im Zeitalter Jesu Christi*, 3 Bände. Leipzig, 1898–1901.

SCHWARTZ, E. 'Zu Eusebius Kirchengeschichte. I. Das Martyrium Jakobus des Gerechten', *Z.N.T.W.* IV (1903).

SCHWEITZER, A. *The Quest of the Historical Jesus*, E.T. London, 1910.

—— *Paul and his Interpreters*, E.T. London, 1912.

—— *The Mysticism of Paul*, E.T. London, 1931.

SCHWEIZER, E. 'Mark's Contribution to the Quest of the Historical Jesus', *N.T.S.* X (1963–4).

SCRAMUZZA, V. M. 'The Policy of the Early Roman Emperors towards Judaism', in *B.C.* V (1933).

The Scrolls and the New Testament, ed. K. Stendahl. London, 1958.

SEZNEC, J. *La survivance des dieux antiques*. The Warburg Institute, London, 1940.

SHERWIN-WHITE, A. N. *Roman Society and Roman Law in the New Testament*. Oxford, 1963.

—— 'The Trial of Christ', *Historicity and Chronology in the New Testament*. S.P.C.K. London, 1965.

SHUTT, R. J. H. *Studies in Josephus*. London, 1961.

SIEFFERT, F. *Der Brief an die Galater*. Göttingen, 1899.

SIMON, M. *Verus Israel: étude sur les relations entre Chrétiens et Juifs dans l'Empire romain (135–425)*. Paris, 1948.

—— *Les premiers Chrétiens*. Paris, 1952.

—— *St Stephen and the Hellenists in the Primitive Church*. London, 1958.

—— *Sectes juives au temps de Jésus*. Paris, 1960.

—— *Recherches d'histoire judéo-chrétienne*. Paris–La Haye, 1962.

SMALLWOOD, E. M. 'The Date of the Dismissal of Pontius Pilate from Judaea', *J.J.S.* v (1954).

—— 'High Priests and Politics in Roman Palestine', *J.T.S.* XIII, n.s. (1962).

—— 'Jews and Romans in the Early Empire', parts I and II, *History Today*, XV (1965). London.

SMITH, C. W. F. 'The Mixed State of the Church in Matthew's Gospel', *J.B.L.* LXXXII (1963).

SMITH, G. A. *Historical Geography of the Holy Land*. London, 1907.

—— *Jerusalem*, 2 vols. London, 1907.

SMITH, P. GARDNER. *The Narratives of the Resurrection*. London, 1926.

SNAPE, H. C. 'The Fourth Gospel, Ephesus and Alexandria', *H.Th.R.* XLVII (1954).

—— 'The Composition of the Lukan Writings: a Re-assessment', *H.Th.R.* LIII (1960).

STAPFER, E. *La Palestine au temps de Jésus-Christ (d'après le Nouveau Testament, l'historien Flavius Josèphe et les Talmuds)*. Paris, 1885.

STAUFFER, E. *Christus und die Caesaren*. Hamburg, 1952.

—— *Jesus and His Story*, E.T. London, 1960.

STEINMETZER, F. X. 'Census', *R.A.C.* II (1954), 969–72.

STENDAHL, K. *The School of St Matthew and its Use of the Old Testament*. London, 1954.

—— 'Matthew', *Peake's Commentary*, 2nd ed.

STRECKER, G. *Das Judenchristentum in den Pseudoklementinen*. Berlin, 1958.

STREETER, B. H. *The Four Gospels*. London, 1924.

—— *The Primitive Church*. London, 1929.

—— 'The Rise of Christianity', ch. VII, *C.A.H.* XI (1936).

STUMPF, A. 'ζηλόω, ζηλωτής', *Th.Wb.* II, 884–90.

TAYLOR, V. *Behind the Third Gospel*. Oxford, 1926.

—— *The Formation of the Gospel Tradition*. London, 1945.

—— *The Gospel according to St Mark*. London, 1952.

TCHERIKOVER, V. A. 'The Decline of the Jewish Diaspora in Egypt in the Roman Period', *J.J.S.* XIV (1963).

TELFER, W. 'Was Hegesippus a Jew?', *H.Th.R.* III (1960).

THACKERAY, H. ST JOHN. 'Josephus', art. in Hastings's *Dictionary of the Bible*, extra vol., Edinburgh, 1904 (*see also under* Josephus *in* Bibliography I).

—— *Josephus: the Man and the Historian*. New York, 1929.

THOMSON, J. E. H. *The Samaritans*. Edinburgh, 1919.

TROCMÉ, E. 'Jésus Christ et le Temple: éloge d'un naïf', *R.H.P.R.* 44 (1964).

VAN UNNIK, W. C. *Evangelien aus dem Nilsand*. Frankfurt-am-Main, 1960.

—— 'Jesus the Christ', *N.T.S.* VIII (1961–2).

VARDAMAN, J. 'A New Inscription which mentions Pilate as "Prefect"', *J.B.S.* LXXXI (1962).

DE VAUX, R. *L'Archéologie et les manuscrits de la Mer Morte* (Schweich Lectures, 1959). London, 1961.

WEISS, J. *Urchristentum*. Göttingen, 1914.

—— *Earliest Christianity*, 2 vols. E.T. of *Das Urchristentum*, 2 vols. New York, 1959.

WERNER, M. *Der Einfluß paulinischer Theologie im Markusevangelium* (Beihefte I, z. *Z.N.T.W.*, 1923).

—— *Die Entstehung des christlichen Dogmas*, 2. Aufl. Bern–Tübingen, 1941.

—— *The Formation of Christian Dogma*, E.T. by S. G. F. Brandon. London, 1957.

WILLIAMS, C. S. C. 'The Synoptic Problem', *Peake's Commentary*, 2nd ed.

WILLIAMSON, G. A. *The World of Josephus*. London, 1964.

WILSON, R. MCL. 'Mark', *Peake's Commentary*, 2nd ed.

WINDISCH, H. *Der Messianische Krieg und das Urchristentum*. Tübingen, 1909.

—— 'Der Untergang Jerusalems (Anno 70) im Urtheil der Christen und Juden', *Theologisch Tijdschrift*. Leiden, 1914.

—— *Der zweite Korintherbrief*. Göttingen, 1924.

—— *Die katholischen Briefe*. Tübingen, 1930.

WINTER, P. 'The Cultural Background of the Narrative in Luke I and II', *J.Q.R.* XLV (1954).

—— *On the Trial of Jesus*. Berlin, 1961.

—— 'Zum Prozeß Jesu', *Das Altertum*, 9. Band (1963). Berlin.

—— 'The Marcan Account of Jesus' Trial by the Sanhedrin', *J.T.S.* XIV, n.s. (1963).

—— Review of M. Hengel, *Die Zeloten*, in *R.Q.* IV (1963).

WOOD, H. G. 'The Conversion of St Paul: its Nature, Antecedents and Consequences', *N.T.S.* I (1955).

—— 'Interpreting This Time', *N.T.S.* II (1955–6).

YADIN, Y. *The Scroll of the War of the Sons of Light against the Sons of Darkness*. Oxford, 1962.

—— 'Masada: Herod's Fortress-Palace and the Zealots' Last Stand', *I.L.N.* (31 October 1964), pp. 693 ff.

—— 'The Excavation of Masada—1963/64. Preliminary Report', *I.E.J.* XV (1965).

—— *The Excavation of Masada, 1963/64*. Jerusalem, 1965.

—— *Masada: Herod's Fortress and the Zealots' Last Stand.* London, 1966.

ZEITLIN, S. 'The Crucifixion of Jesus Re-examined', *J.Q.R.* XXXI (1940–1).

—— *Who Crucified Jesus?* New York, 1942.

—— 'The Warning Inscription of the Temple', *J.Q.R.* XXXVIII (1947–8).

—— 'The Hoax of the "Slavonic Josephus"', *J.Q.R.* XXXIX (1948–9).

ZUNTZ, G. *The Text of the Epistles* (Schweich Lectures, 1946). London, 1953.

Addenda

DANIEL, C. 'Esséniens, zélotes et sicaires et leur mention par paronymie dans le N.T.', *Numen*, XIII (1966). Leiden. [The author makes the interesting suggestion that the reed given to Jesus as a derisory symbol of royalty was actually a Zealot symbol: 'Par suite il nous faut conclure que le roseau *qana* était un symbole ou un signe assez connu à cette époque pour indiquer le Zélote *qana*. Et le roi "Zélote" devait être accompagné du signe qui désignait cette secte ou ce parti politique si l'on veut, le roseau' (p. 97).

KECK, L. E. 'The Poor among the Saints in Jewish Christianity and Qumran', *Z.N.T.W.* 57 (1966). [In this article, which has appeared since this book was set in type, the author acknowledges the seriousness of the case against the Pella-flight tradition, p. 65, n. 36.]

KÖBERLE, A. 'Versuchung', *R.G.G.*[3], VI (1962).

KOEP, L. 'Chronologie', *R.A.C.* III (1957), 48–51.

KOLLWITZ, J. 'Antiochia am Orontes', *R.A.C.* I (1950), 461–9.

MICHL, J. 'Engel II (jüdisch)', *R.A.C.* V (1962), 60–97.

OSSWALD, E. 'Moses', *R.G.G.*[3], IV (1960).

SCHUBART, W. 'Alexandria', *R.A.C.* I (1950), 271–83.

INDEX

I. ANCIENT LITERARY SOURCES

(The figures in parentheses indicate notes.)

Josephus, *Antiquities* (*cont.*)   PAGE

XII. 253	88(3)
XII. 388	292(4)
XIII. 63	292(4)
XIII. 69	293(4)
XIV. 72	89(1)
XIV. 159	28(4)
XIV. 482–3	89(1)
XV. 339	86(2)
XV. 403–5	80(4)
XV. 417	237(4)
XVII. 1–21	29(5)
XVII. 3	30(1)
XVII. 4–6	30(2)
XVII. 18, 219–27	27(3)
XVII. 159	47(1)
XVII. 191	27(1)
XVII. 213	27(1)
XVII. 213–18, 237	78(3)
XVII. 221–3	27(4)
XVII. 261–4	29(3)
XVII. 267	28(1)
XVII. 271–2	28(3)
XVII. 272	29(1)
XVII. 295	1(4), 29(2)
XVII. 304–14	28(2)
XVII. 317–18	65(1)
XVII. 342–4, 355	29(4)
XVIII. 1–10	33(2)
XVIII. 4	49(1)
XVIII. 4–5, 23	48(3)
XVIII. 4, 9, 23	37(4)
XVIII. 5	51(3), 54(5), 83(1), 87(2), 137(3)
XVIII. 6	52(1), 68(1)
XVIII. 6–10, 24–5	31(2)
XVIII. 6–10, 25	36(4)
XVIII. 10	68(1)
XVIII. 11–22	94(2)
XVIII. 18–22	46(3)
XVIII. 23	33(3)
XVIII. 23–4	38(1), 56(4)
XVIII. 23–5	34(3)
XVIII. 26	67(1)
XVIII. 31	66(4), 84(2)
XVIII. 34–5	67(3)
XVIII. 35	68(4)
XVIII. 55	232(2)
XVIII. 55 ff.	69(1, 2)
XVIII. 55–6	66(5)
XVIII. 55–62	362(2)
XVIII. 56	69(4), 70(1)
XVIII. 57	70(2)
XVIII. 58–9	71(1)

Josephus, *Antiquities* (*cont.*)   PAGE

XVIII. 60	76(1)
XVIII. 60–2	75(2), 360(3)
XVIII. 61–2	76(3)
XVIII. 63–4	77(1), 116(4), 360(2)
XVIII. 64	364(1)
XVIII. 65 ff.	362(3)
XVIII. 79	362(4)
XVIII. 85–9	80(1)
XVIII. 90–5	80(4)
XVIII. 95	81(1)
XVIII. 109–15	81(2)
XVIII. 118–19	97(2)
XVIII. 120	81(2)
XVIII. 121	81(3)
XVIII. 122	81(4)
XVIII. 123	82(1)
XVIII. 124	82(2)
XVIII. 143–236	83(2)
XVIII. 237	83(3)
XVIII. 240–55	83(4)
XVIII. 256	84(1)
XVIII. 257–61	84(2)
XVIII. 261–2	85(1)
XVIII. 262	89(3)
XVIII. 263–77	85(5)
XVIII. 263–78	87(5)
XVIII. 271	147(1)
XVIII. 272	89(3)
XVIII. 274	88(1)
XVIII. 278–88	85(6)
XVIII. 285	89(3)
XVIII. 289–301	86(1)
XVIII. 302	88(1)
XVIII. 302–9	86(3)
XVIII. 306	86(4)
XIX. 265–6, 274–5, 309	95(1)
XIX. 274–5	93(1)
XIX. 284–5	84(1)
XIX. 326–7	95(2, 3)
XIX. 328, 330–1	93(3)
XIX. 338–42	96(1)
XIX. 343–50	93(5)
XIX. 360–3	99(2)
XIX. 366	104(3)
XX. 5	99(4)
XX. 6–15	101(3)
XX. 15	101(3)
XX. 97–9	18(3), 100(1)
XX. 100	103(2)
XX. 102	52(4)
XX. 102–3	103(3)
XX. 105–13	104(3)
XX. 113–17	105(1)

II. MODERN WORKS

(The figures in parentheses indicate notes.)

III. NAMES AND SUBJECTS

(The figures in parentheses indicate notes.)